State of
the Environment

The Conservation Foundation is a nonprofit research and communications organization dedicated to encouraging human conduct to sustain and enrich life on earth. Since its founding in 1948, it has attempted to provide intellectual leadership in the cause of wise management of the earth's resources.

State of the Environment

An Assessment at Mid-Decade

A Report from
The Conservation Foundation

Washington, D.C.

State of the Environment:
An Assessment at Mid-Decade

Cover design by Sally A. Janin

Typography by Rings-Leighton, Ltd., Washington, D.C.

Printed by R.R. Donnelley & Sons Company, Harrisonburg, Virginia

5 4 3 2 1

The Conservation Foundation
1717 Massachusetts Avenue, N.W.
Washington, D.C. 20036

Library of Congress Cataloging in Publication Data
Main entry under title:
State of the environment: an assessment at mid-decade.

    Includes bibliographies and index:
    1. Environmental protection—United States.
2. Environmental policy—United States. I. Conservation Foundation.
TD171.S74   1984   363.7'00973   84-12651
ISBN 0-81964-084-3

We are deeply grateful for the support
of the Richard King Mellon Foundation,
which made this report possible.

Contents

PART 2: ISSUES

Figures

Acknowledgments

In preparing this report, The Conservation Foundation sought the advice of a variety of outside experts and drew heavily on its own interdisciplinary staff of scientists, economists, lawyers, political scientists, and policy analysts. Panels composed of industry, environmental, government, and academic representatives helped chart the direction of the four issue chapters and provided useful criticisms of chapter drafts. Many other outside experts also reviewed and commented on chapter drafts.

Edwin H. Clark, II, senior associate at The Conservation Foundation, directed the project. The principal authors of the chapters were: Steve C. Gold (Natural Resources); Rice Odell (Identifying Issues); J. Clarence Davies (Risk Assessment and Risk Control); Frances H. Irwin (Controlling Cross-Media Pollutants); Philip C. Metzger (Water Resources); and Richard A. Liroff and Daniel S. Miller (Intergovernmental Relations and Environmental Policy). Additional Foundation staff who contributed to the report include Virginia Coull, Julia L. Doermann, Jennifer A. Haverkamp, Robert G. Healy, Cynthia S. Herleikson, Michael Mantell, Robert L. Peters II, Barbara K. Rodes, Mary H. Ruckelshaus, Carolyn Rumery, William E. Shands, Pamela J. Sutherland, and Grant P. Thompson. Daniel B. Tunstall, an outside consultant, also provided assistance. The report was edited by staff members Robert J. McCoy and Bradley B. Rymph, with assistance from freelance editors Ira Brodsky, Bethany Brown, and Nancy Heneson.

The experts who served on the panels for each chapter include Edwin L. Behrens, Ron Brickman, Harold Elkin, Richard Fortuna, Robert Harris, Joshua Menkes, Robert Mitchell, and Richard Morgenstern (Risk Assessment and Risk Control); D.C. Anderson, Hope Babcock, Dan Beardsley, Joel Jacknow, Allen V. Kneese, Sam A. Madonia, Langdon Marsh, William Moomaw, and Ronald Outen (Controlling Cross-Media Pollutants); Brent Blackwelder, John Boland, Harold Brayman, William Eichbaum, Joan Kovalic, Steve Schatzow, Kyle Schilling, A.G. Smith, and Victoria J. Tschinkel (Water Resources); and Anne M. Blackburn, James Bowman, Michael Freedman, Michael Harvey, Audrey Hoffer, Jonathan Lash, George H. Pain, Phillip D. Reed, David B. Walker, and John Weingart (Intergovernmental Relations and Environmental Policy).

Additional outside review or assistance was provided by Ernest B. Abbott, Richard N.L. Andrews, George Arras, Robert C. Barnard, William S. Becker, Hugh Black, Jim Bossi, Lee Brown, Danny Bystrak, Don R. Clay, Richard H. Cowart, Geraldine V. Cox, Nan Evans, Sally K. Fairfax, H. Thomas Frey, Sanford E. Gaines, John Grandy, Sam Gusman, Susan Hadden, William F. Hunt, Helen M. Ingram, Carol Jolly, Dale Jones, Michael Kraft, R.W. Kutz, Edward T. LaRoe, Thomas E. Lovejoy, Frances Lynn, William C. Malm, Guy Marchessault, Michael Martin, David Morell, Alden C. Pierce, Paul Portney, James Rochelle, Irene Rothenberg, David Sarokin, Christine M. Schonewald-Cox, Carleton B. Scott, Maitland B. Sharpe, Richard A. Smith, Edward Stone, Marlene Suit, Nancy Tessaro, Merle Van Horne, Norm Vig, Rae Zimmerman, and several people who declined to be recognized by name.

Neither the members of the panels nor the other outside reviewers bear any direct responsibility for the contents of the report. The diversity of their backgrounds was intended to, and did, produce a diversity of views that stimulated exploration of topics. We are very grateful to them for the time and effort they contributed to the report.

The manuscript was typed with great patience under tight deadlines by Jenny E. Billet, Anthony C. Brown, Deborah C. Dorofy, Gwen C. Harley, Debbie K. Johnson, Fannie Mae Keller, and Marsha G. White. The challenge of an extremely tight production schedule was then met by Rings-Leighton, Ltd., of Washington, D.C., typesetters, and R.R. Donnelley & Sons Company of Harrisonburg, Virginia, printers.

Executive Summary

In assessing the state of the environment two years ago, The Conservation Foundation found progress, new problems, and institutional stresses in environmental agencies, particularly at the federal level. Our new report continues to record progress—attributable to policies implemented five, seven, or ten years ago. In addition to offering up-to-date information on environmental conditions and trends, as we did two years ago, we look in this report at the state of the environment in a longer-term perspective. Our assessment at mid-decade is not so much intended to be a snapshot as it is a search for insights and understandings of the issues that will characterize the 1980s and beyond.

The report is divided into two parts. The first three chapters describe environmental conditions and trends.

- Chapter one deals with *underlying trends*, primarily population growth and economic conditions.
- Chapter two covers *environmental contaminants*—toxic substances, hazardous waste, air and water pollutants, and overall waste production.
- Chapter three deals primarily with *natural resources*—water, land (including cropland, forestland, rangeland, wildlands, and critical areas), wildlife, energy, and recreation.

The second part of the report analyzes several long-range issues that cut across the traditional categories used to describe environmental problems.

- Chapter four reports on several studies that have tried to identify *future environmental problems* and discusses the factors that are relevant for establishing priorities among these problems.
- Chapter five explains the methodology used in *assessing environmental risks*. It focuses primarily on analyzing the risks of chemicals in the environment, but the methodology discussed is also applicable to most of the other environmental risks.
- Chapter six analyzes the extent to which toxic substances move from air to water to land and the policy implications of such movement. The key question is whether a more *integrated, cross-media approach to pollution control* is necessary.

- Chapter seven covers *water quality and water quantity* problems, the interrelationships between them, and issues related to the management of this vital resource.
- Chapter eight explores the intricacies of the relationship between the federal government and the states in implementing environmental policies, and it examines what we have learned about *intergovernmental relations and environmental policy* from the experience of the past decade.

Chapter 1: Underlying Trends

Population and *economic growth* fundamentally influence environmental quality—both the generation of environmental contaminants and the consumption of natural resources. The way people react to current conditions and perceived trends—the force of *public opinion*—is in turn an underlying factor molding society's responses to these environmental conditions.

The trends for all three of these factors have some positive implications for environmental quality in the United States. The population growth rate, now less than 1 percent per year, continues to fall. Some trends in the distribution of population growth established during the 1970s appear to be reversing. Many large cities and metropolitan areas that were stagnant or even losing population at that time have begun to grow again. And the rate of population growth in nonmetropolitan areas has declined substantially. But many states in the Northeast and North Central regions continue to lose population to the West and South, which can create environmental problems in the growing states and economic and social problems in the declining states. Internationally, population growth in developing countries continues to be a cause for concern.

The pattern of economic growth has the potential for reducing environmental stresses, with new plants and new industries having the ability to emit fewer pollutants and consume fewer resources than the "smokestack" industries in which employment is projected to decrease. In the short term, the recession of the early 1980s probably improved environmental quality trends because lower production levels meant fewer pollutants emitted and fewer resources consumed. On a global scale, however, a return to economic growth appears necessary to allow developing countries to avoid serious environmental degradation.

Public opinion favors stronger environmental programs more emphatically than it has at any time since the early 1970s. This is reflected both in the responses to public opinion polls and in the significant increases in the membership of environmental groups.

The only clearly negative underlying trend is in *environmental expenditures*. From 1972 to 1982, the United States spent $436 billion for pollution control, approximately $2,000 per person. Many investments still need to be made; yet, in both current and constant dollars, U.S. expenditures for pollution control are falling. The Environmental Protection Agency's operating budget has, in real terms, fallen to the level of 1972 and 1973, approximately a third lower than its peak in 1979. Total federal environmental expenditures are, in real terms, 23 percent less than the 1979 peak and have fallen to approximately the level they were in 1976. The biggest decrease in overall expenditures has been in water-pollution control, where real expenditures have fallen 23 percent since 1978. This decrease reflects reductions by the federal government, state and local governments, and private business.

Chapter 2: Environmental Contaminants

Toxics. Available information on human and environmental exposure to selected toxic substances clearly indicates that at least some past regulatory efforts have been successful. Data on contamination levels of substances such as lead, cadmium, DDT, dieldrin, and PCBs show lower concentrations in air, water, food, fish, birds, waterfowl, and shellfish, as well as in the blood and tissue of U.S. citizens. But these encouraging results are counterbalanced by the realization that very little is known about substances that have not been regulated. The monitoring programs focus primarily on those substances that have already been controlled rather than attempting to identify those substances that may need control in the future.

Even more disturbing, knowledge about the potential hazards of many of the substances to which people are exposed is extremely limited. There is sufficient information to allow a complete health-hazard assessment to be made for less than 2 percent of the chemicals used commercially, and for only 14 percent of the chemicals is there sufficient information to support even a partial hazard assessment. Even for drugs and food additives, there are more substances that lack any hazard information than there are substances for which the existing data are minimally adequate. For 70 percent of the 67,000 chemicals in commerce, there is no information on possible human health effects except, possibly, for confidential data that may be in company files.

Hazardous Wastes. Progress in controlling the risks caused by hazardous waste has been very slow. Recent studies have resulted in substantially increased estimates of the amount of hazardous waste being generated—five to six times higher than was thought in 1980. The current estimates suggest that approximately 2,500 pounds of hazardous waste, as defined by the Resource Conservation and Recovery Act (RCRA), are generated for each person in the United States annually. More than 16,000 sites now contain hazardous wastes that either cause or have the potential to cause contamination.

Given this situation, progress on permitting hazardous waste facilities and cleaning up risky sites appears painfully slow. EPA estimates that as many as 8,500 firms may require a permit to manage wastes under RCRA, excluding thousands of small firms and firms that, for other reasons, were not considered to require a permit. However, only 122 waste-management facilities had received permits as of February 1984; between 500 and 600 facilities have been denied permits or have withdrawn permit applications. Similarly, EPA has put 546 abandoned waste sites on the Superfund priority list and estimates that the total number likely to be placed on that list eventually may be as high as 2,200. Work had begun on 267 of these sites by the beginning of 1984, but EPA expects to clean up only 100 sites with the money currently authorized under the Superfund law. The agency also expects at least 100 additional sites to be cleaned up by private parties. Only six of the Superfund priority sites had been cleaned up completely by January 1984.

Air Quality. Air-quality trends show a much more encouraging picture. Air quality in urban areas in the United States continues to improve, at least in terms of the major, large-volume pollutants. For 23 American cities, the number of days in which air quality is considered hazardous has dropped to an average of only 0.13 days per year. The average number of days in which the air is considered bad enough to cause any health risk has declined by 50 percent since 1974 to approximately 44 days a year. The most dramatic improvement has been in sulfur dioxide and carbon monoxide concentrations, although ozone and total suspended particulate levels have also declined about 15 percent since 1975. Reductions in automobile emissions have been responsible for most of the improvement in carbon monoxide and ozone levels, and reductions in stationary source emissions for lower levels of sulfur dioxide. The reduction in total suspended particulate concentrations has occurred only since 1980, primarily as a result of lower emissions from industrial processes, a trend that may be linked to the economic slowdown.

Contrasting with this good news is increased information about the possible seriousness of problems that are not being adequately addressed—for example, acid rain, carbon dioxide buildup in the atmosphere, and indoor air pollution.

Water Quality. The information on water quality is less encouraging. Although there are many notable success stories, and the majority of the nation's waters are of adequate quality to support the uses that have been designated for them, most water bodies show little change in quality. Some modest improvements can be found in the quality of streams and the quality of estuaries, although in both cases there are also some areas of deterioration. For lakes and reservoirs, however, almost four times as much area has degraded in quality as has improved since 1972.

Probably the most important reasons for the lack of progress in controlling many water pollutants are that: very little effort has been made to control nonpoint sources such as stormwater runoff from cropland and urban streets; many municipal treatment plants still have not been completed; and many of the plants that have been built are apparently not being operated properly. Industrial firms have, on the whole, a much better record for controlling their discharges.

While the quality of surface water may be at least holding its own, groundwater quality may be deteriorating. There is almost no information that would support any firm conclusions about groundwater trends. However, there is increasing evidence that groundwater contamination from a variety of sources is being experienced in almost every state.

Waste Production. For the United States as a whole, as much as 60,000 pounds of waste are generated per person per year. Most of this, however, is produced in agriculture and mining and normally creates relatively minor environmental damage. Pollution-control efforts prevent many other wastes from entering the environment to cause damage. Nevertheless, the amount that continues to enter the environment is cause for concern.

Chapter 3: Natural Resources

Water. As society produces large volumes of waste, it also consumes large amounts of resources. For instance, an average of some 2,000 gallons of water per person per day is withdrawn from U.S. surface water and groundwater, 450 gallons of which is consumed. In the West, per capita withdrawals are almost twice the level in the East, and per capita consumption is 10 times as high. The high levels of withdrawal and consumption are creating substantial problems of instream flows and ground-water depletion. In the southern Colorado River basin, more water is consumed annually than is being naturally replenished.

Two-thirds of all the water withdrawn is supplied by freshwater streams, lakes, and reservoirs. One-fifth of the supply is groundwater. The remaining sources are saline water and a small percentage from reclaimed sewage. In many parts of the country, groundwater with-drawals, used primarily for irrigation purposes, exceed supplies, thus causing saltwater intrusion, other threats of contamination, land sur-face subsidence, and other alterations in the natural hydrologic cycle.

Land. The United States is relatively rich in land, with nearly 10 acres per capita—about 1.4 times the global average and several times more than in most developed countries. Nearly a third of this land (over 700 million acres) is owned by the federal government and an additional 7 percent is owned by state governments. The largest land uses are: forest, 30 percent; pasture and range, 29 percent; cropland, 17 percent; parks and recreation and wildlife areas, 9 percent; and built-up uses, 4 percent.

Land-use patterns vary both in space and in time. On the national scale, however, changes are quite gradual. Urban and built-up areas continue to expand, and the 1970s saw rapid increases in areas devoted to transportation, reservoirs, and park and recreation uses; nevertheless, as a percentage of national area, these uses remain small. A difficult to quantify but significant problem may arise as incompatible land uses are increasingly located adjacent to each other.

There is continuing concern about efficiency in land management. Cropland erosion continues to occur at an average annual rate of eight tons per acre. In some areas, however, including some of the most valuable agricultural lands, the erosion rate is much higher. The use of soil-conserving, reduced-tillage systems, however, has increased.

Croplands, Forests, and Rangelands. Croplands, forests, and rangelands contribute on the order of a quarter of a trillion dollars worth of products annually to the American economy. Crop production is well in excess of domestic demand, though the volume of agricultural ex-ports has fallen off since 1980. Much of the increase in total crop pro-duction and, more dramatically, labor productivity since 1965 has resulted from greater use of agricultural chemicals, irrigation, and machinery; crop output per acre of land and per unit of all inputs has increased as well, though not as rapidly nor as steadily as production per hour of labor.

Forests produce more timber than is cut each year. However, soft-wood species may be nearing the point at which they cannot sustain increases in demand. Forest damage by insects has been very high since the late 1970s, and a combination of pollution and natural factors may be implicated in a widespread slowing of tree growth in the eastern United States.

American rangeland is in very poor condition, with more than 60 percent of it producing forage in amounts less than half its natural potential; there is no evidence that rangeland quality is improving.

Special Areas. Wetlands, an extremely productive and valuable resource, have been destroyed at a rapid rate. Between the mid-1950s and mid-1970s, the area of freshwater vegetated wetlands dropped by over 11 percent, principally as a result of conversion to agriculture. Dredging and urbanization were the greatest causes of a nearly 8 percent reduction in saltwater vegetated wetlands. Riparian zones are particularly vulnerable, and the last addition to the Wild and Scenic River System was in January 1981. On the positive side, development of coastal barriers may be significantly slowed by the 1982 Coastal Barrier Resources Act, which eliminated federal flood insurance for development on such lands.

Wildlife. An encouraging note with respect to natural resources in the United States is the admittedly fragmentary and uncertain evidence that populations of many wildlife species may be slowly increasing. Information on wildlife status and trends is limited and imprecise. Reasonably good data are restricted to species of commercial or recreational interest. It is more difficult to assess the prospects of the vast majority of animals and plants, which do not enjoy special management programs.

Populations of many of the large mammals for which national figures are available are remaining stable or are increasing from previously diminished numbers. A smaller number of species is declining. The Interior Department's Breeding Bird Survey suggests that most bird species are maintaining stable populations, 12 percent are increasing, and 8.3 percent of bird species show declining trends.

The United States has a smaller percentage of endangered or threatened species than Europe. Approximately one-third of the U.S. species listed as endangered have recovery plans, some of which, like that for the whooping crane, show considerable promise. However, extinctions are still occurring in the United States and many species, particularly plants, that may require protection are not yet on the Federal Endangered Species list.

Landings of U.S. marine fisheries and shellfish stocks by U.S. vessels were worth $2.3 billion in 1982. Although the Fishery Conservation and Management Act of 1976 significantly lowered the foreign catch of U.S. marine stocks, overfishing is a present or potential problem for a number of species. The world-wide catch of marine species continues to rise despite the collapse of several important commercial stocks.

Some 190 million acres in the United States are protected in state and national parks and wildlife refuges. The expansion of these systems has slowed markedly since 1980, with no corresponding increase in private acquisitions for conservation purposes.

Energy. Since the oil embargo of 1973, patterns of energy consumption and production in the United States have shifted substantially. A steady increase in domestic production and consumption through the 1950s and 1960s, combined with falling real energy prices, was replaced in the 1970s by a leveling off of production and sharp reductions in consumption in response to price shocks in 1973-4 and 1979. Production of coal, nuclear power, and hydropower increased, while petroleum and natural gas production declined in the decade 1972 to 1982.

Energy consumption in 1983 has declined since the 1979 peak level by 12 percent. In the past two years, the United States has consumed less coal, petroleum, and natural gas, but more nuclear power and hydropower. Petroleum still contributes the largest share of energy usage, accounting for 43 percent of all energy used in 1983. Depressed economic activity and improved efficiency of energy use both played major roles in reducing total energy demand. U.S. dependence on imports has declined since 1978, particularly shifting away from OPEC supplies.

Recreation. Trends in outdoor recreation reflect growing interest in nature and changing attitudes toward leisure. Eighty-nine percent of Americans participated in one or more forms of outdoor recreation in 1982. Participation rates for most activities have increased slightly or moderately since 1960, and some activities, such as bicycling, camping, and jogging recorded substantial increases. Disparities in participation associated with race, age, sex, and income still exist, but are smaller than in 1960. Visitation to state and federal parks and recreation areas has increased dramatically since 1960; much of the increase is due to growth in the number of such areas.

Chapter 4: Identifying Issues

A society confronted with an assortment of environmental issues needs to take stock, to sort out and assess those issues. It needs an overall sense of what must be done and what priorities should be set. This chapter seeks to explore the kinds of problems that are most important and the characteristics that distinguish them.

Among the important characteristics that serve to define an issue are the seriousness of its adverse effects, the type of risk, its immediacy, the trade-offs or benefits associated with the risk-producing activity, the preventability or controllability of the threat or its effects, and the irreversibility of the effects.

The chapter uses six studies to distill a list of 47 major environmental problems. These are divided into four categories: (1) war, accidents, and natural disasters, (2) population growth and distribution, (3) contaminants, and (4) natural resource depletion. In addition, institutional problems were found to be of prime importance in dealing with problems in each of the categories, especially since it is often the case that technological solutions are known or available.

One of the studies, by the Swedish Royal Academy of Sciences, produced a list of the 10 most important issues: management of hazardous chemicals, processes, and wastes; depletion of tropical forests; desertification due to overgrazing; control of pathogens from human waste; river basin management; population growth and urbanization; acid deposition; species loss; protection of the marine environment; and the fuelwood crisis.

Chapter 5: Risk Assessment and Risk Control

Government today is being asked to control many more risks than it was asked to control in the past. Also, the types of risk it is attempting to control are more varied and more difficult to assess. Therefore, the methods used to perform risk assessments have drawn greatly increased attention in the past several years.

Risk assessment is the process of determining the adverse consequences that may result from the use of a technology or some other action. It typically includes three principal elements: (1) an estimate of the probability of a hazard occurring; (2) a determination of the types of hazard posed; and (3) an estimate of the number of people, wildlife, or other environmental elements likely to be exposed to the hazard and the number likely to suffer adverse consequences.

Almost all risk assessments are plagued by inadequate data. Adequate toxicity data are not available for the vast majority of chemicals now in use. As a result, even when data exist on the toxicity of a particular chemical, analysts often do not know whether taking regulatory action on the chemical will increase or reduce risk, because they do not know the toxicity of the substitutes that will be used if regulatory action restricts use of the chemical under examination.

The data on the exposure part of a risk assessment are likely to be even worse than for the hazard part. Exposure to air and water pollutants is not measured directly, but is usually calculated from mathematical models of typical sources. The mathematical models often lack accuracy, and the calculation of exposure usually ignores such important factors as the amount of time that people spend indoors or the fact that people change their place of residence. Current data on exposure in workplaces tend to be more accurate, but historical data on occupational exposures usually are either nonexistent or else based on very rough guesses.

A key to understanding and improving the risk-assessment process is to distinguish between those aspects of the process that are scientific and those that are matters of policy or personal values, and to appreciate their complex interrelationships.

Policy elements enter into a typical risk assessment in several ways. The lack of adequate data requires that assumptions be made about what data to use. In many regulatory agencies, the general rule is to use "worst-case" assumptions, in other words the data that result in the highest estimate of risk. The decision to use such assumptions is a policy decision. In the course of conducting a risk assessment, there are a number of specific decisions that must be made, such as how to extrapolate from toxicity tests on mice or rats to toxic risks for humans. For many of these decisions, scientific knowledge is not adequate to decide the correct course of action, and yet the choice may have a crucial effect on the outcome of the assessment. Because these decisions cannot be made on a scientific basis, they must be made on the basis of policy or personal values.

Priority-setting introduces still another set of policy elements into the risk-assessment process. The risk-assessment agenda—what risks to assess and how many resources to expend in the assessment—is usually a product of policy as much as science. So little is known about how priorities are actually set that it is difficult to tell what kinds of policies are involved or how often the policies are made explicit, but it seems certain that both science and policy are involved in the priority-setting process.

Although policy decisions will continue to play an important part in risk assessment, more data and better scientific knowledge would significantly improve the ability to assess risks. Tens of billions of dollars are being invested to comply with environmental standards, but little, comparatively, is being invested to improve the scientific basis for the standards, even though an improvement in risk assessment would be a major step in ensuring that compliance money is well spent.

Chapter 6: Controlling Cross-Media Pollutants

Pollutants may move from one medium to another, causing damage in each. Sulfur dioxide released to the air changes form and is deposited as acid rain on water and soil. Leaking landfills and surface impoundments contaminate air and water. U.S. environmental control laws and programs, however, seek to control pollutants as if they remain in the same medium. This narrow focus can undermine the effectiveness of the laws.

The cross-media approach has four dimensions paralleling the stages of pollution control: release from a source, waste management, cycling in the environment, and exposure of people and the environment.

The Source. An industrial plant often releases the same pollutant to more than one medium. But permits to control air emissions and water discharges are written at different times by different people, making it difficult to determine how risk from the pollutant can be reduced at the least cost.

Waste Management. End-of-the-pipe controls transfer some pollutants from one medium to another rather than reducing the amount of waste or placing pollutants in the medium where they will do the least damage. A treatment plant removes organic pollutants from the water by bubbling them into the air. Controls under air and water laws produce 118 million tons of sludge each year. Much of this sludge is put on the land, from which some pollutants then leach into groundwater or volatilize into the air.

Cycling. Once released from a factory or waste site, pollutants cycle through the environment. Standards governing pollutants do not reflect this movement. PCBs and metals deposited from the air are a major source of water pollutants in the Great Lakes. Increased air emissions of CO_2 may result in temperature changes that would, in turn, affect both land and water.

Exposure of Receptors. People may be exposed to the same pollutant in more than one way. A person may absorb a solvent through direct contact, breathe it in the air, and ingest it with drinking water, for example. Yet standards usually are based only on the ambient quality of air or water; they do not reflect the total exposure of a person, plant, animal, or ecosystem to a pollutant.

The U.S. Environmental Protection Agency was created in 1970 in an attempt to match the organization of U.S. pollution control efforts more closely with the growing perception of the environment as a single system. However, a desire to clean up air and water pollution quickly has reinforced the legal focus on separate controls for air and water.

The need to control toxic substances that move among media is again encouraging a more integrated approach to environmental control. This approach requires changes in research and monitoring, in pollution-control methods, and in environmental policy and institutions. Some changes can be made fairly easily; others will require longer-term efforts. Research and monitoring would concentrate on identifying the ways in which pollutants move, degrade, or accumulate. The focus of policy would shift from limiting releases into a single medium to reducing risk from a source, from a pollutant, or in a geographical area. Controls would encourage changing products or processes, segregating and recycling waste, treating waste, or securely containing wastes, rather than collecting pollutants and putting them on land. Institutions may need to be modified to carry out a cross-media approach. Three options are improved coordination, reorganization of environmental agencies, and consolidation of environmental laws.

Chapter 7: Water Resources

American water policy has entered a period of fundamental change. This change may be deceptive because it is gradual, sometimes imperceptible, and often at variance with public rhetoric. But cumulatively it adds up to a distinct departure from past practices and mindsets. The nation is moving from an era of water development to an era of water management. The change is forcing reexamination of three basic questions: What purposes will water be used for? Who will decide on the uses? And who will pay for the decisions?

Scarcity and competition are forcing the reallocation of water to different uses, in contrast to the traditional approach of developing new water supplies and facilities to meet new demands. Water facilities also are being modified to accommodate broader or newly recognized values.

These changes are specific responses to local problems, not coordinated answers developed out of any overriding theory or national policy. Given diminishing federal water budgets, state and local governments are turning, of necessity, to the least-cost, more comprehensive alternatives that national water-policy analysts long urged to no avail. Similarly, the user-pay philosophy is winning adherents not by force of rationality but by unavoidable budgetary and practical necessity. Change is stemming simply from adaptation to new conditions. The United States no longer has the unending water surpluses, overflowing capital budgets, or clear policy consensus to continue as before. With new participants, limited funds, and overcommitted water resources becoming common across the country, the individual areas affected are crafting answers responsive to local conditions.

This process of change is generating substantial and often heated conflicts among user groups. The search for resolutions to these conflicts, involving least-cost, user-supported actions that integrate quality and quantity, and sometimes transcend jurisdictional boundaries, cannot be mandated from Washington, D.C. But it can be either stimulated or discouraged by federal programs, and either nurtured or ignored at the state and local levels. The challenge today for policymakers at all levels is to recognize the validity of, and learn about the potential of, the shift to water management, and to understand how management often can harmonize the three basic values of water use—efficiency, equity, and environmental quality. Policymakers can then see how best to apply these broader lessons to the particular water problems each area faces.

Chapter 8: Intergovernmental Relations and Environmental Policy

Tension is inherent in intergovernmental relations, as governments at different levels pursue goals that often conflict. Tension is also exacerbated by the uneven distribution among governments of the benefits and costs of various programs. But there is also much cooperation. For as goals often conflict, they often coincide, and, in many programs, governments need one another's assistance to achieve their objectives.

Eliminating all intergovernmental conflict is an unrealistic goal. But conflict can be used to forge creative solutions to difficult problems. Techniques are needed to reduce intergovernmental tensions without losing their constructive and creative aspects.

Pragmatism reigns supreme in intergovernmental arrangements for environmental protection. The federal system has developed a wide variety of intergovernmental arrangements for controlling pollution and managing natural resources. The form the arrangements take often is a consequence of the nature of the problem being addressed and the relative strength of the interest groups influencing legislation.

It is evident that there are some tasks that either the federal government, on one hand, or state and local governments, on the other, are best suited to carry out. But there is no single framework for intergovernmental relations that guarantees the success of programs. Environmental problems differ too greatly, and too many uncontrollable variables are at work. Bargaining and politics are major influences on how successfully programs are implemented; the attitude of government officials, agency structure and administrative procedures, litigation, and available funding all shape the impact programs will have.

Greater realism in the planning and overseeing of environmental programs would make those programs more effective and enhance intergovernmental relations. Better procedures are needed for giving states a role in the development of federal regulations that guide delegated programs. In general, greater experimentation and risk taking by federal agencies in oversight and delegation is needed.

Many existing environmental programs seem to depend on litigation and other adversarial methods to resolve conflicts. In recent years, attention has shifted to nonadjudicatory approaches, such as mediation and negotiation, for resolving environmental disputes. Experience gained under some recently enacted state statutes should provide useful insights into how such approaches can best be used.

In the management of federal lands, the federal government needs to address the question of how much bargaining leverage to give to state and local governments. The degree of state and local influence should be determined by the nature of the lands involved, with less state and local influence appropriate for Defense Department lands and national parks than for multiple-use lands administered by the Bureau of Land Management. By the same token, state and local governments can help to promote national goals for federal lands and resources, as when national parks are threatened by developments on adjacent lands that are under the regulatory control of state or local governments.

Federal funding has played a key role in the success of U.S. environmental programs. Future federal deficits—even though environmental programs are but a miniscule portion of the federal budget—may severely compromise the effectiveness of both federally managed programs and state programs that receive federal assistance. If states are unable to do a good regulatory job because they have been given added responsibilities and fewer funds, the result could be a wide variation among states in applying environmental requirements—a result unacceptable to all interests affected by environmental regulations.

Overview

Environmental policy at mid-decade is suspended between old problems and new, between progress and retrogression, between cooperation and polarization.

It has become increasingly clear that the understanding of environmental problems in the early 1970s, when the framework for current governmental programs was established, has been superseded by knowledge gained during the past decade. The nation's environmental policies were formulated according to specific media—air, water, and land—and relatively circumscribed approaches to pollutants and their sources. In this report, we describe important changes in the nature of environmental problems and suggest broader, more inclusive ways of thinking about them. We suggest that the nation's environmental laws need readjusting as more is learned about how pollutants actually behave in the environment and as measuring capabilities improve to detect minute traces of toxic chemicals.

The chapters on cross-media analysis, risk assessment, water resources, and intergovernmental relations provide examples of more comprehensive ways of thinking about the environment that help to redefine environmental problems. New types of information and new policies will be needed to respond to these problems; yet not much new information is being collected, and the nation is just beginning to think about new policies.

The United States has made significant progress in many, if not all, environmental areas where laws and institutions have been explicitly devised to address specific problems. Most of the conventional air pollutants no longer pose a health threat to nearby communities; the majority of the nation's rivers are suitable for fishing and swimming; exposure to some specific toxic substances—lead, PCBs, chlorinated hydrocarbon pesticides such as DDT—has declined; the populations of many wildlife species are increasing. Progress on these problems should be a source of significant encouragement. The broad decline in exposure to some toxic substances, as shown by data compiled for the first time in this report, represents a clear success story for past regulatory efforts.

1

But the progress made should not obscure the many points of controversy and vulnerability in on-going environmental programs. Budget cuts at both the federal and state levels over the past few years have weakened environmental programs. In fact, the Environmental Protection Agency's (EPA's) budget in real terms and its staff levels are what they were in the early 1970s, before major new missions were added to the agency's mandate. Environmental monitoring and research are inadequate to evaluate existing programs or to identify new problems. Many potentially harmful toxic substances are not adequately monitored and thus there is no way to assess their risks.

The deadlines for reauthorizing each of the major federal pollution control laws have expired, but there has been little or no progress in revising and reauthorizing them. Temporary reauthorizations have extended the statutes from year-to-year or month-to-month. The lengthy congressional debates over the Clean Air Act and the Clean Water Act have not produced any new legislation, and the debate has not started on some of the other statutes.

Lack of progress on reauthorization reflects an underlying political stalemate at the national level. The two major contending forces—the concerned industrial and environmental groups—each have sufficient power to block new legislation. Neither has enough political strength to pass legislation. The good side of this stalemate is that it has encouraged dialogue between industry and environmentalists, because only on those matters where there is agreement can progress be made. The bad side is the lack of congressional action, with the resulting uncertainty about existing programs and failure to develop new ones.

THE NEED FOR NEW ENVIRONMENTAL POLICIES

The acid rain problem vividly demonstrates the need for new approaches to environmental management. Rather than an aberration, acid rain is probably the prototype of the new environmental problems that increasingly will confront the nation. It is typical in at least three respects:

- Neither the data nor the scientific knowledge exists to delineate the causes or effects of acid rain with precision. There is sufficient evidence regarding both cause and effect to persuade many people that action to remedy the problem should be taken now, but the evidence is far from certain or precise.
- The possible costs of either action or inaction are very large. Most of the control plans for acid rain would cost billions of dollars per

year. But the cost of not taking action may be as great or greater. If, in fact, acid rain will eliminate life in many lakes, stunt or kill forest growth, permanently alter the ecology of large areas, and pose potential threats to human health, then the costs of not dealing with the problem are extremely high.

- Existing laws and institutions are not adequate to deal with the acid rain problem. The Clean Air Act is designed to deal with air impacts of pollutants in the vicinity of pollution sources. In contrast, acid rain involves water and soil impacts in areas hundreds or thousands of miles away from the pollution sources. Furthermore, acid rain is an international problem for the United States, directly and indirectly—directly in that pollution emitted in the United States affects Canada and vice versa, indirectly in that action or the lack thereof by the United States has an impact on whether other nations will do anything to curb the causes of acid precipitation. International institutions for cooperation, such as the Organisation for Economic Cooperation and Development (OECD) and the International Joint Commission, have not been adequate to deal with the problem.

Uncertainty about cause and effect, large costs of action or inaction, inadequacy of laws and institutions—these three characteristics are the hallmarks of the new environmental problems facing the United States and many other nations. New policy initiatives will be necessary to deal with them.

Throughout this report, we have identified the need to reexamine the existing institutional structures for dealing with environmental problems. Not only are new institutions necessary to deal with a new set of problems, but existing institutions may need to be overhauled to promote greater integration and efficiency and to reduce unnecessary conflict.

One of the underlying themes of this report is that existing institutions are inadequate because they are too fragmented. Efforts to provide adequate supplies of water are handicapped because there is little relationship between water-supply programs and water-quality programs, with the result, for example, that unchecked groundwater pumping can lead to saline intrusion in coastal areas. Efforts to deal with pollution from toxic substances are undercut by isolated institutions created to deal with air, land, and water pollution, without recognition of the cross-media nature of the toxics problem. There is a discordant lack of correspondence

between the ecological unity of the natural world and the fragmentation of the institutions that have been developed to deal with that world.
The discord poses a threat to the effectiveness and efficiency of current
environmental programs.

Many have criticized the lack of efficiency of environmental programs,
and rightly so. Improved monitoring and research would improve their
efficiency. Institutional changes would also. For example, in several environmental areas, such as water allocation and energy conservation, use
of market pricing or other market-like mechanisms would significantly
improve both the efficiency and the effectiveness of current efforts.

Toxics and the Cross-Media Problem

The fundamental shift in concern from a few large-volume conventional
pollutants to the numerous toxic substances (organic chemicals and
metals) that started about ten years ago has been accepted in theory
but has yet to be fully implemented. Very few national standards for
toxic substances exist, and most permits for individual pollution sources
do not cover these substances. The implications of the new focus are
just beginning to get attention.

The inadequacy of information about toxics is a problem of fundamental importance. Not only are there very few monitoring data on toxics
but information on the toxicity of new and existing chemicals is frequently lacking. A 1984 report by the National Academy of Sciences
(NAS), the first systematic attempt to analyze the availability of toxicity
data on chemicals, showed that less than 2 percent have been sufficiently
tested to allow a complete health-hazard assessment. No toxicity information at all is available for more than 70 percent of commercial
chemicals. Chemical industry representatives claim, however, that the
NAS report exaggerates the lack of data because it does not cover confidential test data in the possession of chemical firms.

The focus on toxic substances has raised a number of other policy
questions. Probably of greatest importance is the continued viability
of the existing medium-specific approach to pollution control, in which
air pollution regulations are formulated in isolation from water pollution regulations and neither air nor water programs adequately consider
land-disposal problems. The tendency of toxics to be found in more
than one part of the environment and to be readily transferable from
air to water to land casts doubt on the effectiveness of a medium-specific
approach. Scientific findings are increasingly revealing that major water-
pollution problems are due to air pollutants being deposited in water;

at the same time, studies in Philadelphia and elsewhere are revealing that municipal plants to treat water pollution are major sources of air pollution from volatile organic chemicals. Instead of reducing human and environmental exposure to toxics, much of the existing control effort may simply be shifting pollutants from one part of the environment to another.

Water

Overall, the U.S. water challenge can be summarized by asking whether the quality, quantity, and rate of consumption of water can be managed so as to meet water needs efficiently and equitably. This overall formulation covers a number of separable but interrelated policy challenges. How is water quantity to be related to water-quality concerns? How is groundwater contamination to be prevented? How should adequate instream flows be preserved for recreation and fish and wildlife protection? How is nonpoint source water pollution to be controlled? How safe is the nation's drinking water and what, if anything, should be done to make it safer?

These are mostly management and policy problems, not technical ones. With the notable exception of methods for cleaning contaminated groundwater aquifers, technology is available to address these problems.

For many aspects of the water problem, however, there is currently an institutional and policy vacuum. The institutional framework for planning, evaluating, and funding water-resource projects was eliminated in 1981 and no new framework has been proposed. There is no policy for dealing with groundwater at either the national or state level, although a few states, such as Arizona, have adopted innovative groundwater policies. The first hesitant steps for controlling nonpoint-source water pollution were considered in Congress in 1983, but there is still no policy.

Land

Land uses in many parts of the United States are changing in response to new economic and demographic movements. A heightened sense of place-consciousness in large and small cities has resulted in unprecedented conservation and rehabilitation of old buildings. Reinforced by higher comparative costs of new construction and favorable federal tax incentives, preservation efforts are finding new uses for old buildings—electronics firms have moved into the 19th-century factories of

Massachusetts' mill towns.

Farmland losses to parcelation for country living and to low-density urban development around cities are changing the landscape, population mix, and regional economies of innumerable areas of the country. Some of the most beautiful and distinctive pastoral landscapes, from Loudoun County, Virginia, to the flower farms of San Diego County, California, are already characterized by speculator landholdings that make significant use changes inevitable. The growing popularity of agricultural districts, programs to provide easements on farmland or purchase development rights, and land trusts is creating new possibilities for many rural areas to conserve farms and forestlands.

Parts of the nation's most productive agricultural lands, in the Mississippi Valley, for example, are suffering severe soil erosion, although the most serious soil losses are confined to a minority of the nation's cultivated land. Growing awareness of the significance and costs of soil erosion, estimated to total upwards of $3 billion per year in off-farm impacts alone (through sediment loading of streams and rivers, accelerated obsolescence of dams and navigation aids, and so on), combined with widespread interest in curtailing farm production surpluses, creates new potential for integrating soil conservation efforts with such production-reducing measures as land set-asides. However, experience with the Payment-in-Kind (PIK) program, in which much land withdrawn from production saw heavier erosion as wind and water battered the unplanted acreage, reveals the need for effective measures to ensure that cover crops or grasses are grown on temporarily withdrawn lands. Some highly erodible land should be permanently planted in trees, and federal policy should discourage plowing or clearing of new land that is likely to be subject to high rates of soil erosion.

One-third of the land in the United States is owned by the federal government; the management and use of that land has provoked controversy for more than 200 years. Although the Reagan administration has succeeded in quelling the "sagebrush rebellion," there are still basic disputes about the purpose and direction of public land management.

The state role in decisions about federal lands has generally increased over the past decade. It was dealt a setback in 1984, however, when the Supreme Court ruled that federal sales of oil leases on the outer continental shelf are not subject to state review under the Coastal Zone Management Act. This decision, combined with the recent weakening of the planning processes for public lands instituted in the 1970s, has created more uncertainty about the role of the states than has existed in the past decade.

The management of public lands in Alaska is a uniquely important concern. When the Alaska National Interest Lands Conservation Act was passed by Congress in 1980, the issue of federal lands in Alaska faded from the national agenda. There is, however, a real possibility that conservation opportunities may be lost incrementally but irreversibly by the way roads are planned, uses are assigned, and the land is managed. The resources and beauty of the state are too valuable to allow this to happen through lack of attention.

The states and the federal government play vital roles in providing outdoor recreation. The recreation planning functions of the federal government have been disbanded, but there remains a pressing need to review the federal, state, local, and private resources available for outdoor recreation and how they relate to present and projected demands. In this, as in many other policy areas, decisions are being made on an *ad hoc* basis, without adequate knowledge of the current situation or a clear vision of the goals of public policy.

International Issues

Three basic types of international environmental issues face the United States. These are: (1) dealing with domestically important issues that require the cooperation of other nations to solve; (2) dealing with areas of the world that are under some sort of international jurisdiction; and (3) helping less-developed countries grapple with their environmental problems.

An increasing number of issues that pose a threat to the U.S. environment can only be dealt with internationally. Potential threats to global climate, such as ozone depletion and carbon dioxide build-up, are the clearest examples. Actions by the United States alone will be insufficient to deal with these problems: they require concerted action by a number of nations. International action is also necessary to deal adequately with items that are traded in international commerce, such as toxic chemicals.

Several regions of the world, such as oceans and the Antarctic, are in whole or part international territory. These areas are becoming increasingly important as more is learned about their potential as sources of strategic materials. Balancing environmental concerns with the economic advantages of development and exploitation will be a major, continuing issue for these areas.

Helping less-developed nations to deal with the immense environmental problems that they face is not just a matter of morality or altruism.

The implications for the United States of environmental degradation in the third world are very direct. To take only one prominent example, ecological instability contributes to political instability in Central America. As long as population growth outstrips the capacity of less-developed countries to support their people, as long as soil erosion undermines their capability to provide enough food, and as long as forest destruction deprives the local population of fuel, the citizens of these countries will be a potential source of revolutionary discontent.

ASSESSING CURRENT EFFORTS TO IMPROVE ENVIRONMENTAL QUALITY

The turbulence and disorder in federal environmental agencies has subsided in the years since we issued *State of the Environment 1982*. The administration of national environmental laws has stabilized. The turnaround at the EPA from conditions of two years ago is particularly noteworthy. William D. Ruckelshaus presides over a reinvigorated agency whose morale and integrity have been restored by one of the most impressive rescues on record. At the Department of the Interior, Secretary William P. Clark has reopened lines of communication to members of Congress, the press, and environmentalists, and he has reconsidered controversial policies on outer-continental-shelf oil and gas leasing, land purchases for national parks, and coal leasing.

Within the context of an administration still committed to reducing regulatory burdens on the economy and to severely reducing expenditures for a variety of environmental programs, something like a return to normal patterns of management and communication has occurred. That national environmental goals and environmental standards emerged largely unscathed from the first two years of the Reagan administration is itself a measure of the depth of the nation's commitment to environmental progress and public support for the nation's basic environmental charters. In fact, as opinion polls clearly show, there is greater public support for environmental goals now than at any time since the early 1970s.

The justification offered for many of the cuts in federal expenditures has been to encourage states to do more. In the final chapter of this report, we examine the federal system to shed light on the kinds of issues to which state responses are possible and appropriate, as well as on the structure of federal policy necessary to ensure uniformity where 50 separate policies would be impractical. Although no conclusive data are available, it appears that federal cuts are weakening state programs rather than strengthening them. However, the withdrawal of federal support for water-resource planning and the decline in federal aid for water-resource development projects may be one factor forcing states to explore management options largely considered anathema in the past.

Quantitative Indicators of Environmental Quality

The quantitative indicators of environmental quality presented in this report show a picture very similar to that depicted in *State of the Environment 1982*. This is not surprising, for most major changes in the natural environment take much more than two years to occur.

In reviewing the data, one should keep in mind the long time lag between policy changes and changes in the data. Typically, it will take at least a year or two before changes in policy result in changes in behavior by polluters or others whose activities determine environmental quality. It may be several more years before the changes in behavior result in environmental changes. And it takes at least two years to collect, analyze, and report data on environmental changes. Thus, the data in this report are probably more reflective of the environmental policies of past administrations than of the Reagan administration, although some of them reflect the downturn in industrial production resulting from the 1981–82 recession.

Air quality has continued to improve, and most areas of the country are in compliance with the primary standards for most of the traditional pollutants. There are 94 million people, however, living in areas that still exceed the ozone standard.

Water quality, on balance, has remained constant, as has been true for the past decade. As with air, this finding is based on the traditional measures of pollution and does not take into account pollution from toxic substances. There are simply not enough monitoring data to know whether the toxics problem is getting better or worse.

Although land-use patterns can change rapidly in particular localities, overall national land trends tend to conceal these local shifts. One notable exception is the decline in wetlands. Between the mid-1950s and mid-1970s, the area of freshwater vegetated wetlands dropped by over 11 percent, principally as a result of conversion to agriculture.

The status of wildlife in the United States is mixed, and reliable information on many species is not available. Populations of game birds and animals are generally doing well, in part because of the success of wildlife management programs. A number of species of plants and animals, however, continue to be in danger of extinction, and many are not being adequately protected.

Compliance with Existing Environmental Laws

In the absence of progress on environmental legislation, compliance with existing regulations determines the direction and pace of ongoing programs. There are no adequate data nationwide to indicate the extent of compliance with existing pollution-control regulations. EPA figures show that more than 90 percent of industrial facilities are in compliance with air and water regulations. But these figures fail to take account of the size of the facility, and they also consider being on schedule in meeting a compliance order the same as being "in compliance," so they are not very helpful in ascertaining the true state of affairs.

Recent studies by the General Accounting Office (GAO) show substantial noncompliance. A GAO survey of wastewater dischargers found widespread, frequent, and significant noncompliance wth Clean Water Act permit limits. Of the dischargers surveyed, 82 percent exceeded their permits at least once during an 18-month period. About 30 percent were in significant noncompliance, exceeding one or more permit limits by 50 percent or more in at least four consecutive months. Municipalities were almost twice as likely to be in significant noncompliance as industries.

EPA Administrator Ruckelshaus has expressed major concern about the inadequacy of current federal enforcement efforts. Even if EPA enforcement activity resumes its pre-1981 pace, major problems will remain. Enforcement is still focused on getting companies and municipalities to install pollution-control equipment. Monitoring to ensure that the equipment is operated correctly and continuously is often neglected. As the number of pollution sources that have installed equipment rises, the neglect of operation and maintenance requirements becomes an ever greater problem.

Need for Data and Scientific Knowledge

Knowledge and information are the bedrock on which sound environmental policies must be based. This bedrock, however, currently is not adequate to evaluate existing environmental policies or to formulate new ones.

The most obvious problem, and perhaps the most serious, is the inadequacy of the programs for monitoring the condition of the nation's environment. In *State of the Environment 1982*, we discussed the shortcomings of monitoring data and programs. The situation has not improved in the two years since that report. If anything, budget cuts have weakened still further the ability to assess the current status of environmental conditions and whether conditions are improving or deteriorating.

Research on the causes and effects of environmental problems is similarly neglected. In EPA, the research program is in better shape than it was two years ago, and Administrator Ruckelshaus has recognized the need to fund research on problems that are not on the immediate regulatory agenda. But the disparity between the effort expended to comply with environmental regulations and the effort expended to ascertain whether the regulations make sense remains great. Meanwhile, the government and the public will continue to be caught unaware by new issues until the research effort is adequate to anticipate new problems and to assess the relative importance of the problems that have been identified.

Policy-oriented research is as necessary for environmental programs as is pure scientific research. For example, as the risk-assessment chapter in this report shows, assessing the risk of chemical hazards in the environment involves both scientific knowledge and policy decisions. Research on what these policy decisions are and how they should be made is as important for improving risk assessment as is scientific research. Similarly, policy-oriented research is necessary to evaluate the implementation of current programs, to find out whether they are really working. Very little of this research is now being done.

POLARIZATION AND COOPERATION

The nation needs new models to break the gridlock of environmental policymaking in a variety of areas. Cooperation between the public and private sectors and between business leaders and environmentalists is no longer desirable simply to reduce the shrillness and stridency of disagreement. Increasingly, it is essential if anything is to get done.

Part of the inefficiency of environmental programs is due to the amount of conflict they engender. Siting hazardous waste facilities or even cleaning up existing hazardous waste dumps, for example, is an inefficient process because every step is fraught with argument and conflict. Part of the solution is to develop improved institutions and methods for dealing with conflict. In the past few years, experiments with such methods as mediation and negotiation have demonstrated that improved ways of dealing with conflict are possible. In the international arena, improved ways of dealing with conflict are desperately needed, but there has not been the same experimentation, and new ideas and institutions have not been forthcoming.

New policy approaches also are necessary to reduce conflict. They must include the recognition that simple, single-thrust strategies for improving the environment are insufficient. An exclusive emphasis on regulatory approaches is no more adequate to present circumstances than is an exclusive emphasis on creating incentives for better environmental performance without backing up such incentives with strong enforcement. The efforts of the public and private sector must be harnessed so that they work toward the same goals.

It will not be easy to bring such new approaches to fruition. Since 1981, environmental protection has become a partisan political issue to a degree that it never was before. The climate is not conducive to reexamination of existing programs or to policy innovations, though both are badly needed.

Environmental quality *should* be a political issue, although in a quite different sense than as a tool for partisan jockeying. It should be political in the sense that it demands the collective attention and resources of the body politic and the wisdom and dedication of political representatives. Addressing environmental problems can be a challenge that calls forth a sense of common purpose and shared interest among diverse institutions and nations. The effort to improve environmental quality has the potential to create more unity in the human community, in the United States and in the world, and to bring forth the best qualities of political institutions. Environment as an issue is a challenge to the human spirit as well as an effort to protect natural surroundings.

The intent of this report is to help understand and meet the environmental challenge. In essence, its message is that the nation needs to recognize a new configuration of environmental problems that calls for novel responses. The United States must acknowledge the deficiences of some existing environmental programs without in any way abandoning the goals that characterize such programs and without overlooking the fact that experience with these programs has allowed us to understand the state of the environment much more clearly than we did a decade ago.

William K. Reilly
President
The Conservation Foundation
June 1984

PART I
Status and Trends

Chapter 1
Underlying Trends

Like the ever-presence of death and taxes, population size and economic health underpin any social trend, including those of resource consumption and environmental degradation. The number of people and the size and structure of the economy in any society determine how much water, energy, and land are used and, in that usage, how much and what type of wastes are generated—in short, the overall demands placed by a society on its environment. Although the trends since 1981 are an aberration, over the long term the way people react to current conditions and perceived trends—the force of public opinion—in turn determines the vigor, in both policies and moneys, of governmental response.

Thus, an assessment of environmental status and trends starts with a review of the underlying forces shaping environmental conditions—population growth, economic development, public opinion, and environmental expenditures. How these underlying forces manifest themselves in the United States helps explain present environmental conditions, but the situation in this country cannot be examined in isolation. Increasingly, national borders become less relevant; indeed, many environmental issues the United States faces, such as carbon dioxide buildup and extinction of migratory wildlife species, are global in nature—they cannot be solved by one nation alone. Hence, international economic and population phenomena are of concern for what they portend for environmental quality not only in other countries but in this country as well.

POPULATION

In 1983, the U.S. population reached an estimated 234.2 million, as the population growth rate reached its lowest level since the 1930s.[1] Since 1981, the growth rate has been less than 1 percent per year (figure 1.1). Immigration accounts for about one-fourth of the annual population growth, up from one-tenth in 1960.[2] The increase in immigration's

13

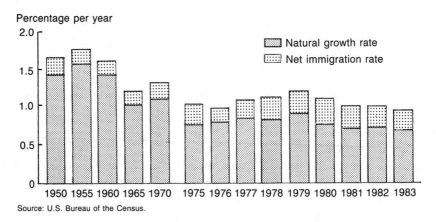

Figure 1.1
U.S. Population Growth Rates,
1950–1983

Source: U.S. Bureau of the Census.

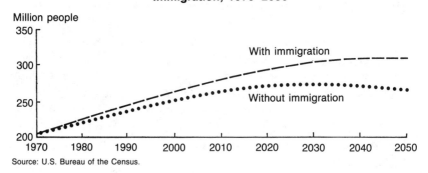

Figure 1.2
U.S. Population Projections, with and without
Immigration, 1970–2050

Source: U.S. Bureau of the Census.

share arises less from increased immigration rates (the net immigration only increased from 0.18 percent of the population to 0.20 percent of the population in the two decades between 1955–1959 and 1975–1979, although it jumped to 0.24 percent in the 1980s) than from reduced "natural" growth rates.*[3] American women continue to bear fewer children than their mothers did.

Since 1972, in fact, the average number of children born to an American woman during her child-bearing years (the "total fertility rate") has been smaller than the number (2.1) required to eventually reach zero population growth or population replacement.[4] In 1983, the U.S. total fertility rate was approximately 1.8.[5] However, with so many women still in their child-bearing years, another 40 to 50 years of similarly low fertility rates are needed for the natural growth rate to fall to zero (figure 1.2). If net immigration continues at about half a million people per year, zero population growth will be delayed an additional 30 to 40 years. Therefore, the chances of the United States reaching zero population growth until well into the next century are slim.

Worldwide, the average population growth rate is 1.8 percent per year (figure 1.3), equivalent to adding more than the entire population of the United States to the planet every three years. However, the average growth rate, like any average, masks significant differences between more-developed and less-developed countries. All of the more-developed countries show low population growth rates. In Western Europe, for instance, the population growth rate has remained under 0.7 percent per year for the past 34 years. In 12 European countries, the current growth rate is less than 0.2 percent, and in half of these it is zero or negative.[6] The less-developed countries, by constrast, continue to experience very high fertility and population growth rates, although these too have diminished a bit during the past decade. On average, the birth rate in less-developed countries is 2.2 times that of their more-developed counterparts.[7] The natural population growth rate approximates 2.1 percent per year, 3.5 times the rate in more-developed countries.†

As a result, 92 percent of the increase in the world's population between 1983 and 2000 is projected to occur in less-developed countries.[9]

---

* A country's natural growth rate is the number of births minus the number of deaths occurring during a year, divided by the total population.

† China is one of the few less-developed countries that successfully controls its population growth. If China is not included in the statistics for less-developed countries, their average natural growth rate increases from 2.1 to 2.4 percent per year and their birth rate averages 2.5, rather than 2.2, times that of more-developed countries.[8]

They will contain about four-fifths of the world's total population by then, about 5 billion people, up more than 1.3 billion from 1983 (figure 1.4). By 2020, population increases of over 80 percent are projected for developing nations as a whole.

Distribution

Within the United States are two major population-distribution trends. The first is regional shifts—people moving primarily from the North Central and Northeast states to the South and the West. During the 1970s, Wyoming, Arizona, Nevada, Texas, and Florida grew most rapidly, whereas New York, the District of Columbia, and Rhode Island all experienced net decreases in population.[10] Since 1980, Alaska, Florida, Nevada, Texas, and Oklahoma have grown fastest, while Michigan and the District of Columbia have lost over 3 percent of their population; eight other states, all but one of which are in the central region, have lost more than 1 percent.[11]

The second trend relates to flight from larger cities and larger metropolitan areas. A change may have occured in this trend since 1980. During the 1970s, although the percentage of people living in the 318 areas designated as standard metropolitan statistical areas (SMSAs) did not change appreciably—about 75 percent—there were significant shifts from the larger to the smaller areas.* The larger SMSAs, particularly those located in the northern and eastern parts of the country, grew slowly if at all.[13] The smaller SMSAs, particularly those located in the western and southern regions, grew faster.

The number of people living in cities with more than 10,000 people dropped from 53 percent to 49 percent of the total population between 1970 and 1980.[14] Again, the trend was most apparent in the largest cities. Cities with a population over 500,000 dropped from 15.7 to 12.5 percent of the total population during this period. Smaller cities—with populations between 10,000 and 250,000—lost only 0.6 percent, falling from 25.0 percent to 24.4 percent.

Between 1980 and 1982, these trends seem to have modified. The New York metropolitan area, for instance, gained 0.3 percent in population after losing 3.6 percent during the decade of the 1970s.[15] Overall, those SMSAs having more than 5 million people have almost doubled their rate of growth (and those in the north are growing again after

---

* Between 1970 and 1980, 75 additional SMSAs were designated. If they are excluded, only 68.6 percent of the 1970 population lived in SMSAs designated as such in that year.[12]

Figure 1.3
World Population Growth Rates,
by Regional Groupings, 1983

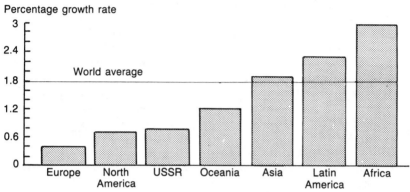

Source: Population Reference Bureau.

Figure 1.4
World Population Projections,
by Regional Groupings, 1983–2020

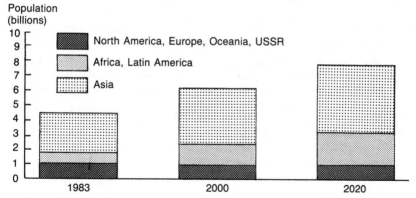

Source: Population Reference Bureau.

losing population during the 1970s). Those containing 1 to 5 million people are growing somewhat faster than they did during the 1970s, those containing 100,000 to 1 million people are growing somewhat more slowly, and those containing less than 100,000 people are generally growing about a third faster than they did during the 1970s.[16] It is not only the larger metropolitan areas that are performing better but generally their central cities as well. On the average, these cities are gaining population, after suffering net losses during the 1970s.[17] Even in the North, the rate of flight from the larger central cities has dropped significantly from its earlier levels.[18]

Population growth patterns in cities and metropolitan areas are reflected by trends in suburban and nonmetropolitan areas. The counterpart of the decline of central cities during the 1970s was in part a flight to the suburbs.

From 1970 to 1980, the average population increases for the 318 SMSAs were only 0.2 percent for the central cities versus 18.2 percent in the suburbs.[19] The most dramatic shift, however, was in nonmetropolitan-area growth: For the first time in the nation's history, nonmetropolitan areas grew faster than the total U.S. population grew, increasing 15.1 percent from 1970 to 1980.[20] But these trends have also changed. From 1980 to 1982, the growth rate in nonmetropolitan areas fell substantially from the levels it had reached in the 1970s.[21] The drop was steepest in those counties adjacent to metropolitan areas.[22] They are now growing at about the same rate as the country as a whole.

What trends will occur in the future? To some extent the answer depends on who is asked. The U.S. Bureau of the Census, for example, tends to make population projections that assume future trends will be the same as those experienced in the recent past. The bureau, then, sees the West and the South continuing to blossom, and the Northeast and North Central regions continuing to wilt.[23] The National Planning Association (NPA) also makes population projections but bases its projections on both economic and demographic factors. The NPA is more optimistic about the potential for employment growth in the Northeast and North Central states and more impressed by the constraints placed on growth by scarce water supplies in the arid Southwest.[24] Thus, NPA projects that growth rates in the West and the South will taper off, while those in the rest of the country will rebound slightly from the low rate of the past decade.

In other parts of the world, the trends in distribution appear to be less ambiguous. In the less-developed countries, only 29 percent of the population currently lives in urban areas (compared to over 70 percent in more-developed nations), but people are flocking to the cities.[25] The population of metropolitan Mexico City increased 64 percent (from 9.2 million to 15.1 million) between 1970 and 1980 and is now about the same size as the New York City metropolitan area.[26] If current trends continue, Mexico City will be the world's largest city by the year 2000, bulging with 25 to 30 million people.[27] Similarly, São Paulo, Shanghai, Beijing, and Rio de Janiero may well double their populations by the turn of the century.[28]

Implications of Population Trends

For the United States and similar countries, the environmental implications of population trends are both positive and negative. On the positive side, reduced growth rates auger well for lowered resource consumption, crowding, and pollution. In the United States, the shift in population distribution means fewer people living in the larger central cities where the highest pollution levels have been experienced in the past. The new booming Sunbelt regions are also those that tend to house less industrial manufacturing; even where such plants are constructed, they tend to be newer and, therefore, less polluting. However, as is indicated in chapter 2, it is no longer the industrial pollutants that are creating the most serious pollution problems but smog often caused by automobile emissions. The southern and western cities are as likely to experience these problems as the older cities in the northeast, and may be even more likely.

The shift is also placing stresses on limited water supplies. Many of the fastest-growing states are already short of water. For instance, as is pointed out in chapter 3, Arizona and the rest of the southern Colorado River basin consume more water than is naturally available. The region will have trouble reaching a hydrological balance even with substantial imports from the rest of the the Colorado River. This population dispersion is also eating up prime farmland and valuable wildlife habitat, through housing and commercial conversions, and creating conflicts with other rural land uses.

In less-developed countries, few positive implications of current population trends exist. The high population growth rates put severe pressure on natural resources, economic growth, and social and political stability in these countries. Problems of rapid deforestation and significant erosion, caused in large part by population pressures, cry for solutions.[29] And the monumental crowding in cities such as Mexico City already produces severe air pollution, water pollution, and water scarcities.[30] The struggle with these immediate problems threatens any real progress for these countries in economic growth and enhanced quality of life.

THE ECONOMY

The U.S. economy has begun to grow again after suffering the most severe recession since the end of World War II.[31] Although the nominal value of U.S. gross national product (GNP) passed 3 trillion dollars in 1982, that year and the next saw more people in the United States unemployed than at any time since the 1930s—over 10.5 million.[32]* The rate of economic growth (as measured by real, inflation-adjusted GNP) has averaged less than 1 percent a year since 1979. However, the recession did significantly reduce the inflation rate. The rate of change in the consumer price index dropped from over 13 percent in 1979 to under 4 percent in 1982 and 1983.[34]

The recovery has not come about quite as expected.[35] Under the economic policies espoused in 1981, substantial tax cuts, particularly for higher-income earners, were supposed to enhance savings that would be used, by businesses, to finance new investments (which also received substantial tax breaks). These new investments, in turn, were to stimulate increased production, improved productivity, and, eventually, lower prices. The second act of the policy script called for reduced government expenditures to free more funds for business investment as well as remove some perceived obstacles to business growth. The expected denouement was lower-than-normal government expenditures and a spurt in business investment.

In fact, however, savings rates did not increase after the enactment of the Economic Recovery Tax Act of 1981.[36] People apparently preferred to spend their additional disposable income rather than save it, in spite of historically high interest rates. And government expenditures—especially for defense and social security—reached new highs and created record deficits. As a result, it has been not business investment, but rather unusually large consumer and government expen-

---

* Inflation pushed the nominal value of GNP over 3 trillion dollars in 1982. When the statistics are adjusted to remove the effects of price changes, the real GNP actually fell from 1981 to 1982.[33]

ditures that have led the economy.[37] Business investment has been trying hard to regain its normal level.

Few informed observers have much hope that the large deficits will disappear soon.[38] Demographic and economic realities argue for continued threats of deficits in the income security programs. Social Security and Medicare together now comprise nearly one-half of federal nondefense spending (and are projected to account for over three-fourths of the increase in budget outlays over the next five years).[39] The increased emphasis on defense means steadily higher defense expenditures as recently initiated programs now begin to mature. The fastest-growing area of expenditure, interest on the size of that debt, can only grow more rapidly because of the unprecedented size of that debt. And the 1981 changes in the tax code will keep the growth in federal revenues below its level of the past two decades.

Obviously, the U.S. economy has an uncertain future. Some economists project slow growth rates until the high budget deficits are brought under control.[40] The Congressional Budget Office, however, projects little change in average annual growth rates (absent such economic shocks as energy embargoes or crop failures); their "baseline projection" shows a real GNP growth rate of between 3.3 and 5.4 percent per year through 1989, similar to those of the past two decades.[41]

Implications of Economic Trends

What do these trends imply about environmental conditions? At the aggregate level, an answer is difficult. The economic slowdown, for all of its costs, may have temporarily benefited the environment. Lower industrial production probably resulted in less industrial pollution and less energy consumption. Reduced production in the "smokestack" industries is reflected in an employment loss of 565,000 jobs (29 percent) between 1979 and 1983.[42*] Only half of these are expected to be regained by 1987. Reduced income presumably forced people to drive less, again lessening automobile emissions and lowering gasoline consumption (figure 1.5). On the other hand, budget reductions significantly hampered some environmental agencies and programs.

How any future economic growth affects environmental quality depends on the pattern of growth. To support a viable growth path,

---

* The smokestack industries in this analysis include motor vehicles and equipment; steel-mill products; aluminum; primary copper, lead, and zinc; farm machinery; and machine tools.

Figure 1.5
Miles Traveled and Gasoline Consumed by
Passenger Cars, 1967–1982

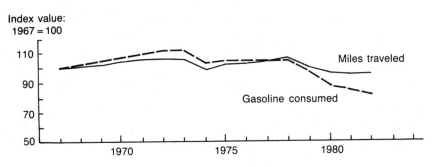

Source: U.S. Department of Energy.

Figure 1.6
Growth in U.S. Industrial Output, by
Industrial Category, 1974–1982

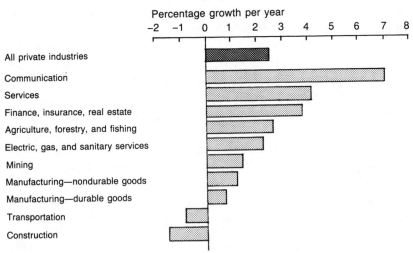

Source: U.S. Department of Commerce.

business investment will have to grow rapidly.* The increased investment by businesses, if realized, should have mostly positive environmental implications. Much new money will likely be invested in relatively
"clean industries"—communications, services, finance, and trade, the
fastest-growing economic sectors (figure 1.6). Even within the manufacturing sector, the growth should be primarily in the clean, technology-
based industries, such as computers and communications equipment,
rather than in smokestack industries (figure 1.7).† And new plants built
in the smokestack industries should be cleaner than the old plants because
of federal pollution-control requirements.[44]

The possible negative environmental implications of a period of strong
growth would result primarily from the probable sites of new facilities.
These may be built outside established industrial areas, sometimes consuming large amounts of prime agricultural land or wildlife habitat.
However, recent evidence suggests that employment in nonmetropolitan
areas is, like population, growing less rapidly than it did during the
1970s.[45]

The slow growth of the traditional industrial base in the Middle Atlantic and North Central states may nevertheless continue to create some
severe economic hardships in these areas.[46] The region made up of
Michigan, Ohio, Indiana, Illinois, and Wisconsin has 50 percent of the
nation's smokestack employment. The employment loss experienced
between 1979 and 1983 is not expected to have been overcome by 1987.
And even where there is compensating growth in the high-technology
industries, these may not be readily accessible to the unemployed workers
because of different job-skill requirements and because the new jobs
will be located in different locations, even within the same region, than
were the old jobs.[47]

The relatively high economic growth rates projected for the western
states also imply increased pressure on water supplies and other environmental attributes in that region. Nor are the technology-based in-

---

* The concern about the nation's crumbling roads, bridges, water-supply systems,
and other such "infrastructure" suggests that public infrastructure investment and
maintenance expenditures will also have to grow rapidly. This will be difficult, given
the current tight budget outlook.

† The high-technology industries include: plastic materials and synthetic rubber;
drugs; computing and office equipment; communication equipment; electronic components and accessories; aerospace; engineering, scientific, measuring, and controlling instruments; medical and dental instruments and supplies; optical instruments
and supplies; and photographic equipment and supplies.[43]

Figure 1.7
Projected Annual Average Employment Changes in U.S. High-Technology and Smokestack Industries, by Region, 1979–1987

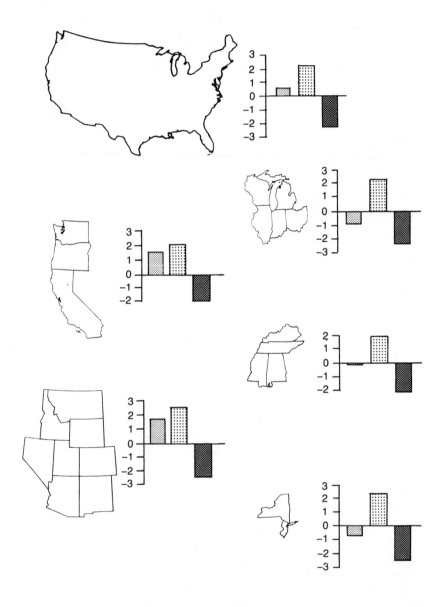

Source: U.S. Department of Commerce.

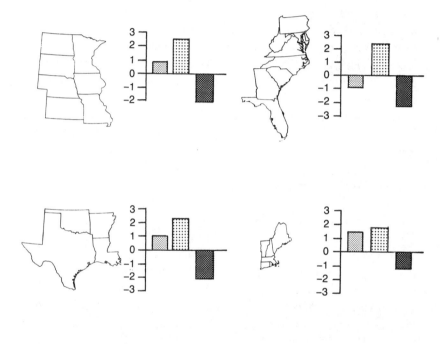

All selected industries

High-technology industries

Smokestack industries

Employment changes indicated as annual percentages.

dustries always clean. They may emit less conventional air and water pollution, but they sometimes use potentially toxic substances that can be released to the environment. Thus, residents of the Silicon Valley, the prototype of the new industries, have concerns about hazardous contaminants entering groundwater.[48]

Economic conditions in other countries are as unsettled as they are in the United States, and their effect on the environment even more uncertain. All countries suffered severely from the most recent recession. The 1982 average unemployment rate in industrialized countries was 8 percent, equivalent to 30 million workers.[49] Real economic growth rates in many developing countries were hurt even more than those in more-developed countries because of foreign currency exchange problems caused by higher prices for energy imports and much lower prices for raw-material exports.[50]

The prices that developing countries receive for raw materials are, in real terms, at a historic low.[51] These low prices combine with reduced export demand and high interest payments to create extremely serious foreign exchange and debt-servicing problems for many lower-income nations. To recover from these problems, some countries may be pushed to aggressively exploit their natural resources. Such exploitation, along with the increased demand for firewood stimulated by population growth and the high cost of energy imports, accelerates the destruction of tropical and other forest lands, increasing flooding, droughts, and soil erosion.[52] According to one estimate, the annual loss of forests is already equivalent to an area the combined size of Austria and Albania.[53] These local trends also threaten to exacerbate the buildup of carbon dioxide in the atmosphere, leading to possibly large changes in the world's climate (see chapter 2).

The World Bank concludes that, for the remainder of the decade, "most developing countries should be able to regain their growth momentum" but, even so, that "the outlook for some of the poorest countries is somber."[54] This relatively optimistic assessment depends, however, on sustained growth in the more-developed countries and substantial improvements in economic management and resource utilization in all countries. But the World Bank also evaluated the implications of a low-growth-rate case, and, even though many of the assumptions used in this case were "optimistic," it concluded that:

> It is easy to envisage a downward global economic spiral emerging from the Low case, with catastrophic consequences for the developing countries. Indeed, it would be difficult to forestall such a global crisis if the industrial countries' recovery were to taper off into a decade of very slow growth.[55]

Another observer, concerned about the possibility of "a decade of economic stagnation," identifies the underlying problem as the way in which the world is depleting its renewable and nonrenewable natural resources, particularly its petroleum, soil, water, and forests:

> In our preoccupation with monthly economic indicators we have lost touch with the environmental resource base on which the economy rests. We keep detailed data on the stock of plant and equipment while virtually ignoring the condition of soils, the health of forests, and the level of water tables. Only when environmental deterioration or resource depletion translates into economic decline do we seem to notice it.[56]

PUBLIC OPINION

As important as a healthy environment is to a healthy economy, aggressive government programs are usually needed to conserve and protect that environment. And in most countries, the viability of these programs depends on strong public support.

The durability of this public support is one of the remarkable characteristics of environmental programs in the United States. Since Earth Day in 1970, many observers and politicians have predicted that public attention would quickly fade as some new fad caught the public's fancy.[57] This was apparently the assumption held by President Reagan and his appointees at the U.S. Environmental Protection Agency (EPA) and Department of the Interior (DOI) when they took office in 1981. Much to their surprise, and partially stimulated by the administration's environmental policies, the public's support for environmental programs appears to be "stronger than ever."[58]

When President Reagan assumed office, there was a gradual, but discernible, upward trend in the number of people who thought the environmental-protection programs had "gone too far" (figure 1.8). Since then there has been a dramatic break in this trend. The number of people who think environmental-protection laws and regulations have gone too far is almost as low as it was in 1973 at the beginning of the environmental decade. Almost half the people think these laws and regulations have not gone far enough; this proportion had never exceeded over one-third previously. And positions seem to have hardened. The percentage who "don't know" is smaller than at any time during the 1970s. The events of the past 3 years appear to have firmly crystalized people's opinions, but not necessarily in the manner expected.

Other recent public opinion polls clearly reinforce these conclusions. A November 1983 Harris poll found that only 13 percent of the res-

Figure 1.8
Public Support for Environmental Programs, 1973–1983

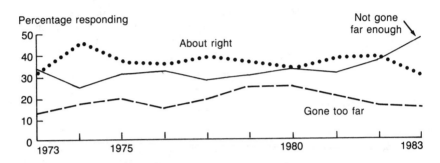

Responses are to the following question:

There are also different opinions about how far we've gone with environmental protection laws and regulations. At the present time, do you think environmental protection laws and regulations have gone too far, or not far enough, or have struck about the right balance?

Source: *Public Opinion* and The Roper Organization.

pondents thought that "controls on dangerous air pollution from a factory should be suspended in order to keep the factory open and thus save jobs."[59] This percentage was down from 17 percent at the beginning of the year. *Business Week* declared the results "astonishing," "considering that the nation is coming out of a wrenching recession in which thousands of industrial jobs were lost."[60] These results were confirmed by a 1983 ABC News/*Washington Post* poll that concluded, "even though the large majority of Americans believe compliance with anti-pollution laws costs business firms at least a fair amount of money, more than three out of four say those laws are worth the cost."[61] And a 1983 *New York Times*/CBS poll found that 58 percent of the people agreed with the statement that "protecting the environment is so important that requirements and standards cannot be too high and continued environmental improvements must be made regardless of cost."[62] Again, this represented a substantial increase over the 45 percent who agreed with the statement in 1981.

On the other hand, people do not necessarily identify pollution and other environmental issues as the most serious issues facing the country.[63] Concerns about the economy and peace usually head this list. Are these results inconsistent with the results summarized above? One expert explains why they are not by distinguishing between the *salience* of the environmental issue and its *strength*. Salience, according to this analysis, "has to do with how much immediate, personal interest people have in the issue," whereas strength "refers to the degree to which people regard the issue as a matter of national concern and are committed to improving the situation or solving the problem."[64] According to this analysis, although people feel very strongly about environmental issues, for very few are they at the top of their immediate concerns. This distinction is emphasized by the results of the 1983 ABC News/*Washington Post* poll, in which three out of four respondents showed strong support for environmental programs, yet most of those polled "don't think that air pollution, unsafe drinking water, or toxic wastes are serious problems in the area where they live."[65]

Membership in some environmental organizations, another measure of the public support for environmental programs, reflects people's increased environmental concern (figure 1.9). Between 1981 and 1983, membership in 11 environmental organizations increased by about 250,000 people (13 percent). This was equivalent to the number of members added between 1970 and 1974. Some organizations have, in particular, taken advantage of the renewed interest. The Sierra Club

Figure 1.9
Membership in Selected U.S. Environmental
Organizations, 1968–1983

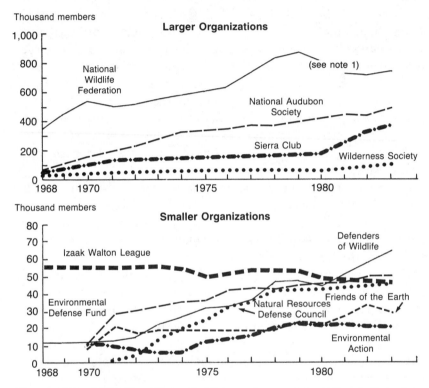

Thousand members

Larger Organizations

National
Wildlife
Federation

(see note 1)

National Audubon
Society

Sierra Club

Wilderness Society

1968   1970   1975   1980

Thousand members

Smaller Organizations

Defenders
of Wildlife

Izaak Walton League

Environmental
-Defense Fund

Natural Resources
Defense Council

Friends of the Earth

Environmental
Action

1968   1970   1975   1980

¹ Between 1980 and 1981, changed its membership-accounting procedure, which resulted in a reduction of their membership totals.

Source: Robert Mitchell.

and the Wilderness Society have essentially doubled their memberships since 1980. Defenders of Wildlife has increased by 50 percent, Friends of the Earth by 38 percent, and the National Audubon Society by 18 percent (almost 25 percent since 1979). And these organizations receive strong backing from many Americans who are not actually members. Over 60 percent of people asked think of themselves as either active in or sympathetic toward the environmental movement.[66] In a similar vein, the Chamber of Commerce discovered in a 1981 poll that almost twice as many people would trust recommendations by environmental groups, over those of business and industry, for changes in the Clean Air Act.[67]

Other countries also feel this support for environmental programs. Europeans place concern about the environment third in a list of issues of greatest concern; in some countries, it is ranked second.[68] And over 87 percent of the Japanese consider environmental problems a serious threat—a higher percentage than in the United States.[69] The rapid growth in several developed countries of political parties based on environmental platforms reflects this worry. Developing countries too show new interest in these issues. In Mexico, for instance, environmental quality was recognized as a political issue for the first time in 1983 in President Miguel de la Madrid's campaign.

ENVIRONMENTAL EXPENDITURES

The environmental programs enacted during the 1970s with strong public support stimulated significant increases in environmental expenditures by both government and the private sector. Total pollution-control expenditures rose to almost 2 percent of GNP in the United States by 1975 and maintained that level through the the decade, falling off somewhat after 1980 (figure 1.10).* Business was responsible for approximately 60 percent of the expenditures, government for approximately 30 percent, and individual consumers for the rest. By 1982, however, government's share had dropped to 23 percent, and consumer's

---

* Very little information is available on pollution-control expenditures in other countries, although information collected by the Organization for Economic Cooperation and Development indicates that, in the mid-1970s, Japan was investing in pollution-control equipment at twice the rate—relative to the size of their economy—of the United States.[70] The European countries for which data were available were investing at about half the U.S. rate. In terms of expenditures per capita, however, countries such as Sweden and West Germany may actually be spending more than the United States.

Figure 1.10
Pollution-Abatement and -Control Expenditures, as
Percentage of GNP, 1972–1982

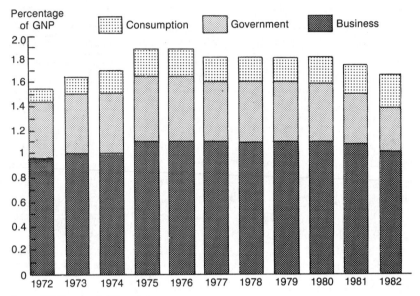

Source: U.S. Department of Commerce.

Figure 1.11
Pollution-Abatement and -Control Expenditures,
in Constant 1972 Dollars, 1972–1982

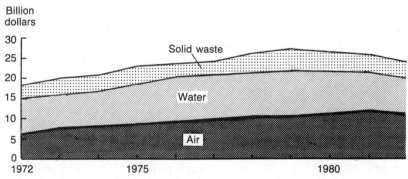

Source: U.S. Department of Commerce.

share had risen to 15 percent. Business' share, though decreasing in terms of the absolute amount of expenditures, remained at 61 percent of the total.

The fall in spending after 1979 was felt primarily in water pollution control (figure 1.11), reflecting decreases in both business and public investment in water-pollution-control devices (figure 1.12 and 1.13). In real terms, expenditures for water pollution control peaked in 1978, while those for controlling air pollution and solid waste peaked in 1981. Since they reached their peak, real expenditures for water pollution control have fallen 23 percent, and both air pollution and solid waste expenditures have both dropped by 5 percent.

During the 11 years from 1972 through 1982, the United States spent a total of $436 billion for pollution control, equivalent to $626 billion in constant 1983 dollars. Forty-three percent of this was for water pollution control, and 41 percent was for air pollution control.

The decreases in pollution-control expenditures reflect, to some extent, a catching up with the backlog of investments made to comply with industrial-effluent limitations. To some extent, they probably also reflect the slowdown in economic growth and total business investment during this period. To what extent the private spending cuts are a reflection of the new policies adopted by the Reagan administration is not clear.

What is clear, however, is that there is ample evidence that many investments still need to be made. This need is indicated by the relatively high degree of noncompliance by municipal and industrial dischargers (see water-quality section in chapter 2)[71] and by the relatively small investment made to pretreat industrial wastes discharged into municipal sewers,[72] as well as by the results of EPA's most recent survey of the amount of investment needed to bring the nation's municipal treatment plants into compliance with the law.[73] Municipalities, however, have cut back sharply in their investments in response to tight budgets. Their situation will not be eased by the decision, in 1982, to reduce the federal share of expenditures on municipal sewage plants from 75 percent to 55 percent.[74]

The federal government has reduced its funding not only for municipal wastewater-treatment plants but for pollution control in general. EPA's operating budget, when adjusted for inflation, peaked in 1979, at just over twice the 1971 level (figure 1.14). Since 1979, operating funds have fallen to the level of 1972 and 1973, leaving EPA's 1983 operating budget roughly two-thirds the 1979 level when adjusted for inflation.

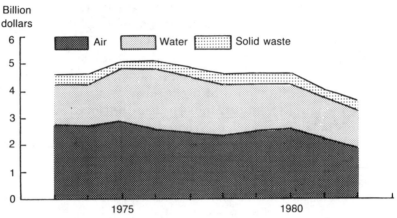

Figure 1.12
Business Investment in Pollution Control, by Medium, 1973–1982
(in constant 1972 dollars)

Source: U.S. Department of Commerce.

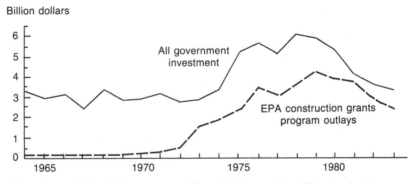

Figure 1.13
Government Investment in Wastewater-Treatment
Facilities, 1964–1983

EPA outlays are funds the agency transfers to states and localities to reimburse them for constructing wastewater-treatment facilities.

Source: U.S. Department of Commerce and U.S. Environmental Protection Agency.

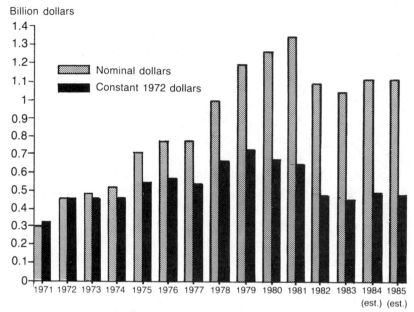

Figure 1.14
U.S. Environmental Protection Agency Budget Trends,
in Nominal and Constant Dollars, 1970–1985

Billion dollars

Nominal dollars
Constant 1972 dollars

1971 1972 1973 1974 1975 1976 1977 1978 1979 1980 1981 1982 1983 1984 1985
(est.) (est.)

Source: American Environmental Safety Council.

Figure 1.15
Federal Expenditures for Environmental Programs,
Fiscal Years 1973–1982

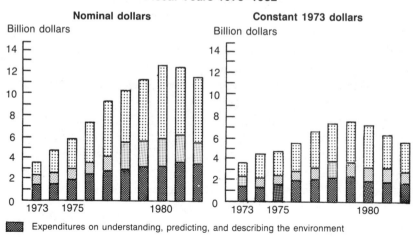

Nominal dollars
Billion dollars

Constant 1973 dollars
Billion dollars

Expenditures on understanding, predicting, and describing the environment

Expenditures on protection and enhancement (includes expenditures for recreation, wildlife, historic preservation, etc.)

Expenditures for pollution abatement and control (including wastewater-treatment grants to municipalities)

Source: Council on Environmental Quality.

One effect of these budget cuts has been a significant reduction in enforcement. That decline has lead one observer to note, "It appears that during the present dearth of government enforcement, private enforcement of traditional environmental laws is more frequent than EPA enforcement."[75]

Indeed, citizen suits are now the predominant federal judicial enforcement mechanism under the Clean Water Act.[76] The Natural Resources Defense Council is one of the principal movers behind this "law and order campaign" by environmentalists.[77] With the Connecticut Fund for the Environment, it has sued 10 major water polluters in Connecticut and is negotiating with 17 others. With the Sierra Club, it plans at least 18 other suits in New England, and with the Chesapeake Bay Foundation it has filed 1 suit in Maryland.

EPA's budget cuts have been echoed throughout all the federal environmental programs (figure 1.15). Even in current dollars, expenditures were reduced in 1981 and 1982 (data for 1983 are not available). In real dollars, 1982 expenditures were 23 percent less than their 1979 peak. The reductions have taken place in pollution abatement and control (23 percent in real terms from 1980 to 1982), protection and enhancement activities (40 percent in real terms from 1978 to 1982), and, perhaps most troublesome in its long-term implications, research and monitoring (17 percent in real terms from 1979 to 1982).

Similar budget reductions also appear to have taken place at the state and local level (see chapter 8). Given the Reagan administration's desire to continue reducing the federal budget for domestic programs, coupled both with its commitment to continue increasing defense expenditures and strong political pressure to reduce the federal deficit, there appears to be no prospect for the environmental programs to regain in the near future the resources they had available in the late 1970s. These budget constraints may well have a more lasting impact upon the quality of the U.S. environment than any policy shifts that the administration has implemented. Still, it is not possible to predict what will finally result from the conflicting trends in increased pressures on the environment resulting from population and economic growth, increased support for strong environmental programs expressed in public opinion polls, and decreasing resources available to government agencies to respond to these pressures.

Chapter 2

Environmental Contaminants

The pollution problem did not suddenly spring full bloom in the 1970s. Cities, including Dickens's London, have dealt with severe air and water pollution problems for centuries. By the 1960s, many areas of the United States had begun vigorous efforts to clean up years of accumulating, indiscriminate pollution. The available monitoring data actually show that urban air quality improved more dramatically during the last part of that decade than it has at any time since.[1] The 1960s also saw the beginning of major efforts to clean up the Willamette River and other highly fouled water bodies. These became the water quality "success stories" of the environmental programs in the 1970s.[2]

But the 1970s witnessed a fundamental shift: environmental quality elevated from a predominately local issue to one of the most important national issues. Beginning with the Clean Air Act in 1970 and the 1972 amendments to the Federal Water Pollution Control Act (since renamed the Clean Water Act), Congress enacted a series of stringent statutes to quickly and decisively control environmental contaminants in air, in water, and on land.[3*]

These statutes focused primarily on cleaning up "conventional" pollutants—smoke and sulfur oxides in the air, oxygen-depleting discharges to the water, and solid wastes on the land. But as the decade ended, emphasis shifted from these pollutants, which, no matter how much they degraded the environment, presented limited direct health risks except at very high concentrations, to a new focus on hazardous

---

* Most of these legislative initiatives were actually amendments to existing federal environmental statutes, some of which had existed for decades. The changes made during the 1970s were so extensive in both philosophy and scope that the common perception of these amendments as entirely new laws is, for practical purposes, more accurate than their technical status.

Figure 2.1
Federal Pollution-Control Statutes, 1970–1983

Statute	Year passed
Statutes Focusing on "Conventional" Pollutants	
Clean Air Act Amendments	1970
Resource Recovery Act (Amendments to the Solid Waste Disposal Act)	1970
Water Pollution Control Act Amendments	1972
Noise Control Act (Amendments to the Federal Aviation Act)	1972
Ocean Dumping Act (A title of the Marine Protection Research and Sanctuaries Act)	1972
Noise Control Act Amendments	1976,1978
Statutes Focusing on "Toxics"	
Federal Environmental Pesticide Control Act (Amendments to the Federal Insecticide, Fungicide and Rodenticide Act)	1972
Safe Drinking Water Act (Amendments to the Public Health Service Act)	1974
Resource Conservation and Recovery Act (Amendments to the Resource Recovery Act focusing on hazardous wastes)	1976
Toxic Substances Control Act	1976
Clean Air Act Amendments	1977
Clean Water Act (Amendments to the Water Pollution Control Act)	1977
Federal Insecticide, Fungicide and Rodenticide Act Amendments	1978
Comprehensive Environmental Response, Compensation and Liability Act (more commonly, Superfund)	1980

pollutants and toxic substances, which could threaten human health even at very low concentrations (figure 2.1).

Toxic Substances

Humans can be exposed to toxic substances in many ways: through the air they breathe, the water they drink, the food they eat, and the cosmetics, drugs, and other products they use. The workplace may qualify as the riskiest environment, because of the many hours spent there and the relatively high levels of exposure to toxic substances. But exposure in other settings and through other activities is also common.

Exposure to a substance at toxic levels can induce either immediate or long-term problems, or both. "Acute" effects include more or less immediate manifestations of contact—rashes, burns, illness, or poisoning. "Chronic" effects, such as lung diseases, cancer, or genetic effects, by contrast, may appear years after a person's first exposure to an adverse substance. Concern about substances capable of stimulating unsuspected overt or covert effects led to the adoption of laws and new administrative policies in the middle and late 1970s to control toxic (or hazardous) substances.*

But what is a toxic substance? The answer is not always clear, and the implicit definition may change from time to time and from program to program. Many normally benign substances, even some that are necessary in small amounts for maintaining health, become toxic in large amounts. Thus, toxicity is only meaningful, at least for regulatory purposes, when related to likely exposure levels.

To begin the job of classifying toxic substances, various laws and government agencies have established registries of such substances. The National Institute of Occupational Safety and Health (NIOSH) Registry of Toxic Substances has almost 60,000 entries.[4] However, this includes every substance that NIOSH knows to have any toxic effect at any level of exposure. The regulations issued by EPA to implement the Resource Conservation and Recovery Act (RCRA) list more than 700 process wastes and

* The terms *toxic* and *hazardous* are essentially synonymous. The same chemical will be called a toxic in one statute (for instance, the Clean Water Act or the Toxic Substances Control Act) and hazardous in another (for instance, the Clean Air Act and the Resource Conservation and Recovery Act).

specific chemicals as hazardous[5] and define as hazardous any wastes with the characteristics of ignitability, corrosivity, reactivity, and "EP Toxicity."* The Clean Water Act, as amended in 1977, lists 129 specific chemical compounds as "priority toxic pollutants."[6]

Chronic effects are much more difficult to identify and, obviously, to categorize. The National Toxicology Program lists 117 chemicals as potential human carcinogens;[7] an International Agency for Research on Cancer Ad Hoc Working Group of experts reviewed 54 chemicals, groups of chemicals, and industrial processes and indicated 36 as probable human carcinogens.[8] But, in the United States, the only substances routinely tested for chronic, generally carcinogenic or mutagenic effects are drugs, food additives, and pesticides (see discussion of toxicity testing below). Industry and the federal government may also test other chemicals suspected of toxicity.

However, only a tiny percentage of the over 66,000 chemicals currently used commercially in the United States have been adequately tested, at least for human health effects.[9]† That is not to imply that the untested compounds are toxic; probably, most of them are not toxic at the low levels to which humans might normally be exposed. Because the potential toxicities of so many substances remain untested, the only real definition of a toxic substance is its classification as such in a statute or regulation.

MONITORING PROGRAMS FOR TOXIC SUBSTANCES

To what extent is the population being exposed to such substances? The answer, for the majority of substances, is still unknown. For a few of them, government agencies collect data on how much of the substance is produced and used in the United States. The U.S. Bureau of Mines, for instance, collects data on mineral production and consumption.[11] The U.S. International Trade Commission accumulates information on imports, exports, and domestic production of a variety of substances.[12] These data, although gathered for reasons unrelated to estimating toxic risks, are available for environmental analysis of amounts and areas of release and the likelihood of human exposure.

----

* "EP Toxicity" is a term used solely in the RCRA regulation to identify wastes that in specific extraction procedures leach hazardous concentrations of any of 14 contaminants—for example, lindane and mercury.

† One reason for this is cost. The cost of carrying out the tests required to register a new pesticide can total $6 million or more.[10]

For some of the suspect substances, various federal, state, and local agencies monitor concentrations in air, bodies of water, drinking-water supplies, and food. Generally, those agencies primarily monitor conventional pollutants in air and water; there is much less monitoring of toxic contaminants. Each year, the federal Food and Drug Administration (FDA) administers "Adult Total Diet Studies" to estimate the average dietary intake of potentially toxic substances by people in the United States.[13] The agency purchases representative shopping baskets of food (currently including more than 200 items) from supermarkets and analyzes them for over 200 potential contaminants. In carrying out its responsibilities under several statutes, the U.S. Department of Agriculture also continually measures the concentration of some substances in meat products.[14] The U.S. Bureau of Marine Fisheries similarly evaluates commercial fish.[15]

Several other agencies also systematically monitor the accumulation of certain substances in fish and other wildlife. The National Pesticide Monitoring Program checks residue levels of selected toxic compounds in wildlife.[16] This program, initiated in 1964, is a cooperative effort by numerous federal agencies. It determines how pesticide residues in birds and freshwater fish vary by geographical region and over time. Selected species are sampled every two to three years from over 100 different sites throughout the United States.* The samples are tested for some 18 to 20 environmental contaminants, many of which are organochlorine pesticides or their metabolites. PCBs (polychlorinated biphenyls), some heavy metals, and other potentially toxic substances, such as selenium and arsenic, also are measured but not consistently.

The U.S. Mussel Watch Program, conducted by the U.S. Environmental Protection Agency (EPA) between 1976 and 1978, was a marine-pollution-monitoring program that assessed water quality along the U.S. coastline.[17] Often, the concentrations of toxic substances in surface water are too low to be detected by normal monitoring equipment. But some animals, such as bivalve mollusks, accumulate substances in their tissues, which allows easier quantification. The Mussel Watch Program analyzed mussels and oysters from more than 100 sites along the Atlantic, Pacific,

---

* The indicator species for birds are the starling, a terrestrial songbird, and the mallard and black ducks, native waterfowl. The fish sampled include bottom-dwelling species such as carp, suckers, and catfish and predaceous species such as trout, walleye pike, and bass. Ducks have been tested since 1965; fish and starlings were first sampled in 1967.

and Gulf coasts for the presence and concentrations of pesticide residues, PCBs, heavy metals, and selected other potentially toxic substances. The results both demonstrated the persistence of contaminants and helped identify toxic "hot spots," such as the generally elevated levels of contaminants near urban centers. Unfortunately, EPA stopped funding this program in 1979, and subsequent work has been continued only at a few locations, supported by states such as California.[18] The Ocean Assessment Division in the National Oceanic and Atmospheric Administration currently has a proposal to reestablish this program on a national scale.[19]

Such programs, however, do not directly measure the total amounts of the substance to which people are exposed. To better illustrate total human exposure, the National Human Monitoring Program (NHMP) was initiated in 1967 as an activity of the U.S. Public Health Service and later transferred to EPA. It consists of two major surveys, the National Human Adipose Tissue Survey (NHATS) and the National Health and Nutrition Examination Survey (HANES II).[20] Both survey persons of all ages, races, sexes, and socioeconomic statuses nationwide to estimate the proportion of the U.S. population harboring selected toxic residues and their average concentrations. NHATS monitors pesticides and PCBs in adipose (fat) tissue, an accumulation site, to indicate cumulative human exposure to such fat-soluble substances. HANES II monitors bloodstream concentrations.

The Global Environmental Monitoring System (GEMS) of the United Nations (UN) also assesses cadmium and lead levels in human blood.[21] Whereas adipose samples tend to show cumulative exposure, blood samples more strongly reflect recent exposure because other body organs remove the metals from the blood. Ten nations currently participate in this project, which collects and analyzes blood samples from elementary school teachers.* However, with the exception of India, the subjects all live in one city in each country (the U.S. subjects live in Baltimore), so the results may not truly represent national averages.

Although these major detection programs collect much useful information, they give only a glimpse of total exposure to toxic substances for a number of reasons. First, the monitoring programs are best suited for measuring environmentally persistent, bioaccumulating toxic substances. Second, they do not provide information on rapidly degrading

---

* Elementary school teachers were chosen because their occupational exposure to the metals of concern is thought to be low.

substances, even those with high initial toxicities. Finally, most programs focus on substances, such as DDT (dichloro-diphenyl-trichloroethane), lead, and PCBs, the deleterious effects of which are already recognized and at least partially controlled. Thus, the existing monitoring programs judge the success of those past control efforts rather than determining what additional substances need to be controlled.

TOXIC METALS

Many metallic elements indispensible to a modern industrial society—such as lead, copper, cadmium, zinc, aluminum, and mercury—can be toxic to humans and wildlife. For instance, mercury discharged from industrial manufacturing plants or copper compounds deposited from urban stormwater runoff can poison estuarine shellfish and the people who consume them.[22] The Clean Water Act lists 11 metals as toxic contaminants.* Two of the most important are lead and cadmium, because they have clearly demonstrated deleterious effects on human health and often exist at relatively high environmental concentrations.

Lead

Acute ingestion of lead, a heavy metal, can cause convulsions, anemia, and neurological and renal (kidney) disorders; chronic exposure can cause anemia, convulsions, kidney damage, and brain damage.[23] The primary uses of lead are in automobile batteries, gasoline additives, and pigments and paints. Humans are primarily exposed to lead in food and air, although people living in older buildings may also be exposed via lead-based paint applied years before.

Lead consumption in the United States gradually increased up to the early 1970s but, since then, has decreased over 40 percent, primarily because of regulations limiting the lead content in gasoline and the reduced manufacture of lead-based paints (figure 2.2). Lead use per capita is currently under six pounds per year. In the United States, approximately 675,000 children between six months and five years old (4 percent of that age group) have high blood-lead levels.[24] (Older children and adults tend to have lower blood-lead levels and less risk of physiological impairments.)

* The 11 metals are antimony, berylium, cadmium, chromium, copper, lead, mercury, nickel, silver, thallium, and zinc.

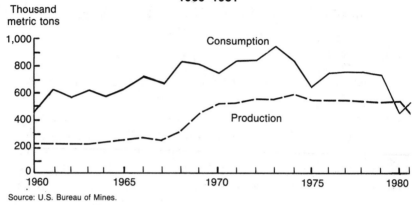

Figure 2.2
U.S. Production and Consumption of Lead,
1960–1981

Source: U.S. Bureau of Mines.

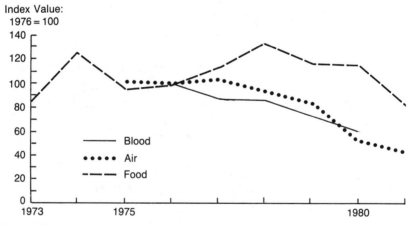

Figure 2.3
Lead in Air, Food, and Human Blood, 1973–1981

Source: U.S. Food and Drug Administration.

Air-quality data from 92 urban monitoring sites in 11 states reveal a substantial decline (64 percent) in average ambient concentrations of lead between 1977 and 1982 (figure 2.3).[25] The decline parallels the reduced use of lead in gasoline, which plummeted 68 percent between 1976 and 1981 as a result of federal regulations.[26] This decline is expected to continue for the next few years as the older, leaded-fuel cars are eliminated from the fleet.

Excessive lead in surface water also seems to be diminishing. The U.S. Geological Survey has measured lead concentrations at 313 water-quality monitoring stations for at least eight years.* A quarter of these stations show statistically significant decreasing trends in lead over this period, fewer than 3 percent show increasing trends, and the remainder show no statistically significant trends.[27] The only two regions with rising lead concentrations are the Texas-Gulf Coast region and Alaska. These trends were confirmed by a study of bottom deposits in 40 lakes in the Northeast. After increasing exponentially over the past 100 years, the deposition of lead in bottom sediments has leveled off or declined in the past 5 years.[28]

Unlike the air- and water-quality studies, adult total-diet studies show no particular trend (figure 2.3). The amount of lead detected in American food (usually the largest portion of total lead intake) fluctuates as much as 50 percent from one year to the next. An anticipated steady downward trend of lead in food, expected because of the reduced use of lead solder in tin cans is not evident.[29] Why this decrease has not materialized is unclear, but, even so, since the FDA began keeping records, the average American daily food intake has never exceeded 22 percent of the acceptable daily intake set by the Joint Food and Agriculture Organization/World Health Organization Expert Committee on Food Additives (JECFA).[30] The U.S. dietary lead intake is about average for countries reporting diet information. Japan's figures are somewhat lower, and Guatemala's and New Zealand's are much higher.

Apparently, the only wildlife-monitoring program that tests for lead is the Mussel Watch Program, but it does not provide national time-series data on lead concentrations. In California, which has collected such data since 1977, some areas show decreases, but other areas evince no noticeable trend (figure 2.4).

---

* See the section on water quality in this chapter for a description of the Geological Survey's monitoring system.

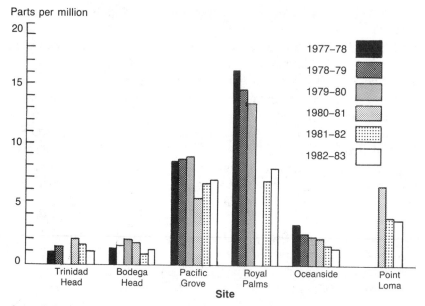

Figure 2.4
Lead in California Mussels

Parts per million

Legend:
- 1977–78
- 1978–79
- 1979–80
- 1980–81
- 1981–82
- 1982–83

Sites: Trinidad Head, Bodega Head, Pacific Grove, Royal Palms, Oceanside, Point Loma

Site

Source: California Department of Fish and Game.

The Price of Lead In Gasoline

EPA has recently completed an analysis suggesting that the amount of lead should be reduced still further if not eliminated altogether.

Lead is added to gasoline to increase its octane, but there are other means to that end. EPA now estimates that those alternatives would not increase the cost of manufacturing gasoline by more than 1 percent, although additional valve wear also could result in some trucks and older cars.

Compared to these costs, estimated to amount to something over $691 million a year, EPA estimates that lead-free gas would provide annual benefits amounting to almost $1.4 billion a year, plus health benefits that the agency cannot express in monetary values. The major monetary savings would result from reduced automobile maintenance—less frequent tune-ups, oil changes, and exhaust system replacements. The agency also has estimated monetary savings that could result from reductions in medical costs and cognitive damage for children with high levels of lead in their blood. The analysts have been unable, however, to place a value on the health damage caused by low blood lead levels.

Industry has extensively criticized the EPA estimates, and it is unclear whether they will result in any further regulatory action.

(Source: Joel Schwartz et al., "Costs and Benefits of Reducing Lead in Gasoline," EPA Draft Final Report [Washington, D.C.: U.S. Environmental Protection Agency, Office of Policy Analysis, March 1984].)

The only monitoring for lead contamination in humans, the HANES
II blood-sampling survey, shows lead levels in the U.S. population declining by 38 percent from 1978 to 1981—the period of air-quality improvement (figure 2.3). The UN study of lead blood levels places U.S.
citizens in about the middle of the 10 surveyed countries.[31] The highest
levels, occurring in Mexico, are three times the lowest levels, found in
Japan and China. The difference again seems to stem from lowered
automobile lead emissions. Mexican gasoline contains 9,000 times as
much lead as Japanese gasoline.[32] In China, 75 percent of the gasoline
is unleaded, and cars are less common.[33]

The fate of lead exemplifies how controls placed on one source of
exposure reduce contaminant levels elsewhere as well. EPA's strictures
on lead in gasoline helped decrease lead levels throughout the environment. Unfortunately, these improvements will not entirely solve the
problem of lead toxicity in children, because the highest levels tend
to be found in children who ingest leaded paint from deteriorating
buildings.[34] But the controls should provide these children a greater
chance.

Cadmium

Cadmium is a metallic element found in various chemical forms
throughout the environment. It accumulates in the body and primarily affects the kidneys, which normally contain about one-third of the
accumulated metal, and the liver.[35] Commercial use of cadmium for
paint pigments, additives for rubber and plastics, batteries, catalysts,
and antiseptics and fungicides expanded rapidly during the 1940s and
fluctuated thereafter (figure 2.5).

The general population in the United States is exposed to cadmium
mainly through food and cigarette smoke. Direct air and water exposures
total less than 10 percent.[36] Leafy vegetables, especially prone to taking
up cadmium from the soil, are a major dietary source of cadmium.[37]
Cadmium accumulates in soil via routes such as phosphate fertilizers,
sludge application, and air deposition.[38]

Measurements of cadmium in air are few, and none indicate trends
over time. In water, about 10 percent of the U.S. Geological Survey's
water-quality monitoring stations detect statistically significant increasing cadmium trends; about 2 percent show decreasing trends; the rest
report no significant trend.[39]

The adult total-diet studies, by contrast, reveal a decline over the
past decade in the amount of cadmium contained in food (figure 2.6).

Figure 2.5
U.S. Production and Consumption of Cadmium,
1958–1979

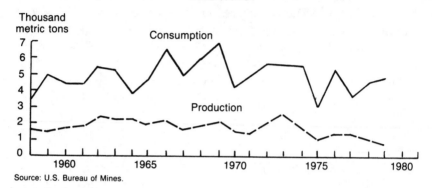

Source: U.S. Bureau of Mines.

Figure 2.6
Cadmium in Human Diet, 1973–1981

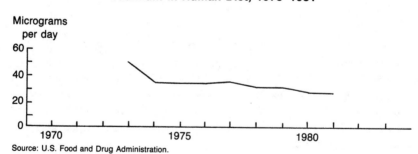

Source: U.S. Food and Drug Administration.

The estimated average daily intake in the United States is about half of the JECFA acceptable level.[40]* Japan, Guatemala, and Canada report somewhat higher levels of dietary intake than the United States, while New Zealand and Hungary report lower levels; but the differences are unexplained.

Only two wildlife programs report any monitoring for cadmium, and only California's Mussel Watch Program provides time-series data.[41] These data, however, demonstrate no significant trend.

HANES II human-blood data indicate that cadmium levels of U.S. residents dropped between 1973 and 1981.[42] And the UN blood analyses confirm that residents of the United States have among the lowest cadmium levels of the countries included in the survey.[43] India is the only other country as low, with Mexico and Yugoslavia showing the highest levels—over three times the U.S. average. Although the survey offers no explanation for these differences, they do show the importance of smoking: smokers show 1.2 to 9 times as much cadmium as nonsmokers.

ORGANIC TOXIC CHEMICALS

Toxic effects of many naturally occurring compounds have been known for so long that their uses are part of civilization's lore. Arsenic's poisonous properties have been exploited for centuries. Lewis Carroll's Alice had seen "mad hatters" before one appeared in her Wonderland: Hat makers were frequently poisoned by the mercury compounds used to form felt hats.[44]

The recognition of synthetic organic chemicals' potential toxicity is more recent. Most organic compounds, of course, are not toxic. The term *organic* only means that they contain carbon. But some organic chemicals, depending on what other elements they contain and how these associate with carbon atoms in the compound's molecular structure, can be toxic. Chlorine is a frequent culprit. Pesticide manufacturers have known for many years that combining chlorine, hydrogen, oxygen, and carbon creates chlorinated hydrocarbon compounds, such as DDT, that effectively kill insects.[45] What they did not realize until recently was the concomitant harm to wildlife and humans.

Many of the advances of modern chemistry—advances substantially improving the quality of life—result from a chemist's remarkable ability

---

* However, very little air- or water-quality monitoring is conducted to confirm this.

to formulate new organic compounds with precise properties. What has not kept pace is testing of these formulations, quickly and cheaply, to determine their toxicity.

More than 90 percent of the 117 substances listed as potential human carcinogens by the National Toxicology Program are organic compounds.[46] Of the 129 toxic substances EPA addresses in its Clean Water Program, 114 are organic compounds.[47] However, this section considers only chemicals registered for use as pesticides and two other widely used compounds—PCBs and benzene.

Pesticides

Pesticides control plants, insects, animals, and fungi classified as pests. They are used widely in the United States for crop protection (both before and after harvest), to control weeds, as wood preservatives, and in paints.[48]

Some 1,400 different active pesticide ingredients are registered by EPA for use in the United States.[49] Many of these, however, are not used extensively.[50] Nevertheless, these relatively few active ingredients are mixed with other substances (some of which may themselves be toxic) to create the estimated 35,000 commercially available pesticide formulations.[51]

Not all of the active pesticide ingredients are organic compounds, but most are. Until the pervasive harm of DDT and related compounds was discovered, emphasis was on developing ''persistent'' pesticides that did not readily decompose, provided long-lasting protection, and required fewer applications. More recently the emphasis has been on developing more short-lived compounds—which are highly toxic when first applied, are used in smaller quantities per unit area, and break down rapidly.[52]

Even brief exposure to high concentrations of some pesticides can provoke acute health effects including vomiting, dizziness, and neurological disorders; exposure even can be fatal.[53] Some compounds cause cancer, miscarriages, birth defects, and genetic mutations.[54] People applying pesticides and working in areas of pesticide manufacture are exposed the most, but everyone is exposed to these compounds at low levels in food, drinking water, or air.[55] EPA is responsible for setting standards ensuring that no exposure levels are high enough to cause problems.[56]

Over the past 30 years, the United States has substantially increased production of organic pesticides, particularly herbicides.* From 1960 to 1980, herbicide production increased almost 700 percent (99 percent between 1970 and 1980) as chemicals replaced mechanical methods of controlling weeds. This expanded production reflects both more intensive and more widespread use of herbicides. In 1971, approximately 71 percent of all U.S. farmland acreage devoted to row crops and 38 percent of all U.S. acreage planted in small grain crops had herbicides applied.[58] By 1982, these figures had risen to 91 percent and 44 percent, respectively. However, 85 percent of the herbicides and 70 percent of the insecticides used in U.S. agriculture are applied to only four crops: corn, cotton, soybeans, and wheat.[59]

In the past few years, however, all pesticide production in the United States has fallen sharply. In fact, insecticide production was only 4 percent greater in 1982 than in 1960, and fungicide production was 39 percent lower (figure 2.7). The 1982 falloff in production is attributed primarily to the bad economic conditions experienced by the U.S. farm sector in 1982.[60] The curtailment probably continued through 1983 because of the continued unfavorable economic conditions and the large amount of land taken out of production under the payment-in-kind (PIK) program (see chapter 3). The U.S. Department of Agriculture (USDA) reports, however, that "farm demand for pesticides, especially herbicides, will climb substantially [in 1984], as row-crop acreage is expected to rebound from 1983's PIK-reduced level to about the level planted in 1982."[61]

These overall trends in production do not show shifts in the types of pesticides produced—for instance from highly persistent organochlorine pesticides (60 percent of insecticides in 1963, down to 27 percent in 1976) to less-persistent but generally more concentrated and more acutely toxic compounds such as carbamates and organophosphates.[62] The recent decline in total insecticide production results in part from greater use on cotton of recently introduced pyrethroids, which are applied at about one-tenth the rate of traditional cotton insecticides.[63] This shift in formulation also was a major reason for the drop in the amount of insecticides applied to major U.S. field and forage crops (a 45 percent decline between 1976 and 1982).[64] In general, the newer

---

* U.S. export of pesticides annually accounts for about 25 to 35 percent of pesticides produced.[57]

insecticides (organophosphates and carbamates) are more toxic to vertebrate animals than are the organochlorines but, because of their more rapid degradation, are often safer to use around humans and wildlife.[65]

Predicting what pesticide formulations will be used in what amounts in the future is difficult. However, the increased use of conservation tillage on American farms (see chapter 3) to control soil erosion and reduce tillage costs will probably increase herbicide use. And a few recently developed biological insecticides—species-specific parasites and viruses, pheromones, and hormone regulators effective against target pests but generally harmless to other living organisms—may find farmers' favor.[66]

Discovering the environmental fate of chemical pesticides is as difficult as predicting trends for their future use. There is very little monitoring of pesticides in the air, surface water, or groundwater. However, FDA and USDA carry out relatively extensive monitoring for pesticides in food.

The FDA studies of pesticides in food products show a significant decline in average daily dietary intake of the organochlorine pesticides DDT and dieldrin (both were banned for use in the United States in the mid-1970s) with some year-to-year fluctuations (figure 2.8). However, malathion intakes have remained constant; parathion levels have fluctuated almost threefold over the past decade. But, even for these compounds, the World Health Organization sets the acceptable average daily intake at a level 80 to 200 times higher than the U.S. average.[67]

The data from USDA show consistently low levels of DDT and dieldrin in cattle and sheep from 1978 through 1983, although up to 30 percent of the samples continue to show DDT concentrations of over 0.01 parts per million or more.[68] Fewer than 11 percent of the samples indicate the presence of dieldrin at that concentration.

Neither the FDA nor USDA programs, however, monitor anywhere near all of the pesticides of concern. For instance, neither program provides information about concentrations of EDB (ethylene dibromide), which was found in sufficient concentrations in groundwater, grains, and semiprepared foods that EPA suspended many of the chemical's uses in 1983 in only the second emergency suspension that the agency has ever issued.[69] (The first, in 1979, was for certain uses of the herbicide 2,4,5-T.) And, in a California study, the Natural Resources Defense Council found that numerous fruit and vegetable samples contained residues of several different pesticides.[70] A total of six different pesticides were found in oranges sampled, and five in strawberries and

Figure 2.7
U.S. Production of Pesticides, by Type,
1960–1982

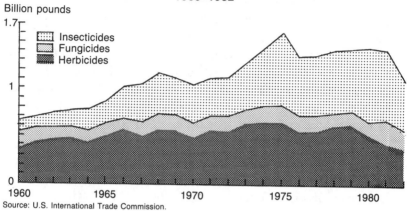

Source: U.S. International Trade Commission.

Figure 2.8
Selected Pesticides in Human Diet,
1970–1982

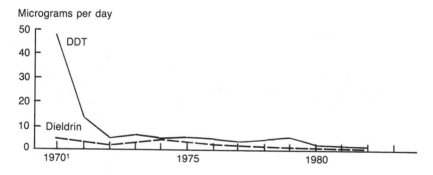

[1] 1970 values represent mean of values measured from 1965 to 1970.

Source: U.S. Food and Drug Administration.

carrots. However, in none of the measurements did the amount of residue exceed the EPA limit.[71]

In 1975, the U.S. Geological Survey established a Pesticide Monitoring Network containing 160 to 180 surface-water sampling stations. This network also collects and analyzes sediment samples from the bottoms of rivers.[72] This survey has detected one or more pesticide residues in less than 10 percent of the 3,000 samples it has tested and in less than 20 percent of the 1,000 sediment samples. Organochlorine and organophosphorous insecticides were found in 1.2 percent or less of the water samples (herbicides were detected with a frequency as high as 4.8 percent).[73] The frequency of detection of the insecticides was much higher—up to 17 percent—for the sediment samples.[74]* In both types of samples, the presence of organochlorine insecticides "appears to have erratically but gradually decreased during 1975-1980."[75]

All of the wildlife-monitoring programs also have found persistent DDT and dieldrin residues years after they were regulated, although levels have dropped substantially since the early 1970s (figure 2.9). The National Pesticide Monitoring Program found DDT and its metabolites in 99 percent of all starling samples tested in 1979.[76] DDT residues also occur in detectable amounts in 100 percent of duck samples, with higher concentrations found in the Atlantic and Pacific flyways than in the more central ones.[77]

More surprisingly, a recent study by the U.S. Fish and Wildlife Service reported elevated levels of DDT in Arizona, California, New Mexico, and Texas.[78] The report states:

> The data collected in this study suggest that there is a major source of DDE [a metabolite of DDT] contamination to wildlife in the Rio Grande and Pecos River Drainages...Kingbirds had significantly higher levels [of DDT residues] after 2 months than when they arrived from Latin America; some resident, non-migratory house sparrows and lizards had elevated DDE levels; young bats at Carlsbad Caverns had DDE levels 13 times higher than bats from a relatively clean area in Texas; and DDE residues in black-crowned night-heron eggs were significantly higher at 2 sites on the Pecos River in New Mexico than at a control site in Texas.[79]

The cause of the residue increase is thought to be use of the pesticide dicofol (Kelthane) as a foliar miticide (an agent to kill mites on leaves)

---

* These differences reflect the physical and chemical characteristics of the compounds. The organochlorines, because they are hydrophobic, would not be expected to be found mixed with water. These compounds do, however, adhere to sediment particles.

Figure 2.9
Trends in Levels of Dieldrin and DDT
in Wildlife, 1968–1979

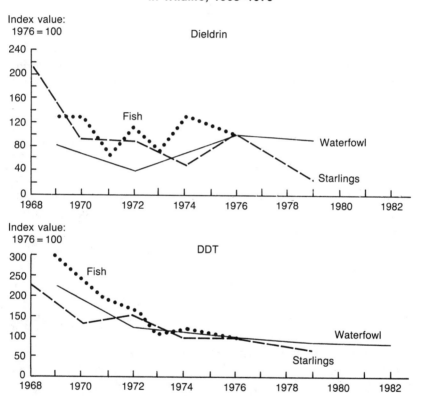

Source: U.S. Fish and Wildlife Service.

for cotton and citrus crops.[80] Dicofol, originally registered as a pesticide in 1957, contains from 9 percent to 15 percent DDT and DDT analogs. Another possible explanation for the residue increase would be the illegal import of DDT from Mexico, where that pesticide still is used.

The adipose-sampling program confirms the rapid decline in DDT concentrations in human fat tissues (figure 2.10). Dieldrin levels have also shown large percentage declines. Heptachlor and chloradane levels remain constant, although those levels always have been quite low. However, the number of samples that continue to contain residues remains high. In 1981, over 95 percent of the samples tested showed the persistence of DDT and dieldrin. HANES II data also show DDT in essentially all blood samples taken, although the frequency of dieldrin, heptachlor, and chlordane occurrence is less than 10 percent.[81]

PCBs (Polychlorinated Biphenyls)

PCBs, among the most stable compounds known, were used extensively until the 1970s as insulating fluids in electrical transformers and capacitors and in the manufacture of plastics, hydraulic fluids, lubricants, and inks. They cause such acute effects as skin rashes, vomiting, abdominal pain, and temporary blindness and are suspected of causing birth defects, miscarriages, and cancer.[82]

Because of concern over these health effects, producers agreed to limit the sale of PCBs in 1971, and Congress prohibited production completely in the Toxic Substances Control Act (TSCA) of 1976 (figure 2.11).[83] However, a substantial portion of all PCBs ever produced remain in transformers, capacitors, and other electrical equipment throughout the United States.[84]

Before the toxicity and persistence of PCBs were understood, the chemical was commonly disposed of by dumping it into sewers or onto land. The bed of the upper Hudson River and Lake Michigan's Waukegan Harbor still contain large PCB concentrations, which bottom-dwelling fish pick up, making the fish unsafe to eat.[85] PCBs also slowly evaporate from landfills; air deposition is probably the largest source of PCBs entering Lake Superior and possibly the other Great Lakes (see chapter 6). However, there are few attempts to monitor PCBs in the air or water, and hence no data following the change in levels over time are available.

A substantial decline in PCB levels from the early 1970s, with minor fluctuations up and down over the past decade, is shown by the FDA diet studies (figure 2.12). The FDA data, as well as those collected by

Figure 2.10
DDT and Dieldrin in Human Adipose Tissue, 1970–1979

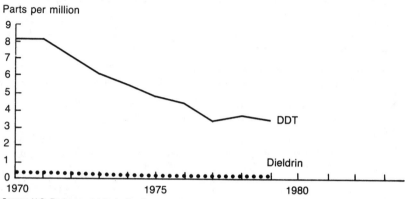

Parts per million

Source: U.S. Environmental Protection Agency.

Figure 2.11
U.S. Production of PCBs (Polychlorinated Biphenyls), 1960–1983

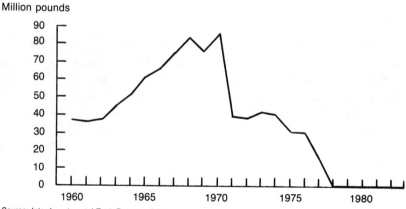

Million pounds

Source: Interdepartmental Task Force on PCBs.

USDA, reveal virtually no PCBs in most products in which the chemical is expected to accumulate. And PCB levels in the United States are substantially lower than those reported by other countries.[86]

One reason for the fluctuations may be that a relatively small amount of the substance entering the food chain can become distributed widely. This was demonstrated in 1979 when a PCB-containing transformer sprang a small leak in a meat-packing company in Billings, Montana.[87] The scraps from this facility were collected and converted into a supplement for chicken feed. This was shipped to poultry farms in six western states, where it was fed to both broilers and laying hens. In the latter case, the PCBs passed through to the eggs and appeared in the newly hatched chicks. By the time the problem was discovered, contaminated eggs and chickens were showing up in at least six states, and millions of eggs, 400,000 chickens, 40,000 pounds of egg products, and about $280,000 worth of cake mixes had to be destroyed or quarantined.

Several wildlife-monitoring programs show PCB concentrations decreasing (figure 2.12), although the trends have not all been consistent. In some samples, residues have increased. The data from mallard ducks demonstrate some geographical differences. Ducks from the heavily populated and industrialized Atlantic Flyway show both the greatest frequency of detection (100 percent) and the highest PCB residues; the concentrations there are more than twice those in waterfowl in the Central Flyway.[88] There are no data available to indicate the PCB trends in mussels either nationally or in California. The Mussel Watch Program has concentrated instead on identifying PCB "hot spots"—typically in the harbors of industrial cities.[89]

Measurements of PCBs in humans show patterns similar to those for wildlife—generally decreasing trends for the concentrations of PCBs in human fat (figure 2.13), but an increase in the proportion of samples found to contain the substance.[90] By 1981, PCBs were being found in virtually every sample tested. The increased frequency of detection may partially be explained by improved analysis methods but also reflects the way in which such a persistent chemical gradually works its way through various physical, chemical, and biological cycles until it appears everywhere.

Benzene

Benzene is a lightweight hydrocarbon derived from petroleum and used as an intermediary in the manufacture of such a wide variety of products as plastics, dyes, nylon, detergents, pharmaceuticals, and pesticides.[91]

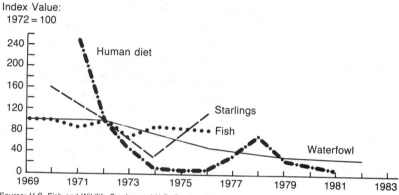

Figure 2.12
PCB (Polychlorinated Biphenyl) Residues
in Wildlife and Human Diet, 1969–1982

Source: U.S. Fish and Wildlife Service and U.S. Food and Drug Administration.

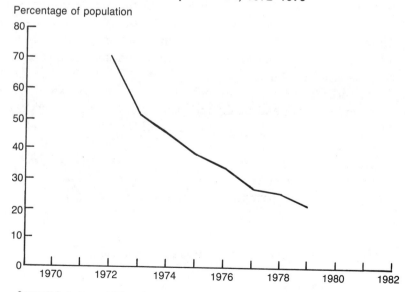

Figure 2.13
Percentage of U.S. Population with
PCB (Polychlorinated Biphenyl) Residues Greater
than 1 Part per Million, 1972–1979

Source: U.S. Environmental Protection Agency.

It also is a component of gasoline. Benzene's production increased substantially between 1960 and 1980 but has declined sharply since then (figure 2.14).* Approximately 300,000 metric tons are released to the environment every year in the United States.[92]

Exposure to benzene can cause leukemia and other chronic blood disorders in humans. However, no air pollution controls have been issued by EPA.[93]† The greatest exposure to benzene for humans apparently occurs from petroleum- and chemical-plant emissions, gas stations, and automobile exhaust, although drinking water, food, and cigarette smoke also are sources of human exposure.[95] However, very little information exists on how high exposures to the chemical are or how they have changed over time.

None of the other monitoring programs relied upon for information about exposure to toxic substances provides any useful information about benzene. The reason is that this substance does not accumulate anywhere in animal or human bodies. Being a very volatile compound, benzene, given the opportunity, quickly evaporates into the atmosphere and disperses. However, this characteristic does not make the chemical any less toxic, just more difficult to find.

ASBESTOS

Asbestos—a generic group of naturally occurring fibrous minerals that are nonflammable, heat resistant, durable, flexible, and strong—was first used in the United States in the early 1900s as a thermal insulator for steam engines and later as fireproofing and insulating material.[96] Currently, asbestos is used mostly in industry in the manufacture of brake and clutch linings for motor vehicles, of furnace and kiln linings, and of paper and plastic products, as well as in the production of cement, plaster, paints, plumbing supplies, and roofing and flooring tiles.

Asbestos, however, is one of the few substances with essentially irrefutable evidence demonstrating that it causes cancer in humans. When inhaled by humans, asbestos fibers stick in and damage the lungs. At

---

* These data do not include benzene mixed with gasoline.

† In December 1983, EPA proposed a regulation controlling leaks from gasoline-storage tanks and other dispersed sources and announced that it would propose controls for refineries and chemical plants in 1984.[94]

high exposure levels, this inhalation can cause asbestosis, a chronic lung disease.[97] And, after 20 to 40 years, a form of cancer, called mesothelioma, which affects the lining of the chest or abdomen, may develop. This type of cancer is only known to occur in people exposed to airborne asbestos.

Although asbestos-caused illnesses at first were related primarily to occupational exposure (people working in World War II shipyards were at particularly high risk), recent concern centers on exposures experienced by the general population and, in particular, by schoolchildren.[98] Deteriorating structures, especially school buildings, are a particularly dangerous exposure source because age and physical damage can disperse asbestos fibers into the air. Exposed children are at greatest risk because the average latency between exposure to asbestos fibers and the development of asbestos-induced disease is 10 to 40 years.[99] The length of the latency period varies with the amount and duration of exposure, but asbestos-induced lung cancers can occur after even relatively short, low-dose exposure.

Some of the highest asbestos concentrations have been found in schoolrooms (figure 2.15). About nine out of every million people can expect to develop lung cancer from a lifelong exposure to typical asbestos levels in outdoor air. But the risks increase over sixfold if people spend their school days in classrooms with deteriorating asbestos surfaces.[100]

EPA and the U.S. Department of Health, Education and Welfare (HEW, now the Department of Health and Human Services) created a program in early 1979 to help schools identify (and if necessary correct) crumbling asbestos construction materials.[101] In 1980, EPA issued a regulation requiring all schools, which had not voluntarily done so, to inspect their buildings for asbestos problems by June 1983.[102] The agency estimates that over half of the schools in the United States failed to carry out the required inspections and that as many as 14,000 public and private school buildings in the United States may need attention.[103] At least 3 million schoolchildren and 250,000 to 650,000 staff are exposed to asbestos currently. The cost of an inspection is usually less than $55, and the U.S. Department of Education estimates that the average cost of correcting problems, if they are found, is $100,000 per school.[104]

Asbestos is another substance for which the monitoring programs provide no information on the extent or intensity of exposure. The problem in measurement in this case is not that the substance is volatile. It is not. The reason probably lies in the difficulty of its detection other than in the air and in its having no demonstrated harm except when inhaled.

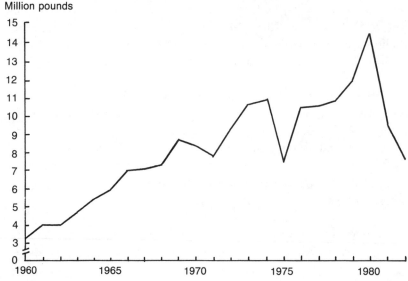

Figure 2.14
U.S. Production of Benzene, 1960–1982

Million pounds

Source: U.S. International Trade Commission.

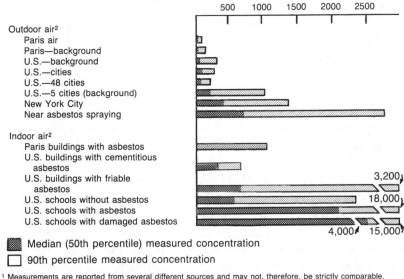

Figure 2.15.

Asbestos Measurements in Outdoor and Indoor Air[1]

Fiber concentration
(thousand fibers per cubic meter)

500   1000   1500   2000   2500

Outdoor air[2]
  Paris air
  Paris—background
  U.S.—background
  U.S.—cities
  U.S.—48 cities
  U.S.—5 cities (background)
  New York City
  Near asbestos spraying

Indoor air[2]
  Paris buildings with asbestos
  U.S. buildings with cementitious
    asbestos
  U.S. buildings with friable
    asbestos
  U.S. schools without asbestos
  U.S. schools with asbestos
  U.S. schools with damaged asbestos

3,200
18,000
4,000   15,000

■ Median (50th percentile) measured concentration
□ 90th percentile measured concentration

[1] Measurements are reported from several different sources and may not, therefore, be strictly comparable.
[2] See figure reference for full description of characteristics of measurements.
Source: U.S. Environmental Protection Agency.

TOXICITY TESTING

All of the chemicals described above have been determined, through tests on animals or epidemiological studies of exposed human populations, to be toxic. But what of other chemicals? There are over five million chemical substances listed in the Chemical Abstracts Service Registry.[105] This presumably defines the universe of "known" chemicals, although it does not necessarily include all substances that occur in nature or as a result of the degradation of synthetic chemicals once they are released to the environment. A National Academy of Sciences (NAS) committee concluded that humans may be exposed to almost 66,000 of these that are used in the United States as food additives, pesticides, drugs, cosmetics, or for other commercial uses (figure 2.16).[106]* And 400 to 600 new chemicals are being brought into commercial use every year.[109]

How many of these chemicals may be creating risks to human health or the environment? The simple answer is that no one knows. Making this determination requires knowing whether the chemical is hazardous (that is, whether it can cause detrimental effects if exposure occurs) and, if it is hazardous, how intense any exposure to it may be (see chapter 5). The NAS committee evaluated a representative sample of these chemicals to determine the adequacy of the testing done to measure possible human toxicity. They found that less than 2 percent of the chemicals have been sufficiently tested to allow a complete health hazard assessment to be made. For only 14 percent is there sufficient information to support even a partial hazard assessment. Adequate testing is most likely to have been conducted for drugs and pesticides, but, even

---

* The committee arrived at its estimate of 65,725 chemicals by adding together five separate lists of chemicals. However, the same substance could occur on more than one of these lists. The committee estimated that eliminating such duplication would result in about 53,500 distinct chemical entities.[107]

There are, however, four reasons why the NAS tabulation may be too low. The first is that they did not include over 1,400 new chemicals that have been produced since the lists the committee used were assembled. The second is that one of the lists was updated after the committee made its assessment, adding about 15,000 additional chemicals.[108] The third is that some of the entries on this list are actually categories of chemicals, such as categories of petroleum distillates, which include a number of different chemical substances. Finally, none of these lists include either natural chemical substances that are not used for commercial purposes or degradation products for those that are. Both can cause human exposure.

Figure 2.16.
Availability of Health-Effects Information for
Categories of Chemicals

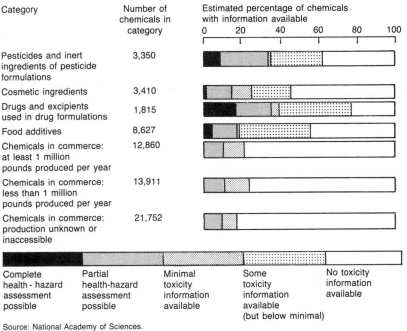

Source: National Academy of Sciences.

for those substances, complete or partial health assessments only have been carried out on only about one-third of the chemicals. And, for most categories, the number of substances lacking any data is much greater than the number for which the data are considered to be minimally adequate. In short, the committee found that for 70 percent of the 60,000 to 70,000 chemicals to which Americans are exposed, there is no information on possible effects on human health. For another 14 percent, there is some information, but it is less than the amount needed for a hazard assessment. Chemical industry officials claim that these figures exaggerate the lack of data because the NAS study did not include confidential test data in company files.

In addition, the committee found that the frequency and quality of testing are unrelated either to the production volume or to the degree of concern felt by the committee members about a substance's potential toxic effects based on their assessment of the substance's physiochemical properties.[110] For 20 percent of the substances, the committee members had a high concern about potential adverse human health effects, and, for another 32 percent, moderate concerns.[111]

The situation with respect to exposure information is even worse than the information on toxicity testing.[112] The committee made a number of efforts, beyond reviewing the data readily available to them, to obtain some information that would allow some estimate of exposure. But "even the simpliest of the relevant data (e.g., reliable annual production rates) could not be obtained in most cases."[113] With such a lack of information, even if an adequate health-hazard assessment could be carried out, there is insufficient information to estimate the amount of human health risk actually associated with the substances.

Moreover, none of this discussion pertains to risk to the nonhuman environment, since the NAS committee only looked at human health risk. In general, there is much less information available on environmental hazards and exposure for wildlife than there is even on human health risks.

CONCLUSIONS

For the most part, how to determine, or to adequately measure, many of the effects that toxic substances have on people or on the environment remains a mystery. The continuing discovery of previously unsuspected hazards from various chemicals and other substances underscores this point. The environmental and human health effects of even those substances identified for priority consideration, in general, have not been adequately studied. Moreover, until the present decade, testing of suspected toxic substances was confined largely to acute effects. Only in the last few years have the chronic, long-term effects of exposure to many of these substances been understood. Knowledge of environmental effects, how chemicals are transported through the environment, what biological pathways they follow, and where they ultimately end up is still lacking for most suspected toxic materials. A shortage of trained personnel and the absence of a comprehensive system for storing and analyzing information aggravate the scientific bases for government inaction.

Shortcomings in the nation's scientific-research knowledge and capabilities are by no means the only factors inhibiting the full and adequate implementation of protective or preventive measures, however. As in the case of EDB, failure to understand a substance's potential pervasiveness confounds prevention action. Even when the toxic properties and potential of a substance are relatively well known, technical obstacles, disjointed legal and administrative jurisdictions, industry resistance, bureaucratic inertia, and legal complexities often delay or effectively prevent instituting protective measures.

Hazardous Wastes

When disposed of on the land, wastes containing potentially harmful substances are called *hazardous*.* It used to be thought that this form of disposal was reasonably safe, based on the implicit assumption that the substances would either degrade into harmless products or at least stay where they were put. Both assumptions were wrong. Many of the wastes do not degrade, degrade very slowly, or degrade into substances that also are hazardous. Often, the wastes do not stay put. Instead, they seep into groundwater or are moved by wind or by storm water and floods to other locations.

---

* As with toxic substances, a waste's "hazard" is a matter of regulatory and legislative definition.

The sad lesson has been learned: Such wastes can create substantial risks for people long after their disposal. Some of the substances in the wastes can cause birth defects, cancer, genetic effects, neurological effects, or liver damage, to name a few. However, it is hard to estimate exposure to wastes and to link this exposure to specific effects.

Recent reports provide a much clearer picture of the amount of hazardous waste generated in the United States, the ways in which it is managed, and the number of sites that need to be cleaned up. Nevertheless, data are not yet adequate to identify *trends* in the amounts generated or in management practices. Estimates of the amount and location of previously disposed hazardous wastes that now need to be cleaned up are being refined. However, the difficulty of determining standards to define *clean* means it is equally difficult to know the extent to which past problems are being remedied.

Estimating how much hazardous waste is being generated, managed, and cleaned up is a knotty problem for three reasons. First are the many problems of definition: When does a material become a waste? Is it a waste if it is going to be recycled? What characteristics make a waste hazardous? Can the differences in hazard between concentrated (small volume but probably more of a hazard) and diluted (large amounts but probably less of a hazard) be taken into account? How should wastes of unknown hazard be considered? That 32 states use definitions different from the one used by the U.S. Environmental Protection Agency (EPA) illustrates the predicament.[114]

A second problem in developing data on hazardous waste is logistical. Different types or forms of hazardous waste are regulated under different laws, with no common definition or information system linking the programs that administer those laws. Nuclear wastes are regulated under the Atomic Energy Act; discharges into water are covered by the Clean Water Act; emissions into air, by the Clean Air Act. Only those wastes regulated under Subtitle C of the Resource Conservation and Recovery Act (RCRA) are included in the hazardous-waste data collected by EPA.

A third obstacle is enforcement verification. Only rarely can accurate information about illegally handled hazardous waste be obtained, and those amounts for which no accurate data exist are obviously beyond estimation.

Despite the dearth of reliable information, surveys and studies are delineating the scope of the hazardous-waste problem and providing a base from which to measure trends in the future. Two laws passed to address the problem mandate some record keeping and reporting of data. Under RCRA, industrial facilities must keep records of the amount and types of wastes they generate and manage. EPA is now undertaking its first biennial survey of generators and managers under RCRA. The survey will provide information on the quantities of hazardous waste generated and on processes used to store, treat, or dispose of those wastes. Findings for 1983 will be available in late 1984.[115]

The Comprehensive Environmental Response, Compensation, and Liability Act (CERCLA) of 1980 created the Superfund to help pay the cost of cleaning up hazardous-waste sites. Under CERCLA, EPA collects information about sites that need emergency or longer-term cleanup as well as about the nature of problems found at those sites.[116]

GENERATION OF WASTE

According to the most recent estimate, industries in the United States generate about 2,500 pounds of hazardous waste per capita annually. This estimate, however, ignores waste from firms generating under 1,000 kilograms (2,200 pounds) a month, as well as household waste, sewage discharged into municipal treatment plants, nuclear waste, agricultural waste, mining waste, and waste from Superfund sites. The Office of Technology Assessment (OTA) speculates that hazardous wastes not included in that estimate may be as large as the amount that is included.[117]

Attempts to quantify the amounts of waste produced also are tied to definitional matters. RCRA defines hazardous waste as solid waste that, when managed improperly, causes an increase in morbidity and mortality or poses a substantial threat to human health or the environment.[118] As was mentioned in the previous section, EPA identifies ignitability, corrosivity, reactivity, and toxicity as characteristics of hazardous waste. If a substance has these characteristics, it is considered hazardous unless exempted. In addition, the wastes listed by EPA as hazardous include some (but not all) carcinogens, an effect for which EPA does not consider reliable testing protocols available.[119] Hazardous wastes may be in any physical form—solids, liquids, semiliquids, or gases. However, EPA interprets RCRA to exempt solid or dissolved material in domestic sewage.[120] Currently, recycled hazardous wastes are exempt from RCRA, although some hazardous wastes slated for recycling, such as sludges, listed wastes, and mixtures containing listed wastes, are subject to transport and storage regulations.[121] Exempting recycling may encourage its use, but recycling also can cause pollution.

Four studies, prepared since RCRA was passed in 1976, have estimated the amounts of hazardous waste generated annually in 1980 or 1981 (figure 2.17). The estimates range from 41 million tons to 264 million tons. The differences result from both the types of wastes included and the sources of information used.

As part of its environmental-impact assessment on the implementation of RCRA issued in 1978, EPA collected information from states and performed studies of the major industries generating hazardous waste. Based on these data, EPA estimated that 56 million tons of hazardous waste were likely to be generated in 1980, 61 percent of it from industrial sources. EPA had not yet issued its definition of hazardous waste when this estimate was made.[122]

A second estimate of the amount of hazardous waste generated in 1980 was made by a contractor for EPA as part of a study of commercial capacity to manage hazardous waste. This estimate of 41 million tons, published in 1980, covers only industrial waste. It is based on extrapolations from model plants and state reports of industry rates of waste generation, many of which used different definitions of hazardous wastes. The focus is on wastes from processes in industries such as metals, electric equipment, paper, transportation, chemicals, and petroleum. Among wastes not included in the estimate are discarded or off-specification products, mining wastes, small-volume generator wastes, or wastes from abandoned sites or spills.[123]

In April 1984, EPA released, as part of a national survey of hazardous-waste generators and management facilities, a third estimate of the amount of hazardous waste generated annually in the United States. At 264 million tons, the estimate was more than six times the 1980 estimate. It also was much higher than the 150-million-ton figure used in the preliminary results of the survey, issued in 1983.[124] This figure is the actual amount of waste generated in 1981 that was subject to RCRA, based on reports by samples of generators and managers of hazardous waste. Since EPA's definition of hazardous waste was used, the estimate does not include small-volume generators, mining, or Superfund wastes. Nor does it cover releases to sewage-treatment plants, treatment in tanks with permits under the Clean Water Act, or wastes beneficially used or recycled at the factories where they were generated.[125] The 1984 survey attributes the differences between its preliminary figure of 150 million tons and its final figure of 264 million tons to the difficulty of sampling generators. A few major plants generate and manage very large amounts of waste. In the initial sample, one plant alone generated 40 million tons, for example.[126] The wastes of these large generators are primarily mixtures of hazardous wastes and nonhazardous wastes.[127] The 1980 estimate of 41 million tons focused on commercial waste management and shipment of wastes from generators to those facilities. The 1984 survey concludes, "The major differences between the conclusions of this and earlier studies appear to be related to the previously unobserved activities of large hazardous waste generators with on-site TSD [treatment, storage, and disposal] facilities."[128]

A fourth survey, based on state estimates of the amounts of hazardous waste generated, was performed for OTA in 1983 by the Association of State and Territorial Solid Waste Management Officials. It came up with a very similar number to the 1984 EPA estimate, but at least partially for different reasons. States used their own widely varying definitions of hazardous waste and data for 1981 or 1982. The total estimated amount of hazardous waste generated by 40 states and 3 territories was 250 million tons. If the remaining states were added, the total might range from 255 million to 275 million tons, OTA suggests. In this estimate, just five states accounted for 85 percent of the total waste generated, at least partly because they included wastes not now regulated by RCRA, such as fly and bottom ash, demolition wastes, and mining and oil-field waste. Georgia alone accounted for 38.6 million tons, of which over 99 percent were dilute wastes neutralized on-site and discharged into sewers or water.[129]

Adding to the confusion are some indications that the amount of hazardous waste being generated actually is declining, although the newer estimates show much more waste subject to RCRA regulations than originally thought and more waste generated than subject to RCRA. About 15 percent more generators recycled wastes after 1981 than had done so before.[130] The Chemical Manufacturers Association reported that a survey of 70 chemical companies showed an 8 percent reduction in the amount of hazardous waste actually disposed of on a wet-ton basis between 1981 and 1982.[131] Lower levels of industrial activity may explain some of the reduction.

Overall estimates of hazardous-waste generation may well continue to increase in the future, however, if additional wastes become subject to RCRA. Among possible candidates are small-volume-generator wastes, wastes burned as fuels, and some recycled wastes. In addition, waste now legally released to sewage-treatment plants might become hazardous waste with implementaion of pretreatment standards. Massachusetts estimates that the quantity of hazardous waste generated in the state would increase by 50 percent in such a case.[132]

The results of EPA's first biennial survey, mentioned earlier, should help clarify the amounts and types of hazardous wastes actually being generated, although these figures will apply only to the hazardous wastes regulated under RCRA. Thus, for example, they will not include PCBs (polychlorinated biphenyls), now handled under the Toxic Substances Control Act (TSCA). Some states may collect data using other definitions than those set down by EPA under RCRA.

The biennial survey also will identify the number of hazardous-waste generators. Although as many as 70,000 firms originally notified EPA that they were possible generators or handlers of hazardous waste, the number of firms affected under RCRA now appears to be much lower, for many reasons: for example, confusion about who needed to notify EPA as a generator; the changes in definition of hazardous waste; and the removal of some wastes from the list. Moreover, generators producing fewer than 1,000 kilograms a month are exempt. EPA puts the number of such small generators at between 500,000 and 1 million.[133]

The 1984 survey estimates that 14,098 generators were active in 1981. The chemical and petroleum industries together account for about 20 percent of the generators and 71 percent of the volume of hazardous waste generated, according to this study. The metal-related industries account for 45 percent of the generators but only 22 percent of the waste volume[134] (figure 2.18).

TREATMENT, STORAGE, AND DISPOSAL FACILITIES

Under RCRA, hazardous waste may be managed by treatment, storage, or disposal. In some cases, a waste may go through all three stages. And a process such as a surface impoundment may be used for all three purposes.

Two sets of data provide estimates of the number of facilities now managing wastes. One is the file of facilities that reported to EPA in 1980 in "Part A" applications that they managed or intended to manage hazardous wastes. In early 1984, EPA put the number of valid Part A applications at 7,549. Of these facilities, 5,255 only store and treat waste; 279 incinerate waste and may also store and treat it; and 2,013 dispose of waste in landfills, surface impoundments, and injection wells or use other processes that require groundwater monitoring, such as waste piles.[135]

In contrast, the 1984 EPA national survey discovered that 4,818 facilities actually treated, stored, or disposed of waste in 1981. There

Figure 2.17
Volume of Hazardous Waste Generated in
the United States: Four Estimates

Estimate in million metric tons	*Explanation*
56	Environmental Protection Agency (EPA) estimate (circa 1978) of volume of hazardous waste likely to be generated in 1980; 61 percent expected to come from industrial sources.
41	EPA contractor estimate in 1980 of industrial hazardous waste likely to be generated that year, with possible range set between 28 and 54 million metric tons.
250	Office of Technology Assessment (OTA) estimate in 1983 based on survey of states. If all states and territories were included, OTA suggests annual generation might range between 255 and 275 million tons.
264	EPA contractor estimate of hazardous waste in 1984 that was generated in 1981. Preliminary estimate was 150 million tons. Difference is due to difficulty of sampling because a few large plants generate and manage very large amounts of waste.

Figure 2.18
Distribution of Hazardous-Waste Generation,
by Industrial Sector, 1981

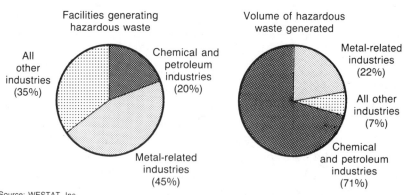

Facilities generating
hazardous waste

All other industries (35%)

Chemical and petroleum industries (20%)

Metal-related industries (45%)

Volume of hazardous
waste generated

Metal-related industries (22%)

All other industries (7%)

Chemical and petroleum industries (71%)

Source: WESTAT, Inc.

are several reasons for the smaller number. The 1980 number includes those generators storing wastes for under 90 days, for example. Some facilities may not have handled hazardous waste in 1981; some of these may do so in the future, or they may stop handling hazardous waste permanently.[136]

The national survey found 1,495 sites treating waste (including incineration), 4,299 storing waste, and 430 facilities—landfills, land-treatment sites, injection wells, and surface impoundments—actually disposing of waste during 1981 (figure 2.19).[137] Tanks and surface impoundments handled the bulk of hazardous waste treated and stored, according to the survey. And, of the 55 million tons of hazardous waste disposed of under RCRA in 1981, more than half (32 million tons) were injected into underground wells, with another third (19 million tons) handled in surface impoundments. Both these disposal methods were used for large amounts of liquid wastes. Three million tons of hazardous waste went into landfills. Although much less waste went into landfills, the national survey shows more than twice as many landfills as sites with injection wells.[138] (Wastes containing hazardous materials, but not managed under RCRA, may also have been legally placed in municipal landfills or sewers or burned as fuel.)

Geographically, the largest number of facilities managing waste in 1981 was found in EPA's Great Lakes region, followed by its two southern regions and the New York-New Jersey region. Few sites were located in the Northwest (figure 2.20).[139]

Relatively little of the waste was transported from the site where it was generated, according to the survey. Indeed, as much as 96 percent of the *volume* of hazardous waste managed under RCRA is handled at its generation site. Large generators of hazardous waste tend to manage it on site. Nevertheless, more than 80 percent of all generators in the study ship at least some of their hazardous waste to off-site facilities.[140]

PERMITTING OF FACILITIES

Any method of handling hazardous waste can create health and environmental risks. The permitting of facilities that treat, store, or dispose of hazardous waste, required by RCRA, is intended to limit the risk by specifying operating and design practices.

Facilities that existed before November 1980, notified EPA of their activities, and submitted initial ("Part A") permit applications have interim permits. These permits require monitoring, record keeping, personnel training, emergency planning, and closure procedures. Non-

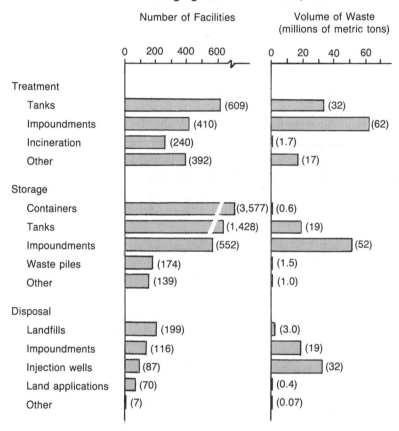

Figure 2.19
Facilities Managing Hazardous Waste, 1981

Source: Westat, Inc.

Figure 2.20
Regional Distribution of Hazardous-Waste Management
Facilities, 1981

Estimated total number of active facilities in 1981: 4,818

Source: Westat, Inc.

compliance with some provisions of interim permits apparently has been high. Of 65 facilities subject to groundwater-monitoring requirements in Illinois and North Carolina, 78 percent were not in compliance as of June 1983. The cost and complexity of locating and operating the monitoring wells were cited by state officials as the reason for the lack of compliance.[141]

Facilities are now applying for "Part B" permits that require adherence to design and operating standards, such as liners for landfills. Until a decision is made on a Part B permit, facilities can operate under interim permits. As of February 1984, only 122 facilities had received Part B permits. The permitted facilities include 112 storage and treatment sites, 7 incinerators, 2 landfills, and 1 waste pile. However, between 500 and 600 facilities have been denied or have withdrawn their permit applications (figure 2.21).[142]

EPA plans to check 8,500 facilities that notified it in 1980 of their intent to manage hazardous waste, to determine whether permits are needed. The 1984 figure of 4,820 facilities managing hazardous waste in 1981—about half the 1980 number—and the rate of EPA's permit-application withdrawals may indicate that many facilities are deciding not to manage hazardous waste in the future. On the other hand, some of these sites may also be storing wastes for under 90 days, which does not require a RCRA permit; however, such sites originally were required to notify EPA. Other sites may need to be closed according to RCRA requirements.

It is not yet clear to what extent waste management capacity will be affected by the implementation of RCRA. The national survey found that capacity appears to be ample, at least for the 1981 levels of hazardous waste. Nationally, only 23 percent of the treatment, 36 percent of the disposal, and 64 percent of the storage capacity were in use. Unused capacity tends to be greatest at the larger facilities. Half of unused treatment capacity is in the Great Lakes region, and another 30 percent is in the South. Sixty percent of the unused disposal capacity is in the Southeast. The Northwest had no unused disposal capacity, according to the survey, but this was based on only two reporting facilities. The ten EPA regions of the United States had average treatment-, storage-, and disposal-facility capacity-utilization rates of between 45 and 65 percent in 1981.[143] Other reports also indicate that there may be adequate capacity in many areas. Members of the Hazardous Waste Treatment Council report unused capacity of 30 percent to 50 percent.[144] A 1984 report by the New York State Hazardous Waste

Figure 2.21
Permitting of Hazardous-Waste Facilities, 1980–1984

Item	Number of firms	Gn	Tp	St	Tr	Ds	Description
1	400,000	•	•	o	o	o	Firms that EPA identified as possible handlers of hazardous waste and sent letters in 1980, seeking responses from those considering themselves subject to RCRA.
2	70,000	•	•	o	o	o	Firms that notified EPA that they were or might be handlers of hazardous waste under RCRA.
3	60,000	•	o				Firms in item 2 that only generated hazardous waste.
4	10,000		•	•	•	•	Firms in item 2 that were not located at the same site as a generator.
5	15,000	o	o	•	•	•	Firms that submitted "Part A" applications in 1980 indicating they intended to treat, store, or dispose of hazardous waste under RCRA.
6	14,000	•	o	o	o	o	Contractor's 1984 estimate of firms actually generating hazardous waste in 1981.
7	8,500	o	o	•	•	•	Firms in item 5 that EPA found required an interim permit to manage wastes under RCRA.
8	4,818	o	o	o	o	o	Contractor's 1984 estimate of firms that managed hazardous wastes in 1981—under RCRA definition.
9	4,299	o	o	•	o	o	Facilities in item 8 that stored hazardous waste for over 90 days in 1981.
10	1,495	o	o	o	•	o	Facilities in item 8 that treated hazardous waste in 1981 (includes incineration)
11	430	o	o	o	o	•	Facilities in item 8 that disposed of hazardous waste in 1981
12	500–600	o	o				Part B permits denied or sites withdrawing from permitting process as of February 1984.
13	122	o	o	•	•	•	Storage, treatment, and disposal facilities that had received Part B permits as of February 1984.
14	7	o	o	o	•	o	Number of incinerators in item 13.
15	3	o	o	o	o	•	Number of disposal facilities in item 13 (two landfills and a waste pile)

• Activities that are primary focus of estimates

o Other activities in which firms included in estimate could also be engaged

Gn—Generation
Tp—Transportation
St—Storage
Tr—Treatment
Ds—Disposal

Source: U.S. Environmental Protection Agency.

Treatment Facilities Task Force found no "readily apparent" crisis related to treatment capacity and siting issues.[145] Across the country, 22 new management facilities have received Part B permits.[146] States and regions are experimenting with various siting processes. For example, Southern California is developing an integrated regional plan that sites some type of facility in each county.[147] It is not yet clear how effective state siting processes for commercial facilities will be. Commercial facilities, defined as private or public facilities receiving more than half of their waste from off-site, in 1981 had less than 1 percent of the nation's total treatment capacity, 3 percent of the storage capacity, and 6 percent of disposal capacity.[148]

A good bit of attention has been given to the need to limit the types of substances placed in landfills and the use of protective measures such as liners and monitoring, although these steps are still in the preliminary stages of implementation.[149] However, less attention has been paid to other methods of land disposal—in particular, surface impoundments and deepwell injection, which the national survey surprisingly showed are used to dispose of over 90 percent of the waste.

Impoundments often have been the source of pollution problems in the past. Almost one-third of the sites on EPA's National Priorities List for Superfund are surface impoundments.[150] An earlier EPA study, done before the RCRA definition of hazardous waste was established, identified 180,000 existing impoundments used by industry, agriculture, mining, municipal government, or oil and gas extraction. It found little relationship between protection practices that impoundments use, such as liners and monitoring, and the likelihood of damage due, for instance, to proximity to aquifers used for drinking water.[151] An environmental group in Maryland traced records on 17 impoundments in the state that the EPA study listed as "worst-case" because of type of waste and location. Only six had monitoring wells, and five of these showed groundwater degradation. Eleven were on EPA's list of sites to be evaluated for Superfund. Three more that were not on the list to be evaluated showed evidence of groundwater degradation.[152] California, where 10 of the top 15 Superfund sites are impoundments, is considering a bill that would close any impoundment within a half mile of a potential drinking-water source and would require soil and groundwater testing for others. Leaking impoundments would have to be retrofitted with a double liner and leak-detection system.[153]

Underground injection, already the disposal method used for almost 60 percent of the volume of waste disposed of, may well grow if restrictions on landfills and surface impoundments are increased, as some proposed RCRA amendments provide. Wells used for hazardous waste may be Class I or Class IV wells under the federal classification system. Class I wells discharge below the deepest underground source of drinking water. Class IV wells discharge into or above drinking-water sources. Early state estimates put the number of operating Class IV wells in the United States at about 300, but many of these turned out to be other types of wells. An EPA staffer estimates that 20 Class IV wells may now be operating. All Class IV wells that inject directly into underground sources of drinking water have been banned. All state programs have indicated their intention to ban the remaining Class IV wells, and in May 1984 EPA banned the remaining wells in states that have not been delegated authority to run the underground-injection program.[154]

Initial RCRA notifications in 1980 showed about 160 Class I and Class IV wells. By 1982, RCRA was estimating 133 Class I wells at 74 sites.[155] The 1984 EPA national survey found 87 sites with injection wells.[156] EPA's Office of Drinking Water is also surveying Class I wells. As of May 1984, its survey had identified 215 active wells (171 continuously operating and 44 that inject waste intermittently) at 118 sites. One reason for the larger number in the Office of Drinking Water's survey may be that states used their own definitions of hazardous waste in responding. Only 4 new Class I wells were built in 1983, down from a peak of 18 in 1976.[157] However, there are some indications that this number may increase again.[158]

Injection wells are used to dispose of liquid waste—for example, acid or alkaline solutions, solutions containing metals, and solvents. The wastes are pumped into underground strata where they are assumed to be contained by impermeable rocks. The average depth of the active wells found in the Office of Drinking Water survey is 3,800 feet.[159] Although the technology of underground injection has seen extensive use in the oil and gas industry, the possible effects of its use for hazardous-waste disposal have not received detailed analysis. There have been problems at a number of sites. An injection-well site in Erie, Pennsylvania, formerly used for pulp-mill waste, is on the Superfund list and may be contaminating an aquifer serving parts of Pennsylvania, Ohio, and possibly Canada.[160] More recently, leaks have been found in injection wells operated by an active liquid-waste facility in Sandusky County, Ohio.[161] Neither of these facilities was being operated in accordance with current regulations. There are also concerns whether present regulations are adequate. The pressure and injection rate in wells are now monitored; some engineers say the effectiveness of this monitoring in detecting leaks has not been demonstrated. The groundwater penetrated by the well may not be monitored.[162] Responsibility for problems that might occur after a well is closed is not yet clear in the regulations.[163]

CLEANING UP HAZARDOUS-WASTE SITES

EPA estimates that between 16,000 and 22,000 sites across the United States harbor hazardous wastes that either cause or have the potential to cause contamination (figure 2.22).[164] The Comprehensive Environmental Response, Compensation, and Liability Act (CERCLA) created a fund, popularly known as Superfund, to clean up problem waste sites. To qualify for cleanup under Superfund, a site must be placed on the National Priorities List (NPL). An exception is emergency actions, which are evaluated separately for Superfund cleanup. In addition, some states have their own cleanup programs.

To determine whether they belong on the NPL, sites are ranked by their potential impacts on health and the environment through air, groundwater, and surface water. About 900 sites have been evaluated so far by EPA for possible inclusion on the list for Superfund cleanup. The often large variety of substances at waste sites and the many routes of exposure make it very tough to assess actual health and environmental effects. So far, 444 toxic pollutants have been found at these sites. The 10 most commonly found substances are lead, trichloroethylene, toluene, benzene, PCBs, chloroform, phenol, arsenic, cadmium, and chromium. Some of these substances can cause immediate poisoning. Virtually all of them can damage health as the result of low-level, long-term exposure, particularly through drinking water. Seven are believed capable of causing cancer; seven, birth defects; and five, genetic effects. The risk resulting from being exposed to more than one of these substances at the same time is not known.[165]

As of March 1982, 115 sites had been designated NPL sites.[166] A total of 546 are now on the list,[167] and EPA believes that the list may eventually include between 1,400 and 2,200 sites.[168] Each state may designate a top-priority site for the list; other sites are placed on the list by their ranking in the assessment. New Jersey tops the list with 85, followed by Michigan (48) and Pennsylvania (39).[169] (Figure 2.23).

Hazardous substances are known to exist in the groundwater at 75 percent of the sites now on the NPL, in surface water at 56 percent, and in the air at 20 percent.[170] An analysis of documented damage cases

Figure 2.22
Cleaning Up Hazardous-Waste Sites

Number of sites	Description
16,000–22,000	EPA's 1983 estimate of the sites that may cause hazardous waste problems.
7,113	State officials' 1983 estimate of sites requiring cleanup.
1,400–2,200	EPA's estimate of sites likely to be eventually placed on the National Priority List (NPL), which makes a site's cleanup eligible for Superfund financing.
546	Sites on or proposed for NPL as of April 1984.
267	Sites on NPL at which work had started as of January 1984.
100	NPL sites EPA expects to cleanup with current Superfund authorization.
100–170	NPL sites EPA expects to be cleaned up by those who contributed waste to site.
196	Sites at which emergency removals had taken place as of January 1984.
33	Sites not on NPL at which states completed long-term cleanups in 1981, 1982, and part of 1983.
6	NPL sites that had been cleaned up as of January 1984.

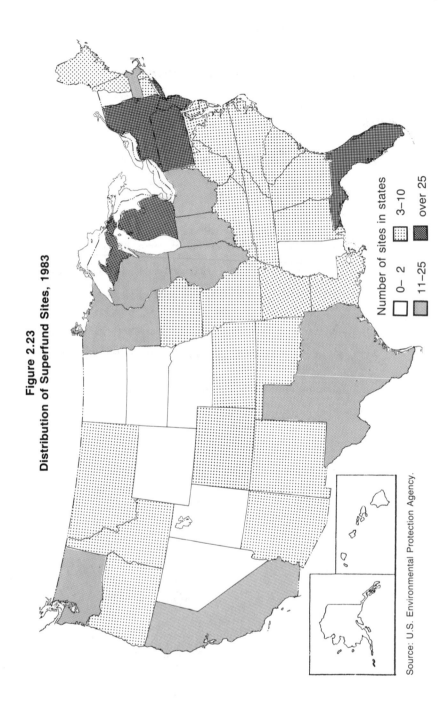

Figure 2.23
Distribution of Superfund Sites, 1983

Number of sites in states

0– 2   3–10

11–25   over 25

Source: U.S. Environmental Protection Agency.

at active and inactive hazardous-waste-management facilities found 34 percent involved drinking water; 29 percent, property; 25 percent, animals and plants; and 12 percent, effects on human health and the food chain.[171]

Two types of cleanup actions can be taken with Superfund financing: emergency actions and longer-term cleanup. Dangers of fire, explosion, or acute effects from direct contact are considered for possible emergency action under Superfund. As of January 31, 1984, 196 such actions had been taken. They involved such situations as abandoned factories or treatment facilities, accidents at operating plants, and illegally dumped wastes. Of these actions, 75 took place at NPL sites that still remain eligible for long-term remedial action.[172]

Longer-term cleanup is moving very slowly. As of January 1984, just six sites on the NPL had been completely cleaned up. Some work had begun at 267 more. Remedial action such as removal, treatment, or containment had started at 24 of these sites; initial measures such as building fences had been initiated at 32 sites. Data collection, feasibility studies, or detailed design of remedial measures were underway at the remaining sites.[173] EPA expects to complete clean up at only about 100 sites on the NPL with the $1.3 billion that Superfund is likely to generate before the tax on petrochemical feedstocks and other chemicals authorized by CERCLA expires in 1985. An additional 100 to 170 NPL sites may be cleaned up by the generators, transporters, and site owners and operators.[174] Thus, current resources will fund remedial work at only a small fraction of the several thousand sites likely to end up on the NPL.

The numbers of sites needing cleanup may grow larger than expected, given how many are withdrawing from the RCRA permitting process. Federal facilities and additional mining-waste sites may also be placed on the NPL. Sites not selected for the list will need to be cleaned up with other resources. A survey of state officials estimates that at least 7,113 sites will require some remedial action.[175] The thousands of municipal landfills that may contain hazardous wastes present a special problem. Cities now have little incentive to encourage listing on the NPL of these sites because they must pay half the cleanup cost.

EPA estimates that cleaning up all the sites on the NPL will cost between $8 billion and $16 billion, although the General Accounting Office suggests that these estimates may be low.[176] The cost estimate skyrockets when restoration of contaminated groundwater is needed. A study for the Chemical Manufacturers Association (CMA) put the price of conducting engineering studies and removing and containing waste at $4 million to $6 million per site. Usually, containment is less expensive than cleanup, but it requires long-term monitoring. If restoration of contaminated aquifers is necessary, total costs, as estimated by the CMA study, increase to $17 million per site.[177]

The "how clean is clean" issue is a major one. There are no standards for many substances found at waste sites. Only 20 maximum-contaminant levels are set under the Safe Drinking Water Act, for example.[178] EPA decides on a site-by-site basis how to get the most cleanup for the least cost. The balancing test required by Superfund in choosing remedial methods at a site now often means that containment methods such as capping are selected. If longer-term costs are included, the choice might shift at many sites to methods that actually treat the waste to decrease its volume, mobility, or hazard.[179]

Congress, state and local governments, and private groups are all taking steps to speed the cleanup process, which now looks as though it will take at least another decade. Debate has started in congressional hearings on the form an extension of Superfund might take, particularly on its size and whether taxes should be placed on wastes as well as feedstocks.[180] Since 1981, states have completed long-term cleanup at 33 sites and started work at 100 more sites, one survey shows. None of these sites are on the NPL.[181] Some states are developing their own hazardous-waste cleanup plans and funding methods. New Jersey, which has both a Spill Compensation and a Hazardous Discharge Fund to help pay for cleanups, has scheduled remedial action at 106 sites, including 41 not now on the NPL. Its master list includes 900 sites known or suspected to contain hazardous waste, but most of these sites must still be evaluated. The state lists 70 sites as cleaned up; most involved only removal of drums of waste, however.[182]

Leaders in the environmental community and the chemical industry have worked for nearly a year, under the auspices of The Conservation Foundation, to find a way to accelerate the process of cleaning up sites. To complement Superfund, the group has proposed creation of a nonprofit organization supported by foundation and corporate funds. To overcome major barriers to more rapid cleanup, the organization would: (1) help potentially responsible generators and transporters of waste and site operators and owners to negotiate fair allocations of financial liability for cleaning up individual sites; (2) monitor and certify cleanup proposals and activities; and 3) provide management skills to oversee complex multiparty cleanups, particularly those involving some public money.[183]

CONCLUSION

The amounts of hazardous waste and methods used to manage it on land, in the past and at present, can now be described and action taken to lessen the risk. But no one can yet detect trends in generation or in treatment, storage, and disposal with any certainty. Thus, the disparity between a 1970 estimate of 9 million tons of industrial waste generated[184] and the OTA estimate of as many as 275 tons annually in the early 1980s presumably results mainly from differences in definition and increased knowledge about generators of hazardous waste, particularly larger on-site ones.

Only by looking at the handling of waste in all media—emissions to the air and discharges to groundwater, surface water, and wastewater-treatment plants as well as wastes managed under RCRA and Superfund—and not just on land will an understanding be gained of where hazardous wastes go, how they are handled, and whether the amounts actually are being reduced, management practices improved, and the risk lessened.

Air Quality

Air quality in the United States continues to improve, at least in terms of previously identified and monitored pollution problems, caused by so-called conventional pollutants, in urban areas. The battle, however, is far from won. Many areas of the country continue to experience episodes when air pollution levels create human health risks. Finishing the cleanup in these areas may well prove more difficult and expensive than it was in areas that have already attained standards.

In addition to these obstinate areas of urban pollution, other air pollution problems are being discovered that current control efforts do not address.[185] Little has been done to control "hazardous" and other "nonconventional" air pollutants. Existing sulfur oxide controls appear to be inadequate to protect lakes and forests against the problems of acid rain. The inexorable buildup of carbon dioxide in the atmosphere threatens large-scale climatic changes. And there is essentially no effort being made to control the level of air pollution indoors, where most Americans spend the majority of their time.

Even for conventional pollutants, the significance of the improvement can be questioned because the data lack authority.[186] No national system exists for monitoring air quality. Instead, the monitors are operated by different states and localities. Although the U.S. Environmental Protection Agency (EPA) has tried to improve the quality of these data, the task is hard: the number and location of the monitors have changed over the period of record; many records are incomplete; the data have been collected using varying monitoring techniques; and the quality control and verification of monitoring results have not always been satisfactory.[187]

Interpreting these data is likewise difficult. Year-to-year improvements in air quality occur for a number of reasons aside from pollution-control efforts. Some major sources of pollution may have closed or moved elsewhere, increasing pollution levels at the new site. Temporary economic slowdowns may have caused an equally temporary reduction in industrial emissions. Or climatic conditions may have changed for the better, with steady breezes dispersing the pollutants, for instance. Monitoring data are not adjusted to account for any of these changes.

For these reasons caution should be exercised in interpreting any year-to-year variations in air quality. However, when the data show consistent changes over several years, the trends can be interpreted more confidently.

AMBIENT AIR QUALITY

Efforts to control air pollution have traditionally focused primarily on improving ambient air quality in urban areas for five "conventional" pollutants: total suspended particulates (TSPs), sulfur oxides, nitrogen oxides, carbon monoxide, and ozone. However, many cities and states began controlling particulates and sulfur oxides before the 1970 Clean Air Act. As a result, many major emitters switched to cleaner fuels (for example, from high-sulfur coal to oil or natural gas) or adopted control technologies (such as electrostatic precipitators or bag houses) during the late 1960s—often with impressive results. Available data indicate that ambient urban-pollution levels decreased 23 percent for particulates from 1960 to 1971 and 58 percent for sulfur oxides between 1966 and 1971.*[188]

Further dramatic improvements appear unlikely, but continued progress has been made since 1970. EPA estimates that emissions of the conventional pollutants from most of the major sources have either

---

* The data for particulates are based on 92 monitors, and those for sulfur dioxide, on 32 monitors, all in urban areas.

declined or held steady despite increased economic activity in each of the polluting sectors (figure 2.24). U.S. cities continue to benefit from cleaner and less unhealthful air—at least for these conventional pollutants.

Pollution Standards Index

The air quality in large American cities, as measured by the pollution standards index (PSI), has improved consistently and significantly over the past decade (figure 2.25). The PSI measures how frequently the air quality is bad enough to create health risks.* The average reading of the 23 metropolitan areas included in the national index for 1981 shows 0.13 days in the hazardous category (PSI greater than 300), down from 1.8 days in 1974; 11.3 days in the very unhealthful category (PSI of 200 to 300), down 65 percent from 1974; and 33 days in the unhealthful category (PSI of 100 to 200), about half of the number experienced during most of the 1970s. The greatest drop in the very unhealthful category occurred between 1976 and 1978, whereas the drop in the unhealthful category has happened primarily since 1978.

The cities showing the most significant improvements are Chicago; Portland, Oregon; and Philadelphia—which registered decreases of 92 percent, 78 percent, and 77 percent, respectively, in the number of days in the unhealthful category since 1974. Houston, Los Angeles, Sacramento, and San Diego are 4 of the 23 cities with increased PSIs over the last decade.

Trends for Particular Pollutants

Trends in the average pollution levels for particular pollutants generally show less dramatic decreases than the PSI (figure 2.26). One reason is that the PSI only measures the frequency of serious air pollution episodes, not average air quality. The goal of the air-pollution-control program is to eliminate these serious episodes; less attention is paid to reducing emissions if the air quality is already better than the standards. Thus, the frequency of serious episodes will decrease more rapidly than

---

* The PSI is used to compare air-quality monitoring data in metropolitan areas around the country to the health-related standards established by EPA as mandated in the Clean Air Act. If the air pollution level at a site exceeds the standard for any one of the five criteria pollutants, then the index will be given a value of 100 or more for that day. In theory, the higher the index reading, the more severe the pollution and the greater the threat to human health.

Figure 2.24
Air Emissions, by Source and Type of Pollutant,
1970 and 1981

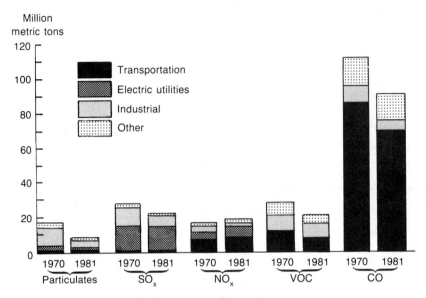

Source: U.S. Environmental Protection Agency.

Figure 2.25
Air Quality in 23 Metropolitan Areas, as Measured by the
Pollutant Standards Index (PSI), 1974–1981

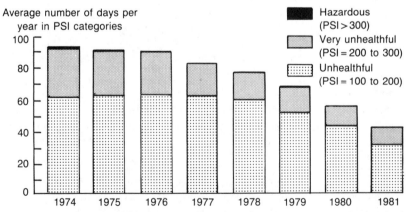

Source: Council on Environmental Quality.

Figure 2.26
U.S. Trends in Ambient Air Quality
for Five Pollutants, 1975–1982

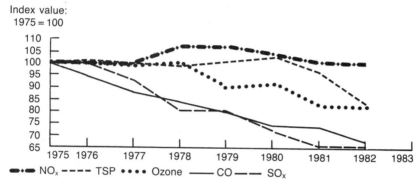

Index value:
1975 = 100

●–● NOₓ ---- TSP •••• Ozone ——— CO —— SOₓ

Source: U.S. Environmental Protection Agency.

Figure 2.27
U.S. Air Pollutant Emissions, 1970–1982

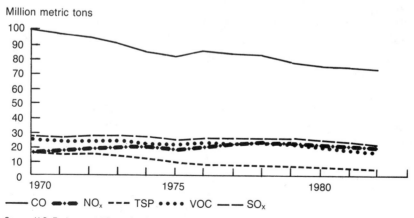

Million metric tons

——— CO ●–● NOₓ --- TSP •••• VOC —— SOₓ

Source: U.S. Environmental Protection Agency.

average air-quality levels. Also, most of the serious episodes are caused by one pollutant—ozone (or smog)—and its average has fallen in a pattern similar to the PSI.

Ambient air quality is only monitored extensively for six pollutants. Three of these, TSPs, sulfur oxides, and volatile organic compounds come principally from "stationary" sources such as industrial sites and electric power plants (figure 2.24). Two others, carbon monoxide, and lead emanate principally from motor vehicles.* The sixth, nitrogen oxides, is produced by both sources.

Total Suspended Particulates†

In 1981, TSP levels dropped sharply at about three-fourths of all monitoring sites, the first measured decline in 10 years (figure 2.26).[189] However, the change may represent only a temporary improvement resulting from the cutback in industrial production during the 1981-82 recession.[190]

EPA estimates that TSP emissions declined by about half during the past 10 years (figure 2.27). However, residential emissions increased, thanks to the popularity of wood-burning stoves for home heating, and now cause serious local air-quality problems in enclosed valleys during winter months.[191]

Why hasn't air quality improved if emissions have fallen so much? There are three major reasons. First, EPA's estimates are just that: estimates. They are based on assumptions about the rate at which particulates are emitted and how successful firms are in controlling them. Second, the estimates ignore such essentially uncontrollable sources as wind-blown dust. And, third, the larger, heavier particles, which probably are being eliminated most effectively, may never have reached the monitors, which can be located many miles away from the particles' source. These larger particles tend to settle to earth in the area around their source.

If the third reason explains the discrepancy to any extent, then the results are not nearly as encouraging as they might seem. Increasingly, small particles, those less than 0.3 micron in size, are recognized as presenting the most serious health risk because they are breathed and easily embedded into the lungs.[192] These particles can carry with them other pollutants such as toxic metals. The large particles create black

---

* The data on lead are in the toxic-substances section, above.

† TSPs are measured as suspended particles up to 25 to 45 microns (a millionth of a meter) in size.

smoke, but are apparently relatively benign in terms of their effects on human health. Because of this difference in health effects, EPA proposes revising the particulate air-quality standard so that it would apply solely to small particles.[193] Environmental groups generally oppose EPA's proposal because it could allow total particulate emissions to increase.[194]

Despite the absence of a clear downward trend in average TSP levels, the total health risk from TSP has lessened because fewer days are recorded when the ambient concentration exceeds the level deemed to pose a health hazard.* No data spell out the actual exposures people are experiencing, but weighting the ambient measurements by the populations of the counties in which the measures are taken indicates that the potential exposure of the U.S. population to suspended particulates continued to decline during the 1970s and in the first years of the 1980s.[195]

In the mid-1980s, 75 percent of the U.S. population lives in counties with no measured days above the TSP standard.[196] When examined on a city-by-city basis, the people living in the Denver-Boulder area have the highest exposure rates—more than 30 days per year above the standard. (Although much of this exposure may result from wind-blown dust that, being composed of larger particles, is not thought to create a health hazard.)

Data on suspended particulate matter (equivalent to TSPs in the United States) collected by the U.N. Environmental Program (UNEP) suggest that, except in arid countries where wind-blown dust may be a problem, particulate levels in other countries are remarkably similar to those in the United States.[197] European cities have relatively low, and falling, levels. Asian and Canadian cities are somewhat higher, in the same range as St. Louis and Houston. Of the cities with information on trends, about half show no change over a 5- to 10-year period, although a third show air-quality improvements. The cities improving air quality the most are: Zagreb, Yugoslavia; Brussels, Belgium; London, England; and São Paulo, Brazil.

Sulfur Dioxide

Sulfur dioxide (SO_2) is a pungent, though colorless, gas that, when present in high concentrations, aggravates respiratory diseases, irritates eyes,

---

* This conclusion is based on the original standards, relating to TSPs rather than on the concentration of fine particulates. Insufficient information is available to determine whether this conclusion would still apply if only fine particulates were taken into account.

corrodes metals and stone, reduces plant growth, and injures aquatic life.[198] It can also form sulfuric acid in the presence of water.

In the United States, SO_2 concentrations in the air declined steadily from 1976 through 1982. The drop was approximately 33 percent over this period.[199] EPA estimates that SO_x emissions declined about 15 percent over the same period, or 20 percent since 1971 (figure 2.27). For SO_2, the emission estimate and ambient measurements more closely parallel one another than in the case of TSP because most of the emissions come from sources (electric utilities and other industrial fuel-combustion facilities) controlled under current programs and included in EPA's estimates.

Electric utilities (primarily those burning coal) are the largest source of sulfur dioxides, emitting an estimated 15.6 million tons annually (figure 2.24). This estimate is slightly lower than it was in 1971, despite an 85 percent increase in coal consumption by utilities since then.[200] This trend reflects the use of more low-sulfur coal, the adoption of coal washing, and the installation of flue-gas desulfurization devices. The largest reduction in SO_2 emissions, however, has been achieved by sulfuric acid plants and copper, lead, and zinc smelters.[201]

Only 2 percent of the U.S. population lives in counties where SO_2 concentrations ever exceed the health-based standard.[202] No county exceeded the standard for more than six days in 1981, making the exposure of the U.S. population to excessive SO_2 concentrations a relatively rare occurrence.

In some European cities, SO_2 trends show an even more dramatic improvement (figure 2.28). Sulfur dioxide levels are relatively high for some sites in Europe, South America, and Asia, with the highest values reported in areas of extensive coal and high-sulfur oil burning. In 1978, the average annual concentration at about one-third of the sites exceeded the long-term guidelines set by the World Health Organization to protect human health.[203] About 61 percent of the sites report declines in SO_2 concentrations between 1975 and 1980; 17 percent, no change; and 22 percent, increases. The most noticeable improvements in SO_2-related air quality are found in Zagreb, Yugoslavia; London, England; Frankfurt, West Germany; and Brussels, Belgium. Increases have been monitored in São Paulo, Brazil.

Nitrogen Dioxide

Nitrogen dioxide (NO_2), a pungent brownish-red gas at high concentrations, aggravates respiratory illnesses and is a precursor, along with volatile organic compounds, of photochemical oxidants.[204] Nitrogen dioxide, like SO_2, can combine with water to form an acid—in this case nitric acid—harmful to plants and animals.

EPA reports no increase in the average concentration of NO_2 from 1975 to 1982 (figure 2.27). This seven-year trend, however, masks two distinct trends: an increase of 7 percent between 1975 and 1978 and a decline of 7 percent from 1979 to 1982. EPA estimates a similar reduction in emissions since the late 1970s. Total stationary-source emissions have changed relatively little, with decreases in the industrial sector being offset by increases in the electric-utility sector.[205] The recent decrease, therefore, apparently results almost entirely from adopting more stringent automobile-emission controls.

Exposure to unhealthful nitrogen dioxide concentrations is limited almost entirely to people living in southern California, where they were exposed to NO_2 concentrations above the standard for 18 days in 1981.[206] This rate represents a substantial improvement over the 43-days-per-year average registered in 1974 through 1976.

Carbon Monoxide

Carbon monoxide (CO), a colorless, odorless gas, forms when fossil fuels, principally gasoline and diesel fuel, combust incompletely. Carbon monoxide has immediate health effects (drowsiness, slowed reflexes) at high exposure levels because it reduces the blood's capacity to carry and circulate oxygen.[207] Very high concentrations cause death.

Carbon monoxide concentrations in air declined an average of 31 percent from 1975 to 1982, with 88 percent of the 196 monitoring sites recording declines.[208] The decline in estimated emissions is less dramatic: only 11 percent over the same period (figure 2.27). Both declines result from the estimated 17 percent reduction in emissions from highway vehicles, the major source of human exposure to carbon monoxide, related to control technology—the catalytic converter.[209] With catalytic convertors, most CO emissions occur when a car is started. By the time drivers reach congested areas (where the monitors are located), the catalyst has heated up and is converting CO to carbon dioxide. Some states, such as New Jersey, also credit their automobile-emission inspection and maintenance programs with improving urban air quality because these programs test the catalysts' effectiveness.[210]

Exposure to CO depends on where and how people live, work, and commute. The number of people exposed to CO concentrations above the national standard is large, but declining rapidly. However, four metropolitan areas—Denver, Albuquerque, Los Angeles, and Las Vegas—continue to experience CO levels more than twice the health-based standard.[211]

EPA, in 1983, completed the first detailed study of human exposure to CO pollution.[212] The study, which had a group of Washington, D.C., residents wear personal-exposure meters, shows that about 3.9 percent of the population was exposed to levels above the CO standard.[213] Virtually all persons with readings above the standard either had high occupational exposures (for instance, because they were parking-lot attendants) or spent more than 16 hours a week commuting to work. The peak exposures for every test subject occurred during the morning and evening weekday rush hours (figure 2.29).

Ozone

Ozone, a principal component of smog, is produced by chemical reactions between nitrogen dioxide and volatile organic compounds (VOCs) in the presence of oxygen and sunlight. Photochemical oxidants such as ozone impair breathing; irritate the eyes, nose, and throat; reduce visibility; and damage crops and other vegetation.[214]

Measured ozone concentrations declined by 18 percent between 1978 and 1982 (figure 2.26). Preliminary data collected by state and local agencies around the country indicate further improvements in 1982 (though 1983 may show an increase because of generally higher temperatures and less precipitation in the summer and fall).[215] At 241 sites, the ozone air-quality standard was exceeded an average of four days in 1981, down 40 percent from 1975.

This improvement results principally from emission controls on automobiles, which have reduced emission of VOCs by an estimated 40 percent between 1970 and 1981, even though the number of vehicle-miles traveled increased 37 percent.[216] In contrast, industrial VOC emissions (now 50 percent to 70 percent higher than vehicle emissions) and emissions from natural sources have not declined.[217]

Violations of the photochemical oxidant standard affect more people than any other source of outdoor air pollution in the United States. About 94 million people live in 187 counties with at least one day of excessive exposure levels per year.[218] This still constitutes a substantial reduction from the 140 million people exposed to unhealthful levels in 1977. More important, the number of days of very unhealthful photochemical oxidants (PSI greater than 200) has declined on average to fewer than one-half day per year.[219] Southern California continues

Figure 2.28
Sulfur Dioxide Concentrations in Selected European and U.S. Cities,
1973-1980

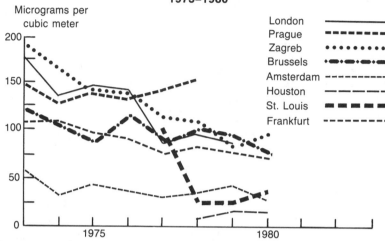

Data are annual averages.

Source: United Nations Environment Program and World Health Organization.

Figure 2.29
Exposure to Carbon Monoxide in Washington, D.C.

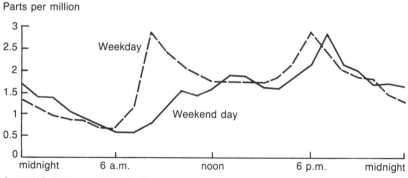

Source: U.S. Environmental Protection Agency.

to have the most serious problems; people there experience some 134 days per year above the unhealthful standard (PSI greater than 100). On 52 of those days, the air quality is more than twice as bad as the standard.

LONG-RANGE TRANSPORT

Although the Clean Air Act has focused primarily on air quality in urban areas near major pollution sources, some air problems result from the transport of small pollution particles over hundreds of miles. Two of these are acid precipitation and visibility impairment. In each case, sulfates and, to a lesser extent, nitrates appear to be the major culprits.*

Acid Precipitation

Acid precipitation is increasingly recognized as a problem in both Europe and the United States and may be occurring elsewhere as well. It is blamed for sterilizing lakes in the northeastern United States, eastern Canada, Sweden, and Norway; for killing trees in Germany's Black Forest and in eastern Europe; and for crumbling facades of historic buildings, such as the ancient cathedral in Cologne, Germany.[220]

The problem results from sulfates and nitrates reacting with moisture in the atmosphere to form dilute sulfuric and nitric acids. These aerosols then carry back to earth as rain or snow (some also settle to earth without precipitation). In some areas, the acid is "buffered" by the earth's natural alkalinity and apparently causes little, if any, damage. In other areas, the acid reacts with soil, leaching important nutrients and freeing other, potentially toxic compounds, or it drains off the land and accumulates in ponds and lakes, substantially damaging these waters' ecology. Many lakes, for instance, are so acidified that they now support no fish or other aquatic wildlife.[221]

In the United States, acid precipitation data have been collected systematically for only seven to eight years. Successful control of sulfur dioxide emissions during this period (see above) appears to have prevented the acidity of rainfall in the Northeast from worsening: no trend—either up or down—is discernible in rainfall acidity measurements

---

* Sulfates and nitrates are small particles created when the gases sulfur dioxide and nitrogen dioxide combine with oxygen either during combustion or in the atmosphere.

taken during this period.[222] And water-quality measurements in head-waters of streams over 10 to 15 years actually show a slight decrease in sulfate levels in the Northeast, although most of the South and West show increases.[223] However, rainfall in the Northeast remains highly acidic—more than six times as acidic as rain falling in isolated locations around the globe.*[224] The likely cause of the Northeast's acid rain is sulfur dioxide emissions. Except for Missouri, the states with the highest emission densities are all east of the Mississippi River (figure 2.30).

Visibility Impairment

In clean air areas, particularly in the western United States, a major effect of air pollution has not been on health but on visibility. Where mountains were commonly visible 200 to 300 miles away, fine particles in the air now interfere with such vistas; some days a visitor can hardly see across the Grand Canyon.

The National Park Service sponsors research into and monitoring of visibility in some national parks. In 1984, some of the first results from these studies were released.[225] They show that visibility problems are significantly worse in the summer than in the winter (figure 2.31).

This pattern of worse visibility in the summers is true for the Grand Canyon. In urban areas such as Los Angeles, just the reverse is true; the visibility is worse in the winter months.[226] Apparently, Los Angeles is the cause of both problems.[227] The southern California area around Los Angeles is a major source of sulfates. During the winter, these pollutants are trapped in the Los Angeles basin, clouding visibility there; but in the summer they can carry high into the atmosphere, move hundreds of miles, and obscure the Grand Canyon vistas.

The trend in relative visibility during the summer has deteriorated in two out of three years since measurements began in 1978 (figure 2.31). In summer months, the average visual range is under 75 miles in both Grand Canyon and Big Bend national parks. And the Grand Canyon is in a relatively good area. The best standard visibility occurs in the area where Nevada, Utah, and Idaho meet (figure 2.32).

---

* Precipitation in the Northeast has a pH of 4.4 compared with that which falls in isolated locations around the globe with an average pH of about 5.2.

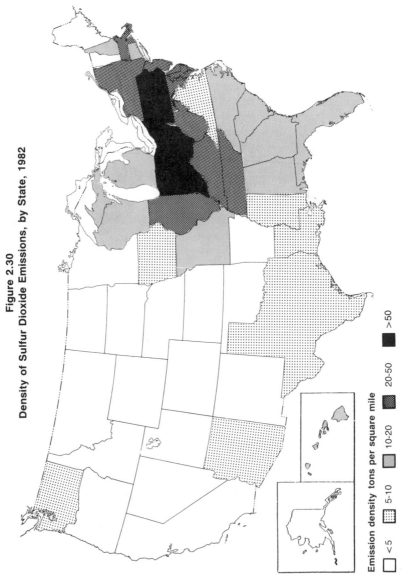

Figure 2.30
Density of Sulfur Dioxide Emissions, by State, 1982

Emission density tons per square mile

<5   5-10   10-20   20-50   >50

Source: U.S. Department of Energy.

Figure 2.31
Visibility in Grand Canyon and Big Bend National Parks, 1979–1982

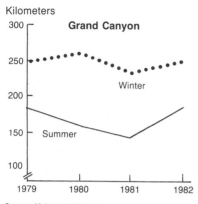

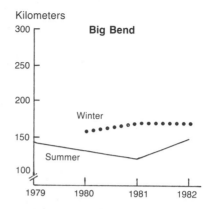

Source: Malm and Molenar.

Air Pollution and The Olympics

Air pollution became a major concern in planning the 1984 Summer Olympics in Los Angeles. That city experiences more days in which air quality is worse than health-based standards than does any other city in the United States. In fact, those standards are surpassed in Los Angeles almost daily during the summer months. The most serious pollution problems typically occur in inland areas removed from ocean breezes and in the afternoon between noon and 4 o'clock. Increased traffic associated with the Olympics could make these problems worse.

Some doctors speculate that athletes, because they breathe more deeply and therefore inhale more ozone than the average person, may be particularly affected by the pollution. At the least, those doctors predict that problems of painful and shallow breathing, throat irritation, and headaches will be common, especially in endurance sports. The concern among the coaches and athletes is the extent to which these reactions affect performance.

The planning committee for the games attempted to take into account potential pollution problems in scheduling the site and time of the events. Recognizing that afternoon, inland sites pose the highest risks, most outdoor events were scheduled for morning or evening times and nearer to the coast. Indoor events were less of a concern because ozone breaks down quickly once inside a building.

A second thrust was to attempt, through voluntary measures, to reduce pollution emissions by promoting use of rapid transit and car pools, recommending that power plants burn natural gas, and encouraging residents to avoid nonessential driving and reduce electrical energy consumption.

Whether or not these efforts succeed, Los Angeles officials point out that this is not the first Olympics to face air pollution problems. Mexico City (1968 Olympics) and Tokyo (1964 Olympics) suffered serious air-quality problems as well. So does Greece, which some are proposing as the permanent site of the games.

(Source: Coalition for Clean Air, South Coast Air Quality Management District, and the *Los Angeles Times*.)

Figure 2.32
Standard Visual Ranges, Western United States

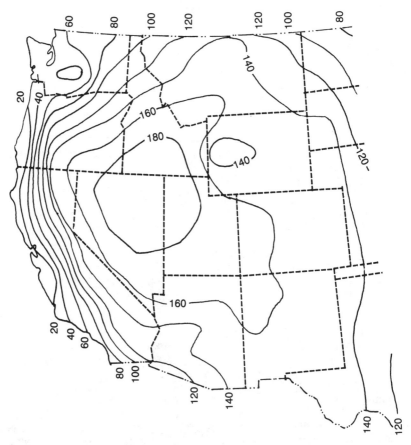

Numbers along lines indicate distance in miles that a person can see under normal conditions if there are no obstructions.

Source: Malm and Molenar.

UPPER ATMOSPHERE PROBLEMS

Some potentially serious air pollution problems are not even occurring near the earth. Pollutants can escape to the upper atmosphere where they may, over time, change the globe's whole energy balance and climate.

Carbon Dioxide

Carbon dioxide (CO_2) in the atmosphere is unquestionably increasing. Readings at Mauna Loa, Hawaii, have increased an average of 0.4 percent per year since 1958 (figure 2.33). Comparable data from CO_2 measurements at the South Pole and other locations show similar results.[228]

These increases have resulted primarily from human activities. In the past, the amount of CO_2 produced when humans burned fuels represented a tiny addition to the natural CO_2 release, but these amounts have multiplied incredibly over the past century as industrial societies have used more and more fossil fuels (coal, petroleum, and natural gas) (figure 2.34). Combustion CO_2 emissions increased over 5,300 percent between 1860 and 1980. Approximately half of this CO_2 is thought to remain in the atmosphere.[229] Tropical deforestation compounds the problem, for these forests are important in reverting atmospheric carbon dioxide to oxygen. Current rates of deforestation correspond to a 33 percent increase in fossil fuel consumption.[230] Projections (assuming continued growth of 1 to 2 percent per year in the production and use of fossil fuels) suggest that CO_2 concentrations will double preindustrial levels by the year 2065, and lead to a gradual warming of the earth and global climate changes.[231]

The National Academy of Sciences (NAS) estimates that there has been a marked increase in the Earth's temperature over the past 100 years, with the mean global temperature reaching a level comparable to the peak reached during the last interglacial period (figure 2.35). In the Northern Hemisphere, the average temperature was about one-half degree (Celsius) warmer during the 1970s than it was 90 years earlier.[232] Temperatures in the Southern Hemisphere have increased by a similar amount. By the middle of the 21st century, a 2° to 3° C increase is expected, resulting in average temperatures higher than any for hundreds of thousands of years.[233]

What is not clear is how this trend will affect weather patterns and what damages will result. Various studies have suggested that the buildup

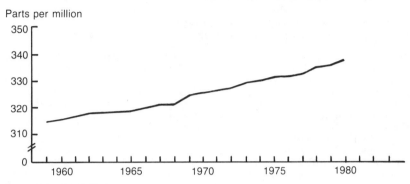

Figure 2.33
Atmospheric Concentrations of Carbon Dioxide, 1959–1980

Parts per million

Source: *Carbon Dioxide Review.*

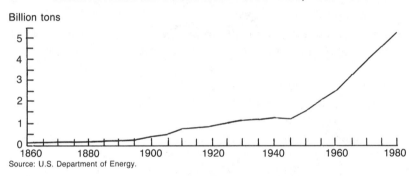

Figure 2.34
Carbon Dioxide Emissions from Fossil Fuels, 1860–1980

Billion tons

Source: U.S. Department of Energy.

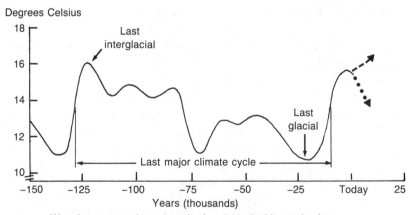

Figure 2.35
Mean Global Temperatures, 150,000 B.C. to Present

Degrees Celsius

Last interglacial

Last glacial

Last major climate cycle

Years (thousands)

——— Warming expected as a result of carbon dioxide production
•••• Cooling expected absent carbon dioxide production

Source: U.S. Department of Energy.

could result in ice-cap melt at the North or South pole, leading to a rise in sea level, drowning out many coastal cities, and large shifts in weather patterns that would turn agricultural areas, such as the Great Plains of the United States, into deserts and seriously affect world food production.[234] The NAS report concludes that the impact may not be as serious as others fear, although many factors still need further investigation.[235] But an EPA report suggests that the damages could be very significant; however, the latter report is resigned to the impracticability of preventing those damages.[236] Other commentators feel that the most constructive response would be for everyone to prepare to adjust to the changes rather than to try to prevent them.[237]

Ozone Layer

One potential problem that recent analyses suggest may not be as serious as once was feared is the depletion of the Earth's atmospheric ozone layer. Ozone is depleted by the continuous release of chlorofluorocarbons (CFCs) into the environment. A diminished ozone layer could reduce agricultural productivity and increase the incidence of skin cancer.

An NAS report released in 1984 indicates that ozone levels are unlikely to fall more than 4 percent, as opposed to the 18.6 percent figure cited in the academy's 1979 report.[238] This brighter prospect results not from reduced production of CFCs but rather from a better understanding of the atmospheric sciences. Although CFCs were banned from use in aerosols in the United States in 1977, they still are used widely as refrigerants and for other purposes.[239] In fact, worldwide industrial production of CFCs is rising.[240]

Nor are the projections about the ozone levels entirely encouraging. The relatively small overall change is the net result of projected "dramatic" decreases in concentrations in the upper atmosphere coupled with equally large increases in the lower atmosphere—a combination that one expert refers to as a "precarious balance."[241] And the NAS panel points out that "increasing concentrations of ozone in the lower atmosphere ... pose potential risks to air quality over the surface of the globe."[242] It could also affect atmospheric transport processes and climate, perhaps reinforcing the greenhouse effect caused by the increasing CO_2 trends.[243]

INDOOR AIR QUALITY

Air pollution is not an exclusively outdoor problem. Six air pollutants—nitrogen oxides, carbon monoxide, radon, formaldehyde, asbestos, and passive tobacco smoke—particularly affect human beings indoors because their concentrations are often far greater inside buildings than outside. Since most people spend the bulk of their time indoors (about 90 percent of the time, on the average), these high concentrations may be causing serious human health risks.

Trends in indoor air pollution are difficult to judge because data are not available. No indoor-air-monitoring program is established in the United States comparable to federal, state, and local outdoor-air monitoring. However, several factors indicate that indoor-air quality may be getting worse.[244] One, ironically, is energy conservation. Conservation practices in homes, offices, and other buildings (sealing cracks and installing insulation) reduce the escape of indoor air and allow pollutant concentrations to build up. Second is the popularity of alternative fuels in the home, especially wood and kerosene, which when burned release a variety of hazardous air pollutants. Third is the expanded use of synthetic chemicals, such as formaldehyde and volatile organic resins, in home construction and furnishings; some of these substances are believed to be toxic to humans under normal conditions and use.

Indoor-air-pollutant concentrations may exceed health-based standards established for outdoor air, regardless of actual outdoor concentrations. For example, some studies show nitrogen dioxide levels in indoor environments at two to seven times higher than outdoor standards.[245] Nitrogen dioxide is a by-product of gas cooking, which can also produce excessive levels of carbon monoxide in improperly ventilated homes.

CONCLUSIONS

Air pollution presents both one of our major environmental successes and one of our greatest environmental problems. The efforts undertaken over the past two decades have produced some significant air-quality improvements. But these efforts now appear to have been too narrow in scope. By focusing on nearby pollution sources, they have missed the problem of long-range transport. By focusing on outdoor air, they may have missed the more serious problems created by pollutants indoors.

The problems that the United States has not addressed are proving to be much more difficult to deal with than those that it has addressed.

In many cases, they cannot be resolved—at least with existing technologies—by the single installation of a pollution-control device on the source of an emission. How—and whether—these problems will be handled is now very uncertain.

Water Quality

Unlike the nation's relatively consistent and widespread improvements in air quality, success in cleaning up surface waters has been mixed. Many streams have improved, some of them dramatically: the "dying" Great Lakes, Erie and Ontario, are reviving, with fewer algae blooms and growing fish populations; Atlantic salmon have returned to New England's Connecticut and Penobscot rivers; and shellfish-bed and public-beach closings due to dangerous bacteria levels have become less frequent.[246] But water quality in some streams and many lakes appears to be degrading, and in most there has been little change since the early 1970s.

The trends in the quality of the nation's groundwater are probably even less encouraging. New contamination problems seem to be discovered almost daily. However, for groundwater there is virtually no information documenting water-quality changes.

No firm evidence exists on why only limited progress has been made in the nation's water-quality-improvement efforts. Unfortunately, the federal Environmental Protection Agency (EPA) maintains no records and makes no estimates of the quantities of pollutants discharged by different types of sources to either ground or surface water. One possible reason is that the job has proven more difficult than originally thought, as evidenced by repeated failures to meet the deadlines established in the Clean Water Act. In particular, cleaning up discharges from municipal sewage-treatment plants has been much more expensive and proceeded much more slowly than originally scheduled; even when the plants are built, they may not be operated properly.[247] Another reason is that some major sources of pollution, particularly storm-water runoff from agricultural land and city streets, have been largely ignored. The problem of groundwater contamination also was largely ignored until the late 1970s, and there still is no comprehensive program to address the problem. It may well prove to be more difficult to deal with than surface-water pollution because of the extremely long time it can take groundwater aquifers to purge themselves once they become polluted.[248]

Because water-quality conditions can be assessed according to several definitions, some subjective and others objective, problems of interpretation are further compounded. In addition to measuring quality by concentrations of specific contaminants, water quality can be defined either by the extent to which a water body supports the uses for which it has been designated* or simply as "improving" or "degrading" as judged by water-quality officials.

SURFACE WATER

In 1984, the Association of State and Interstate Water Pollution Control Administrators (ASIWPCA) released what is probably the most comprehensive assessment of changes in water quality that has been undertaken.[250] In each state, the pollution-control agency was asked to estimate both whether the quality of the state's streams, lakes, and estuaries was adequate for whatever use (for example, drinking water, recreation, irrigation) had been designated for that body and how the quality had changed since 1972. The survey concludes that the large majority of U.S. surface waters satisfy their designated uses.[251] As of 1982, 64 percent of the U.S. stream miles fully supported their designated uses, 22 percent partially supported them, and 5 percent did not support them. Of the 16.3 million acres of lakes and reservoirs assessed, 84 percent supported, 10 percent partially supported, and 3 percent did not support their designated uses.

The survey also concludes that most of the surface water did not change appreciably in water quality between 1972 and 1982 (figure 2.36). This is largely because much of the water was already relatively clean at the start of this period, and its cleanliness has been maintained. For streams and estuaries, quality improved in somewhat more water bodies than it degraded during the decade, but lakes and reservoirs got worse— only 0.4 million acres improved, while 1.7 million acres degraded.

The ASIWPCA conclusions were based primarily upon sometimes subjective assessments by the agency personnel. Actual water-quality-monitoring results were used in these assessments for only 22 percent of the stream miles and 29 percent of the lake area.[252] Water-quality

---

* Most of the U.S. surface waters have "fishable-swimmable" as their designated use. Some, including 120,000 stream miles, have more stringent use designations such as for drinking or food processing.[249] Another 32,000 stream miles have less-stringent designations, such as for navigation or agricultural uses.

changes in almost half of the surface waters were not even assessed sub-
jectively, either because the current quality was unknown, the quality
10 years ago was unknown, or the state agencies would not supply the
information.*

A similar picture of general, though modest, improvement in stream
water quality was provided by the 1982 EPA summary of state water-
quality reports required by Section 305(b) of the Clean Water Act.[254]
Of the 35 states providing overall trend information to EPA, 21 cited
continuing improvements in water quality. Fourteen states reported
generally stable trends. No states reported statewide trends of degrading
water quality, although 29 of the states reported some local degradation.

A third source, the National Fisheries Survey, gives similar results.[255]
Conducted by EPA and the U.S. Fish and Wildlife Service in 1982-83,
the survey assesses the "fishable" component of water quality—that
is, the biological condition of U.S. waters as demonstrated by the
capability to support fish life. According to the survey, 73 percent of
the U.S. inland waters are clean enough to support sport fish, such as
largemouth bass and rainbow trout. However, low-flow levels and pollution threaten aquatic life in many areas, as evidenced by stunted growth,
reduced populations, and outright fish kills, a situation little changed
over the past five years.

Another source of nationwide water-quality trend information is the
U.S. Geological Survey's (USGS) National Ambient Stream Quality Accounting Network (NASQAN).[256] NASQAN provides the most consistent and comprehensive information available on specific contaminants. It is a system, currently with over 500 ambient monitoring
stations located in river basins and subbasins throughout the country,
that has collected information on the same pollutants since 1974.

The USGS attempts to adjust the results measured by the NASQAN
system to take account of differences in stream flow from one year to
the next and then analyzes these adjusted data to identify statistically
significant increasing or decreasing trends in a pollutant's
concentration.[257]

Although NASQAN is the most comprehensive continuous quality-
monitoring system available, its data still do not necessarily measure
water quality where it is most likely to affect people.[258] Originally
established to measure the quantity of surface-water flow, NASQAN

* Louisiana, one of the states unable or unwilling to supply information on changes
since 1972, reported having approximately 300,000 miles of streams—almost as many
as all other states combined.[253]

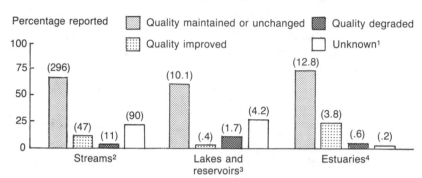

**Figure 2.36
U.S. Water-Quality Changes, 1972–1983**

Percentage reported — Quality maintained or unchanged — Quality degraded — Quality improved — Unknown[1]

Streams[2]   Lakes and reservoirs[3]   Estuaries[4]

[1] Includes only water bodies for which states reported that they did not know whether water quality had changed. Water bodies for which states did not respond are not included in these tabulations.
[2] Numbers in parentheses indicate thousand stream miles
[3] Numbers in parentheses indicate million acres
[4] Numbers in parentheses indicate thousand square miles
Source: Association of State and Interstate Water Pollution Control Administrators.

Progress in the Great Lakes

The Great Lakes, containing one-fifth of the world's freshwater supply, show promise of being a major environmental success story, although many serious problems remain. The lakes have suffered water-quality problems since settlers first reached their shorelines over 100 years ago, and one of them, Lake Erie, was thought by many to be beyond saving. Uncontrolled sewage discharges, high concentrations of chemicals and toxic substances, and advanced eutrophication were a few of the problems being faced.

Although not all those problems have been corrected, controls implemented over the past decade on point sources of pollution, such as industrial and municipal discharges, have resulted in significant improvement. However, completing the job is likely to require that additional controls be placed on nonpoint sources of pollution, such as stormwater runoff from agricultural lands and urban streets. These sources are thought to contribute as much as 11 million tons of sediment to the lakes each year, along with substantial amounts of heavy metals, other toxic contaminants, nutrients such as phosphorous and nitrogen, bacteria, and other pollutants.

The Great Lakes states and Canada have been in the forefront of efforts to address such problems. For example, to control fertilizer runoff from farmland, some farmers in the countries along Lake Erie's western shores have been provided with planting equipment and technical assistance for development plots using conservation tillage or no-till farm operations. Initial results of this project are encouraging—yields are as good as county averages, and farmers could save money through reduced labor, energy, and capital costs associated with conservation tillage. Because most of the farmland is suitable to this type of farming, erosion could be reduced by up to 50 percent in the eastern basin and 70 percent in the western basin. Measurable water-quality improvement would also be expected in Lake Erie if these conservation practices become widely accepted and well used.

(Source: The *Conservation Foundation Letter* [Oct. & Nov. 1983]; the International Joint Commission.)

stations are generally located at the downstream end of a watershed—often upstream of, or too far downstream from, major pollution sources to record locally severe problems. NASQAN stations are limited further because they do not measure all pollutants (including most of the potentially toxic organic chemicals) and because, in many cases, monitoring equipment may not be sophisticated enough to measure pollutants at low concentrations that are nonetheless high enough to be of concern.

Trends for Key Pollutants

According to the NASQAN information, the years 1974 to 1981 saw little change in water quality with respect to the conventional pollution indicators: dissolved oxygen, fecal coliform bacteria, suspended sediment, dissolved solids, and phosphorus.[259] For each of these, the vast majority of monitoring stations show no significant change in pollutant concentrations between 1974 and 1981, with those showing trends of increase balanced by a comparable number of decreases (figure 2.37).

Shifting the focus from national trends to local problems, EPA's Section 305(b) report indicates that conventional pollutants remain a problem.[260] The 35 states included in that report most often cite bacteria, dissolved oxygen, and nutrients, followed by toxic substances, suspended solids, and metals, as the parameters responsible for pollution problems in their "waters of concern."*

Dissolved Oxygen

Dissolved oxygen, usually present in clean waters at levels of five parts per million or more, is necessary for fish and other aquatic life to survive. The decomposition of organic pollutants, such as those in municipal sewage, depletes the natural oxygen levels. Ten percent of U.S. inland lakes and rivers have levels of dissolved oxygen low enough to affect fish communities adversely, according to the National Fisheries Survey.[261]

The great majority of NASQAN stations show no changes in dissolved oxygen levels since 1974.[262] Improved conditions (that is, higher oxygen levels) are being witnessed in parts of New England, the Ohio-Tennessee and Missouri river basins in the Midwest, and in the South Atlantic-Gulf (figure 2.38). Decreasing oxygen levels have been observed in the Pacific Northwest and in California.

---

* "Waters of concern" are the water bodies a state identifies as possessing unresolved water-quality problems. These bodies are selected either by states as those waters that do not meet assigned use classifications or water-quality standards, or by other various statewide priority-ranking schemes.

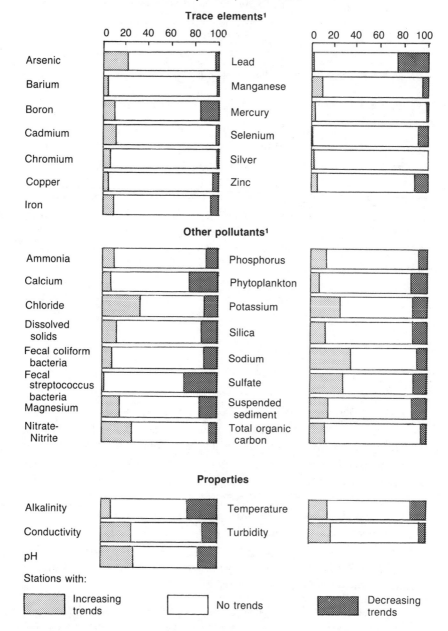

Figure 2.37
Water-Quality Trends for Selected Pollutants
and Properties, 1974–1981

Trace elements[1]

Arsenic, Barium, Boron, Cadmium, Chromium, Copper, Iron

Lead, Manganese, Mercury, Selenium, Silver, Zinc

Other pollutants[1]

Ammonia, Calcium, Chloride, Dissolved solids, Fecal coliform bacteria, Fecal streptococcus bacteria, Magnesium, Nitrate-Nitrite

Phosphorus, Phytoplankton, Potassium, Silica, Sodium, Sulfate, Suspended sediment, Total organic carbon

Properties

Alkalinity, Conductivity, pH

Temperature, Turbidity

Stations with:

Increasing trends

No trends

Decreasing trends

[1] Increasing trends indicates deteriorating quality

Source: U.S. Geological Survey.

Figure 2.38
U.S. Geological Survey Water-Resources Regions

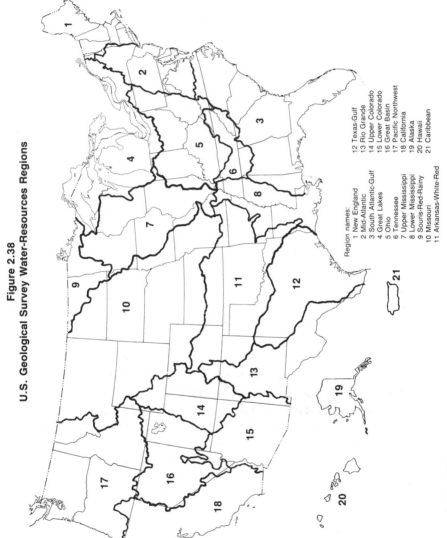

Region names:
1 New England
2 Mid-Atlantic
3 South Atlantic-Gulf
4 Great Lakes
5 Ohio
6 Tennessee
7 Upper Mississippi
8 Lower Mississippi
9 Souris-Red-Rainy
10 Missouri
11 Arkansas-White-Red

12 Texas-Gulf
13 Rio Grande
14 Upper Colorado
15 Lower Colorado
16 Great Basin
17 Pacific Northwest
18 California
19 Alaska
20 Hawaii
21 Caribbean

Source: U.S. Geological Survey.

Bacteria

Many bacteria are harmless, but the concentration in water of fecal coliform and fecal streptococcal bacteria from human and animal wastes indicate the potential for infection and disease. High bacteria counts force officials to close public swimming beaches and restrict shellfishing in contaminated waters. It was the discovery that oysters contaminated by urban sewage were carriers of typhoid fever that prompted Baltimore to construct America's first sewage treatment plant in 1914.[263]

Although the majority of NASQAN stations record no change in fecal coliform counts, stations showing overall improvements outnumber those with increasing coliform concentrations.[264] The improvements are most apparent in the southern United States, in the South Atlantic-Gulf, and the Arkansas-White-Red water-resources regions.

The decreases in fecal streptococcal counts are more marked.[265] Reduced fecal streptococcal counts are observed in every region, but especially in the South Atlantic-Gulf, Upper Mississippi River, and Missouri River basins.

Suspended Solids

Brown, turbid water caused by suspended solids such as soil sediment and other solid particles can significantly reduce beneficial uses of water by people and harm aquatic wildlife. These particles can also carry nutrients, pesticides, bacteria, and other harmful substances. Many rivers have always carried high sediment loads because of natural erosion occurring in their watersheds. But erosion from cropland, construction sites, rangeland, and forestland has elevated sediment to a major water pollutant.[266] The National Fisheries Survey cites turbidity as the most important pollutant affecting fish life in 34 percent of the waters surveyed.[267] Nationwide trends of suspended-solids analysis at NASQAN stations show little change over the decade.[268] Most stations record no change; of the rest, almost an equal number show increases as decreases.

Dissolved Solids

Total dissolved solids (TDSs) is a measure of all the inorganic salts and other substances dissolved in water. High levels of dissolved solids can make water unfit to drink, adversely affect fish and other freshwater aquatic life, accelerate corrosion in water systems and equipment that uses water, and depress crop yields.[269] These problems are more likely in regions with low annual rainfall, such as the Southwest and the High

Plains, whereas lower concentrations occur in New England, the mid-Atlantic, the Southeast, Alaska, Hawaii, California, and the Pacific Northwest, regions with relatively high precipitation.

Two-thirds of the NASQAN stations report no significant change in TDS concentrations between 1974 and 1981 (figure 2.37). A slight majority of the remainder showed increasing (worsening) rather than decreasing trends. The Great Lakes, Rio Grande, and Upper Colorado River water-resources regions show the most improvement. Degrading trends are more prevalent in the Missouri River, Arkansas-White-Red River, and Pacific Northwest regions.[270]

Trends vary for some of the specific dissolved solids, including sodium, chloride, calcium, and sulfate.[271] Sodium and chloride concentrations in surface waters appear to be rising, particularly in the mid-Atlantic, Ohio-Tennessee, Missouri, and Arkansas-White-Red water-resources regions.*

Calcium concentrations, in contrast, appear to be declining.[274] Many NASQAN stations throughout the United States report decreasing trends (83 decreasing versus 23 increasing; 198 show no change), with most of the improvement occurring in the New England, South Atlantic-Gulf, Texas-Gulf, Rio Grande, and Upper Colorado water-resources regions.

The NASQAN data pertaining to the acidity and alkalinity of surface waters provide an unclear message.[275] The direct measurement, pH levels, suggests that either acidity is decreasing in the more acid waters or alkalinity is increasing in the alkaline waters. But two other measurements show apparently contradictory trends. Alkalinity is decreasing in many more stations than it is increasing, and the concentration of sulfates, which are responsible for much of the nation's acid rain, is increasing in more stations than it is decreasing. Sulfate levels are increasing most commonly in the central United States (the Missouri, Arkansas-White-Red, and Texas-Gulf regions), the Southeast, and the Pacific Northwest.

A special USGS study of acidity shows small declines in stream sulfate concentrations in the Northeast and small increases in sulfate in the

---

* One possible culprit, road salt, seems to be innocent. Although almost 10 million tons of road salt was used for snow and ice control in 1982-83, research studies report that chloride concentrations in raw water before being treated have declined since 1972.[272] In addition, a preliminary USGS analysis of sodium and chloride concentrations at NASQAN stations does not show a significant seasonal correlation—for example, with spring snowmelt—as might be expected.[273]

Southeast and West.[276] In the Northeast, this slight decrease follows a trend of increasing acidity in New England and New York's lakes from the 1930s to the 1970s, whereas in the southeastern United States available data suggest that surface-water acidification dates its increase to the 1950s. The study notes that these trends correspond with trends in air pollution from sulfur dioxide, with substantial declines in emissions in the Northeast and northern Midwest between 1965 and 1980, while emissions were increasing in the Southeast and west of the Mississippi River.[277]

Nutrients

Nutrients, such as phosphorus and nitrogen, can stimulate algae blooms and growth of nuisance water plants, accelerate eutrophication (the aging of lakes and reservoirs), and cause problems with oxygen depletion as the plants die and decompose.[278] Nutrient overenrichment in the Chesapeake Bay produces algae growth that blocks the sunlight from reaching submerged aquatic vegetation, thereby killing off valuable nursery habitat for finfish and shellfish.[279] The primary sources of nutrients are fertilizer runoff from croplands and urban lawns, and discharges from municipal wastewater-treatment plants.[280]

Over three-fourths of the NASQAN stations show no significant change in phosphorus concentrations since 1974.[281] A slight majority of the rest show increasing levels (figure 2.37). Two-thirds of the stations measuring nitrate-nitrogen levels also show no change; however, a quarter show increasing trends compared with only 8 percent registering decreasing trends.[282] Most increases occurred in the eastern United States (the New England, mid-Atlantic, South Atlantic-Gulf, and Ohio-Tennessee water-resources regions) and the Pacific Northwest. The National Fisheries Survey reports that nutrient surpluses are hurting fish communities in 12 percent of U.S. surface waters.[283]

Metals and Toxic Substances

Although conventional pollutants were the original focus of most water-quality-improvement programs, heavy metals and toxic organic chemicals have become of increasing concern. But, unfortunately, few ambient monitoring data of toxics are available. NASQAN does monitor for total and dissolved concentrations of 13 metals; however, it does not collect information on the majority of widely used pesticides and organic chemicals.[284] In most cases, toxic pollutants found in surface waters, fish tissues, and bottom sediments come primarily from industrial and municipal sewers, agricultural runoff, spills, and solid-waste disposal.[285]

State officials listed toxics as the fourth most frequent cause of continuing pollution in "waters of concern";[286] 30 out of 35 states cite resulting violations of water-quality standards or use impairments. In the ASIWPCA study, 41 states perceive toxic materials as a major problem, with at least 14,000 miles of streams and rivers (39 states reporting), 638,000 acres of lakes (16 states reporting), and 920 square miles of estuaries in 8 states affected.[287] (These figures are likely to be underestimated, because the officials reporting tend to focus on hot spots or known acute situations.) The National Fisheries Survey reports toxic contamination of fish populations in 10 percent of all waters.[288]

For most of the metals they monitor, the vast majority of NASQAN stations show no significant change in concentrations since 1974 (figure 2.37). Lead is the salient exception. A quarter of the stations register significant decreasing trends, with fewer than 3 percent showing increasing trends. Selenium, too, showed more decreases than increases, whereas arsenic concentrations appeared to be on the increase.

GROUNDWATER CONTAMINATION

Despite the paucity of information on the extent of groundwater contamination and on trends in groundwater quality, there is widespread agreement that groundwater pollution is a serious problem that is growing worse. Newspapers contain frequent accounts of newly discovered local problems, many sufficiently serious that wells must be closed. The Council on Environmental Quality attempted a national survey of groundwater contamination in 1980 and found, in areas from Maine to Hawaii, hundreds of episodes (affecting millions of people) of well closures because of contamination from toxic organic pollutants.[289] The Environmental Assessment Council reviewed the situation in 10 states and found adequate documentation for a total of 869 incidents of well contamination, approximately half of which had affected drinking-water supplies and another 15 percent of which were reported as threatening such supplies.[290] Even for these states, "anecdotal data" had to be relied upon because comprehensive surveys had not been completed.[291]

Much of the current attention is being given to contamination by toxic compounds, particularly those leaking from existing or abandoned hazardous-waste-disposal sites. Arizona and New Jersey cited this type of problem as the one most frequently found, but in none of the states did it account for a majority of the documented cases.[292]

Saltwater contamination is another frequent problem. It can result from natural causes, from saline waters being sucked into an aquifer by excessive freshwater pumping, from deicing salts applied to roads, or from irrigation water that dissolves salts in the soil and carries them down to the aquifer. In a 1983 USGS report, 22 states reported salinity contamination as a serious problem.[293] High salinity levels can make water unfit to use for any purpose except cooling, and even low levels can create health problems for individuals who may suffer from high blood pressure.[294]

Bacteria and viruses are also frequently found contaminants and can cause serious intestinal illnesses. The source is often improperly operating septic tanks or municipal sewage disposal.[295]

Nitrates are being increasingly found in groundwater underlying agricultural areas, septic tank fields, or areas where municipal sewage is disposed of. A survey of 4,350 wells in Nebraska found nitrate contamination affecting 16 percent of them.[296] Many other states (for example, New York, Iowa, Washington, Michigan, Washington, and Hawaii) also report problems of nitrogen contamination.[297] The major health risk from nitrates is apparently for children who face the threat of methemoglobinemia.

Radioactive contamination from natural sources, mine tailings, or radioactive-waste disposal also is cited as a problem in several states.[298] Other types of frequent contamination include pesticides seeping into the ground from agricultural land and gasoline or other petroleum products leaking from storage tanks.[299] All can cause serious chronic or acute health problems.

In most cases of serious contamination, the least-cost response is often to stop using the well. However, this may be only a temporary solution. Increased pumping from other, nearby wells may only speed the flow of the contamination through the aquifer.[300] Many rural residents may have no feasible safe alternative to using their wells; about 44 million people in rural areas obtained their drinking-water supplies in 1980 from their own wells.[301] Treating well water before it is used may be economically infeasible. And some treatment systems, even if they are installed, cannot be counted upon to remove all of the different types of contaminants that may be in the water.

A national study of rural water conditions, which included distribution systems in rural communities as well as individual wells, found bacteria to be the most common problem, occurring in 42.1 percent of the households served by individual systems (predominantly wells).[302] Other frequently found contaminants included iron, total dissolved solids, manganese, sodium, lead, selenium, cadmium, and mercury, all of which were observed in over 10 percent of the households.[303] In the majority of those cases, the contamination levels were higher than the standard (maximum contaminant levels) established by EPA in its Safe Drinking Water Program.

SOURCES OF WATER-QUALITY PROBLEMS

Sources of surface-water pollution are categorized either as "point" sources, such as manufacturing industries or municipal wastewater-treatment plants that discharge directly into surface waters, or "nonpoint" sources, such as runoff from agricultural fields, urban streets, timbered lands, and construction sites, leakage from septic tanks, and deposition of atmospheric pollutants.[304] The same distinction is often made for sources of groundwater pollution, although a nonpoint source in one case can be classified as a point source in the other.

Point-Source Discharges

The nation's pollution-abatement efforts have primarily focused on reducing discharges to surface water from industrial and municipal point sources.[305] For industries, EPA sets nationally applicable effluent limitations based on the availability of pollution-abatement technologies and whether firms in the industry can afford to install the technology. Municipal wastewater-treatment plants are required by statute to achieve secondary treatment or better. Each discharger must obtain a National Pollutant Discharges Elimination System (NPDES) permit specifying the amount of pollution that the particular facility can discharge.

Municipal Wastewater Discharges

Municipal wastewater discharges continue to contribute a significant portion of the pollutants carried in U.S. rivers and streams, in spite of Clean Water Act amendments in 1972 that called for secondary treatment at all municipal sewage-treatment plants by 1977 (with some extensions up to 1983).[306] When ASIWPCA asked state officials for the primary causes preventing their streams from supporting their designated uses, municipal discharges ranked first in 19 states (only nonpoint sources ranked higher) and second in another 20.[307]

Municipal wastewater disposal, along with septic tanks, is also frequently cited as a source of groundwater contamination.[308] The problem can result from leaking sewer pipes (often a problem in older communities), the use of lagoons for treating wastewater after it has been collected, or the disposal of a system's effluent or sludge after treatment has taken place. This is the case where a conflict may exist between protecting surface-water and groundwater quality unless care is taken in planning, constructing, and operating the waste-treatment system. Treatment in lagoons or by land application is often recommended as an economical way of preventing surface-water pollution. But part of the unseen cost of treatment may be the contamination of groundwater supplies.

In addition to the high volumes of water and sewage flushed daily from homes and businesses, wastewater-treatment plants must handle everything else poured down toilets, sinks, garbage disposals, floor drains, and bathtubs: wastewater carrying a formidable array of food wastes, household cleaning solvents, soaps, and other household and commercial chemicals. They also must handle wastewater from industries hooked into municipal systems. In many older cities, particularly those in which sewage systems were built before 1900, stormwater runoff is also carried in the same leaky sewer pipes, resulting in overwhelming volumes of waste being delivered to treatment plants during wet weather.[309] During heavy storms, in fact, combined sewers must be allowed to overflow, spewing raw sewage directly into receiving waters. A 1978 EPA report estimates that 38 million people, mostly in the Northeast, the upper Midwest, and the Far West, are served by combined sewer systems.[310] Correcting combined sewers would cost an estimated $35.7 billion nationwide.[311]

Pollutants from municipal wastewater discharges consist primarily of suspended solids, oxygen-consuming organic matter, nutrients (phosphorus and nitrogen), and smaller amounts of heavy metals and organic and inorganic chemicals. According to one estimate, municipal discharges are responsible for 82 percent of all phosphorus, 74 percent of all biological oxygen demand, and 55 percent of all suspended solids discharged into surface waters from point sources.[312] (Their percent contribution decreases, of course, when nonpoint-source loadings are included as well.) They are also frequently cited as a possible cause of nitrate contamination in groundwater.

The availability of effective wastewater treatment to the U.S. public has increased dramatically since 1960, especially since passage of the Clean Water Act in 1972 (figure 2.39). While the proportion of the population served by some sort of sewer system, with or without treatment, has remained relatively constant at around 71 percent since 1970 (with the remaining 30 percent who are "not served" relying primarily on septic tanks), the number receiving at least secondary treatment or better has risen from 2.2 percent in 1960 to almost 54 percent in 1982. This trend is likely to continue over the next several years as municipalities not yet in compliance with the Clean Water Act complete work on facilities currently under construction. Only 1 percent of the population served by some form of sewage system receives no treatment of their wastes, down from 39 percent in 1960.[313] Over four million people are now served by systems that discharge no effluent to surface water, up from two million in 1978. Such systems, usually regarded as alternatives to tertiary treatment, use the wastewater for such purposes as irrigation, watering golf courses, or recharging groundwater aquifers, rather than releasing it into a stream or lake. This again, however, can lead to groundwater contamination.

The septic tanks and other on-site disposal systems relied upon by 30 percent of the population not served by a municipal system are frequently cited as a major source of groundwater contamination.[314] EPA estimated that there are 16.6 million septic tanks in the United States receiving 800 billion gallons of water a year.[315] These tanks are probably the primary cause of bacteria being the most common contaminant found in rural households served by individual water-supply systems.

Although less progress has been made in abating pollution from municipal sources than was originally expected,, the progress that has been made is important. For example, ASIWPCA estimates that the amounts of oxygen-demanding pollutants leaving municipal plants decreased by 46 percent between 1972 and 1982, while the amounts entering the plants increased by 12 percent.[316] Pollutants leaving municipal treatment plants would have been almost twice as high as the amount actually discharged in 1982 if there had been no improvement to the facilities that existed in 1972.

Industrial Discharges

Industries appear to have been much more successful than municipal facilities in reducing the pollution loads they discharge into surface waters. EPA estimates that, on the whole, industries reduced their discharges of most conventional pollutants by 70 percent or more from 1972 to 1977.[317] Although metal loadings also have been reduced (by an estimated 78 percent), industrial sources are still thought to be responsible for 26 percent of lead loadings, 43 percent of copper, and 30 percent of cadmium.

Little information exists on industrial responsibility for other toxic pollutant loadings. Many priority pollutants, including pesticides, toxic organic compounds, and less-common metals, are by-products of

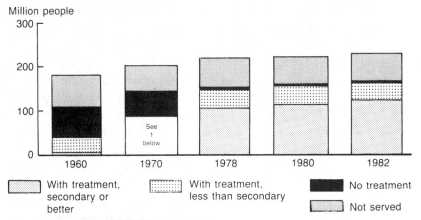

Figure 2.39
U.S. Population Served by Municipal Wastewater
Systems, by Level of Treatment, 1960–1982

Million people

	With treatment, secondary or better		With treatment, less than secondary		No treatment
					Not served

[1] Available data for 1970 do not distinguish between types of treatment.

Source: Council on Environmental Quality.

Figure 2.40
Estimates of Pollutant Loadings from Non-Point Sources

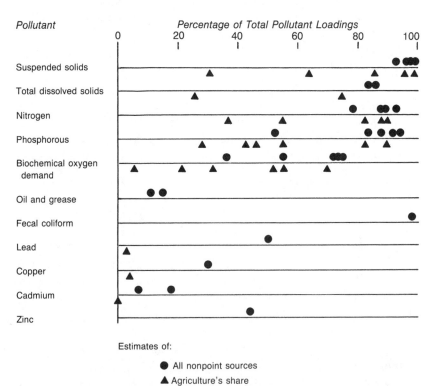

Estimates of:

● All nonpoint sources
▲ Agriculture's share

Source: The Conservation Foundation.

specialized manufacturing or handling processes and consequently are found infrequently or in the discharges of only a few facilities. Their potential impacts on surface waters, however, can be acute, and EPA currently is issuing effluent guidelines for controlling these discharges from the most significant sources.[318]

Even less information is available about the extent to which industrial wastes contaminate groundwater. Such contamination can result from accidental spills, land disposal of waste, injecting liquid wastes deep into the ground as a disposal method, or seepage from areas where raw materials are stored.[319] Many of the more threatening practices are no longer used, but the legacy of early actions can remain. For instance, as is described in chapter 7, major problems have been caused by a plant near Tucson, Arizona that dumped cleaning agents on the ground for decades before the resulting contamination of the city's water supply was discovered.[320]

As indicated in the discussion of hazardous wastes, industrial-waste lagoons also are a significant threat to groundwater supplies. A joint EPA/state survey of waste-disposal sites (called the Surface Impoundment Assessment), located almost 11,000 sites, containing about 26,000 impoundments, used for disposing of industrial wastes.[321] Those impoundments covered 430,000 acres and received an estimated 54 billion gallons of wastewater per day.* Of the 8,163 industrial impoundments that were actually examined, over 70 percent were found to be unlined. Approximately 30 percent were also found to be located in permeable materials and to overlie usable aquifers; in turn, one-third of those sites were within one mile of a water-supply well. Less than 10 percent of the sites had any groundwater monitoring, and only half of those were regularly sampled. How many of these impoundments contained hazardous wastes was not clear, but many of them posed a risk of some kind of groundwater contamination.

Other Point Sources

Numerous other types of point discharges can cause serious problems for both surface water and groundwater, at least in local areas. With EPA's focus being predominantly on municipal and industrial discharges

---

* These estimates, however, may be too high since the U.S. Geological Survey estimated that total water withdrawals by the category ''industry and miscellaneous'' was only 40 to 50 billion gallons a day in 1975, and the rate of withdrawal was not increasing then.[322]

to surface water, many of these other types have received less attention and may be officially included among the uncontrolled "nonpoint" sources.

Mines provide one example. Acid drainage from mining operations can seriously affect both surface water and groundwater. Radioactive mine tailings are identified as a problem by at least one state—New Mexico—and may be a problem in others.[323]

Waste-disposal sites are another example. Hazardous-waste sites have received the most attention, but landfills can also cause contamination.[324] Some 24 states identify landfills as a significant current or potential source of groundwater contamination. Particularly if they are located in a flood plain, they can pollute surface waters as well.

EPA has controlled surface-water pollution from animal feed lots. This may be one reason why USGS reports improving trends in fecal streptococcal bacteria in U.S. rivers.[325] However, this again is an instance where, if care is not taken, surface water can be protected to the detriment of groundwater. Pollution of surface water usually is controlled by preventing stormwater from leaving a site. But, as is explained later in this chapter, this may result in the stormwater's seeping instead into the ground with its heavy pollution loads.

Municipal and Industrial Permit Compliance

Studies by the U.S. General Accounting Office (GAO) and EPA show significant numbers of both municipal and industrial facilities failing to comply with their permits specifying allowable discharges to surface waters.[326] No such national permitting system exists to control most discharges to groundwater (underground injection and hazardous-waste disposal being the major exceptions).

A GAO study reports that noncompliance with NPDES permit limits is "widespread, frequent and significant."[327] For example, 82 percent of the study's sample of major industrial and municipal dischargers exceeded their monthly average permit limits at least once during the 18-month period GAO surveyed. Some 31 percent of the dischargers exceeding their permit limits were in "significant noncompliance," defined as "exceeding permit limits for one or more pollutants by 50 percent or more in at least four consecutive months."[328] The percentage of municipal systems (38 percent) in significant noncompliance was almost twice that of industrial sources (21 percent).[329]

Nonpoint-Source Pollution

As point-source discharges have been reduced, the importance of non-point sources as a cause of surface-water pollution has become increasingly recognized. Although information on the actual magnitude of pollutant loadings and the magnitude of the problem they cause is scanty, various estimates suggest that nonpoint sources account for up to 99 percent of suspended solids and usually between 50 to 90 percent of other conventional pollutants (figure 2.40).

When ASIWPCA asked state officials for the primary causes preventing their streams from supporting their designated uses, most cited nonpoint sources.[330] Nonpoint sources ranked first in 26 states and second in 13 others. Forty states reported that nonpoint sources need to be controlled if water quality is to continue to improve.[331]

The ASIWPCA survey found nonpoint-source pollution from agriculture to be a more significant problem than urban nonpoint-source pollution (figure 2.41).[332] Urban runoff, however, can also cause serious local problems. In addition, mining and land disposal of wastes frequently were cited as causing localized problems.

Nonpoint-source pollution's impact on surface-water aquatic life is substantial. Nonpoint sources adversely affect fish communities in 30 percent of the nation's lakes and rivers, with agricultural sources the most frequent culprit.[333] In contrast, point sources harm fish in only 20 percent of the waters.

Many nonpoint sources also threaten groundwater quality. In some cases, they are the same sources that are polluting surface waters, creating the same types of potential conflicts between surface water and groundwater protection mentioned under point sources. Compared with point sources, which produce regular, year-round discharges, significant nonpoint-source pollution usually occurs only during major storms or when the snow melts.[334] Because the pollutants are carried off with large volumes of water, their impact on surface-water quality may not be immediately evident. However, they can accumulate downstream in lakes, reservoirs, and estuaries, causing serious problems there.

Agricultural Sources

Although the United States has recognized soil erosion as a serious agricultural problem for 50 years, only recently has much attention been given to how this problem affects surface waters. Agricultural lands are the most pervasive nonpoint pollution problem, in themselves con-

Figure 2.41
Severity and Extent of Nonpoint-Source Pollution
Problems for 45 States, 1982[1]

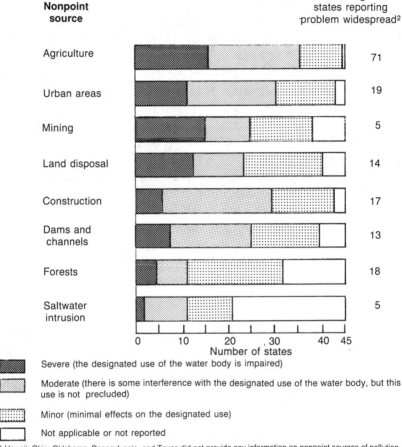

Nonpoint source

Percentage of states reporting problem widespread[2]

Nonpoint source	Percentage
Agriculture	71
Urban areas	19
Mining	5
Land disposal	14
Construction	17
Dams and channels	13
Forests	18
Saltwater intrusion	5

Number of states (0, 10, 20, 30, 40, 45)

■ Severe (the designated use of the water body is impaired)

▨ Moderate (there is some interference with the designated use of the water body, but this use is not precluded)

▦ Minor (minimal effects on the designated use)

☐ Not applicable or not reported

[1] Hawaii, Ohio, Oklahoma, Pennsylvania, and Texas did not provide any information on nonpoint sources of pollution.
[2] The nonpoint source is considered to cause a widespread problem if it affects 50 percent or more of state's waters.

Source: Association of State and Interstate Water Pollution Control Administrators.

tributing most of the sediment, nitrogen, phosphorus, and BOD entering U.S. surface waters (figure 2.40). They are also major contributors of pesticides, bacteria, and dissolved solids.

The heavy nutrient loadings from agricultural lands are one obvious suspect in the search for the cause of the degradation of U.S. lakes and reservoirs. Such traditional water-quality concerns may not, however, be the biggest problem caused by agricultural sources. The biggest costs may be in terms of the sediment filling in lakes, valuable reservoir capacity, navigation channels, and harbors—impacts usually ignored in water-quality-planning efforts.[335] The total costs of these and other impacts are estimated to run into billions of dollars a year.

Agricultural lands also are a significant cause of groundwater contamination. If the pesticides, fertilizers, and other pollutants are not carried off the land during heavy storms, they may be leached into the soil by moderate rainfall or irrigation water. In a Nebraska survey of nitrogen contamination in groundwater, nonpoint sources—predominantly fertilizer—were the cause of the contamination in 82 percent of the wells where nitrogen was found.[336] States from Florida to Washington and Maine to Hawaii cite such agricultural sources as a cause of groundwater pollution.[337]

Agricultural regions relying on center-pivot irrigation using groundwater supplies face a unique threat. In many of those systems, pesticides and fertilizers are fed into the irrigation water before it is sprayed on the field. But the back-flow valves on these devices may not operate properly, resulting in the materials being sucked back down the well directly into the aquifer when the pump is turned off.[338]

Urban Runoff

Urban runoff, long viewed primarily as a source of flooding, is now understood as a water pollution problem as well. Recent information shows that high concentrations of heavy metals—particularly lead, copper, zinc, and cadmium—are carried from streets and parking lots into receiving waters during rainstorms.[339] Coliform bacteria, organic chemicals, oxygen-demanding substances, suspended solids, and nutrients also can occur at significant concentrations.[340]

The most comprehensive U.S. attempt to analyze urban nonpoint-source pollution to date is EPA's National Urban Runoff Program (NURP), completed in early 1984.[341] EPA, in cooperation with USGS, monitored pollutant concentrations in stormwater runoff, analyzed the runoff's impacts on designated uses of receiving surface waters, and studied the effectiveness of selected control measures at 28 urban sites across the country.

Results of the five-year study indicate that heavy metal concentrations at the point of discharge (that is, prior to dilution in the receiving stream, lake, or estuary) frequently exceed limits set by EPA water-quality criteria (figure 2.42). Lead, copper, zinc, and cadmium exceeded the freshwater "chronic" criteria in half or more of the NURP monitoring samples, and copper and lead exceeded "acute" levels in 47 percent and 23 percent of the samples, respectively. In fact, all 13 of the metals included on EPA's list of priority pollutants were detected in NURP samples, and all but 3 at frequencies higher than 10 percent. At the Denver NURP site, for example, levels of lead, zinc, copper, and cadmium exceeded ambient criteria for freshwater aquatic life during almost every storm.[342] Copper is particularly a problem in the South and Southeast, and somewhat less in the Northeast.[343]

Organic pollutants are detected in urban runoff less frequently and at lower concentrations than are heavy metals.[344] However, 63 of EPA's 100 organic priority pollutants were found in the NURP samples. The most commonly observed were selected compounds used in making plastics and certain pesticide compounds, although these compounds were found only at some of the sites.

Urban runoff also carries heavy loads of animal (primarily pet) wastes and their associated bacteria. The NURP study found that the runoff for these wastes exceeded recommended bacterial counts at virtually every site whenever it rained.[345] In many cases these wastes were found to seriously impair water quality in bays and estuaries with important shellfish industries and recreational beachfronts.

No such comprehensive study has been conducted for urban-runoff contamination of groundwater, and only one state, Texas, identified it as a problem in the USGS survey.[346] However, many northern states did identify highway-deicing chemicals as a contamination source.[347]

Other Nonpoint Sources

Other nonpoint sources of pollution can cause serious problems in some regions and in localized areas. Construction sites, at which erosion rates can exceed 150 tons an acre, are probably the most intensive sources of sediment. If construction is occurring on an abandoned plant site or waste-disposal area, the soil can carry with it other serious pollutants as well. Twenty-three states identified construction sites as a nonpoint-source pollution problem in EPA's survey.[348] In addition, mine drainage

Figure 2.42
Frequently Detected Pollutants in Urban Runoff, 1983

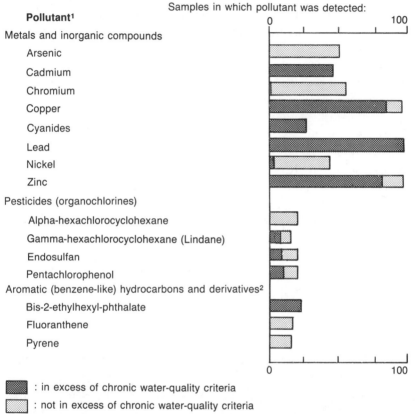

: in excess of chronic water-quality criteria

: not in excess of chronic water-quality criteria

[1] Only those pollutants that were detected in 15 percent or more of the samples are listed.

[2] Aromatic compounds are organic chemicals containing at least one benzene subunit. Fluoranthene and pyrene contain several such subunits and are classed as "polycyclic" compounds.

Source: U.S. Environmental Protection Agency.

is identified as a nonpoint source in terms of surface-water protection; its impacts were described earlier. In one EPA survey, 29 states reported mining as a surface-water problem.[349] Finally, timbering operations in forests can create serious erosion problems. The impact of this type of nonpoint-source pollution may be particularly noticeable because forest streams frequently are particularly clear and stable in their natural condition. In EPA's survey, 20 states identified silvaculture operations as a problem.[350]

Except for mines, quite different sources are cited as groundwater-contamination problems. Several states cite, as a cause, oil and gas wells, which may contaminate an aquifer directly by allowing brine from a saline aquifer to seep into a freshwater supply.[351] They, along with abandoned water wells, also can provide an easy path for pollutants at the ground surface to enter an aquifer. Another potentially serious threat in many localized areas is posed by underground storage tanks, which gradually corrode and can begin to leak without anyone being aware of it until nearby water wells suddenly begin pumping a combination of water and gasoline. EPA estimates that "100,000 tanks nationwide are leaking gasoline or other chemicals."[352]

Both surface water and groundwater also are affected by natural sources of pollution, particularly salt deposits. Such deposits provide the majority of the salt entering the Colorado River (see chapter 7), and saline groundwater is, as indicated earlier, a frequently cited contamination problem. Natural radioactivity and other natural sources, too, cause problems in some areas.

Finally, contaminated surface water and groundwater can pollute one another.[353] Much of the water replenishing groundwater aquifers comes from stream channels, and if a stream is polluted, the water entering the aquifer will be too. During dry periods, when stormwater runoff is minimal, groundwater can flow back into stream channels, providing much of its water supply at low flow. Again, if the groundwater is contaminated, the low flow will be too.

CONCLUSIONS

Over the past 10 years, the United States has been quite successful in achieving one of the major goals of its water-pollution-control program, reducing industrial discharges of conventional pollutants. Progress in abating municipal discharges also has been significant, though much remains to be done. The nation is just beginning to address some of the problems that it previously had not adequately dealt with—

particularly discharges of toxic substances from industrial sources, and nonpoint sources of pollution. Until those problems are adequately handled, surface-water-quality improvements will likely continue to occur slowly, and many of the benefits of the substantial investments already made will be delayed. Still, the public support that existed for the original goals remains. Public opinion polls show that efforts to improve water quality continue to be among the most strongly supported environmental programs.[354]

With respect to groundwater contamination, there is even less encouraging news to report. No national program to protect this valuable resource exists, and EPA admits that its existing authorities can only do part of the job.[355] The agency has had substantial problems developing a coherent groundwater-protection policy, having made its third attempt in almost as many years in 1984. In part because the problems are potentially so significant, in part because the existing programs can deal with at least some of the problems, and in part because groundwater has traditionally been almost entirely a state—not a federal—concern, Congress is proceeding very tentatively in attempting to address this problem.

Waste Production

Substantial amounts of waste are generated in the United States, perhaps as much as 60,000 to 65,000 pounds per person per year (figure 2.43). Most waste materials are relatively innocuous, and many others are removed from the waste stream before the stream enters the environment. Still, the depiction of the United States as a waste-producing society has validity.

Estimates of the amounts of the different types of wastes produced by U.S. society often are only rough approximations, however, and could easily be 20 percent too high or 20 percent too low. Some double counting has occurred—for instance, some of the industrial or residential solid wastes may be burned in incinerators, generating air pollutants.

Nevertheless, comparisons of different waste types are instructive. The largest amounts of wastes are produced by the agricultural (25,900 pounds per person in 1980) and mining sectors (20,000 pounds) and are generally harmless.[356] Over 90 percent of the agricultural wastes are recycled within the agricultural sector, helping to build up soil fertility.[357] However, an estimated 2,000 pounds per person are not recycled, and, as indicated earlier in this chapter, are important as nonpoint-source water pollutants.

With the implementation of the Surface Mining Act, some mining wastes also are being recycled as strip-mined lands are returned to their original contour and replanted.[358] Two types of environmental degradation caused by the remainder of the mining refuse are, again, nonpoint-source water pollution (included in figure 2.43) and "diffuse"-source air pollution—that is, air pollutants that are not released from smokestacks or other "point" sources (not included in figure 2.43).

Air pollutants from point sources constitute the third largest category of residuals (4,200 pounds per person).[359] (The amount would be much higher if carbon dioxide releases were included.) But almost 70 percent of these point-source pollutants are removed from wastes before they are released to the environment.[360] Unfortunately, this removal process may only involve converting one type of pollutant to another. The extraction of pollutants from air waste, for example, may create solid waste and sludges, which are then disposed of on land. For instance, electric utilities with scrubbers were estimated to be producing approximately 350 to 700 million metric tons of scrubber sludge in 1977 (approximately 3,500 to 7,000 pounds per person).[361] (Some of these wastes created in the process of abating air pollutants reappear in figure 2.43 as industrial solid wastes, hazardous wastes, or water pollutants.)

Industrial solid wastes (2,900 pounds per person), hazardous wastes (2,500 pounds), and residential and commercial solid wastes (1,300 pounds) are disposed of predominantly on land.[362] Many of these wastes used to be discarded in open dumps or burned in open fires, but these practices have declined substantially over the past decade. Sanitary landfills now are much more prevalent for most solid-waste dumping.[363] (And, as indicated earlier, substantial efforts are under way to reduce the risks associated with the disposal of hazardous wastes.) Some wastes disposed of in landfills do decompose over time, but this decomposition generates methane and carbon dioxide, which are likely to be released to the atmosphere—another "diffuse" source of air pollution.[364]

Nonpoint waste sources, as indicated previously in this chapter, are the largest category of pollutant loadings to water (1,500 pounds per person). Very few nonpoint-sources are currently controlled. Point-source water pollutants, however, are more thoroughly controlled: over 85 percent of the approximately 1,000 pounds per person per year of these wastes are estimated to be removed by pollution-abatement facilities,[365] although removing these pollutants often results in little more than their transfer to some other medium (see chapter 6). Organic wastes may be converted into carbon dioxide (which is released into the atmosphere) or, along with

Figure 2.43
Estimated U.S. Waste Production, 1980

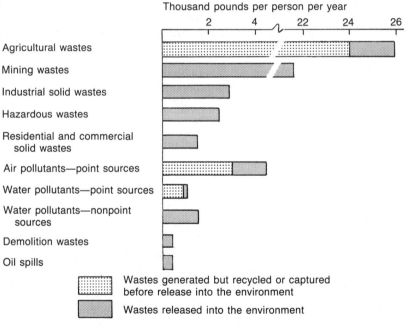

Thousand pounds per person per year

Source: U.S. Environmental Protection Agency.

other pollutants, removed from treatment facilities as sludge.

An estimated 30 to 40 million metric tons of sludge were produced in 1980 by municipal treatment plants (nearly 290 to 390 pounds per person), most of which was disposed of on land.[366] A wastewater-treatment plant can be relatively inefficient. For example, some systems can require several pounds of chemicals to be added to the water for every pound of pollutant removed, and create substantial amounts of sludge.[367] Some of this wastewater-treatment-plant sludge is dumped in the ocean along with oil spills (400 pounds per person) and demolition wastes (375 pounds).[368] Still, the ocean receives less waste directly than the air, surface streams, or the land.[369] Of course, many of the wastes released to surface waters or the air ultimately end up in the ocean.

It must be stressed, however, that none of these estimates of the amounts of different types of waste generated can indicate how much damage pollutants cause or how much risk they create. The increased amounts of waste generated by municipal wastewater-treatment plants, for example, may well cause less environmental damage and reduced health and environmental risks than the smaller, original pollutant loads would have caused if they had been released to surface water. These two factors—environmental damage and health and environmental risks—matter most, not the total amount of waste created.

Chapter 3

Natural Resources

The nation's concerns about how it uses its natural resources, like its concerns about contaminants, have undergone a substantial change in recent times. Here the shift has been from policies that primarily emphasized the exploitation of resources to policies emphasizing conservation and even preservation. The United States has recognized that, as abundant as its natural resources are, they are not limitless. The era of water development is giving way to increased emphasis on managing water use. A land ethic emphasizing settlement and development is being replaced by new policies focusing on conserving farmland, wetlands, and wilderness. Fish and wildlife programs, which for most of their life focused on bolstering populations of game and commercial species, are increasingly concerned with protection of those species that are rare and endangered, regardless of direct economic value. And the energy "crunch" of the early 1970s dramatically shifted the nation's attention to the need for using available energy supplies more wisely.

At the same time, increased population and economic growth (see chapter 1) are creating increased demands for the consumption of natural resources. The production of wastes and use of hazardous substances is affecting the quality of many resources. And people through their participation in outdoor recreation place yet additional stresses on resources, at the same time generating increased demands for their preservation.

These increased pressures affect not only the resources themselves, but the policies, management approaches, and institutions created to deal with natural resources. Changes in both policies and the condition of resources tend to be gradual, but, as the information summarized in this chapter indicates, some shifts are beginning to occur.

Water

The United States is, on the average, a water-rich country, receiving about 18,000 gallons of rainfall per person every day (figure 3.1). The majority (65 percent) of that rainfall quickly returns to the atmosphere through evaporation or transpiration, less than a third reaches the oceans through surface or subsurface flow, and only 2.5 percent is consumed.

Averages, however, are always misleading, and nowhere more so than in the case of water. East of the Mississippi River, the average rainfall is 44 inches per year; in the Great Plains, it drops to 20 inches; and in some parts of the Southwest, it falls to 4 inches.[1]

Even where water is most plentiful, it is not always available in the right amounts of the right quality at the right time. Most of the current concern focuses on projected water shortages resulting from rising demands bumping against limited supplies. Yet the dryest part of the country—the West—has suffered from substantial floods during the past two years: In the spring of 1983, rapid melting of a record-breaking, heavy snowpack caused the Colorado River to flood.[2] While torrential rainstorms were battering the West Coast in 1983, the Midwest was suffering a drought.[3] The Great Salt Lake is at its highest level in 100 years, flooding many valuable shore properties and wetlands.[4] Such regional variations occur every year, and an area that floods one year can experience a drought the next. Looking at longer-term trends, however, the major problem across the United States will be ensuring that sufficient water of adequate quality is available to satisfy the nation's growing thirst.

TRENDS IN WATER USE

The amount of water used in the United States has continued to increase steadily throughout this century. The two common measures of water use are "withdrawal" and "consumption." Water is withdrawn when it is taken from a ground or surface source and is conveyed to the place of use. Water is consumed when it is no longer available for use because it has been removed from available supplies by evaporation or transpiration, for use in agriculture or manufacturing, or for food preparation and drinking.[5] Withdrawals and consumption refer exclusively to offstream uses of water; that is, uses that depend on water being taken out of the stream channel, impoundment, or groundwater aquifer

Figure 3.1
Water Budget of the Coterminous United States

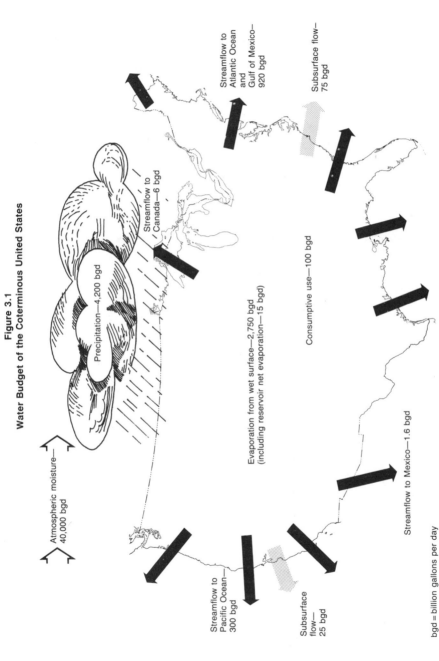

Atmospheric moisture—40,000 bgd

Precipitation—4,200 bgd

Streamflow to Canada—6 bgd

Streamflow to Atlantic Ocean and Gulf of Mexico—920 bgd

Subsurface flow—75 bgd

Evaporation from wet surface—2,750 bgd (including reservoir net evaporation—15 bgd)

Consumptive use—100 bgd

Streamflow to Pacific Ocean—300 bgd

Subsurface flow—25 bgd

Streamflow to Mexico—1.6 bgd

bgd = billion gallons per day

Source: U.S. Geological Survey.

through which it naturally flows. By contrast, instream uses—for example, hydroelectric-power generation, aquatic life, navigation, and wastewater dilution—utilize water without removing it from the source.

Increasing withdrawals are seriously reducing the amount of water available for instream uses in many parts of the country. For instance, the 1983 National Fisheries Survey reported that low water levels are adversely affecting fish communities in 68 percent of U.S. inland water bodies.[6] Much of the Southwest has insufficient water flows to support many instream uses in an average year, and, in dry years, the problem of inadequate stream flows is experienced in much of the Great Plains as well.[7]

Water Withdrawal

Water withdrawal in the United States rose 22 percent between 1970 and 1980 (figure 3.2). That was a somewhat lower rate than the 37 percent increase that occurred between 1960 and 1970, but it still was about twice the nation's population growth rate.[8] In 1950, Americans withdrew, on the average, 1,200 gallons of water per person per day for all uses; by 1980, that average had grown to about 2,000 gallons per person per day.[9]

Steam electrical generation has grown most quickly, surpassing irrigation as the largest water user in the 1960s (figure 3.3). But irrigation has increased as well, about 7 percent in both the amount of water used and the total irrigated acreage since 1975.[10] An average of about 2.9 acre-feet of irrigation water was applied to each of 58 million acres of farmland in 1980.[11] Some of the most rapid increases have been in areas that traditionally depended on rainfall but are now adopting supplemental irrigation systems to avoid damages caused by droughts.

In addition, public water supplies, which support some industrial as well as most residential and commercial uses, have increased significantly, up 15 percent since 1975.[12]

Water Consumption

Consumption, like withdrawal, has grown continually for most water uses. Most of the water withdrawn—78 percent—is soon returned to surface-water or groundwater supplies, rather than irretrievably consumed.[13]

The proportion of withdrawal eventually consumed varies quite a bit among categories of use. For example, out of 100 gallons withdrawn from a river for cooling steam electric utilities, over 98 gallons are usually

Figure 3.2
U.S. Water Use, 1900–1980

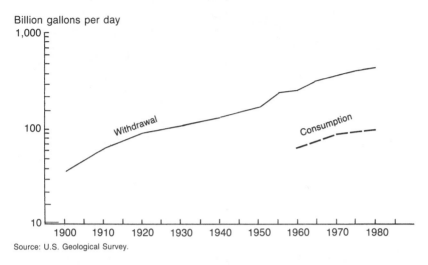

Billion gallons per day

Source: U.S. Geological Survey.

Figure 3.3
U.S. Water Withdrawal, by Use, 1950–1980

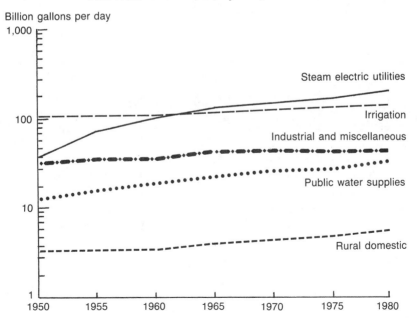

Billion gallons per day

Source: U.S. Geological Survey.

returned almost immediately to the river; fewer than 2 gallons are consumed through evaporation.[14] In contrast, irrigation consumes an average of 55 percent of all irrigation water withdrawn and accounts for 83 percent of the total water consumed in the United States.[15] Fifty-nine percent of water withdrawn for rural domestic use is consumed,[16] as is 21 percent of the water withdrawn for public supplies.[17] Self-supplied industrial users (not including electric utilities) consume only 13 percent of their withdrawals, although this figure is rising because industries are reusing more of their water,[18] in part to avoid the high costs of wastewater treatment.

On the average, the growth in water consumption appears to be slowing down: between 1970 and 1980 consumption increased by only 14 percent, compared with a 44 percent increase for the previous decade (figure 3.4).

SOURCES OF WATER

Most U.S. water withdrawn (64 percent of total withdrawal, 77 percent of freshwater withdrawal) is from freshwater streams, lakes, and reservoirs.[19] Groundwater is the source of 20 percent of total supplies and 23 percent of freshwater supplies. Almost all of the remaining withdrawals are saline water (about 99 percent of which is taken from bays and estuaries).[20] One-half billion gallons a day (about 0.1 percent) are reclaimed sewage. During the early 1970s, withdrawal of both groundwater and saline water increased much faster than did withdrawal of surface fresh water.[21] Between 1975 and 1980, however, these trends changed substantially, with the use of surface water increasing more rapidly than the use of either groundwater or saline water. The use of reclaimed sewage declined slightly.

From 1950 to 1975, groundwater withdrawal increased approximately twice as quickly as did surface-water withdrawals. Much of the newly pumped groundwater was used for irrigation (for instance, in the High Plains of Texas)[22]; indeed, 67 percent of current groundwater use is for irrigation (figure 3.5). Public water supplies and industry each account for about 13 percent of groundwater withdrawal.

Not surprisingly, over the years, groundwater withdrawal rates have closely reflected trends in the use of groundwater for irrigation. Between 1975 and 1980, the growth rate of groundwater use for irrigation slowed, perhaps because of farmers' efforts to hold down the cost of pumping water from deep aquifers. Those costs have resulted from both increased

Figure 3.4
U.S. Water Consumption, by Use, 1960–1980

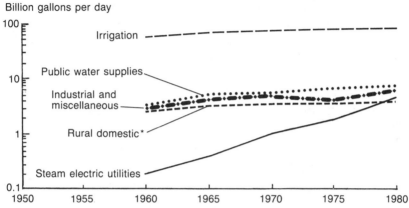

Billion gallons per day

Estimates of consumptive use were not tabulated before 1960.
* Includes livestock watering as well as household use.

Source: U.S. Geological Survey.

Figure 3.5
U.S. Groundwater Withdrawals, by Use, 1950–1980

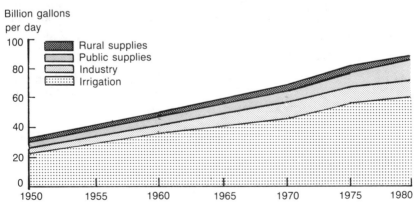

Billion gallons
per day

Source: U.S. Geological Survey.

energy costs and the fact that groundwater levels are declining by between 0.5 and 6.6 feet per year under 15 million acres of land irrigated by groundwater.[23]

Groundwater depletion continues to be a serious problem in many parts of the United States. Nationally, a quarter of the amount of groundwater withdrawn is not replenished.[24] In the Texas-Gulf region, however, the proportion rises to 77.2 percent.[25] In 1975, the latest year for which information is available, two-thirds of the nation's water-resources regions were experiencing overdrafts.[26] Groundwater levels have declined substantially in many parts of the country: 100 feet in the past 10 years in Alabama; 400 feet in 50 years southeast of Phoenix, Arizona; 300 feet since the early 1930s in southern Arkansas; 200 feet since 1950 along the California coast; more than 850 feet in 116 years in northern Illinois; and as much as 20 feet per year throughout large areas of the Columbian Plateau in Washington.[27] In addition to causing pumping costs to climb, these declines can reduce surface stream flow during periods of low rainfall, draw saltwater into aquifers and speed the spread of other contaminants, and cause land subsidence that can damage structures, interfere with the drainage of streams and sewers, and increase the threat of flooding.

Traditionally, when water supplies have become tight in the United States, either new reservoirs have been built or more wells have been installed to satisfy the rising demands. But, for a variety of reasons discussed in chapter 7, the rate at which reservoir capacity is being added in the United States has fallen off dramatically.[28] And, in many areas of the country, additional reservoir capacity—by itself—would not increase the available water supply substantially, since increased reservoir construction is accompanied by increased evaporation. Reservoir evaporation in the United States is already equivalent to 15 percent of the total amount of offstream water consumption.[29] At some point, additional evaporation from new reservoirs built in a watershed may significantly decrease the amount of water that can be continually withdrawn (figure 3.6).[30]

Other water sources—saline water and reclaimed sewage—can be used only for specific purposes. Saline water can be used in coastal facilities to generate electricity, and reclaimed sewage can provide water to irrigate golf courses, lawns, and nonfood crops. Reclaimed sewage is, however, a relatively expensive source of water compared with the surface water and groundwater the United States is accustomed to using.

Some proposals have been made to develop ''new'' sources of water, such as towing icebergs down from the Arctic, diverting Canadian and Alaskan rivers to flow south into the United States, or pumping water

from the Great Lakes to irrigate the Great Plains. These would be extremely expensive projects. As is indicated in chapter 7, better management of what water is available seems more efficient than hoping for
such new sources.

Regional Patterns

Although water shortages will be experienced more and more frequently
throughout the United States, it is in the West that the conflicts are
greatest. The West receives the least rainfall of any section of the
country,[31] and almost 70 percent of the nation's runoff occurs east of
the 95th meridian (the north-south line running at approximately the
western boundary of Minnesota, Iowa, Missouri, Arkansas, and
Louisiana).[32] The Pacific Northwest is responsible for 13 percent of the
runoff; only 1 percent occurs in the Colorado River basin.

Although only 30 percent of the runoff in the United States occurs
west of the 95th meridian, about 80 percent of the nation's water is
consumed there. The 17 contiguous states west of the 95th meridian
withdraw an average of 2,900 gallons per person per day and consume
1,200 of these (figure 3.7). By contrast, the consumption rate in the
East is only 120 gallons per capita per day—one-tenth of the amount
that is consumed in the West.

As a result, many areas in the West are already consuming much of
their available water (figure 3.8). In many portions of the eastern United
States, average consumption levels are only 1 to 2 percent of the
renewable water supply. In the West, consumption levels equal to 30
percent or more of the renewable supply are common, and, in the lower
Colorado River basin, consumption already exceeds renewable supply.[33]
As a result, except during unusual floods, the Colorado River never
reaches its natural mouth in the Gulf of California, ending instead 14
miles away in a saline pond.[34]

The Colorado River is not the only river so exploited that there is
no water left during much of the year. Yet population and economic
growth in its basin continue to occur faster than in most of the rest
of the country (see chapter 1), placing still greater demands on the water
that is left. With very limited prospects for obtaining increased supplies, the emphasis in the future will have to be on better management
of what water there is rather than on new development. One encouraging
example is the proposal that the Los Angeles Metropolitan Water District
pay for lining irrigation canals in the Imperial Valley to conserve water
now being lost by seepage and evaporation and use the water saved—

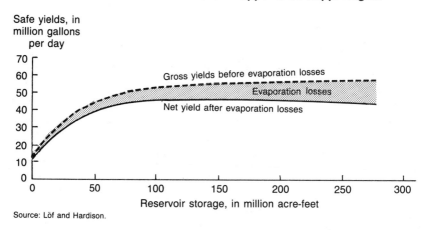

Figure 3.6
Potential Yields of Reservoirs in Upper Mississippi Region

Source: Löf and Hardison.

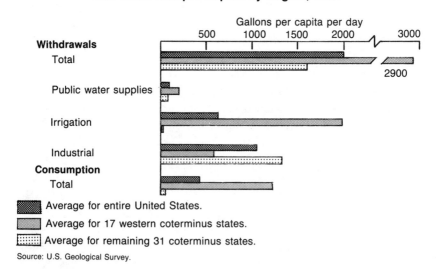

Figure 3.7
U.S. Water Use per Capita. by Region, 1980

Source: U.S. Geological Survey.

Figure 3.8
U.S. Water Supply and Consumption, by Region, 1980

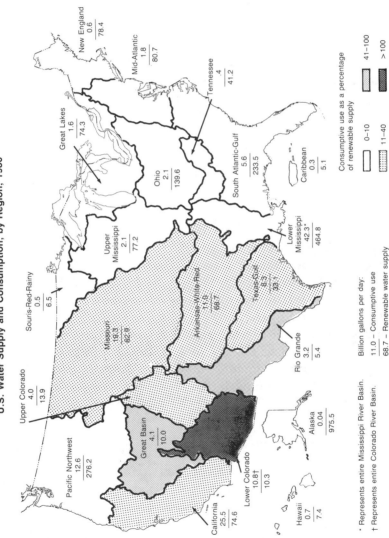

New England
0.6
────
78.4

Mid-Atlantic
1.8
────
80.7

Tennessee
.4
────
41.2

Great Lakes
1.6
────
74.3

Ohio
2.1
────
139.6

South Atlantic-Gulf
5.6
────
233.5

Caribbean
0.3
────
5.1

Upper
Mississippi
2.1
────
77.2

Lower
Mississippi
42.3*
────
464.8

Souris-Red-Rainy
0.5
────
6.5

Missouri
19.3
────
82.9

Arkansas-White-Red
11.0
────
68.7

Texas-Gulf
8.3
────
33.1

Upper Colorado
4.0
────
13.9

Rio Grande
3.2
────
5.4

Great Basin
4.1
────
10.0

Pacific Northwest
12.6
────
276.2

Lower Colorado
10.8†
────
10.3

California
25.5
────
74.6

Alaska
0.04
────
975.5

Hawaii
0.7
────
7.4

Consumptive use as a percentage
of renewable supply

0–10

11–40

41–100

>100

Billion gallons per day:

11.0 – Consumptive use
────
68.7 – Renewable water supply

* Represents entire Mississippi River Basin.
† Represents entire Colorado River Basin.

an estimated 438,000 acre-feet a year—itself.[35] The cost of this water could be less than potential additional water supplies made available from the California State Water Project, and the newly available water would just offset the loss from the Colorado River that Los Angeles faces when the Central Arizona Project is completed. Other benefits that could result from the conservation project include slowing the rise of the Salton Sea, which currently is causing substantial damages in the valley, and providing the valley with a modern irrigation system at no cost to the valley's residents.

Such innovative responses will be needed more and more in all parts of the United States as increasing stress is placed on both surface-water and groundwater supplies. These issues are discussed at length in chapter 7.

Land Use

The United States is relatively rich in land. With 2.2 billion acres of land surface (not including 0.1 billion acres of inland water bodies),[36] the amount per capita is 1.4 times that of the world as a whole. In cropland (2.7 times), pasture and rangeland (1.4 times), and forestland (1.3 times), the U.S. per capita acreage also exceeds the global average. Compared to nearly every other industrialized nation, these advantages are even greater: the United States has at least 300 percent larger acreage per capita for all land types.[37] But U.S. land, with all its riches, is not an unlimited resource; the relative wisdom of land-use trends is of crucial concern to all Americans.

LAND OWNERSHIP

One legacy of the United States' territorial expansion is federal ownership and oversight of an enormous area of land. Indeed, for much of the 19th century, considerable economic and political energy was spent seeking to dispose of these lands. Between 1781 and 1982, over a billion acres of public land were sold or granted to homesteaders, states, railroad corporations, and other entities.[38] Nonetheless, over 700 million acres of the United States, especially in the West and in Alaska (figure 3.9),

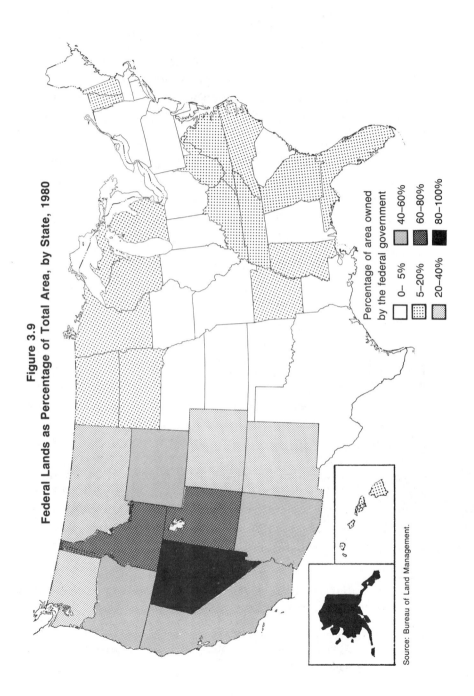

Figure 3.9
Federal Lands as Percentage of Total Area, by State, 1980

Percentage of area owned
by the federal government

0– 5%   40–60%
5–20%   60–80%
20–40%   80–100%

Source: Bureau of Land Management.

remain in federal ownership,* representing 32 percent of the nation's land.[40] Other significant public landowners are the states (7 percent of total area) and Native American Indian tribes (3 percent).[41]

Of the land in private hands (59 percent of the total area of the United States), two-thirds is owned by individuals and married couples. An additional 16 percent of the privately owned land is held by other family groups, including family corporations. Nonfamily corporations and partnerships (13 percent) and miscellaneous deed holders (4 percent) own the remainder.[42] Distribution of private land title is uneven: 40 percent of privately owned land is in the hands of just 0.5 percent of the landowners, whereas 78 percent of private landowners hold deeds to only 3 percent of the private land.[43]

As with federal ownership, patterns of private land ownership vary greatly from state to state. For example, although individuals and married couples own 67 percent of the private land nationwide, in the Pacific region less than half the private land is in such ownerships. In the Corn Belt and Lake States regions, single and joint title holders hold more than 80 percent of the private land.[44]

CATEGORIES OF LAND USE

Land without human-built structures on it is generally classified by its vegetative cover—trees, grasses and/or shrubs, or cultivated crops. The three largest land classes—forests, rangelands, and croplands—constitute 77 percent of the area of the United States (figure 3.10).†

Forestland, the largest of the three categories, comprises 703 million acres. Next, pasture and rangeland, dominated by forage grasses and shrubs, but also including 76 million acres of cropland used only for pasture, covers 663 million acres. Another 395 million acres are lands used for crops (369 million acres) or idle croplands (26 million).[46]

The remaining 23 percent of the U.S. land area is usually grouped into two broad categories, "special uses" and "other." Special uses in-

---

* The federal agencies responsible for nearly all of this land are the Bureau of Land Management (343 million acres), Forest Service (184 million), U.S. Fish and Wildlife Service (82 million), National Park Service (68 million), and U.S. Department of Defense (30 million, including some acreage, such as lands administered by the U.S. Army Corps of Engineers, which is not used for military purposes.)[39]

† The most recent analysis of major land uses in the United States is for 1978. A revision using 1982 data is in preparation; no major changes are expected, except for large reclassifications of land to park and wildlife areas in Alaska.[45]

Figure 3.10
Major Uses of Land in the United States, 1900–1978

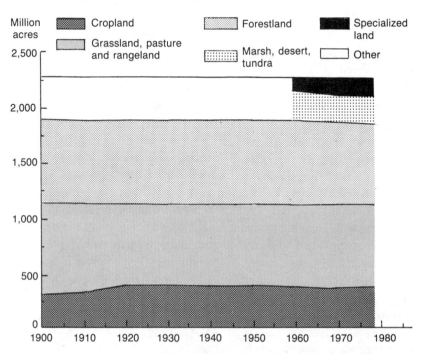

"Other" land (pre-1959) includes specialized land uses and marshes, deserts, tundra, and other lands of undetermined use.

"Specialized" land includes urban and built-up areas (cities and towns, rural highway and road right-of-way, railroads, airports, and public institutions in rural areas) and nonurban special-use areas (parks, recreational areas, federal and state wildlife refuges, national defense sites, flood-control areas, federal industrial areas, farmsteads, and farm roads).

Forestland excludes reserved forestland in parks, wildlife refuges, and other special-use areas.

Source: U.S. Department of Agriculture.

clude parks, recreation areas, and wildlife areas (98 million acres), non-farm transportation uses (27 million acres), defense (25 million acres), and farmsteads and farm roads (8 million acres).[47] Many of these areas, if not dedicated to specialized uses, would be placed in other categories. Some 33 million acres used for parks, recreation, and wildlife conservation, for example, are forested,[48] although reserved from commercial exploitation. The "other" class includes areas of miscellaneous vegetation, such as desert, marsh, and tundra, and urban and built-up areas. This classification encompasses 345 million acres in the United States, about two-thirds of it in Alaska.[49] Some 47 million acres (just 2 percent of the total area) is in urban areas, as defined by the U.S. Census Bureau.[50]*

These estimates of land-use areas come from many sources which use different statistical sampling techniques with various degrees of error. Although the rough estimates are an adequate gross representation of the uses to which land is being put, they are not precise. For example, the urban area is almost certainly overstated because city limits, being political boundaries, do not coincide with actual land character. On one hand, undeveloped and rural land may exist within city limits, and be considered "urban." On the other, built-up areas in towns of under 2,500 residents are not classified as "urban."[52] Furthermore, the character of spaces within each land-use category varies tremendously. The downtown skyscrapers of a large city, clustered single-family homes in a suburban subdivision, and the main street of a small town all occupy urban land. Land devoted to dairying is quite different from the land on a cotton plantation; both are categorized as agricultural.

National statistics have another shortcoming: they obscure the kinds of regional patterns shown in figure 3.11.

CHANGES IN LAND-USE PATTERNS

Land use, whether considered on the smallest or the grandest scale, is not static. Individuals see a subdivision being built on what had been a neighboring farm, a new office building rising on a formerly vacant lot, a former woodlot that now grows crops. Yet national trends in land-

---

* The terms "urban" and "urban and built-up" are often used interchangeably, but they are not the same. The urban and built-up category used by the U.S. Department of Agriculture incorporates smaller settlements and more facilities than the urban category used by the Bureau of the Census. The 1977 Agriculture Department classification listed 89 million acres as urban and built-up land.[51]

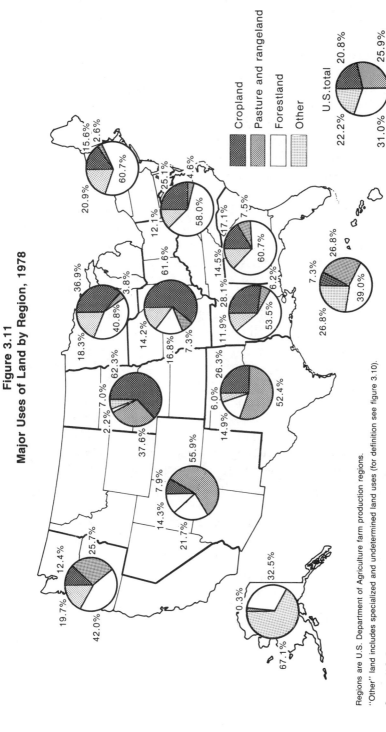

Figure 3.11
Major Uses of Land by Region, 1978

Regions are U.S. Department of Agriculture farm production regions.
"Other" land includes specialized and undetermined land uses (for definition see figure 3.10).

Source: U.S. Department of Agriculture.

use change are difficult to identify or confirm, especially in the short term. Even seemingly clear trends are difficult to support with conclusive data, because definitions of land-use categories change, making year-to-year comparisons problematic.

Historically, the gradual settlement of North America by Europeans is associated with large-scale and dramatic changes in land use and cover. Conversion of huge tracts of forest, and then prairie, to agricultural crops affected the most acreage. But even on nonagricultural land, intensive logging and livestock grazing, as well as the spread of towns, represented major departures from Native American patterns of crop production, animal husbandry, and settlement. By the beginning of the 20th century, the current pattern of land use on the North American continent had pretty well emerged. Certain trends, such as an increase in urbanized land, continue, but the changes in this century have been gradual and, compared to the nation's total land area, relatively small (figure 3.10).

The slowly changing totals mask considerable shifting back and forth among the different land-use categories. Land use tends to shift to and from all categories except "urban and built-up," which gains land more or less irreversibly from all other categories. The shifts may be very large, even if they result in small net changes. For example, the net change of cropland acreage was less than 10 percent between 1967 and 1975, but the number of acres converted to or from cropland during that period amounted to nearly 30 percent of the cropland base.[53] Furthermore, regional distribution of land use has changed considerably. Again using agriculture as an example, large amounts of land have been taken out of crops in the East, while drainage—of bottomland forests in the Mississippi Valley, prairie potholes in North Dakota, and marshes in Florida—and irrigation in the Texas High Plains, central California, and the Snake River Valley created new concentrations of cropland (figure 3.12).[54]

Amid all of this shifting of land among uses, some changes, such as building roads and cities, or inundating areas by constructing reservoirs, are basically irreversible and represent conversions to "specialized" uses. Specialized land use showed the largest percentage increase of any category during the 1970s. Nearly 3 million acres per year that were transformed into urban and other built-up uses between 1967 and 1977 account for most of the increase.[55] New roads and highways, especially the interstate highway system (which occupies 1.8 million acres of land), add to this total both by direct consumption of land and by easing ac-

Figure 3.12
Areas with Increases and Decreases in Cropland Acreage, 1949–1976

Increases

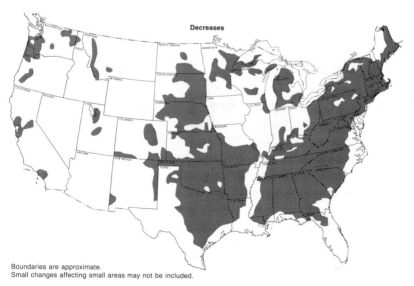

Decreases

Boundaries are approximate.
Small changes affecting small areas may not be included.

Source: United States Department of Agriculture.

cess to undeveloped areas.[56]* Dam building, begun on a large scale in the 1930s, has inundated millions of, generally agricultural, acres, especially in the Tennessee Valley, Missouri River Basin, and Columbia River Basin.[58] (One significant additive shift in specialized land uses, designation of public areas for recreation, wildlife, and wilderness, is not irreversible and often merely reflects added legal protection rather than actual land-use or vegetative-cover changes.)

Care should be taken in extrapolating from past rates of increase in specialized lands. Much of the expansion, especially of reservoirs and roads, is no longer occurring at previous rates. Yet rising demands for land uses such as urban development, public recreation areas, pipelines, and powerlines may result in a modest continuation of these trends.

EFFECTS OF INTERSPERSED USES

A significant class of land-use problems, growing in importance, stems from conflicts between incompatible, but adjoining, land uses. The classic example pits farmers against the residents of newly suburbanized areas. Farmers complain of children and pets who destroy crops or harass livestock and of rising property taxes pushed up by newcomers' services. Nonfarmers get equally irate about farm machinery operating early in the morning, manure odors, and pesticide spraying. Farmers eventually lose such battles because, as urban fringe areas develop, nonfarmers come to outnumber the farmers and to dominate local government. One analyst describes the result as the "zone-out" process—suburbanites gain a numerical majority, incorporate the area, then enact zoning regulations to ban "objectionable" agricultural uses.[59] Farmers have counterattacked in state legislatures, and since 1971 about 30 states have enacted "right-to-farm" laws, which exempt preexisting agricultural uses from nuisance suits. Few of these laws have yet been tested in the courts, and they may prove easier to pass than to implement.[60]

Conflicts between uses involve not only cropland, but also forestland, as new rural residents object to clearcutting of timber, burning of logging residues, and aerial application of herbicides.[61] Particularly in the West, nonfarm rural settlement has been associated with a greater incidence of forest fires and more difficult fire management once a blaze starts.[62]

---

* The total amount of land actually used by all nonfarm roadways has risen only slightly, even with the construction of the interstate highways, from 19.8 million acres in 1954 to 21.5 million acres in 1978.[57]

It is likely that inter-use conflicts will continue to expand in rural areas. In spite of decreased growth rates in nonmetropolitan areas (see chapter 1), people will continue to settle at the urban fringe and far into the countryside. However, intensified rural land uses, including greater use of chemicals, more land in active production, larger machinery, and more frequent timber harvests, are as much involved in inter-use conflicts as is increasing concentration of residences on rural land.

The land produces a myriad of goods and services, some easily quantifiable in economic terms, others not. Many of these outputs, such as crops, timber, and wildife, are renewable if managed wisely. The following two sections discuss the current status of and trends in the condition of lands used for renewable resource production.

Cropland, Forestland, and Rangeland

Despite the Industrial Revolution and the recent shift to service industries, a tremendous amount of American economic activity is still rooted in the land. More than 77 percent of the U.S. land area is devoted to growing crops, trees, or forage.[63] In 1982, the market value of crops produced was over $85 billion,[64] and livestock and their products were worth almost $42 billion,[65] exclusive of value added during processing.* There is no comparable figure for the value of raw timber, but the forest products manufacturing industries had shipments in excess of $127 billion in 1981.[66] These figures do not include other values that accrue from crop-, forest-, and rangelands such as recreation and wildlife habitat.

Because these lands are so important to the economy, most readily available information about them concerns their marketable products. However, to report only on the quantities of goods extracted from the land is to take an incomplete view. Productive use of the land and its vegetation may affect its quality and the renewability of its yields.

---

* The value of shipments by the manufacturing industries, classified as food and kindred products, tobacco products, and textile mill products, was $335 billion in 1981. This figure double counts the raw values of those agricultural commodities that underwent manufacturing processes and excludes the raw value of those farm products that did not.

CROPLAND

All three renewable resource industries alter land from its "natural" state, but agriculture has, to date, most transformed natural ecosystems over the greatest area. The replacement of North America's natural vegetation by agricultural crops was the major ecological change that resulted from European settlement. Huge areas of forest, especially in the East and South, were cleared to allow agricultural planting. As settlement moved westward, crops replaced native grasses; only isolated vestiges remain of the tall-grass prairie that once covered some 140 million acres of the plains.[67] But by 1920, the amount of cropland (including that not currently used to grow crops) had more or less stabilized near its current total of 471 million acres.[68]

Productivity

The amount of food grown on all this land has increased steadily, particularly since World War II (figure 3.13). Agricultural production in the United States now far exceeds domestic demands. Periodic large surpluses have depressed prices and caused economic cycles for farmers, whose net income from 1980 through 1982, when corrected for inflation, was substantially less than in 1965 and averaged only about a third of the level reached in the peak year of 1973.[69] A variety of price-support and land-idling programs attempt to buffer farmers from these cycles. The latest program, called PIK (payment-in-kind), which offered farm operators stored grain from previous surpluses if they idled cropland, induced farmers to leave 80 million acres of cropland fallow in 1983.[70]

Agricultural production still exceeds domestic demand, however, in part because of the emergence (with government encouragement) of a large and rapidly growing export market for American produce. Between 1970 and 1980, the volume of U.S. agricultural exports more than doubled (figure 3.14).[71] During that decade, more than half of American production of such major crops as wheat, soybeans, and rice was sold to foreign countries.[72]

Agricultural export volume remained high in 1981 and 1982, despite dropping somewhat relative to 1980.[73] Foreign policy issues such as the state of relations between the United States and the Soviet Union, the debt capacity of developing countries, and the strength of the dollar relative to foreign currencies all affect farm exports and have contributed to their recent decline.[74] Yet, even though the era of large year-to-year

Figure 3.13
Crop and Livestock Production, 1967–1982

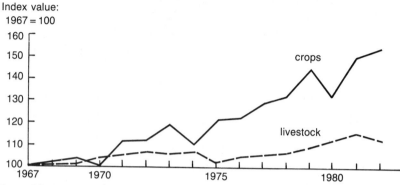

Source: U.S. Department of Agriculture.

Figure 3.14.
Volume of U.S. Agricultural Exports, 1967–1982

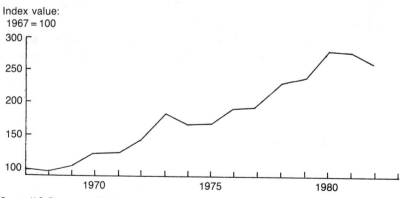

Source: U.S. Department of Agriculture.

increases in agricultural exports may be past, nearly a third of all harvested crop acreage in America is needed to fulfill export demands.[75]

What accounts for the great increases in production, which turned the United States into the world's breadbasket? American agriculture has been tremendously intensified in the last 40 years. The amount of land in crops has not increased very much, but the heavy use of new technologies, particularly pesticides, fertilizers, and improved seeds,* has made each acre produce more. As more and more reliance has been placed on chemicals, irrigation, and machinery, agricultural production has demanded less and less human labor (figure 3.15). For each American employed principally in agriculture, there exist over 200 acres of cropland; this is 5 to 15 times the amount of cropland per farmer in Western Europe, about 100 times that in Japan, and more than 200 times that in China.[76]**

Despite the reduction in farm labor requirements and the very real gains in total agricultural production, gains in productivity have been uneven. Sometimes an apparent increase in return from one input results from use of another input as a replacement. Over the past 15 years, for example, more and more yield has been coaxed from each unit of labor (figure 3.16). However, the yield increase per unit of land has been much smaller, and when *all* resources used in agriculture are considered, the productivity gains have been slightly smaller still—only 15 percent between 1967 and 1980. ('Estimated'' 1982 and ''preliminary'' 1981 figures show substantially higher overall productivity in those two years, which have only a small effect on the long-term trend.)[78] In general, this growth has slowed (and become more expensive to accomplish) in recent years, suggesting that agriculture, like any industry, is experiencing diminishing returns on its inputs. Continued variations in yields from year to year further demonstrate that, despite modern technology, farmers are still vulnerable to the vagaries of disease and weather (figure 3.17). For example, the 1970 leaf blight outbreak, and

---

* In some parts of the country, particularly central and southern California, the dry western Plains states, and, recently, double-cropped areas in the South, irrigation water has been a critical input.

** These ratios are based on data from the United Nations Food and Agriculture Organisation, which reported that the United States in 1980 had an ''agricultural population'' of 2.2 million economically active persons engaged principally in agriculture. The U.S. Department of Agriculture reported that about 5 million Americans did some work on farms in mid-July 1982.[77] Factors such as distribution of farm ownership and crop mix, as well as use of technology, affect the comparison among nations.

Figure 3.15
Resources Used in Agricultural Production, 1964–1983

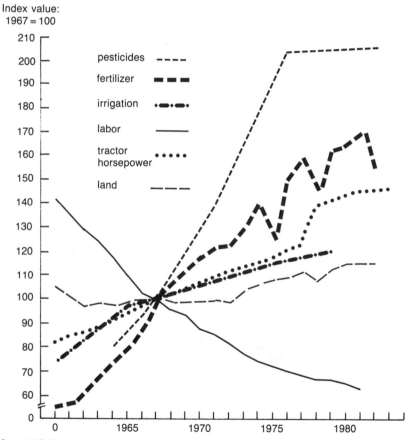

Index value:
1967 = 100

Source: U.S. Department of Agriculture.

Figure 3.16
Agricultural Productivity, 1965–1982

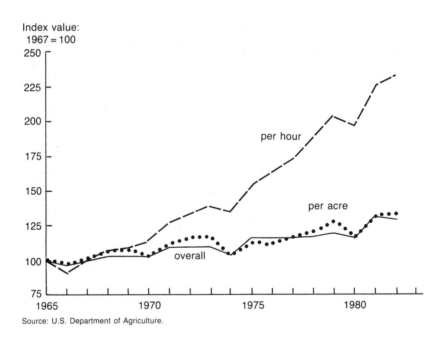

Source: U.S. Department of Agriculture.

Figure 3.17
Yields per Acre, Selected Crops, 1965–1982

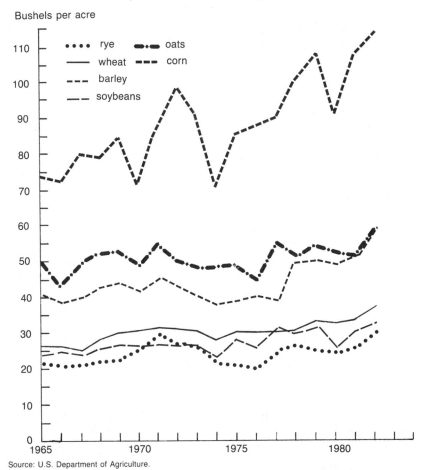

Bushels per acre

Source: U.S. Department of Agriculture.

the farm belt droughts of 1974, 1980, and 1983, were all reflected in severely reduced corn yields.[79]

The greater use in crop production of inputs produced off the farm means farmers are also vulnerable to disruptions in supply of those inputs. The oil embargo of 1973, together with limited natural gas supplies and energy price controls, created a temporary shortage of nitrogen fertilizer;[80] in 1975, with controls lifted and nitrogen prices climbing to more than double their levels of two years before, farmers cut back on fertilizer use, and yields did not return to normal that year, even though the weather did (figure 3.17).[81]

Productivity changes associated with improved technology and greater application of purchased inputs make it difficult to ascertain any trend in productivity of the most fundamental agricultural input: the soil. There are indications that both the amount of this vital resource and its quality are at risk.

Farmland Conversions

Even though the total amount of land classified as cropland has remained relatively constant, some cropland is being converted to other uses as an offsetting amount of new land is brought under cultivation. Much of the cropland lost, unfortunately, is probably of somewhat higher quality than the new land that is taking its place.* According to one estimate, between 1967 and 1975 about 875,000 acres of land suitable for crops (600,000 actually used as cropland at the time) were paved over, built on, or flooded by dams each year.[83] (Estimates of the current rate of farmland loss will not be available until data from the Agriculture Department's 1982 National Resources Inventory are fully analyzed; the preliminary data suggest that earlier estimates of rates of farmland may be somewhat too high.[84]) An unknown, but significant, additional area of usable cropland already is subdivided, for future development, into parcels too small to farm efficiently, if at all.[85]

Although even a million acres is less than 0.3 percent of the crop area harvested annually, and a still smaller fraction of the nation's total arable land, this land loss is significant because it is essentially irreversible and, therefore, cumulative. In addition, when farmers see their

---

* This may not always be true. Enough relatively poor land is now in cultivation to suggest that changes in the cropland base might have no net effect on overall productivity.[82] Unfortunately, there is no information available that would allow a direct comparison between the land being converted out of and into agriculture.

neighbors' lands being sold, they may begin to feel that conversion is inevitable, and consequently avoid making needed investments in their farms.[86] Investments in soil conservation practices are a good example.

Soil Erosion

Soil erosion is a potential major threat to the continued productivity of American agriculture.* Erosion—the movement of soil by wind or water—is a natural process, but human disturbance of the soil surface generally increases the amount of erosion. In the United States, sheet-and-rill erosion (soil carried off by flowing water) on cultivated cropland averages 4.82 tons per acre per year;[89]† wind moves about an additional 3.3 tons per year.[91]

To put this in perspective, consider that an inch of topsoil covering an acre of ground weighs about 150 to 165 tons; this means that, on the *average*, 0.03 to 0.05 inch of topsoil is eroded away each year, yet only about 10 percent of that loss is replaced by natural soil-formation

---

* The exact degree to which erosion reduces soil productivity is neither clearly established nor easy to determine. The depth of topsoil, a critical factor in the effect of erosion on productivity, varies widely in the United States. Other variations in soils, the crops grown on them, and the technologies applied to them makes it difficult to reach firm conclusions from studies that compare observed yields from ''eroded'' and ''non-eroded'' land. Different definitions of ''eroded'' make it tricky to compare these studies to each other. Controlled scientific experiments are expensive, difficult, and extremely time-consuming to conduct.

Most studies show small (on the order of 4 percent to 10 percent yield reductions) cumulative losses of productivity resulting from moderate erosion rates over a period of years. Most authors agree, as well, that, since World War II, any productivity loss related to erosion has been hidden, and far outstripped, by yield improvements based on technological innovation, at least in the United States.[87] This may be less true in the rest of the world, particularly in developing countries, in which expensive inputs are less accessible and population pressures force farmers to use marginal cropland and forgo conservation measures.

There is very little data on erosion in countries other than the United States. However, the Worldwatch Institute, extrapolating from direct and indirect measures of soil loss in the United States, U.S.S.R., India, and China, estimates that over seven tons of *excess* erosion (above natural soil production) occurs each year on an average acre of cropland in the world.[88]

† This is slightly below the average (5.07 tons per acre per year) reported in 1977, though this difference is at best barely statistically significant and may reflect improved measurement rather than an actual reduction in erosion rates.[90]

processes.[92] Of course, not all the soil moved by wind and water is "lost"; much of it is deposited farther downslope or downwind. Eventually, though, the soil is moved off the field, generally into a stream. And even before that happens, the area from which it was moved may become less productive, because the organic and finely grained mineral matter most beneficial to plants is removed most readily by erosive agents. On some lands, the soils left behind are coarse and poor in nutrients, although this is less of a problem in regions of deep, rich soils.

The average figures presented thus far obscure the tremendous variation in erosion from site to site, depending on the slope of the land, type of soil, crops grown and cropping system used, and the use of soil conservation techniques. In the United States, two-thirds of all soil erosion from cropland in 1982 took place on less than one quarter of the land (figure 3.18).[93] Extremely severe erosion tends to be a highly localized problem, which limits the usefulness of aggregate statistics. The average annual erosion rate, for example, on all cropland in Tennessee in 1977 was 14.11 tons per acre. Most of this came from the state's 17 westernmost counties, in 8 of which erosion exceeded 20 tons per acre. Some sites had erosion rates of nearly 100 tons per acre.[94] Even in places with soil thick enough to remain productive under such conditions, the gullying of land and muddying of streams that result from extreme erosion represent serious problems (see chapter 2).

Soil Conservation

Methods of controlling soil erosion are available, but some are expensive, either in direct cash outlays or by reducing areas available for cropping. These costs, which seldom seem balanced by productivity gains (particularly in the short term), are a prime reason that soil-conservation practices are in place on only about half the nation's farmland.[95] For example, on a Tennessee farm in 1979, installing nearly a mile of terraces, three sediment basins, two grassed waterways, and grading and stabilization structures cost almost $500 per acre—more than a third of the cost of the land itself.[96]

Farmers may have misconceptions about the effectiveness and cost of soil conservation practices. Conservation tillage, a group of techniques that disturb less of the earth (and less often) than conventional tillage, is a good example. In conservation tillage, crop residues are left on fields, helping to hold the soil and protect it from erosion. In addition, reducing the extent of tilling generally cuts down on fuel and labor costs. Nonetheless, of the farmers in a government survey who did not practice con-

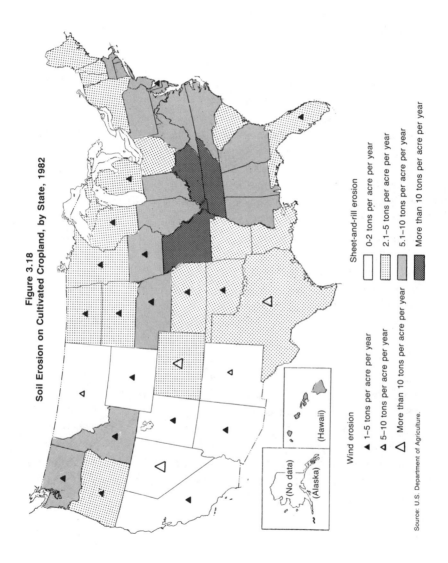

Figure 3.18
Soil Erosion on Cultivated Cropland, by State, 1982

Sheet-and-rill erosion

☐ 0-2 tons per acre per year

▨ 2.1–5 tons per acre per year

▨ 5.1–10 tons per acre per year

■ More than 10 tons per acre per year

Wind erosion

▲ 1–5 tons per acre per year

◮ 5–10 tons per acre per year

△ More than 10 tons per acre per year

(No data)

(Alaska)

(Hawaii)

Source: U.S. Department of Agriculture.

servation tillage, half felt that it would not reduce erosion and one-fifth felt it would increase time and labor requirements and reduce profits. These perceptions were held by three times as many nonusers of conservation tillage as users.[97]

It does appear, however, that more and more farmers are adopting conservation tillage. It is difficult to establish a precise use trend, because groups that collect tillage data use widely differing definitions. A national survey by the Conservation Tillage Information Center in 1982 indicated that over 94 million acres—24 percent of the nation's cropland—was tilled using methods that left at least 20 percent of the crop residues on the field. No-till farming, in which seeds are planted directly in the previous crop's stubble with no plowing at all, is the most unconventional conservation tillage method. It was used on over 10 million acres in 1982, an increase over the 7 million or so acres planted that way in the late 1970s.[98] In 1983, much cropland was idled because of PIK; the 87 million acres in some form of conservation tillage, while a slight reduction from 1982, represented almost a third of that year's cultivated crop acreage. The number of acres under no-till was virtually unchanged between 1982 and 1983.[99]

Conservation tillage and other soil-conserving practices offer the possibility of maintaining the natural fertility of the land, regardless of the limits or potentials of new technologies. It must be remembered that technology is not stagnant and possibilities of increasing production are constantly being explored. Biological research going on today may revolutionize agriculture in much the same way that organic chemicals synthesized after World War II did. If successful hybrids can be made using a newly discovered perennial corn, or if genetic engineering can be used to develop nitrogen-fixing abilities in the major cereal grains, the effects may be dramatic. There is no way to predict how great the gains will be from this new technology, nor how quickly they will come about. Nonetheless, for the foreseeable future, crops will still require good soil in which to grow.

FORESTLAND

The sheer magnitude of American forests overwhelmed the first European colonizers. Seeing what appeared to be a nearly infinite and invaluable resource, the colonists immediately began to cut the forests for firewood, building materials, masts, and, especially, to clear land for growing crops.[100] As settlement expanded, so too did the clearing of forests, continuing through the 18th and 19th centuries. Finally, around the time of World War I, the clearing slowed. The total amount of land covered by forests has been relatively steady, with some increases, ever since.[101]*

The amount of land that grows trees, however, is not a complete indicator of the health of forest resources. The size of individual stands, age (and therefore size) distribution of trees within stands, the diversity of species, and density of the canopy all affect the usefulness of a forest, whether as a sample of undisturbed nature, a home for wildlife, a place for solitude and recreation, or a supplier of wood products. Both natural processes and human activities that affect forests' conditions, therefore, merit attention.

Timber Product Production and Consumption

There has been a long-term general increase in both the production and consumption of forest products, although this has been subject to some fluctuation in response to economic conditions. Poor economic growth, and, in particular, declines in housing construction associated with recessions, tend to depress the forest products market. The general increase in consumption has been relatively smooth and gradual (figure 3.19). A major exception is the use of fuelwood, which the U.S. Forest Service estimates has quintupled since 1976.[103] Because only a small fraction of the wood is marketed commercially, the amount of fuelwood used is difficult to determine; because much of the fuelwood is taken from dead or very small trees, often on odd woodlots in or near urban areas, the actual effect of fuelwood harvesting on forests is hard to estimate. Nevertheless, if this use of timber continues to grow at recent rates, it could begin to affect supplies, particularly of hardwoods.†

Consumption of forest products (though not of raw timber; see below) is greater than their production in this country (figure 3.19). The balance is made up by net imports, which, on a volume basis, have remained fairly steady over the last 30 years. The United States is a net importer of wood products partly because of shipping costs—it is often cheaper,

---

* It is worth noting that, on a global scale, forest clearing, especially for agriculture, is continuing. The Food and Agriculture Organisation of the United Nations estimates that between 1970 and 1980 the amount of forestland and woodland in the world declined by nearly 300 million acres (3 percent), with an equal percentage increase (of 100 million acres) in the amount of cropland.[102]

† In general, hardwoods are deciduous trees; softwoods are conifers.

for instance, to ship timber products to the northeastern United States from eastern Canada than from Washington or Oregon. The same factor could operate in favor of exports. For instance, shipping logs to Japan from the Pacific Northwest can be cheaper than shipping them to New York.[104] The National Forest Products Association sees the potential for the United States to become the world's "woodbasket,"[105] but the actual growth in exports has been fairly slow (under 3 percent per year over the last decade),[106] and the U.S. Forest Service believes this country will remain a net importer of forest products.[107]

Shipping costs make importation economically sensible, but there is now enough wood growth in the United States to meet domestic needs. Despite the increasing amount of timber harvested, American forests in general grow more new wood each year than is removed. In 1976, the last year for which national figures are available, total growth was nearly double total harvest.[108] It would seem that, so long as new growth exceeds harvest, there is no need for concern about the renewability of forest resources. But not all trees are alike. Newly grown hardwood in 1976 was 124 percent greater than the amount cut, while for soft-wood, which includes the species most in demand for lumber and paper, growth surpassed harvest by only 22 percent.[109] State surveys carried out by the U.S. Forest Service's experiment stations indicate that, although no very dramatic changes have been observed, this disparity might have become even greater in the past eight years, with softwood harvests close to or exceeding net growth in many areas.[110]

In addition, comparisons of aggregate growth and cut mask important changes, such as damage to particular harvested acreages, changes in the species and size composition of the standing forest, the amount of time needed for trees to grow to the sizes needed for some uses, and changes in the nature of the forests covering whole regions. Specific instances include:

- The almost unmanaged growth of overcrowded, commercially underproductive woods in New England, after large-scale clearing and harvesting, which began in colonial times, had reduced forest area, altered species composition, and all but eliminated the largest trees.[111]
- The redevelopment of forestry in Michigan, which had ceased by 1900 after the state's once-extensive forests had been completely destroyed. Only now are trees again reaching commercially useful size.[112]

Figure 3.19
U.S. Timber-Product Production and Consumption, 1950–1980

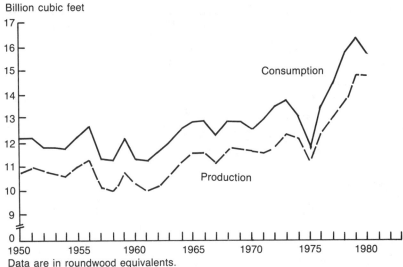

Data are in roundwood equivalents.
Source: U.S. Forest Services.

Figure 3.20
Forest Acres Damaged, Planted, and Seeded, 1950–1982

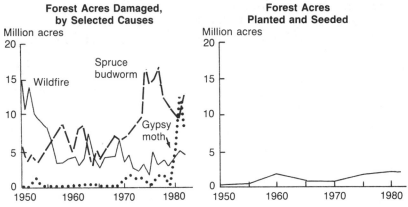

Source: U.S. Forest Service.

- The loss by drainage of valuable bottomland hardwood species in the South, while acres of pines and other conifers, once cut, regenerate naturally to hardwood species of less commercial value.[113]
- The steady decline in old growth ('virgin forest') in the Pacific Northwest, meaning that less of that region's most valuable timber product—large softwood logs—will be available, at least until restocked trees reach merchantable size.[114]
- The increasingly apparent, but unexplained, slowing of growth in numerous eastern forests, particularly among conifer species. The decline in growth has been observed in both northern and southern forests, especially at higher elevations. Atmospheric pollution, including acid precipitation, is a suspected cause, perhaps acting in tandem with natural stresses.[115]

Forest Protection and Management

Forest productivity depends both on natural processes and management practices. Some potential sources of damage to forests are relatively easy to control; others are not. Major efforts to protect forests from fire have reduced the number of acres burned each year to about a third of what it was in the 1950s. However, the decrease in burning appears to have bottomed out; some forest fires are inevitable.* Insect pests are a more serious problem; they (and tree diseases) accounted for 60 percent of the mortality of standing trees in 1982.[117] The imported gypsy moth, for years the scourge of northeastern forests, is still increasing its range and has been found in 30 states.[118] It and the spruce budworm, two of the most destructive forest pests, have generally been defoliating more and more acres each year, although insect populations tend to fluctuate widely (figure 3.20). The amount of defoliation caused by other major pests, such as the many varieties of pine beetles, is not tabulated precisely, but these pests also tend to show periodically serious outbreaks.[119]

The second panel of figure 3.20 shows how many acres of forest were seeded or planted each year since 1950. When a forest is cut, the natural succession of vegetation from the bare site usually ends up producing another forest, but the process can take a long time, and the forest that

---

* Foresters' attitudes toward fire are changing as they recognize the ecological role of small, naturally caused fires, which reduce litter buildup, encourage reproduction of some species and enhance the diversity of the forest. Some fires are now allowed to burn themselves out, and, in some cases, fires are set and controlled to achieve management goals. Such controlled burning may, in fact, take place over many more acres than are burned by uncontrolled wildfire.[116]

grows up may be very different from the one it replaces. Artificial planting is an important tool for protecting clear-cut areas from erosion, and, from the timber harvester's viewpoint, for ensuring that the desired species will continue to be available. Forest planting has been rising slowly but fairly steadily over the past 20 years.[120]

Well over half the acres planted and seeded each year are owned by forest-industry companies.[121] But private, "nonindustrial" landowners— typically a farmer or investor with a woodlot—hold title to 58 percent (1977 data) of the commercial forest in the United States,[122] while, in a typical year, they are responsible for fewer than one third of the acres planted,[123] a symptom of generally less-intense management of private nonindustrial forests.

Although such lands have the biological capacity to produce as much timber per acre as similarly situated industrial timberland, in most parts of the country average production of private nonindustrial forest is far less.[124] The forest products industry is trying to promote intensive management on nonindustrial lands in the hopes of increasing total timber production. But nonindustrial owners are often not interested in their forests as sources of income from timber sales. They may want to use the woods in other ways, such as for hunting and recreation, from which intensive, even-aged, stand management would detract.[125] In addition, forest management requires more effort and outlays than many owners are willing to expend, especially since returns are often years away. A recent study of nonindustrial forest landowners in the South who had harvested pine finds that 35 percent of clearcut and six percent of partially cut acres were replanted; the two reasons cited most frequently for *not* replanting were the belief that the pine would regenerate naturally and that reforestation was too expensive.[126] The way in which nonindustrial owners of woodland choose to manage their land remains an important variable influencing the overall condition of American forests.

RANGELAND

The range is land that has natural productivity too low to support crops or trees, generally because of aridity. In its natural condition, range is typically grassland, although various types of shrubby and desert vegetation also constitute rangeland. The amount of rangeland in the United States—about 587 million acres, most of it in the West—has remained pretty much constant, with some decreases since 1920.[127] There is very little available data characterizing range resources. Mineral extraction, a major use of the range, is well quantified, but does not depend directly on the renewable resources of the land. The recreational and wildlife values of rangeland are difficult to evaluate in economic terms. And for the major, economically quantifiable, renewable resource use of rangeland—livestock grazing—there is no comprehensive government data-gathering organization parallel to those for agriculture and forestry.

Even definitions of rangeland are elusive. In government land classifications, some harvested and grazed pastures, though used to grow livestock feed, are counted as cropland,* and often are used to grow crops either seasonally or in some years. In fact, over the past 60 years about 60 million to 90 million acres of cropland have been used exclusively for pasture in any given year.[129] Yet the relatively small cropland acreages used to grow forage nevertheless provide more food value than the vast, but far less productive, range. Although some pastures are fertilized and quite intensively managed, there is considerable potential for improving forage yields from most of the nation's grazed pasture should economic conditions warrant it.[130]

Ecological Effects of Grazing

Although range grazing is not the most important source of livestock feed, on the nearly 600 million acres of range the ecological effects of livestock grazing are a dominant influence. The interests of wildlife and of livestock ranchers, to some extent, come into direct conflict on the range. An example was the fence put up (and, after negotiations, breached) by a Wyoming rancher in late 1983, which kept a herd of pronghorn antelope from its winter feeding ground.[131] But even absent such human actions, the mere presence of livestock affects wild game.

One significant effect is direct competition for food. The primary productivity (plant growth) possible by native forage plants is more or less fixed and will support only a limited population of grazing animals indefinitely. Any forage eaten by a domestic grazer is unavailable to a wild one. A highly speculative estimate suggests that domestic cattle and sheep consume more range forage than the huge herds of bison,

---

* Historically, the classification of pasture as cropland stemmed at least in part from planting of pasture with non-native grasses; the "open range" grew native grasses and was not fenced, as pastures were. However, a mix of native and non-native grasses is not uncommon in less intensively managed pastures. History and natural land productivity seem to shape the definitions. For example, intensively managed range is still considered range, rather than range converted to "cropland" (pasture).[128]

elk, antelope, and bighorn that roamed freely before the introduction of livestock. These herds have been so reduced that big-game forage requirements in the western United States are now only about 5 percent of domestic livestock's.[132]

Livestock grazing not only reduces the amount of forage available to wildlife, it changes the type of vegetation as well. Those plant species most preferred by cattle and sheep tend to disappear, because they are consumed more quickly than they can grow back. Less-palatable plant species replace them, and the new plant community provides food and habitat for different animal species. The widespread replacement of grasses by shrubs in much of the West, for example, while harmful to wild grazing species, has resulted in substantial deer populations where there had been few or no deer before.[133]

Rangeland Condition

The changes in quantity and quality of rangeland plants just discussed are classic symptoms of overgrazing. Grazing too many animals on a given range reduces the number of animals the range can sustain, and the only way to bring the carrying capacity back up to previous levels is to reduce, temporarily, the amount of grazing pressure on the plants.

Although there are no up-to-date national statistics on the amount of range grazing by livestock, it is generally agreed that overgrazing is an ongoing problem. The most recent estimate of forage consumption by livestock, made in 1976, was 213 million "animal unit months" per year, virtually unchanged from 1970.[134]* In 1977, the U.S. Forest Service estimated that over two-thirds of U.S. rangeland was in only fair, poor, or very poor condition—producing less than 60 percent of its natural potential of useful forage. Twelve percent of the land was producing less than a fifth of its biological potential.[136] In 1982, the Soil Conservation Service, which uses a slightly different rating system,**

---

* An "animal unit month," the standardized measure of food consumption by livestock, is the amount of forage required to feed a 1,000-pound cow for one month. Beef production increased substantially in the early 1970s, but range grazing by cattle did not, because of the shift to grain concentrates, pasture grasses, and harvested plants.[135]

** The U.S. Forest Service noted in its assessment: "For many years the Forest Service has rated rangelands into five condition classes—excellent, good, fair, poor, and very poor... The Soil Conservation Service and the Bureau of Land Management have used four condition classes—excellent, good, fair, and poor... In order to use existing Forest Service data in this Assessment, the five condition classes were reduced to four by combining the excellent and good classes into the good class. The resulting four classes are considered to be essentially equivalent to the four classes used by the Soil Conservation Service and the Bureau of Land Management."[137]

rated over 60 percent of rangeland fair or poor—producing less than half of its biological potential—and only 4 percent as excellent—producing more than three-fourths of its potential (see figure 3.21).[138] Although the data are not strictly comparable, it is clear that very little, if any, improvement has taken place in the condition of rangelands.

Wildlife, Wildlands, and Critical Areas

The economic importance of land as a source of food and fiber cannot be disputed. Yet the significance of other renewable "outputs" of land—wild animals and plants, places for quiet and solitude, nurseries for fish and shellfish, purification of air and water by natural processes—is gaining recognition.[139] It is difficult to place monetary values on the products and services of wildlife and wild places, yet the growing awareness of their importance has led, especially in the past two decades, to numerous government and private protection programs.

Determining the current status of, and future prospects for, wildlife, wildlands, and ecologically critical areas* in the United States is difficult. About wildlife, in particular, both the extent and reliability of available data are extremely inadequate. Determining the amount of protected and undeveloped land is, while not easy to do precisely, relatively straightforward; however, it is often difficult to ascertain how well a protected status actually ensures that the ecosystems involved function properly. Because natural systems cannot be adequately described by measuring one or a few units of production, any analysis of their condition is predicated on data with severe limitations.

WILDLIFE

Historically, the greatest concern for, and therefore the most information about, wildlife has focused on a relatively small group of species—those commercially valuable or taken for sport (for example, salmon and deer), those with special aesthetic appeal to amateur naturalists (birds, butterflies), or those especially awesome or cute (whales, owls,

---

* By this term we refer to special ecosystems that serve unique functions and are small in area or unusually fragile relative to others.

Figure 3.21
U.S. Rangeland Quality, 1982

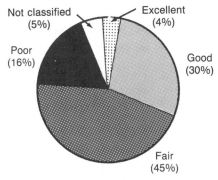

Not classified (5%)

Excellent (4%)

Poor (16%)

Good (30%)

Fair (45%)

Data pertain only to nonfederal land.

Source: U.S. Department of Agriculture.

Rangeland Problems in Arid Lands

The data presented above show that large amounts of American rangeland have been seriously degraded. The loss of productivity on arid and semi-arid lands is sometimes denoted by the general term *desertification*. Desertification is a serious ecological problem in parts of the United States; yet the loss of rangeland productivity currently does not have a major effect on livestock production, because most of the food consumed by livestock consists either of harvested grains and forage crops or of grazed cultivated pasture. In arid, developed countries, such fallbacks do not exist, and the ecological damage caused by overuse of marginal lands is easily translated, particularly during drought years, into large-scale human tragedies.

One estimate made several years ago was that upwards of 50 million people dependent on crop or livestock raising for their livelihoods were living on arid or semi-arid lands that were deteriorating rapidly. Reducing overgrazing in such regions is not a simple matter of governments imposing limits on herd size. Reduced herds mean a reduced food supply and, in many cultrues, substantially reduced wealth and status as well. Yet proper policies for land conservation, using both indigenous and internationally provided resources, are essential. If desertification remains unchecked, "the ecological problem becomes a pressing human one as millions of people see the whole basis of their livelihood placed in jeopardy. . .the deterioration of the world's marginal lands. . .may well result in the creation of a vast army of marginal people, living in totally inacceptable [sic] conditions."

(Source: Mohammed Ayyad and Gisbert Glaser, "Marginal Lands," *UNESCO Courier* 1981(4):19-20, 21.)

grizzly bears). Therefore, most readily available data on wildlife are on vertebrates, particularly mammals and birds, and especially game species. Far less is known about the status of amphibians, reptiles, invertebrates, and plants, except in a few cases, even though these groups may have considerable potential value or play very important roles in the ecosystem. One indication of how game species dominate in the allocation of resources to wildlife programs is that in 1980 11 state fish and wildlife agencies devoted no money at all to nongame programs. In only one case did such an agency allocate more than a tenth of its budget to nongame species.[140]*

Of course, protecting the habitat of game species benefits some associated nongame organisms. On the other hand, actions that benefit (purposefully or not) some particular species inevitably harm certain other creatures. Because alteration of ecosystems is more common than their complete obliteration, in most instances some species will be on the increase while others are declining; the complexity of wildlife communities makes gross assessment difficult. The clearest conclusion emerging from a survey of wildlife data is that more are needed. Nevertheless, the available information provides some insights on the status and trends of wild organisms in the United States.

Large Game Species

Wildlife management originated largely in response to the destruction or near destruction by hunters of such species as the bison and passenger pigeon.[142] Since the turn of the century, many game species, once depleted in numbers, have recovered dramatically. Deer, for example, were estimated to number less than half a million around 1890, and could not be found in much of the eastern United States; [143] recent

---

* Although the general emphasis on game species in fish and wildlife programs cannot be disputed, some caution should be used when interpreting this information. Eight states, some of which spend significant amounts on nongame species, did not break down their programs by type of wildlife.

Spending for management of nongame wildlife has almost certainly increased since 1980. One reason state wildlife agencies emphasize game species is that they draw large fractions of their budgets from taxes and fees paid by hunters and anglers. Innovative funding techniques have increased the flexibility of these agencies. Of the 40 states with income taxes, 31 now permit voluntary donations to wildlife programs by marking the state tax forms. Funds from these "check-off" programs are earmarked primarily, in some cases exclusively, for nongame species; all but 2 of these programs began in or after 1980, including 11 new ones in 1983.[141]

figures indicate that, in states east of the Mississippi, more than three times that number are now taken by sport hunters each year.[144] Similarly, the wild turkey, which had been reduced by 1930 to a remnant 20,000, has been reestablished in many areas by transfer from regions where the birds had survived.[145] In 1980, more than a quarter of a million turkeys were harvested.[146] The current population of the wild turkey, found in every state but Alaska, is estimated at 2 million.[147]

Data collected by the U.S. Forest Service show that, on its lands, the population of most large animals has been relatively stable since 1960 (figure 3.22: note that not all the species may be legally hunted; some are endangered or threatened). The most obvious exception is the timber wolf, now found only in Alaska and northern Minnesota, which experienced a drastic decline in the early 1970s, but now appears to be declining more slowly or perhaps even stabilizing at its new low level. In Alaska, the U.S. Forest Service's admittedly crude estimates of wolf numbers show a fall of over 50 percent from 1970 to 1974 and relatively small fluctuations since then; the legal wolf harvest on Alaskan lands managed by the Forest Service has been 77 to 125 wolves annually. In Minnesota, the trend is less clear, but still generally downward.[148] In this case, the Forest Service blames the reduced numbers on the wilderness status accorded to the Boundary Waters Canoe Area in 1978, noting that, with timber cutting banned, the denser forest supports fewer deer and, hence, fewer wolves.[149]*

It is important to note that the data shown in figure 3.22 only pertain to lands managed by the U.S. Forest Service and are not necessarily representative of nationwide population trends. Indeed, a majority of the land in the United States is privately owned, and development pressures that render habitat unsuitable for big game are manifest primarily (though not exclusively) on private land.

No data are collected to describe precise animal population trends on all lands on a national scale. The U.S. Forest Service, as part of its assessments of renewable resources, collects population estimates from state wildlife agencies. The most recent data show that, between the mid-1950s and mid-1970s, a number of major game species increased in most reporting states, while others, notably the mule deer and ring-necked pheasant, generally declined (figure 3.23). These data are in-

---

* A management plan, proposed by the U.S. Fish and Wildlife Service, which would make management of Minnesota's timber wolves a state responsibility and permit, under certain conditions, sport trapping of wolves, was found illegal by a federal district court in January 1984. The Interior Department has appealed.[150]

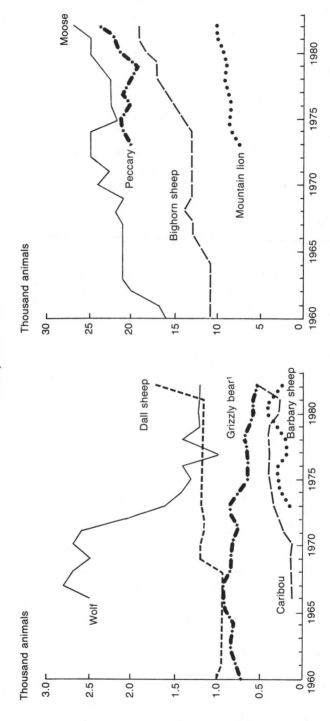

Figure 3.22
Populations of Selected Large Animals on U.S. Forest Service Lands, 1960–1982

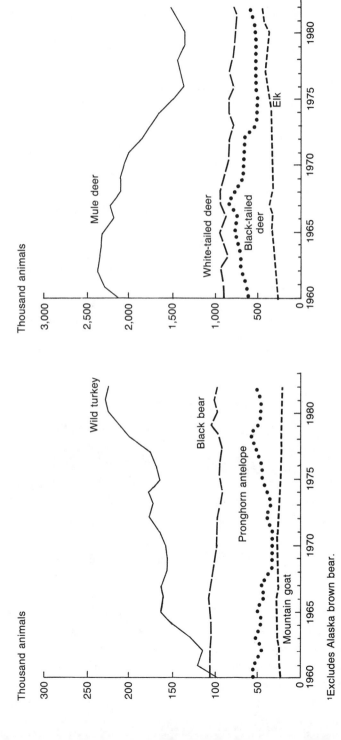

Thousand animals

Thousand animals

[1]Excludes Alaska brown bear.

Source: U.S. Forest Service.

Figure 3.23
Population Trends for Selected Game Animals, as Reported
by States, mid-1950s to mid-1970s

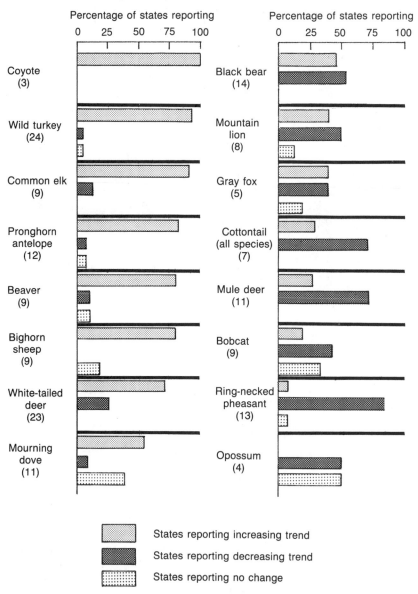

Number in parentheses for each species is number of states
actually reporting trends.

Only states having significant populations of an animal are included.

Source: U.S. Department of Agriculture.

complete both with respect to species and states included in the reports, but they provide a general sense of the direction of change for several species.

Birds

The Breeding Bird Survey, conducted by the Interior Department's Patuxent Wildlife Research Center, has collected data on birds found along a group of standardized routes since 1965. The data are particularly useful for determining *trends* in population (the sampling method does not permit estimation of actual population size) and range changes.[151]

Most of the bird species sampled by the survey show no statistically significant* upward or downward trend in population (figure 3.24). Twelve percent of the species show significant increases, and 8.3 percent show significantly declining trends. Some patterns are apparent. Nonnative, introduced species, for example, have been successful. The population of rock doves (pigeons) is rising, especially in the East, where another species, the house finch—native to the West and South Central states but introduced to the Atlantic Coast—is also spreading. The starling population may be stabilizing, but its earlier success is blamed for declines observed in such natives as the eastern bluebird and the flicker.

Habitat modification, particularly increased cropping, has caused significant declines in populations of loggerhead shrikes, prairie warblers, and some native sparrow and bunting species. The regrowth of eastern forests has also led to regional declines in grassland species, which had moved east when the forests were cleared. For instance, the brown-headed cowbird, which spread northward and eastward from the Plains as forests were cleared for farming, decreased in the Northeast and increased in the Southeast during the survey period, presumably reflecting the changes in amount of cleared land in those regions. Many warbler species which prefer woodland habitat are on the increase in the East.

These warblers, as well as other species—notably robins and hawks— have also benefited from the reduced use, since 1970, of chlorinated

---

* A number of large changes in species populations, especially weather-related declines in the late 1970s, are not statistically significant either because they are short-term reversals of previous trends or are part of a series of up-and-down fluctuations. Conversely, some of the statistically significant trends are relatively small in magnitude. Some species which are rare or which naturally occur in small or isolated areas were not sampled sufficiently to permit statistical analysis.

Figure 3.24
Population Trends for Species
of Breeding Birds, 1968–1981

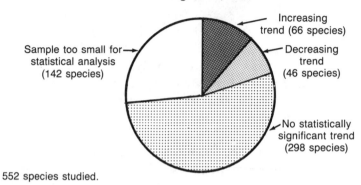

552 species studied.

Source: U.S. Fish and Wildlife Service.

Figure 3.25
Duck Populations in North America, 1955–1982

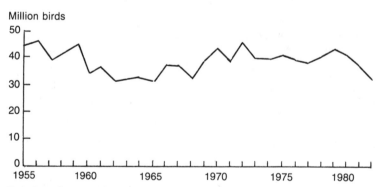

Data based on population surveys at breeding grounds.

Source: U.S. Fish and Wildlife Service.

hydrocarbon pesticides, which had been responsible for reductions in many bird populations.* The cliff and barn swallows have also been on the increase, in part because the overpasses built to carry interstate highways also make good nesting sites for these birds.

The Breeding Bird Survey gives some indication of an upward trend in waterfowl populations, but these species are not well sampled by the survey. Other estimates of breeding duck populations made by the U.S. Fish and Wildlife Service show oscillations since 1955, with the most recent trend for ducks as a group being downward (figure 3.25), though individual species may be increasing.[152]

Endangered and Threatened Species

The Breeding Bird Survey offers an unusual opportunity to spot declining populations of a species before it becomes at risk of extinction. Special attention is paid to most nongame species, however, only when they are in danger of extinction ('endangered') or likely to become endangered ('threatened').

Since 1880, over 160 animals and plants are known to have become extinct in the United States, not including the destruction of Hawaii's endemic flora and fauna (over 140 extinctions since 1850).[153] Although the Endangered Species Act[154] seems to have slowed the rate at which species disappear in the United States, in 1982 and 1983 three fish and one bird were removed from the endangered species list because they were presumed extinct; early in 1984, one extinct mussel was removed from the list as well.[155]†

The number of species listed as endangered or threatened (figure 3.26) has increased steadily in recent years.[156] The significance of this trend is unclear. Formally adding a species to the list is a regulatory act that sometimes lags behind biological reality, depending on the resources and priorities of the Fish and Wildlife Service. (Many states maintain endangered and threatened lists, and, in most, a majority of the species identified do *not* appear on the federal lists.[157]) The preponderance of vertebrates, especially birds and mammals, on the federal list reflects

---

* The large spruce budworm outbreaks of the 1970s, while a bane to foresters, were a further boon to the warblers, which received a very large source of food.

† It should be noted that removal is an administrative change that need not reflect *current* extinction rates. For example, the last known specimen of the longjaw cisco, a once common Great Lakes fish, was seen in 1967; it was declared extinct in 1983. No one can be certain when the species actually disappeared.

Figure 3.26
Endangered and Threatened Species in the United States, 1984

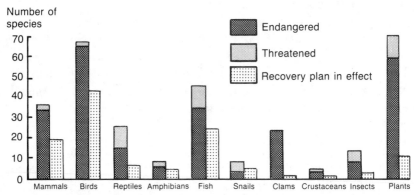

Data do not include species if only foreign populations are endangered or threatened.

Source: U.S. Fish and Wildlife Service.

Figure 3.27
Status of U.S. Vertebrates, 1984

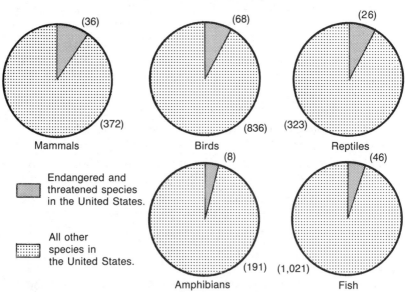

Numbers in parenthese indicates number of species.

Source: U.S. Fish and Wildlife Service and Council on Environmental Quality.

the high priority placed on these species and the superior information about them, but does not necessarily imply that only a handful of invertebrates face extinction. The plant kingdom (70 listed species) is grossly underrepresented on the lists when compared with animals (231 species).[158] Only 5 new plant species were listed from January 1983 to March 1984. An additional 23 are proposed for listing.[159] But the Fish and Wildlife Service has identified 2,560 native vascular plants as candidates for listing.[160]

It is even unclear, then, whether a long list should be viewed as a bad sign (lots of species in trouble) or a good one (lots of species enjoying protection). By itself, the number of species on official endangered and threatened lists is surprisingly uninformative. Nevertheless, it is worth noting that a relatively small fraction of U.S. vertebrate species is endangered or threatened (figure 3.27). In European nations, with their smaller areas and longer history of development, much higher percentages are at risk. For example, 41 percent of all known vertebrate species in West Germany are endangered or threatened. The available data show a range from 6 percent of the birds in Finland to 86 percent of the reptiles in the Netherlands.[161] Data for invertebrates and plants are not presented, because reliability of estimates of the total number of species and comprehensiveness of endangered lists are in doubt.

The U.S. Endangered Species Act requires, in addition to *protection* of listed species, that attempts be made to help species *recover*. Approved management plans aimed at recovery from endangered or threatened status are in effect for 113 of 298 listed species that are found in the United States.[162] Over half of these are birds and mammals, which, except for snails, have the highest percentage of listed species covered by plans (figure 3.26).

A number of the recovery plans have been striking successes. Painstaking efforts to increase the rate of whooping crane reproduction led to a 10-fold increase in the bird's population since 1941—albeit, only to 148 individuals.[163] Transplantations and breeding efforts are helping birds of prey return from the brink of extinction. Peregrine falcons, for example, can now be found nesting on the Verrazanno-Narrows Bridge in New York City,[164] and 95 bald eagles have been relocated to New York State since 1976, 3 of which are known to have reached maturity and to be nesting.[165] Less spectacular efforts have been successful as well. The simple act of building a wall around an acre of habitat may be sufficient to save the Robbins cinquefoil, a plant found only near the peak of Mt. Washington, New Hampshire.[166]

One of the best known recoveries is that of the American alligator. The alligator's recovery under strict protection not only reduced its danger of extinction (it is now listed as threatened, rather than endangered, in Florida, Louisiana, and Texas, as well as in coastal Georgia and South Carolina); in some areas, the animal has become so abundant that limited hunting and "nuisance animal control" programs are in effect.[167]

WILDLANDS AND CRITICAL AREAS

The protection provided by game and endangered species laws is crucial for the continued well-being of wildlife species. However, these laws may go for naught if sufficient suitable habitat for plants and animals is not maintained. For example, species such as the northern spotted owl that require or strongly prefer mature (older than 200 years) conifer forests may be imperiled unless some of these forests are left unharvested.[168] It is important, therefore, to consider the status of protected "wild" ecosystems. Among the most significant habitats are a number of wet environments that, because of their relative scarcity, special functional role, or both, can be considered "critical" areas.

Protected Lands

Protected wildlife habitat is found in state and national parks and other preserves, wildlife refuges, wilderness areas, and private preserves. Many of these areas are used for purposes other than wildlife protection, especially recreation.

Reserved Public Lands

The total acreage of state and federal parks and wildlife refuges grew, though at variable rates, more or less continuously through the 1960s and 1970s (figure 3.28). In 1980, the formal classification of huge tracts of the federal estate in Alaska, under the Alaska National Interest Lands Conservation Act,[169] more than doubled the acreage of the National Park System and National Wildlife Refuges and increased by nearly fourfold the amount of land in the National Wilderness Preservation

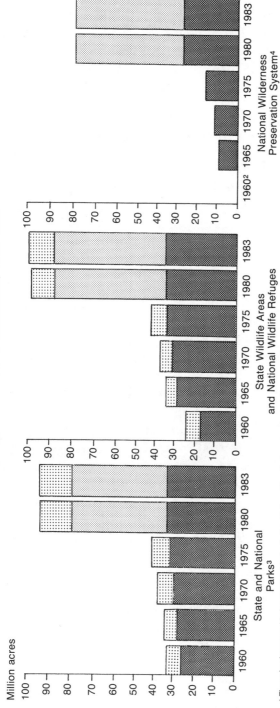

Figure 3.28
Parks, Wildlife Areas, and Wilderness, 1960–1983

Million acres

State and National Parks[3]

State Wildlife Areas and National Wildlife Refuges

National Wilderness Preservation System[4]

State
National Lands in Alaska, added in 1980[1]
National

[1] These lands were added under the Alaska National Interest Lands Conservation Act, enacted on December 2, 1980.
[2] The National Wilderness Preservation System was created in 1964.
[3] Some overlap may exist between state parks and wildlife areas in states in which a single agency administers both types of land. 1980 and 1983 data for state parks may not be strictly comparable, perhaps overstating increases; see figure references.
[4] The National Wilderness Preservation System (NWPS) is composed of areas managed by four federal agencies. In 1983, the system includes national parks (35.3 million acres), national wildlife refuges (19.3 million acres,) national forests (25.3 million acres), and lands managed by the Bureau of Land Management (about 10,000 acres). Acreages shown above for the NWPS include some land also counted in parks and wildlife refuges.

Source: U.S. Department of Agriculture, National Park Service, and state park agencies.

System.* Very little new land has been added to state and national parks, refuges, and wildernesses since 1980.†

Parks. No two sets of aggregate figures on state parks agree, because the states use a variety of designations for land that could be considered "parks." By any definition, however, little land has been added to state parks in the past few years. The National Association of State Park Directors noted an 83 percent decline in land acquisition, from 404,000 acres acquired in 1979-80 to only 70,000 acres in 1981-82.[170]

Many state parks are heavily used for recreation, and undoubtedly a considerable (but indeterminable) portion of their acreage is developed or too disturbed by humans to be called a "natural ecosystem."[171] To a certain extent, the same is true of the National Park System. Lands administered by the National Park Service, and depicted in figure 3.28, include, for example, the White House, the Statue of Liberty, and the home of President Adams. The great bulk of the system, however, clearly does represent conservation of natural areas.‡ Fewer than 60,000 acres have been added to the National Park System since 1980.[173]**

Whatever their merits as largely natural areas, state, national, and even municipal parks in urban and suburban areas often provide enough variety in the landscape to shelter some species, tolerant of humans, that might be absent or less numerous but for the park.[175]

Wildlife Refuges. After rapid growth in the late 1970s, the amount of land in state wildlife areas has hardly changed since 1980.[176] A small amount has been added to the National Wildlife Refuge System, which in September 1983 included 418 refuges and 149 Waterfowl Production Areas.[177] The overwhelming majority of the refuges and much of the total refuge acreage, at least in the contiguous states, is managed primarily for migratory birds, especially waterfowl.[178]

---

* The lands protected by the act were very similar in area and location to those that President Carter sheltered from development in a 1978 executive order.

† As this book went to press, bills designating new wilderness areas in some 19 states were expected to be acted on by Congress in its current session, which would greatly increase the size of the wilderness system.

‡ In 1970, well before the huge addition of wild Alaskan lands, the National Park Service categorized 83.8 percent of the acreage under its control as "natural" rather than "historical" or "recreational."[172] The service no longer uses that classification method.

** The National Park Service reports larger increases since 1980, but these are primarily the result of upward revisions of the estimated area in certain parks, especially in Alaska.[174]

Wilderness. Designation of an area as part of the National Wilderness Preservation System provides the greatest degree of protection from human disturbance. Created in 1964 by the Wilderness Act[179], the system includes lands "untrammeled by man . . . retaining [their] primeval character and influence."[180] The lands are managed by a variety of federal agencies, principally the U.S. Forest Service, the National Park Service, and the U.S. Fish and Wildlife Service. Of the 264 Wilderness Areas designated through January 1983, 66 (33 of them in Alaska) were added in 1980. No new areas were designated in 1981, 2 in 1982, and 4 in 1983.[181]*

These relatively extensive systems of protected lands make the United States one of the few countries in the world with more than 5 percent of its area in "conservation areas" recognized by the International Union for the Conservation of Nature and Natural Resources (figure 3.29). Worldwide, 3 percent of the land area is in conservation areas (2.7 percent if the large and mostly unprotected land mass of Antarctica is included). Many large nations protect less than 1 percent of their land, and a number of important, biologically distinctive regions—including, for example, the Argentine pampas and Malagasy thorn forest—have little or no protected land within their boundaries.[182]

Other Wildlife Habitat

The extensive holdings of the U.S. Forest Service and Bureau of Land Management, though not strict nature preserves, must by law be administered for "multiple use," including the maintenance of wildlife habitat as a major objective. Other types of government holdings, from reservoir watersheds to military bases, may shelter wildlife as well.

A majority of the nation's land is privately owned, and private land-protection programs, although comparatively small, play an important role in protecting areas that, for one reason or another, are excluded from government programs. In 31 years, through 1982, The Nature Conservancy completed over 3,000 projects protecting over 1.9 million acres, emphasizing areas of unique ecological importance, such as virgin forest along Wisconsin's Brule River.[183] The Trust for Public Land, started

---

* Since many Wilderness Areas are included in the National Park and National Wildlife Refuge systems, it is incorrect simply to add wilderness acres to park and refuge acreages; however, the total acreage receiving this highest level of protection is of interest.

Figure 3.29
Protected Natural Areas as a Percentage of
Total Area, by Country, 1982

1	Less than 1%
2	1- 5%
3	5-10%
4	More than 10%

Alaska, Hawaii, and Puerto Rico treated separately from contiguous United States; Greenland treated separately from Denmark; Spitsbergen treated separately from Norway.

Source: Harrison, Miller, and McNeely; International Union for the Conservation of Nature and Natural Resources.

in 1973, has assisted public agencies in the acquisition of over 45,000 acres (including some city parks) and helped private nonprofit organizations to protect 16,000 acres of agricultural and scenic land.[184]* The National Audubon Society owns or leases nearly 80 sanctuaries, which are used for education as well as preservation, covering about a quarter of a million acres.[185]**

Obviously, not all privately owned wild land is on tracts maintained by preservation organizations. Rural land, which is not developed by its owners, or which is developed using practices (for example, hedgerows or small-grain cover crops on farms, shrubs and bird feeders near homes) conducive to wildlife, is a significant, if unquantifiable, natural resource. For example, 23 young eagles released to the wild in New York State in the summer of 1983 were set free on private land.[187] A project of The Nature Conservancy, which notifies landowners of important natural features on their holdings, has led over 200 owners to agree voluntarily to protect these features; the program is now in effect in five states.[188] The registry of a similar program, the National Natural Landmark Program, is maintained by the National Park Service. By 1981, 51 individual and corporate landowners (other than conservation groups) had entered into nonbinding agreements to preserve the character of over 23,000 acres identified on the registry. Nearly a quarter of a million other privately held acres were included in the listing with no owner agreements to protect them.[189]

Protected land, whether in private or public ownership, is subject to pressures from the development of nearby areas. The extent and severity of the problem is difficult to quantify. One indication that it may be quite significant, however, was provided by a recent survey of National Wildlife Refuge managers. Seven of the 14 most frequently reported management problems related, at least in part, to land-use practices outside the refuges themselves. Similarly, the National Park Service found that a majority of the pressures on natural resources inside the National Parks come from activities on lands outside them.[190]

---

* The Nature Conservancy does maintain nearly 700 of its own properties, but the bulk of its acquisitions, and all of the Trust for Public Land's, are turned over to government agencies for management; therefore, it is not accurate simply to add these lands to the governmental totals.

** There is no evidence that increased private protection is in any way making up for the reduced rate of increase in federally protected land. The Nature Conservancy, for example, protected more acreage in 1980 (143,000 acres) than in either 1981 or 1982 (86,000 and 106,000 acres, respectively).[186]

Watery Habitats: Critical Areas

Watery habitats are uniquely productive and important resources. Such habitats include: inland areas—river channels, lakes, and "palustrine" wetlands (ponds, mud flats, marshes, and swamps); coastal wetlands—intertidal marine (saltwater) and estuarine (partially freshwater) areas; and offshore waters—submerged estuarine and marine habitats out to the beginning of the deep ocean. Despite unprecedented measures over the last decade or so to conserve critical areas, particularly wetlands,[191] many of these ecosystems continue to face serious threats.

Inland Palustrine (Freshwater) Wetlands

Inland wetlands include small ponds, marshes, and swamps, such as New England's cranberry bogs, the South's bottomland hardwood forests, and the Midwest's prairie potholes. Along the major migratory bird flyways, wetland resources are crucial to waterfowl; their vegetation helps to control floods and purify water;[192] and wetlands produce direct economic values, such as timber, fish, and game.

Notwithstanding the value of these lands, vast amounts have been paved, ditched, drained, or flooded. The U.S. Fish and Wildlife Service estimates that over 11 million acres* (11.1 percent of the 1950s total) of vegetated palustrine wetlands were converted into some other type of land between the mid-1950s and mid-1970s (figure 3.30). Conversion to farmland accounts for nearly all of this loss, with the balance due to urbanization (about 750 thousand acres, an area larger than Rhode Island) and minor conversions to other land or flooding to make ponds and lakes. The conversions were greatest in the lower Mississippi Valley. Other large losses occurred in Minnesota, the Dakotas, and Nebraska; in Florida and North Carolina; in California; and in Texas (see figure 3.12 to relate this geographic distribution to changes in agricultural land).[193]

This loss, over just two decades, comes after a long period of essentially unrestricted drainage, the extent of which cannot be precisely quantified. One estimate is that nearly half of the original wetlands (including both inland and coastal areas) in the United States are gone.[194]

Riparian lands—those wetlands along riverbanks that are regularly flooded—shelter specialized plant and animal communities and, par-

---

*Actually, this figure is the net result of about 15 million acres lost and 4 million acres added; most of the added acreage had been nonagricultural land.

ticularly in the arid West, make vital contributions to river nutrient supplies and wildlife habitat. They have been altered with particular rapidity and to an especially great extent. An estimated 63 percent of the bottomland hardwood forests lining the great river systems of the southern United States have been cleared; studies of three rivers in Arizona and California have shown losses of natural vegetation ranging from 28 percent over 43 years to 98 percent over 130 years.[195]*

The National Wild and Scenic Rivers System, created in 1968, protects some unaltered rivers and their shorelines (figure 3.31). Of 356,000 miles of major river segments (longer than 24 miles), 214,000 miles (60 percent) were found to be too developed for inclusion in the Wild and Scenic Rivers System.[196] And, of the 142,000 potentially suitable miles of streams, fewer than 7,000 are designated wild and scenic.[197]

There are a few exceptions to the overwhelming trend of destruction of inland watery habitats. In the two decades since the mid-1950s, the acreage of nonvegetated palustrine wetlands nearly doubled, to almost 5 million acres. Most of the increase resulted from construction of ponds with undetermined value to fish and wildlife.[198] Deep-water lakes, which are not wetlands but are an important water resource, expanded by 1.4 million acres, primarily due to damming. Of course, such gains in lake acreage are offset by losses of the lands that are flooded, which resulted in a net loss, to lakes, of 311,500 acres of palustrine vegetated wetlands.[199] The loss, from all causes, of palustrine vegetated wetlands, is in any case much larger than the gains in acreage of freshwater lakes and non-vegetated wetlands.

Coastlands

The meeting of land and sea produces not only spectacular scenery but productive and protective ecosystems. It is also the location of the densest concentrations of human residences, industries, and commercial activities. This combination has resulted in severe stresses on very important coastal environments, especially estuaries and barrier islands.

Estuaries. Estuaries, the tidal areas where freshwater rivers meet the salt oceans, are among the most productive areas of the earth, when viewed from a biological standpoint. Virtually all the shellfish and many of the fish species used by humans for food or by-products require

---

* This discussion considers only acres of inland wetlands lost. It does not consider alterations, such as polllution, that affect the quality of wetland resources.

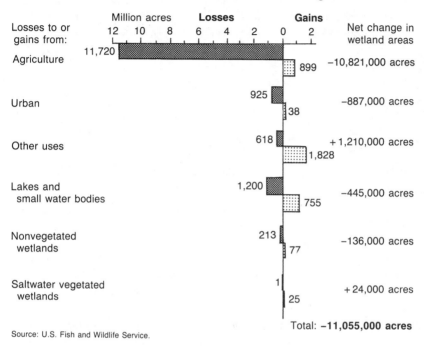

Figure 3.30
Freshwater Wetland Conversions, mid-1950s through mid-1970s

Source: U.S. Fish and Wildlife Service.

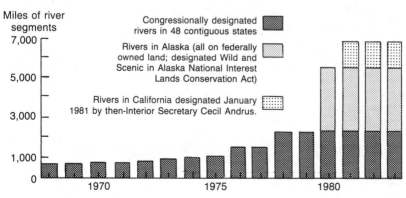

Figure 3.31
National Wild and Scenic River System, 1968–1983

Source: National Park Service.

estuarine environments for at least part of their life cycles, not to mention shorebirds and other animal species from amphipods to turtles to otters, and a whole community of specially adapted plants. The marshes and waters of the Chesapeake Bay, the largest estuary* in the United States, yielded 117 million pounds of oysters in 1879—more than five times present harvests from the bay and more than double the present U.S. *total*.[200]

Estuarine (saltwater**) wetlands are, on one hand, being dredged to create navigable waterways and, on the other, being filled to create *terra firma*. The U.S. Fish and Wildlife Service estimates that, between 1950 and 1969, dredging and filling destroyed over 640,000 acres (4.1 percent) of the estuarine habitat the service identified.[201] The more recent estimate of changes from the mid-1950s to the mid-1970s, although not strictly comparable because of differences in definitions and methodology, confirms the general trend, showing a loss of 372,000 acres (7.6 percent) of intertidal, vegetated estuarine habitat (figure 3.32).† Almost two-thirds of this was converted (by dredging and erosion) to subtidal parts of the estuaries, which, while valuable, are less productive than the intertidal areas. And fully 106,500 acres were lost to urban development. Most losses of saltwater wetlands occurred in Louisiana and Florida.[202]

In addition to outright destruction, estuaries (like inland wetlands) are threatened by degradation resulting from human activities. Rivers draining into estuaries may be charged with eroded soil, which gradually fills the estuary. Chemical contaminants may be borne down rivers, arrive with the tides from spills at sea, or fall from the sky. If fresh water is diverted for human use and not allowed to reach the estuary, the intrusion of salt water from the ocean may upset the balance by which estuarine productivity is maintained.

---

* Definitions of *estuary* generally include not only wetlands but also subtidal areas, which are always submerged, so long as there is some interaction between fresh and salt water. This section focuses on estuarine wetlands but of necessity refers to some deep-water resources: for example, shellfish may require wetland habitat but are harvested primarily from open water.

** "Saltwater wetland" is not strictly accurate, because estuarine wetlands, by definition, receive freshwater flows and are less salty than the ocean.

† The study's category, "estuarine wetlands," excludes subtidal areas. It also includes a relatively small amount of coastal wetlands that are not at river mouths, although they are subject to freshwater runoff; strictly speaking, such areas are not parts of "estuaries."

Limited information is available to help judge the significance of estuary degradation. The National Shellfish Register, a survey of coastal waters no longer undertaken, found in 1974 that over a quarter of the shellfish-producing waters in the United States were closed because of public health risks (usually bacterial contamination and occasionally chemical contamination).[203] Comparable current information on a national scale does not exist. However, 1980 data for the classified shellfish area of 39 Gulf Coast estuaries from Florida to Texas show 26 percent (over 1,200 square miles) closed.[204] Furthermore, a study of Chesapeake Bay, completed in 1984, documents significant water-quality problems, including nutrient overloading, low oxygen levels, and heavy metal and organic chemical pollution. The harm to biological resources, particularly freshwater fish and oysters, is manifest; the once prodigious oyster harvest, referred to above, has fallen more than fivefold in the last century, although aquaculture techniques have helped stabilize it since the mid-1960s.[205]

Coastal barriers. Coastal barriers (some, attached at one end to the mainland, are not islands) are deposits of sand and other sediments eroded by the action of winds and waves. By their nature coastal barriers are impermanent, constantly being reshaped by the same forces that formed them. The beach, dune, and lagoon communities formed by these barriers support a diverse flora and fauna, including 20 or more endangered species. The barriers also protect the productive estuarine environments to their landward side, and, as their name implies, partially shield structures on the mainland from the full force of storms.[206] They are found almost entirely on the Atlantic and Gulf coasts.

Development on coastal barriers is inherently risky because of the inevitability of storms and the likelihood that erosion will undermine any built structures. Attempts to correct these problems, by building groins or seawalls, disrupt the geological and ecological processes that maintain and modify the barriers, causing serious erosion and reducing wildlife populations.[207] (These efforts may also be counterproductive in a purely human sense, by encouraging added development because of a false sense of security.)[208]

The Department of the Interior has estimated that nearly 140,000 acres of coastal barrier land were urbanized or built up between the 1950s and the early 1970s, bringing the total developed acreage to nearly 230,000 acres (13.6 percent). By 1982, nearly 40 percent of the barrier mileage, on a beachfront basis, had been developed (figure 3.33).[209] Despite the surge of development in the 1960s, over a third of the beach-

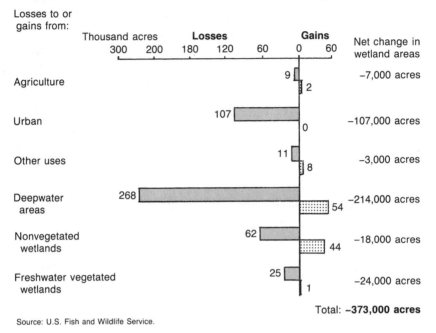

Figure 3.32
Saltwater Wetland Conversions, mid-1950s through mid-1970s

Source: U.S. Fish and Wildlife Service.

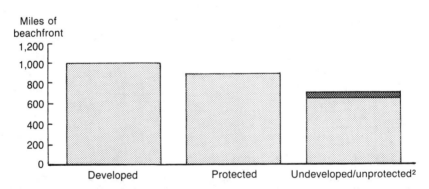

Figure 3.33
Status of U.S. Atlantic and Gulf of Mexico
Coastal Barrier Islands, 1983[1]

[1]Also includes other coastal barriers such as peninsulas.

[2]The miles of beachfront indicated by the darker shading are undeveloped and unprotected barriers that are *not* subject to the Coastal Barrier Resources Act's cutoff of federal support for development activities.

Source: U.S. Department of the Interior.

front not protected by federal or state ownership is still undeveloped. The Coastal Barrier Resources Act,[210] enacted in 1982, prohibits any federal support, including flood insurance, for development on over 90 percent of this land.[211]

Offshore Lands and the Continental Shelf

Lands that are always under ocean water fall far outside normal definitions of "wetlands." Yet the continental shelves, covered by a relatively thin coat of water (fewer than 200 meters or 700 feet, compared to a typical ocean depth of about 4000 meters), are geologically distinct from the ocean floor; they are extensions of the continental land mass. The shelves are vast, having been variously estimated at 8 percent to 18 percent of the earth's surface, and they are rich in physical* and biological resources.[212]

Marine fisheries (including those for shellfish) are a biological resource of major economic importance. Landings of fish and shellfish by U.S. commercial vessels in U.S. waters (within 200 miles of shore) in 1982 were worth $2.3 billion.[213]† Just about half the catch was for human consumption, with the rest being processed for such products as meal and oil, although the food fishery provides 94 percent of the revenues to the fishing industry.[214] Per-capita consumption of commercial fish and shellfish (including imports) rose steadily through the 1960s and 1970s, peaking in 1978 at 13.4 pounds; it has declined slightly since, but at 12.3 pounds (1982) is still well above historical norms.[215]

The total fish catch in U.S. waters has declined since the early 1970s,‡ a result of dramatic drops in the catch by foreign fleets since the 1976 enactment of the Fishery Conservation and Management Act (figure 3.34).[216] This act extended United States jurisdiction to a "fishery conservation zone" between 3 miles and 200 miles offshore** and imposed

---

* The enormous energy sources submerged beneath the country's coastal waters are discussed elsewhere. This section is concerned with the renewable, living resources of the continental shelf.

† Values are based on ex-vessel prices, that is, those paid to fishermen upon landing.

‡ Aggregate figures are unavailable for years prior to 1969 because data on catches by foreign vessels are lacking.

** Waters within 3 miles of shore are under the jurisdiction of the various coastal states. In 1982, 61 percent (4.3 billion pounds) of the fish and shellfish caught by U.S. vessels were taken less than 3 miles from shore; 33 percent in the fishery conservation zone; and 6 percent from beyond 200 miles or off foreign shores. Of course, some species are caught almost entirely near the shore and others almost exclusively in deeper water.[217]

severe restrictions on foreign fishing within that zone. The increased catch by U.S. vessels has only partially offset the reduction in foreign fishing. In part, the reduction in overall catch results from the exercise of management authority, under the Fishery Conservation and Management Act, designed to limit overfishing.

Absent management, overexploitation—a natural result of economic forces—is endemic to the fishing industry. Each fishing concern has an economic incentive to catch as many fish as possible, but, if the sum of all these individual efforts increases the total catch beyond the ability of the fish stock to replace the loss, the fish population begins to decline. This leads, ultimately, to a total catch far below that which could be sustained if the population were maintained at an optimal level—while the incentive to overfish still exists for individual firms.[218]* An overfished stock may disappear almost completely, or it may persevere at a chronically reduced level.

A number of American fisheries appear to be overfished,** but determining that can be quite difficult, because marine habitats are particularly inhospitable places in which to conduct animal censuses. Often, the only directly observable fact about the fish population is how much of it gets caught.

The American lobster provides a good illustration. The catch of this species has increased steadily over the last four decades, with 1982's record harvest more than triple 1942's (figure 3.36). To catch these lobsters, though, harvesters need to set over eight times as many traps as in the 1940s. The steady decline in catch per trap, reflecting increased difficulty in finding lobsters, is one reason biologists believe the lobster population is overfished. Since most of the lobsters are caught close to shore and in their first year of adult life, there is a risk that a single year of recruitment failure (defined as low reproduction and/or little migration coastward from offshore) could devastate the fishery.[219]

The vulnerability of a fishery to a single poor year is dramatically evidenced by the king crab fishery in Alaska. The population collapsed in 1981, and landings, which had risen from 76 million pounds in 1973

---

* Overfishing can lead to economic inefficiencies even if the biological status of the fish population is not threatened. But that issue is beyond the scope of this discussion.

** Total catch, as given in figure 3.34, masks considerable variation from fishery to fishery. It is necessary to analyze individual species, and in some cases individual stocks (for example, bay scallops from New England, Long Island Sound, and Chesapeake Bay), to determine the extent of overfishing.

Figure 3.34
Commercial Catch of Marine Fish and Shellfish
in U.S. Waters, 1969–1982

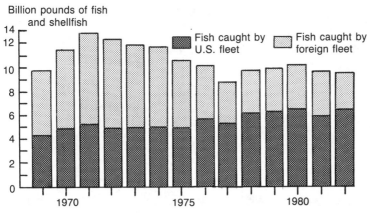

Source: National Marine Fisheries Service.

Figure 3.35
Global Commercial Marine Fish Catch, 1951–1981

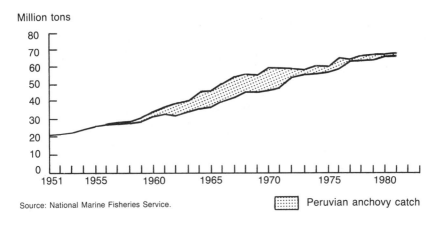

Source: National Marine Fisheries Service.   Peruvian anchovy catch

Figure 3.36
American Lobster Fishery, 1942–1982

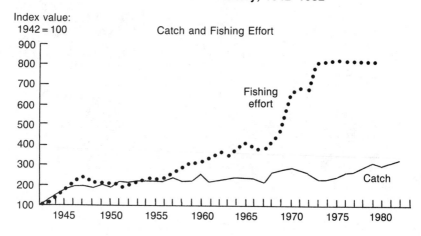

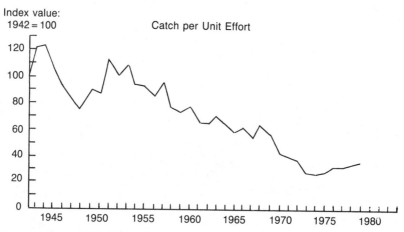

Source: New England Fishery Management Council.

to 180 million pounds in 1980, plummeted to fewer than 90 million pounds in 1981 and under 40 million pounds in 1982.[220] Figures for 1983 are expected to show a continued decline, and the recruiting stock for 1984 is small as well.[221] The reasons for the king crab's decline are not well understood. The National Marine Fisheries Service believes subtle changes in the physical environment and predatory fish species are more responsible than overfishing.[222] But the run of bad years would undoubtedly have produced smaller biological and economic consequences had harvests not increased so rapidly beforehand.

Finfish, as well as shellfish, are vulnerable to overexploitation. Harvests of the anadromous river herring fell by 90 percent between 1969 and 1981, primarily because immature fish were and are being taken by offshore trawlers, which began operating in the late 1960s.[223] The stock of Atlantic menhaden, in recent years second only to its Gulf cousin in total pounds landed, collapsed in the mid-1960s and then recovered after about five years of extremely reduced catch; its reproductive stocks remain low.[224] Yellowtail flounder, which was seriously overfished before the Fishery Conservation and Management Act, had fallen to an estimated 60 percent of the optimum population size by 1976. The catch dropped 37 percent between 1972 and 1974;[225] the first significant increase in harvest since the act, in 1982, just possibly heralds a recovery.[226]

It should be noted that not *all* fish and shellfish species are overfished, and that even high levels of fishing pressure can often be sustained for a long time. Three shrimp species harvested in the Gulf of Mexico, for example, have provided a total catch of 170 million to 270 million pounds annually since 1963, with relatively mild year-to-year fluctuations.[227] Some species, in fact, because of high biological potential, low market demand, inadequate harvesting technologies, or some combination thereof, are quite underexploited. For example, calico scallop landings averaged a little under 1.5 million pounds in the mid-1970s (1973 to 1977), then exploded to nearly 15 million pounds in 1981.[228] The National Marine Fisheries Service is currently trying to encourage the development of commercial fisheries for Alaskan groundfish, including pollack and Pacific cod, and Atlantic coast squid.[229]

The fish catch on a global scale continues to increase steadily[230], despite the boom and bust of major stocks such as the well-known Peruvian anchovy, which collapsed as a result of climatic factors and overexploitation[231] (figure 3.35). Certain stocks, such as rock lobsters in New Zealand[232] and yellowfin tuna in the southwestern Indian Ocean,[233] have shown evidence of overfishing, even while increasing global demand has supported a rise in aggregate catch. Fisheries management, particularly for species harvested internationally, is difficult. Available estimates of critically important biological parameters are often little more than guesswork. Yet proper management of marine fisheries in the United States and abroad is a key to continued renewability of a very important resource.

Energy

Energy consumption has a strong impact on the environment, although the connection is no more rigid than the one that exists between energy use and the gross national product (GNP). Choices about the fuels people consume, the technologies in which the fuels are converted to useful work, and the means selected to deal with the waste products of fuels may have profound and lasting effects on the environment, including human life and health and the global climate. This is especially true of some of the most heavily used fuels, like coal. For these reasons, the trends that drive energy use yield important environmental information.

In addition to the direct environmental effects of energy production, use, and waste disposal, fossil fuels also represent resources that, once consumed, are gone forever. Use of these resources, formed over millions of years, in a period of a few hundred years raises concerns about the sustainability of a high-energy world economy and underlines the need to plan for an orderly transition to renewable energy resources.

ENERGY CONSUMPTION

Since the oil embargo of 1973, patterns of energy consumption and production in the United States have shifted substantially. A steady increase in domestic production and consumption through the 1950s and 1960s, combined with falling real energy prices, was replaced in the 1970s by a leveling off of production and sharp reductions in consumption in response to price shocks in the winter of 1973-74 and in 1979.[234]

Consumption by Fuel Type

Since its peak in 1979, U.S. energy consumption has dropped steadily each year. People are using less of every form of energy, save hydroelectric, coal, and nuclear power, which have increased slightly in recent years (figure 3.37). Most dramatic has been the shift in oil consumption, which dropped 6 percent from 1973 to 1975, and almost 21 percent between its historical high in 1978 and 1983. In 1983, the 30.0 Quads* of energy consumed from petroleum was the lowest amount since 1970.[236] Consumption of natural gas in 1983 was 24 percent below its historical peak of 1972; on the other hand, coal consumption increased 23 percent between 1973 and 1983, and is projected to increase by 6.4 percent in 1984 over 1983. Recent coal-consumption increases are due partly to a surge in electric power sales, resulting from a recovering economy and severe weather during the last half of 1983.[237]

Electricity generation during 1983 was up 7.3 percent over 1982.[238] The same year continued the trend, begun in the mid-1970s, of a decrease in the total amount of energy consumed in the economy, but a higher proportion of that energy was consumed as electricity.

Consumption by Economic Sector

Consumption shifts are evident in every energy-consuming sector of the economy (figure 3.38). The greatest reductions took place in the industrial sector, which in 1983 used 26 percent less energy than in 1979. Industry was responsible for the greatest volume reduction in petroleum use, cutting back 2.8 Quads, or 26.8 percent of total petroleum use, by all sectors since 1979.[239] The residential and commercial sectors' total energy use has remained essentially constant in recent years.[240] This fact masks important shifts in per-capita residential use: despite an increase in the total number of households, total residential energy consumption did decline slightly.[241]

Residential energy users have been changing the kinds, as well as the amounts, of energy consumed in their homes. The number of households heated primarily by fuel oil dropped from 26 percent to 18 percent of

---

* A Quad is the unit measurement of quadrillion BTUs. A BTU (British thermal unit) is the amount of energy required to raise the temperature of one pound of water one degree Fahrenheit. In one barrel of crude oil, there are approximately 5.8 million BTUs.[235]

Figure 3.37
U.S. Energy Consumption, by Type of Fuel, 1960–1983

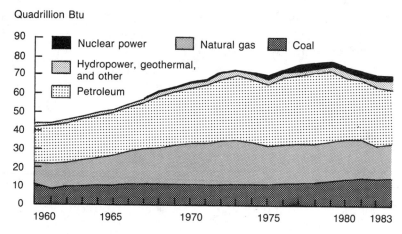

This figure excludes many important types of energy—wood used for home heating, passive solar building designs, windmills, and energy self-generated by industry from waste products. Taken together, these and similar noncommercial sources may be a significant component of energy consumption.

Source: U.S. Department of Energy.

Figure 3.38
U.S. Energy Consumption, by Sector, 1950–1983

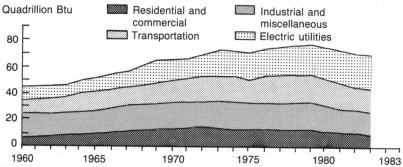

Electric utilities, shown in this figure as a separate sector, supply energy to the other sectors. In 1981, with electricity distributed, the transportation sector used 18.7 Quads; industrial and miscellaneous, 29.3 Quads; and residential and commercial, 26.4 Quads.

Source: U.S. Department of Energy.

the nation's total between 1970 and 1980, while households using electric heating increased from 8 percent to 18 percent.[242] Natural gas, despite rapid price increases over the past couple of years, continues to be the most widely used residential heating source, representing 56 percent of all households in 1981 (figure 3.39).[243]

The transportation sector reduced its energy consumption by 7.8 percent between 1978 (highest year) and 1983; but in the decade since 1973, that sector actually increased its consumption of energy by just over 2 percent (2.1 percent).[244] Recent reductions are attributable to a number of factors, including more efficient cars and people taking fewer and shorter trips.

The use of public transportation, however, has been disappointing to those who saw in it a solution to energy and air-pollution problems. Eighty-six percent of the American work force used private modes of transportation to get to work in 1980, up from 81 percent in 1970 and 70 percent in 1960.[245] Only 6 percent used public transportation in 1980, down from 10 percent in 1970 and 17 percent in 1960.[246]

Primary energy consumption by electric utilities (electricity from which is then distributed among the industrial, residential and commercial, and transportation sectors), unlike the other sectors, climbed steadily throughout the late 1970s. Between 1981 and 1982, however, consumption dropped by 1.9 percent, the first decline since 1957–58. Yet consumption was on the upswing again between 1982 and 1983, rising 2.9 percent.[247]

Two fundamental factors contributed to the changes in the rate at which Americans use energy. First, the American economy grew at a slower rate, causing slower growth in energy consumption. The recent economic recession undoubtedly dampened consumption, though by how much is not clear. Second, higher energy prices (and, in some cases, temporary shortages) made consumers aware of energy prices in their daily habits and buying decisions: some people did without, while others found more efficient ways to carry on. The 1982-to-1983 upswing reflects a healthier economy.

ENERGY EFFICIENCY

Perhaps the most encouraging trend over the past 12 years is a realization that, although economic activity and energy consumption bear a relationship to one another, they are not as tightly coupled as many once believed was the case. In 1973, the American economy consumed

Figure 3.39
Fuels Used for Residential Heating, 1978–1981

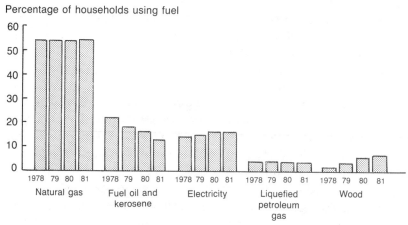

Percentage of households using fuel

Source: U.S. Department of Energy.

Saving Energy in Davis, California

Some municipalities, such as Davis, California, have been very successful in promoting energy conservation on the community level. Davis has enacted building codes specifying maximum permissible amounts of heat gain and loss for all new housing and requires that the same standards be met by existing homes before they can be sold on the market. The city has supplemented these code requirements by providing technical assistance to building and home sellers on how to meet them. Davis also is promoting more energy-efficient transportation by creating extensive bike lanes and increasing the availability of public transit (including the use of double-decker buses).

The program is estimated to have resulted in "drastic energy savings," showing the significant role that local governments can play in promoting increased energy efficiency.

Other actions taken include building two housing complexes with solar heating and cooling as a demonstration for local builders, requiring pools in apartments and motels to be solar heated, encouraging narrower streets (saving land, asphalt, and fuel), promoting the use of shade trees, and implementing material-recycling programs.

(Source: James Ridgeway, *Energy Efficient Community Planning: A Guide to Saving Energy and Producing Power at the Local Level* [Emmaus, Pa.: JG Press for the Public Resource Center, undated].)

59.2 thousand BTUs to produce a single dollar of GNP (1972 dollars); by 1983, it took only 45.9 thousand BTUs to produce that same (1972) dollar of GNP.[248] The drop, in thousands of BTUs, of *oil and gas* consumed to produce a (1972) dollar is from 45.7 in 1973 to 30.9 in 1983; in contrast, for all other energy forms, the ratio actually rose slightly (from 13.5 in 1973 to 15.0 in 1983).[249] Because the price rises in petroleum and natural gas have been substantially higher than for other energy forms (especially coal, and, therefore, electricity), the explanation for the more efficient use of oil and gas and less efficient use of other energy forms may lie in simple economics.

More efficient energy use can be seen in every sector of the economy (figure 3.40). In 1981, the average household used 13 percent less energy than it did in 1972; over the same period, energy consumption per square foot in commercial buildings dropped by about 10 percent; industrial energy use per unit of output fell by more than one-quarter; and fuel consumption per mile for automobiles declined by 13 percent.[250]

The causes of increasingly efficient use of energy are not yet well understood. It remains to be seen what proportion of the efficiency gains is permanent, because of such capital investments as purchasing cars with better mileages or installing new storm windows, and what is ascribable to potentially short-term behavioral modifications, such as joining a carpool or lowering the thermostat.[251] It is known that, whereas in 1973 at least 85 percent of all households set thermostats higher than 70 degrees in the winter, by 1981 that figure had dropped to 50 percent.[252] However, factors not related to conservation also contributed to the decline in household consumption, including a 10 percent reduction in the number of persons per household, a population shift away from the cold Northeast and North Central states to the South and West, and an increase in households in which both members of a couple worked, reducing daytime heating.[253]

The industrial sector led the way in efficiency improvements, measured as energy use per dollar of GNP or unit of output. Many industries greatly reduced consumption by replacing old machinery, such as traditional blast furnaces, with more efficient systems, such as electric arc furnaces in the steel industry. However, industrial efficiency gains may not be so great because some improvements were gained by production shifts to less energy-intensive products (for example, ''smokestack'' industries to high-technology firms) or by fuel switching from petroleum to electricity (which itself consumes fossil fuel's primary energy at 33 percent efficiency). Finally, the movement of energy-intensive industries overseas

Figure 3.40
U.S. Energy Use Intensity, by Sector, 1970–1982

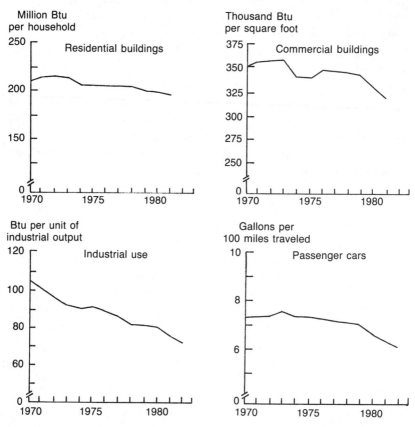

Source: Motor vehicle data, Federal Highway Administration; all other data, Oak Ridge National Laboratory.

may hide real energy consumption, as the United States imports its energy hidden in the form of mineral ores and petrochemicals.[254]

U.S. industry is still far from the energy efficiency it can ultimately attain. Some experts argue that modernization of production systems can reduce consumption another 15 percent to 20 percent over the next decade.[255] The perceived glut in oil supplies and accompanying price reductions, however, are slackening management's sense of urgency to conserve energy, so improvement may not continue at its past rate.

ENERGY PRODUCTION AND SUPPLIES

As the world's greatest energy consumer,[256] the United States is fortunate to possess large domestic reserves to feed its energy appetite. Estimated U.S. coal reserves are enormous, comprising, at 280 billion tons, one-quarter of the world's total,[257] and its natural gas and petroleum reserves are plentiful compared to those in most industrialized countries. In 1983, domestic production accounted for 86.6 percent of U.S. energy consumption,[258]* a situation unparalleled by most Western trading partners. Domestic production of all energy types has remained relatively constant since 1970 (figure 3.41). In 1983, domestic production totaled 61.0 Quads, down slightly from 1982 and 2.4 percent below 1970's total.[259] In 1981, America retained its status as the world's largest producer of all forms of energy combined, with 23 percent of the total.[260] Even for crude oil, widely perceived as the Achilles heel of the U.S. energy mix, the United States led world production until 1974, when the Soviet Union became the leading producer.

Coal production has grown significantly in recent years, up 25 percent between 1978 and 1982, with most of the growth attributable to more mining in western states. The growth rate slowed in the years 1982 to 1983, with a 7.1 percent decrease in production. (Yet consumption increased during the same year by 3.7 percent.)[261] Between 1970 and 1981, the percentage of coal mined west of the Mississippi River leapt from 7 percent to 33 percent. (Most western coal is extracted by surface-mining techniques.) Coal exports jumped from 41 million tons in 1978 to 106 million tons in 1982, but dropped off in 1983 to 78 million tons.[262]

Despite the vast reserves and increasing production trends, it is not clear that coal will readily replace more strategically sensitive fossil fuels.

---

* The figure does not include consumption of wood fuel.

Figure 3.41
U.S. Production of Energy by Type of Fuel,
1960–1983

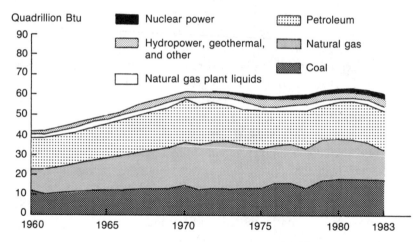

This figure excludes many important types of energy—wood used for home heating, passive solar building designs, windmills, and energy self-generated by industry from waste products. Taken together, these and similar noncommercial sources may be a significant component of energy production.

Source: U.S. Department of Energy.

Coal's role in the future U.S. energy supply is clouded by such uncertainties as the current glut of petroleum, higher railroad transportation costs for bringing coal to market, the lack of interest in synthetic-fuels plants, and the environmental costs of acid rain, acid mine drainage, strip mining, and mineworker's safety.[263] A 1983 report by the Department of Energy, on the other hand, predicted that coal use would grow faster than the economy, 2.6 percent as compared with 2.5 percent, respectively, per year, through 1990.[264]

While U.S. petroleum production has been relatively constant since 1970, American dependence on imports has lessened (figure 3.42). The steady decline in oil imports, begun in 1978, continued through 1983. Since the 1977 high of 8.8 million barrels a day, imports have dropped 43 percent to 5 million barrels a day in 1983. U.S. imports from Middle-Eastern OPEC nations have plummeted, from 18.5 percent of all petroleum consumed in 1977 to only 4.3 percent in 1983.[265] Concurrently, the importance of oil from the non-OPEC nations of Mexico, the United Kingdom, and Canada has grown.[266]

Some argue that such shifts in supply away from Arab "trouble spots" are not equivalent to a reduced energy vulnerability. Although the United States may be decoupling its energy fate from the politics of the Middle East, its important allies in Europe and Japan continue to depend heavily on Arab oil and to look to the Siberian natural gas pipeline for gas supplies.

Renewable Fuels

While media attention is no longer focused on the energy crisis and the development of renewable fuel sources, progress has nevertheless continued in selected alternative-fuel industries.

Biomass

Organic substances (biomass) can be burned, converted by bacteria, or broken down to form energy. Approximately 2.6 Quads of biomass energy were used in the United States in 1982.[267] One example is ethanol fuel, sometimes known as gasohol (when mixed in a 1:9 ratio with gasoline). Produced from biomass, primarily corn and other grains, but potentially from such disparate sources as cheese whey, citrus fruit peels, and forestry residues, ethanol's share of the transportation-fuels industry has grown steadily since its introduction in 1977.

Total gasohol consumption in 1981 was 47,000 barrels per day and is projected to increase in the future.[268] In 1984, ethanol production is expected to exceed 5 percent of the total gasoline market.[269] Further, alcohol fuels, such as ethanol, provide a more environmentally benign substitute for lead as an octane-improving additive, and are likely to increase their market share as lead additives are phased down.[270] Finally, in 1982, 20 percent of the alcohol used by industry was made from biomass.

Also, municipal garbage could be converted into energy. Despite the 150 to 300 million tons (see chapter 2) of solid waste generated in the United States each year, less than 1 percent is being used to generate energy. In comparison, several Scandinavian countries convert up to 40 percent of their municipal garbage into usable energy.[271]

Solar

Solar energy systems are widely used in the United States today. The Department of Energy estimates that up to 600,000 households use solar collectors, predominantly for swimming pool heating, space heating, and domestic water heating.[272] There are two basic types of solar energy collectors: solar thermals, which use the sun's heat for heating, and photovoltaics, which use solar cells to convert sunlight directly into electricity. Thermal solar systems are the most widely used and the most advanced of the solar technologies.

The Department of Energy estimates that a million square feet of solar collector provides energy equivalent to .201 trillion BTUs per year.[273] As of January 1982, approximately 85 million square feet of collectors were in use; thus, 17 trillion BTUs were being generated. The number is expected to continue increasing.[274] In 1974, 1.28 million square feet of solar collectors were produced, and by 1981 that figure had jumped to 19.95 million square feet (figure 3.43). During the same period, the number of solar collector manufacturers rose from 45 to 342.[275] However, by 1982 the surge in residential collector sales had flattened, mainly because of a decline in housing sales. Nonetheless, other solar technologies, photovoltaics in particular, continue to increase exponentially in use.[276]

Other Renewable Energy Sources

The adoption of most other renewable energy alternatives steadily increases. In particular, businesses, industries, and utilities are realizing that renewable energy technologies are wise investments.

Figure 3.42
Sources of Petroleum Consumed in the United States, 1970–1983

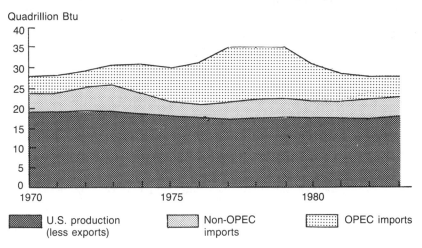

Quadrillion Btu

- U.S. production (less exports)
- Non-OPEC imports
- OPEC imports

Source: U.S. Department of Energy.

Figure 3.43
U.S. Production of Solar Collectors, 1974–1981

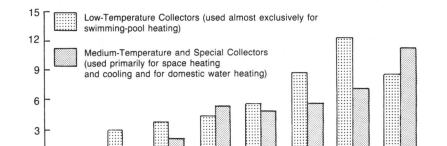

Million square feet

- Low-Temperature Collectors (used almost exclusively for swimming-pool heating)
- Medium-Temperature and Special Collectors (used primarily for space heating and cooling and for domestic water heating)

Source: U.S. Department of Energy.

Geothermal heat is a vast, largely untapped source of electricity. In 1960, geothermal sources produced 33 million kilowatt hours, or .766 trillion BTUs. This production has risen steadily to 4,843 million kilowatt hours, or 105 trillion BTUs in 1982.[277] The main source of geothermal energy in the United States is in northern California, where the Geysers Geothermal Field has a capacity sufficient to meet the electrical demands of the city of San Francisco.[278] Untapped geothermal resources have the potential to provide up to 1.5 Quads by the year 2000.[279]

Hydroelectric power has contributed to U.S. electricity stores since the 19th century. Hydropower production has increased steadily over time, rising from 1.47 Quads in 1952 to 3.5 Quads in 1983.[280] However, this rate of increase is not likely to continue because most of the prime, high dam sites have been used and the remaining major sites are not economically, environmentally, or physically possible to use. Nevertheless, small-scale energy generation from low-head sites,* both abandoned and newly created, may help satisfy energy needs in some sections of the country.[282]

The use of wood-burning stoves and fireplaces for heat is popular again, particularly increasing after the oil price shocks of the 1970s (figure 3.44).[283] Residential firewood use in the United States more than doubled between 1972 and 1981,[284] and up to 31 percent of American households now use wood as an energy source, mainly for space heating.[285] Firewood provides an average of 8 percent of the energy consumed in each of those households.[286] Industries (especially forest-products industries) and utilities are also moving toward using wood and wood waste for energy generation in lieu of costly petroleum.[287]

The growing use of wood stoves and fireplaces can bring its own problems, such as local air pollution and, when improperly installed or maintained, fire hazards. In Maine and Vermont, 96 deaths from wood-stove fires were reported in 1979, when none had been reported a few years before.[288] And in Missoula, Montana, where wood smoke has fouled the air, residents who burn wood during air-pollution alerts can be fined up to $100.[289] Also, the future of large-scale, wood-generated energy is uncertain because availability of large supplies of wood may be limited, and thus the price will be higher.

Wind-powered electrical generation has become a reality in the state of California, where an estimated 4,600 wind turbines in wind farms

---

* The vertical distance between the water level in the reservoir and the turbine below is called head. Low-head hydro is water held less than about 250 feet above the turbine.[281]

can generate 300 megawatts of electricity, approximately 6 trillion BTU. This is enough to satisfy the residential electrical needs of 120,000 people. Ninety-five percent of the turbines were installed during 1982 and 1983.[290]

ENERGY PRICES

The most striking change in the energy picture of the 1970s and 1980s has been in the prices people pay for energy. Price hikes in all fuels, but particularly in petroleum products resulting from the 1973–74 oil embargo and 1979 OPEC price increase, have combined with fears of shortage to stimulate most of the shifts in production, consumption, and efficiency discussed above, and have focused attention on energy's impact on the world's economic structure and political arrangements.

Energy Prices by Fuel Type

In real terms, the price rise for most forms of energy has been less than consumers might think (figure 3.45). Although the price of gasoline at the pump rose 146 percent between 1974 and 1981, when adjusted for the general rate of inflation, the real price increase was only 38 percent. Between 1976 and 1981, however, the real price of residential fuel oil rose by 89 percent.[291]

In recent years, the picture has changed somewhat. Real prices of gasoline and heating oil have actually declined by 20 percent and just over 13 percent between 1981 and 1983, respectively. In current dollars, the average price for a gallon of gasoline dropped from $1.39 per gallon at its peak in March 1981 to $1.23 at the end of 1983.[292] These figures are a response to the 18 percent decrease in current prices of crude oil between 1981 and 1983, dictated in part by OPEC price reductions in response to the decline in the demands for petroleum products because of the worldwide recession.

Price decontrol within the United States, a process completed in 1981, permitted world prices to be felt directly and immediately by domestic consumers. In other countries, oil prices did not moderate as they did within the United States, because international oil prices are denominated in U.S. dollars, a currency that has been highly valued during the period in question.

The prices of electricity and natural gas, in contrast, continued to increase. While still at a level below the 1963 average, residential electricity prices have climbed steadily, up 13.8 percent in real terms, be-

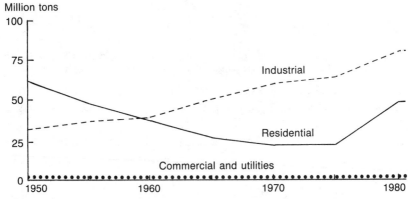

Figure 3.44
U.S. Wood Energy Consumption, 1950–1981

Source: U.S. Department of Energy.

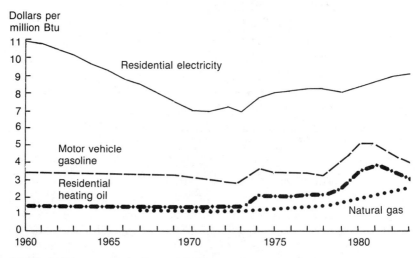

Figure 3.45
Cost of Fuels to End Users, 1960–1981
(in constant 1972 dollars)

One million Btu is the energy contained in approximately 8 gallons of gasoline, 6.7 gallons of heating oil, 293 kilowatt hours of electricity, or 981 cubic feet of natural gas.

Price deflator: Consumer Price Index for all items less energy.

Source: U.S. Department of Energy and The Conservation Foundation.

tween 1979 and 1983.[293] Fuel switching by utilities during the 1970s reduced fuel oil's share of electricity generation, helping to moderate prices. But as new plants, especially nuclear, are completed and their construction costs are added to customers' bills, electricity prices are likely to continue to rise in many parts of the country.

Sharp increases in natural gas prices marked the winter of 1982–83, rising by as much as 25 percent nationally from the previous winter.[294] Natural gas prices vary significantly among regions. In November of 1982, for example, people heating their homes with gas in Boston paid $8.18 per thousand cubic feet, while those in St. Louis paid $6.12, and in Los Angeles, $4.81.[295] Such variations arise from a variety of factors, including the relative amounts of low, price-controlled versus new, decontrolled gas the region's pipeline company has contracted for from gas producers. It is unclear what natural gas prices will be in the future, as Congress continues to debate the schedule for lifting certain wellhead price controls, now slated for January 1985, for newly discovered gas.

Residential Energy Prices—Responses

In the residential sector, sharp increases in the price of fuel oil (144 percent in current-dollar terms between 1978 and 1981) prompted both conservation and a switch to less expensive fuels.[296]

From 1979 through 1981, 3.6 million households switched from fuel oil to another heating source; in comparison, 12.2 million households in 1981 still relied primarily on fuel oil.[297] Fifty-six percent of those switching chose natural gas; 31 percent switched to wood. Such fuel switching, saving money over the short term, did not necessarily entail saving energy as well.[298] And the cost savings with gas become less significant as gas price decontrol, combined with dropping real prices for fuel oil since 1981, brings the prices of oil and gas closer together.

The Northeast, the region in which 44 percent of the households rely on fuel oil and that saw a 61 percent increase in average home-heating expenditures between 1978 and 1981, was also the region most likely to practice conservation measures. Almost 45 percent of northeastern households in 1981 took such conservation measures as caulking or weatherstripping, installing storm windows or doors, adding insulation, and using automatically adjusted thermostats, compared to 39.1 percent in the North-Central states, 27.6 percent in the South, and 25.3 percent in the West (figure 3.46).[299]

Figure 3.46
Conservation Measures Taken in Single-Family Housing Units, by Region, in 1981.

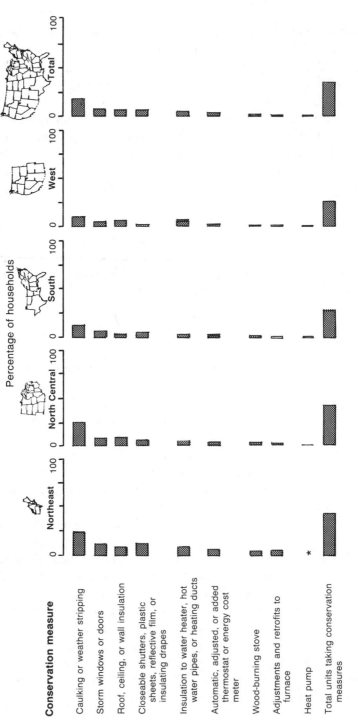

* Data withheld because of a large variance.
Source: U.S. Department of Energy.

International Energy Price Comparisons

International energy prices vary widely according to the type of fuel used, the tax levied on the fuel, and the sector in which it is used.

Petroleum prices greatly affect efficiency in the use of oil. The United States and Canada have the lowest gasoline prices ($1.30 and $1.38 per gallon in 1982, respectively) worldwide, while Italy has the highest prices, at $2.91 a gallon in 1982. France, West Germany, the United Kingdom, and Japan also had prices well over $2.00 a gallon in 1982.[300] Over time, real gasoline prices rose steadily between 1978 and 1980 in all countries. These price differences among countries reflect, in large part, differing policies toward gasoline taxes.

Prices of other petroleum products, such as light fuel oil used in the industrial and household sectors, have also gone up steadily in current dollars since 1978. Canada has consistently had the lowest prices, while the higher U.S., Japanese, and Western European countries' prices have been fairly comparable to one another.[301]

Natural gas is used as an energy source primarily in industry, households, and in the electricity-generation sector. In all use-sectors, Japan has far and away the highest natural gas prices. In the industrial sector, for instance, natural gas was almost $11.00 per thousand cubic feet in Japan in 1982, while the United States and Western European average prices were less than half that ($3.00 to $5.00 per thousand cubic feet in the same year).[302]

Similar discrepancies can be seen in the household sector. In 1982, 1,000 cubic feet of natural gas cost an average of almost $14.00 in Japan, yet only about $4.00 in Canada and about $5.00 in the United States.[303] Over time, there have not been substantial price increases (in constant U.S. dollars) within most countries since 1978. Yet, despite the general slowing of price increases in parts of Western Europe, U.S. prices continue to increase more rapidly as the effect of domestic price decontrol serves to bring American gas prices nearer to market levels.

Electricity is predominantly used in industry and households. Its price is determined mainly by its sources: coal, hydropower, and nuclear power are all used to generate electricity. These fuels vary in efficiency and availability; thus, the end price of the electricity will differ accordingly. Canada has the lowest electricity prices in both industrial and household sectors (about $0.03 per kilowatt hour in 1982), while Japan has the highest ($0.09 to $0.12 per kilowatt hour in 1982).[304] Electricity prices in the household sector have risen steadily in all countries since 1978 (figure 3.47). The United States and the United Kingdom have shown the greatest increases since 1978 (60 and 52 percent increases, respectively), while France's prices have remained the most stable (an 8 percent increase).[305] Because public control or public ownership of electricity systems is virtually universal, price changes reflect policy choices more strongly than in most other energy forms.

Coal is an important fossil fuel in electricity generation and is used by industry as an energy source. The prices of both metallurgical coal (used by the steel industry) and steam coal (used by industry and electricity generators) are lowest in the United States (from $35.00 to $63.00 per short ton) and highest in France and West Germany (from $70.00 to $112.00 per short ton in 1982).[306] Coal prices are lowest in the United States because of relatively easily extractable and plentiful supplies as compared to other nations.

INTERNATIONAL CONSUMPTION

Worldwide, Canada is the biggest per-capita consumer of total energy, using 256 million BTUs per person in 1981. The United States was a close second, consuming 193 million BTUs per person. However, the United States leads the world in total energy consumption, with 51 Quads in 1981, with Japan (10 Quads) and West Germany (7.6 Quads) a distant second and third in the same year.[307]

The United States is the world leader in total consumption of refined petroleum products (17.06 million barrels a day in 1982), with the nearest competition coming from the USSR and Japan, whose total-barrels-per-day consumed were 8.91 million and 4.96 million, respectively. Historically, the United States also leads per-capita consumption of refined petroleum products, with Canada a close second. However, between 1975 and 1980, Canada surpassed the U.S per-capita consumption (29.5 barrels a year versus 27.3 in the United States in 1980)[308] (figure 3.48).

Future international consumption of energy will be determined by a complex mixture of domestic and international politics, domestic and international economics, and, in the long run, the supply of various fuels. As for so many other aspects of environmental policy, the dimensions of future problems will be defined by a combination of natural forces and public policy.

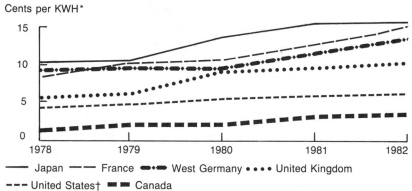

Figure 3.47
Price of Electricity in the Household Sector,
by Country, 1978–1982

Cents per KWH*

—— Japan —– France ●•● West Germany •••• United Kingdom
––– United States† ■ ■ Canada

* U.S. dollars converted at 1978 exchange rate: apparent relative prices in subsequent years may not accurately reflect current exchange rates.

† Price excluding tax

Source: U.S. Department of Energy.

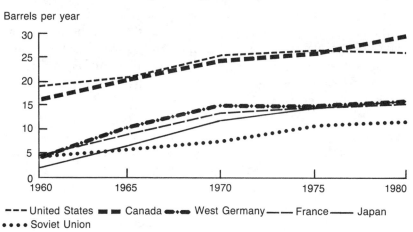

Figure 3.48
Per Capita Consumption of Refined Petroleum Products,
by Country, 1960–1980

Barrels per year

––– United States ■ ■ Canada ●•● West Germany —– France —— Japan
•••• Soviet Union

Source: United Nations, U.S. Bureau of the Census, and U.S. Department of Energy.

Recreation

Outdoor recreation is tremendously important for Americans. A 1982 survey reveals that 89 percent of U.S. residents had participated in some form of outdoor recreation during the previous year.[309] Another survey conducted in 1980 reports that nearly 100 million people—50 percent of the U.S. population—participated in one or more wildlife-associated recreational activities.[310] Visits to private, state and local, and federal parks and recreation areas have gone up dramatically since 1960, and money spent on recreation-related equipment also has increased in that time.

Outdoor recreation affects many aspects of American life. It contributes to physical well-being and mental health,[311] generates substantial economic activity,[312] and helps build ties between people and their natural environment.[313] Outdoor recreation activities also have many environmental implications. Some adversely affect the environment. For instance, off-road vehicles can irreparably damage fragile ecosystems such as dune grasses or alpine tundra.[314] Excessive use of backcountry campsites by backpackers can transform those areas from pristine to trampled, unsightly areas devoid of ground cover.[315] In each case, the amount and type of recreational activity, the type of land it is conducted on, and the supply of such land must be known if the resource is to be properly managed for recreational use with minimal resource degradation.

Participation in outdoor recreation also influences popular interest in nature and environmental concerns. It warrants consideration when formulating environmental policies, particularly for such programs as the Land and Water Conservation Fund. Although participation is only a rough proxy for demand, the available information suggests strong support for programs that will increase or enhance available outdoor recreational activities.

Trends in outdoor recreation also have implications for managing those federal, state, local, and private lands open for recreational uses. For example, both the U.S. Forest Service and the Bureau of Land Management must administer their lands for "multiple uses."[316] The amount and type of recreational use in a particular area may determine whether it is managed for recreation, for another renewable resource (such as grazing), or for nonrenewable resource extraction (such as coal mining). If the area is designated for recreation, the agency must still decide whether to develop visitor facilities or leave the area in its primitive state.

The National Park Service constantly faces the same management difficulty. For years, the service has struggled to balance its competing mandates to manage the parks for the enjoyment of present visitors, while conserving park resources and providing that those resources remain unimpaired for the enjoyment of future generations.[317]

Unfortunately, most public and private recreation managers must make do with information that is often sketchy, unreliable, or not comparable over time. Although the available information allows some general observations to be made, its limitations clearly illustrate the need for greater efforts in data collection.

PARTICIPATION IN RECREATION

More and more Americans are participating in outdoor recreational activities. They do so for a variety of reasons. The 1982 National Recreation Survey shows that 76 percent of respondents "particularly enjoyed" engaging in one or more outdoor recreational activity.[318] Of that 76 percent, 68 percent indicated that they liked those activities because of the opportunity to enjoy nature and get outdoors, 56 percent because the activities enabled them to get away from day-to-day problems, and 47 percent because of the quiet and peacefulness associated with their recreational activity (figure 3.49).[319]

Several factors have contributed to the dramatic increase in recreation observed since 1960. These include rising amounts of disposable income and leisure time, technological innovation in the recreational equipment industry (for example, the development of lightweight backpacking equipment or waxless cross-country skis), and a new awareness of the benefits of physical fitness.[320]

Precise data on participation rates and trends in particular outdoor activities generally do not exist. Public agencies that keep track of visitation frequently do not collect data on particular activities, or base such data on general estimates made by field personnel. Proxies for participation, such as the value of equipment purchases or number of licenses issued, tend to be crude. Perhaps the most comprehensive sources of information about participation in outdoor recreation are survey results. But few national surveys have been made (and some of these are not comparable), so detailed trend analysis of recreation is essentially impossible.

Despite this uncertainty, the available data all point to a sizeable increase in outdoor recreation. Many activities show slight-to-moderate

Figure 3.49
Reasons People Engage in Their
Favorite Outdoor Activity, 1982

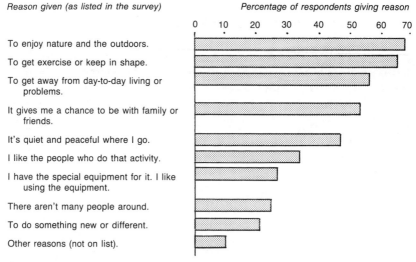

Reason given (as listed in the survey)   *Percentage of respondents giving reason*

Percentages based on those respondents (76 percent of the total) who cited one or more activities they ''particularly enjoyed.''

Source: National Park Service.

gains from 1960 to 1982, while others show dramatic increases. Visits to state parks and federal recreation lands soared between 1960 and 1982. Sales of outdoor recreational equipment also are up markedly.[321] National recreation surveys, conducted in 1960 and 1982, show increasing participation.

Technological Innovation and Fitness

Some factors influencing participation in outdoor recreation affect certain activities more than others. For instance, the growing national awareness of physical fitness and technological improvements in footwear combined to yield, in 1982, a nation in which 26 percent of the people 12 and over run or jog at least once a year.[322]* In 1960, jogging was not popular enough to be included in that year's National Recreation Survey. The same forces—the desire to be physically fit and technological innovation—have helped raise participation in bicycling from 9 percent in 1960 to 32 percent in 1982 (figure 3.50).[323] Moreover, bicycling is no longer a "kid's sport." In 1960, fewer than 5 percent of adults 25 years old and older bicycled once or more a year;[324] in 1982, bicycling participation rates were 37 percent for those 25 to 39 years, 22 percent for those 40 to 59 years, and 7 percent for those over 60 years of age.[325] The fitness boom apparently has not affected participation in such activities such as hunting, fishing, and nature study (figure 3.50).

Technological advancements play a large role in the increase of certain outdoor recreation activities. For example, too few people used off-road vehicles in 1960 to include that activity in the national survey; in 1982, 11 percent used off-road vehicles (not including snowmobiles, which 3 percent of the population used) (figure 3.50). U.S. Forest Service figures indicate that off-road vehicle use on Forest Service lands increased by about a third between 1975 and 1983.[326] Similarly, improvements in downhill and cross-country ski equipment, and a dramatic increase in the number of ski areas during the 1960s and early 1970s, contributed

---

* All 1960 and 1982 participation data are from the 1960 and 1982 National Recreation Surveys, and all refer to people 12 years old and older. Data on the number of days spent participating in particular activities are not yet available for the 1982 survey. For 1960 data, percent participation refers to the percentage of respondents who participated one or more times in the activity during the summer months (June through August), except hunting (September through November) and skiing (December through February). 1982 data include participation within 12 months preceding the survey. Therefore, 1960 participation is somewhat understated relative to 1982 data.

Figure 3.50
Participation in Selected Outdoor Recreation
Activities, 1960 and 1982

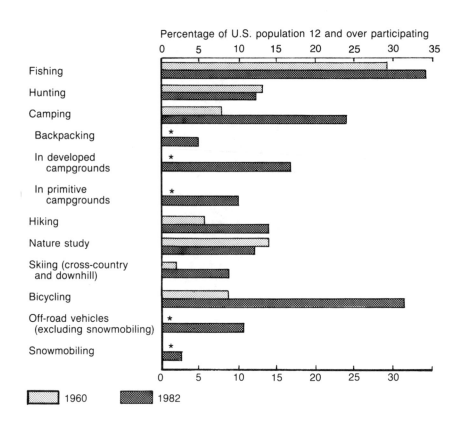

* No 1960 data available

1960 data based on participation during summer months only (June-August), except hunting (September-November) and skiing (December-February). 1982 data based on year-round participation. Thus, increases from 1960-1982 may be somewhat overstated.

Source: National Park Service.

to a rise in skiing participation from 2 to 9 percent.[327] Skiing, perhaps more than other outdoor activities, depends on favorable weather— that is, sufficient snow cover. The year 1980 was a poor one for snow, and the number of downhill skier visits that year dropped by roughly 20 percent from 1979 levels.[328]

Wilderness Appreciation

Trends in camping and hiking reflect Americans' changing attitudes toward natural and wilderness settings.[329] Camping participation rates tripled between 1960 and 1982, from 8 percent to 24 percent (figure 3.50). Indeed, camping at many National Park System campgrounds increased so much that the Park Service adopted use restrictions to stem resource damage.[330] Backpacking, closely tied to a strong appreciation for wilderness values, was not common enough to merit treatment in the 1960 survey; in 1982, 5 percent of the population had backpacked at least once in the last year (figure 3.50). National Park Service data from 1972 to 1983 show a steady increase in the amount of backpacking in National Park System units. Overnight backcountry stays increased 73 percent in that time period, from 1.5 million to 2.6 million.[331]

Hiking, like backpacking, reflects an appreciation for natural environments. Hiking participation rates more than doubled from 1960 to 1982, rising from 6 percent to 14 percent.[332] Like bicycling, hiking expanded from being primarily an activity associated with youth to encompass older segments of the population.[333] The U.S. Forest Service has estimated the number of recreation visitor-days (RVDs)* spent in various activities on U.S. Forest Service lands. Although these estimates are very rough, the figures for hiking and mountain climbing show a substantial increase from 1977 to 1983 (22 percent), twice the rate of increase for all types of recreation combined on U.S. Forest Service lands.[336] However, hiking still accounts for a small percentage of total recreational activity on these lands (about 5 percent), far behind the two main activities, camping and mechanized travel (largely people driving through national forests), each of which account for about 25 percent of total recreational activity.[337]

---

* One recreation visitor-day is a measure of recreation use that is equivalent to one person engaged in some kind of recreational activity for 12 hours. It may entail one person for 12 hours, six people for 2 hours each, or any equivalent combination, either continuously or intermittently.[334] It contrasts with a "visit," which is essentially the entry of a person onto federal land or water, generally for recreational purposes, without regard for time.[335]

Fishing and Hunting

As noted earlier, participation rates for fishing increased only slightly between 1960 and 1982, from 29 percent to 34 percent (figure 3.50). Still, fishing is one of America's most popular outdoor activities. In 1980, 42.1 million people aged 16 years and over spent an average of 20 days each fishing (for a total of 858 million days);[338] about 36.4 million Americans fished in freshwater. The most popular freshwater fish sought were bass, panfish, catfish, and trout.[339] Approximately 12.3 million people aged 16 years and over went saltwater fishing.[340]

Hunting participation rates were about the same in 1960 (13 percent) and 1982 (12 percent) (figure 3.50). In 1980, 17.4 million hunters aged 16 years and over spent 330 million days hunting.[341] Small-game hunting was the most popular type, with 12.4 million hunters spending 151.2 million days; 11.8 million big-game hunters made that category the second most popular, with 112.8 million days spent hunting; 5.3 million hunters spent nearly 43 million days hunting migratory birds.[342]

LOCATION OF RECREATION

The nation's vast outdoor recreation estate includes private, local, state, and federal land. The availability and quality of visitation data vary significantly among these categories. On a national scale, only federal agencies compile statistics that are at all reliable. Reliability varies among the various federal agencies as well. Consequently, the relative contribution of each category of land—private, local, state, and federal—to total recreational opportunities is difficult to assess. All, however, contribute significantly. Moreover, each serves a different function—for example, national parks may preserve areas of scenic beauty and historical significance, U.S. Army Corps of Engineers reservoirs provide water-based recreation, and local parks host team sports and picnic lunches. The fact that there are many providers of recreation means that each should consider the existence of the others when formulating its management policies. For instance, a national forest campground may relieve pressures on a nearby national park, reducing the need to develop more facilities at the park.

Private Recreation Areas

The private sector plays a major, if imprecisely quantified, role in supplying outdoor recreational opportunities. There are 740 million acres of privately held range- and forestland in the United States, about one-third of which is open to public use.[343] Private recreation lands are particularly important for outdoor recreation in the eastern United States, because over 90 percent of the forestland and rangeland in federal ownership are in the West.[344] In 1980, there were 16 federally owned forest and range acres per person in the western United States, but only 0.1 acres per person in the northern states and 0.3 acres per person in the southern states.[345] In 1981, roughly 7,900 private campgrounds hosted close to 300 million camper days.[346] Two-thirds of all hunting in 1980 occurred on private lands.[347]

State Parks

State park data are complicated by variations in reporting by state park agencies, some of which manage only state parks, while others manage parks, historic sites, fish and wildlife reserves, and forests.[348] Thus, the aggregate data do not include the entire base of state-provided outdoor recreational opportunities. Even so, the data reveal that state parks support a large and growing amount of recreation.

In 1981, state park systems (excluding Alaska, where the state park system includes nearly 3 million acres) contained 6.4 million acres, roughly one-fourth of the acreage of the National Park System (again excluding Alaska, which has roughly 54 million acres). But state parks registered over twice as many visits as the National Park System, some 631 million.[349] In 1983, state parks reported 645 million visits.[350]

The presence of state forestland and rangeland helps offset the dearth of federal lands in the eastern United States, particularly in the Northeast and North-Central regions. These two areas contain 9.6 million and 11.8 million acres of state-owned forestland, respectively, and the Southeast and South-Central regions contain 1.6 and 3.3 million acres, respectively.[351] Adding state-owned lands increases the per-capita distribution of forestland in the north from 0.1 to 0.3 acres per person.[352]

Federal Recreation Areas

By far the best visitation data available are those put out by the three major federal recreation agencies, the U.S. Forest Service, the U.S. Army Corps of Engineers, and the National Park Service. However, even figures for these agencies are based on varying combinations of actual counts, educated estimates, surveys, and outright conjecture, so comparisons must be made with caution. Reliability varies not only from agency to agency, but also over time within a given agency.[353] Because National

Park Service data permit greater analysis, visitation to the National Park System is discussed here in comparatively great detail, even though it represents a relatively small share of total recreational activity on federal land.

In fiscal year 1982, 553.6 million recreation visitor-days (RVDs) occurred on all federal lands. Although many people commonly think of the National Park Service as the primary federal recreation agency, lands administered by the U.S. Forest Service actually receive more recreational use than those of any other federal agency. In 1982, 42 percent of all RVDs on federal lands occurred on U.S. Forest Service lands, 25 percent on U.S. Army Corps of Engineer lands (mostly reservoirs), while the Park Service ranked third, with only 18 percent.[354] Other federal agencies that manage lands with a significant amount of recreational activity are the Bureau of Reclamation (9 percent of total federal RVDs in 1982) and the Bureau of Land Management (5 percent of total federal RVDs in 1982).[355]

Forest Recreation

The U.S. Forest Service has been the leading recreation agency in terms of visitation for some time (figure 3.51). Its visitation has risen fairly steadily over the last several years, roughly 11 percent since 1977. Nearly one-fourth of the service's 1983 visitation occurred in California, and another 9 percent occured in Colorado.[356] Oregon, Arizona, Washington, and Utah were the next most-visited states in the National Forest System. Together, these western states accounted for 60 percent of total visitation on U.S. Forest Service lands, while states east of the Mississippi River accounted for only 16 percent.[357] This distribution reflects the geographic distribution of Forest Service lands.[358]

Winter use of U.S. Forest Service lands more than doubled between 1971 and 1981.[359] This increase largely reflects the growth in capacity of ski areas located on the Forest Service's lands during that time.

Water-based Recreation

Total visitation to reservoirs and waterways under the jurisdiction of the U.S. Army Corps of Engineers has climbed dramatically in the past two decades, reflecting an increased interest in water-based recreation and an increased number of reservoirs. However, the rate of increase has fallen off rapidly. Between 1965 and 1971, the number of "recreation days" (a unit of measure that is analogous to the "visit," since it does not account for time) on areas under the Corps' jurisdiction increased 83 percent, from 169 to 310 million; between 1971 and 1977, the increase was 37 percent, to 424 million; and between 1977 and 1983, the increase was only 13 percent, to 480 million.[360] In fact, 1983 figures showed almost no change from 1982.[361]

The Corps also keeps a set of statistics that measures only recreation at developed areas, thus excluding dispersed recreational activities such as backpacking and hunting. Recreation at developed areas only, measured in RVDs, fell 16 percent between 1977 and 1983 (figure 3.51). Since total recreation at areas under the Corps' jurisdiction rose, while recreation at its developed sites fell, it is likely that there was an increase in dispersed recreational activities such as hunting and backpacking. However, because the figures for total recreation and recreation at developed sites are based on different units of measure, this conclusion cannot be made with certainty.[362]

National Park System

Between 1970 and 1983, total visitation to lands administered by the National Park Service nearly doubled, from 172.0 million visits to 335.6 million visits.[363] But these figures overstate the increase in visitation to the parks, because they include nonrecreational visits (such as entries by persons owning land within a park's boundary going to and from their property, entries by tradespeople with business in the park, and through traffic) as well as recreational visits. Additionally, the system's tremendous expansion during the 1970s contributed greatly to the increase in visitation, and makes trend analysis difficult.

Recreational and nonrecreational visits have different management implications, and the number of nonrecreational visits is substantial—in 1983, there were 243.6 million recreational visits and 92.0 million nonrecreational visits.[364] It is sometimes difficult to determine whether a visit is recreational, particularly in the case of parkways, because it simply is not feasible to stop all cars and inquire whether the passengers are driving in the park for business or pleasure. The Natchez Trace Parkway unit, for instance, which had 19.2 million total visits in 1983,[365] simply assumes that one-third of these are nonrecreational.[366] The accuracy of this method is certainly open to question, but alternatives are scarce. Indeed, the idea of a recreational visit to a parkway highlights the variety of experiences that fall within the measure of a "visit." Because a recreational visit can be nearly anything, from an arduous hike to and from the bottom of the Grand Canyon to a brief glimpse

Figure 3.51
Recreation at Lands Managed by Three Federal
Agencies, 1977–1983

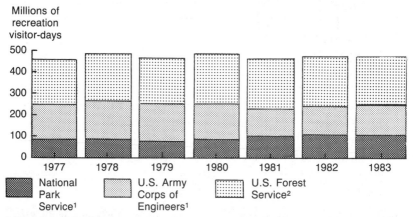

Millions of
recreation
visitor-days

| National Park Service[1] | U.S. Army Corps of Engineers[1] | U.S. Forest Service[2] |

[1] Based on calendar year.
[2] Based on fiscal year.

Source: National Park Service, U.S. Forest Service, and U.S. Army Corps of Engineers.

Figure 3.52
National Park Service Recreation Visits, 1972–1983

Millions of recreation visits

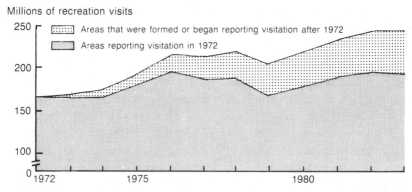

Areas that were formed or began reporting visitation after 1972

Areas reporting visitation in 1972

Source: National Park Service

over its rim, the visit, as a unit of measure, may be too general for many park-management purposes. Moreover, the National Park System is a diverse collection of natural, historical, and cultural areas. Therefore, aggregate visitation statistics provide only a rough guide for park-system management decisions.

Aggregate visitation statistics overstate the growth in visitation to individual units of the National Park System because of the system's tremendous expansion during the 1970s. That decade saw an influx of urban-oriented parks, such as Golden Gate National Recreation Area and Gateway National Recreation Area, that draw huge numbers of visitors. In 1983, these two parks had a total of 27.9 million recreational visits—11.5 percent of total system visitation that year.[367] System-wide visitation totals for 1983 show a 47 percent increase over 1972 totals. But, when the visits to parks that began reporting after 1972 are removed from the 1983 totals, the 1983 increase over 1972 drops to only 14 percent[368] (figure 3.52).

Golden Gate National Recreation Area (GGNRA), added to the system in 1972, significantly affected system visitation totals. GGNRA, which contains several distinct units, has added "new" units to its counting totals almost every year since it was added to the system. One of the "new" units, Aquatic Park, had already operated for several years. When added to the reporting totals in 1980, Aquatic Park's 5,638,000 visits alone accounted for 41 percent of the *system-wide* increase from 1979 to 1980.[369] That same year, GGNRA had the most recreational visits of any park—18.4 million. Adding new areas complicates visitation trend analysis by enlarging the counting base. The U.S. Army Corps of Engineers' data share this problem.[370]

In sum, nearly 70 percent of the National Park System's increase in recreational visitation from 1972 to 1983 is due to the addition of new parks, predominantly located near urban areas, rather than to increases in visitation at the older units of the system (figure 3.53). Nevertheless, both the dramatic increase in visitation for the system as a whole and the smaller increase in visitation for existing units indicate a strong interest in outdoor recreation and cultural and historical preservation, and have important implications for the national parks.

USER CHARACTERISTICS

Participation in outdoor recreation generally decreases with age and increases with income. Of the 11 percent of Americans who did not participate in outdoor recreation in 1982, two-thirds came from households

Figure 3.53
22 Most Popular National Park System Units, 1982
(with 1960 and 1982 visitation)

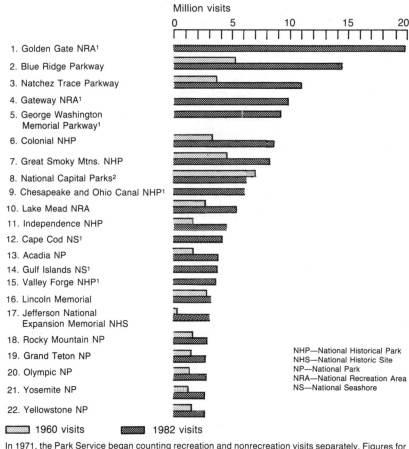

Million visits

In 1971, the Park Service began counting recreation and nonrecreation visits separately. Figures for 1982 include only recreation visits; thus 1960 visitation is slightly overstated relative to 1982.

[1] Established after 1960.
[2] National Capital Parks had higher visitation in 1960 than 1982, due to redesignation of several units formerly included in National Capital Parks as separate units of the park system.

Source: National Park Service.

with incomes under $15,000. Twenty-seven percent of nonparticipants were between the ages of 40 and 59 years, and another 54 percent were 60 years of age or older. Nonparticipation was more frequent among blacks than whites (18 percent versus 10 percent) and among women than men (14 percent versus 8 percent). People living in central cities in standard metropolitan statistical areas (SMSAs) had a higher non-participation rate (15 percent) than those living in suburbs (8 percent) or outside SMSAs entirely (12 percent).[371]

Some activities did not follow these trends, and, generally speaking, disparities among different groups decreased between 1960 and 1982.[372] For example, nearly equal percentages of men and women bicycled, and more women than men rode horses, walked or drove for pleasure, went sightseeing, or had picnics. Participation rates for birdwatching and other nature-study activities were slightly higher for those over 60 years of age than for any other group, although the difference may not have been statistically significant. A higher percentage of blacks than whites ran or jogged (30 percent versus 26 percent).[373]

In other cases, the general trend was particularly exaggerated. Men's participation in golfing was three times that of women (20 percent versus 7 percent). And while 22 percent of men hunted once or more, only 3 percent of women did so. Ten percent of whites skied, but only 1 percent of blacks did.[374]

Place of residence—urban, suburban, or rural—affects participation in recreational activities. This is especially apparent for hunting and fishing. In 1980, 69 percent of hunters lived in small towns and rural areas, 26 percent in small cities (population range of 2,500 to 499,999), and only 5 percent in big cities.[375] Looked at another way, participation rates in small towns and rural areas were four times higher than in big cities (16 percent versus 4 percent). Fishing had a similar pattern of urban-rural participation, with 55 percent of fishermen coming from rural areas or small towns, and only 8 percent from big cities.[376]

CONSTRAINTS ON RECREATION

People's participation in outdoor recreation is frequently constrained by a variety of factors, and this is one reason that participation is only a rough proxy for the demand for outdoor recreation opportunities. The participation figures cited above indicate that advancing age and lack of income may prevent many people from participating in outdoor recreation. Even those who do participate, and who particularly enjoy one or more outdoor activity, find constraints to greater participation. The 1982 Nationwide Recreation Survey reports that the most common constraints to greater participation for this group of people are lack of time (mentioned by 56 percent of respondents), lack of money (20 percent), and lack of available facilities (19 percent).[377] Only 13 percent felt that overcrowding of areas curtailed their participation.

Similarly, a 1977 national recreation survey of the general population found the most common constraints to greater park visitation were lack of time (mentioned by 52 percent of respondents), overcrowding (40 percent), and lack of money (37 percent).[378] The 1977 respondents also frequently cited pollution problems and poorly maintained facilities as constraints (25 percent and 20 percent, respectively).

For technical reasons, both surveys likely underestimate the constraining effects of lack of time, lack of money, overcrowding, and so forth, on the general public's recreational activity.[379]

Looking at visitation statistics for only those National Park System areas that reported visitation before 1973 reveals how external events influence park visitation. Declines in visitation in 1974 and 1979 correspond with the gasoline price increases and economic recessions of those years (figure 3.52). In 1976, many parks hosted special events to celebrate the nation's Bicentennial, and the system recorded its highest visitation of the decade. It is from this perspective that 1977's visitation decline must be viewed.

Predicting future trends in recreation is difficult at best. Participation is affected by a host of social, economic, and demographic factors. As the "baby boom" ages, recreation participation rates may decline. Continued migration to the Sunbelt will affect regional demand for outdoor recreation. Changes in personal income, energy prices, and personal tastes will all affect participation, but cannot be predicted accurately. Given the importance of recreation to environmental policy formulation, there is clearly a need for more basic research on recreation— more detailed studies of user characteristics, more accurate information on participation rates and trends, and better assessment of recreation's environmental consequences.

PART II
Issues

Chapter 4

Identifying Issues

In the early 1970s, as the United States initiated many new environmental programs, it still had a relatively simplistic view of what needed to be done. Concern about pollution focused on about half a dozen air pollutants and a similar number of water pollutants. Other environmental issues were considered—for instance, threats to parkland and wildlife and the dangers of pesticides—but in general the problems seemed relatively straightforward. The nation even was able to establish a goal of eliminating, by 1985, all pollutant discharges to our waterways.

Over the ensuing years, more has been learned about those problems. Several have been found to be less straightforward than had been thought, and many others have been discovered. The newspapers seem to report some new environmental threat almost daily. Citizens and government officials alike are more than a little confused and intimidated by this unnerving variety of perceived and potential problems. They want a clear picture of where the real dangers lurk, how serious they are, and what should be done about them. They particularly hope to begin anticipating and avoiding the most unpleasant surprises, rather than responding to them after they strike.

Government and private groups have rushed to sort out existing and future environmental problems to clarify the current situation and to help organize responses more effectively. These efforts have been characterized by such phrases as *management priorities*, *risk assessment*, *foresight capability*, and *critical-trends assessment*.

During the past year or so, half a dozen surveys—by the Royal Swedish Academy of Sciences, the U.S. Environmental Protection Agency (EPA), the French government, the University of Michigan (in cooperation with EPA), the Congressional Clearinghouse for the Future, and The Conservation Foundation[1]—have attempted to identify and, to some extent, rank the major current and future environmental issues. They have done this principally by soliciting scientists and other knowledgeable people for their expert, albeit fairly subjective, opinions. (See box.)

237

Six Surveys Identifying Major Environmental Issues

The results of the following six surveys are used in this chapter to define the major environmental issues confronting society:

Swedish Symposium

The Royal Swedish Academy of Sciences convened a group of 35 independent scientists from different disciplines and different countries to discuss and select "a strategic set" of priorities for environmental research and management in the 1980s. The conference was held in Rättvik, Sweden, in November 1982. The result was a list of 10 *research* priorities requiring urgent attention and a second list of 10 *management* priorities.

As part of an elaborate procedure before and during the conference, the participants were asked to focus on three questions: (1) What environmental problems are inadequately understood and urgently require scientific research? (2) What problems are well understood on a scientific basis but urgently require new management efforts? and (3) What are the priorities among these problems for both environmental research and management in the 1980s?

Thirty key environmental issues were identified by the scientists before the conference. Each scientist also submitted a personal list of up to 10 priorities for research and 10 for management. These lists were compared and consolidated. The consolidated list was sent to each scientist for review; each then returned a new personal list of priorities. The lists were further discussed and refined at the conference itself.

Some problems were included on both the research and management lists. Conference director R. D. Munro said that for these issues the scientists felt that "further research on some specific aspects of the problems was urgently required but enough scientific knowledge and information was already available for management actions to be taken *now* as a matter of priority."[1]

EPA/Coates Study

The U.S. Environmental Protection Agency commissioned a study to develop a domestic environmental agenda for EPA for the rest of this century. Although the emphasis was on U.S. issues, a good many of them have international scope.

Participants were asked to identify issues in two categories: the most important continuing problems and new or newly important problems.

The study was based on results obtained from seven workshops and surveys. These were conducted among groups of federal officials; staff members of Congress; members of the World Future Society (Washington, D.C., chapter); and participants at national meetings of three organizations, the National Association of Environmental Professionals, the International Association for Impact Assessment, and the American Association for the Advancement of Science.

The groups were asked to rank the top environmental problems by impact and importance. For example, at a workshop of two dozen EPA people involved in research or long-range planning in the environmental field, the individuals gave scores to emerging problems and continuing problems, according to their likelihood and their importance. The firm of J. F. Coates Inc. then integrated the results of the workshop with those of the other workshops and surveys to develop comprehensive, but unranked, lists of the top problems.

The EPA/Coates study concluded that the federal officials were more sophisticated in their analyses than the other participants because, in addition to recognizing the substantive problems, they highlighted critical institutional issues such as management, integration across levels of government, multi-agency communication, communication with Congress, and so forth.

French Survey

The French government conducted a "consultation on environmental trends," a survey of experts in the field. A total of 295 people—most of them in France —responded to an elaborate questionnaire sent to 1,100 people in spring 1982 by the Ministry of Environment and the Ministry of Urban Planning and Housing. The experts surveyed included university professors and researchers, people in industry and agriculture, government officials, consulting firms, associations, and the like.

The respondents were asked to rank, in order of importance, the problems that, in their view, will arouse greatest concern in the future. They were given a list of 20 problems to choose from but could add any others they wished.

The survey and analysis provided a distinction between problems of the "everyday" environment and those associated with the "naturalistic and scientific" concepts of the specialists. In the first category were such issues as safe drinking water, noise, and urban planning; the second category included ecosystem protection, resource depletion, and similar subjects.

Related to this was a second distinction between the perceptions of the experts and those of the community at large, which the respondents were also asked to assess. As the study report summarized it, "According to the experts, the community, too concerned with its lifestyle, does not pay sufficient atten-

tion to the major environmental problems because of a lack of information."[2] It underestimates the importance of such issues as the deterioration of the Third World environment, protection of endangered species, and so forth. The community, in contrast, would "overestimate" the seriousness of such problems as "the cleanliness of cities."

EPA/Michigan Study

The University of Michigan, under a cooperative agreement with EPA, has sought to identify a short list of the most important emerging problems of concern to EPA.

The program included a small survey conducted in 1983 and two workshops, one each in the two previous years. The results were not integrated. For example, the 1981 workshop produced a draft list of 38 problems of widely varying types. The 1983 survey, which included only 10 respondents, identified eight domestic concerns, a number of management concerns, and eight global problems.

Congressional Clearinghouse for the Future Survey

The Congressional Clearinghouse for the Future compiled a comprehensive list of major environmental issues identified by staff members of the committees and subcommittees of the House of Representatives. Called "Environment: The Future Agenda," it linked issues with the 21 subcommittees responsible for dealing with them.

The list noted or briefly discussed several concerns, including a mixture of substantive and institutional, domestic and international, current and emerging problems. They ranged from rural migration to the effects of the expiration of the Clean Air Act, from regional resource conflicts to the future of Antarctica. The study did not evaluate the relative serious-ness of the different issues.

The Conservation Foundation Solicitation

The Conservation Foundation, as part of its preliminary work on this volume, solicited a wide range of people for their opinions on the major environmental issues. Respondents were requested to list issues that were likely to become more important over the next decade and that tended to cut across traditional program and institutional boundaries. Some 500 requests were sent out, with a response rate of about 33 percent. While no attempt was made to select a statistically valid sample, there was an effort to include representatives from different levels of government, the business community, environmental groups, other public interest groups, the press, and research and academic institutions. The questions were open-ended, and respondents could send in as many suggestions as they wished. A relatively high proportion of the responses focused on institutional problems such as inadequate funding and intergovernmental relations.

This chapter is devoted to assessing the results of these surveys and discussing ways of analyzing environmental threats and setting priorities, based on the seriousness, imminence, certainty, controllability, and irreversibility of the threats' effects.

What can one say about the overall results of the six surveys? Is there a consensus on the most dire threats facing society, or even a list of serious problems? There appears to be some rather broad agreement on the most significant and difficult issues. For instance, three problems, broadly defined, appear in all six surveys—chemical contamination, agricultural land losses, and deforestation.

Since the seriousness of a problem is a function of the breadth, as well as the intensity, of its ill effects—that is, the number of people or the extent of the environment affected—it seems logical to rank global or international problems highly. In fact, the survey by the Royal Swedish Academy of Sciences finds 10 top management priorities for the 1980s that generally have international implications—though the most immediate effects typically are local. The 10 issues are:

Management of hazardous chemicals, processes, and wastes
Depletion of tropical forests
Population growth and urbanization
Acid deposition
Species loss
Desertification due to overgrazing
Control of pathogens from human waste and their aquatic vectors
River-basin management

Protection of the marine environment

Fuelwood crisis

In addition, the Swedish study lists 10 priorities for research. Five are the same or virtually the same as the first five management issues in the above list. The other five are cryptic spread of mutant genes, droughts and floods, carbon dioxide buildup and climate change, loss of productive land because of salinization, and insufficient energy for current and future needs.*

EVALUATION

What is the usual approach in deciding which environmental problems are most critical for society to manage? The logical first step is to determine which problems are likely to involve the most hazardous effects. In some cases, however, other factors may dictate against aggressive control of a problem even if it poses a serious risk. The problem may result from activities that are highly valued and cannot be controlled without

---

*The French experts expect the following problems, listed in order of importance, to arouse their greatest concern in the future:

The campaign against waste (using less energy or raw materials)

Drinking-water quality (including health effects)

Protection of the countryside and architectural heritage—conservation of our heritage for future generations (including agricultural lands)

The campaign against environmental degradation in developing countries

The campaign against noise (including health effects)

Reduction of pollutants that are toxic or widespread or that appear in trace quantities

Food quality (including health effects)

Overcoming the problems of the biosphere (hazards linked to changes in climate, the loss of genetic diversity, etc.)

The campaign against classic air and water pollution

Any other qualitative element of growth

In the most recent, small survey under the University of Michigan program, the respondents give the most votes to these 10 issues, in approximate descending order of importance:

Toxics and hazardous-waste management

Groundwater contamination

Acid rain

Loss of agricultural land

Indoor air pollution

Competing uses of water

Declining urban environment

Nuclear-waste disposal

Depletion of forests

Carbon dioxide buildup

eliminating the benefits as well. The problem may be temporary, or it may involve effects that can be remedied.

Then there is the question of whether anything can be done to reduce the risk. In some cases, no remedy exists; in others, the social, economic, or political difficulties are overwhelming.

Assessing the Risk

Risk assessment has been identified as a major problem because of its importance in environmental protection and its difficulty. There is, in fact, much disagreement about how to conduct risk assessments of environmental problems because they often involve great uncertainty about the degree and the nature of the risk as well as highly subjective judgments. This subject is discussed in greater detail in the following chapter.

In some cases, the severity of the environmental effects may be very obvious—an example is desertification in the Sahel region of Africa. But for most problems, there is uncertainty—sometimes extreme uncertainty—about the effects, about the number of people exposed, and even about whether the impacts will occur at all. Opinions differ about the effects of chemicals like dioxin, about nuclear-waste disposal, about acid rain. There are uncertainties about the full impacts of tropical deforestation, oil spills, and population growth. The loss of plant species offers additional illustration. Some tropical plants, for example, have proved to have considerable medicinal value. It seems logical, therefore, to assume that others of similar merit exist in the tropics and are vulnerable to extinction because of widespread deforestation. Yet it is virtually impossible to estimate with any accuracy the number of useful species being lost or their true medicinal values.

The degree of uncertainty grows if a particular condition is not intrinsically dangerous but is capable of causing or exacerbating other problems. A prime example is population growth, which is not necessarily a problem per se but can contribute significantly to resource depletion, pollution, conflict, and so forth. It is impossible, however, to assess the extent of the potential problems—for example, the extent to which food shortages increase the prospect of nuclear conflict.

As noted, another important consideration in assessing a risk is the number of people or the amount of environment likely to suffer. A pervasive threat such as population growth might be considered ahead of a problem like nuclear-waste disposal, which is more severe but threatens fewer people. On the other hand, there are certain environments and perhaps population groups (for example, children) that society may consider particularly valuable. If these are threatened, the risk may be considered serious even though its damage will be limited. Presumably, if two problems are judged to be equivalent in severity and extent, the one more likely to occur deserves a higher priority.

In any case, certain assumptions must be made when characterizing effects and risks. For instance, is nuclear war assumed to be a simple exchange of minor bombs or a broader, more devastating conflict? Is a nuclear-plant accident assumed to be far more damaging than, say, the one at Three Mile Island—perhaps a core meltdown? Further, while a localized event does not warrant the same consideration as a dire, far-reaching threat, a localized event, such as contamination from an abandoned hazardous-waste site, can occur in so many places that it becomes a widespread problem.

Similarly, droughts can be fairly localized or can blight the Sahel, North America, or several continents at the same time. Should risk assessors be concerned about a common drought—the type that occurs annually somewhere with serious but localized effects? What of the drought that occurs once in 100 or 500 years and that is extensive enough and of sufficient duration to severely reduce world food supplies and cause widespread starvation and malnutrition?*

Should problems be assessed in a global or long-term context rather than a domestic or short-term context? For example, one typically thinks of conventional air pollution in terms of the United States and its regulatory problems. But conventional pollutants can plague other developed countries and Third World countries as they are exposed to more industrialization, vehicle emissions, and the like.

The more one attempts to evaluate the seriousness of the problems, the more one runs up against difficulties in defining exactly what the problems are.

---

*Courts in the United States have generally concluded that environmental-impact statements prepared in adherence to the National Environmental Policy Act must include a discussion of the effects of an action under a "worst-case" scenario. For example, the Fifth Circuit U.S. Court of Appeals, assessing the U.S. Army Corps of Engineers' impact statement for a deep-water port at Galveston, Texas, said the corps had wrongly failed to consider the results of a loaded supertanker sinking in Galveston Bay.[2]

The Council on Environmental Quality (CEQ) in 1983 proposed a guidance memorandum for federal agencies advising them to skip the worst-case analyses unless the effects could be considered likely enough to pass a "threshold of probability." After receiving many negative comments, however, CEQ withdrew its proposal.[3]

Another important determination is the *nature* of the effects. Direct impacts on human health clearly rate more serious attention by society than amenities or, except perhaps in extreme cases, ecological stability. A problem that spread famine or disease to a large number of humans would be rated highly. Of the 10 issues on the Swedish list, at least 5 can be said to involve human health directly or indirectly. Eight involve direct or indirect effects on the adequacy of at least one essential human resource—food, water, or energy.

These are some of the primary considerations needed to assess the seriousness of risks. There is no good way to rate or rank them according to a coherent, combined set of criteria. Nevertheless, people often seem to agree on which problems are most serious. This is demonstrated to some extent by the degree of consensus in the six surveys.

Trade-offs

Some risks that seem very serious result from activities that create highly valued benefits. For example, fuelwood used by the Third World poor, for all its unfortunate contributions to ecological degradation, clearly offers immediate benefit to those poor. The discharge of sulfur dioxide, and the resultant fallout of acid rain, is largely caused by the generation of relatively cheap and much-needed electricity. Even the risks of war can be associated with important benefits, such as the preservation of liberty under a democracy.

Problems usually occur as by-products of efforts to obtain benefits—efforts to get critical resources such as water, food, and energy and efforts to make money. Tropical forests are wiped out by subsistence farmers desperate for land and by cattle operators seeking to make money selling to the U.S. hamburger market.

It would be wonderful, of course, if the risks could be eliminated without affecting the benefits. But this is rarely the case; usually, risks must be weighed against benefits.

As individuals, of course, people do this all the time, deciding whether to ski, drive to work, smoke, or do many other activities. But weighing social risks is often very difficult.

People may disagree greatly over whether a product containing a toxic chemical is of substantial or very little benefit to society. Farmers might consider a pesticide to be critical to crop production, while others view it as hardly worth the financial and environmental costs, perhaps because a biological alternative is available. A more complex example is mass migration, such as that from Mexico to the United States. There probably is a fair amount of agreement over the unwanted effects. But some see the benefits as very substantial not only for the Mexicans involved and their families at home but for the economy and well-being of the United States. Others disagree on that point.

The distribution of benefits also may affect how highly people rate problems. The benefits may be broadly distributed among the general population (firewood or electricity), or they may be limited primarily to an individual firm or a small part of the population (as with a toxic chemical made by a single company and needed for a health treatment by only a few people).

Irreversibility and Immediacy

Another consideration is whether or not damages can be reversed if they do occur. Many damages are physically irreversible. An extinct species cannot be replaced. Many direct effects on human health or safety are physically irreversible, for example, mutagenesis, cancer, and starvation. Similarly, a person suffering from a pathogen-caused disease cannot have its effects wiped off the slate.

On the other hand, some problems may be essentially irreversible for institutional—economic, social, or political— reasons, even if technological means are available. Soil erosion, tropical deforestation, and pathogens from human waste are examples of serious problems that seem to be institutionally irreversible. Much of the impact of drought could be alleviated by installing irrigation works in advance—if sufficient water were available for storage. But the economic costs could be prohibitive. The fuelwood and desertification crises could be ameliorated, in theory, by halting overexploitation of these resources, but the countervailing socioeconomic obstacles are enormous, as is the problem of enforcement.

The time factor is important. Overgrazed land, as in the Sahel region, can lead to ecological collapse and starvation—effects that are, for the many people immediately affected, irreversible. But the Sahel region, over a long period of time, probably can be returned to ecological health.

Certain types of damage can be dealt with after they occur; others cannot. Medical care may be able to mitigate the effects of a disease. For instance, squamous-cell and basal-cell skin cancers are relatively easy to treat and rarely fatal, while melanoma, another skin cancer, is difficult to treat and frequently fatal. It, therefore, would seem reasonable to place a higher priority on preventing melanoma.

Remedial efforts, however, tend to be expensive as well as politically difficult to arrange. For example, solving the fuelwood problem—whether by reforestation, energy imports, or furnishing solar or kerosene stoves—would be very difficult to manage both socially and economically. A dollar of prevention usually is worth many dollars of cure.

Preventing problems that entail irreversible damages—whether physical or social—should generally be assessed a higher priority than preventing problems with injurious effects that can be remedied or mitigated.

A final consideration is the immediacy of the threat. Most of the problems cited are occurring now. Others, such as carbon dioxide buildup, are threats in the future. The common reaction is to deal first with those problems nearest at hand. The short-term planning horizon that typically influences political decision making can reinforce this approach. It may make better sense, however, for society to devote more resources to preventing future problems, even if that means postponing the mitigation of existing damages.

Controllability

After all the risks have been evaluated, a problem may appear to be a prime candidate for action yet still end up near the bottom of the list of priorities because nothing can be done to prevent it. Some problems, at least for the present, are technologically uncontrollable. Scientists cannot control mutant genes or prevent drought, earthquakes, hurricanes, and volcanoes. (While heavy downpours cannot be prevented, whether or not they result in damaging floods depends to a great extent on water resources and floodplain management in the area.)

Of course, a problem that already has occurred is no longer controllable. For an existing hazardous-waste dump, it is too late; future dumps, however, can be prevented. And it is often possible, given the desire, to prevent other types of future mistakes such as contamination from a new bioengineering process.

Some situations are essentially uncontrollable for institutional reasons. For example, a well-patrolled electric fence along a border could technologically prevent mass migration but might not be feasible for political, social, or economic reasons (if, for example, the patrolling and fencing would be too expensive). Another likely example is the increasing level of carbon dioxide in the atmosphere. This problem could be controlled by substantially reducing the amount of fossil fuels burned, but the social and economic impacts of such a program would be unacceptable.

In some cases, controllability is reduced because a control system is vulnerable to human fallibility. In strictly technical terms, a nuclear power plant could be made totally safe from serious accident; but a human error in welding, supervision, operation, or some other function could lead to an accident. Furthermore, the threat of sabotage also must be taken into account.

In other cases, human error need not be part of the assessment. For example, tropical deforestation could be prohibited by law and therefore not subject to human error. There is, however, another human element that must be considered: disobedience of the law. Deforestation laws would be rendered ineffective if enough people disobeyed them. Then the problem of control would be institutional (Are there enough enforcement personnel and funds to make control feasible?) rather than technological. In China, for example, population-control regulations are extremely rigorous; yet it is possible that in the long run, they will fail for institutional reasons.

It should be stressed that most problems are susceptible to technological control. Even nuclear war is totally preventable. All that must be done is to stay away from the button, tear out the wires, or remove the warheads from the missiles. And population growth also can be controlled—with pills, intrauterine devices, condoms, and so forth. While aspects of acid rain are sharply disputed, there is fairly wide agreement that a reduction in power-plant sulfur dioxide emissions—which is technologically feasible with scrubbers, use of low-sulfur coal, and so forth—would produce roughly the same reduction in acid deposition.

In some cases, the prime means of preventing or controlling a threat is to dispense with whatever product or activity generates the threat. A toxic chemical might be scratched from production or a very noisy type of airplane might be forbidden to fly.

There are second lines of technological defense. If it is considered dangerous, a chemical in production and distribution can be subjected to strict usage controls. Homes near airports can be soundproofed to protect against noisy overflights, or people can be moved away. But these types of controls, while technologically sound, are somewhat less effective because of problems in implementing them.

In between the clearly preventable and the unpreventable are a number of problems for which technological control could be possible but extremely difficult—desertification, the spread of pathogens, toxic pollution in air and water, carbon dioxide buildup in the atmosphere, and nonpoint-source water pollution, to name a few.

If a threat *cannot* be prevented technologically, there is no need to ask whether prevention is institutionally feasible. Of course, society must select the best ways of ameliorating the effects of an unpreventable problem. In the case of drought, for example, reserves of water can be stored. But if a technological method of prevention is available, its institutional feasibility must then be assessed. Such an assessment typically requires a large measure of subjective judgment.

Consider nuclear war. As noted, it is technologically preventable. Prevention also happens to be virtually free of cost (and could, in fact, have strong positive economic consequences). Other institutional questions, however, are very tricky.

How will relations between the superpowers evolve? What are the prospects for arms control? Will a seemingly minor, faraway confrontation escalate? What are the dangers of general nuclear proliferation around the globe? What are the prospects for adequate inspection and enforcement? Might a nuclear exchange be triggered by a small country's use of a nuclear weapon or by terrorism?

Already noted, too, is the fact that population growth is technologically easy and inexpensive to control. The problems, clearly, are socioeconomic and political—the former because of cultural, religious, and economic factors; the latter because of, say, the reluctance of leaders to push birth-control programs.

For some problems, the economic, social, or political obstacles are not overwhelming; it is just that no institution is capable of doing the job. Unfortunately, this is frequently the case with international problems. Individual nations will not give up authority to an international organization yet, by themselves, can do little or nothing about the problem. And because the costs and benefits of an action are rarely distributed evenly to all countries, there is little incentive for them to act in consort.

A. Maurice Strong, former head of the United Nations Environment Program, speaking at the Swedish conference, said, ''The limits we are beginning to confront today are not primarily physical. They are limits of political and social will and of adequate institutional means to assure careful use of the earth's resources and equitable distribution of benefits and costs resulting from their use.''[4]

A SORTING OUT

Refining and consolidating the results of the six surveys resulted in a list of 47 major environmental issues confronting society. (See box.) It should be quickly noted, however, that any such summary or integration must be loose and arbitrary in several respects, partly because the surveys differ in various ways. Some surveys are oriented to domestic problems, some to global problems, and some to both. Different terminologies are used to describe essentially the same issues. Different surveys use different time frames; some are based largely on present knowledge, while others distinguish between current problems and those problems with the potential for being discovered as more serious; some deal with issues of prime significance up to the year 2000, and some deal with issues not expected to become critical until the next century. Also, the Swedish study distinguishes between research and management problems, but, for many issues, this distinction is difficult to maintain. In distilling the list of 47 problems, this distinction was not made.

In a sense, the list excludes many of the specific problems listed in the surveys. Some problems were particularized aspects of larger problems and were included on the list by implication. Some problems seemed clearly not as serious as the others and were excluded. Some were geographically specific, for example, environmental deterioration in the Third World, threats to Antarctica, mineral development of Alaska, water conflicts in the western United States, Sunbelt growth, and ecological modification of the Southwest. These were not listed because the type of threat involved is covered under broader issues such as firewood depletion, soil erosion, and population growth.*

The problems on the list of 47 fall into four different categories as follows.

Wars, Accidents, and Natural Disasters

This category includes both nuclear and conventional wars, a wide variety of serious accidents, and natural disasters such as volcanoes, droughts, and floods. The damage from many of these is confined to local areas, but some obviously can have severe global consequences—nuclear war (or even a large-scale conventional war) and widespread drought or temperature cooling from short-term or long-term climate change. The largest volcanic eruptions, such as those of Tambora and Krakatau, also have the capability of altering climate over much of the earth's surface.

It should be noted that none of the six surveys discussed here list nuclear war—with its obvious devastating environmental consequences

---

*For the same reason, the "work environment" is not included. It was felt unnecessary to distinguish between the effects of, say, chemical contaminants and noise pollution in the general environment and in the workplace.

47 Issues

Wars, accidents, and natural disasters
Wars
Nuclear accidents, terrorism
Chemical plant explosions
Failure of aging infrastructure (for example, dams, reservoirs, navigation channels, water-supply systems, water-treatment systems, sewers, highways, and bridges)
Intentional weather modification (unintentional effects)
Droughts
Floods
Earthquakes, volcanoes, and other natural disasters
Population growth and distribution
Population growth
Crowding and impacts of urbanization
Sprawl problems
Mass migration, immigration

Contaminants (chemical, physical, and biological)
Radioactive waste disposal (including decommissioning of nuclear power plants)
Debris from space (especially, radioactive debris scattered by satellites reentering the atmosphere
Microwave radiation[a]
Electronic pollution[b]
Solid-waste disposal (including municipal waste management; landfills, incineration, and ocean disposal; sludge disposal or treatment; reduction at the source, resource recovery, and recycling; and littering and city cleanliness)
Noise
Pathogens from human wastes[c]

Proliferation of biological organisms, bioengineering wastes, and mistakes
Genetic mutation[d]
Carbon dioxide accumulation in the atmosphere (caused primarily by deforestation and the burning of fossil fuels; widely expected to absorb much of the solar heat escaping the Earth's surface, thereby making the climate significantly warmer through the "greenhouse effect")
Acid deposition
Depletion of the ozone layer#
Hazardous-waste management
Conventional pollutants, ambient air
Toxic pollutants in air
Indoor air pollution (including carbon monoxide from stoves, heaters, and appliances; formaldehyde insulation; radon gas from building materials; and chemicals in household cleaners)
Conventional pollutants in water, from point sources
Nonpoint-source water pollution (including agricultural runoff of sediment, fertilizers, pesticides, and animal wastes; nonpoint municipal and industrial discharges; acid mine drainage; accelerated runoff from urban streets; storm-water and sewer overflows)
Toxic pollutants in surface water
Groundwater, drinking-water contaminants
Pesticides
Chemical fertilizers
Chemicals in food chains
Natural-resource depletion
Water scarcity

Loss of agricultural land because of salinization, desertification, or urbanization
Soil erosion and overexploitation of agricultural soils
Ocean fisheries depletion
Plant and animal species loss
Energy scarcity
Critical-materials scarcity
Damage to the marine environment (including damage caused by oil spills, ocean dumping, and ocean mining)
Loss of tropical forests
Degradation of coastal areas
Loss of wetlands
Degradation of wilderness areas, parks, and wild and scenic rivers

---

[a] Microwave communications and heating have increased and, with them, the incidence of nonionizing radiation.

[b] Electronic office equipment of various kinds emits ozone from corona discharge. The EPA/Coates study notes, "Exposure to concentrations of 1.0 parts per million causes chronic lung damage to small animals."[1] (See numbered references under box title in chapter references preceding index.)

[c] As noted in the Swedish study, this problem refers to the fact that many pathogens (viruses, bacteria, protozoa, and parasites) leave humans through excretion; contaminate water sources, soils, foods, and other objects; and are then transferred back to humans, where they manifest themselves with a wide range of diseases affecting hundreds of millions of people.[2]

The EPA/Coates study, in suggesting that the problem of viruses in water is likely to have a high priority on future agendas, said, "Biomedical research is revealing a new pattern of diseases associated with viruses. . . . Of particular interest are the slow viruses that may cause disease 20 years or more after they enter the body . . . There is a steady flow of hints that other major and minor public health disorders, such as Alzheimer's disease, are viral in origin."[3]

[d] According to the Swedish report, many chemicals (as well as ionizing radiation) can increase the mutation rate of genes from one form to another: "Mutagenic agents can affect any cell of the body. Mutations occurring in somatic cells may lead to cancer or other degenerative diseases in exposed individuals, and a fetus may have congenital malformations. If mutations occur in a germ cell, however, they may be transmitted to the next generation and give rise to an individual all of whose somatic cells carry the mutant gene. This individual may then transmit the mutant to his offspring and later generations. Thus an increase in mutation rate will lead to an accumulation of harmful mutant genes in the population, and this in turn to increased incidence of hereditary diseases and a decrease in general health and well-being."[4]

[e] Chlorofluorocarbons (used in aerosols, refrigerants, industrial solvents, and so forth) and nitrogen oxides (released by fertilizers) cause destruction of ozone molecules in the stratosphere, thereby depleting the ozone layer that screens the Earth from most of the sun's ultraviolet radiation. The fear is that this could increase skin cancers, harm crops, disrupt the marine ecosystem, and cause climate changes.

—as an environmental issue. This is, of course, chiefly a matter of definition. As explained by Alf Johnels, president of the Royal Swedish Academy of Sciences, the experts gathered for the Swedish survey "recognized that nuclear war, although it is perhaps the primary political issue of our time, cannot be the subject of environmental management as usually defined."[5] Nevertheless, because of the environmental ramifications, nuclear and conventional wars are included here as one of the threats that should be analyzed.

The point about management is important, however. None of the threats in this category is traditionally thought of as an environmental problem. Almost all lie outside the normal responsibilities of environmental agencies. In addition, they typically involve such serious and direct threats to life and safety that the ensuing environmental impacts are of secondary consideration, if they are considered at all. Yet these environmental impacts can be enormous.

A good example is the Vietnam War, which was fought without much appreciation of the overall environmental destruction involved—destruction from bombing, defoliation, and plowing, not to mention the effects of dioxin. As one expert put it, "Vietnam's renewable resource base has been devastated."[6]

Recently, there has been much concern and many expert warnings about the environmental effects of nuclear warfare. But modern conventional warfare can be horrific enough, as World War II, Vietnam, and other conflicts make clear. Said one commentator, "We must not allow our understandable fear of a nuclear war to blind us to the increasingly awesome destructiveness of conventional weapons. Conventional weapons killed 15 million in World War I and over 54 million in World War II."[7]

Another current example of the linkage between war and the environment has been brought up by Russell E. Train, president of the World Wildlife Fund U.S. Train criticized the "extraordinary oversight" of the National Bipartisan Commission on Central America (chaired by Henry Kissinger) which did not include any natural-resource expertise:

It seems clear that the development of a reasonably harmonious relationship between human populations and their natural resource base will be a critical and perhaps even a decisive factor in bringing about political, economic and social stability throughout the Third World. . . . When one looks at El Salvador and its exploding human population, destroyed forests, devastated watersheds, and eroding soils, it is hard not to conclude, as in Haiti, that we have an ecological disaster of major dimensions on our hands and that such an ecological disaster is one of the root problems of the area. I am not so naive as to suggest that a few ecologists can solve the problems of Central America, but I do find it incredible that resource experts are not at least part of the effort to find long-range solutions.[8]

The same theme was sounded by Peter S. Thacher of the World Resources Institute. He said the Kissinger commission report "does not show awareness of the relationship between social inequality on the one hand and misuse of natural resources like land, forests, and water on the other." Pointing to commercial agriculture policies that deprive peasants of lands that are good for crops, Thacher said, "This forces them into higher and steeper areas where they are driven by poverty to clear forests and plant on erosion-prone lands. This, I suggest, is the start of the real 'falling dominos,' whereby deforestation leads to downhill soil erosion, loss of watersheds, siltation, floods, and all of the attendant social and economic hardships, which lead to instabilities that invite foreign intervention of all sorts."[9]

Population Growth and Distribution

Population problems have always been high on the environmentalists' agenda. Population growth, in general, has been perceived as a great underlying cause of other problems and potential problems with disastrous long-run effects—especially the depletion of critical resources such as water, land, and food.

Other long-standing concerns have related to land use and crowding as well as to the possible implications of population growth for economic inequality, loss of freedom, and political conflict—up to and including war.

Over time, new manifestations of the population problem have appeared and grown more serious: mass migration and refugee problems, immigration, population redistribution, crowding, urbanization, and sprawl.

The overall problem of population growth—which shows some limited signs of improvement—clearly will be here for a long time to come, especially considering its built-in momentum and the many years required for stabilization even under the most optimistic estimates of control. The population problem, for all its intractability, is at least readily understandable and measurable. Moreover, it does not threaten, by and large, to present unanticipated ramifications.

Contaminants (Chemical, Physical, and Biological)

The number and variety of contaminants is almost staggering; it is certainly intimidating. Even so, considerable progress has been made in recognizing and controlling some types of contamination. The surveys recognize that in some respects the conventional or "standard" air and water pollutants no longer present the problems they once did or will not remain serious problems much longer. Much has been accomplished in controlling such pollution, at least in developed countries. The traditional contaminants are by no means satisfactorily regulated everywhere, of course; the air pollution in cities like Mexico City is evidence enough of that. Control of point sources of water pollution is another area of success, although the problem of nonpoint sources such as agricultural and urban runoff remains unsolved.

Of course, new manifestations of pollution keep the issue very much alive and can be expected to continue doing so indefinitely. This is partly because of the ubiquitous use of chemicals in modern society, but it also results from knowledge derived from current research on the effects of pollution; from new, sophisticated measuring techniques; and from increased monitoring. In addition, as time goes by, delayed and accumulated effects surface—as with long-buried hazardous wastes that leach out into water supplies or nuclear wastes that proliferate beyond storage capacity.

The picture changes in other, often surprising ways. Indoor air pollution becomes a "new" problem. Pollutants are transformed, or interact, in ways unknown before. They follow paths and pass into different media (air, water, land) in ways that are not well understood. They increasingly cross boundaries—inadvertently in the case of acid rain; deliberately, in the case of pesticides exported to other countries.

Natural-Resource Depletion

Natural resources can be renewable or nonrenewable. But the distinction is not always simple. Consider a water aquifer. It may be renewable in the sense that, even if severely depleted, it will be replenished by surface water. But this process might take so long that, for all practical purposes, it is irrelevant. Similarly, a tropical forest that has been slashed and burned might eventually return to some kind of forest, but the process could take many decades.

In most cases, the loss or degradation of a natural resource is manifest; there is no doubt about what is happening. A land area rendered infertile because of salinity is clear to behold, as is a mountain denuded of its fuelwood or an aquifer contaminated. However, the full implications of such losses can be hard to understand. For example, the ominous long-term consequences of tropical deforestation, soil erosion, and water depletion still have not been fully assessed. It seems clear, however, that problems of natural-resource impoverishment, already serious, generally are getting worse, considering the increasing demands generated by population growth and rising material expectations.

INSTITUTIONAL PROBLEMS

The issues discussed so far are substantive problems—for example, the effects of acid rain and what methods of control are available. They do not involve the political difficulties of reaching international or interstate agreements on a solution or meeting the costs of control. Institutional problems—including their political, social, and economic aspects—clearly can be more daunting than anything else. In addition, institutional factors can cause or contribute to substantive environmental problems. For example, political-economic action by the OPEC oil cartel had much to do with the momentous energy scarcity of recent years.

Indeed, some survey respondents rated institutional problems as more serious than many of the threats in the substantive categories. There are four general types of institutional concerns.

Underlying Conditions and Constraints

Some survey respondents seemed concerned that underlying economic, social, and political conditions prevent society from coming to grips with environmental problems. Many of these conditions result from basic inequities—the unequal distribution of wealth, influence, natural resources, environmental quality, and environmental damage, both within the United States and internationally. These inequities are problems in themselves; they may interfere with efforts to defuse some environmental threats if they intensify social and political polarization. One specific equity problem is that victims of environmental degradation typically are not compensated for the injuries or losses they suffer.

Or consider a poor country that is ill equipped to deal either with its own environmental problems or those exported by others. This is at the heart of the long-standing "North-South" political struggle between developed and developing countries.

Some survey respondents also emphasized the need for providing the public with a better understanding of environmental threats. Yet, while some respondents thought the problem was too little knowledge, others worried about the confusion and "hysteria" resulting from "information overload."

Ability to Identify Issues

A second concern relates to the ability of existing institutions and programs to identify clearly the important issues. This concern grows in part, from inadequate monitoring and research and the resulting lack of information. Without basic information, the responsible institutions have difficulty determining how serious a problem is, what its causes are, and what should be done to control it. Survey respondents cited the new awareness of acid rain and other long-range pollution transport problems as evidence of this knowledge gap.

Respondents also expressed concern about the ability—and sometimes the willingness—of agencies to properly assess the seriousness of various threats. Inconsistent risk assessment and inadequate technology assessment both fell into this category.

Ability to Implement Programs Effectively

A third area of concern involves the capacity of existing political systems to respond to problems. Survey respondents were most strongly concerned about global and international problems because of conflicts among nations and the instability of many Third World governments. However, a number of respondents mentioned problems and disputes involving intergovernmental relations in the United States, particularly in terms of political and economic changes that have occurred during the past four years.

In other words, can agencies implement control programs even after they have decided to take action? What can be done to prevent discord among different levels of government and different governmental functions from impeding effective program implementation?

Other factors identified as hamstringing programs were inadequate resources, the difficulty government agencies have in attracting and retaining good staff, and a general lack of good leadership. Respondents frequently cited inadequate enforcement as an implementation problem.

Efficiency

Worries over the efficiency of current programs were almost as frequent as concerns about their effectiveness. Some specific concerns included the need to coordinate environmental programs with economic and social goals, to develop more efficient systems for allocating scarce natural resources among potential users, and to modify traditional regulatory approaches to allow more cost-effective responses.

A specific problem is the need to develop efficient procedures for siting unpopular facilities—for instance, hazardous-waste sites, radioactive-waste facilities, and new industrial plants. Although no one wants these near them, they have to be sited somewhere. Existing institutions, fragmented as they are, seem unable to make these decisions.

The concern about making such decisions efficiently seems to have triggered an interest in modifying the way decisions are made. Are there alternatives to the common approach of confrontation and litigation? What of increased reliance on negotiation and mediation?

SOME FINAL THOUGHTS

The most serious environmental problems probably are the global or international ones. Their effects are, by definition, widespread; they affect more people and more, larger ecosystems. They are apt to be less manageable financially and politically. They are likely to be ignored by domestic agencies like EPA, while international institutions for dealing with the problems typically are weak, if they exist at all.

Clearly, society has not been very astute in anticipating problems so far. In some ways, this is not surprising. It would have been difficult indeed to foretell the complex transformation and transportation of chemicals in the atmosphere that has given us not just local emissions of sulfur dioxide but distant deposition of acid rain. In other ways, however, society's relative blindness is perplexing. For one reason or another, it was a well-kept secret that huge volumes of chemical wastes stored and dumped indiscriminately had an obvious potential to come back and haunt society.

Clearly, it is important to develop better foresight capability and to build up the institutions that might be able to provide it.

Far from failing to anticipate problems, society sometimes ignores problems that are already here. Joseph F. Coates, president of J. F. Coates Inc., says that, while everyone is greatly concerned about chemical pollution, no one worries about noise—"yet the likelihood of damage is far higher from noise than from chemicals." Exposure to loud rock-and-roll music is a prime example of rampant, damaging noise. 'It's a pure and simple matter of denial,'' says Coates.[10] Of course, there is also massive denial of the hazards of smoking.

Another example is the distraction of romance, says Coates. "The romance of fireplaces and stoves has blinded people to the tremendous environmental stresses of burning wood."

Few problems are likely to be ignored altogether. But some deserve special emphasis and this emphasis should not be allowed to induce a complacency in society toward lesser but still serious threats. Some observers regard "issues overload" as a substantial problem. But it can be dangerous to use the lack of funds and manpower as an excuse for neglecting the less immediate or less threatening problems. There are so many uncertainties, that it is difficult to be sure that a problem relegated to the bottom of the list may not in fact turn out later to be a prime threat.

Interactions between humans and their environment are complex and unpredictable. They are full of surprises and synergistic effects. It can be argued, therefore, that society must find the wherewithal to understand and protect itself simultaneously from all serious and potentially serious dangers, and to do so even when it is impossible to achieve a consensus for action.

John Naisbitt, author of the popular book *Megatrends*, says, "Societies, like individuals, can handle only so many concerns at one time. . . . A person can keep only so many problems and concerns in his or her head or heart at any one time. If new problems or concerns are introduced, some existing ones are given up."[11]

While there is truth in this, it seems far from the whole truth. Naisbitt illustrates his reasoning with the concept that the amount of space a newspaper devotes to news is pretty much constant, for economic reasons; therefore, if a new issue gains "market share," another issue must lose it. (Naisbitt says that when the amount of space allocated to environmental problems accelerated dramatically, news about civil rights was forced to yield a comparable amount of space.)

Newspaper coverage, of course, does not tell us everything that is going on, though it may be a decent measure of public concern. And the fuel of public concern typically is necessary to drive the engines of research and reform. Also, the comparison of society and an individual is not entirely valid. Society is made up of many individuals, and many individuals can handle many problems simultaneously. And they do, regardless of whether or not their efforts are publicized in newspapers.

David J. Rose, a professor of engineering at the Massachusetts Institute of Technology, has written of "selective inattention" and its counterpart, "selective attention." In the case of selective inattention, people who are faced with "the complexities and paradoxes of real problems . . . selectively ignore vital aspects and concentrate on only one or a few simple features, as if those were the whole."[12]

Rose said, "Civilizations grow and collapse partly as a result of this selective attention or inattention, a combination of chance and social purpose." Perhaps it should be added that selective inattention can involve whole issues as well as details of a particular issue. A civilization or society could collapse if it concentrated too much on certain environmental problems while selectively ignoring others.

General or selective inattention can result from apathy or feelings of hopelessness. These, in turn, can be caused by public perceptions that there is a depressingly long list of problems without real solutions. But invariably there are solutions. And there have been a good many environmental successes. Complacency and lack of attention and funding—these are perhaps the most dangerous underlying issues of all.

FURTHER READING

A variety of reports and studies provide more or less comprehensive digests of the major pending environmental issues, either global, domestic, or both. Some of these reports are:

Center for the Study of Social Policy, *Assessment of Future National and International Problem Areas*, Vol. 1, prepared for National Science Foundation (Washington, D.C.: U.S. Government Printing Office, 1977).

"EPA Memorandum and List of Candidate Priorities for Agency Activities in Fiscal 1985," *Environment Reporter—Current Developments*, September 30, 1983, p. 942.

Global Tomorrow Coalition, "Action Packet" (Washington, D.C.: Global Tomorrow Coalition, 1983).

International Union for Conservation of Nature, *World Conservation Strategy* (Ann Arbor: UNIPUB, 1980).

U.S. Congress, House, Committee on Science and Technology, *Survey of Science and Technology Issues Present and Future*, Staff Report, 97th Congress, 1st sess., June 1981.

U.S. Environmental Protection Agency, Research and Development, *Research Outlook 1983* (Washington, D.C.: U.S. Environmental Protection Agency, February 1983).

Chapter 5

Risk Assessment and Risk Control

Is the manufacture of toxic chemical X to be permitted or prohibited? Should nuclear power plant Y be built? What about requiring air bags in automobiles or limiting smoking areas in office buildings? Does a town need to increase the size of its police force? How much of a worry are the threats to the world's climate? What should be done about the threatened extinction of rare animal species?

These questions have at least one thing in common: answering them requires an assessment of risk. The methods used by government to perform risk assessments have drawn greatly increased attention in the past several years, which is not surprising. The results can lead to decisions on how strictly to protect public health or the environment. They can lead to regulations that require the expenditure of hundreds of millions of dollars or threaten the viability of entire industries.

Government today is being asked to control many more risks than it was asked to control in the past. Also, the types of risks it is attempting to control are more varied and more difficult to assess. Less is known about the nature of these risks, and there may be no way to control them without creating serious economic effects, interfering with different social goals, or imposing other, perhaps more serious, risks on society.

Some participants in the debate over risk assessment have taken extreme positions. At one end are those who argue that no formal risk assessment should be conducted prior to a regulatory decision because society already knows there is a risk and that risk should simply be eliminated. At the other extreme are those who argue that before any regulation, assessment should be undertaken until the nature and extent of the risk are clarified beyond any doubt—that is, dead bodies and smoking guns must be discovered.

This chapter rejects such extreme positions. Rather it assumes that: (1) the government will continue to be asked to control a large variety of possible risks; (2) decisions about these risks will have to be made under conditions of substantial uncertainty; and (3) some process of risk assessment by government is necessary to ensure that any actions taken are reasonable and, in fact, are likely to result in the betterment of society.

Under these assumptions, questions like the following arise: Which risks should be assessed? How is their seriousness to be gauged? What are the roles of science, values, politics, and public perceptions in the risk-assessment process? And, most fundamentally, how can risk assessment contribute to public policy decisions?

It would take several large volumes to explore these questions fully. (Indeed, several of these volumes have already been written: see the section on further reading at the end of this chapter.) The purpose of this chapter is not to formally answer all of them but, rather, to provide the reader with a better understanding of risk-assessment issues.

The Changing Nature of Risks

One of the primary functions of government is to protect its citizens against certain kinds of risks. Police offer protection against risks to life and property; armies, against the risk of foreign invasion; government engineers, against the risks of floods. Over time, however, government has been asked to control a growing number and greater range of risks, not only those involving immediate danger to health and safety. There are programs that offer protection against economic risks, against risks to the stability of the environment, to the survival of individual species of animals, and, indeed, to the entire range of conditions and activities that contribute to the quality of life.

In these cases, and many others, some form of risk assessment is necessary before the government acts. In the past, many risks seemed so obvious that no formal analysis was required—a reasonably clear understanding existed of what the risks were and what needed to be done to control them. Now this is seldom true. The risks of an exploding boiler are much clearer than those that may, or may not, be associated with the use of a pervasive chemical such as formaldehyde or benzene.

The basic logic underlying risk assessment is essentially the same for all types of activity. The focus here is primarily on assessing risks to public health, particularly those risks linked to the release of chemical substances into the environment. There are at least three reasons for this focus:

Boilers versus Carcinogens

The following comments by Donald Kennedy are excerpted from a speech to the 22d Annual Education Conference, Food and Drug Law Institute, Washington, D.C., December 5, 1978. Kennedy was, at that time, a commissioner of the U.S. Food and Drug Administration:

The way we regulate the complex and refractory must, unfortunately, differ from the way in which we regulate the comparatively straightforward.

To show you what I mean, let me refer you to the very first federal regulatory agency.

That agency—the Steamboat Inspection Service—was founded in 1836. It was called into being to address a specific problem: exploding boilers on steamboats. This was what one might call an unequivocal problem. Boilers exploded, or they did not. Given the explicit nature of explosions, the results were inescapable: there was noise, fire, usually followed quite rapidly by the lapping of water around one's ankles. I hope you don't take it as an extreme statement if I say that people detested having the boilers on their steamboats explode. There was no constituency that favored, let's say from motives of overwhelming ennui, the excitement that followed your run-of-the-mill boiler explosion. No one had organized the survivors into a committee for freedom of choice. And the causes of these unfortunate occurrences were well understood: too much steam pressure unfairly competing with inferior types of iron and copper boilers. Indeed, even private enterprise saw clearly that one might anticipate a larger passenger revenue if people were given some assurance that a trip to New Orleans might not terminate unexpectedly in the middle of the Mississippi River, causing one to miss all kinds of connections with the not unlikely exception of that with one's maker.

So, there we have the father of federal regulation, just oozing common sense.

Today, people fear cancer more than, I imagine, our floating ancestors feared boiler explosions. But we do not have a single agency dealing in a comparatively straightforward way with the problem. Nor are we aware of the initiation of the carcinogenic process; we are not really certain how it happens; we do not by any means have a complete inventory of the environmental causes; we do not understand the matrix of reactions between outer and inner environment; we understand practically nothing about interaction among carcinogens and co-carcinogens, potentiation of carcinogens by other substances, and a host of other complex problems of this nature; nor do we have any real proof about threshold or linearity, and if we did we could not be sure that your threshold was the same as mine due to differences in genetic background and our inventory of habits, bad and good.

public health is the arena in which much of the current controversy over risk assessment is played out; the assessment of chemical risks starkly defines most of the principles and issues involved in all risk assessment; and assessing the potential risks of chemicals in the environment is inherently important.

Only for the past 15 to 20 years have industrial societies worried about the possibility of increased risk of cancer from environmental pollutants and from chemicals. Before about 1965, the major hazards from water pollution were considered to be its threats to fish and wildlife; in the case of air pollution and occupational exposures, concern focused on "acute" health effects—that is, those effects manifest within a few minutes or at most a few days. Rarely were chemicals tested for their potential to cause cancer, birth defects, genetic changes, or other "chronic" health effects. Now, concern over possible chronic adverse health effects is the primary rationale for controlling environmental pollutants. Since the early 1970s, most proposed federal regulations to limit exposure to chemicals have been based on grounds that the chemical is a carcinogen.

Earlier, it had been generally agreed that if "conventional" pollutants, that is, a half dozen air pollutants (the "criteria" pollutants) and a similar number of water pollutants (fecal coliform, suspended solids, biochemical oxygen demand, nitrogen, and phosphorus), were successfully controlled, there would be no pollution problem. However, once chronic health effects became the focus of concern, the universe of pollutants exploded. Hundreds of chemicals and metals are now or have been candidates for regulatory action. These pollutants, the so-called toxic substances, are found in all parts of the environment—air, water, and land—and often in very small amounts compared with the conventional pollutants.

The large number of toxic substances, their ubiquity in the environment in very small amounts, and their potential for causing chronic health effects make more explicit risk assessment an important part of regulatory decision making. Deciding which chemicals to regulate, at what levels, and where in the environment requires a careful effort to define not only the various risks involved but also the benefits of the chemicals to society.

Trade-offs Required

For many toxic substances, there seems to be no threshold exposure level below which no adverse effects will occur. That is, exposure to *any* amount of the substance may involve some degree of risk. Advances in the ability to detect chemicals at extremely low levels have forced regulators and citizens alike to come to grips with the implications of a "zero threshold." One implication is that exposure to toxics is so widespread and, in fact, inevitable in an industrialized society, that zero risk is not an attainable goal. The risk from some individual toxic substances may be reduced to zero—for example, by banning them—but eliminating all risks from toxics is not feasible.[1]

There are risks associated with taking regulatory action as well as with not taking action. Nuclear power plants, even if designed, constructed, and operated with the utmost of care, pose some small but finite risk; eliminating this risk by banning such plants would result in more electricity being generated by coal-fired power plants, which also create risks. Banning nitrites from food would increase the risk of botulism or might lead to substitution of another chemical with risks of its own. In these cases, therefore, eliminating the source of the problem would not eliminate all risk; it would change the nature of the risk and might even result in a more serious threat.

Moreover, it is necessary to trade off risks against such social values as economic growth. The need for these trade-offs has been reinforced by the poor performance of most Western economies in recent years.

For these reasons, making trade-offs is critical to assessing and controlling risks. And it increases the amount of information required. However, while the need for information increases, current knowledge about the specific nature and magnitude of risks remains woefully inadequate.

Pervasive Uncertainty

Virtually all elements of risk assessment are clouded with uncertainty, basically of two kinds. First, the various scientific disciplines involved in assessing risk are not sufficiently developed either to explain the mechanisms by which particular causes produce particular effects or to provide good quantitative estimates of cause-and-effect relationships. Second, the data needed to analyze particular risks are usually not available. Typically, it is not known how many people are, or will be, exposed to a hazard, how much of a toxic substance will be present in a specific part of the environment, how a new technology will perform in practice, or how much it actually would cost to reduce a given hazard by a given amount of money.

The pervasive uncertainty about risks and risk reduction has, somewhat ironically, reinforced the importance of risk assessment and intensified the emphasis on it. Much risk-assessment methodology involves decision rules for dealing with uncertainty. Because the process relies so heavily on assumptions and guesswork, it is particularly important that all steps be clearly documented. Only in this way can an assessment's credibility rest on some base other than the reputation of the risk assessor.

In the face of scientific uncertainty and inadequate data, some interested parties magically invoke the term *risk assessment* in an effort to bring authority and confidence to an uncertain process. (The term *cost-benefit analysis* was similarly invoked several years ago.) Insofar as it focuses attention on an important field of study and leads to improvements in methodology, this is useful. However, to the extent that it deludes politicians or the public into thinking that the analytical process of risk assessment can eliminate the need for more scientific knowledge or more adequate data, it leads to misplaced confidence and false expectations of certainty. The use and misuse of the term *risk assessment* make its careful definition particularly important.

Some Definitions

Risk Assessment

As the popularity of the term *risk assessment* has increased, varied interpretations of its meaning have proliferated. At one extreme, the term is used loosely to encompass all of the societal functions related to risk, from identification that a risk exists to implementation of risk-reduction measures. At the other extreme, the term has been limited to embrace only the methods used to quantitatively extrapolate human cancer risks from toxicological studies on animals.*

Risk assessment is defined here as *the process of determining the adverse consequences that may result from the use of a technology or some other action.* A risk assessment typically includes three principal elements: (1) an estimate of the probability of a hazard** occurring; (2) a determination of the types of hazard posed; and (3) an estimate

---

* In the literature, all of the terminology related to the field of analyzing, assessing, managing, and controlling risk is in a state of almost hopeless confusion. As just one example, a number of researchers have defined *risk analysis* as one component of *risk assessment*, while a recent National Research Council committee defined *risk assessment* as a component of *risk analysis*. And Congress, in the proposed Risk Analysis Research and Demonstration Act of 1982 (H.R. 6159), identified *risk assessment* and *risk evaluation* as the two components of a risk analysis, and then rather inconsistently called *comparative risk analysis* a procedure for risk evaluation.

** The use of the terms *hazard* and *risk* is also confused and inconsistent in the literature. Generally, in the United States *hazard* means the nature and likelihood

of the number of people, wildlife, or other environmental elements likely to be exposed to the hazard and the number likely to suffer adverse consequences. The different elements of this definition of risk assessment (which is the same as that used by the National Academy of Sciences in a recent report[2]) are indicated in figure 5.1. Although the definition was first developed in studies assessing the risks of toxic substances, it is broadly applicable to other types of risks as well.

Risk assessment can be used for several different purposes—to establish priorities for further risk assessment or for research; to help inform the public about risks; and, as part of the regulatory process, to help decide which risks should be regulated and what the content of the regulations should be. A determination of the actions needed to control a risk is not part of risk assessment but of what is called *risk management*.

Risk Management

Risk management encompasses all of the actions taken to affect a risk. First comes a decision on whether any actions are necessary and, if so, what the actions should be. These decisions must be based not only on *measurements of risks* but also on *judgments about their acceptability*—"a matter of personal and social value judgment."[3] Implementation of decisions and evaluation of their effect are also part of risk management.

Risk-management decisions are always grounded in some sort of risk assessment, although this may be no more than a decision maker's implicit assumption about the seriousness of the risk. However, as discussed in greater detail later in this chapter, a risk-management decision requires consideration of a number of factors in addition to the nature of the risk itself.

---

of an adverse effect, and *risk* includes the likely magnitude of the effect, that is, measuring the risk of a chemical includes not only its inherent toxicity (its hazard) but also the number of people likely to be exposed to it. In Europe the terms are usually used in the reverse way, with *hazard* meaning what *risk* does in the United States. See, for example, The Royal Society, *Risk Assessement* (London, The Royal Society, 1983), p. 22. For an examination of U.S. and European approaches to risk control, see Sam Gusman et al., *Public Policy for Chemicals* (Washington, D.C.: The Conservation Foundation, 1980).

Figure 5.1
Elements of Risk Assessment and Risk Management

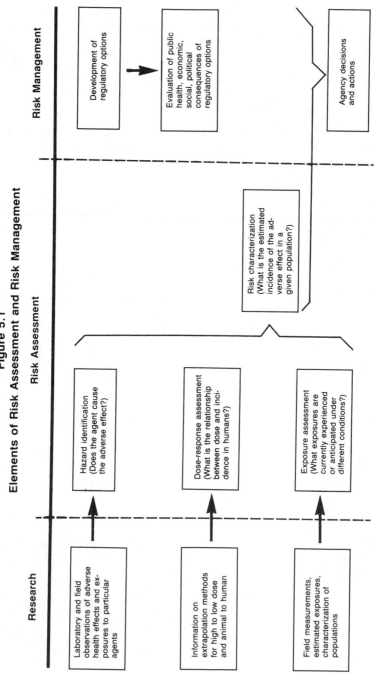

Source: National Research Council.

Priority Setting

Far more potential risks exist than can ever be thoroughly assessed, and usually there are more risks assessed than can be considered for management action, at least for action by the government. Thus, setting priorities for both risk assessment and risk management is a crucial and inescapable element in the process of risk control.

Yet priority setting usually is not explicitly examined. In discussions of risk control, the implicit assumption is made that the agenda is rational and that all appropriate chemicals or other types of risks are on it. There have been very few examinations of how risks actually get on the government's agenda.[4]

Risk Control

No generally accepted term describes the entire process—priority setting, risk assessment, and risk management—for dealing with risk. This chapter uses the term *risk control* (which is not meant to imply that positive actions can or should be taken to control all possible risks) to characterize the process.

The three elements of risk control are more interactive than sequential. Although a risk must get on the agenda before it is assessed, the agenda itself is based on some comparative evaluations of risks. Similarly, although risk management depends on some form of risk assessment, exposure is a key element of risk assessment, and the amount of exposure is determined by risk-management decisions. A rough and intuitive assessment may put a risk on the agenda for a more elaborate assessment; the more elaborate assessment may then result in a decision to reduce the risk, and that decision may in turn result in a still more elaborate and sophisticated assessment. Thus, each of the three elements of risk control may be repeated several times in varying forms during the course of deciding what to do about a particular risk.

PRIORITY SETTING: WHICH RISKS SHOULD GOVERNMENT ASSESS?

Any government agency involved in risk control will likely face a larger number of potential risks than it can effectively work on at any one time. Thus, one of the most critical questions an agency must answer is, Which risks will it deal with first? There is, however, little agreement on how priorities should be established and only limited understanding of how they actually are established.

How the Agenda Is Set

Scientists might be expected to be the key actors in setting priorities, and scientific discoveries to be the driving force in changing the agenda. In many situations, especially where the priority-setting process has been routinized, scientists do play the leading role in initial decisions about which hazards to assess. For example, under the U.S. Toxic Substances Control Act (TSCA), an interagency committee, composed primarily of agency scientists, has responsibility for recommending to the federal Environmental Protection Agency (EPA) which existing chemicals industry should be required to test.[5] The agency is supposed to decide within a limited time whether it will issue regulations requiring the testing of nominated chemicals. Although in many cases EPA has rejected particular committee suggestions, the committee nonetheless basically has determined the agenda for testing existing chemicals under TSCA.

Once an initial assessment has been made by scientists from government, academia, or industry, the role of scientific information in setting the agenda rapidly diminishes. The risk-management agenda of a regulatory agency is prone to be influenced more by lawsuits or the daily press than by scientific journals or panels. And the risk-management agenda, in turn, becomes a dominant factor in establishing the risk-assessment agenda, because if an agency is considering regulating a risk, it likely will want more information about and analysis of that risk.

As one report puts it, "Scientific evidence of harmful health effects does not in and of itself explain why some chemicals are regulated and others are not." Based on case studies of five chemicals, the report concludes that, at least for these cases, "union and public concern over harmed workers distinguishes the regulated from unregulated substances."[6]

Pressures from nongovernmental groups may be particularly influential on agencies that have not established adequate internal priority-setting mechanisms. The Occupational Safety and Health Administration (OSHA) is a case in point. A recent article notes: "OSHA's absolute interpretation of its mandate to protect and its consequent resistance to quantitative methods and cost considerations has militated against its considering any mechanisms for choosing and ranking regulatory candidates. Although OSHA has mustered scientific evidence to show a health risk, the agency has never formally compared one risk to another to target the worst."[7]

Sometimes Congress or a court establishes a partial agenda. Under TSCA, for instance, Congress instructed EPA to restrict the manufacture and use of PCBs (polychlorinated biphenyls) within one year and gave the agency authority to regulate any of the other 60,000 chemicals currently in commerce.[8] The agency began at once to regulate PCBs but has taken only a few actions on other existing chemicals in the nearly eight years since the statute was enacted.

An environmental group, the courts, and Congress established an agenda for controlling toxic discharges under the Clean Water Act. The Natural Resources Defense Council (NRDC) felt that EPA was not doing all it should to promulgate regulations governing discharges of toxic effluents as required by the act. In 1975, NRDC sued EPA. This led to a court-approved agreement that contained a detailed timetable for issuing the regulations and lists of the toxic substances and industries to be covered.[9] Congress later incorporated this agreement into the 1977 amendments to the law. The agency is currently issuing effluent guidelines to implement these requirements.[10] In this way, an organized public, not a panel of scientific experts or even the responsible agency, established the priorities for risk management.

The experience with hazardous air emissions illustrates the problems an agency can have in defining priorities even when it makes an explicit attempt to do so. In 1977, EPA focused on a list of 37 air pollutants to determine which, if any, were potentially hazardous. In 1981, however, EPA contracted with Argonne National Laboratory to develop a revised method for ranking air pollutants, and only 18 of the original candidates were in the first 37 ranked by Argonne.[11]

In recent years those charged with setting priorities have agreed on one standard—that chemicals or processes believed to cause cancer be given the highest ranking. In many regulatory programs, such as the one for pesticides, the focus on carcinogens has dominated all other health and environmental concerns. Of the 76 pesticides reviewed by EPA for possible cancellation of their registration (the "rebuttable presumption against registration" process), 62 had their registration questioned on grounds that they might be carcinogens. Most of the others were suspected of being mutagens, and thus were also under some suspicion of being carcinogens.[12] How does an assessor evaluate the validity of this priority?

A variety of measures can be used to compare the relative importance or significance of a disease or adverse effect. The simplest measure is the number of deaths it causes. By this measure, cancer ranks second only to heart disease.[13] But simply counting deaths does not take into account the age at which death occurs. The number of years of potential life lost is important because society generally values the life of a 25 year old more highly than the life of a person who is 90. By this measure, cancer and heart disease lead all other causes, together accounting for almost half of all potential years of life lost.[14] A number of other measures could be used, such as workdays lost, number of days of hospital use accounted for by the disease, and economic cost to society.

A different kind of measure, but a crucial one in the context of agenda setting, is the degree of public concern about various diseases. At least since 1939, the public has consistently ranked cancer as the disease it dreads most.[15]

Thus, by many measures the priority accorded to reducing the incidence of cancer is rational. But in ranking risks, how can the importance of cancer be compared with other threats—mutagenicity, for instance? Genetic changes affect individuals from the time of birth and can be passed to future generations. But the extent to which mutagenicity is really a problem is unknown: How many individuals are affected, what are the causes of genetic changes, or how does one assess adverse effects actually resulting from genetic changes? In comparing cancer to mutagenicity, a known, dread disease is compared with a problem that science, at the present time, is unable to explain satisfactorily.

The present risk-assessment agenda probably is not, and may never be, thoroughly rational. There are many agendas and differing definitions of what constitutes a rational agenda. At most, society can evaluate the processes used to set priorities and hope that if the processes become more rational, the results will also.

What Factors Should Determine Priorities?

Criticizing existing priority-setting systems is easy, but designing a better system is hard. One might suppose that the ideal system would employ an independent group of scientists to sift through all available information on relative risks and then to rank the risks in a preferred order of assessment. Although such a scheme sounds attractive, it probably is neither possible nor desirable.

There is no way, for example, to reach even a crude estimate of the relative risk of each of the more than 60,000 chemicals now used in the United States. And any judgment on the extent or severity of risk posed by a particular chemical depends on assumptions about the number of people exposed and the intensity and duration of that exposure. These factors, in turn, depend upon assumptions about how and to what extent the substance is used or misused.[16]

As an official of the Materials Transportation Bureau in the Department of Transportation stated, "You can take isolated pieces of our business and apply risk analysis—specific commodity, specific containment system, specific pathway—and the minute you change any one of those three things, that risk analysis is gone. So what I'm dealing with here is not billions, but trillions of permutations. And nobody has shown me the methodology to be applied generally."[17]

The concept of a purely scientific assignment of priorities runs into other problems. One is that alternative scientific methodologies for ranking risks may produce quite different results.[18] Yet there may be no sound scientific basis for choosing from among these methodologies. The choice of methodology, therefore, is a policy, rather than a scientific, question.

Likewise, science provides no means of comparing and ranking essentially incommensurate types of risks. For instance, how does the risk of 100 people contracting lung cancer compare with the risk of 50 deformed births, or the risk of 1,000 injuries resulting from automobile accidents to the risk of two fish species becoming extinct? But these are exactly the types of risks that somehow must be compared when setting priorities.

Risk assessment also may be discouraged by some who see it as a means of imposing elitist views on the public. One investigator interviewed workers exposed to hazardous chemicals in various occupations and found that, "while scientific assessment could enhance regulatory decisions, our interviews suggested that workers are not likely to accept risks solely on the basis of expert risk-benefit calculations. They believe that risks cannot be objectively measured and balanced, that personal dangers must be avoided at any cost. They want a greater voice in decisions that may affect their health."[19] Although these findings apply primarily to risk management, rather than risk assessment, they indicate that opinions other than those based on pure science need to be considered when setting priorities.

Public Perception of Risk

How the public perceives a risk can be an important consideration when setting priorities. Studies of this issue reveal that there are systematic biases in the public's estimates of the degree of risk from given causes.

As figure 5.2 shows, the public does correctly perceive the approximate rank order of various causes of death. However, the public is often incorrect—sometimes by two orders of magnitude—when asked to estimate the actual number of deaths from a particular cause. For example, according to the data in the figure, the public estimates that several hundred people die each year from botulism poisoning, whereas the actual number is fewer than five. At the other end of the scale, the public estimates that deaths from all diseases total 100,000 per year, whereas the actual figure is more than a million. In general, the public overestimates the number of deaths from rare, dramatic risks and underestimates the number from common, undramatic causes.

The public's factual errors in quantifying various risks may have little to do with how serious it considers those risks to be. There are many other, less quantifiable aspects of risk besides the number of deaths or injuries, and there is some evidence that these are important determinants of the public's views. For example, in one study, samples of both students and members of the League of Women Voters gave nuclear power the lowest fatality estimate of 30 activities and technologies but rated it as the highest perceived risk.[20]

The study found that the public's rating of risks can be explained mostly by two underlying sets of risk characteristics. The first, which the study termed *unknown risk*, applies to risks that are new, unknown, involuntary, and delayed in their effects. The second, *dread risk*, is associated with events whose consequences are seen as certain to be fatal, often for large numbers of people. These characteristics help to explain why the public considers some technologies, such as nuclear power, more risky than the experts consider them.

Relative Risk

Public subjectivity notwithstanding, a key factor in judging the priority and acceptability of a given risk is how it compares to other risks. Sometimes the comparison is explicit, sometimes not. But like most aspects of risk assessment and decision making, weighing relative risks is not a simple matter.

One method compares the risk in question to a similar risk that occurs naturally. This is in part the basis for U.S. radiation exposure standards, which limit increases in radiation exposure from human activities to some percentage of natural background radiation.[21]

A more common method is to compare the seriousness of different sources of risk that exist in modern industrial society. Such an analysis

Figure 5.2
Public Perception of U.S. Annual Death Rates from Selected Causes

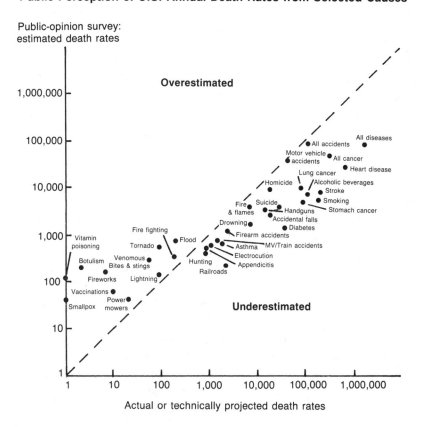

Source: Edward V. Lawless, and Paul Slovic, Baruch Fischhoff, and Sarah Lichtenstein.

can be used to focus attention on serious risks or to pull attention away from risks that, by comparison, appear minor.

Although these comparisons can be useful, they are not straightforward. How should sources of risk be categorized—all accidents together or just automobile accidents or just automobile accidents caused by mechanical failure? The risk of using a particular chemical may seem small compared with the risk from all accidents but large compared with the risk of automobile accidents caused by mechanical failure. In what units should risk be measured—lives saved, years of life saved, lives and injuries combined? Should aspects of risk that are important to the public—such as whether the risk is undertaken voluntarily—be taken into account? The answers to such questions will have a major effect on the outcome of any comparison among risks. For example, using only lives lost as the basis of comparison would equate 1,000 accidents each causing only one death with one accident that caused 1,000 deaths. However, it is clear that society is much more concerned about the one accident that would cause 1,000 deaths.

The data used to compare risks are likely to be highly uncertain. One expert, attempting to fit into a single framework a variety of risk estimates from different sources, finds wide disparities in the estimates made by different people for the same risk. For example, the probability of premature death from a motorcycle accident was estimated to be 3.5 chances in 100,000 by one source and 1,800 chances in 100,000 by a different source. Similarly wide ranges were found for many other types of risk.[22]

Another difficulty is that a comparison of risks has many limitations as a method for judging the acceptability of a given risk. Risk comparison ignores the benefits derived from the risk-creating technology. It tends to assume that risks endured in the present or past are acceptable, a proposition that would certainly be disputed by many. And it fails to deal with the cumulative impact of many small risks.[23]

Controllability

Another nonscientific consideration in establishing priorities is the feasibility of controlling a risk, even if it is serious. If a government agency can do nothing to prevent or reduce the risk, why should the agency devote valuable resources to assessing it?

Some risks—for instance, volcanic eruptions—cannot be prevented. Even if such eruptions were a major source of air pollution, there would be little reason for an air-pollution-control agency to assign them a high

EDB

EDB (ethylene dibromide) is an organic chemical currently used as an additive in leaded gasoline and as a pesticide. Its use as a gasoline additive to prevent lead deposits in car engines began in the late 1920s. It was first registered under the Federal Insecticide, Fungicide and Rodenticide Act as a pesticide in 1948 and, until the recent bans and restrictions, was widely used to kill nematodes (roundworms) and soil insects.[1]

Until those constraints were enacted, approximately 300 million pounds of EDB were used in the United States each year.[2] About 13 million pounds were used in soil-treatment applications before crops were planted, and 7 million pounds were devoted to other insect-control uses.[3] Almost all the rest (more than 90 percent) continues to be used as an antiknock agent in leaded gasoline.[4]

In 1956, EDB was exempted from Food and Drug Administration regulations on pesticides in food because it was believed that EDB would not leave residues in food.[5] In 1974, preliminary results from a National Cancer Institute (NCI) study reported EDB to be a powerful carcinogen, causing cancer in laboratory animals.[6]

However, it took almost 10 years from the time that study was completed until the federal government took any effective regulatory action to limit the uses of EDB. Part of the delay was due to questions about the NCI study, so that additional testing was necessary, but part also was due to the reluctance of the government to take regulatory action.

What put EDB on the priority agenda for the federal government was action by the state of Florida. In 1983, EDB was discovered in Florida groundwater, and the state began a recall of food products found to contain EDB at the minimal detectable level of 1 part per billion.[7] Florida's action received a great deal of press attention and prompted action by the U.S. Environmental Protection Agency (EPA) and a number of other states.

In September 1983, EPA issued an emergency ban on the use of EDB in soil and ordered the phase-out of certain fruit and vegetable fumigation uses by September 1984.[8] EPA took no action to deal with the use of EDB in leaded gasoline, in part on the grounds that, because leaded gasoline was being phased out, this use of EDB eventually would be halted without additional regulation.

EPA also set safety guidelines for the amount of EDB allowable in food products. Massachusetts, Maine, and New York set more stringent standards than the federal guidelines, each of them different. Those states and four others forbade the presence of any amount of EDB in baby foods. The patchwork of standards resulted in food products pulled from grocery shelves in states with stringent EDB restrictions being redistributed in states that had adopted the federal standards or that were not aggressively testing for EDB residues.[9]

Most of the substitutes for EDB as a pesticide potentially pose health risks as significant as EDB's. The most commonly used substitute for fumigating citrus fruit, for example, is methyl bromide. Some evidence exists that methyl bromide also may be a carcinogen and may pose various other hazards as well.[10]

The EDB case is, in many respects, typical. Although some scientific evidence of its risks existed for many years, an incident that the federal government had nothing to do with put it on the federal government's risk-management agenda. For a short time, the chemical received a great deal of press attention, which resulted in a variety of uncoordinated actions being taken. In light of ignorance about the substitutes for the chemical, as well as uncertainties about the risk of EDB itself, it is not clear to what extent restricting the use of EDB will actually reduce risks to human health.

priority for risk assessment. (This would not necessarily be true for an emergency response agency, which would want to know the volcanoes most likely to erupt and how violently in order to plan evacuation and rescue operations efficiently.)

This points to a second factor affecting controllability: Does an agency have the legal authority to take action on a risk? If not, the agency probably would assign a low priority to a risk assessment. For example, the risks from indoor air pollution have not been adequately assessed because no agency has a clear legal mandate to regulate the problem. In some cases, control responsibility will belong to other agencies. But the point is that any risk will have different priorities for different agencies depending upon their legal mandates.

Social, political, or economic reasons may explain why a risk cannot be controlled and, therefore, does not rate as an urgent priority. Smoking is probably the best example. Although there is broad agreement that smoking is the greatest single health risk in American society today, it is not high on the government's risk-management agenda. The unhappy precedent of liquor prohibition (and also of narcotic drug prohibition) has revealed all too clearly the difficulty of trying to regulate the personal habits of people.

The economic benefits of a technology or product also may influence its priority on the agenda. For example, the benefits of the automobile are considered so valued by the public that attempts to assess or control the associated risks are often foiled. EPA discovered this when it tried, for pollution-control reasons, to impose transportation-control plans on selected cities. It encountered overwhelming opposition from Congress and citizens.[24] Offsetting this factor is the knowledge that widespread benefits may be associated with widespread exposure: the more people who use a product and benefit from it, the more who are exposed to its potential hazards. For example, the widespread use of artificial sweeteners explains both the large effort mounted to assess their risks and the controversy surrounding the regulatory decisions on saccharin and aspartame.

Both the comparative ease with which an activity can be regulated and the benefits derived from the activity are closely related to the political strength of the forces with an interest in a risk-producing activity. Government agencies and even academic scientists may be reluctant to face the political risks of trying to control the health or environmental risks from a product supported by powerful interests in society. Thus, the political, economic, or social constraints can be just as intractable as the technological ones.

International Implications of the Risk Assessment Agenda

Decisions in the United States about which risks the government should deal with influence the priorities established by most other countries in the world. (The effect of U.S. priorities on those of the Soviet Union and the Eastern European countries is not clear.) Very few developing nations have the scientific and administrative capacity to identify environmental health risks. Even the capacity and interest of many of the developed nations are quite limited. To a remarkable degree, the U.S. agenda is the world's agenda.

In a few important cases, another country has identified a risk and led the United States to make it a national priority. Mercury and cadmium assumed importance as environmental problems in the United States in part because of work done by Swedish researchers.[25] The Swedes and Canadians were the first to identify and analyze the acid rain problem. An incident in Japan involving food contamination by PCBs, and subsequent research by Japanese scientists, led the United States to focus attention on PCB contamination.[26]

It is likely that the agenda-setting process for chemicals will become increasingly international in the future. The Organization for Economic Cooperation and Development (OECD), which includes most of the noncommunist developed countries, is attempting to establish a framework for setting priorities for assessing the risks of existing chemicals. If the OECD effort comes to fruition, it may lead to a formal international agenda for chemical risk assessment.

Of the many examples of international cooperation today, there is the United Nations Environment Program, which established an International Register of Potentially Toxic Chemicals (IRPTC). The register provides information on the effects of individual chemicals and also on national regulations pertaining to them.[27] The IRPTC may become the vehicle for international exchange and dissemination of the results of chemical risk assessments. The International Institute for Applied Systems Analysis, an international research institute for scholars from both communist and noncommunist countries, has done extensive research assessing the risks from various forms of energy generation.[28]

COMPONENTS OF A RISK ASSESSMENT

A complete risk assessment is composed of three interrelated but conceptually separate components. First comes an assessment of the probability that the risk-causing event will actually occur. While some threats seem certain to occur or are occurring already, others have not and require that some estimate of their likelihood be made.

The second component is a determination of the anticipated effects of the event if it occurs and *if* people or the environment are exposed to the risk. This component is frequently termed *hazard assessment*. It involves identifying the types of danger inherent in a chemical, a technology, or a form of behavior, and the severity of those dangers. Thus, for a chemical, a hazard assessment includes a determination of the health or environmental effects the chemical is capable of causing and the potency of the chemical in relation to each of its effects. For example, can the chemical cause cancer; if so, how strong a carcinogen is it compared to other chemicals?

The third component is an estimate of the amount of exposure that will result if the risk-producing event takes place. This includes an estimate of the number of people (or portion of environment) exposed, the intensity and duration of the exposure, and the extent to which particularly sensitive segments of the population or environment will be exposed.

The Probability of the Event Occurring

In many risk assessments a key step is calculating the probability that an event which creates risk will occur—that a plant component will malfunction, that a girder on a bridge will snap, or that war will be declared. This step is not as relevant for risk assessment of chemicals, especially when chronic hazards are involved, because chronic hazards usually result from exposure to a chemical over a long time rather than from a discrete event.

The probability can be estimated in two ways: actuarially and statistically. Actuarial probabilities are assigned to risks on the basis of previous experience with the same situation. A good example is the way an insurance company estimates the chance of someone having a car accident. Its estimate is based on voluminous data on the frequency of auto accidents, perhaps including such factors as the sex and age of the driver, previous driving record, and how the vehicle is used. An insurance company will combine these data with information on accident costs and then establish insurance rates—a very explicit result of risk assessment.

Statistical probabilities are based not on actual experience but on statistical models that suggest how such a risk would be realized. This approach must be used to assess the risks associated with new technologies. When there is not enough experience with the technology to support an actuarial assessment, engineers and ''systems analysts'' must try to identify everything that could go wrong, the probability of each of these failures occurring, and then the probability of various combinations of them taking place. Some of the early work in this field was performed for the nation's program to land a person on the moon. It involved estimating the likelihood of different types of mechanical failures that would interfere with the mission. Where the probability of failure was too high, the design was modified or backup systems were installed to reduce the risk to an "acceptable" level.

Perhaps the best-known statistical analysis of an environmental and public health risk is the Rasmussen study published in 1975 by the U.S. Nuclear Regulatory Commission (NRC).[29] It was the most extensive study of potential nuclear power plant hazards ever conducted; it involved an exhaustive analysis of permutations and combinations of engineering failures. However, a high-level committee convened by the NRC to review the Rasmussen report found that it was "inscrutable, and that it [was] very difficult to follow the detailed thread of any calculation through the report."[30] While the committee approved the basic methodology used in the report, it stated that, "We are unable to define whether the overall probability of a core melt given in WASH-1400 [the Rasmussen report] is high or low, but we are certain that the error bands are understated. We cannot say by how much. Reasons for this include an inadequate data base, a poor statistical treatment, an inconsistent propagation of uncertainties throughout the calculation, etc."[31]

Both statistical and actuarial probabilities are only that— probabilities—and thus either can be misleading when applied to specific cases. Generally, actuarial probabilities are more reliable than statistical probabilities because they are based on experience. But the fact that there is an average of one fatality per 36-million miles driven[32] does not mean that you will not be in a fatal accident when you drive half a mile to buy some milk. Had an actuarial assessment of the risk of a serious accident in a nuclear power plant been completed the day before the Three Mile Island accident, the report would have concluded that the likelihood of such an accident was extremely small, if not close to zero.

Hazard Assessment

Assessing the hazards associated with a technology or an event may be relatively straightforward. This is so if the link between exposure and effect is very clear (the hazard, for example, of burns from a defective electrical cord).

For many of the risks that the government is currently attempting to control, however, neither the nature nor the potency of the hazard is clear. Perhaps the link between exposure and effect is indirect, or perhaps there is no empirical evidence about the effects of exposure. In these cases, the hazard assessment can become a very complicated process, and the accuracy of the assessment may be very uncertain.

Methods for Assessing Hazards

There are many methods for assessing hazards (figure 5.3). When it comes to details, probably no two assessments use exactly the same methodology. A number of techniques for assessing engineering and chemical hazards are well developed, although all have numerous shortcomings. Methods for assessing hazards to the natural environment are less well developed.

It is generally agreed that the more an assessment can be based on empirical evidence of effects on people or environments exposed to the hazard, the better the assessment will be. Thus, the strongest evidence of a chemical's toxicity is actual toxic effects experienced by people exposed to the substance. Laboratory studies of humans cannot be used to detect severe hazards, such as death or cancer, for obvious ethical reasons. But tests that do not cause permanent damage sometimes can be useful in assessing, for example, an air pollutant's interference with respiratory functions.

In many cases, the only empirical evidence available about effects on humans comes from statistical analyses, usually epidemiological studies, of human populations actually exposed to the hazard. A group of people that suffers from a common disease or disability can be examined to find the cause; or a group that has been exposed to a suspected hazard (a chemical, a life-style habit, a technology) is examined for signs of excessive susceptibility to some disease or disability.

Epidemiological studies may take a long time to complete; they are expensive; and they are very difficult, often impossible, to conduct properly. Accurate data about the extent or intensity of exposure are usually not available; it may be impossible to pinpoint a single cause from among all the potential causes; and it is frequently hard to identify an appropriate control group that permits an estimate of whether the disability rate in the exposed population is unusually high. In addition to these problems, very large numbers of people must be studied to obtain information adequate for regulation.

For example, when attacking a proposed Consumer Product Safety Commission (CPSC) ban on urea-formaldehyde foam, the formaldehyde

Figure 5.3
Methods and Techniques for Forecasting and Hazard Assessment

Analogies

    Barometric (indicator) analysis
    Case studies
    Historical comparisons
    Horizontal information flow
    Human/societal needs/desires appraisal
    Tort liability analysis
    Structure-property correlations
    Structure-activity correlations
    Substitution forecasting
    Technosocial similarities search

Trend analysis

    Simple extrapolation
    Trend projection
    Time series analysis
    Curve fitting
    Statistical modeling
    Box-Jenkins pattern recognition
    Substitution curves

Probabilistic approaches

    Actuarial data analysis
    Bayesian statistics
    Epidemiological methods
    Carcinogen acceptable-dose
      calculations
    Markov steady-state analysis
    Monte Carlo simulation
    Sensitivity/parametric analysis

Tracing and cause-effect methods

    Econometric modeling
    Event tree analysis
    Fault tree analysis
    Feedback loop analysis
    Input-output analysis
    Relevance tree analysis

Simulation methods

    Panel testing
    Physical modeling
    Role playing/moot court
    Structural modeling
    Surrogate testing
    Toxicological testing/interspecies
      extrapolation

Survey methods

    Authority opinion
    Brainstorming
    Checklists
    Conjecture
    Delphi technique
    Monitoring (e.g., media interest,
      legislation, environmental quality)
    Panel survey
    Public preferences
    Synectics

Holistic methods

    Alternative futures
    Decision and policy-science methods
    Divergence mapping
    Morphological analysis
    Scenario construction
    Values forecasting

Source: Edward V. Lawless, and Paul Slovic, Baruch Fischhoff, and Sarah Lichtenstein.

industry placed some importance on epidemiological studies that show no significant increase in the number of cancers among workers exposed to formaldehyde. But the 11 epidemiological studies introduced in court by the industry covered a total of only 10,000 workers, while the CPSC ban was based on a risk of one case of cancer for every 20,000 people exposed. Thus, there was no conflict between the CPSC's estimate of risk and the negative epidemiological studies, because the studies did not cover enough people to challenge the CPSC estimate.[33] Epidemiological studies that show a positive correlation are usually given more weight than those failing to show such a relationship because it is more likely that epidemiological studies will err on the side of not showing a cause-effect relationship.

If the empirical data are insufficient, a hazard assessment must be based on some other type of evidence or analysis. For instance, the hazard posed by a core meltdown in a nuclear power plant can be assessed only by a theoretical engineering analyis of what is liable to happen under certain circumstances combined with a medical and biological assessment of plausible health and environmental effects.

In the absence of direct evidence from human experience, the standard method for determining whether a chemical can cause cancer is a long-term animal study, known as a bioassay. Such a study, which involves feeding very high doses of the chemical to 100 or more rats or mice for approximately two years, is difficult to conduct properly and can cost as much as $1 million. Despite these obstacles, most scientists agree with the Office of Technology Assessment (OTA) that ''a substantial body of experimentally derived knowledge and the preponderance of expert opinion support the conclusion that testing of chemicals in laboratory animals provides reliable information about carcinogenicity.''[34]

Short-term studies on animals long have been used to determine the acute (short-term) toxicity of chemicals. Within the past decade, a number of studies also have been developed for ascertaining whether a chemical can pose chronic hazards, such as mutagenicity. Many of the short-term tests for chronic effects use bacteria, yeast, or cultured cells to indicate if a chemical can provoke a specific effect.

The reliability of short-term tests in determining the likelihood of chronic hazards in humans has generated great controversy. Such tests are now commonly used by both government and industry as screening devices to decide whether further testing should be done. Their low cost (compared to long-term animal studies) provides a major incentive for developing new short-term testing schemes.

When even short-term test results are not available, a chemical's molecular structure may be compared with that of other chemicals for some indication of potential hazards. For example, some categories of structurally similar chemicals (aromatic amines, for instance) are known to contain a high proportion of potential carcinogens. But comparisons based on molecular structure can provide only a very rough indication of hazard. OTA cites the example of the chemical 2-acetylaminofluorene, a known carcinogen, and the very closely related 4-acetylaminofluorene, which, based on all available evidence, is *not* a carcinogen.[35]

Physical characteristics of a chemical also can be important indicators of hazard. The Japanese government, when it establishes regulatory priorities, emphasizes the persistence of a chemical in the environment.[36] Chemicals that do not degrade rapidly or that can accumulate in humans or animals result in greater exposure and thus greater risk.

Generally, at present, evidence from structural analysis is considered weaker than evidence from short-term tests; evidence from short-term tests is considered weaker than evidence from bioassays; and evidence from bioassays is considered weaker than epidemiological evidence. The problem is that assessment can be based only on the available data, and the information available is often from the weaker end of the scale.

Assessments of hazards to the natural environment are even more difficult to make than assessments of human health hazards because environmental assessments are apt to involve a wide variety of hazards and to engage numerous scientific disciplines. Environmental hazards can range from threats to a particular species of plant or animal to changes in the upper atmosphere that affect climate. Among many relevant academic disciplines, the science of ecology potentially could be the most useful and could provide an integrated framework for assessing natural hazards. But ecology is not sufficiently developed to serve these functions well. One report summarizes the situation with the comment, "environmental assessments may, at times, require much more data than a health effects assessment, yet provide an answer that is more tenuous or at least less quantitative."[37]

Probabilities and Hazards

Hazard assessment involves still other problems. In many cases, there is some probability that a person or environment exposed to a hazard will not actually suffer the predicted effect. Toxic chemical hazards again provide some clear examples.

The sensitivity of individuals to a health hazard usually varies substantially throughout a population. Only some people catch the cold going around the office. More than 25 percent of Europe's population in the 14th century survived the plague even though virtually everyone was exposed.[38] In the same way, only some persons contract cancer or other ill effects as a result of chemical hazards. Scientists know very little about the reasons for these differences. Even in animal bioassays that use only pure strains of a test animal (that is, all the test animals are bred to be as nearly identical as possible), only some of the animals develop tumors. Much greater variations can be expected in the heterogeneous human population.

To predict the probability of a chemical causing cancer in humans, analysts use techniques based on animal bioassays. These methods are very controversial. If animal studies show no significant increase in the cancer rate of the exposed animals, then it is assumed that the chemical will not cause cancer in humans. But if a study shows a significant increase, the question remains, What is the probable cancer rate in the human population attributable to the chemical?

The estimation of human cancer risks from bioassays involves two basic steps: extrapolating from the test animal (usually rats or mice) to humans and extrapolating from the high doses used in the bioassay to the low doses to which humans are typically exposed. High doses are used in the bioassays to offset the comparatively small number of animals tested. If the attempt is to detect a risk of one cancer in 100,000 or in 1 million by using only a few hundred animals, it is necessary to use high doses of the substance under study.

Both steps in the extrapolation from bioassays are subject to controversy because, within limits, scientific knowledge is not well enough developed to certify what method is the correct one to use. Which statistical models to use to extrapolate from high doses to low ones is especially controversial. A number of statistical models have been developed, and some of these models have been discarded as scientists learn more about the mechanism of cancer causation in humans. But at least four or five of the models are consistent with scientific knowledge about cancer causation, and each model produces quite different results. Thus, the choice of model can make a significant difference in the outcome (and thus in what regulatory action, if any, is taken), but there is no scientific basis for selecting one model over another.

In choosing a dose-response extrapolation model, as well as in making other decisions affecting human health, some regulatory agencies argue for the use of "worst-case" assumptions—in other words, models or decisions that predict the highest probability of the hazard occurring.[39]

This may produce regulatory decisions that err on the side of preventing adverse effects rather than on the side of preventing unnecessary control expenditures. In 1983, three separate federal court decisions held that government agencies must refrain from spraying certain herbicides pending completion of a worst-case analysis of the health risks.[40]

Others, frequently the groups that have to pay the initial cost of reducing the hazard, argue that the worst-case approach is unscientific because it fails to make the best use of available information. Like so many aspects of risk assessment, the resolution of this controversy must be essentially a political decision about how much risk is acceptable and how much society is willing to pay to reduce it.

Exposure

Most of the disputes over risk assessment center on estimating the probability of an event or on evaluating the hazards created by the event. Determinations about actual exposure, however, are equally important and, if anything, even tougher to assess. Estimating exposure involves a complex definition of the number of people exposed, the level or degree of their exposure, the relevant characteristics of those exposed, the route by which they are exposed, and the effect that exposure to other hazards might have on the risk of the hazard under examination.[41]

Gauging exposure is difficult because of both the number of factors to consider and the general lack of information. Even for existing risks, information about the number of people exposed and the degree of their exposure is rarely adequate. In the case of chemicals, large manufacturers usually keep records of workers exposed to possible hazards, but data on the level of exposure to particular chemicals usually are not precise.

Taking steps to prevent harm from hazards contained in food (such as food additives or pesticides) requires knowing how much of a given type of food is eaten by those people exposed to the hazard. Yet figures on typical food-consumption patterns are imprecise, and even if they were accurate, researchers still would need to know the range and the highest levels of consumption to estimate risk. To regulate a pesticide used on citrus fruit, for example, the officials would want to know not only how many oranges a typical person eats but also how many people eat a large number of oranges, because the latter group would be the population at greatest risk. To estimate the risk from a nuclear attack, the analyst would need to know not only where the bombs would drop but also, among other things, which way the wind would blow and

Zero Risk from Natural Disasters?

Many processes in nature, although normally benign, may at random or unpredictable times produce extremes that carry substantial risks. Examples are earthquakes, volcanoes, fires, pest and disease outbreaks, floods, and droughts. Planning to deal with natural disasters involves an important element of risk assessment.

If one does plan, the question becomes, *for what* is one planning? Droughts come in diverse shapes and sizes. Managers typically take a conservative approach and plan to take on the largest known disaster—the so-called 100-year flood or drought of record. For example, water systems are designed, at least in theory, so that their "safe yield"—the amount of water they can be expected to deliver under the worst conditions ever experienced—is at least equal to the anticipated demand.

Obviously, planning for the worst conditions ever recorded is useful only if the record is both accurate and long enough to have captured nature's most unusual extremes. But even if the records are good, they suffer simply from being mere empirical descriptions of random events. Flood recurrence intervals are based solely on experience; a flood so great as to be expected only once in 100 years becomes a 50-year flood if it is exceeded by the discharges of the 101st year. Northeastern water systems designed to provide adequate water under Dust Bowl conditions seemed fine until the mid-1960s drought exceeded that of the 1930s both in severity and duration. If climate or other factors underlying natural disasters are changing, using data stretching many years into the past may be folly rather than prudence. And of course, even if plans are adequate for dealing with one worst-case event, there is every reason to believe that from time to time two such disasters will occur back-to-back.

The worst conceivable case is limited, of course, only by an ability to conceive. It may seem desirable to protect the public from the worst disaster that can be imagined, but protection carries costs. Is it worthwhile to forgo development of an area because it is expected to be inundated every 200 years? Every 100? Every 10? Must all water uses continue uninterrupted no matter how severe a drought?

Water-supply capacity sufficient for the drought of record is by definition well over capacity nearly all the time. Considering the dollars spent, the economic opportunities forgone, and the environmental damage perpetrated when building water systems (especially dams and reservoirs), does it make sense to try to protect against all drought? It may be more reasonable to plan for relatively frequent droughts while recognizing that truly severe ones will inevitably cause harm and dislocations. The challenge then becomes to devise management strategies that mitigate the damage—such as ensuring water supplies for critical uses, preparing phased and equitable conservation steps, and aiding those most seriously affected.

Such an approach seems just as reasonable as the present practice of arbitrarily planning for the worst, and it can result in substantial savings. For example, several jurisdictions in the Washington, D.C., metropolitan area now are coordinating their water use, and are basing their planning on accepting a 5 percent risk of not being able to meet the normal demand for water. When normal demand cannot be met from existing supplies, a variety of water-conservation measures will be instituted.[1] This scheme eliminates, for the foreseeable future, a previously identified "need" for new dams to provide water in drought years.

whether it was day, when people were at work, or night, when they were home.

One of the most important exposure factors—although one that only rarely can be calculated with any precision—is which populations are most sensitive to the hazard and the extent to which these populations are likely to be exposed. Some regulatory laws mandate the protection of sensitive populations. For example, Clean Air Act provisions regarding promulgation of primary air-quality standards have been interpreted to require consideration of the impact of pollutants on "sensitive or susceptible individuals or groups."[42] Although an adequate risk assessment needs some consideration of particularly sensitive populations, any governmental mandate to protect all sensitive people probably cannot be implemented short of a total prohibition of the pollutant or activity in question. In the case of air pollution, people with asthma are more sensitive than the general population. People who have both asthma and weak hearts are more sensitive still. For heavy smokers with asthma and weak hearts, any pollution at all may pose a significant risk.

Exposure to multiple hazards often results in portions of a population becoming more sensitive to any single hazard. We are all exposed to a wide variety of hazards—from food, from smoking, from industrial pollutants, from driving and flying. Some hazards are "antagonistic"—that is, the effect of one hazard cancels out or mitigates the effect of another. But in many cases the hazards are "synergistic"—one hazard increases the risk from another. Workers who smoke are far more likely to get cancer from asbestos than workers who do not.[43] Exposure to both excess particulates and sulfur oxides is more likely to be harmful than exposure to either air pollutant by itself.[44] Exposure to synergistic hazards greatly complicates a risk assessment because most assessments focus on a single hazard. Similarly, the cumulative effect of many individual hazards poses major difficulties for risk assessment because it is difficult enough to assess an individual hazard without trying to account for the interactions among many hazards.

The task of estimating exposure is complicated not only by the number of hazards but by their sources. As shown in the cross-media chapter of this report, a person can be exposed to a single hazard from multiple sources. Exposure to lead, for example, can come from air, food, and water. A parallel problem arises when different people are exposed to the same hazard at various stages in the processing or handling sequence. One group of workers may be exposed to a chemical when it is first produced, a second group when the chemical is incorporated into a product, and a third group (including consumers) when the product is used. Assessments of the total risk of exposure must take into account each of these sources and each of these stages.

These controversial aspects of exposure analysis are apparent in the diverse methodologies of studies comparing the risks of different electricity-generating techniques. Some analyses consider the full chain of risks, from mining the fuel to consuming the electricity. Others consider only the risks associated with generating the power, as in coal-fired or nuclear plants. The two types of analysis may produce different conclusions about which forms of electricity generation are safer.[45]

The same difficulties exist when assessing hazards to natural systems. For example, any single stress on a wildlife population or an ecosystem may not be sufficient, by itself, to cause major damage. But when one stress combines with other stresses, the result can alter dramatically.

Uncertainty and Values

Pervasive uncertainty is one of the fundamental characteristics of many risk assessments. The analyst may be uncertain how often, if ever, the event creating the risk will occur, how serious the hazard is, and how many people will be exposed. Frequently, personal or policy value judgments must substitute for certainty.

One of the most important weaknesses, and the one hardest to detect, is that analysts may ignore some of the potential hazards, either because they overlook hazards, they think hazards are unimportant, or they shy away from hazards that are difficult to assess. The scope of a risk assessment often predetermines its conclusion about the seriousness of the risk.

Examples of bias or inadequate problem definition are, unfortunately, easy to find. For instance, the International Institute for Applied Systems Analysis reviewed a series of studies of the risk from liquid natural gas (LNG) facilities. None of the studies examined the hazard from deliberate sabotage of LNG facilities, even though such hazard must be considered real given current world conditions.[46] Another example is provided by the chemical industry, which for many years determined the safety of a chemical only on the basis of acute toxic effects. Chronic hazards, such as cancer, mutagenicity, or sterility, were simply not considered in hazard assessments. Nor were chronic hazards considered by the scientific and regulatory communities.

Another pervasive problem in hazard assessment arises from the inadequacy of scientific knowledge to provide clear methods for appraising certain types of hazard, especially the cancer hazards of chemicals. A committee of the National Research Council identified 50 separate components, or decision-points, in a typical risk assessment for carcinogenicity. It found no scientific consensus about how to deal with many of these components: "Policy considerations inevitably affect, and perhaps determine, some of the choices."[47] The committee concluded that "the choices encountered in risk assessment rest, to various degrees, on a mixture of scientific fact and consensus, on informed scientific judgment, and on policy determinations."[48]

The impact that such choices have on risk estimates is illustrated by a study of perchloroethylene (PCE), a solvent used in dry cleaning. The study looked at three crucial steps in assessing the risks of cancer from PCE—the choice of which test animal to use (mice or rats), the choice of methodology for extrapolating from animals to humans (by body surface area or body weight), and the choice of a dose-response model (linear or quadratic) to extrapolate risk from high doses of the chemical to low doses. For none of these choices is the state of scientific knowledge sufficient to offer guidance as to which option should be picked. If the risk assessment used mice, surface area extrapolation, and a linear model, the risk from PCE was assessed to be 347 cancer cases annually. If the assessment used rats, body weight extrapolation, and a quadratic model, the risk was assessed to be 0.01 cancer cases annually.[49] Thus a set of choices for which science could provide little or no guidance changed the assessment of risk by a factor of approximately 35,000.

If the major choices about the conduct of risk assessments, at least for cancer, are left exclusively to scientists, then much will depend on the institutional affiliation and personal values of the scientists doing the assessment. A recent study of 136 scientists shows consistent and systematic differences among scientists affiliated with industry, government, and universities.[50] For example, although 80 percent of industry scientists agreed that thresholds exist for carcinogens, only 60 percent of the academic scientists and only 37 percent of the government scientists agreed. Similarly, the majority of government (69 percent) and academic (52 percent) scientists agreed that "a substance which is shown conclusively to cause tumors in experimental animals should be considered a carcinogen, thereby posing a risk to humans."[51] Only 27 percent of the industry scientists agreed.

Like most human endeavors, risk assessment is as much art or philosophy as science. However, an explicit and quantitative assessment lets society see and weigh the limitations of the technique. An intuitive assessment of risk, based only on the instincts of a scientist, engineer, or decision maker, is likely to have more problems and limitations, and the problems and limitations will be less visible.

Scientific versus Legal Standards of Proof

When examining risk assessments made in a regulatory context, a scientific determination of what constitutes a hazard requires a different type and degree of proof from a legal determination. Scientists do not have to make decisions; they can wait patiently for added evidence and certainty. A regulator, however, cannot wait. A regulator must decide to regulate or not regulate. Waiting for more evidence is, in reality, a decision not to regulate.

The tension between science and regulation is most apparent in assessing cancer hazards. For most toxicologists, a chemical is not a human carcinogen until epidemiological evidence proves that it has caused cancer in humans. The International Agency for Research on Cancer (IARC) has stated that "at the present time a correlation between carcinogenicity in animals and possible human risk cannot be made on a scientific basis, but rather only pragmatically, with the intent of helping regulatory agencies in making decisions related to the primary prevention of cancer."[52] For most regulators, delaying regulation until direct evidence proves a chemical causes human cancer would be irresponsible. Appropriate evidence from animal studies must be considered a sufficient basis for regulating a chemical as a human carcinogen.[53]

Most scientists express the evidence about a chemical in terms of the *probability* that it is a carcinogen. Regulators translate probabilities into certainties because they need to make decisions and defend them. This is nicely illustrated by the decision-making scheme for regulating toxic air pollutants used by the state of Michigan (figure 5.4). This approach begins with an absolute yes-no decision about whether a substance is a carcinogen. In general, regulators are reluctant to reveal the probabilities that their findings are correct, in part out of fear that a reviewing court will strike down any conclusion based on less than certainty.

Not coincidentally, the public view is similar to that of the regulators. The public does not have a good grasp of the meaning of probabilities. It tends to demand certainty. As one study put it, "They [the public] want statements of fact, not probability."[54]

The public's view is stimulated and encouraged by the popular press, which tends to have little tolerance for the complexities and uncertainties of scientific explanations. Thus, the courts' need for certainty about risk, as perceived by the regulators, is reinforced by pressures from the public and the press.

Figure 5.4
Michigan Decision Tree for Processing Permits

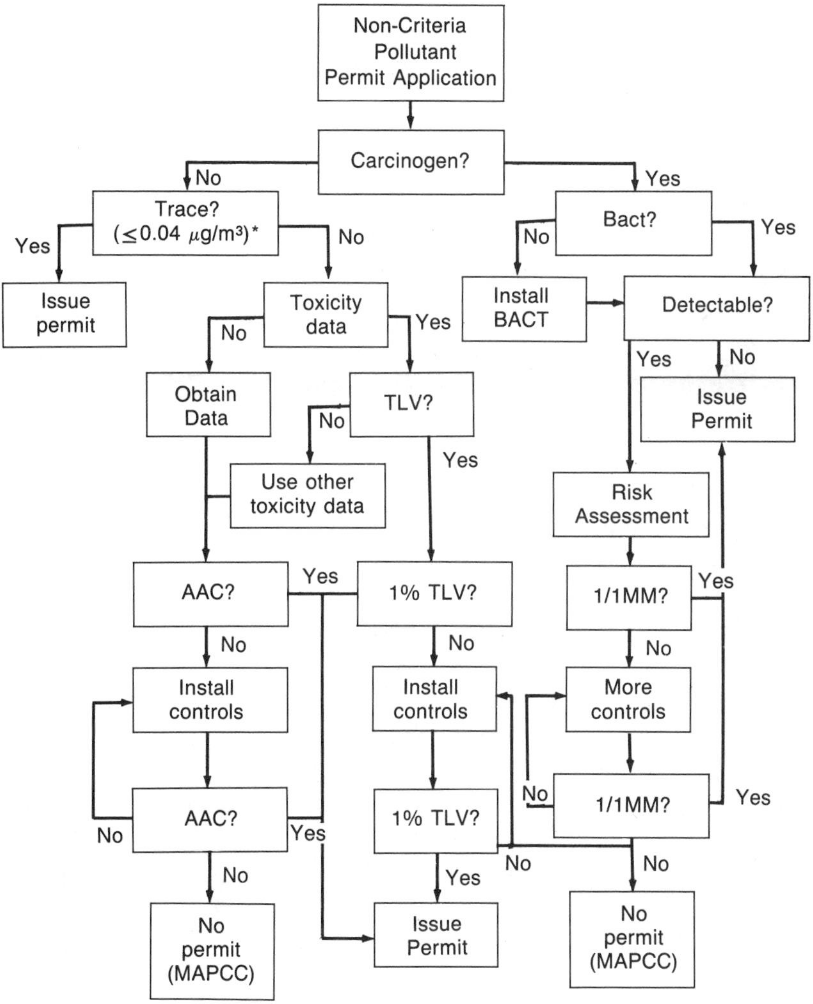

AAC—Acceptable ambient concentration
BACT—Best available control technology
1MM—1 million
MAPCC—Michigan Air Pollution Control Commission
TLV—Threshold Limiting Value (legal limit at which damage to health will occur).

* Trace amount defined as less than equal to 0.04 micrograms per cubic meter.

Source: Su and Wurzel.

INSTITUTIONAL ARRANGEMENTS FOR RISK ASSESSMENT

Because of the complex interrelationship among science, law, and policy in risk assessment, and because of the many uncertainties in method and data usually involved, the institutional arrangements for conducting risk assessments are of great importance. Three institutional questions need to be addressed in the risk-assessment process: (1) Who should do the assessment? (2) Should there be standards for each assessment, and, if so, who should determine these standards? (3) How much independent review should there be and by whom, and what authority should the independent reviewers have?

Who Should Do the Assessment?

Some risk assessments are undertaken by health or science agencies with no regulatory authority—primarily to increase scientific and public understanding of a risk. But most are undertaken in anticipation of regulatory action to control the risk.* In such cases, there has been substantial controversy about who should be responsible for the assessment. Alternatives range from the office responsible for implementing the regulatory program to a completely independent group of risk-assessment specialists. Currently, each of the federal regulatory agencies has established its own institutional arrangement for conducting assessments. Within an agency such as EPA, the arrangements differ widely among different programs.[55]

Much of the testing required for risk assessments is done by the regulated industries or the National Toxicology Program (NTP), which is an amalgam of institutions, including the National Institute of Environmental Health Sciences and the National Center for Toxicological Research. Risk assessments for the regulation of occupational hazards are performed by the National Institute for Occupational Safety and Health (NIOSH). But in practice, OSHA, the regulatory agency for occupational hazards, never has paid much attention to NIOSH's assessments. Most agencies do not have a separate unit for making risk assessments.

There are several advantages to having a regulatory program office do its own assessments. The assessment process will be better coordinated with the regulatory program, leading to administrative efficiency. If the

---

*Many chemical firms and some other types of companies use risk assessments to determine the safety of products and processes. The discussion here, however, focuses on governmental institutions.

two functions are completely independent, the regulatory process may be stymied while waiting for a risk assessment to be completed. A second advantage is that "in-house" assessments should be better tailored to regulatory needs. OSHA, for example, has often redone NIOSH assessments because they were not sufficiently relevant to the rule-making process.

But there also are strong arguments against a regulatory program office performing assessments. One is the fear that lawyers, rather than scientists, will dictate how an assessment is done and mold the process to fit regulatory needs at the expense of "scientific" method. Then there is the question of duplication of effort and inefficient use of valuable scientific talent if each program office conducts its own assessments.

Agencies have tried to meet these criticisms by setting up separate assessment offices supervised by scientists within the agency. In 1976, EPA established the Carcinogen Assessment Group (CAG) to do cancer risk assessments for all of the agency's programs. EPA recently took steps to centralize in one office all risk assessments for the entire agency. Some of the EPA divisions, however, such as the Office of Toxic Substances, do their own risk assessments without using the centralized office.[56] The National Highway Traffic Safety Administration similarly relies on assessments undertaken by four offices that report to the associate administrator for research and development.[57]

Regulatory agencies also have tried to blunt criticism by establishing nongovernmental review panels and scientifically acceptable standards for conducting assessments. The agencies, however, have resisted strongly proposals to give assessment responsibility to completely independent organizations such as the National Science Foundation or the National Academy of Sciences.

Risk-Assessment Standards

Different agencies and offices use diverse procedures and standards in assessing different types of risks. The results vary widely depending on the purpose of the assessment, on the type and quality of data used, and even on the biases of the scientists performing the work.

The basic postures of the agencies range from EPA's extensive, systematic attention to carcinogenic risk assessment to OSHA's general aversion to any risk assessment at all. Many things account for this disparity, but one key factor appears to be the extent to which the agency's statutory authority requires it to balance the health benefits of a regulation against its economic costs.

Attempts to bring about greater uniformity among the agencies usually have taken the form of guidelines, particularly guidelines for conducting and interpreting assessments of potential carcinogens. In 1979, the Interagency Regulatory Liaison Group (IRLG), composed of the five major regulatory agencies, proposed a set of guidelines.[58] Although never formally adopted, these guidelines were generally accepted by the agencies until the Reagan administration took office and disbanded the IRLG. Under the Reagan administration, the Office of Science and Technology Policy (OSTP) has proposed new guidelines for cancer assessment.[59]

Meanwhile, William Ruckelshaus, the administrator of EPA, has initiated a plan to bring the regulatory agencies together into a broader version of the IRLG for the purpose of coordinating risk-assessment and risk-management activities.[60] The Interagency Risk Management Council, the result of this effort, plans to draft its own cancer policy.[61] (The effort devoted to creating and recreating guidelines for assessing carcinogenic risks contrasts sharply with the virtual absence of effort brought to evaluating other risks, such as mutagenicity, teratogenicity, and immune effects.)

The need for specific standards and guidelines has been strongest for regulating chemical risks because the same chemicals may be regulated by several different agencies; it seems reasonable that all agencies be consistent. In programs such as automobile, airline, or nuclear power safety, in which all assessments and actions are by a single agency, formal procedural documents apparently are considered less important; if the same regulators are responsible for all of the assessments in an area, they tend to develop unwritten standards.

The guidelines that have been prepared are described as scientific, not policy, statements. This distinction is the focus of much of the debate on risk assessment. It is, however, a largely false dichotomy. Guidelines are necessary because, in many areas, there is no single scientific answer to how an assessment should be conducted; choosing from among several alternatives becomes largely a policy question. By developing guidelines, the agencies force agreement on how these policy questions will be answered. If the guidelines do not accomplish this, policy determinations remain in the hands of the different agencies or of individual scientists.

Ironically, then, risk-assessment guidelines are apt to be controversial. If they succeed in addressing the important problems, they will contain major policy statements that cannot be defended on the basis of science alone.

Independent Reviews

Once an assessment is complete, there are further thorny questions regarding its review: Who should review it? At what point in the risk-control process? On what basis? And what authority should the reviewers have to require modifications?

At some point in the risk-control process, all interested parties are given an opportunity to review and comment on a risk assessment, because it is included in the rule-making package for a proposed rule. Where no rule making is involved, the assessment usually is made available, at least to those people most likely to be concerned. If the assessment is part of a proposed rule, the Administrative Procedure Act requires the responsible agency to consider any comments submitted before the final rule is promulgated.[62] But the key question is whether some parties will have an opportunity to review and influence the risk assessment earlier, in other words, before it is released as part of a *proposed* regulation, and thus whether some parties will have more influence than others. The principal parties involved in this controversy are independent scientists, the public (including industry), other federal agencies (particularly the Office of Management and Budget [OMB]), Congress, and the courts.

Scientific Peer Reviews

The chief technique for ensuring quality in scientific research is "peer review" by qualified scientists who themselves have not participated in the research work under consideration. Because the quality of science used in support of regulation and public policy often has been questioned,[63] many groups and individuals have recommended that the regulatory agencies institute peer review as a normal part of their regulatory process.

Peer review is not often part of that process now, though a notable exception is the development of the criteria documents that form the scientific basis for national ambient air-quality standards. Statute requires that these documents be reviewed by the Clean Air Scientific Advisory Committee, a group of experts on air pollution effects.[64] Other exceptions are the scientific studies used to develop hazardous air pollutant standards, which are reviewed by the EPA Science Advisory Board,[65] and major pesticide regulations, which must be reviewed by the pesticide Science Advisory Panel.[66]

Other decisions by regulatory agencies are reviewed from time to time by agency science advisory committees, by the National Academy of Sciences, or by ad hoc panels of government or nongovernment scientists. But, in most cases, the scientific information that goes into a decision has not been peer reviewed.

The Public

Because the public's perception of risk may be substantially different from that of the experts, it can be argued that the public should have a voice in risk assessment. Under current procedures, however, the results of risk assessments are rarely subject to public hearings or other forums for public participation—until the results are incorporated in a proposed regulation. As noted, public comments must then be considered by the agency.

Public comment on risk assessment takes various forms. Organized groups that represent the public or segments of it frequently comment critically on the scientific findings used to support proposed regulations. Industry, labor, and environmental organizations (such as the NRDC, the Environmental Defense Fund, and the National Audubon Society) have staff scientists, or hire outside scientists, and their comments are a form of peer review, albeit review from a particular perspective.

The unorganized public usually does not have a major voice in public policy. In recent years, however, this public has become vociferous about decisions creating possible risks for local communities. The siting of nuclear power plants, hazardous waste dumps, and some types of industrial facilities has encountered major local opposition. One study concluded that, "Public opposition to the siting and operation of hazardous waste management facilities is so widespread that it might be thought to be unavoidable."[67]

Local opposition is a form of public risk assessment. The opposition is based on a view that the risks of the proposed facility are unacceptably high. By the definition used in this chapter, however, such public action is really a judgment about risk management, because the *acceptability* of a risk is part of risk management, not risk assessment. But most of the public does not clearly separate these two functions; the public's assessments of the nature and degree of a risk tend to be embedded in a judgment about its acceptability.*

---

*The public's judgment also may hinge on the *distribution* of the risks and benefits of a proposed action. Who benefits and who bears the risks are important questions in risk management. Another often crucial factor is the general public's mistrust of government.

Other Federal Agencies

One of President Reagan's earliest actions was his promulgation, on February 17, 1981, of Executive Order 12291,[68] giving the OMB in the Executive Office of the President authority to review all proposed regulations and to delay their issuance for an indefinite period. All major regulations submitted to OMB were to be accompanied by an analysis showing that the benefits of the proposed regulation exceed the costs.

The major effect of the executive order has been to greatly increase OMB's power to change, delay, or veto regulations. Its effect on the quality of analyses performed for regulatory purposes is less clear. It seems likely that the order has increased the importance of economics and economists in regulatory analysis, but there is little evidence that it has affected the quality of risk assessments.

The Reagan executive order is only the latest in a long series of efforts to define how regulations proposed by one federal agency can be reviewed by other federal agencies. Under the Carter administration, the agencies regulating chemical risks agreed to share (and, in some cases, to work jointly on) risk assessments before they were made public. During the Nixon and Ford administrations, most important regulations were subjected to a "Quality of Life Review" under OMB's direction. This allowed any other agency to review and comment on the risk assessment underlying a proposed regulation before the lead agency could make the regulation final.[69]

None of these procedures is without controversy. Interest groups seeking increased government control over risks have challenged the right of OMB and other agencies to review regulations and risk assessments before they are promulgated. They particularly question reviews that focus more on policy than on science and that take place outside the normal administrative procedures established to protect the rights of all parties.[70]

Congress

Congress rarely attempts to review an individual risk assessment. It has, however, expressed concern about the risk assessment process. Members of Congress have held hearings and introduced bills that would establish independent assessment review boards or even assign assessment responsibilities to an independent agency.

On the other hand, Congress has attempted to become more involved in deciding the reasonableness of proposed actions based on risk assessment. In some cases, Congress has required that one or both houses be allowed to veto a proposed regulation before it is promulgated.* In other cases—as with PCBs under TSCA or toxic chemicals under the Clean Water Act—Congress has specifically concluded that certain risks must be controlled by an agency. In still other situations, such as banning saccharin, Congress has decided that action should *not* be taken to control a risk and, therefore, has prohibited an agency from doing so statutorily or, to much the same effect, has forbidden it to spend any money on regulatory efforts.[71]

The Courts

In recent years, three federal court decisions have had a potentially significant impact on risk assessment in the regulatory agencies. The first decision dealt with a proposed OSHA standard for benzene;[72] the second with an OSHA standard for cotton dust;[73] and the third with the proposed CPSC ban on urea-formaldehyde foam insulation.[74] All three cases were decided in the context of a continuing debate about the extent to which the federal courts should second-guess the reasoning and conclusions of agency regulations dealing with potential risks.[75]

In the benzene case, a badly splintered U.S. Supreme Court struck down the proposed benzene standard on grounds that OSHA had not performed either a quantitative risk estimate showing the benefits of the proposed standard or an analysis showing that the benefits bore a reasonable relationship to the cost of control. Four of the nine justices disagreed with this conclusion, arguing that the act did not require such analyses. The majority of five justices produced three separate opinions, each of which contained a different line of reasoning.

The primary impact of the benzene case was to require OSHA (and, by implication, the other regulatory agencies) to conduct explicit risk analyses for proposed regulations. The decision, however, gives less than helpful guidance about the form that such analyses should take. Justice John Paul Stevens' plurality opinion states that OSHA must make a threshold determination that a significant risk exists before it regulates. Such a determination should not be a "mathematical straitjacket," and it does not have to be supported "with anything approaching scientific certainty." But, Stevens states, it must be quantitative and supported by "substantial evidence." Political scientist Norman Vig observes that "the criteria which Stevens offers for establishing risk significance are

---

*Such requirements were ruled unconstitutional by the Supreme Court on June 23, 1983, in *Immigration and Naturalization Service* v. *Chadha* (776 F.2d 317 [1983]).

kindly described as unclear.''[76] Chief Justice Warren Burger, after noting Stevens' opinion that the agency's factual finding of risk must be ''quantified sufficiently to enable the [agency] to characterize it [the risk] as significant in an understandable way,'' commented, ''Precisely what this means is difficult to say.''[77]

A year later, in a decision upholding OSHA's standard for cotton dust, the Supreme Court decided five to three that the Occupational Safety and Health Act did not require OSHA to conduct a cost-benefit analysis of its proposed regulations.[78] This settled a basic point that had been left unclear by the benzene ruling, but the cotton-dust decision did not clarify what kind of risk analysis the agency must perform.

An April 1983 decision by the Fifth Circuit Court of Appeals striking down CPSC's ban on urea-formaldehyde foam insulation did address the kind of risk analysis that should be performed, but it did so largely by telling CPSC what (in the court's opinion) it did wrong rather than by giving any positive guidance about what type of analysis should be conducted.[79] CPSC had, in the court's words, used ''an exacting, precise, and extremely complicated risk assessment model.'' But, ''the predictions made by the risk assessment model are no better than the data base. We have concluded that this base was inadequate.'' The court found that the two studies used by CPSC to gauge the levels of formaldehyde in a home were methodologically flawed, and it criticized as ''not good science'' CPSC's reliance on a single study involving 240 rats for evidence of formaldehyde's carcinogenicity without evaluating other available studies.[80]

The formaldehyde decision is unprecedented in the degree to which the court undertook a detailed review of the substance of a regulatory risk assessment. However, the Reagan administration's Justice Department declined to appeal the decision to the Supreme Court. It is too early to tell whether the decision will have a major impact on the way regulatory agencies perform risk assessments. In the short run, though, it is likely to place a heavier burden of proof on the agencies to show that a significant risk exists.

RISK MANAGEMENT AND RISK ASSESSMENT

The final step in the risk-control process is *risk management*. A thorough discussion of this stage is beyond the scope of this chapter. But some interactions between the assessment and management functions are inescapable. They also are controversial.

Some scholars and practitioners consider a risk-management decision to be an integral, inseparable part of risk assessment; others insist that they are totally distinct. To some extent, the argument is based on differences in definition, but there is more to it than that.

Those who believe in separating the two functions note that risk assessment is scientific, whereas risk management obviously involves policy considerations.[81] The fallacy in this distinction has been pointed out earlier: policy decisions also are made in the assessment process, particularly in deciding how to deal with uncertainty; the basic questions are not whether these *are* policy decisions but who should make them, should they be open and explicit or hidden in the analysis, and should they be made in a consistent fashion.

The Tacoma Smelter

One of the most publicized risk-management decisions faced by the U.S. Environmental Protection Agency (EPA) in recent years involved the Asarco copper smelter in Tacoma, Washington. EPA presented the people of Tacoma with the results of the agency's risk assessment and sought public comment on what action the agency should take. The case raises important questions about quantitative risk assessments.

Arsenic emissions from the Tacoma smelter became a priority for EPA because of a lawsuit against the agency by the state of New York.[1] The court decision required EPA to publish proposed emission standards for inorganic arsenic by July 1983 under the provisions of Section 112 of the Clean Air Act. On July 20, 1983, EPA proposed hazardous-air-pollutant standards for arsenic emissions from copper smelters and glass plants.[2] The plant most affected by the proposed standards was Asarco's Tacoma smelter, which, the agency estimated, emitted 310 tons of arsenic per year, or 23 percent of all arsenic emissions in the United States.[3]

The Clean Air Act directs EPA to set emission standards for hazardous air pollutants at a level that will protect public health with "an ample margin of safety."[4] At the time the arsenic standard was proposed, EPA estimated that, even if the Asarco smelter installed the best-available-technology controls, the maximum lifetime risk of lung cancer to the most-exposed persons would be about 2 in 100. The risk to people living closest to the plant was estimated to be about 00.2 chances in 100 and to a typical Tacoma resident, 0.004 in 100.[5] EPA calculated that, if the plant were closed, 1,300 jobs and $20 million in local revenue would be lost.[6]

All of these numbers were uncertain. The cancer risks were estimated on the basis of a hazard assessment by EPA's Cancer Assessment Group[7] and a model of air emissions from copper smelters by EPA's Office of Air Quality Planning and Standards.[8]

The hazard-assessment document noted that arsenic "exists in various chemical states, e.g., tri- and pentavalent inorganic arsenic and methylated organic arsenic, with each having differing toxicological potential. In man, experimental animals and other organisms, arsenic undergoes a variety of transformations, the full signi-

The types of policy considerations involved in risk-assessment are, however, different in several respects from those involved in risk management. Both hinge on basic policy views about how cautious or conservative to be about risk. But risk assessment policy involves a choice about the general methodology to be used for assessing certain kinds of risks. Once this choice is made, it can be applied consistently to all such assessments. In contrast, many of the policy considerations involved in risk management are unique to a particular decision. The political, economic, and social costs and benefits differ in each case.

Those who espouse the separation of risk assessment and risk management are concerned that the political, social, and economic considerations associated with a specific management decision will improperly

ficance and mechanisms of which are as yet not well understood. Furthermore, there appears to be a nutritional requirement for low levels of arsenic. . . . All of these factors complicate the analyses of the toxicological effects and the risk for human health. . . ."[9] To extrapolate the human dose-response relationship, an appropriate model had to be chosen. Several different models fit the available data, and the risk estimates that were produced by these models ranged from 1 cancer to 136 cancers in 10,000 exposed people.[10]

The exposure part of the risk assessment was based on a general model of air emissions from copper smelters. When EPA later did a specific model of emissions from the Tacoma smelter, the emission estimate was reduced by more than half.[11] Actual exposure is still unknown, the estimates being based on mathematical computer models of how the arsenic from the plant is distributed in the atmosphere.

Even the estimates of economic impact were far from certain. Articles in the press reported the number of jobs that would be lost as 1,300,[12] 800,[13] 575,[14] and 500.[15] EPA Administrator William Ruck-

elshaus announced that the agency would hold public hearings in Tacoma on the proposed arsenic standards and would provide the local public with maximum information on health risks and economic losses associated with alternative courses of action. The choice facing Tacoma citizens was widely billed as "jobs versus health," although Ruckelshaus denied that the trade-off was so stark.[16] Many environmental groups attacked the administrator's strategy of maximum public involvement on grounds that the decision was solely his and that the provisions of the Clean Air Act did not allow him to consider the economic effects of the proposed standard.

EPA issued a revised estimate of emissions from the smelter just before the November 1983 public hearings in Tacoma. The revision reduced the previous estimate by about 50 percent, and seems to make it possible to avoid the starkest choice between significant cancer risks and closing the plant. However, EPA has yet to issue a final standard for arsenic emissions. The uncertainties about all the factors in the tradeoff remain, and they are typical of most risk-control decisions.

influence the assessment process. They worry, for example, that a zealous regulator who wants to ban a chemical will pressure the assessors to exaggerate the risk of the chemical or will distort the findings of the assessment. This is a valid concern, although the extent to which such abuses actually occur is disputed. In the absence of policy guidelines for conducting risk assessments, a regulator can make a risk assessment support any view—and do so without violating the tenets of acceptable science.

There are, however, beneficial ways in which risk-management policy can influence the risk-assessment process and, therefore, should be closely related to it. The criteria and analytical procedures used in a risk-management process can help clarify the type of risk assessment needed. They also may suggest how closely the risk-assessment process should be tied to the management process. If a management decision is to be based on technology alone, there is little reason to produce extensive risk assessments. A virtually complete separation between the two functions should cause few problems.

The more the management criteria emphasize "reasonable" risk, however, the more reason for close integration. For example, to reduce the risk of a chemical, regulatory options short of a total ban will involve making choices about the number of people exposed to the chemical, the length of time they are exposed, and the amount of the chemical to which they are exposed. Each of these choices will affect the assessment of the risk posed by the chemical, and the identification of management options will, in turn, be affected by the estimates of risk for each option. Thus, a high degree of interaction between risk managers and risk assessors in a regulatory agency will be necessary if management options are to be adequately defined and evaluated.[82]

Criteria for Reducing Risks

The purpose of risk management is to reduce risks. The major question the risk manager has to decide is: How much? The first answer to this question is provided in the statutory language under which the risk manager operates. As figure 5.5 shows, the different statutes specify widely varying degrees of allowable risk. The degrees can be classified in three categories: (1) zero risk; (2) technology-based risk; and (3) reasonableness of risk balanced with benefits.[83]

Only a few statutory provisions mandate or imply the achievement of zero risk. The most important are the Delaney Clause of the Food, Drug, and Cosmetic Act,[84] which prohibits the use of food additives shown to cause cancer in appropriate animal tests; the provisions of the Clean Air Act relating to the establishment of primary air-quality standards;[85] and Section 112 of the Clean Air Act, which covers regulation of hazardous air pollutants.[86]

Many have argued that a goal of zero risk is irrational and undesirable, if not impossible. It is usually politically necessary to take economic factors into account. The combination of scientific findings that for many hazards there is no threshold of risk and the scientific advance in detection methods, allowing detection at the parts-per-trillion level, means that a total ban on a chemical often would be the only way to achieve zero risk.

In fact, regulatory agencies only rarely implement the literal meaning of zero-risk statutory provisions. The Food and Drug Administration (FDA) has used the Delaney Clause sparingly, relying instead on other, less stringent provisions of the law.[87] Peter Hutt, former general counsel of the FDA, has stated flatly that "repeal of the Delaney Clause, without revision of the other food safety provisions in the law, would not change any action that the FDA has taken in the past or may take in the future."[88] EPA has managed to implicitly account for the economic impact of the primary air-quality standards by choosing which sensitive populations to consider and by adjusting the margin of safety so that thinner margins are set for the pollutants that require more expensive control measures. To deal with hazardous air pollutants, EPA, in several instances, has abandoned the zero-risk concept altogether and resorted to technology-based standards.

A second type of legal requirement directs the agency to focus on the effectiveness and costs of alternative control technologies rather than on how control actions could affect risks. The Clean Water Act, for example, requires industries to install the "best practicable control technology" for reducing water pollution.[89] Technology-based controls are particularly appropriate to problems such as industrial water pollution, where installation of a single control system can reduce the risks from a variety of different pollutants.

Most provisions, however, require some balancing between the degree of risk and the economic cost of controlling the risk. Under the Toxic Substances Control Act, EPA is required to regulate only those risks that are "unreasonable,"[90] and under the Safe Drinking Water Act, it is supposed to regulate contaminants "to the extent feasible," taking costs into consideration.[91] One of the most difficult problems in risk management is deciding how this balancing should be done and when the balance is "reasonable."

Figure 5.5
Federal Statutory Directives Concerning Hazardous Materials

	Federal Insecticide, Fungicide and Rodenticide Act	Consumer Product Safety Act	Toxic Substances Control Act	Federal Food, Drug and Cosmetic Act					Occupational Safety and Health Act
Statute	§136a(b)(1972, as amended 1975) Cancellation & Change in Classification. 7 U.S.C. §136a (1947, as amended 1972) Pesticide Registration	15 U.S.C. §§2056(a), 2058(b) (1972, as amended 1976)	15 U.S.C. §2605 (1976)	21 U.S.C. §346 (1938) Tolerances for Poisons in Food	§346a(b) (1938) Pesticide Tolerances	§348(b)(c)(3)(A) (1938, as amended 1962) Carcinogens in Food (Delaney Clause)	§355(d) (1938, as amended 1962) Drug Products	§360b(d)(2) (1968) Animal Drug Products	29 U.S.C. §655(b)(5) (1970) Occupation Exposure to Toxic Substances
Directive	Register pesticides which, in addition to other requirements, will not cause "unreasonable adverse effects on the environment" (§136a(c)(5)(C)(D)). The term refers to "any unreasonable risks to man or the environment taking into account the economic, social and environmental costs and benefits of the use of any pesticide" (§136(bb)).	The commission is to establish such standards as are reasonably necessary to prevent or reduce an unreasonable risk of injury associated with a consumer product. (§2056(a)) Consider relevant available product data including the results of research, development, testing, and investigation activities conducted generally. Also consider and take into account the special needs of elderly and handicapped persons to determine the extent to which such persons may be adversely affected (§2058(b))	Take action if a substance "presents or will present an unreasonable risk of injury to health or the environment." Consider: the effects of such substance on health and the environment and the magnitude of the exposure of human beings and the environment to such substance; the benefits of such substance for various uses and the availability of substitutes for such uses; and the reasonably ascertainable economic consequences of the rule, after consideration of the effect on the national economy, small businesses, technological innovation, the environment, and public health.	Take into account the extent to which the use of such a substance is required or cannot be avoided in the production of each article, and the other ways in which the consumer may be affected by the same or other poisonous or deleterious substances.	Regulate the use of pesticides on agricultural commodities to the extent necessary to protect the public health. Give appropriate consideration, among other relevant factors, 1) to the necessity for the production of an adequate, wholesome, and economical food supply; 2) to the other ways in which the consumer may be affected by the same pesticide chemical or by other related substances that are poisonous or deleterious; and 3) to the opinion submitted with a certification of usefulness.	In assessing the safety of a food additive, consideration of the extent to which... the probable consumption of the additive and of any substance formed in or on food because of the use of the additive, the cumulative effect of such additive in the diet of man or animals, taking into account any chemically or pharmacologically related substance(s) in such diet, and safety factors which in the opinion of experts qualified by scientific training and experience to evaluate the safety of food additives are generally recognized as appropriate for the use of animal experimentation data.	Approve a drug if it is safe for use under the conditions prescribed, recommended, or suggested in the proposed labeling and it is shown to have the effect it purports or is represented to have.	Consider among other relevant factors 1) the probable consumption of such drug and of any substance formed in or on food because of the use of such drug; 2) the cumulative effect on man or animal of such drug; 3) safety factors which... are appropriate for the use of animal experimentation data, or suggested in the proposed labeling, are reasonably certain to be followed in practice.	Set the standard which "most adequately insures to the greatest extent feasible that no employee will suffer material impairment of health or functional capacity."
Agency	EPA	CPSC	EPA	FDA					OSHA
Specificity of guidance directing agency in evaluating relevant decisional factors	General guidance identifying types of relevant considerations.	A list of relevant factors is provided; no priorities are provided	A list of relevant factors is provided; no priorities are provided	Decision based on single factual policy finding.	A list of relevant factors is provided; no priorities are provided	A list of relevant factors is provided; no priorities are provided	A list of relevant factors is provided; no priorities are provided	A list of relevant factors is provided; no priorities are provided	Guidance on considerations is provided.

	Federal Water Pollution Control Act	Marine Protection Research and Sanctuaries Act	Safe Drinking Water Act	National Environmental Policy Act	Resource Conservation and Recovery Act	Clean Air Act				Hazardous Materials Transportation Act
Statute	33 U.S.C. §§1314(b)(1), 1314(b)(2) (1972) Best Practicable Technology, Best Available Technology Effluence Limitations	33 U.S.C §1412 (1972, as amended 1974) Ocean Dumping	42 U.S.C. §§300g-1(a)(2), 300g-5(a) (1974) Drinking Water Contaminants	42 U.S.C. §4321 et seq (1969)	42 U.S.C. §§6921a, 6922, 6923(a) (1976) Generators and Transporters of Hazardous Waste	42 U.S.C. §§7408, 7409 (1970, as amended 1977) National Ambient Air Quality Standards	§7410 (1970, as amended 1977) SIP Approval	§7411 (1970, as amended 1977) New Source Performance Standards	§7412 (1970) National Emissions Standards for Hazardous Air Pollution	49 U.S.C §1801 et seq. (1975)
Directive	*Total costs, age of equipment and facilities, processes involved, engineering aspects, environmental factors, and energy are to be taken into account in assessing Best Practicable Technology and Best Available Technology Du Pont v. Train (4th Cir. 1976) among others held that no cost benefit analysis is required.* Listing: Maintain a list of toxic pollutants taking into account the toxicity of the pollutants, its persistence, degradability, the usual or potential presence of the affected organisms in any waters, the importance of the affected organisms, and the nature and extent of the effect of the toxic pollutant on such organisms. Standard Setting: Though not exclusively the case, the administrator may publish more stringent (than BAT) effluent limits at the level which (s)he determines provides an "ample" margin of safety. §1314(a)(4).	Issue permits allowing ocean dumping only where such dumping will not "unreasonably degrade or endanger human health, welfare, or amenities, or the marine environment, ecological systems, or economic potentialities." Consider the effect on human health and welfare, including economic, aesthetic and recreational values, and the effect on fisheries resources, plankton, fish, shellfish, wildlife, shore lines and beaches, and the effect on marine ecosystems, particularly with respect to several specified...	Protect health to the extent feasible using technology, treatment techniques and other means, which the administrator determines are "generally available (taking costs into consideration)" §1412(a)(2). (A state with enforcement responsibility may exempt a public water system upon finding that due to compelling factors (including economics) the state is unable to comply and that the exemption will not result in an "unreasonable risk" to health.) §1416(a).	Federal agencies are required to assess the expected effect of a proposed action on the environment and evaluate possible alternatives to the action. In Calvert Cliffs Coordinating Committee v. AEC (D.C. Cir. 1971) the D.C. Court of Appeals interpreted NEPA to "require a balancing analysis" in which economic and social benefits are to be weighed against environmental costs.	Listing: Develop criteria for identifying and listing hazardous wastes taking into account toxicity, persistence, and degradability in nature, potential for accumulation in tissue, and other related factors such as flammability, corrosiveness, and other hazardous characteristics (§3001). Standard Setting: Set standards for hazardous waste transporters "as may be necessary to protect human health and the environment" (§§3002, 3003).	Listing: Maintain a list of air pollutants which in the administrator's judgment cause or contribute to air pollution reasonably anticipated to endanger public health or welfare (§108 (a)(1)(A)). Standard Setting: Set standards to "protect the public health" allowing an adequate margin of safety."	The factors to be considered, listed in §110(a)(2), involve the effectiveness, efficiency, procedural fairness of the SIP. Union Electric v. EPA (U.S. 1976) held that consideration of economic or technical feasibility	Standards are based on the level of technology which has been "adequately demonstrated." Consider the costs of compliance as well as any non-air quality health and environmental impacts, and energy requirements. Portland Cement v. Ruckelshaus (C.A.D.C. 1973) held that a cost-benefit analysis is not required.	Listing: Maintain a list of hazardous air pollutants for which the administrator intends to establish an emissions standard. Standard Setting: Once a substance is placed on the list the administrator is to prescribe as emissions standard at a level which in his judgment "provides an ample margin of safety to protect the public health" barring a finding that the pollutant is "clearly not hazardous."	Upon a finding that transportation of a particular quantity and form of material in commerce may pose an unreasonable risk to health and safety or property (§1803) the secretary may regulate any aspect of the transportation of such "hazardous materials" as he deems necessary or appropriate (§1804).
Agency	EPA	EPA	EPA	All Government Agencies	EPA	EPA	EPA	EPA	EPA	DOT
Specificity of guidance directing agency in evaluating relevant decisional factors	A list of relevant factors is provided; no priorities are provided.	A list of relevant factors is provided; no priorities are provided.	§1416 Exemptions: no guidance (beyond reasonableness). §1412: guidance in weighing considerations is provided.	General guidance identifying types of relevance considerations.	Listing: A list of relevant factors is provided; no priorities are provided. Standard Setting: Decision is based on single factual and/or policy finding.	Listing and Standard Setting: Decision is based on single policy finding.	A list of relevant factors is provided; priorities are provided.	General guidance identifying types of relevant considerations.	Listing: no guidance (beyond reasonableness). Standard setting: Decision is based on single factual and/or emissions policy finding.	No guidance (beyond reasonableness).

Source: Gregory Wetstone.

The diversity of statutory mandates is a source of concern to many people. William Ruckelshaus, in a major statement on "Science, Risk, and Public Policy," recently said: "It is my strong belief that where EPA, OSHA, or any other social regulatory agency is charged with protecting public health, safety, or the environment, we should be given, to the extent possible, a common statutory formula for accomplishing our tasks."[92]

The basic reason for the diversity in the statutes is that they were formulated by different congressional committees, at different times, operating under different political pressures. There are, however, logical reasons for some of the differences. As noted above, technology-based requirements may make more sense than those based on individual pollutants if a single technology can control a number of different pollutants. In some cases, it can be argued that Congress, in the language of the statute itself, already has weighed, at least intuitively, the relevant costs and benefits. For example, the Delaney Clause has been defended on grounds that it represents Congress's explicit view that the benefits of any food additive would clearly be outweighed by any risk of cancer.[93]

Although it would be neater and simpler to have greater uniformity among the statutes, it is not clear how much actual difference it would make in the risk-assessment and risk-management processes. The context of Ruckelshaus's comment, quoted above, indicates a primary concern not so much with uniformity as with a desire to change the zero-risk statutory provisions to allow consideration of the economic costs of control. Changing zero-risk provisions would give greater leverage to industry and less to environmental groups in arguments over standards. But given that agencies generally circumvent such provisions anyhow, it is not clear how standards actually would differ if economic considerations were permitted by law.

A study reveals wide disparities in agency policy decisions when measured by the cost per life saved or cost per life-year saved. These decisions have resulted in consideration of regulations that involve net additional costs to society, ranging from zero dollars per life saved to $169 million per life saved. The study concludes that there are systematic differences among the agencies: the median OSHA program was 400 times more expensive per life-year saved than the median program of the National Highway Traffic Safety Administration.[94] In listing possible reasons for these disparities, however, one author of the study does not even mention the statutory mandates of the agencies. He attributes the differences to the nature of the problem being regulated (whether the victims are identifiable, for example) or to the political forces that affect the agency.[95]

The emphasis in recent years on the use of cost-benefit analysis in making risk-management decisions is in part an effort to promote consistency. But, particularly for health and safety decisions, there is usually little or no quantitative information about many of the factors that must be analyzed, and many of the most important factors cannot be translated easily into dollars. Given these and numerous other obstacles, it is not surprising that, despite all the theorizing about cost-benefit methods for risk management, there are very few examples of their actual use in the regulatory process.[96] In short, given the differences in the types of problems regulated and in the political factors at work, a greater degree of uniformity or consistency with respect to risk management does not seem in the cards.

Greater consistency in risk-assessment practices does seem both possible and desirable. The National Academy of Sciences recommends that the regulatory agencies adopt uniform guidelines for risk assessment,[97] and, as noted earlier in this chapter, several efforts are under way to develop such guidelines. It is hard to justify the existing differences in risk-assessment methodology on grounds other than the greater flexibility it gives to the regulators.

The Risks of Risk Management

Decision makers often are faced with the problem of choosing between competing risks. The FDA approves life-saving drugs that pose risks otherwise intolerable in any other context (risks, for example, of cancer or other chronic diseases). Officials in charge of drinking-water systems add chlorine to the water to reduce the risk of bacterial diseases, even though chlorine can combine with other chemicals in the water to produce potentially cancer-causing compounds.[98] In parts of Asia, Africa, and Latin America, DDT (dichloro diphenyl trichloroethane) is still widely used because the risk of malaria is considered greater than the risk of any genetic problems that the pesticide might cause; in the United States, where malaria is not a problem, DDT was banned because the genetic risks were considered greater than the benefits from its use as an insecticide.[99]

Regulatory decisions can sometimes increase the degree of risk to which society is exposed by failing to deal with competing risks. Regulations governing the flammability of children's sleepwear encouraged the use of the flame-retardant, Tris, which turned out to be a potent carcinogen.[100] More typically, new chemicals or products are subjected to greater regulatory scrutiny than those already on the market. The result may be that a new pesticide or dye or solvent is banned even though it is less harmful than the older products it would replace. The reason for such decisions usually is a dearth of reliable information about the risks posed by the older products.

In some cases, as discussed in the cross-media chapter, a risk-management decision in one program office will only result in transferring the problem somewhere else—and may even result in a net increase, rather than reduction, in risk.

All of these considerations should be taken into account in managing risks, regardless of particular legislative criteria. Where the criteria call for what is "reasonable," it would appear to be mandatory to take competing risks into account.

How Much Does Risk Assessment Help Risk Management?

Those who discuss risk assessment and risk management have a tendency to overestimate how systematic and rational the regulatory process is in practice. Typically, regulatory decisions are made in an intensely political environment, under conditions of great uncertainty, by people who have very little time to weigh or analyze the relevant evidence and options. Two experts, after reviewing a variety of regulatory decisions, concluded that "anyone asserting that scientific evidence determined the regulation simply did not have the correct information."[101]

In many cases, there is little need or opportunity to develop rigorous risk assessments before taking some action. An engineer building a bridge or a manufacturing firm installing a new process will rarely give explicit consideration to the acceptable degree of risk. Standard formulas and rules of thumb provide the only form of risk analysis.[102] Even life-and-death decisions for individuals or society rarely have the benefit of extensive formal analysis. The operator on duty at the control panel of Three Mile Island had to act quickly and, to a great extent, intuitively. The top-level officials debating U.S. policy during the Cuban Missile Crisis had the benefit of various intelligence analyses, but the decision-making process itself could not be described as analytical; the debate had proceeded for a number of hours before Secretary of Defense Robert McNamara made the daring suggestion that the participants write down their options and the reasons for them.[103]

All of these largely intuitive forms of risk-management decision making can be described as "professional judgment," whether the professional involved is an electrician, an architect, an engineer, or a senior government official. There are many occasions when the lack of time or information, or the cost of doing an analysis, makes professional judgment the appropriate method for making risk decisions.

The government spends a lot of time and resources gathering and analyzing risk data, but the results are often ambiguous. Very rarely are the analyses dramatic or decisive enough to motivate action or to clearly indicate what should be done. The coin used in the regulatory market is primarily political and economic, not toxicological or engineering.

This is not to say that scientific data are unnecessary. As the two experts cited above put it: "A more realistic assessment of the role of science and scientists is that they help in the formulation of the right questions, the search for the best data and judgments, and identification of the range of uncertainty. Putting more weight on the role of science would not only lead to the gathering of scientific information more useful to the regulatory process, but would also improve regulations by correctly reflecting the uncertainties involved."[104]

Improvements in scientific knowledge will improve the ability to analyze and deal with risks. But political and economic factors are likely to dominate not only risk-management decisions but also the rate at which new risks are created.

SCIENCE AND POLICY IN RISK ASSESSMENT

A key to understanding and improving the risk-assessment process is to distinguish between those aspects of the process that are scientific and those that are matters of policy or personal values, and to appreciate their complex interrelationships.

Inadequate Data

Almost all risk assessments are plagued by inadequate data. Adequate toxicity data are not available for the vast majority of chemicals now in use.[105] Thus, even when data exist on the toxicity of a particular chemical, analysts often do not know whether taking regulatory action on the chemical will increase or reduce risk because they do not know the toxicity of the substitutes that will be used if regulatory action restricts use of the chemical under examination.

The risk from a particular chemical is primarily a function of hazard and exposure. The determination of hazard is usually based on tests conducted on rats or mice, because working with other kinds of animals is too expensive. Some people question the validity of these types of tests for telling anything about hazards to humans. But even assuming their validity for hazard assessment, the tests are difficult to do correctly and, thus, the data may be open to question simply because the test was not done right. Even when valid test results are available, the inadequacy of scientific knowledge is a basic handicap in interpreting what the test results mean in terms of human hazard. Because the mechanism of cancer causation in humans, for example, is poorly understood, there is uncertainty about how to translate findings into standards to protect people from cancer. In the case of other potentially serious threats, such as chemicals that affect genes, even less is understood. No one knows what kinds of diseases or defects, if any, will be produced by mutagenic chemicals.

Even when data on *human* exposure to a chemical are available, they often are not very helpful. The purpose of such data is to demonstrate a cause-effect relationship between exposure to a chemical or some other potential hazard and adverse effects on humans. But causation is hard to determine because people are exposed simultaneously to a multitude of chemicals and other potential hazards, making it difficult or impossible to isolate a single causative factor. The effect part of the puzzle is similarly difficult because the same effect usually can be produced by a variety of different causes. The exceptional cases, where human data have been able to show a cause-effect relationship, such as with asbestos or vinyl chloride, mostly involve substances that produce rare or unique effects. Vinyl chloride, for example, causes a very rare form of cancer.[106]

The data on the exposure part of a risk assessment are likely to be even worse than for the hazard part. Exposure to air and water pollutants is not measured directly, but is usually calculated from mathematical models of typical sources. The mathematical models often lack accuracy, and the calculation of exposure usually ignores such important factors as the amount of time that people spend indoors or the fact that people change their place of residence. Current data on exposure in workplaces tend to be more accurate, but historical data on occupational exposures usually are either nonexistent or else based on very rough guesses.

Intermingling of Policy and Science

The lack of adequate data and the scientific uncertainty about questions like the biological mechanisms of cancer result in risk assessment being a mixture of science and policy.

A key policy decision is which data to use in risk assessments. At least until recently, EPA has used worst-case assumptions; in other words, it has used the data that produce the highest estimate of risk. For example, in calculating air pollution exposure to benzene from chemical plants, EPA used meteorological data from Pittsburgh because the Pittsburgh weather conditions resulted in the highest exposure.[107] The decision to use worst-case assumptions has been attacked as being "unscientific." But in reality the decision does not relate to science—it is a policy decision to err on the side of risk avoidance, albeit a policy decision that produces risk estimates that sometimes may be six or seven orders of magnitude (a million or 10 million times) greater than the theoretical "best" estimate.

Using worst-case assumptions is a general decision rule. There are a number of specific steps in quantitative risk assessment in which a policy decision has to be made about how to do the assessment. For example, in extrapolating the risks from the results of animal studies to human exposure, the analyst can use either the ratio of the animal's weight to the average human weight or the ratio of skin surface area. There is no scientific basis for choosing between the two. Federal regulatory agencies generally use the surface-area method which, for tests conducted on mice, increases the risk estimate by a factor of 13 over using the weight method.[108] Like the worst-case rule, the choice of the surface-area method is a policy decision about how conservative to be in estimating risk. It is not a scientific decision, because at present scientific knowledge is not adequate to choose between methods.

Priority-setting introduces still another set of policy elements into the risk-assessment process. The risk-assessment agenda—which risks to assess and how many resources to expend in the assessment—is usually a product of policy as much as science. So little is known about how priorities are actually set that it is difficult to tell what kinds of policies are involved or how often the policies are made explicit, but it seems certain that both science and policy are involved in the priority-setting process.

Separation of Policy and Science

The basic role played by policy decisions in risk assessment should not obscure the facts that the purpose of an assessment is to answer empirical questions about the nature of reality and that answering such questions is usually considered to be the domain of science. Furthermore, many aspects of risk assessment for things like chemicals are well established scientifically and are not subject to dispute among scientists.

It is important that those aspects of risk assessment for which there are accepted scientific methods or answers not be subjected to the pressures of politics or policy. Otherwise, the credibility of both policy makers and scientists will be jeopardized, and, because the risk assessment will be distorted, the resulting policy is likely to be faulty. Policy decisions should be made by policy makers, but scientific decisions should be made and reviewed by scientists. A risk-assessment process that is defensible from both a scientific and a policy standpoint must accurately identify which aspects of assessment are policy and which are science. The difficulty is that both scientists and policy makers tend to define their realms in the broadest terms.

Toward Better Science

More data and better scientific knowledge would significantly improve the ability to assess risks. Tens of billions of dollars are being invested to comply with environmental standards, but little, comparatively, is being invested to improve the scientific basis for the standards, even though an improvement in risk asssesment would be a major step in ensuring that compliance money is well spent.

An effort to improve the scientific basis of risk assessment for chemicals should concentrate on three areas:

- The data base for determining hazard should be improved. The authorities contained in the Toxic Substances Control Act to require testing of both new and existing chemicals should be used much more than they have been. When regulatory action is being considered to restrict use of a new chemical, testing of likely substitute chemicals should be required to ensure that the regulatory action actually reduces human risk.
- Research to understand better the biological nature of adverse effects would greatly improve the assessment of risks and probably also would lead to more efficient methods of testing for toxicity. A great deal of research is being conducted to understand the biological mechanisms of cancer. But much less work is being done on mutagenesis, teratogenesis, immune deficiencies, neurological disorders, or other health effects of concern. There also is little work on adverse effects on wildlife or ecosystems.
- Exposure data tend to be even more inadequate than hazard data. The system for monitoring chemicals in the environment is plagued with many problems and, in reality, is not a system at all: there is little or no coordination or compatibility among different monitoring efforts. No monitoring data exist for most toxic substances. In addition, knowledge of how pollutants are transported in the environment and of how ambient levels of pollutants relate

to actual human exposure needs improvement.

Toward Better Policy

Better scientific knowledge will not by itself solve all of the problems of risk assessment. Several policy steps are also necessary:

- Explicit quantitative risk assessment for important decisions should be encouraged. Anyone who has read this chapter should be under no illusions about the accuracy of the numbers resulting from such assessments. However, being both explicit and quantitative allows the assumptions and data underlying an assessment to be critically examined and lays the basis for improving the process.
- Guidelines should be promulgated by the regulatory agencies for the risk-assessment decision rules that involve both science and policy. Both scientists and policy makers should be involved in the formulation of the guidelines.
- Risk assessments used as the basis for regulatory actions (including major decisions not to regulate) should be peer reviewed by nongovernment scientists. The review should limit itself to those aspects of the assessment in which there is scientific agreement about what is scientifically correct and should not second-guess the policy-science matters that are subject to guidelines.
- More study and attention need to be devoted to the priority-setting process for assessing and managing risks from chemicals and other sources. Choosing which are the most important risks to assess and manage is an essential part of the risk-control process, but it is the least well understood part.

Even if all of these scientific and policy steps were implemented, risk assessment would remain an inexact science, and there would still be a significant policy element in every assessment. However, given the multitude of potential risks society faces, given the need to sort out important risks from insignificant ones, and given the major investment being made to manage risks, improved risk assessment should be high on the nation's agenda.

Today's world is one in which the age-old risks of humankind— drought, floods, communicable diseases—are less of a problem than ever before. They have been replaced by risks of humanity's own making—the unintended side effects of beneficial technologies and the intended effects of the technologies of war. Society must hope that the world's ability to assess and manage risks will keep pace with its ability to create them.

FURTHER READING

The initial and classic work on contemporary risk assessment is William W. Lowrance, *Of Acceptable Risk: Science and the Determination of Safety* (Los Altos, Calif.: William Kaufman, 1976). Lowrance's book is dated in some respects, but it is still a very readable and important introduction to the field. Another pioneering work, more complex than Lowrance's, is William D. Rowe, *An Anatomy of Risk* (New York: Wiley Interscience, 1977).

Perhaps the best general introduction is Baruch Fischoff et al., *Acceptable Risk* (New York: Cambridge University Press, 1982). As the title implies, the focus is primarily on what this chapter calls risk management, but the volume summarizes a good deal of information about risk assessment and contains excellent analyses of the entire risk-control process. Two collections of papers also provide an overview of risk control, although from differing perspectives. Christoph Hohenemser and Jeanne X. Kasperson, eds., *Risk in the Technological Society* (Boulder: Westview Press, 1982) is based on papers presented at a 1980 symposium of the American Association for the Advancement of Science. The authors are a broad mixture of scholars and activists; the diverse range of topics includes failures in managing technological risk, the structure of technological risk, and defining tolerable risk levels. Susan G. Hadden, ed., *Risk Analysis, Institutions, and Public Policy* (Port Washington, N.Y.: Associated Faculty Press, 1983) contains papers primarily by political scientists and, as the title suggests, focuses on the institutional and political aspects of risk assessment.

The National Academy of Sciences recently issued two significant reports on risk assessment. *Risk Assessment in the Federal Government: Managing the Process* (Washington, D.C.: National Academy Press, 1983) examines alternative institutional arrangements for risk assessment and the mix of policy and science in assessments. *Risk and Decision Making: Perspectives and Research* (Washington, D.C.: National Academy Press, 1982) focuses on the means available to deal with uncertainty in risk assessment.

Lester B. Lave, ed., *Quantitative Risk Assessment in Regulation* (Washington, D.C.: The Brookings Institution, 1982) provides a good analysis of the regulatory use of risk assessment, as well as six case studies of the use of scientific risk information in regulatory decisions. A useful summary of the field from a British perspective is *Risk Assessment: A Study Group Report* (London: The Royal Society, 1983).

There is a Society for Risk Analysis, 1340 Old Chain Bridge Road, Suite 300, McLean, VA 22101. The society issues a quarterly journal, *Risk Analysis*, published by the Plenum Publishing Corporation (233 Spring Street, New York, NY 10013).

Chapter 6

Controlling Cross-Media Pollutants

Lake George long has been a favorite New York recreation area. The desire to keep its waters clean was demonstrated early in the century when a law was passed prohibiting the discharge of any wastes into the lake. Nevertheless, in the mid-1970s, fish had accumulated such high levels of mercury and PCBs (polychlorinated biphenyls) that the state advised against eating them. The source of these pollutants is not certain, but it appears likely that they were emitted into the air by industrial or power plants and then deposited on the water or on land from which they washed into the lake. Prohibiting direct discharges into Lake George water was not enough to protect it from pollutants.[1] Therein lies an important lesson.

U.S. environmental-protection laws seek to control pollutants as if they remain in the same medium—the air, water, or soil—to which they are initially released. But many pollutants are discharged into more than one medium, and few remain in a single medium. They cross and recross medium boundaries, change form, and have harmful effects in media other than the ones into which they are first released.

The medium-specific approach that is now the basis of government regulatory programs may be ineffective in some respects. In some cases, it has created costly problems rather than provided the most cost-effective reduction of health and environmental risk. In a cross-media approach to pollution control, managers and regulators ask, "What is the optimum form of control to reduce risk from a pollutant in the environment as a whole?"

Pollutants move about for many reasons. Manufacturing plants, agricultural production, and other sources release pollutants into the air, water, and soil. Pollutants are intentionally moved among these media through the management of wastes—including residues removed from the air and water by pollution-control equipment. Pollutants also move among the media through natural processes such as leaching and deposition. Pollutants may change into more, or less, hazardous substances as they move through the environment. They may accumulate in places called sinks for long periods of time but then move again. People often are exposed to the same pollutant through more than one medium—by breathing air, drinking water, eating food, or absorbing it through the skin.

There is nothing novel in the concept that the environment is a system composed of air, water, soil, and biota through which elements and pollutants cycle. The U.S. Environmental Protection Agency (EPA) was created in 1970 in an attempt to match the organization of U.S. pollution-control efforts more closely with the growing perception of the environment as a single, interconnected system.[2] But amendments to the air and water laws reinforced a contrary focus on separate controls for air and water pollutants to reach cleanup goals rapidly.

Now, over a decade later, the interest in taking a more unified approach to pollution control is emerging again. Recent experience emphasizes the extent to which pollutants do indeed move among the air and water and land. Acid rain is a dramatic example: sulfur dioxide is controlled only for its adverse health effects as a local air pollutant, but, in chemically altered form, it is proving to be a major water and soil pollutant as well.

About 66,000 chemicals are in commercial use.[3] Relatively little is known about how most of them behave in the environment or about their potential effects, but that some chemicals can have serious adverse effects on humans at very low levels of exposure is known. Leaching of pollutants from waste sites into drinking water shows that some of our waste-management practices amount to little more than soil pollution, which eventually becomes water or air pollution. Recent regulation of land disposal has begun to close the "last frontier" for disposing of wastes. Both government regulators and waste generators are now beginning to ask what *should* be done with a pollutant. It is no longer possible merely to say where a pollutant *should not* go, on the assumption that some "safe" place for disposal is available.

Attempts to organize pollution-control practices to take into account the interrelationship of air, water, and soil pollution have been labeled *integrated, intermedia, multimedia,* and *cross-media.* These terms emphasize the importance of the transfer of pollutants among the media. In the sense of "channel" or "vehicle," *medium* is a useful term to describe the function of air, water, and soil in relation to pollutants.

However, it is a term more familiar in other uses, such as communication media or the media used by an artist, than in its environmental sense. The term *integration* describes efforts to coordinate individual air, water, and waste programs, particularly for toxic substances. This chapter uses *cross-media pollutants* to mean pollutants that are released initially in one medium but cause damage in a different medium. Although the term is sometimes used only for those transfers resulting from controls under the Clean Air and Clean Water acts, it is used here for both natural and intentional movement of pollutants among media.

IDENTIFYING CROSS-MEDIA PROBLEMS

The cross-media problem can be looked at in a number of ways. Perhaps the most straightforward is to follow the pollutants from their creation to the point at which they are no longer of concern—either because they have been rendered innocuous or because they are contained in some way that no longer creates health or environmental risks. This process may be very short—the pollutants may be turned into nonhazardous materials soon after they are created. Or it may have no end—the pollutants may (for all practicable purposes) never be contained, and may pose potential risks in perpetuity.

To help the reader understand the various dimensions of the cross-media problem, this section will focus on four stages in this process (figure 6.1): (1) the initial creation and sources of the pollutant; (2) the pollutant's fate when controls are applied; (3) the pollutant's physical, chemical, and biological transformations after its release into the environment; and (4) the various ways humans and the environment can be exposed to the pollutant.

The first stage looks at a source's release of a pollutant to air, water, and soil and determines how to achieve the greatest risk reduction at the least cost. The second stage focuses on residues from air- and water-pollution-control processes and other wastes, raising such questions as how control practices can be prevented from simply moving wastes from one medium to another without actually reducing the risk of exposure to them, and which media can be used for handling each waste with the least risk. The third stage follows the pollutant's movement and behavior after release from a factory, waste site, or other source, asking where the pollutant moves, whether it degrades into more harmful or less harmful products, and whether it accumulates and, if so, where. The fourth stage relates pollutants to their receptors. It attempts to deter-

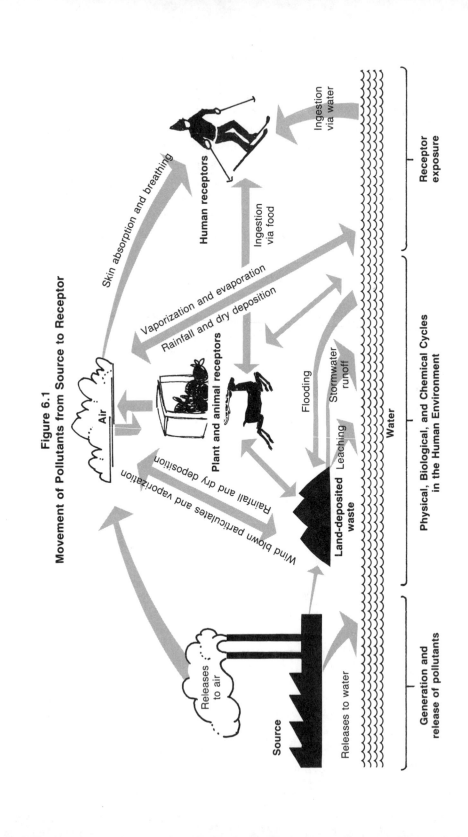

Figure 6.1
Movement of Pollutants from Source to Receptor

mine how much of a pollutant reaches humans, plants, or animals from the three media and in what form; the extent to which receptors are exposed simultaneously to many pollutants from different media; and how receptors react to exposure to multiple pollutants from multiple media.

For each of these stages, two basic questions are asked: (1) What is the traditional approach to the issues dealt with at that stage and (2) What are the cross-media perspectives on these issues?

Sources

Although the definition of a source is sometimes vague and has been the subject of many court suits, the concept of an initial pollution source is commonly accepted. A source is some human activity or structure—be it a steel manufacturing facility, an automobile, a mine, or a sewer pipe—that would, if no action were taken, release pollutants into the environment. The particular substance that becomes a potential pollutant may not be created as the source—it may, for instance, be a raw material manufactured elsewhere and shipped to the source in a tank car. The point of release of a substance into the environment, not necessarily the point of creation, defines the source.

The Traditional Approach

Many sources, if uncontrolled, will release pollutants to all three media. For instance, contaminants in metallurgical ores may be released to the atmosphere during smelting, washed off into wastewater during quenching, and dumped into a landfill as waste material. The traditional approach deals with each of these releases separately. They are dealt with under separate laws that are implemented independently, sometimes by different agencies.

The present process of granting permits for releases makes choosing among releases to different media, to achieve the greatest reduction of risk at the least cost, difficult. At the federal level, most emissions into the air come under the Clean Air Act; discharges into the water, under the Clean Water Act; and disposal of waste on land under the Resource Conservation and Recovery Act (RCRA). Each of these laws was designed and implemented essentially to reduce the release of pollutants to a single medium. A facility receives permits for releases under each of these laws independently and at different times. Thus, when an agency prepares a permit for a discharge to water, the permit is based on the use of a particular technology to achieve a reduction of the pollutant to meet the allowed concentration in that medium. It takes little account of possible transfers to other media or, for that matter, the same medium in another location. Often the regulators do not know the requirements of permits for releases into media other than the one being regulated at the time, and, because different systems are used to identify permit holders by different media programs, it is difficult to find out.

Also, financially pressed industries may have the resources to address only the first, but not necessarily the most serious, pollution problem identified by regulators. Release of a toxic pollutant to the air, for example, may turn out to be the greatest risk from an industrial plant, but, by the time that release is identified and regulated, the plant already may be spending large amounts to control lesser risks and thus have limited capacity to deal with the more serious ones.

A Cross-Media Perspective

Under a cross-media perspective, an environmental-control agency assesses simultaneously the risks caused by discharges into different media and develops the most efficient and effective mix of control requirements to reduce the assessed risks.

The cross-media approach considers the way in which different pollution-abatement devices interact. As one engineer observed:

> This [pollution-control] process has been evolutionary and, by its very nature of promulgation along single medium lines, has forced both emission control vendors and users to develop and install various control technologies along single medium lines. The result of this is that the design of today's technologies, in general, does not consider the effects of one control process upon another. This, in turn, results in duplicate treatment steps with increased costs. For these reasons, the systems engineering approach . . ., which considers interactions among various control technologies, has the potential of improving overall design and performance of existing control systems to result in significant cost savings to the industrial community.[4]

The choices of control equipment for emissions from an incinerator illustrate how different options can affect the amount of waste handled in each medium and, thus, the overall risk. One choice is between a dry scrubber and a wet scrubber. Use of a dry scrubber instead of a wet scrubber reduces the scrubber residue of a rotary kiln incinerator from 130 tons of wastewater per day to only 20 tons of wastewater per day.[5]

A study of residual-substance management in the New York region, published in 1968, first demonstrated the physical, technical, and economic interrelationships among all types of wastes and the importance of considering these relations simultaneously.[6] Later studies of petroleum refining, steel production, and pulp and paper manufacture prepared by Resources for the Future (RFF) explored the differences in form and amount of residual wastes released to air, water, or land under different assumptions about product characteristics, manufacturing processes, and pollution controls. The study of the pulp and paper industry points out that different types of products require different inputs of chemicals, water, and energy, all of which affect the amount and type of residuals. Reducing the brightness of the paper (and thus the amount of bleaching needed) cuts leftover sulfur dioxide in half, dissolved solids by over 85 percent, and biochemical oxygen demand by almost 80 percent. Different forms of processing also change the wastes.[7]

EPA is experimenting with a cross-media perspective, focusing on sources, in its Integrated Environmental Management Division. The agency has developed an industry-specific cross-media pollution-abatement model that also estimates the reduction in human health risks attributable to adopting various sets of abatement measures. The model has been applied to the iron and steel industry. The results of these analyses are helping the agency decide which regulatory actions of those currently under consideration should have the highest priority.[8]

With a cross-media perspective, regulators as well as plant managers can look at what substances are being released and where. Hence, they can first consider possible product design, raw material, or process changes to modify the type or form of pollutants emitted or to avoid releasing some pollutants at all, as well as different types of control equipment or different mixes of controls. Then, they can determine the combination of pollutant releases to different media, within some minimum standard, that reduces the most risk at the least cost.

For industry, then, the advantage of a cross-media approach to regulating pollutants at the source is one of cost. It allows the managers to choose the least expensive way to meet standards. From an environmental-risk regulator's point of view, the cross-media approach is an opportunity to reduce risk more efficiently and probably more effectively.

Although relatively few cross-media analyses have been undertaken, those completed demonstrate cost savings. The EPA analysis of the iron and steel industry, mentioned above, shows that controls on releases to some media are more efficient than others in controlling risk. Likewise, analyses of a 1,000-megawatt coal-fired power plant, a 1,000-ton-per-day Kraft pulp mill, and a 3-million-ton-per-year integrated iron and steel mill, completed 10 years ago for EPA by Battelle Columbus Laboratories applied a methodology to determine the optimum mix of pollution controls across media.[9]

The cost of a cross-media approach can be less for both government and industry because risk reduction across media augments efficient use of pollution controls. In addition, companies are able to save money and staff time by performing analyses of their processes and needed controls comprehensively rather than for each medium. Enforcement is cheaper because separate inspections for each medium can be replaced by a single integrated inspection.[10]

Waste Management

Much of the pollution abated under current practices involves changing the location of pollutants. The amount of pollution may actually increase when chemicals and other materials are added during treatment.[11] Current waste-management methods may reduce the risks created by a pollutant through such methods as stabilization. But, in other cases, the pollutant may just reenter, in a different place, the medium from which it was originally removed. The effort to clean up the environment can be most inefficient if regulators are unaware of cross-media problems arising at the pollution-abatement, or waste-management, stage.

The Traditional Approach

Some traditional pollution-abatement devices just transfer pollutants to another medium rather than chemically or physically changing them into nonpollutants. A precipitator installed to control air pollution is one example. Other devices increase the volume of waste substantially. For instance, with air pollution scrubbers, from three to six tons of scrubber sludge may be produced for every ton of sulfur dioxide removed from the flue gas, depending on the efficiency of the system, the composition of the major wastes, and the percentage of moisture remaining.[12]

Because the Clean Air and Clean Water acts limit emissions into the air and discharges into water, the land has borne the brunt of pollution in the form of sludge. Pollution controls now generate about 118 million dry metric tons of sludge annually. About four-fifths of the sludge comes from air pollution controls on industrial and power plants; the rest, from water pollution controls—water treatment, industrial wastewater treatment, and municipal sewage treatment.[13]

Some pollutants are transferred from water to land or air when sludge from wastewater-treatment plants is handled. Municipal wastewater-treatment plants are projected to produce 10 million dry metric tons of sludge annually by 1990, more than twice the amount produced in 1972, when the Clean Water Act was passed.[14] About two-thirds of all sludge produced by these plants is managed on the land. In some cases, managing sludge on land may transfer heavy metals to water or into the food chain. Metals are of particular concern because they do not degrade. Concentrations of metals are highest in sludges from industrial areas. These can be controlled somewhat by pretreatment requirements. But metals often are present in sludges from other sources of contamination such as plumbing systems, household cleaners, chemicals used in water treatment, and runoff.[15]

Finding new sites near urban areas to handle the increasing amounts of sludge, particularly when it is contaminated with metals or persistent organic chemicals, borders on the impossible. Six New Jersey treatment plants, which together produce half the state's sludge, are discovering that the levels of heavy metals and organic chemicals in the sludge make it difficult to find either land disposal or incineration facilities. Counties in New York and California are among many areas wrestling with similar sludge-disposal problems.[16] Incineration is used in some cities, but fuel is expensive and pollutants may still be transferred to the air through emissions or to the soil through residues. Sludge is increasingly used in reforestation and in reclamation of strip mines to provide nutrients and improve water retention and aeration. Uncertainty about the effects of contaminants continues to make use on food crops controversial.[17]

Treatment plants release pollutants to the environment through other means than sludge. Recent EPA studies in Philadelphia indicate that treatment plants may be as large an air emission source of volatile organic chemicals as industrial plants, perhaps because smaller-scale facilities, such as dry cleaners and small chemical plants, often discharge directly into municipal treatment facilities, which then remove these pollutants from the water by "bubbling them off."[18] A recent report shows that nearly one-fourth of 48 small-quantity generators sent their hazardous wastes to municipal sewer systems.[19] Factories that produce under 1,000 kilograms of hazardous waste are not covered by EPA's current RCRA regulations. Nor are hazardous wastes mixed with domestic sewage subject to RCRA.[20]

Treatment or disposal of waste on land can also lead to transfers to other media. One study of 27 of the approximately 200 chemicals found at Love Canal shows that 18 of the 27 were identified in air, water, and soil.[21] An assessment of case histories at various types of waste sites shows that 32 percent of the media transfers related to groundwater, 31 percent to soil, 29 percent to surface water, and 8 percent to air.*

Contamination of groundwater is a major problem from land management of wastes. (See box.) Although there is no national survey of groundwater contamination, state data show that more than one-fourth of reported incidents of groundwater contamination in Arizona and Illinois were caused by leaching from landfills.[23] A survey of surface impoundments, conducted between 1978 and 1980, found that about 40 percent of industrial impoundments used to store and dispose of waste were located in areas with a high potential for groundwater contamination.[24]

Wastes also move from land to surface water or air. In New Jersey, when parts of a landfill located on the banks of the Raritan River were submerged during heavy rains, industrial liquid wastes could wash directly into the river.[25] And, in some cases, the wastes in landfills can end up as air pollutants. For instance, a study of a municipal landfill in New Bedford, Massachusetts, found that airborne transport may be the major means by which PCBs escape the landfill in warmer months.[26]

Incinerating wastes, including sludges, may transfer some contaminants to another medium. The volume and composition of the waste burned and the type of incineration and pollution-control equipment used determine the amount and type of releases and residues. Incinerators emit particulate matter, nitrogen oxides, and sulfur and other acid gases.[27] These pollutants are usually controlled by scrubbers. Depending on the waste being burned and the incineration process used, other pollutants may be emitted. For example, any metals in the waste will not be destroyed by incineration. Rather, they will leave the incinerator as gases or as part of fly ash or other residues.[28]

An incinerator operated under RCRA regulations transfers fewer emissions into the air, however, than blending wastes with fuel and burning it in industrial boilers. The estimated 20 million tons of hazardous waste burned annually as fuel are not now controlled under RCRA. Rather, they are burned in boilers with lower efficiency and with less air-pollution-control equipment. If the waste were burned in incinerators under RCRA regulations, yearly emissions would be 4,000 tons, accord-

---

* However, the sample was not random, so the percentages cannot be projected to all sites with damage.[22]

Shifting Wastes in Tennessee

Experiences at waste sites have illustrated dramatically how pollutants defy the basic assumption that they will remain, in a sort of benign limbo, where they are placed. Instead, pollutants move among the air, water, and soil, causing damage to health and resources in unexpected ways.

In a rural area of eastern Tennessee, solvents and pesticides did not stay in a landfill that followed the "time-honored" practice of burying wastes in shallow trenches. The wastes leached through the soil into the groundwater and contaminated the wells of nearby homes. Residents reported severe headaches, gastrointestinal disorders, and other health problems that studies strongly suggest result from exposure to the pollutants in their water.

The landfill opened in 1964, after a flood washed pesticide wastes out of a dump in Memphis and allegedly caused a major fish kill in the Mississippi. Velsicol, one company that had put its wastes into the Memphis dump, bought a farm east of Memphis in Hardeman County and began burying drums and cartons of wastes from its pesticide production. By 1967, tests showed that some of the wastes in the shallow trenches had contaminated surface water and groundwater near the surface, but a hydrogeologist's report concluded that local wells were not in danger.

During the next three years, the area covered by dumping doubled to more than 40 acres. The residents complained about air pollution. Additional homes were built nearby, and more wells were drilled. A new evaluation found that the wastes were, indeed, likely to move through the aquifer toward the residents' wells. In 1972, Velsicol was ordered to stop dumping at the site, and in 1975 the company finally stopped all dumping. The site was covered with clay and seeded with grass.

The residents, however, found their water tasted and smelled odd; further, the residents had many health problems. Tests of the water in 1978 showed that their wells were contaminated with extraordinarily high levels of organic solvents and pesticide wastes. One well 1,500 feet to the north of the site had concentrations ranging from 9,820 parts per billion (ppb) to 20,000 ppb in the year following November 1978; in 1982, monitoring showed the concentrations had increased to a range of 18,000 ppb to 164,000 ppb.

Carbon tetrachloride is readily absorbed after breathing, eating, or drinking. The most common effects in people exposed to it are liver and kidney damage. It is also a central nervous system depressant. Six of the contaminants found in the wells, including carbon tetrachloride, cause cancer in animals. Five, also including carbon tetrachloride, cause reproductive effects in animals.

Most people living near the landfill stopped using the water in 1978. The movement of the wastes from the soil into the groundwater ruined the drinking-water source for residents; the transfer may also have contaminated the deeper aquifer that supplies Memphis.

Two health surveys suggest that exposure to chlorinated solvents was responsible for numerous health problems among residents. In a 1982 study of 102 people who had lived within three miles of the landfill, 88 percent reported headaches, often associated with showering. This presumably resulted from breathing solvents released from the water into the air. Significant eye problems and liver damage were among the many other types of problems experienced.

Risk estimates indicate that the residents are at high future risk of liver damage and cancer from exposure to carbon tetrachloride. Not enough is known about the interaction among chemicals to make risk estimates that take into account exposure to the different chemicals found in the air and water.

Now, 20 years after it was opened, presumably with the hope of managing wastes more safely, the Hardeman County site is on the Superfund list for cleanup.[1]

ing to one study, whereas emissions from the same amount burned in boilers total 1.2 million tons.[29]

Another way in which waste handling transmits cross-media pollutants is waste oil. California, for instance, estimates that 368,000 tons of waste oils were generated in the state in 1981 from industrial processes and engine/motor oils. Ten percent of the waste oils are sprayed on dirt roads to suppress dusts and can end up polluting both soil and water. Sixty-five percent are reblended with fuel oils and burned without controls, which results in air pollution unless the waste oils are screened for hazardous contaminants.[30] Budget pressures can force fuel users, such as schools and hospitals, to rely on the least expensive fuel, which is usually fuel blended with waste oil, although many users do not realize this is the case.

Risks to human health and the environment can be reduced substantially when pollutants move to another medium. Small particulates probably create more risk in the air than on the ground or in the water. But, as the earlier examples show, transfers may also increase the risk.

A Cross-Media Perspective

A cross-media approach at the waste-management stage raises two basic questions. Are overall risks substantially reduced after all transfers are taken into account? Are there other ways to deal with the problem at the source that will achieve at least as much reduction in net risk at a lower cost?

These aspects of a cross-media perspective are reflected in several analyses of pollution-control programs. RFF's decade-long research program on management of residuals and environmental quality stresses the importance of considering air, water, and solid residuals simultaneously.[31] The National Academy of Sciences, in a 1977 report, recommends a cross-media approach for managing sludge from waste-water treatment to allow the economic and environmental costs of various management options to be assessed and compared before decisions are made.[32] EPA's Sludge Task Force is developing guidelines for managing sludge from municipal treatment plants on this basis.[33] A 1983 survey by the General Accounting Office finds widespread support for such an approach.[34] Britain's Royal Commission on Environmental Pollution recommends implementation of a national integrated policy for waste disposal, one that places waste where it does the least harm rather than where it is under the least control.[35]

Some U.S. laws also encourage cross-media perspectives. The Clean Water Act requires discharge permits for municipal treatment plants to incorporate conditions on the management of sludge. It also provides for the guidelines on sludge management mentioned above.[36] The Marine Protection, Research, and Sanctuaries Act of 1972 mandates that land and ocean options for waste management be compared,[37] and RCRA explicitly recognizes the cross-media perspective in its findings, which state that:

> as a result of the Clean Air Act, the Water Pollution Control Act, and other Federal and State laws respecting public health and the environment, greater amounts of solid waste (in the form of sludge and other pollution treatment residues) have been created. Similarly, inadequate and environmentally unsound practices for the disposal or use of solid waste have created greater amounts of air and water pollution and other problems for the environment and for health.[38]

Some businesses are beginning to recognize the cross-media difficulties caused by conventional approaches to pollution control. They recognize the relative futility of merely transferring the pollutant to another medium, because the generator may then be required to do something with it there. The total cost may well be greater than the cost of eliminating the pollutant in the first place.

This type of thinking has stimulated companies, such as the 3M Corporation, to carefully analyze their production and waste processes to locate opportunities for more efficient waste management. The 3M Company claims savings of $20 million over about three years through process and product changes that have reduced hazardous-waste generation. Hundreds of success stories of firms that have turned waste into a financial asset are chronicled in the Pollution Probe Foundation's *Profit from Pollution Prevention*.[39]

The most obvious advantage of a cross-media approach at the waste-management stage is its ability to help avoid the types of wasteful and counterproductive pollutant transfers described earlier in this chapter. Pollutants would not be shifted unthinkingly and expensively from one medium to another where they might continue to cause problems. The cross-media approach encourages treatment that neutralizes or degrades the waste or contains it more adequately than in the past. The advantages extend beyond greater efficiency in waste management, however, for in many cases a need to reduce hazardous waste implies a need to decrease the use of hazardous substances altogether, if no economically feasible means of treatment can be found. This, in turn, translates into probable risk reduction for workers and consumers.

Cycling of Pollutants

Pollutants move among media not only through handling of wastes but also through many natural processes. They may adhere to particles carried by the wind and later be deposited on the soil. They may erode with soil particles into a stream. They may volatilize into air. They may also change chemically, degrading into other more or less harmful forms. They may accumulate in various locations or in plants and animals. Unless these physical, chemical, and biological processes are taken into account, they can confound society's efforts to clean the air, water, and land.

The Traditional Approach

Traditional systems of pollution control often do not consider the changes that can occur as pollutants move through natural cycles. Allowable releases from individual industrial plants are set so that the concentration of a pollutant in the surrounding air or water will not exceed a certain level. (Many toxic substances are not controlled under this system; only a few toxic air pollutants are regulated, and requirements for controlling toxics under the Clean Water Act are still being implemented.) But a regulatory agency focusing on the amount of a pollutant that a plant releases to a single medium and the concentration of that pollutant near the release point may overlook other potentially serious problems.

Acid rain is perhaps the clearest example. The primary ambient air-quality standard for sulfur dioxide has been achieved in most U.S. air-quality regions. The standard was written to ensure a concentration of sulfur dioxide low enough to prevent health effects from its inhalation in the immediate vicinity of the emissions. However, 24 million metric tons of sulfur dioxide are still discharged into the nation's air each year, and some of these emissions move long distances in the atmosphere physically and change form chemically. Sulfur dioxide as an atmospheric gas can eventually combine with water vapor to form sulfuric acid. The acid vapor falls with rain on land or water, hundreds of miles from the source, damaging plants and wildlife. The acid may also deposit in dry form, as sulfate particles, for example, and, upon contact with water, form sulfuric acid. Monitoring of local sulfur dioxide emissions or concentrations did not disclose this problem; the sulfur dioxide moves high into the atmosphere and then changes into unmonitored forms. The paths and transformations of sulfur dioxide only became apparent after the increased acidity damaged lakes and forests.[40]

A Cross-Media Perspective

A cross-media perspective tries to identify how pollutants might be transported, transformed, and accumulated after they enter the environment. This requires an understanding of major environmental cycles or processes, be they physical, chemical, or biological.

Physical Processes. Pollutants move in many ways among media, but three physical processes are particularly worrisome: leaching from soil to groundwater; volatilization from water or land to air; and deposition from air to land and water.

Leaching is a major means by which pollutants move from waste-management sites on land into groundwater. Some pesticides, particularly those used as soil fumigants, also leach into groundwater. Leaching is more likely to occur in sandy or gravel-laden soils than in clay, which may bind chemicals. But the rate of leaching also depends on the solubility and electrophysical properties of the pollutant.[41] Erosion and flooding also can transfer pollutants from soil to water, usually to surface water.

Pollutants also shift from land or water to the air by becoming volatile. This process, called volatilization, is a concern at hazardous-waste sites. The rate of volatilization is influenced by the ambient temperature, the vapor pressure, the wind speed, the relative local concentration of the pollutant in the air compared with its land or water concentration, the solubility and density of the pollutant, and the electrochemical bonds that the pollutant can form with soil particles. Even if the pollutant forms strong bonds in soil, the compound can physically transfer to the air if the soil or dust particles to which it adheres are picked up and carried by the wind. It also can transform into an aerosol, which is a suspension of particles in water vapor or other gas, and change medium.[42]

Deposition is a key means of transfer between media in acid rain as well as in the movement of many heavy metals and other toxic pollutants from air to land and water. A study of sulfate levels in streams relatively unaffected by land use shows that even small changes in sulfur emissions to the air are reflected in higher water acidity.[43] Deposition from the air is a major source of pollution in the Great Lakes.[44] Figure 6.2 shows the contribution of deposition as a route for four metals entering the Great Lakes. The rate and quantity of atmospheric deposition are influenced by the concentration of the pollutants in the air, the size of the pollutant particles (or the dust particles on which the pollutants are adsorbed), and the amount of rainfall.

Chemical Processes. Various changes in a pollutant's chemical structure are possible as it moves through the environment. As noted, sulfur dioxide transforms into sulfate through several different chemical processes. Sunlight acting on unburned hydrocarbons and nitrogen oxides creates smog.

Some pollutants degrade into products with properties, and effects, quite different from those of the original pollutant. Although DDT (dichloro-diphenyl-trichloro-ethane) is itself toxic, it is one of DDT's degradation products that causes the thinning of birds' eggshells.[45]

Most organic pollutants degrade into other substances eventually. If the resulting products are not pollutants, then the main concern is how long it takes the original pollutant to degrade. Some pollutants persist longer in one medium than in another. For example, cyanide degrades rapidly in water (the half-life is several hours) but persists in air for as long as several months.[46]

Elemental pollutants do not break down, but they may change form. For example, when arsenic oxidizes, it dissolves and becomes relatively stable in water. When it methylates, however, it is volatile and evaporates rapidly.[47]

Biological Processes. Plants and animals influence the permutations of pollutants. Microorganisms basically break down toxic compounds. The rate at which biological degradation and transformation of pollutants occurs depends on many factors, including the natures of the pollutant and the microorganism. The process of biological transformation can take from as little as a few hours to many months.[48] Researchers, taking advantage of the degradation abilities of many bacteria and other microorganisms, are experimenting with strains—through artificial selection and genetic-engineering techniques—that more rapidly convert substances into less toxic forms.[49]

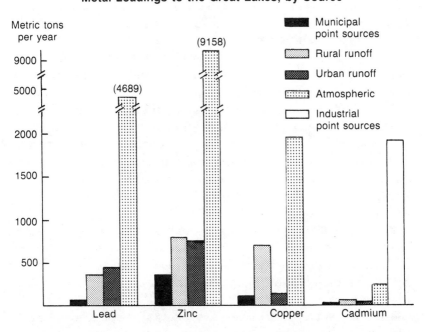

Figure 6.2
Metal Loadings to the Great Lakes, by Source

Industrial loadings are not indicated for lead, zinc, and copper.

Source: Great Lakes Basin Commission and Great Lakes Science Advisory Board.

But a pollutant's toxicity can also be enhanced through microbial transformation. For instance, microorganisms can change mercury into the more toxic methylmercury. This substance bioaccumulates rapidly in fish and animal tissues and is relatively persistent—its half-life is about 40 percent longer than inorganic mercury and about 20 percent longer than elemental mercury.[50]

Bioaccumulation is the process by which increasing amounts of a toxic substance build up in an organism's body. Even if the concentration of a pollutant in water is low, it may still accumulate rapidly, as in the case of methylmercury in fish. When a fish or other organism is eaten by an animal higher in the food chain, some pollutants biomagnify—that is, their concentration increases in successive steps along the food chain. The processes of bioaccumulation and biomagnification are important because, even if pollutant levels in water are very low, plants or people higher in the food chain may be exposed to much greater levels.

Sinks. Pollutants may accumulate in the air, land, or water in places called sinks. Lake bottoms are often sinks for water-borne pollutants. Sediment settles out of the water and carries other contaminants with it. A lake can be a sink for dissolved pollutants, such as nutrients, caught up in the biochemical cycles involved in eutrophication. Land can also provide a sink, at least until the pollutant is carried off by rainwater or evaporates into the air.

Although pollutants sometimes remain in a sink for a long time, most likely they eventually move. Those in river sediments, for example, can be dislodged by microorganisms or by a flood. Turnover of sediments by animals also keeps pollutants in surface layers, ready to move back into the water.[51]

The study of biogeochemical cycles realistically depicts how elements cycle through organisms and the environment. It recognizes that, though a substance may remain in one medium for a few minutes or millions of years, the pollutant is not static but moves dynamically through a cycle or even several differently timed cycles.

Research on biogeochemical cycles focuses mainly on elements essential to life, but the same methods can be used to study the pathways and exchanges—among air, water, soil, and organisms—of other substances of concern, such as pollutants. The Scientific Committee on Problems of the Environment (SCOPE) has taken the lead in work on biogeochemical cycling.[52]

At this stage of pollutant cycling, the advantage of a cross-media approach is not so much in the possibility of near-term reductions in

PCBs Pervade Fishing Port

The chemical compounds called PCBs (polychlorinated biphenyls) came to New Bedford, Massachusetts, in the 1940s when two manufacturers of capacitors moved into the old textile mills on the waterfront of the long-time fishing port.

Capacitors are used to even out the voltage in all kinds of electrical equipment from fluorescent lights to components used in nuclear research. PCBs largely replaced mineral oils in capacitors because they were more efficient insulators, which enabled the capacitors to be smaller and less expensive. PCBs, however, are now known to be both toxic and persistent. People exposed to them may get chloracne, a skin inflammation. PCBs may also cause reproductive effects and cancer.

Millions of kilograms of PCBs were put into capacitors manufactured in the two New Bedford plants before the use of PCBs was stopped. In the process, PCBs also contaminated the water, soil, air, and harbor sediment of New Bedford. Favorite fishing and lobstering grounds have been closed. Some of the 100,000 residents have PCBs in their blood.

PCBs entered New Bedford's air, water, and soil by at least five different routes. Some wastewater contaminated with PCBs was discharged directly into the Acushnut River estuary leading to the Buzzards Bay fishing grounds. Other wastewater was discharged into the sewers; sediments containing PCBs have been found in the sewers and in residues from the sewage-treatment plant. No decrease in the level of PCBs in the waste occurs during treatment, so the PCBs are discharged with water from the plant into the bay. Some are also emitted into the air when sludge from the wastewater-treatment plant is incinerated.

In addition, the PCBs are found in two landfills that were used by the treatment plant to dump sludges, grit, and ash and by the capacitor plants to dump products that did not meet specifications. There are some indications that PCBs may be leaching into the groundwater as well as volatilizing into the air at these two landfills.

Some PCBs were used to suppress dust on roads. Some of these PCBs probably remain in the soil; others may have either eroded into streams or adhered to particles picked up by the wind, eventually settling back on land or water.

Careless handling practices and accidents, especially at railroad sidings where PCBs were transferred from railroad tank cars to truck tankers, also led to contamination. PCBs spilled on pavements may have volatilized.

Once the PCBs entered the environment by these routes, they either found temporary sinks or continued to cycle among media. The harbor is one sink. Harbor sediments have levels anywhere from a few parts per million (ppm) to over 100,000 ppm. The water itself has very low levels of PCBs, but the fish and lobsters contain PCBs at levels 100,000 to 1 million times higher than the water levels.

The harbor and one of the landfills are on the Superfund priority list. The wastewater-treatment facility, which was denied a permit under the Clean Water Act, needs to be upgraded.

New Bedford may have some of the most extensive PCB pollution in the country, but it is not alone. The Hudson River also was contaminated by discharges from two capacitor plants during a 25-year period. High levels of PCBs have been discovered in Waukegan Harbor in Lake Michigan. PCBs are now found in Lake Superior, far from urban or industrial areas, apparently carried by the air.

About 600 million kilograms of PCBs were produced in the United States between 1929 and 1977. More than half are still in use, some in electrical equipment. About 10 percent have been exported, about 20 percent placed in landfills, and maybe 5 percent destroyed. As many as 10 percent may have dispersed in the environment.[1]

pollution-abatement costs as it is in avoiding unanticipated health and environmental risks. This means, however, that a long-run cost savings may be realized.

Certainly, over the past decade, as more has been learned about environmental contaminants, waste-disposal practices once thought adequate have been found wanting, as is the case with many hazardous-waste sites being dealt with under EPA's Superfund program. The Love Canal landfill, for instance, was considered by its owner to be better than many methods of disposal used by industry.* It was lined and capped with clay.[53] The Hughes Aircraft Company used TCE (trichloroethylene) between the 1940s and 1970s to clean aircraft parts. The company dumped the solvent and other wastes into unlined pits and ponds. Apparently little thought was given to what would happen to the wastes once they were placed on the soil. The chemical is now spreading through the aquifer that Tucson depends on for its groundwater.[55]

In all these cases substantial amounts of money are being spent to address problems once thought resolved. And the cleanups are proving to be much more expensive than proper management. Today, to the tune of billions of dollars, the environmental equivalent of the mechanic's warning—"You can pay me now, or you can pay me later" —taunts society. Those extra costs accrued in large part because of insufficient knowledge or recognition of the natural environmental processes and cycles.

The failure to adopt a cross-media perspective may have serious risks. Minimizing potentially serious risks is the major advantage of using a cross-media analysis. Reducing or preventing risks is, after all, the pur-

---

* Hooker, the company that buried the wastes, stresses the role later construction by the city and state played in allowing water to seep into the landfill. However, scientists now generally agree that no land disposal site can provide secure containment over decades.[54]

pose of our pollution-control programs. It is the reason such large investments have been made in pollution control. No programs this large or important can afford to have their purposes thwarted because inadequate consideration was given to natural cycles and processes that might affect the results substantially.

Pollutants and Receptors

Perhaps the most important stage in cross-media-problems analysis is the final one. At this point, actions taken at previous stages coalesce, and the success of a program in preventing or reducing the exposure of the receptors—people and the environment—to harmful substances can be evaluated.

The Traditional Approach

In most cases, the risk assessments, the basis for pollution-control regulations, are limited to risks created by single chemicals causing exposure in a single medium. Regulations issued under the Clean Air Act, for instance, typically consider only the amount of exposure caused by emissions from specific sources through the air. Regulations implementing the pesticide-control statute (the Federal Insecticide, Fungicide and Rodenticide Act, or FIFRA) carefully evaluate the risk to people mixing chemicals, spraying chemicals, and eating foods that contain chemical residues. But they usually do not consider the risk to people who do all three.*

If agencies are unlikely to assess the combined risk posed by one substance because of exposure in several media, then they are even less likely to assess the risk posed by interactions with other substances to which the same people or environments are exposed. Some of these interactions may be antagonistic (that is, one substance tends to cancel out the effects of another), but some are synergistic (when the total harmful effect of exposure to the two substances together is greater than the sum of the individual effects). In either case, such interactions are relevant to pollution-abatement efforts. Unfortunately, in part because of the lack of a cross-media perspective, usually too little is understood about these interactions to identify them.

---

* Regulations to implement the Clean Water Act do not require risk assessments. They are based only on the cost and effectiveness of available pollution-abatement technologies.

A Cross-Media Perspective

The cross-media perspective applied to receptors explicitly recognizes that exposure can occur through all media. All animals, including people, breathe air, drink water, and eat food grown in water and on land. Plants use the air, water, and soil. In developing health and environmental controls, an assessment of exposure to pollutants in all three media is needed because living organisms are the integrators of these exposures. Organisms can be exposed to a single pollutant in several media as well as to many different pollutants that may interact.

Human exposure to pollutants occurs by three routes. A person may inhale a substance, ingest it through water or food, or absorb it through the skin. Air pollutants are inhaled. Pollutants may enter food, to be ingested later, in several ways: they may leach from packaging materials or be deposited on the soil from the air and then incorporated in plants and animals higher in the food chain. The same is true for pollutants entering drinking water. Skin exposure usually occurs during manufacture, use, or transport of a product, although it can also occur at a hazardous-waste site. The effects of exposure may differ depending on the route.

The adoption of a cross-media perspective can produce unexpected results. A study of cadmium exposure in East Helena, Montana, showed that ingestion through locally raised food was the major source of human exposure. The cadmium was deposited on soil and plants from air emissions. In this case, inhalation exposure, the usual basis for a limit on air emissions, caused less risk than exposure through ingestion, although the major release of cadmium was to the air.[56]

Exposure routes for plants and animals are very much the same as those for humans. Absorption is important for plants because of their constant exposure to air pollutants that settle on their surfaces or are transferred by gas exchange. Aquatic animals are constantly surrounded by surface-water pollutants, dissolved and suspended, which can be absorbed through skin or scales or, after filtering directly through gills. In some cases, the major exposure route may be ingestion.

A recent study shows that ingestion of contaminated prey is the primary route by which lake trout accumulate PCBs, accounting for more than 99 percent of the concentration of PCBs found in the fish. Some earlier studies had assumed that the concentration could be estimated by considering water as the principal route of exposure.[57]

A cross-media analysis also tries to account for risks posed by combinations of pollutants. Although clearly much remains to be learned in this area, some information is becoming available. For instance, studies at Argonne National Laboratory recently found that although exposure to sulfur dioxide and nitrogen dioxide individually did not seem to affect crops, exposure to the two air pollutants together lowered soybean yield by 9 percent to 25 percent. The concentrations of both pollutants were below those permitted by air standards.[58]

Adopting a cross-media perspective at the receptor or exposure stage zeros in on the purpose of pollution-control programs—significantly reducing the risks. All the advantages come to naught if this basic goal is not realized. There are few of the economic advantages described for the other stages. In fact, there might well be net costs. Cross-media risk assessments are more difficult, expensive, and time-consuming. They might well show that pollution controls should be more stringent than suggested by an assessment of a single substance in a single medium. In addition, interactions among chemicals must be considered. Fifty or more chemicals might be present at a single waste site,[59] and exposure to any or all of them could occur through inhalation of volatilized substances, through drinking contaminated water, through eating contaminated food, and through skin contact. Only a cross-media approach can paint the broad picture.

EPA is performing some assessments that include several routes of human exposure. In 1981 the air office began preparing health assessments to document exposure by ingestion as well as inhalation.[60] A few attempts are being made to take different routes of exposure into account in evaluating new sources of air emissions. An EPA study examined the potential health hazards of trace toxic metals from 32 planned facilities (8 sewage-sludge incinerators, 14 solid-waste incinerators, 9 conversions of power plants from oil to coal, and 1 coal and refuse power plant). The study notes that, along with direct exposure through inhalation, indirect exposure through ingestion of food and water contaminated by metals deposited from air to water and soil must be considered.[61]

New York State's criteria for ambient drinking-water quality take other pathways of exposure into account by allowing only a portion of the acceptable daily intake of a pollutant to be allocated to drinking water. This portion is determined by scientific judgment. In addition, New York recognizes the need to protect against exposure to multiple substances by limiting the sum of the concentrations of organic chemicals. Discharge permits are to be written to maintain these limits.[62]

SOME QUESTIONS RAISED BY A CROSS-MEDIA APPROACH

Currently, a cross-media perspective on pollution control raises more questions than it can answer. Largely because a cross-media approach has not been used in the past, little solid evidence exists by which to compare its effectiveness and efficiency with that of the traditional approach. But comparisons obviously are important, and they become more important as environmental problems become increasingly difficult and complex.

Where Do All the Toxic Substances Go?

Where do all the toxic and other pollutants go? That they are generated is given. That existing pollution controls are aimed at removing them from the media to which they are first released is true. But, in most cases, no one has a notion about where they eventually end up.

Probably the most straightforward answer comes from a "mass-balance" analysis. This approach identifies not only where pollutants originate but also where they migrate. Thus, it allows the analyst to discern unrecognized sources as well as likely resting places.

A mass balance traces the flow of a pollutant from its sources through the environment to its sink (figure 6.3). As the primary analytical tool for following substance distribution among the media, mass balances have been used in tracing radionuclides for a long time. In the past decade or so, the mass-balance technique has been applied to metals and organic chemicals. A complete mass balance looks at all the air, water, and land releases of a pollutant from its production, use, and disposal. The pollutant is then traced to its sinks. The amount of a pollutant released and the amount in sinks should be the same. If not, then there are sources or sinks as yet unidentified.

A mass balance can be performed on pollutants in any scale of environment, ranging from a small lake to the entire globe. In a mass-balance analysis tracing lead emitted from cars in Los Angeles (figure 6.4), the lead is transferred to other media by deposition or wind. Coastal waters turn out to be a major sink for auto exhaust lead emitted in the Los Angeles Basin.

Gathering information for mass-balance analyses can be a Holmesian task of investigation. A report on mass balances of lead, zinc, cadmium, and arsenic in urban regions notes that developing a mass balance for zinc was blocked by the lack of emissions information on zinc from tire dust, combustion of lubricating oils, and metallurgical operations.

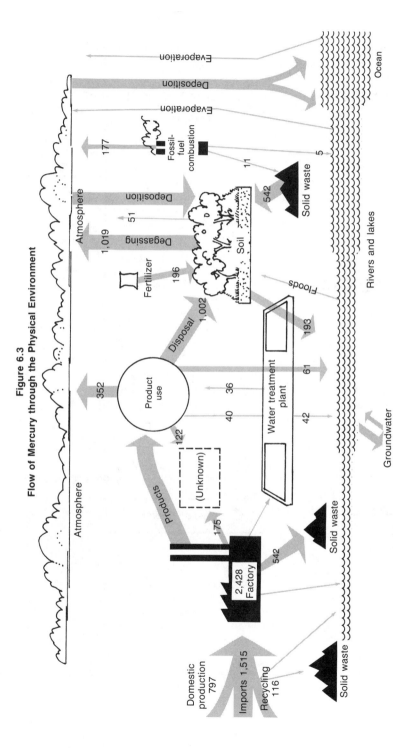

Figure 6.3
Flow of Mercury through the Physical Environment

Numbers signify flow of mercury in the United States in thousand kilograms per year.
Source: The Conservation Foundation.

Figure 6.4
Flow of Lead from Automobiles in Los Angeles Basin
(Tons per Day)

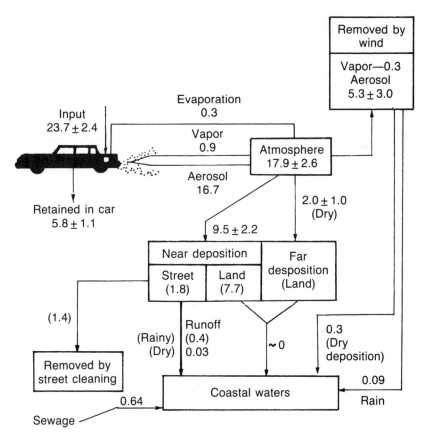

Source: U.S. Environmental Protection Agency.

For cadmium, on the other hand, the study shows more deposited than emitted from known sources.[63]

In preparing a materials balance for benzene, EPA's Office of Pesticides and Toxic Substances could not estimate benzene releases for some large uses such as solvents, or releases to land and water from coal-coking operations.[64] An exposure and risk assessment for lead, prepared by the Office of Water Regulations and Standards, says no data on releases from the production, use, and disposal of lead acid storage batteries exist, despite this being the single largest use of lead.[65] Information on release during product use and waste management is generally sparse in mass balances; therefore, it is not a surprise when the figures for releases to the environment differed as much as 10-fold in three assessments of arsenic.[66]

Discharge may also occur through accidents. For instance, a draft EPA study based on data from four states concludes that the equivalent of one 55-gallon drum of waste is lost for every five trucks shipping hazardous materials. Thus, the expected release from truck transport is 0.35 percent compared to less than 0.01 percent from incinerators. The highest risk of release is from rail transport, according to this study.[67]

Release during accidental burning of products or wastes is a potential transfer mechanism. Fires often cause hazardous substances to be formed; burning of acrylonitrile or its polymers produces hydrogen cyanide.[68]

Mass-balance analyses easily ignore the possibility of such accidents because even predicting their occurrence—let alone the frequency, magnitude, or location of a release—is something of a crap shoot. Sometimes, because of chemical reactions, the substance released cannot be specified.

Data about a pollutant's fate once it enters the environment also are often unavailable because scientists still know very little about how pollutants move through the environment—a subject referred to as "transport and fate."[69] What factors affect a pollutant's movement between media? Does a pollutant degrade? If so, how long does the process take? Are there any hazards associated with the degradation products? If a pollutant accumulates, where? Does it move easily from that locus if disturbed? Will there be any exposure to a pollutant in its sink?

EPA currently funds UCLA's National Center for Intermedia Transport Research. The center studies the ways pollutants move between media. Research projects address wet and dry deposition and processes in the soil that affect transfer to water and air.[70] But support for research on the transfer, degradation, and accumulation of other pollutants must be stepped up if control programs are to take cross-media effects into account.

An integrated approach to pollution control needs to link the releases from sources with pollutant levels in all media and in sinks. Information is needed on transfer rates among media and on releases from sinks. Such monitoring data would provide some information now missing in mass balances.

In sum, Where do all the toxics go? The short answer is no one knows. Nor is such knowledge very close to being found. For the most part, the techniques for analyzing transfers across media that may be useful in calculating mass balances are still in an early stage of development. Not only is little monitoring information available to feed multimedia models, the models themselves are in experimental stages. Furthermore, scientists are really just beginning to unravel the biogeochemical cycles of major elements.

Where Does All the Risk Come From?

As indicated in chapter 5, to predict risk, one must know both the degree of hazard and the extent of exposure. Traditional risk assessments usually focus on a single pollutant with direct exposure occurring through a single medium. But what are the results of looking at exposures through several media and with several pollutants?

The analytical method used to determine exposure to pollutants and to provide a basis for control decisions is called "exposure assessment." An exposure assessment carries mass-balance analysis another step by relating the location of a substance to the likelihood that humans, plants, or animals will be exposed to it, and if so, by what route, at what concentration, and, for what period of time.

A National Academy of Sciences study on halomethanes illustrates how major routes of environmental exposure—breathing, eating, and drinking—can be accounted for simultaneously. In this study, the total intake of halomethanes is estimated by combining estimates of rates of ingestion through food and drinking water and rates of inhalation. Because these rates vary geographically and because of differences in individual behavior, in physiology, and in the efficiency of absorption, three exposure estimates are made. The different routes of exposure are of varying importance, depending on these assumptions about rates of ingestion and inhalation. For chloroform and carbon tetrachloride, absorption leads to equal distribution throughout the body and target organs. Therefore, the totals for each route of exposure are probably additive.[71] If routes of exposure affect various organs differently, then exposures may not be additive. An example is the contrast between exposure to asbestos through inhalation and that through ingestion of drinking water.

The researchers at Oak Ridge National Laboratory, who did the cadmium study, have developed a composite hazard index that links the amounts of a pollutant in different media with the human health risk. The method is applicable to more than one pollutant if the pollutants damage the same organ and have the same biological effects. However, there is generally not enough knowledge about the ways in which pollutants interact or about their biological effects to apply this method.[72]

Even if all exposures could be identified, their hazards in combination still need explication. Most available information, although not abundant, deals with interactions of two chemicals, not the dozens that may be found at a waste site or in some bodies of water. One way to overcome the difficulty of testing chemicals for synergistic effects is to use "biological monitors" such as fish. Mutagenicity testing of mixtures—such as air particles, industrial or municipal treatment effluents, or leachate from hazardous-waste sites—could also be used to explore synergisms.[73]

Also necessary is an expansion of the understanding of how ecosystems work. Most tests for adverse effects of a pollutant now involve single species rather than interactions in a population or ecosystem.[74] One of the most severe effects of pollutants may be to cause an adverse change in the cycle of an element basic to life. But little is known about how these cycles work and how society's pollutants affect them. Long-term ecological measurements are important to distinguish natural climatic, geological, and biological changes from human-induced changes.[75]

Little monitoring data exist on which to base estimates of total exposure. A few programs now provide information on levels of some pesticides, metals, and volatile organics in humans.[76] One example is the EPA National Human Monitoring Program. The U.S. Fish and Wildlife Service measures pesticide residues in fish, starlings, and ducks.[77] The National Center for Health Statistics collects data on health. Usable measurements of ecosystem effects are scant, although New Jersey is developing a biomonitoring system to detect changes in reproduction, feeding habits, and other behavior of aquatic organisms.[78] This information can help identify potential cross-media problems.

Problems at hazardous-waste sites underscore society's limited understanding of how much risk is created by different types of exposure to multiple pollutants at low levels. In short, our understanding of where risks come from is even weaker than that of where pollutants go.

CHANGES NEEDED TO IMPLEMENT A CROSS-MEDIA APPROACH

A cross-media perspective raises questions, not only about the adequacy of our knowledge of what happens under the traditional pollution-control system, but also about the ability of the existing system to address cross-media issues. An integrated approach requires that changes be made in research and monitoring programs, in the focus and methods of analysis, in the types of controls, and in institutions.

Research and Monitoring

A primary obstacle to integrated control of pollutants is insufficient knowledge. More research should be conducted on the movement, degradation, and accumulation of pollutants. Detailed mass balances should be prepared on major pollutants, showing sources, sinks, and rates of transfer among media. Analyzing the behavior of pollutants in sinks is especially important. Under what conditions do pollutants move from sinks? To what extent are receptors likely to be exposed? What methods can be developed to predict the effects of exposure from more than one pollutant at a time?

EPA funds some research and monitoring that addresses the movement of toxic substances across media. For example, EPA helps support the Ecosystems Research Center at Cornell University, which does some work on the transport and fate of pollutants. One study, prepared by the center, reviews the role of wetlands as sinks for heavy metals. This analysis looks at surface water, tidal water, groundwater, and the atmosphere as possible pathways for the addition and loss of metals from wetlands. It concludes that some metals, such as lead, are retained by wetlands, if loading rates are low. However, the majority of heavy metals, such as zinc and cadmium, pass through the ecosystem. Studies also show that metals are removed from sediments in salt marshes through uptake by grasses, which, in turn, are eaten by animals higher in the food chain.[79] Understanding interactions in a single ecosystem is a start. But more knowledge of the interactions among heterogeneous ecosystems (a lake and forest or an estuary and the continental shelf, for example) that make up a regional ecosystem would help researchers compare the effects of managing hazardous waste in a variety of regional ecosystems.[80] One barrier to better research on the behavior of pollutants is fragmentation. Scientists in a dozen government agencies do research which relates to transport and fate questions. Creation of a national center might focus these disparate efforts by providing the critical mass of scientists and the leadership necessary to develop this field more rapidly.[81]

A basic grasp of the biogeochemical cycles of elements, particularly the effect of human-caused emissions on the cycles, is essential. To understand changes in amounts of gases—such as carbon dioxide and methane, which cause the "greenhouse effect"—researchers must explore atmospheric concentrations of gases over geologic time. Analyses of ice cores show that methane was relatively constant until the 17th century. Since then, concentrations appear to have doubled and now are growing at 1 percent or 2 percent a year. However, the relative importance of this increase in biological production and formation in the atmospheric sink eludes researchers.[82] The International Council of Scientific Unions' SCOPE program coordinates some work on biogeochemical cycles. A recent workshop proposed establishing a long-term International Geosphere-Biosphere Program to mesh multidisciplinary research on global change. The National Aeronautics and Space Administration has initiated a Global Biology Research Program. It will focus on global biogeochemical cycling.[83]

For many pollutants, better monitoring information is a prerequisite to conducting better mass-balance analyses. Monitoring tells where pollutants are located and whether efforts to control them are successful; it is needed both to identify problems and to evaluate control programs. To be sure, fairly extensive monitoring is performed. Both air and water permits for industrial and treatment plants require monitoring. But the compounds monitored are not always the toxic pollutants of concern. Also, the monitoring under permits covers only initial releases, not what happens to pollutants after release. Some releases, such as air releases at waste sites, are usually not monitored at all.

A cross-media approach requires not only greater emphasis on monitoring of sinks but also major efforts to make information usable by experts and decision makers in several disciplines. The Council on Environmental Quality's monitoring report points out the need to relate environmental and health data—for instance, data on drinking water and cancer. Particularly important for cross-media analysis is linking data on a product, such as lead in gasoline, with the levels in water, air, soil, and food.[84]

Monitoring information must also be collected and stored so that it is useful at all geographic scales—local, national, regional, and global. The Global Environmental Monitoring System (GEMS), set up under the United Nations Environment Programme, works closely with other international groups in several programs important to cross-media analysis. For example, GEMS tracks the long-range transport and deposition of sulfur dioxide in Europe. This program needs to be extended to other pollutants and other regions.[85]

A Change in Focus

Even the best research and monitoring results will not, in themselves, provide the best regulatory answers. In environmental analyses, as in every other area, the answers one gets depend on the questions one asks. So it is important, in developing a strategy for efficiently minimizing risk, that managers shift the focus of analysis.

Several natural-resource programs already have wrestled with this focal problem. For instance, the U.S. Forest Service has a multiple-use management approach that focuses on the question of how the land can be used most productively. Within this focus, the agency has changed patterns of forest management considerably in response to changed public needs.

Similarly, the Bureau of Land Management used to be governed by innumerable special-purpose laws and requirements. One result: the serious degradation in the quality of public grazing lands. In 1976, the passage of the Federal Land Policy and Management Act (FLPMA) forced the agency to broaden its view of land management, to maximize overall and long-term productivity of a variety of products and services including wildlife habitat, recreation, and water quality and quantity. The focus changed from managing a series of separate land uses to managing the resource in an integrated, coherent manner.

A necessary condition for realizing some of the benefits of cross-media analyses is for pollution-control agencies to adopt such analytical approaches. In 1980, EPA established its Program Integration Project (now the Integrated Environmental Management Division) to find the most useful focus for cross-media problems. Three approaches are being tested. The first asks, How can the risk from a single source of pollution be most efficiently reduced? The second asks, How can the risk from a particular substance be reduced? And the third asks, How can the most efficient risk reductions in a particular geographical area be achieved?[86]

The Marine Protection, Research, and Sanctuaries Act, RCRA, and the Surface Mining Control and Reclamation Act statutorily pose the first question. The first two statutes focus on minimizing risks from wastes. The third law assesses and regulates all the different types of environmental problems that can be associated with surface coal mines.

None of these statutes has been implemented in an effective cross-media fashion. But they have helped broaden the perspective of the responsible agency. For instance, a contractor for EPA developed a cross-media scheme for ranking the relative risks associated with abandoned hazardous-waste-disposal sites to be cleaned up under Superfund. The state of Michigan adopted a modified form of this ranking system to establish priorities for taking remedial action on its hazardous-waste sites. The state uses a number of factors to estimate exposure to a chemical at a hazardous-waste site, taking into account five pathways—groundwater, surface water, air, direct contact, and fire and explosion.[87]

EPA's Integrated Environmental Management Division is experimenting with methods of combining into one assessment all the environmental risks associated with a particular industry. The effort attempts to demonstrate the tradeoffs in economic costs and risk reduction associated with different control options in each medium, while taking into account cross-media residual transfers.* EPA is also attempting to develop techniques for comparing risks in different media to come up with the set of control options most likely to achieve a given degree of risk reduction most efficiently.[88]

Some states have discovered that their permitting programs can be more efficient and effective if they shift focus from releases into individual media to all releases from a particular source. New York's Environmental Quality Act requires state government agencies to minimize all adverse environmental effects in decisions on permits or projects.† This mandate forces the state to consider all pollution-control permit requirements for a source simultaneously, so as to ensure that issuing a permit for releases to one medium does not create problems elsewhere. For instance,

---

* It is perhaps ironic that New York's equivalent of a National Environmental Policy Act (NEPA) forced the state to adopt this cross-media approach. EPA vigorously resisted efforts to apply NEPA to its decisions, in spite of any cross-media benefits that might have ensued, arguing that to do so would cause serious delay and duplication.[89]

† The methodology has been developed by using the iron and steel industry and the chemical industry as examples.

in reviewing permits for fossil-fuel-generating facilities, the state may explicitly consider the tradeoffs between sulfur emissions (which may cause acid rain) and the creation of sludge and its disposal problems if these emissions were reduced. In a recent case, the state decided that the additional 500,000 tons of sludge a year were likely to create a lower risk than the sulfur emissions.[90]

Other states have adopted permit-coordination processes, often at the urging of permit applicants who hope to reduce the uncertainty and delays associated with independent permit reviews. Illinois established a permit-coordinating committee in the state's EPA in 1981.[91] The committee, which includes representatives of the agency's land, air, water, and public water-supply divisions, meets at least every two weeks. If there is sufficient concern about the cross-media problems associated with a specific application, a special group may be created to track that particular permit application.

The Illinois process has identified a number of cross-media problems that otherwise might have been missed. For instance, in reviewing air permit applications, the water division identified a possible air pollution problem with a quenching process in a steel mill; in another case, it discovered groundwater contamination from leaking waste-holding tanks; and, in a third case, it found groundwater contamination and illegal discharges to surface water. In reviewing a land-division permit, the air office discovered that a solvent recycler released potentially toxic pollutants to the air, creating possible risks to nearby residents.[92] Colorado's Joint Review Process, initiated to review and speed permit applications for major new energy and mineral resource-development projects, enhances the likelihood that cross-media problems are identified and resolved.[93]

These are several examples of ways in which cross-media problems can be avoided by shifting the focus away from pollution in a single medium to pollutants from a single source—whether it be a whole industry or an individual facility. A somewhat different approach is to focus on specific pollutants. This focus, which leads to mass-balance analyses and exposure assessment, is done by the Office of Toxic Substances at EPA. It was such an analysis that originally alerted the agency that significant amounts of some volatile organic air pollutants were being released by municipal sewage-treatment plants.

The third possible focus is on a particular environmental asset, geographical area, or group of people at risk. This focus allows an analysis of the total risks to a receptor. An example in the natural-resources area is the Endangered Species Act, under which the U.S. Fish and Wildlife Service is supposed to assess all the risks to an endangered species and outline a comprehensive program for protection and recovery.[94]

The state of New York also implicitly takes this approach in setting groundwater-contamination standards when it takes into account the possibility of people drinking the water also being exposed to the same contaminant in other media. The groundwater standards, then, are set low enough so that the total risk (to people who drink groundwater) from all sources of exposure will not be too high.[95]

EPA also is experimenting with a geographical focus in its Integrated Environmental Management Division. By collecting and analyzing all the available monitoring information for an area, the agency attempts to estimate the total risk to the area's citizens, the major sources of those risks, and the most cost-effective ways of reducing them. The approach, first tried in Philadelphia, is now being applied in Baltimore and Santa Clara County, California.[96] But a political entity, such as a city or a county, may not be the most appropriate geographical focus if significant pollution sources or large numbers of people are located outside its borders. River basins or other naturally formed areas may be more appropriate areas of analysis.

Each of these types of focus has its own advantages and disadvantages. Concentrating on a specific source makes obtaining information on emissions relatively easy. It can also lead to more efficient pollutant controls. On the other hand, the risks associated with these emissions depend on facility location. Moreover, this approach does not necessarily take account of the ways in which pollutants, after their release, move through the environment and create other risks at other locations.

Focusing on a specific substance allows explicit consideration of wider cross-media effects. Its practical benefit is limited because individual substances are rarely released in isolation. Usually, many pollutants are emitted jointly and need to be controlled jointly. It would be inefficient to control them one at a time. The substance-specific focus also suffers from serious information gaps. However, it provides the important benefit of demonstrating what those gaps are and making sure that control efforts undertaken with different focuses have not overlooked serious problems.

Analysis of a specific geographical area or group of people has the advantage of focusing on the ultimate purpose of a pollution-control law—avoiding risks. But it can be very expensive and easily suffers from inadequate information. The area-specific approach requires substantial amounts of monitoring data and other information to determine the entire risk, to identify the origins of that risk, and to develop the most efficient control system. On the other hand, this focus also demonstrates exactly where the serious gaps in knowledge lie.

Which of the three types of focus is best depends on the purpose of the analysis. Often, more than one focus will be needed. The various advantages and disadvantages aside, all three probably come closer to asking the right questions than the traditional technique of separately focusing on releases to different media.

Types of Controls

A shift in the focus of pollution-control analyses might well lead to adoption of different methods to control pollutants. The existing system stimulates media-specific control technologies. Some manufacturers of pollution-control equipment focus on air pollution abatement, others on water pollution abatement, and still others on hazardous- and solid-waste handling. The distinction is sufficiently strong that each group of companies has its own trade association.*

A cross-media focus probably would deemphasize installing boxes to collect wastes at the ends of smokestacks and sewer pipes and finding "safe" landfills to store them in. Rather, it would stimulate development of techniques either to reduce the amount of waste produced or decrease the amount of hazard associated with the waste. Such reductions can be achieved in a number of ways: changing the product, changing the process, segregating the waste, recycling the waste, treating the waste to eliminate or reduce the hazard, and containing the waste. Often, more than one of these methods would be used.

The simplest way to reduce volume and hazard of waste is to change the product or the product characteristics so that the hazardous materials are not used. Industry substituted organic pigments for inorganic ones in some paints and plastics. A change in a product's characteristics may also be the direct result of government regulation. EPA has limited the use of lead in gasoline. The amounts of pollution from substitutes must be taken into account to estimate the overall reduction in volume of hazardous waste or risk, however. Organic pigments do not contain metals but use chemicals posing risks that are less well understood.

---

* There is also a trade association, Environmental Industry Council, that includes manufacturers of different types of pollution-control equipment.

Replacing asbestos pipe with plastic pipe still produces hazardous waste; using clay will reduce the volume of hazardous waste.[97]

Another means of reducing the volume or toxicity of wastes is to change manufacturing processes. Modifications in the process used to make chlorine and caustic soda illustrate how such benefits can occur even if, as is often true, waste reduction is not the primary motivation for the change. The mercury cell was replaced by the diaphragm cell in this process because the diaphragm could use natural salt brines as raw material. The change, however, also eliminated contamination of wastewater with mercury. A membrane cell, developed largely to reduce energy costs and produce a higher-quality product, also eliminates asbestos waste from the diaphragm.[98]

Generally, new industrial plants produce less waste than older ones. One report estimates that new factories cut the amount of hazardous waste in half.[99] The French government recently compiled a description of 100 clean technologies, of which 70 percent involved less expenditure to reduce pollution than add-on controls.[100] There are exceptions. If a synthetic-fuel industry develops, it may provide a cleaner fuel for consumption at the cost of major pollution from production plants.[101]

Segregation of waste reduces its volume, too. Dilution, which increases the volume of waste, is now more common than segregation. Firms dilute wastes to lower pollutant concentration for discharge into a sewage-treatment plant or directly into air or water, or to inject them more easily into deep wells. To save money, small electroplating firms often mix their organic wastes with those containing metals and cyanide before dumping them in the sewer, rather than treating them independently. The sewage-treatment plant can degrade the organic wastes, but the metals and cyanide accumulate in the plant's sludge.[102] A cross-media approach designed to avoid this problem might require the discharger to segregate and treat separately the heavy metals and cyanide to prevent their release.

Once wastes are segregated, they are easier to recycle or treat. One recycler notes that no chemical "process" has a greater impact on the fate of wastes than the method of storing and collecting them. For example, a new waste-handling system enabled an electronics firm to sell some used solvents and recycle other materials because the system separated the materials to avoid mixing and contamination.[103]

Developing additional treatment techniques and applying existing methods are key components of any cross-media pollution-control program. Ideally, treatment by physical, chemical, or biological processes, or some combination, would recycle a material and eliminate both releases to the environment and disposable residue. Several chemical processes have been developed that satisfy these goals. These processes remove PCBs from oil so that the oil can be reused in a transformer or burned without releasing PCBs to the environment.*[104]

Some pollutants can be degraded by biological processes. If refinery wastes are spread on the land, naturally occurring organisms in the soil will break them down. Leaching or runoff may occur before pollutants are degraded, however, so such processes must be carefully controlled. New forms of microorganisms are being developed to degrade wastes that are not degraded by existing forms. Other research efforts focus on speeding the degradation process.

If an organic waste cannot be degraded by other treatment processes, incineration may be used, particularly for liquids. Incineration reduces the volume and hazard, but a residue remains and pollutants can be emitted into the air. Since metals do not degrade, incineration and biological methods are likely to transfer any metals in the waste. For instance, the high temperatures needed to degrade organic compounds in sludge may increase volatile emissions of lead or cadmium.[106] Therefore, air pollution controls must be used. But existing equipment may not catch the small particles.

Stabilizing wastes with high metal content may be an alternative. Although this keeps metals from migrating and so reduces the hazard, it does not eliminate the waste. New methods of high-temperature decomposition may also reduce transfer of pollutants. Metals do not volatilize during pyrolysis but collect in the residue, reducing concern about air pollution.[107]

A cross-media perspective, finally, promotes the adoption of systems for truly containing whatever hazardous materials are left in the wastes. Present methods of disposal often fail to do this. Every landfill has some probability of leaking, even though—through use of liners, covers, and leachate-collection systems—they can be made much more secure, but continued monitoring and surveillance are needed to assure that pollutants do not move. For particularly hazardous wastes, such as dioxin, concrete containment vaults are a possible stopgap measure until treatment methods are further developed. Other forms of possibly accept-

---

* The development of these processes was stimulated by regulations under the Toxic Substances Control Act that control the disposal of PCBs.[105]

able containments include binding the waste into vitrified or concrete blocks and, with care, injecting some types of wastes into deep wells where they are contained by appropriate geological formations.

Of course, not all wastes need to be contained. If a waste is known to transform naturally into harmless substances as it moves from a landfill or surface impoundment, then these means of disposal are adequate, and the natural transformation becomes a treatment technique. However, the waste material and its degradation process must be well understood, which they often are not.

All of these approaches to pollution management would reduce significantly the residual risk associated with hazardous wastes. If such permanent solutions are not adopted, wastes will be little more than moved from temporary storage for shorter or longer periods, in one location or another. In some cases, substantial research and development work must precede the widespread introduction of improved techniques. The signs, however, are encouraging. New bacteria can degrade toxic substances. New membranes are being refined that can separate wastes more easily. One developing technique would transform the nitrous and sulfur oxides emitted from power plants into commercially usable sulfuric acid or fertilizer, instead of the hard-to-use sludge produced by scrubbers.[108] A cross-media focus, by stimulating new permanent types of controls, also stimulates the research needed to perfect them.

Institutional Changes

A final question is institutional. How might existing institutional arrangements be modified in order to encourage the adoption of an effective cross-media perspective? Is better coordination the simple answer, or must these institutions be reorganized? Maybe changes in the basic enabling legislation are necessary.

Improve Coordination

Evidence of substantial progress gained through coordination is seen at the state and federal levels.

Some states coordinate their permit process successfully, as described above. In addition, a federal grants program under Section 28 of the Toxic Substances Control Act helps nine states improve coordination among the parts of state government involved in toxic substance control. Illinois uses "management by objective" to involve different offices in achieving toxic substances control. Maryland depends on its

Science and Health Advisory Group; New Jersey uses coordinating committees. The National Governors' Association's State Integrated Toxics Management Program has analyzed the results of efforts such as these.[109] Its analysis shows that more efficient use of resources, such as skilled health personnel, was a key benefit. Developing working relationships between environmental and health agencies is an important part of these toxic programs.

A recent report by California's Hazardous Substance Task Force calls coordination and cooperation among state agencies "absolutely essential." California has 5 agencies with major responsibilities for managing control of toxic substances; another 17 have some authority in this area. The study recommends joint inspections of facilities by air-, water-, and waste-management personnel or training inspectors to check compliance with regulations in all three media. Other areas that require additional coordination in California are permitting, cleanup of hazardous-waste sites, data collection and management, and development of regulations.[110]

Coordination can be greatly aided by information systems that collect data on releases to all media from a source. New Jersey is taking an industrial survey to collect basic information from plants about the amounts of certain chemicals handled, the amounts released to air and water, the amounts that become solid waste, and the methods used to dispose of waste. The results for toluene use at a New Jersey plant are shown in figure 6.5. In contrast, a search of the numerous files and enforcement records at EPA and at state air, water, and waste offices revealed only one number—the hourly discharge into the air. But even this number was not useful without knowing the number of hours a year the plant operated. Likewise, there was no indication of the amount of toluene wastes burned as supplemental fuel. The industrial survey, however, provides the numbers to plan a cross-media approach.

Data coordination has taken other directions at the federal level. The EPA Toxics Office prepares a guide that lists current EPA actions affecting a chemical in different offices in EPA.[111] The office collects mass-balance information on chemicals. It has also issued guidance documents on 22 intermedia priority pollutants. These include information on the physical and chemical properties; health and environmental effects; releases to air, water, and land; exposure routes; and applicable regulations.[112] It performs some multimedia exposure assessments and, in a few cases, takes actions that limit the risk of exposure on new chemicals across different media. But the office has not been able to

Figure 6.5
Toluene Releases from a Chemical Plant

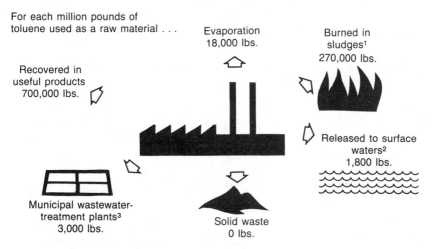

For each million pounds of
toluene used as a raw material . . .

Evaporation
18,000 lbs.

Burned in
sludges[1]
270,000 lbs.

Recovered in
useful products
700,000 lbs.

Released to surface
waters[2]
1,800 lbs.

Municipal wastewater-
treatment plants[3]
3,000 lbs.

Solid waste
0 lbs.

[1] Not covered under Resource Conservation and Recovery Act.
[2] Not included in state and federal wastewater-discharge files.
[3] Municipal treatment plants were not not aware that toluene wastes were being received.

Figures based on a New Jersey plant using 16.5 million pounds of toluene per year.

Source: INFORM, Toxic Substances Program.

regulate existing chemicals to any extent, partly because of the split authorities over them.

Attempts to coordinate control efforts through chemical work groups suffer from lack of interest or priority among media-specific program offices. The work groups have no authority to regulate on their own, and it is not always clear which office would implement regulations proposed by them. Cross-media concerns can also be raised at the final formal review stage by assistant administrators. Often such concerns are not perceived as worth making an issue about, especially if they were not raised earlier.

Even under the coordination option for implementing the cross-media approach, the first priority of media-specific programs will remain cleaning up air, water, or waste sites, rather than reducing risk from all media. In EPA, coordinating groups effectively collect and distribute information about specific chemicals or problems effectively, but these activities do not usually lead to cross-media controls. Although the coordinated permit processes adopted by some states apparently work, a federal attempt to develop a consolidated permit was unsuccessful.[113] Strong leadership emphasizing the need to take cross-media effects into account and sufficient resources combined with increased research presumably could make coordination more effective than it sometimes has been in the past.

Reorganize Pollution-Control Agencies

Coordination by itself, however, may not suffice. It is time-consuming and expensive; it can create some problems; and it is often ineffective. To avoid these pitfalls, some agencies have opted for reorganization. The Iowa State government has, for example, organized a Department of Water, Air, and Waste Management along functional lines, with an Operations Office that handles all permitting. Since the reorganization only took place in 1983, it is too early to tell whether it more effectively takes account of pollutant transfers among media.[114] EPA already is partially organized by functions such as research and enforcement. Reorganization there might create offices to prepare standards and permits on a mixed-media, risk-reduction basis.

The advantage of the reorganization option is that agency structure would encourage staff members to achieve risk reduction across all media. It would force more interaction among narrowly focused technical staff, but the price might be another layer of administration. Reorganization requires only an administrative order. However, unless legislation also were changed, the media-specific goals of existing statutes would continue to receive priority, especially given the strong constituencies for clean water, clean air, and clean waste sites. In such a situation, the benefits of reorganization might not outweigh the disruption.

Integrate Environmental Legislation

The U.S. system of environmental laws has grown piece by piece as understanding of the effects of human intervention in the environment has increased. There are now many pieces. When vinyl chloride was recognized as a hazard in the mid-1970s, five federal agencies would have needed to act under 15 different laws to control all exposures to the substance from manufacture through use to the waste site.[115]

Attempts have been made in the newer laws and in amendments to the earlier ones to induce coordination among pollution controls for different media. Most of these provisions, such as Section 9 in the Toxic Substances Control Act, aim to clarify the jurisdiction among agencies. A few provisions in media-specific laws do require consideration of the effects of an action on other media. For instance, language in the Clean Air Act requires that new source performance standards take into account "any nonair quality health and environmental impact."[116] Both the piecemeal nature of the laws and the specificity of requirements inhibit integrated analysis, controls, and enforcement.

However, integrating the major environmental laws is a mind-boggling task, and there are other obstacles to statutory changes besides the difficulty of drafting the language. At present, no clear constituency exists at the federal level for an integrated environmental law. In contrast, narrower constituencies for clean water, clean air, and Superfund activities have grown up not only in Congress but also among lobbyists and analysts in both the industrial and environmental communities. Also, revising environmental law may seem too all-encompassing and vague a task, particularly to the general public. Among those who have worked hard on passage of and compliance with existing laws, there may well be a feeling that a "devil we know" is better than a new law that might be better—or might not. Companies that have invested in pollution-abatement equipment are not eager to have the rules changed, and they fear additional controls. And environmentalists do not want to risk losing hard-won concrete gains for the sake of what may seem abstract integration.

States may move faster than the federal government toward a cross-media approach. Both environmental groups and businesses at the state level are likely to have a geographic focus rather than a media specialization. They tend to look at environmental programs as wholes and may even be frustrated by the absence of cross-media management for the region they care about. In addition, according to a state environmental official, daily involvement in permitting and enforcement decisions emphasizes the need for practical methods to deal with cross-media problems.[117]

CONCLUSIONS

Some immediate steps can be taken to address the cross-media problem. Managers can insist on analyses that focus on discharges into all media by a source, on the pollutant, or on the receptor—analyses that illuminate the tradeoffs among risks and between control costs and risk reductions. Regulations and permits can be written to require particular methods of managing sludge contaminated with metals or of reducing volatilization of organics at waste-treatment plants. Permits for releases into different media can be coordinated. Impacts of proposed facilities or regulatory programs on all media can be assessed and weighed. Incentives can be used to encourage the adoption of technologies that reduce waste.

As a better understanding of the nature and extent of cross-media problems is gained, society will also find better ways to improve both the effectiveness and efficiency of pollution-control policies. Among alternatives to consider are coordinating mechanisms, reorganizing institutions, and consolidating environmental laws.

FURTHER READING

There is very little literature that addresses cross-media control of pollutants directly. However, the basis for the approach is found in the work of economists, engineers, and scientists.

Resources for the Future (RFF) has contributed a major portion of the research in economics on the linkage among residuals in all media. Its work is summarized in Allen V. Kneese and Blair T. Bower, *Environmental Quality and Residuals Management* (Baltimore: Johns Hopkins University Press, 1979). Earlier publications include Clifford S. Russell, *Residuals Management in Industry: A Case Study of Petroleum Refining* (Baltimore: Johns Hopkins University Press, 1973) and Clifford S. Russell and William J. Vaughan, *Steel Production*

(Baltimore: Johns Hopkins University Press, 1976). At the request of the Council on Environmental Quality and the U.S. Environmental Protection Agency (EPA), Battelle Columbus Laboratories has prepared a report on *Development of Cross-Media Evaluation Methodology* (Columbus: Battelle, 1974). Julian Lowe, David Lewis, and Martin Atkins build on the work by RFF and Battelle in *Total Environmental Control: The Economics of Cross-Media Pollution Transfers* (Oxford: Pergamon Press, 1982).

These books look mainly at how pollutants from industry can be controlled most efficiently. Studies describing how different types of pollution-control methods work can be found in periodicals such as *Environmental Science and Technology* and the journals of the Air Pollution Control Association and the Water Pollution Control Association.

Concern about the widespread distribution of toxic substances led scientists from many disciplines to start tracing pollutants through the environment. An early study is G. M. Woodwell et al., "DDT in the Biosphere: Where Does It Go?" *Science*, 174(4014):1101 (1971). The National Academy of Sciences has prepared a series of assessments of multimedia environmental pollutants for the EPA; *An Assessment of Mercury in the Environment* (Washington, D.C.: National Academy of Sciences, 1978) is an example. Researchers at the California Institute of Technology developed a methodology for preparing mass balance of metals with support from EPA, published as *Mass Balance Determinations for Pollutants in Urban Regions: Methodology with Applications to Lead, Zinc, Cadmium, and Arsenic* (EPA-600/4-78-046) (Las Vegas: U.S. Environmental Protection Agency, Office of Research and Development, 1978). That same year, EPA held a workshop on research needs on the movement of toxic chemicals. Rizawnul Haque edited *Proceedings of the Workshop on Transport and Fate of Toxic Chemicals in the Environment*, Norfolk, Virginia, December 17-20, 1978 (EPA 600/9-81-024) (Washington, D.C.: U.S. Environmental Protection Agency, 1981). The National Center for Intermedia Transport Research at the University of California, Los Angeles and the Ecosystems Research Center at Cornell University are both funded by EPA to continue research in this area.

At the international level, the Scientific Committee on Problems of the Environment (SCOPE) of the International Council of Scientific Unions coordinates work on biogeochemical cycles. A recent publicaton is Bert Bolin and Robert B. Cook, eds., *The Major*

Biogeochemical Cycles and their Interactions (New York: John Wiley & Sons, 1983). The National Aeronautics and Space Administration has sponsored two workshops on global change. The reports are Richard Goody, *Global Change: Impacts on Habitability, A Scientific Basis for Assessment* (Pasadena: California Institute of Technology, Jet Propulsion Laboratory, 1982) and Michael McElroy, *Global Change: A Biogeochemical Perspective* (Pasadena: California Institute of Technology, Jet Propulsion Laboratory, 1983).

Although separate air, water, and waste-control programs dominate EPA, the agency has sponsored some cross-media research. An early example is Ralph Stone and Herbert Smallwood, *Intermedia Aspects of Air and Water Pollution Control* (EPA-600/5-73-003) (Washington, D.C.: U.S. Government Printing Office, 1973).

The need to handle sludge produced by water pollution controls resulted in one of the few cross-media management studies: *Multimedium Management of Municipal Sludge* (Washington, D.C.: National Academy of Sciences, 1977).

EPA's most recent integrated management projects have not yet been documented in published form. Three papers are useful: Jurgen Schmandt, "Managing Comprehensive Rulemaking: EPA's Integrated Environmental Management Project," March 23, 1984, University of Texas at Austin; Michael A. Gruber, "The Industry Approach to Integrated Environmental Management: Rationale, Objectives and Methods"; and Robert Currie, "The Geographic Approach to Integrated Environmental Management: Rationale, Objectives, and Methods." The first paper analyzes integration efforts under the Toxic Substances Control Act. The last two papers describe the work of the Integrated Environmental Management Division of the Office of Policy Analysis at EPA and were presented at a seminar in April 1984.

Chapter 7
Water Resources

Apocalyptic headlines in magazines and newspapers, proclaiming water shortage and contamination, raise the specter of water quantity and quality as the "energy crisis of the 1980s." At the same time, the lives and habits of most Americans remain largely or entirely untouched by water perils or prognostications. Does this prove the doomsayers wrong, or suggest instead that the U.S. "water outlook now is frighteningly reminiscent of the oil outlook a decade ago—affording, cynics say, a matchless opportunity to make the same mistakes again"?[1]

Many experts agree that most water problems do not result primarily from physical limitations or technical inadequacies.[2] Water shortages, while growing in number and seriousness, are still fairly unusual. And, certainly, technical means are available for dealing with most contamination problems—at least of surface water. But, as in the case of energy, water problems could be compounded as a result of imprudent and misguided human choices. Such choices typically are shaped by market imperfections and by unwise government policies, including narrow-purpose programs, long-established subsidies, and inappropriate legal constraints. Because many of today's water crises stem largely from government policies and human desires and habits rather than physical or technological limitations, crises over water often are susceptible to, and prevented by, changes in the ways legal, political, economic, and social institutions deal with water. The real question is whether the institutional adjustments necessary to respond to conditions of increased scarcity can be made before it is too late.

Such changes, necessary as they may be, generate bitter conflict. Farmers, urbanites, industrialists, professional and sport fishers, environmentalists, and officials of different states all find themselves competing for water, the purity and availability of which suddenly carry a high price. Water administrators and legislators accustomed to distributing largess to appreciative constituencies now find that the limited availability of both water and money forces decisions that outrage various parties. In short, water allocation and treatment programs developed under conditions of surplus and subsidy must adapt to conditions of mounting shortages and heated competition.

Water problems, obviously, are most likely to be noticed when they become tangible—be they manifested as groundwater pollution in New Jersey, flooding along the Colorado River, groundwater depletion in Illinois, or the drying up of the Everglades Swamp in Florida.[3] These situations may worsen, and others, less pressing now, are likely to erupt. But underlying all these specific problems are some generic issues relating to water use and management in the United States. Three of the most fundamental issues are: For what purposes are supplies of water to be used? Who should decide how to allocate water? Who should pay for water investments?

These questions, and the range of answers to them, are the focus of this chapter. Future decisions about water supply, allocation, and financing will less and less resemble those of the past because of environmental, political, and financial flux. Among the factors forcing change are the swelling demands for limited water supplies, the unabated desire for improved water quality, the emergence of stronger interests competing for water, recent court decisions limiting the authority of states to manage water, and scarcity of federal money for water development. These trends cloud the forecast for water resources. But clearly many of the stresses are caused by, and thus any resolutions will have to respond to underlying value conflicts.

VALUES IN CONFLICT

Probably no other natural resource carries such varied and conflicting personal and social values as water. 'We made from water every living thing," says the Koran.[4] Water is essential to human life, and this essence can be the source of economic wealth, the creator of beautiful environments, and a telling element of many cultures. A study of six irrigation communities in Spain and the western United States concludes that water usage in them relates to "the justice of institutions—to the relations in irrigation communities among popular control, distributive shares, economic growth, and farmers' concepts of fairness."[5] Plato and Aristotle probably were not the first to recognize that the values to which water is applied have far-reaching implications for the nature of human society.[6]

The Basic Values

The clash of conflicting values is at the heart of most of the battles over water fought in this country and abroad. In the United States, four distinct values have been recognized as legitimate purposes of water-resource development*: economic efficiency, equity, environmental quality, and regional economic development.

The last of these, economic enhancement of an area, even though it was the great motivating force behind the creation of the U.S. Bureau of Reclamation and the Tennessee Valley Authority, has, since the mid-1970s, been discredited as a continuing justifiable purpose for federal investments by successive presidential administrations and some members of Congress.[8] They have realized that benefits generated for one region may not be newly created but rather may merely be shifted from another region (as when the irrigation of western cotton displaces southern cotton). Now, regional development is no longer considered a consensus goal of water investment.

Definitions of the remaining three values—economic efficiency, equity, and environmental quality—vary widely among users and contexts. Each has strong defenders, though those defenders may, at least implicitly, mean different things when using the terms. Economists, for example, traditionally define as efficient those projects with net national benefits that exceed net national costs, regardless of who receives the benefits or pays the cost. Such calculations, however, are easily manipulated, and the result may well depend more on the dullness, imagination, or zeal of the estimator than on any intrinsic worth associated with a proposed project.

Some people use the terms *economic efficiency* and *free-market decisions* interchangeably. They may do so for ideological reasons, because process is confused with result, or because the association happens to serve particular interests. In any case, during a time of water scarcities and tight budgets, the efficiency argument is relied on heavily by project proponents and opponents alike. In fact, substantial economic inefficiencies in the existing system appear to be causing many current

---

* These values, and the conflicts among them, were formally recognized in a federal water-planning document called ''Principles and Standards for Planning Water and Related Land Resources,'' which was developed, after substantial conflict, to guide federal decisions on proposed water-resource developments.[7] The ''principles'' established four separate analytical categories, or ''accounts'': national economic development, environmental quality, social well-being, and regional development.

"shortages" and conflicts.[9] In many regions, the view seems to be that water is so valuable that it should be virtually free; as a result, most water users pay far less than the actual cost of water service. The ultimate result is pervasive waste—leaking water-supply mains left unrepaired, excessive amounts of water spread on low-value crops, and lawn sprinklers left running all night. Society may no longer be able to afford the obvious inconsistency between such waste and the high economic, environmental, and cultural importance claimed for water.

The term *equity* takes on an even greater range of meanings. People who have water offer the equity argument to oppose any action that might result in their receiving less, or paying more for what water they do receive. It is not equitable, the "haves" argue, to change the rules of the game. For example, several western states such as Montana restrict the transfer of water rights, especially out of irrigation to industry, emphasizing the protection of existing cultures or lifesyles.[10] This form of the equity argument may be resorted to even before the game has started. Thus, Congress's past approval (or "authorization") of a project continues to be taken as a promise that the project will be built, even though the conditions may have changed substantially during the decades since the approval occurred (or, in extreme cases, though it may be realized that there is no water to fill the project)[11] or even though many who originally voted in favor of the authorization never really expected the project to be constructed.

But this expedient concept of equity is used only by those who already have, or would obtain, the project's water. The waterless use *equity* to quite a different end, arguing that the term means providing water to those who have none, even if it must be taken from someone else.

Recognizing many inequities is a Solomonic task. For example, is it unfair if downstream residents must pay to treat water because of wastes discharged by their upstream neighbors, even though requiring a city to treat its own wastes does not necessarily increase (and may decrease) net economic efficiency?[12] Should water be saved for all the states in a basin even though only some of those states can use it efficiently at present? Without "equitable apportionment," ad hoc water use may reach a point at which states deprived of water and the resulting economic development feel they are being told, "We've got ours; you're out of luck."[13] Should free-flowing rivers, as wilderness, be preserved so that choices about their disposition can be left to future generations?

Environmental quality also has many guises. For example, it is cited both to defend and oppose the same project because, on one hand, environmental quality will create a favorable reservoir environment for certain types of fish and recreation and, on the other hand, it will drown out a valued natural fishing and boating stream. Similarly, a project may simultaneously create and destroy wetlands.

Many environmental-quality values are easy to recognize in the abstract. For example, clean water is better than dirty water, and more wildlife is better than less. But the value may become much less distinct in specific situations: Are more trout better than more squawfish? Is it desirable to have cleaner water even though there is less of it left in the river?

Of course, project supporters and opponents are likely to use—and misuse—any argument they can. But there is little question that the values of efficiency, equity, and environmental quality, as commonly understood, will be affected, and often diminished, by any proposal to deal with water quality or quantity. Almost all water-resource decisions involve consideration of all three of these values; some involve substantial trade-offs and, therefore, conflicts between them. Harmonization of these values becomes paramount for most projects or programs, because it is politically difficult to take any action perceived as slighting any one of them.

Institutional change, it should be noted, already is under way throughout the United States. Intensive scrutiny of new water projects is now an accepted part of the procedure for winning congressional authorization. Respected observers declare that the day of mammoth new waterworks is over; the time for cost-effective management is at hand.[14] Water-banking schemes, to improve the transferability and thus the market pricing of water, are springing up in a number of states.[15] Charges based on actual use of water are used more often by municipalities for water supply and wastewater treatment. Reorganization of state water agencies along functional lines is more common.

Examples of Conflicts

The sharpest conflict is often over perceptions of efficiency and equity— when the use of water to provide the greatest economic productivity clashes with the expectations of a small or poor group.

The flooding along the lower Colorado River in the summer of 1983 is a classic example. The many reservoirs with huge capacity along the Colorado were built for both water supply (requiring that the dams store water) and flood control (which requires that the dams not store too much water).[16] In response to strong state preferences for the many valuable, water-dependent uses that had sprung up in the river basin, the U.S. Bureau of Reclamation filled Hoover Dam well into the portion of storage capacity historically allocated (under the unamended priorities of the law authorizing the dam) to flood control.

When unusually massive late-spring runoff roared down the Colorado in June 1983, the bureau could only let it surge around the full dams and cause over $50 million of damages to downriver Arizona and California towns, which had been built, at least in part, with the expectation that the dams would protect them from such floods. In defense of the bureau, some cite the western saying that "a flood costs millions; a drought costs billions." However, although the damage likely to result from inadequate Colorado River storage during drought probably would be far greater—justifying on efficiency grounds the tacit decision to overfill the reservoirs—few could argue with the flood victims' claims of unfair treatment.[17]

The problem of how best to use existing reservoir capacity is not only a western one. Growing urban areas in the East and South also seek to fill "empty" flood-control dams for supply purposes. The Washington, D.C., area has congressional approval to reallocate flood storage to urban supply in western Maryland's Bloomington Dam on the Potomac River (figure 7.1). Similar plans are in the works for the Kowanesque Reservoir in Pennsylvania, and more can be expected.[18]

Supply conflicts—and their redress—work both ways, as with the massive allocation (and potential reallocation from existing users) of western water to meet the long-standing claims of American Indian tribes. Because much of the Indians' water will be funneled to marginal agriculture (although some probably will be leased to uses with higher economic values), this allocation is both inefficient and ironic, coming at a time when scarcity is driving western water prices higher and is driving water itself toward urban and industrial applications. It is, however, a redress amply justified by the centuries-old abrogation of Indian resources by non-Indians, and it also upholds equity by recognizing the cultural value of water to the western tribes.

Another example is provided by Charles County, Maryland, where poor, rural residents depend on groundwater from shallow wells. New subdivisions in the county—a growing Washington, D.C., "bedroom" community—can afford to dig deeper wells, drawing the water away from the original residents or spreading contamination through the water that remains. The rights of the original residents are little protected by the "efficient" market solution.[19]

When urban areas seek unallocated water from distant rivers or aquifers for high-value uses, the market suggests that this is efficient. But, to the localities that would lose water, it smacks of theft—especially if there is a cheaper way to obtain the water. For instance, New York City has long imported costly water from the distant Delaware River, creating a problem with ocean water entering Philadelphia's supply. However, several studies show that the Hudson River, which flows past New York City, would be a cheaper, if less reliable, source, and more efficient in the future than sources even more distant than the Delaware.[20] Similarly, Boston proposes diverting water from the Connecticut River to the disadvantage of western Massachusetts, but the city might meet its needs more economically by recapturing the estimated 35 percent of its water that leaks from transmission pipes. (The national average for such leakage is estimated at less than 12 percent.)[21]

Even when water-allocation decisions balance efficiency and equity considerations, their effect on environmental quality can be politically explosive. Many early water developments in southern Florida, for instance, focused on providing drainage for land so that it could be developed for agriculture or housing. A canal was dug in the mid-1960s to cut off the overland flow of water into Everglades National Park, allowing new housing for several hundred residents to be constructed next to the park. Such projects, however, soon began to create serious problems for the Everglades, which can only survive if its water is continually replenished. The Everglades were also threatened occasionally by heavy releases of stormwater into the park, which previously had been spread across the lands being developed for agriculture and housing. Now, initiatives are underway to fill in the drainage canal, and some stormwater runoff has been redirected to flow across the yards of nearby residents, to their understandable distress.[22] Most Americans probably agree that the ecological survival of Everglades National Park is sufficiently important to not allow a few homeowners to use the park as a local water-regulation basin. However, the Everglades' residents did rely on prior government action—as did the flooded Colorado River valley dwellers—before they built their homes.

Of course, attempts to solve problems sometimes harm the environment. The energy crises of the 1970s brought in their wake a raft of plans for low-head (that is, small) hydropower dams, primarily on the West Coast and in New England.[23] But when a dam is operated to maximize power (especially peak power) production—requiring dramatic fluctuations in water releases and, hence, lake levels—the results may include serious harm to users of both the dammed lake and the river downstream.

Figure 7.1
Reservoir Storage Reallocation for
Washington, D.C., Metropolitan Area

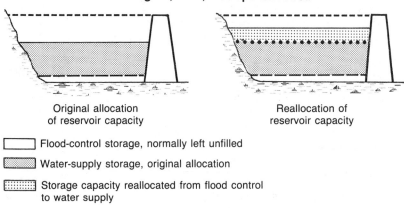

Original allocation   Reallocation of
of reservoir capacity   reservoir capacity

☐ Flood-control storage, normally left unfilled

▨ Water-supply storage, original allocation

▨ Storage capacity reallocated from flood control
to water supply

Source: U.S. Army Corps of Engineers.

Figure 7.2
Economic Costs of Colorado River Salinity, by Sector, 1982

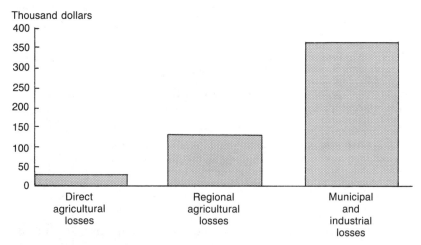

Direct agricultural losses: decreased crop yields, increased water requirements for salt leaching and drainage, increased management costs.

Regional agricultural losses: decreased income to segments of the economy dependent upon agriculture.

Municipal and industrial losses: increased water-treatment costs, accelerated pipe corrosion, and appliance wear, increased soap and detergent needs, and decreased water palatability.

Source: U.S. Bureau of Reclamation.

For example, the townspeople of Swanville, Maine, feared that a new hydropower facility on Swan Lake would destroy the lake's fish as well as their own access to the lake for fishing, swimming, boating, and reliable water supply, and so they intervened in the federal-permit proceeding for the facility. As a result, the permit was not awarded for well over two years after application was made for it—and not until the operator had reached a compromise with the town on lake levels and recreational use. Even then, concern remained that federal jurisdiction over lake operation would enable the operator to abrogate the compromises. In other localities with similar problems, even such tenuous agreements often are not reached.[24]

As the Swanville example suggests, sometimes mutually acceptable compromises between genuinely conflicting values can be struck. However, even resolution leaves these questions: What level of government, if any, decides on water-use proposals, and what interests get to participate in that decision? Is there a means for society to decide whether or not some alternative would be preferable? Who should bear the financial burden of an action—the beneficiaries or taxpayers generally, through government subsidies? The answers to these questions were predictable 15 years ago, but the waves of change that are sweeping across the field of water management are leaving an altered institutional landscape. The "Who Decides?" and "Who Pays?" sections of this chapter explore that landscape in a search for new answers to these questions. Next, however, is a look at one of the most pervasive and difficult problems in water policy today—the relationship between water-quantity and water-quality management—and the powerful but flawed institutional legacy of past solutions to water problems.

The Quality/Quantity Problem

The United States generally has dealt with its two major types of water problems—water quantity and water quality—in different statutes, by different agencies, and at different levels of government. Yet the problems are closely related, and solutions dealing with only one problem often end up exacerbating the other.

To appreciate the quality/quantity relationship, it is essential to understand that pollution is not an absolute concept.[25] Nearly all water is contaminated in some way. Contamination is only a concern when it reaches concentrations that pose a threat to human health or to the uses of water.

The quality/quantity relationship is strikingly demonstrated by the

Colorado River's salinity problems, which have worsened steadily since the 1930s when construction of reservoirs in the river basin began. About half of the salt in the Colorado comes from natural deposits; most of the rest comes from irrigation return flow—water that picks up salt from croplands.[26]

Still, the higher salinity in the river is caused less by greater additions of salt than by consumption of the river's fresh water—water that formerly diluted the salt, keeping its concentration down. Of the 13.5 million acre-feet of average annual flow in the river, some 2.25 million acre-feet evaporate annually from reservoirs in the two basins of the river system; over 750,000 acre-feet are transferred out of the Colorado's upper basin to satisfy the thirst of rapidly growing cities such as Denver, and another 2.1 million acre-feet are consumed in irrigation in the upper basin.[27] Lower-basin diversions which increase salinity concentrations above Imperial Dam, California, just north of the U.S.-Mexican border, include about 950,000 acre-feet diverted to Las Vegas and Los Angeles and several hundred thousand acre-feet for irrigation.[28]

The Colorado's high salinity substantially damages downstream water uses. It depresses crop yields, corrodes equipment, may require costly treatment of water for municipal use, and reduces long-term soil productivity (figure 7.2). Damage is estimated at over half a million dollars for each additional milligram per liter of salt content at Imperial Dam—the increase in concentration that results when 10,000 acre-feet of fresh water are removed from the upper portion of the river.[29]

The Colorado River's salinity problem is a dramatic example of how a single-value water-resource use can impose substantial "externality" costs on users and on taxpayers because decision makers did not consider all relevant factors. In 1974, Congress approved a program to ameliorate the salinity problems that were caused by earlier water-quantity decisions.[30] As part of this program, the United States is building a $234.1 million desalting plant in Yuma, Arizona, to meet treaty obligations with Mexico to deliver each year 1.5 million acre-feet of water with acceptable salinity.[31] The river basin's consumers, of course, pay no more of these costs than do residents of New York or any other region located out of the basin.

Such projects are inefficient, as the then-commissioner of the U.S. Bureau of Reclamation, Robert Broadbent, conceded in 1982 when he testified that "subjecting the Salinity Control Program to a cost-benefit analysis could prevent the units from ever being constructed."[32] Now the bureau and water-development interests in the Colorado basin are finally being forced to come to grips with the need to increase the quan-

Yakima Valley: Dousing the Flames of Conflict

The Yakima River basin in Washington State, known as the "fruit basket of the Pacific Northwest," offers a microcosm of the water-use conflicts and management issues being faced throughout the West and, increasingly, throughout the nation. An arid region located in the "rain shadow" east of the Cascade Mountains, the Yakima Valley owes its remarkable productivity to the energy of its farmers and to the U.S. Bureau of Reclamation, whose projects have liberally watered the valley for over three-quarters of a century. But, following the recent emergence of interests formerly excluded from the competition for water, it appears that the basin's once-lavish water supplies may no longer be adequate if they continue to be managed as they are now.

Yakima Valley farmers are renowned as growers of apples and other orchard fruits. Their hops, for beer, are a major factor in the international hops market. In addition, there has been a recent explosion of grape cultivation for high-quality wines. All these activities have increased pressures to expand irrigated acreage. But the farmers themselves are not a monolithic bloc. Rather, they are commonly divided into "junior appropriators," who mostly are downstream and either have secondary, relatively recent (post-1920s) rights to the river's water, or have benefited from earlier Bureau of Reclamation projects, and the largely upstream "senior appropriators," who have primary, long-standing "natural flow" water rights. The senior appropriators are assured of a full supply of water even during droughts, causing frequent friction between the two groups.

More pressure was added to the al-

ready tense Yakima water-allocation situation when, in the mid-1970s, the Yakima Indian Nation filed suit to claim both treaty rights to flow sufficient for a renewed salmon fishery and federal reserved rights for water to irrigate their croplands and supply their homes. The total yearly anadromous (migrating) salmon run on the Yakima had declined from about 500,000 fish before 1880 to a mere 11,000 in the 1920s, a result of off-stream diversions and inadequate fish-passage facilities (that is, screens and ladders) at the various diversion dams and hydroelectric facilities along the river.

Sparks ignited the dry tinder of this water competition in 1977 when the Bureau of Reclamation predicted a major drought that would effectively eliminate all bureau-project water deliveries to junior appropriators. Although the drought turned out to be much less serious than predicted (the bureau mistakenly had omitted agricultural return flow from its calculations), many farmers had meanwhile taken such costly steps as purchasing emergency water supplies and transplanting entire fields of perennial crops, such as mint, to the neighboring Columbia River basin. Understandably, the 1977 fiasco spurred congressional and bureau inquiries. Subsequently, the farmers' demand for more storage to stabilize and expand the reliable supply and to meet the Indians' demands won a congressional response in 1979—a federal study of possible new storage, the Yakima River Basin Water Enhancement Project (YRBWEP).

In 1980, the Pacific Northwest Electric Power Planning and Conservation Act contributed still more fuel to the flames when it required that steps be taken to resuscitate the Columbia River salmon fishery, for which the Yakima was formerly a prime spawning ground. Implementation of the Yakima's treaty rights would help, but the addition of yet another claimant to the basin's water competition seemed to some to further justify prompt authorization and construction of YRBWEP.

But gaining that new storage remains difficult and uncertain. As of the spring of 1984, no new water project anywhere in the United States had won an appropriation of funds from (or had been newly authorized by) Congress since 1976. Congress would surely take a hard look at YRBWEP's economics before approving more federal water subsidies to a basin that, relatively speaking, is quite prosperous.

And state environmentalists soon raised another objection to the proposals. The largest single element in the storage project would be the enlargement of Bumping Lake from its current 33,000 acre-feet to 458,000 acre-feet. The enlarged reservoir would back up water into the proposed Cougar Lakes Wilderness Area (now a national forest primitive area) just east of Mount Rainier National Park and would be located adjacent to the settlement of Goose Prairie—the favorite home of the late Justice William O. Douglas, a patron saint of many environmentalists.

Environmental groups sharply criticized the bureau's moves to quickly specify final reservoir sites. Instead, they urged the bureau to prepare "at least one nonstructural alternative as a part of the feasibility study," in fulfillment of the NEPA requirement to consider such options. The bureau, together with the state Department of Ecology, did move to consider the

possibility, convening an expert panel in early 1984 to aid in the evaluation of techniques such as water banking, improvements in the efficienty of water use and conveyance in canal systems and on farms, management consolidation, and advanced water supply forecasting and modeling. Such techniques would seem to hold out a promise of easing the basin's water conflicts, although they are greeted with suspicion by many of the existing water users and managers.

What implications does the new openness to these techniques in the Yakima Valley have for the rest of the United States? The interest in using the techniques in the Yakima basin stems largely from tight federal budgets and a growing congressional resistance to further water subsidies, two conditions likely to continue indefinitely. If the technological "fix" of the innovative approaches proves itself in a variety of settings, the means of resolving many present water conflicts across the country could be at hand.

But, while engineers can tell policy makers how much additional water is obtainable through innovative management, those policy makers must in turn tell the engineers how to allocate the water among users. Improved technical administration of water may ameliorate some conflicts, but it will not eliminate the need to address the difficult institutional problems—fragmented management perspectives, unresponsive allocation systems, and wasteful pricing structures—that helped to create such conflicts. In other words, what computer-age technology may have given water policy is at best a breathing space in which to put its affairs in order.[1]

tity of water as a means to reduce salinity; they are supporting an on-farm program run by the U.S. Department of Agriculture to reduce saline return flows and conserve water. As one U.S. senator observed, the more efficient use of scarce western water supplies should be "the cornerstone of the salinity control effort."[33]

In some cases the quality problems can be caused by excessive quantities of water. The drainage of North Carolina coastal wetlands for farming, aided by federal and state agencies interested only in agricultural productivity, has been reducing the salinity of one of the largest estuarine systems on the Atlantic Coast by pouring into it fresh water from the drained wetlands. Faced with the decline of a highly productive and profitable estuarine-fisheries industry dependent on the previous degree of salinity, a gubernatorial task force recommended that drainage practices be limited in a way that would be fair to both farmers and fishermen. In effect, the task force sought a plan that would harmonize economic interests, fairness concerns, and environmental values.[34]

The relationship between quality and quantity is being increasingly recognized as groundwater supplies also become more intensively exploited. If an aquifer becomes contaminated, increased withdrawals speed the spread of the pollution. Similarly, when water is pumped from an aquifer faster than it is recharged (that is, when the groundwater is "mined"), saline water can be sucked in from nearby aquifers or, in coastal regions, from the ocean. Either form of contamination can render the aquifer useless as a continued source of supply.

In recent years, Florida has discovered that a great number of dangerous contaminants—in percolation from waste-disposal sites and in concentrations of pesticides used to protect citrus trees—find their way into its large, shallow, limestone aquifer. Tucson, Arizona, has discovered similarly that it has, for all practical purposes, a closed water system.[35] As groundwater pumping has increased (lowering the water table by 100 to 250 feet in 35 years),[36] a number of contaminated sources have threatened the city's aquifer, on which the city depends for survival. The heavy pumping has caused dumped wastes of the toxic chemical TCE (trichloroethylene) to spread into a six-mile plume in the aquifer, forcing the closure of 23 wells and posing a threat to at least 60 more.[37] Because of periodic floods, heavy metals and landfill pollutants are recharged into the groundwater. Leakage from tailings ponds of copper mines south of Tucson percolates into an area with domestic and municipal wells.

Such areas are finding that there is no clear-cut distinction between water-quality and water-supply problems. Their situation is not unique, and there is every reason to expect that it will become more commonplace in the next few years. Groundwater pumping nationally went up 76 percent from 1960 to 1980, and total consumption of both ground-water and surface water increased nearly 64 percent over the same period.[38] Concerns about the implications of increased consumptive use of fresh water in the Chesapeake Bay watershed has led at least one Maryland state official to fear that ''all of our water quality ... control steps would be rendered ineffective.''[39] Thus, as more water supplies are consumed, pollution from poorly controlled sources—waste and dump sites, farm and urban runoff—will become far more serious.

Institutional Reflections

Governments do not ordinarily act comprehensively to remedy a major problem. More commonly, as was the case with the Colorado River's salinity, a statute is passed initiating a new program to deal with the most obvious or politically sensitive aspect of the problem. The eventual result—as demonstrated in chapter 6—is likely to be a patchwork of often inconsistent laws dealing with different facets of a larger problem and working at cross purposes. In this way, the institutions created to deal with some water problems may first embody one generation's preferences, may later cause other water problems, and may end up complicating the search for comprehensive solutions.

Most of the reasons for institutional conflicts are understandable. All sides of the so-called iron triangle—legislatures, bureaucracies, and interest groups—seek to fit new programs into the mold of existing processes, legislative jurisdictions, and agencies.[40] At the federal level, interest groups ''with a conscious, specialized stake in Washington,'' join with well-placed legislators and ''the bureaucracy [to put themselves] either in control of or in a strong bargaining position vis-a-vis the gamut of values at stake in national policy making.''[41]

These different interests have succeeded in splitting water-development authority among different federal agencies—the Bureau of Reclamation, the Army Corps of Engineers, and the Soil Conservation Service—each of which caters to the desires of its particular constituency. Water pollution programs were placed in the Environmental Protection Agency (EPA) with little meaningful coordination or sharing of missions between it and the other agencies. This fragmentation of power is often duplicated in practice, if not by administrative structure, at the state and local levels—in part, stimulated by a need to mirror the federal structure of grants and mandatory programs.

The same concern for turf protection and other self-interest that generated the one-track problem-solving approach creates an inertia in the participating groups that is very difficult to change.[42] The difficulty in applying cost-benefit analysis—a technique to evaluate the economic efficiency of a project and, potentially, to lay bare its real purposes and inadequacies—to federal water projects is an extreme example. Though such analysis was first required for some projects, strenuous resistance from all three sides of the iron triangle prevented cost-benefit analysis from being made mandatory throughout the government until 1979, when it became part of a continuing effort to integrate efficiency, equity, environmental quality, and regional economic development into a formal project-planning process for all federal agencies.[43] The Reagan administration, however, backtracked in 1982, when it reverted the guidelines to a voluntary status and abolished the interagency Water Resources Council that led the fight for consistency, rigor, and integration within the federal government.[44]

Thus, there tends to be limited support for the more sweeping integration of quality/quantity solutions across agency boundaries: such integration is relegated to politically impotent regional planning and river-basin organizations, if it is addressed at all. As a result, the single-focus-agency approach to quality/quantity issues may fall short on all three goals of efficiency, equity, and environmental quality. The Colorado River salinity example suggests how fragmented decision making forces society to pay twice to solve quality/quantity problems: once to reach the original supply or cleanup objective and once again to deal with problems created by the first "solution."

It is also difficult to contend that single-aim programs provide socially equitable benefits. Programs to build storage dams and other water-supply projects seemed sensible in their earlier years, with their aim to redistribute resources to regions (for example, the West) and social groups (for example, small farmers) that were otherwise disadvantaged. But, over time, some of the formerly disadvantaged have become rather privileged.[45] Besides, water-development programs in practice have not always provided as much help for the poor as intended. For instance, although 91 percent of the landowners receiving irrigation water from the Bureau of Reclamation own fewer than 160 acres (the size limit set in 1902 for irrigation subsidies), under 3 percent of the farms control 31 percent of the land served by bureau projects.[46]

Finally, federal agencies are being forced to recognize that single-mission water policies are often detrimental to environmental quality. The U.S. Army Corps of Engineers was among the federal agencies most frequently sued for failure adequately to consider environmental concerns in their proposals in the first years after the National Environmental Policy Act (NEPA) was passed.[47]

Options for Integrated Solutions

One approach to the quality/quantity quandary is to take direct steps to reduce fragmentation and spur closer integration of the two issues. In fact, numerous measures have been adopted, primarily at the state level and primarily in response to specific local conditions and issues. This contrasts with the way in which federal regulations, grants, and projects often have forced state and local actions into the same mold, regardless of local suitability. Some of the possibilities of these integrated programs, and their difficulties, are discussed below.

Formal Requirement to Consider Effects of an Action. This option represents the least change from business-as-usual. It was instituted throughout the federal government by NEPA and many similar state laws that require some sort of impact-assessment process.[48] Although denigrated by many as relatively trivial, these laws marked a historically significant rejection of compartmentalized decision making by requiring agencies comprehensively to assess the effects of their proposed actions.

However, impact assessment alone is not sufficient to merge water-quality and -quantity goals in agency decisions. Unless an agency has the authority to act on such broader considerations—and reap institutional benefits from doing so—it is not likely to take them into account to any significant degree. The behavior of the Tennessee Valley Authority (TVA) in pressing for completion of the Tellico Dam in Tennessee is illustrative. TVA's actions suggest that the loss of agricultural land and of fish and wildlife caused by the project (which, even from the standpoint of direct costs alone, was uneconomical) were not compelling considerations to TVA, because its statutory mission was limited to flood control, power production, and economic development.[49] The project's local and congressional backers, the other two sides of the iron triangle, shared the same narrow concerns. Mere information and argument generally will not force such groups to recognize broader views.

Institutional Coordination. If simple consideration of effects does no more than raise agency awareness—with limited hope of corresponding action—then perhaps a structured liaison among agencies can be more effective. At the federal level, an interagency memorandum of understanding is the typical method for making coordination formal, but historically this device has been weak unless applied to specific, active projects or to statutes that demand coordination.[50] One interesting state initiative illustrates a pertinent principle.

Minnesota has established a coordinating council, the Groundwater Protection Strategy Work Group, comprised of key staff from the 13 major federal, state, and local agencies responsible for particular aspects of groundwater management. Although the group has no power of its own and operates fairly informally, the political premium that Minnesota citizens place on the plenitude and purity of their water apparently induced the members to seek substantive management agreements to protect groundwater quality and supply and to implement those agreements in their respective agencies. Similar arrangements to coordinate the actions of different water agencies are proposed in Mississippi and Wisconsin, although they are not likely to be as effective unless their state's residents and governor have the apparently strong political commitment to coordinated management that enabled the Minnesota group to be effective without formal statutory authority.[51]

Broader Statutory Mandates. Another alternative being used with increasing frequency is to broaden agency objectives by statute—that is, to permit an agency to consider and act upon wider concerns. One type of provision adopted in several states encourages agencies to act on the commonsense proposition that it is efficient to match an available water supply with users who need water of that quality.

In Florida, for instance, new industries that do not require high-quality water are strongly urged by statute to locate at coastal sites where abundant quantities of briny water can be supplied, leaving inland fresh water for domestic and agricultural needs.[52] Similarly, several localities around the country, some under statutory mandates, use treated effluent from municipal wastewater plants on public golf courses, on farmland, and for the recharge of groundwater supplies.[53] The motivating factor in most of these cases is probably economics. Where "new" supplies are very costly, wastewater already in the system may be the least expensive source of supply.

Administrative Consolidation. The ultimate logical step toward integration is to combine quality and supply responsibilities in the same agency. Such an administrative consolidation seems desirable in principle, but a half-century of failed attempts to establish a unified federal Department of Natural Resources suggest the unlikelihood of creating a federal Department of Water Resources.

Even in the state "laboratories of democracy," where such consolidations have been tried, the results have varied widely. In Washington State, a 1970 consolidation of quality and quantity functions (which had been in two separate, potent bureaus) into a single Department of Ecology was to some degree undone in late 1983, even though, at the beginning, the consolidation had been taken so seriously that many staff members of the original agencies exchanged duties.[54] The reversion was impelled, at least in part, by the state legislature's desire to see specific functions administered individually in a familiar bureau—possibly another example of the iron triangle at work.

More recently, South Dakota successfully combined two active water agencies because of strong gubernatorial prodding and probably because the issues of salinity and effluent reuse were important to both quality and quantity constituencies.[55] Iowa, Mississippi, and Tennessee have each merged a largely advisory or untested water-quantity function with a more dominant water-quality function within the last five years.[56] Although some fear that the smaller quantity function will get short shrift in appropriations and program visibility, in a larger agency it may be better placed politically and substantively to expand if water allocation becomes a hot political issue nationwide.

Evidence of consolidation's clout is apparent in the experience of New Jersey. An ability to deal with severe pollution threats to the state's urban water supplies—and with the lust of Philadelphia and New York City for the vast, pure aquifers of New Jersey's Pine Barrens[57]—has shown the benefits of the integrated review of all water permits that is routine in the state's consolidated Department of Environmental Protection.[58]

Thus, a few states with combined water agencies seem to have put an integrated operation into place, although no such program has really been tested over the long term. But, even when organizational obstacles can be overcome, the possible costs of restructuring, including program disruption (as Washington State's consolidation illustrates), must be recognized. However, a clearly warranted and well-designed consolidation should produce long-term improvements in water policies and program operations that outweigh any short-term costs.

A more serious, seemingly permanent, drawback to integration is that tying water-quantity management more closely to that of water quality makes it more difficult to integrate water-quality programs with air and solid-waste regulation (as discussed in chapter 6). Ending management fragmentation in one problem area may often cause it in another.

Whether consolidation is desirable depends largely on whether it is functionally practical, politically realistic, and appropriate to local conditions. Without these ingredients, consolidation is unlikely to be worth its costs; in such situations, it seems preferable to reduce fragmentation in water management by the other, less drastic means of broadening statutory mandates and coordinating existing institutions. In any case, the most important thing is to have enough administrative coordination to find harmony when a conflict is not irreconcilable (as in the North Carolina drainage case) and to at least recognize the different points of view in a genuine conflict (as in the Everglades flooding).

Concluding Thoughts

The quality/quantity examples discussed here generally appear to involve relatively straightforward relationships between depletion and contamination, but whether these relationships always hold is not known. Despite all the complexities of the administrative adjustments evaluated above, it is easier to suggest such adjustments than to define the actual physical principles that link water quality to water quantity and should guide bureaucratic practice. These principles can be found only through further scientific study, and such study can be gained principally by observing how integrated agency practices and decisions actually affect a physical water resource itself—a sort of Catch-22 situation. Nothwithstanding this uncertainty, a greater degree of integration remains desirable where it can be obtained.

WHO DECIDES ON WATER USE?

In 1976, a farmer named Joy Sporhase started using water from a well on his farm in Nebraska to irrigate some land he owned in Colorado, just across the road. He had been barred from drilling the well in Colorado itself because the land overlay part of the Ogallala aquifer, which was subject to heavy overdrafts and strict control of water withdrawals.[59] Like many states, however, Nebraska had a statute strictly limiting the export of water. It therefore demanded that Sporhase cease piping his Nebraska-drilled water into Colorado. He refused and vowed to defend his position to the limit.

The resulting 1982 U.S. Supreme Court decision—*Sporhase* v. *Nebraska ex rel. Douglas*[60]—shocked the West and has striking implications for the rest of the United States as well: the court held that Nebraska's statute limiting exports was an unconstitutional restriction of interstate commerce in water. If the decision is broadly applied, it could greatly limit states' power to control interstate transfers of water, especially from farms to cities and industries.

The increasing competition for scarce water resources is already stimulating such transfers both within and between states. Today, the challenge for water policy is to resolve these conflicts through sensitive and careful planning and management. This makes the question of *who* resolves the conflicts increasingly important.

In the past, it usually was possible to settle such conflicts simply by developing new water supplies.[61] But, with tighter supplies and tighter money, it will be increasingly difficult to apply such solutions in the future. To supply new claimants, more water will have to be squeezed out of existing supplies by conservation, better management, and, in some cases, transfers from present users. With greater demands on scarce water, will decision makers be able to balance wisely and fairly the demands for efficiency, equity, and environmental quality in water use and allocation?

Growing scarcity and market competition for water are not the only factors changing the traditions of water allocation. As the last drop of water is wrung out of western river systems such as the Colorado's (figure 7.3), and as new industrial and municipal users place unprecedented demands on watersheds in other parts of the country, protests are being raised about reduced water levels and the loss of various resources and activities—riparian and in-stream habitat for fish and wildlife, swimming, boating, fishing, aesthetic values, and the like—that depend on more generous stream flows.[62]

Laws designed to keep water in rivers often are enacted in response to such protests, but, in reality, they set the stage for increased allocation conflicts between in-stream and off-stream competitors. In addition, in many western states, the water claims of American Indian tribes add still another layer of confusion to the water-allocation picture. Many tribes are seeking rights to water as a resource reserved to them along with their reservations, and the amounts claimed may exceed available stream flows.[63] It is clear, in any case, that the varied claimants all want to be included in the decision-making process.

In the arid West, the first region to face full-scale competition among all types of users for a fully allocated water supply, watching the development of a slow but irresistible wave of change is particularly illuminating. The traditional interests—farmers, ranchers, miners, and their lobbyists and allies throughout the government, who long defined the rules under which water was used—are now facing the mounting influence of other

Figure 7.3
Average Annual Water Flow in the Lower Colorado River

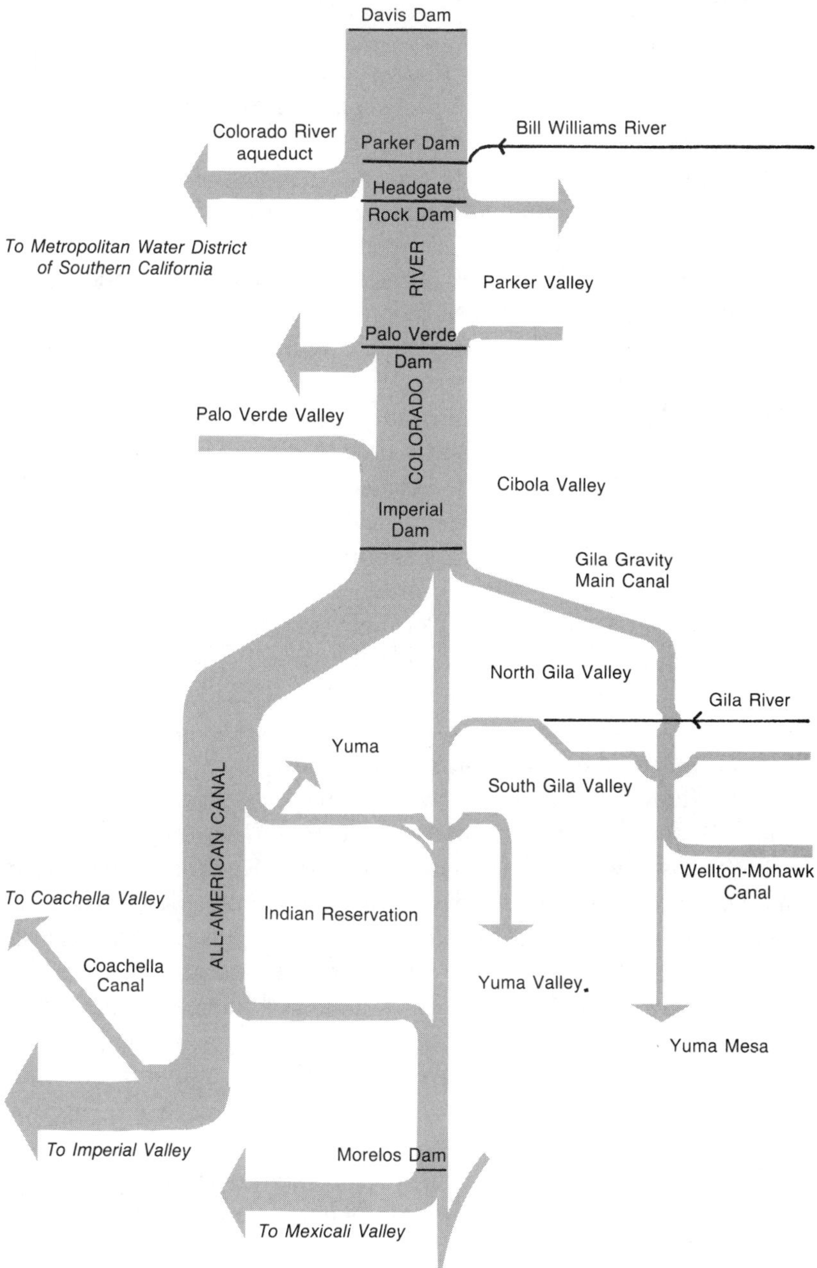

Width of line proportional to average annual flow.

Source: U.S. Geological Survey.

groups such as American Indians, Hispanics, environmentalists, and tax payers associations, in water decisions.

In Arizona, passage of the sweeping 1980 Groundwater Management Act[64] marked the decline of farmers' influence over water allocation and the ascendancy of urban interests. An alliance of traditional user groups in California failed, in 1982, to win voter approval of the state's controversial Peripheral Canal project.[65] In New Mexico and Colorado, special commissions on water law and allocation appointed by the governors have included as members several persons not identified with traditional water interests.[66] In Congress, the emergence of new voices and values has brought a slowdown in the authorization of new projects since 1976.[67]

Water-quality decisions provoke less debate than water-quantity decisions about which constituencies should be involved, probably because the Clean Water Act incorporates public participation. Few decisions can be made without a public hearing or public comment, and those comments go on the record that is used to interpret the law. Thus, no one interested in the issue is excluded.

But the water-quality programs have stimulated substantial debate about which level of government should have primary responsibility to decide.[68] Before 1972, this authority clearly rested with the states or, if they did not exercise it, with local governments. However, the 1972 amendments to the Clean Water Act transferred much authority to the federal government, although it could be delegated back to the states if they demonstrated the capability and willingness to accept it. To regain control, the states had to implement the uniform, national, technology-based effluent limitations set by the federal government. Even then, the feds would look over their shoulders.

In the last few years, the question of how much independence states should have has been debated even more vigorously. When the former EPA administrator, Anne Gorsuch, attempted to give the states greater flexibility in setting ambient water-quality standards, the Senate's Environment and Public Works Committee resisted the move until her successor, William Ruckelshaus, relented.[69] Similarly, a long-standing controversy over who should have primary responsibility for controlling toxic waste discharges into municipal sewers—the municipality that owns the sewers, the state, or EPA—was settled in favor of EPA.[70] These results reflect both a concern that too many states and municipalities are unable or unwilling to exercise effective control over problems that affect their economic growth and a judgment that EPA is better situated politically to deal with such problems.

Interstate Conflicts

The specter of *Sporhase* is threatening to many states because the case could undermine their authority to control their water resources and the economies that rely on them. *Sporhase*-authorized interstate water transfers promise to give government less, and the water market more, control over water allocation. The West has had a quiet market in water rights, but the rapidly growing populations and large energy companies there can afford to pay very high prices for water rights—prices so high that many farmers growing low-value alfalfa are sorely tempted to sell their rights. This market already is becoming more competitive and volatile. But, even as the competitive pressures that create intrastate water conflicts spill over state lines, the *Sporhase* decision puts state power to deal with interstate conflicts in a sort of limbo.

The first major post-*Sporhase* decision, *El Paso v. S. E. Reynolds*, strengthens the concept that state export limits are impermissible.[71] The city of El Paso, Texas—which sought to pump water from the Mesilla Bolson (aquifer) of southern New Mexico as its own supplies became depleted—successfully contested, at the federal district court level, New Mexico's absolute ban on water exports. The court held that *Sporhase* prohibits any export limits other than those that protect the few gallons per day necessary for the "survival" of a state's residents.

Many states are probably largely unaware of *Sporhase*—witness the recent proposals in Michigan to bar any out-of-state water exports.[72] Officials in other states, particularly in the East and South, may assume that *Sporhase* does not apply to their states. But those states may well be proved wrong if they too attempt to limit water exports because of feared local shortages and increased interstate competition that might negatively affect their economic futures. Local protectionism may be a two-edged sword. While New York City longs to store and divert the headwaters of the Susquehanna River—which flows completely across Pennsylvania and is the main freshwater source of the Chesapeake Bay in Maryland—New York State goes to court to restrain Exxon's diversion of Hudson River water to Aruba by oil tankers.[73]

Interstate disputes on the Apalachicola River system (in Georgia, Alabama, and Florida), the upper Missouri River, and the Connecticut River—between municipal and industrial supply and in-stream flow for water quality, navigation, and fishery protection—illustrate that these conflicts affect all parts of the nation.[74] The inexorable pressure throughout the United States for interstate water diversions to support municipal and industrial development will continue to erode unilateral state attempts to control water resources within state boundaries. Indeed, state autonomy over river resources had begun to fade even before *Sporhase*. As one state official commented, "although the States in their constitutions and statutes claim ownership of the water resources within their boundaries, the development of those resources tend to be out of State hands."[75]

The diminishing of interstate water-quality disputes over the past decade by uniform national effluent standards may just be a temporary calm, as states find out-of-state sources responsible for some of their nonpoint-source water pollution. Maryland has discovered already that much of the pollution entering Chesapeake Bay comes from Pennsylvania. Canada clearly has a major stake in the Great Lakes, but a large part of the pollution there results from the United States' failure to further clean up Great Lakes waters as directed in binational agreements.[76]

Among the obstacles to resolving interstate water disputes over quality or quantity, the first and most obvious is simply geography. Few major river systems are contained within a single state; the common use of rivers as state borders guarantees conflict over water allocation and use. Only three state borders in the entire nation—Montana-Idaho, North Carolina-Tennessee, and Virginia's western borders with West Virginia and Kentucky—follow watershed lines for any significant part of their length, and no border does so in its entirety.

Another obstacle is the quality/quantity issue: troublesome under any conditions, it becomes particularly so in interstate conflicts, as in the case of the Colorado River's salinity. Sometimes, quality problems are so intractable they are simply ignored in allocation agreements, which may lead to difficulties later. Sometimes attempts to avoid quality problems lead to supply disputes. This was the experience of El Paso when it turned to the aquifers of southern New Mexico as an alternative to increased pumping of its own groundwater because such pumping would have caused saline intrusion from deeper, poorer-quality aquifers.[77]

Conversely, several factors promote resolution of interstate water conflicts. Any state has the potential to lose as well as win from interstate transfers, particularly if a state shares watersheds or groundwater aquifers with other states. If states recognize this mutual vulnerability, *Sporhase* may stimulate them to cooperate more aggressively in interstate agreements. If states see that they cannot control the water demands of out-of-state users (ranging from cities to mineral or energy developments in remote, rural settings) by themselves, they may seek to limit those demands in concert with other states and Congress. New and more flexible interstate agreements may emerge from this turmoil.

Similarly, federal budget constraints, under which states are forced to share water-development costs with the federal government, create incentives for states that share a common water body to find cost-effective interstate plans for water development and treatment.

Intrastate Conflicts

Although it is perhaps ironic that a lawsuit involving a lone Nebraska wheat farmer could open the floodgates for such a tidal wave of change, the emergence of this dispute now is not a historical fluke. The same water scarcities that caused Colorado to prevent Joy Sporhase from drilling a well on his Colorado farmland are becoming common not only in the West but throughout the United States—and for both groundwater and surface water.[78] The U.S. Geological Survey identifies water availability and, implicitly, the "rising competition for water" as "an issue in every state" and one that is in fair part "a function of the facilities and the institutional arrangements—laws, agreements, and operating rules—for withdrawing the water."[79]

In eastern states, where conditions of water surplus have long been routine, the very definition of water rights, not to mention their quantification and transferability, often has been left quite vague. But with growing demands for inland navigation and irrigation water in the South, for flows to dilute pollution in the North and Midwest, and for municipal and recreational water everywhere, this vagueness is not likely to be politically, economically, or socially tolerable for long. As the Geological Survey noted, "although the competition grows gradually, the resulting scarcity may develop ... suddenly."[80]

Most western states have passed this stage and are in more serious straits. Shortages in some areas are so severe that mandatory water-conservation programs are being imposed for all types of users; in other areas, the cost of extending wells to rapidly receding water tables is leading many farmers to practice conservation and even causing some to reduce the amount of irrigated acreage.[81]

However, neither the western appropriation nor the eastern riparian system of water allocation was designed to resolve competition among users and claimants. Appropriation tends to prefer existing users, while the riparian system fails even to provide a clear mechanism for accommodating competition. The appropriation system requires proof that water-right transfers would cause no harm to third parties. In states under riparian law, water use must be "reasonable,... adapted to the character ... of the stream," and "fair ... [as] between [the user] and his neighbor."[82] Both legal doctrines were well-adapted to their time and purpose of stimulating new water-resources development but—like federal subsidies of regional growth—they may have outlived their usefulness.

This is particularly clear in eastern and southern states, where there often are no tools, or only rudimentary tools, for states' water administration. Often, no mechanism exists to clarify rights to water. In addition, deep-seated political traditions of local autonomy in these states sometimes make effective statewide or regional management of water supply difficult or impossible.[83] For example, when the city of Virginia Beach, Virginia, tried during a 1980-81 drought to acquire groundwater rights from neighboring localities, it was unsuccessful largely because no system of rights transfer existed to define the process and allay local fears. As a result, when the city thereafter sought to find a long-term water supply for its booming population, it decided to spend $180 million for an 85-mile water-supply pipeline to a distant reservoir rather than deal with the uncertainties involved in trying to obtain cheaper groundwater rights from its neighbors.[84]

For western American Indian tribes, the process of defining their own water rights has been particularly troublesome. These rights traditionally were quantified by courts, not states, although the relatively sizable allocations some tribes received on paper through litigation were rarely followed by the financial assistance from Congress that generally is necessary to bring "wet" water to Indian lands. While some tribes have won significant victories by litigation, other tribes have decided to explore a more direct role in managing water resources and to try to secure actual water supplies through negotiation. Some advocates of negotiation argue (not without reason) that that process offers the Indians the best deals they could get, but others are not so sure. Negotiations often may be structured from the start to assure continuity of water supply for non-Indian economic growth and may thereby diminish the breadth of tribal choice on the use of their water. Tribal participation in the settlement process thus may be less meaningful than it appears to be. Accordingly, the settlements sometimes grant water on terms that sharply restrict its use, terms that may press the water toward uses that the Indians lack the time to consider fully and that many Indians do not find to be in their best interests.[85]

Even if such cases are settled, much conflict may remain—between tribes that lease their rights and want to control the uses to which the leased water is put and states that want to mold the use of water in the local economy and to administer Indian water rights within existing systems.[86] This may require states simultaneously to become more sophisticated in gathering data and analyzing water use and to accept more flexibility in controlling water use within state boundaries.

Meanwhile, water-quality conflicts also will intensify within states. Controls on point-source discharges to surface waters (from such sources as industries and municipal sewage systems) are being installed, but (as is indicated in chapter 2) many stream segments still will not attain standards. Should states change the standards or require increased abatement from point sources? Or should states attack problems, such as runoff from agricultural land and urban streets, that have been too controversial and complicated to take on in the past?

In addition, the pollution of groundwater is becoming more serious. Groundwater contamination is difficult to prevent, and, in most cases, is very expensive to clean up. While some states are moving to reduce nonpoint and groundwater pollution, many are not, and there is growing support for federal technical and financial aid to spur nationwide action. If this limited federal role develops, will it stimulate adequate state and local pollution-control responses, or will pressure grow for direct federal intervention in these two problem areas, which are frequently tied to traditionally local land-use decisions?

Mechanisms for Deciding

Thus, the relatively straightforward conditions of past years—supplies that were generally ample for all comers and quality problems that were thought to be restricted to industrial discharges and municipal sewage— are gone, and traditional systems of allocation and interstate coordination may not be adequate for making decisions. What, then, are some possible decision-making mechanisms, and how do they help balance efficiency, equity, and environmental quality?

In assessing different mechanisms, it is necessary to understand that all water claimants, new and old, have important social precedents on their side. Municipal and industrial users, who can best afford to apply their water efficiently and, therefore, set the market price, stake their strongest claims on efficiency. The role of equity can be raised persuasively both on behalf of Indians with historical claims to water but little history of use and on behalf of the rural poor (particularly in Hispanic or Appalachian communities), who have long-standing but often unquantified rights and are least capable of defending them against outside incursions. Even more affluent farmers who can better afford to defend their rights may on occasion find their traditional life-style threatened as their neighbors' sale of water rights for nonagricultural use erodes local farm economies. And in-stream flow claimants can raise valid concerns about environmental quality. Any new market or other allocation proposal that does not explicitly attempt to balance these three competing goals can be expected to fail.

Historically, both the riparian and appropriation systems of state water allocation were regulatory in nature. And, because these systems were developed and interpreted to provide investment security for the principal water-using groups in each region, both systems resist the changes in water use that are being demanded. But some changes are clearly necessary, and some nontraditional allocation systems are being discussed. Any new system will require some degree of regulation to establish the rules under which the system will act. However, the fundamental choice will be among an essentially regulatory and administrative process, a negotiation and mediation approach, or a market concept.

Regulatory Approach

Existing allocation systems in many states take a regulatory approach in theory, but in practice they are rendered incoherent by many antiquated provisions, particularly the obstacles to transfers. Some observers argue that confusion and bureaucratic narrow-mindedness are inherent in all regulation because public-sector managers lack individualized, market-based performance incentives;[87] others find this criticism of the bureaucracy largely theoretical rather than based on reality.[88] And, as noted earlier, the market mechanism alone historically has been weak in evaluating net social benefits of an action, including those of fairness and environmental quality.

Arizona's 1980 Groundwater Management Act represents the closest thing to a comprehensive regulatory approach. It requires inventories of available groundwater resources, sets a long-range goal of sustained yield from aquifers, and gives the state government the authority to specify how much water each user group can consume and to reduce those allocations (without compensation) as necessary to fulfill that goal.[89] Both supporters and critics of the new law agree that the administrative burden of planning, monitoring, and enforcing such a comprehensive water-use structure is immense, and the Arizona state agency responsible has already complained of having less than half the necessary staff for the task.[90]

As an alternative, the state might have been an opportune place to experiment with a pure system of private groundwater rights, but politicians were apparently unwilling to let the farmers—the predominant rights-holders—capture the entire wealth that such a market would have created. Instead, Arizona adopted a regulatory approach that requires water conservation. This approach deals with equity concerns by requiring that all groups share in water-use reductions.[91] It is, however, too early to tell whether this approach (in conjunction with massive new water imports) will allow Arizona to reach its goal of sustained yield.

Regulatory approaches also are used in interstate conflicts. Equitable apportionment is a process whereby the U.S. Supreme Court takes original jurisdiction over water suits among litigating states by assigning shares of a disputed river flow to them.[92] Such an apportionment typically is based on such factors as past water use, potential for future water development, and extent of the watershed located in the respective states. Although some criticize apportionment as being an inadequately informed judicial interference in a fundamentally political issue, a more serious shortcoming is that apportionments only settle existing claims to amounts of water and provide no means for avoiding or resolving future disputes.

A different way to ameliorate interstate friction over water, which was extensively discussed and strongly advocated by the National Water Commission, is federal legislation that allows states to create federally chartered regional corporations to undertake some water-resources operations.[93] Such corporations principally would bring cost-effective coordination to the water-supply and wastewater-management activities now split among federal, state, and local governments; place some limited authority for these activities at the same regional level as planning by a river-basin commission; and, not least, create a background of positive accomplishments that might spur the participants to reach a more difficult consensus on policy.

Territorial jealousies undoubtedly would create obstacles to this approach, but charter authority should only be sought in cases where there is a clear consensus on regional need. At any rate, supra-local authorities may prove able to obtain such operational functions more easily than they can win regulatory powers, which tend to be retained at the state or local levels.[94]

Negotiation

John Folk-Williams, an astute observer of the western water scene, recently noted that "increasing competition for a scarce resource is causing more and more groups to look for settlement methods less costly or protracted—and better suited to deal with on-going management issues—than litigation."[95] Several notable attempts to negotiate settlements to water disputes have occurred in the past three years. For instance, a multi-interest state task force was established in New Mexico to develop agreements on what methods should determine the effects of mining on groundwater systems. In Colorado, 31 elected officials and private citizens from both sides of the Continental Divide reached agreement in April 1983 on principles to guide plans for meeting Denver's future water needs. In Utah and Montana, state officials and Indian tribes have negotiated water-resource compacts, and in Nebraska water users and environmentalists have been negotiating ways to protect minimum stream flows while allowing interbasin transfers.[96]

Other water-related issues that have been settled through negotiations or mediation include a nutrient-control plan for the Patuxent River in Maryland, several low-head hydropower permits in New England, and large-scale hydroelectric disputes such as the proposed Storm King pump-storage project on the Hudson River and the proposed raising of the Ross Dam on the Skagit River in Washington State.

For interstate waters, negotiation is a better established technique. States may negotiate and agree among themselves on the allocation of water in a basin and on the principles and procedures governing conflicts.[97] When such agreements are ratified by Congress, they become legal compacts with much of the force of federal law. But, while compacts allocate rights to river flow and generally set out procedures for resolving disagreements, they rarely set up institutions independent of the signatory states to aid in carrying out the compact. Quantitative allocation is merely a first step in settling interstate water conflicts; follow-up implementation mechanisms also are essential.[98]

A broader approach, which could in theory provide such a mechanism either by itself or in conjunction with compacts or apportionments, is the establishment of an interstate river-basin commission. Two commissions, for the Delaware and Susquehanna river basins, were established by specific act of Congress and the participating states.[99] Also, Title II of the Water Resources Planning Act of 1965 conferred general authority on states to set up interstate river-basin commissions with both federal agency and state membership. This authority has been used six times, although former interior secretary James Watt eliminated federal funding for these commissions in 1981, effectively abolishing most of them.[100]

Most Title II river-basin commissions operated in the absence of any type of interstate water allocation; they had little or no independent authority and were largely concerned with the preparation of basin-wide water-management plans to coordinate with federal plans. They reflected the understandable reluctance of states to relinquish any meaningful part of their powers to an uncontrollable entity of doubtful competence, political sympathies, or permanence. (Historically, the political authority of regional or interstate governing bodies in the United States has been allowed to grow no further than was absolutely necessary.)

In fact, of all the interstate commissions, only the Delaware River Basin Commission (DRBC)—a body created in 1961 by the need to implement the U.S. Supreme Court's 1954 equitable apportionment of the Delaware River—has been effective, allocating water in its metropolitan region through times of plenty and of intense drought.[101] However, many observers feel that the DRBC's performance has been less effective in dealing with water-quality problems and intrabasin fairness issues raised by water diversions. Perhaps, this reflects the narrowness of the apportionment issue that led to the DRBC's formation.[102]

As with the institutional remedies for quality/quantity fragmentation, political and legal power such as that possessed by the DRBC encourages, but is not always essential for, a successful interstate body. The Interstate Commission on the Potomac River Basin (ICPRB) is a purely advisory entity with no regulatory or developmental authority of any kind. Nonetheless, its sophisticated modeling and research on the most efficient ways to meet the water supply needs of the Washington, D.C., metropolitan area were critical in convincing state and local governments that agreeing to cooperate would be to their common advantage.[103] Elsewhere, even since the termination of federal support for the Title II river-basin commissions, states in at least one basin (the Missouri River's) have minimally funded their commission to act as a communication medium and to retain a means of generating regionally defined solutions if major conflicts emerge.[104]

Attention to regional problems on the ICPRB model might be a more fruitful outlet for commission efforts. Indeed, if the states themselves want to structure commissions to be more responsive to regional imperatives, they might also consider creating interstate water tribunals or mediation services within such bodies to contain, negotiate, and resolve interstate water disputes within the region.[105]

Negotiation does not always work, either in setting specific disputes or in coordinating interstate interests, particularly if one of the parties has nothing to gain from an agreement. For instance, this give-and-take approach, which was the basis of the nation's water-quality improvement efforts before 1972, was so ineffective that Congress adopted strong federal standards in the Clean Water Act Amendments. Under the pre-1972 laws, no real penalties existed for dischargers who ignored the negotiation process.[106]

Markets

Reacting to the intractability of most existing systems for the transfer of water rights, some commentators press for the creation of entirely free markets in such rights, permitting the value of water (and presumably the efficiency of its use) to rise unhindered by political obstacles to transfer or by preferences for the retention of certain uses.[107] For example, with respect to groundwater, free-market proponents contend that the definition of private rights to extract specific quantities of water would prevent the kind of free-for-all exploitation of this common resource that often has turned renewable aquifers into nonrenewable ones. Proponents claim that the market would protect environmental values as well.[108]

However, a completely free-market system probably would be inconsistent with basic hydrologic principles. For instance, if market transfers were allowed to take pumping operations spread throughout an aquifer and concentrate them in one corner of that aquifer, it could seriously interfere with neighboring pumpers and greatly reduce groundwater flow to surface streams. A straightforward, but still market-based, corrective to this weakness was adopted in New Mexico, where rights transfers are administratively simple but are contingent on a lack of damage to other surface-water or groundwater rights-holders.[109] Moreover, New Mexico's formula respects the equity value of future generations by barring the mining of water (that is, pumping in excess of recharge) in rechargeable aquifers.

Despite the New Mexico scheme's flexibility and responsiveness to change, those who participate must conform their activities to its demanding legal and technical dictates. Moreover, the elaborate, expensive proceedings used to quantify rights in such a system often are far beyond the means of the rural poor. Case studies in northern New Mexico indicate that the organizational requirements needed to benefit from state or federal water projects—like the establishment of irrigation districts with pooled water rights—may be incompatible with the community structures of historic cultures and may be feared as an attempt to "disenfranchise" small rights-holders (see box on Hispanics, Indians, and Anglos).[110] Is there a tenable middle ground between such equity considerations and the efficiency demands of urban and industrial users who seek new supplies of water? The question is not restricted to New Mexico; it arises whenever poor, rural water claimants (such as American Indian tribes) are forced to contend with the water institutions of the mainstream culture.

The New Mexico scheme also lacks any means to protect or retain water flows in-stream. This is a weakness even in the eyes of some market advocates, who argue for the rights of private citizens or organizations to buy and sell in-stream flows on the model of English fishing rights.[111] In light of the inadequacy of many current state programs to protect in-stream flows in the United States and the relatively easy manner in which private rights to in-stream flow could be integrated into the allocation systems of existing appropriation law, such a market proposal might make sense as a supplement to state protection programs. However, in many rivers with complex water-use patterns, private rights-holders alone could have great difficulty trying to monitor and enforce in-stream rights against competing and often hostile off-stream water users.[112]

If a water market on the New Mexico model does develop in other states, it surely will be accompanied by demands to moderate its narrow orientation to efficiency. Already, market competition among water uses in many states has brought demands for state action to protect existing uses and life-styles that are dependent on water. The resulting conflicts between equity and efficiency have created some strange political bedfellows. Conservative Wyoming and Nevada ranchers, who sought divestiture of federal land to the states and furiously battled local environmentalists in the process, have joined those same environmentalists in opposing water allocations for coal-slurry pipelines and MX missile systems.[113]

The market concept also offers an intriguing solution to some interstate conflicts. If interstate rights granted by compact or apportionment could be sold or leased among states in a basin, in the same manner that intrastate water rights of private owners along a river are transferred, it would increase the flexibility—and thereby both the efficiency and the fairness—of interstate water allocations.

Leases of such rights would be beneficial for several reasons. The incentive of states to press for economically inefficient water projects

Hispanics, Indians, Anglos: A Struggle over Water Rights

A particularly poignant illustration of the conflicts among water-use values is being played out in the Pojoaque Valley in New Mexico, just north of Santa Fe. The Rio Grande and one of its tributaries flow through the valley, providing an invaluable water supply to small farmers, mainly Hispanics and Pueblo Indians. Other demands on the water supply come from predominantly Anglo developers, mining companies, and ranchers. As demands are enlarged, conflict between efficient users (the developers) and traditional water-rights holders (the Indian and Hispanic farmers) is becoming increasingly apparent.

But in addition to this rather typical efficiency/equity conflict, a jarring dispute has arisen pitting two types of "equity" values against each other. The Hispanic and Pueblo Indian populations in the valley have been sharing water there for centuries, but recent increases in water demand and more efficient water-collection techniques have resulted in overallocation of the water. The surface water and groundwater sources no longer supply enough water to fulfill all of the claims made on them by farmers, developers, and participants in the local energy boom. Thus, the Hispanics and Indians are on opposing sides of *New Mexico* v. *Aamodt*, a lawsuit in which the tribes lay claim to 36,000 acre-feet of water per year, more than four times the current average annual flow in the Rio Grande system north of Santa Fe. The fight has become bitter, with each side arguing its ancient historical rights and more recently perceived injustices.

While the Hispanics' claim to the water dates back nearly 400 years,

when the first Spanish colonists arrived in what is now the United States, the Indians claim "prior and paramount" water rights for their thousand years or more of occupation. The Hispanics foresee the death of their culture if their rights to receive water are cut. They accuse the tribes of aspiring to become the state's "water sheiks." The Pueblos in turn assert that they are "just defending their rightful portion against the state and neighbors," that losing the lawsuit would represent another broken federal promise of tribal self-sufficiency, and that "the Spanish people . . . were stealing our water night and day and would not let us irrigate."

Unlike many western water disputes, this one does not directly pit a small, poor, native population against a large, wealthy newcomer. But, sadly and typically, the struggle between the Hispanics and Indians has been spurred by the seemingly irrestible encroachment of modern development upon their communal water supplies. The Hispanics' underlying concern is that the Indians will "sell out" to larger, more powerful Anglo water users such as ski resorts and industries and that the Hispanics' long-time partners in dignified adversity may become the "water bosses" to whom they must come for their water allocations. The Pueblos counter that Anglo interests would soon acquire the region's water rights in any case, that non-Indian farms thus are "probably doomed" regardless of how the lawsuit is resolved, and that Indians would be the best stewards of those water rights for future generations.

The tragedy of the situation in the Pojoaque Valley is that two long-established minorities with sophisticated cultures are being forced to battle each other while it is the well-heeled "newcomers" who are likely ultimately to benefit. If the Pueblos end up with the rights, the costs and benefits to all groups could be balanced if Anglos purchase water rights from the Indians and give (or sell at reduced prices) some back to the Hispanics. Such a solution, however, would require a degree of altruism largely unknown in the competi-tion for water.

Government acquisition of some water rights for the Hispanics may be a somewhat more realistic prospect and one consistent with the tradition of giving federal aid to those displaced by assertions of Indian rights. The cost of such acquisition may be considerable; this suggests how high the stakes in these battles really are and in turn asks American society how highly it values cultural diversity based on historic water use.[1]

simply to keep "their" water within their boundaries could be substantially reduced. States could also regain the development potential of their water resources if and when their economies are ready to absorb it, they could reap some financial gain from the resources in the interim, and in-stream flows would be retained on the way to downstream states leasing upstream rights, thus aiding aquatic and riparian habitat, recreation, water-quality improvement, and the like.*

These are not academic concerns, considering that California withdraws about 20 percent more than its 4.4 million acre-feet-per-year allocation of Colorado River water, and upper basin Colorado River states are seeking new water projects while thousands of acre-feet lie unused in upper basin reservoirs.[115] But the desire for projects threatens to enshrine inefficiency permanently. If new storage is built, however uneconomical the uses of its water may be, that water must be withheld annually to serve those uses. If California (or any downstream state) then tries, under this interstate rights scheme, to pay Colorado (or any upstream state)

---

* This technique might also be used in some cases in which the federal government is asserting a water right, whether directly or in another guise. In the recent case, *Riverside Irrigation District* v. *Andrews*,[114] the Corps of Engineers interpreted its statutory duty under Section 404 (dredge-and-fill) of the Clean Water Act as requiring it, in regulating construction of a dam, to consider the effects in another state, not only on water quality under the Clean Water Act itself, but also on water supplies in downstream wetlands under the Endangered Species Act. Effectively, the federal government is claiming a water right in Colorado (by requiring releases from the dam) for use in Nebraska (the site of the wetlands). The case is controversial not only because the releases are for out-of-state use but also because they are being done through uncompensated regulation.

to send that water downstream again, it is hard to envision Colorado accepting the money to lease its rights. Such a lease would mean letting its long-awaited water projects sit empty—even assuming they contain enough carryover storage from year to year to withhold much water in the first place. Thus, though some might claim that projects are a prerequisite for this scheme, in fact they would probably make it much more difficult to implement.

But there may be other conditions under which interstate leasing could work. One would be where there are competitors lurking for the water. California might be much more interested in entering into a lease if the state thought that another state would divert the water first. Another way would be through Congress, with its power over water-project authorizations and appropriations. The congressional leverage could be applied to require leases for projects that would use more water than a state has been apportioned. In addition, political leverage could be a factor in regional alliances of governors. Such nonphysical leverage is admittedly difficult to assess, but the potential benefits of the interstate-rights concept make it well worth exploring.

Although market approaches are being considered as a way of dealing with allocating water quantities, they also are advocated for implementing water-quality programs. For instance, some economists argue strongly for the adoption of effluent fees, citing their increased efficiency. Such fees were opposed in 1972 by environmentalists (though some now support them) because they implied a right to pollute—which was considered inequitable to the public and bad for the environment. Effluent fees also are opposed by industrialists, largely, some suspect, because the fees may be more effective.[116] At mid-decade, more attention is being given to creating discharge rights, such as those being experimented with in the air-pollution-control programs, which could be bought and sold.

Conclusions

Given the intractability of many present systems of water administration, the lure of a market system is both substantial and understandable. But it can be argued that the process of apportioning uses among competing groups is essentially political and that the government can accommodate equity concerns more harmoniously and with less painful dislocation than a pure market approach can. The challenge to makers of policy in both western and eastern states in the next decades will be to identify, adopt, and harmonize the best features of both the market approach and the regulatory approach. To be effective, any solution must fully acknowledge the implications of interstate or intrastate water allocation on all the values associated with water use—efficiency, equity, and environmental quality.

WHO PAYS?

Traditionally, the answer to the question of who pays for water resources has been based far more on political clout than on economic theory or even on coherent budgetary policy. States and localities have induced the federal government to fund much water development (particularly in the West and South) and water treatment (largely in the Northeast and Midwest).[117] When the federal government has demurred, state and local governments have either paid the tabs themselves or gone without. The goal of capital spending on water has simply been to meet the ever-growing demands of every user group.[118]

But with massive federal deficits and the emergence of concerns about efficient and fair water distribution and its environmental effects, a simple preoccupation with meeting demand now seems profligate and short-sighted. The attainment of a new consensus on goals will be a long and arduous process, contrary to the political expectations of many.

At this point, in any case, federal domination in water-development and pollution-control funding is no longer commonplace. For water-resources projects, a decade or more of real reductions in federal appropriations and a congressional stalemate on funding policy have shifted the fiscal initiative to the states.[119] States also have been under financial strain due to cutbacks in federal assistance and the national economic recession and already have substantially increased taxes.[120] Thus, much of the burden of funding water supply and treatment in the future could fall on users through repayment of capital-bond obligations of local, state, or federal governments. Does this mean that federal spending on water resources will only go to users who can repay in full, or can acceptable alternative criteria for funding be found? Will states choose to subsidize certain users or ignore needs of those who cannot pay? What is the federal interest in funding any water development? Answers are needed to clarify federal spending policies and the stakes in capital water investment.

Historical Perspectives

It might seem ironic that a need for debate on the federal role in water-resources development still exists as the 20th century ends, when federal activity in the field dates from the earliest days of the republic. Yet this is not so strange when one compares the historical rationales for federal intervention in water resources with the contemporary situation. Beginning with the active emergence of the U.S. Army Corps of Engineers in 1824, the federal government, throughout the 19th century, was deeply involved in canal planning and river and harbor improvements to open up vast new expanses of the United States to settlement and commerce.[121]

During the latter half of the 19th century, federal water activities turned to making the newly settled lands more useful and productive. Flood-control programs started this trend. They were joined in 1902 by the Reclamation Act, which was intended to stimulate large-scale agricultural development in the 17 western states.[122] Subsequent programs for water power, flood control, navigation, municipal water supply, and the like were of the same ilk as their 19th-century predecessors: the central, driving theme usually was regional development, and the method of achieving it was a substantial or nearly total financial subsidy of program beneficiaries.[123]

How well did this traditional approach meet the three goals of economic efficiency, equity, and environmental quality? The efficiency of projects has been safeguarded in theory since 1936 by cost-benefit analysis, but the relative cost-effectiveness of many nominally efficient projects is still quite low, and numerous recent projects have failed to provide even the minimal levels of repayment required by law.[124] Equity was protected either not at all or on no systematic basis; the superficially equal opportunity of political deal making gave way in practice to a decided preference for projects in the South and West.[125] And, with the exception of soil conservation, environmental-quality considerations were largely ignored until the advent of impact-assessment and habitat-mitigation programs in the 1970s.

The Present: Political Stalemate

The question of who pays did not really begin to spark controversy until President Jimmy Carter unveiled his water-project "hit list" shortly after he took office in 1977. This was a group of 18 authorized projects for which Carter recommended termination of federal funding on environmental and efficiency grounds. The hit list also provided a way to begin cutting through the backlog of more than 800 approved but unfinished or unstarted projects, for which the 1978 estimated total $33.8 billion price tag had escalated to $60 billion by 1981.[126] The political reaction was immediate and violent: Carter had dared to challenge the near-sacred political consensus that then surrounded water projects. In an attempt to mollify the opposition and deal with the backlog systematically, the Carter administration proposed a cost-sharing policy, under which project construction would proceed promptly if states paid between 5 and 10 percent of the cost "up front."

This proposal did little to soothe the hostility that the hit list created. Advocates of traditional funding policy felt that times had not changed but that "we just are having a terrible problem with the President right now."[127] The traditionalists heartily welcomed the Reagan administration in 1981, believing that all this nonsense would soon be done with.

But, in large measure because of federal budget problems, it was by no means done with. The Reagan administration's policy makers instead sought to up the states' required ante to 35 percent. In response, Senator Paul Laxalt (R.-Nev.), a close presidential ally, and 14 other western Republican senators wrote President Reagan that his cost-sharing proposals were "even more Draconian" than President Carter's and that they would "be painted as 'anti-water'" and threaten the president's western political base.[128] But the new reality in water was slowly dawning, for five other western GOP colleagues—including the chairman of a key Senate water subcommittee, Senator James Abdnor (R.-S.D.)—failed to sign the letter.

Although President Reagan in January 1984 appeared to bow to this partisan pressure by agreeing to treat project cost-sharing on a case-by-case basis and to abandon cost-sharing for dam-safety repairs, it was unclear whether this retreat would actually spur more project authorizations or new construction starts—particularly in the face of $200 billion budget deficits—or, more important, whether the new case-by-case policy would be abandoned after President Reagan's 1984 reelection campaign.[129]

As debates on the advisability of continuing traditional water-development policies rage on, there is little dispute about the political reasons behind the present stalemate: the long-standing national consensus in favor of subsidizing regional development by water spending has disappeared. This disappearance is observed even by a Washington, D.C., representative of traditional user groups, who concludes that, "For 200 years we've been running out and putting a Band-Aid on water problems.... We need to study and reflect, and determine what kind of a program we should have."[130] As a result, no major new water projects have been authorized or begun since 1976, and overall appropriations for water-project construction (excluding municipal wastewater-treatment plants) have plummeted by nearly 70 percent in the eight years since (figure 7.4).[131]

Certainly, the mounting federal budget deficits of the last 10 (and particularly the last 3) years, together with three major national recessions during that period, have played an important part in changing policy. These fiscal constraints, in turn, have highlighted the inconsistencies and inequities in present cost-sharing policies. The proportion of federal project costs that are recovered varies widely, depending on project purposes and agencies, from a federal government average of 6 percent for inland waterways to 64 percent for hydroelectric power and municipal and industrial supply (figure 7.5).[132] The disparities reflect the patchwork nature of present federal water programs, and the resulting inequities make the old policy consensus that much harder to defend. As one environmental lobbyist notes, "Pressures of the budget are going to force a rational evaluation of water project authorizations, and rational evaluation is the antithesis of pork barrel."[133]

An additional, key factor in the demise of the old consensus, however, has been the political objections of northeastern and midwestern congressional blocs to the heavy, almost exclusive weighting of water subsidies to favor the already booming southern and western regions of the country. The older regions have discovered their own need—the repair of crumbling "infrastructure" such as sewage and water-supply systems—which threatens to overwhelm state and local budgets in areas of economic decline. Representatives from these regions see little reason to pay for water infrastructure that would lure still more jobs to the Sunbelt and accelerate the industrial depression of the North.[134]

The Basic Issues

Some observers discern in the decline of new capital investment a loss of national will. They appear to embrace a sort of social catastrophism and to yearn nostalgically for the "good old days,"[135] not unlike some environmentalists' longings for a time of mythical, primitive harmony with natural systems. There is little reason to endorse such a superficial view; indeed, the present "infrastructure crisis" should teach the shortsightedness of always equating politically attractive spending on new construction with wise investment policy.[136]

Predictably, the current political debate is more narrowly focused. The question of how much the federal government should give to whom predominates, with all sections of the country attempting to justify their

Figure 7.4

Federal Appropriations for Construction of Water-Resources Projects, 1968–1984 (in constant 1982 dollars)

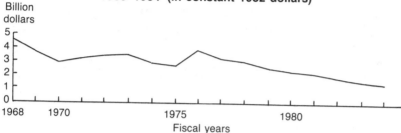

Figures do not include Colorado River Basin Trust Fund expenditures. Fiscal year 1984 figure is from president's budget; actual appropriation will not be known until end of fiscal year.

Source: Congressional Budget Office.

Figure 7.5
Effective Nonfederal Cost Shares of Federal Water-Resources Development, by Purpose and Agency

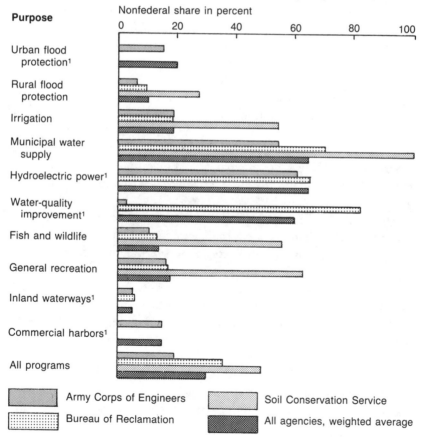

[1] Either activity or cost share not reported by some agencies. See figure references.

Source: Congressional Budget Office.

claims on such grounds as past promises, regional equity, political power, or comparative poverty. The emphasis has been on working out compromises that will get the dollars rolling again, but no proposal seems able to win general acceptance. And, in the process, several basic questions are, for the most part, being ignored. In view of the disappearance of the old funding consensus, no proposal will gain lasting approval until certain questions get direct answers.

Why More Capital Investment?

One of these questions is whether more development really makes any sense. Most of the best dam sites are already used up. Those remaining typically would be much more expensive to develop—as indicated by the rapid increase in the average amount of material that has to be placed in the embankments to create an acre-foot of reservoir capacity (figure 7.6). As a result, most experts concur that few undeveloped sites remain that are both environmentally acceptable and economically efficient.[137] The full exploitation of water resources in many major river systems suggests that the land-settlement and water-resource phases of the nation's development are virtually complete.

The emphasis on building more projects seems even more questionable given the budgetary dimensions of the more than $60 billion project backlog and the current problems in operating and maintaining the investments already made. As one expert observes, there should be a ''rethinking [of] our sense of what capital investment is 'needed,' and overhaul[ing of] the institutions ... that have led to under-maintenance and postponed repairs.''[138]

The problem of inadequate operation and maintenance is probably nowhere better demonstrated than with municipal waste-treatment plants. Congress has appropriated about $38 billion in federal funds alone to construct such facilities over the past decade, but the General Accounting Office estimates that as many as 82 percent of them are not being operated properly.[139] Similar fears were raised with respect to the maintenance of dams when the Teton Dam failed in June 1976. The U.S. Army Corps of Engineers estimated in a subsequent survey that one-third of the dams it inspected were unsafe, and a tenth of those required emergency measures to prevent ''imminent failure.''[140]

The emphasis on capital construction also may prevent dealing with water shortages by other techniques that are more cost-effective. In many cases, existing conflicts may be resolved and substantial amounts of money saved by managing existing supplies more efficiently rather than by developing new ones.

Work done in the Washington, D.C., metropolitan area over the past five years is a dramatic example of these techniques. For decades, there were often bitter disputes about how many dams would have to be built to guarantee adequate water to the area, which has periodically had to declare emergencies because of shortages. No consensus could be reached, however, and sharp population growth caused the shortages to get worse. Finally, some of the major water institutions in the region decided to explore options for better management of existing supplies. The results were striking. After undertaking a combination of measures—improved hydrologic assessments, a conservation-oriented rate structure and education program, more efficient institutional arrangements for operating and connecting different parts of the existing water-delivery system, the reallocation of some storage in Bloomington Dam from flood control to water supply, and the construction of one small reservoir—the parties were able to conclude that existing supplies would be adequate for another 50 years without building the $250 million or more worth of reservoirs that had been recommended (figure 7.7).[141]

One of the leaders of this effort attempted to estimate the implications of adopting similar management improvements more generally. He concluded that it should be relatively easy to achieve a 10 percent to 15 percent improvement in the operating efficiency of federal projects and that such an improvement would be "worth just as much" as 20 years of new construction. The costs of achieving such an improvement would be very modest—probably less than 1 percent of the amount currently spent on new construction—to produce the same benefits.[142]

Similarly, in many instances in which new construction in general and interbasin diversions in particular are demanded, the least-cost means of obtaining the desired amount of water is, instead, to repair old or inefficient water-delivery systems or to subsidize installation of water-saving devices in homes. (Orlando, Florida, has spent over $400,000 for home water-saving devices as a "supply" source.) The demand by various regions of the country for more federal project dollars may snuff out opportunities for cost-effective nonstructural or lower-cost structural investment. Before charging ahead with massive capital-spending programs, it seems wise to ask whether they are necessary.

What Should Users Pay for Water?

A second basic question is how further capital investment in water under the present water-pricing policies can be afforded. Only rarely in the United States does any government treat water as if it were a valuable commodity. In almost every state, unclaimed water is given to anyone who asks for it; the only charge, if any, for making a transfer formal is a permit fee that usually does not even cover the cost of the paperwork. More than 55 percent[143] of water-supply utilities charge by declining block rates, which discount water to large users, especially commercial and industrial classes. Such favorable rates encourage inefficient use, requiring a search for more expensive new supplies and inflating a utility's total costs. In addition, many public companies do not even recover their full costs—they receive tax, interest rate, and sometimes (in the West and South) indirect federal subsidies.[144] Thus, much water is sold for less than it costs to obtain it.

Even when revenues do cover costs, a user may not actually be charged for the amount of water used. If water use is not metered, a household that never waters its lawn may be charged as much as a household that leaves its sprinklers on continuously. Many communities—for instance, New York City (23 percent metered) and Chicago (31 percent metered)[145]—do not have universal metering of individual residences. The many old apartments in those cities require replumbing to meter all residences, and this exacerbates the problem. Still, the demonstrably substantial savings from metering and from rates based on the amount of water consumed point to a need to require metering in future construction, particularly when old apartments are rehabilitated.

Most federal programs are operated on the same basis. On a national average, irrigation water is priced at 19 percent of the real cost of supplying it, and in some cases there is no limitation on the amount of water that may be consumed.[146] However, there often is a limit on the amount of land that farmers may irrigate with that water. Limiting the amount of land irrigated but not the amount of water used clearly eliminates any incentive to stretch supplies through conservation.

Such pricing policies have long been justified by reference to equity principles in various guises. In irrigation, the original idea that reclamation benefits are "national in character" could apply to virtually any economic sector. But at a time when western farming is neither new nor disadvantaged, the system is distinctly inequitable for those farmers (particularly in the West) who lack a water subsidy. The subsidies might or might not be endorsed if Congress addressed the issue directly as

Figure 7.6
Volume of Dam Material Required Per Acre-Foot
of Reservoir Capacity, pre-1920 through 1960s

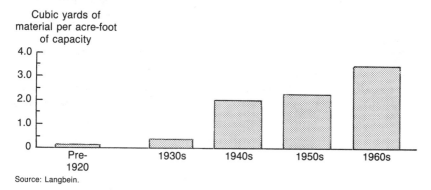

Source: Langbein.

Figure 7.7
Water Remaining in Washington, D.C., Metropolitan Area
Water-Supply Reservoirs after Severe Drought

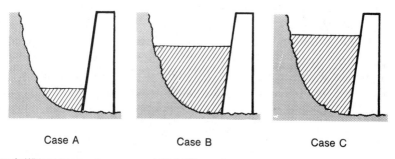

Case A: Without improved management (13.5 billion gallons remaining).

Case B: With improved management. "Improved management" here includes regional cooperation among state and local governments (40.2 billion gallons remaining).

Case C: With improved management and 50 percent of flood control reallocated to supply. Reallocation of 50 percent of flood control to supply storage reduced flood-control benefits by approximately 7 percent (46.1 billion gallons remaining).

Total reservoir capacity is 60.3 billion gallons.

Source: U.S. Army Corps of Engineers.

an element of national farm policy. But at least they are no longer needed to achieve the initial aim of aiding settlement of the West.[147]

Pricing municipal water below real cost, it is sometimes argued, is worthwhile because water is necessary for survival and thus must be available to all in adequate quantities. But under most utilities' water rates, those who use only minimal, "survival" quantities end up subsidizing larger users.

It is not surprising that, even while water is subsidized, much agonizing about how to cope with increasing water shortages and how to pay for new development goes on. A recent study emphasizes that the ability of localities to pay for new water is closely tied to the way they charge for the old; the more they give their water away, the more difficulty they will have in financing new development.[148] This is even more the case with wastewater treatment, for which most utilities have failed to adjust rates adequately to compensate for the recent decline in federal subsidies. One expert observed in 1983 that "heavy reliance on relatively unpredictable subsidies (most prevalent for wastewater systems) exposes the utility to future managerial and financial crises."[149]

In some areas, citizens and their governments may be coming to understand the importance for future economic stability of limiting water depletions. Orange County, California, fashioned a strong local response to the nationwide problem of excessive groundwater pumping by charging water users a $24 tax for every acre-foot of water they consumed (in addition to the well owner's pumping costs).[150] Arizona's Groundwater Management Act permits the state to impose such a charge, although the purpose is to provide funds to operate the management program rather than to reflect the true value of the water. Nevertheless, as breaks with the tradition that water should be given away, both measures should reduce local demand for new water and better enable their jurisdictions to afford supply measures if and when they become necessary.

Why Should the Federal Government Pay?

The third basic question has three parts: Should the federal government help pay for water developments at all? If so, for what purposes? And how much? The "how much?" question is the focus of most of the current debate in Washington, D.C., but it is being treated as the only question, not the last.

Political back-scratching may have worked well enough in a period of established policy consensus and flexible budgets, but it no longer does. The old method of authorizing a discrete and easily comprehensible list of specific projects to fund is defunct. A clear new policy rationale for federal involvement in water funding might win broad political support, but none has yet been developed. In the absence of a clear rationale with local support, any "new" approach that is fundamentally a political-logrolling appropriations scheme (for example, unconditional block grants or loans) is liable to find its support evaporating during any budget squeeze. Some politicians have noted this, arguing that placing the cost-sharing cart before the program-rationale horse is, "to put it mildly, an exercise in futility ... when ... the probability of federal participation now and in the foreseeable future will be nil."[151] This is not, then, a fight over who gets funding—whatever grant or loan formula is chosen decides that—but over whether any budgetary support at all should be expected for a program that lacks clear goals.

So can a supportable goal or underlying rationale be found? One state-level group defined "national interest" in water development as including projects that "address national defense, international and interstate commerce, major energy development, and multi-state or regional problems."[152] An examination of this list illustrates the difficulty of defining national interest, now that regional development is no longer a consensus objective and now that purely local benefits from such development are not seen as automatically enhancing the national interest. Defense certainly is a national goal, and energy development arguably is; but projects to provide water for these purposes are almost inevitably formulated to concurrently provide substantial, strictly local benefits.[153] Some projects may be built solely to meet international treaty obligations (such as the desalting plant in Yuma, Arizona), but they may indirectly subsidize local water users. These projects thus produce local as well as cross-boundary benefits. Other examples are the Great Lakes municipal treatment plants that aid local fishing and water supply while fulfilling U.S.-Canadian agreements.

Interstate or regional problems comprise perhaps the most troublesome category of national-interest goals. Some parties cite, as support for a continuing federal role, the difficulty and duplication involved in organizing several states for a single project.[154] Perhaps, the federal government could buy state cooperation with financial assistance, but this technique would look very much like the subsidies of sectional growth that have lost favor. A never-quite-defunct proposal for a federally funded North American Water and Power Alliance project is a classic example of the sectional dynamic carried to its extreme. The $50 billion to $200 billion fantasy project—to bring water from the Canadian Yukon to the American Southwest by means of transcontinental canals and a 400-mile-long trench reservoir at the U.S.-Canadian border—is clearly an interstate project that, equally clearly, would shovel unprecedented subsidies into the Colorado River basin.[155]

Instead of looking at types of projects that the federal government might help fund, one can look at different types of benefits that projects can produce. This has been the traditional approach, and it accounts, in part, for the wide disparity that has existed in federal cost-sharing policies among programs and agencies (demonstrated in figure 7.5). Perhaps, for instance, the federal government should pay part of the cost of providing benefits if most beneficiaries could not easily be identified and charged. This might apply to water resources devoted to federal lands or to wildlife habitat, particularly that used by migrating wildlife. It certainly would be the case for water used for national defense purposes. It would not, however, apply to water for municipal or irrigation use. This is the view argued by the National Water Commission, which concluded that subsidization should be offered only where "conventional markets and pricing mechanisms cannot be counted on to achieve socially desired benefits." The commission, however, left open the question of what such socially desired benefits might be.[156]

Water pollution control provides probably the most obvious example. Because the pollution usually damages someone other than the polluter—creating a market externality—the federal government stepped in to require cleanup. But just because government has a role does not demonstrate that government should pay the costs. And, in fact, the two major types of point sources are treated differently: industrial polluters must pay essentially all the costs of their pollution-control practices, while the federal government provides a large share of the pollution-control costs of municipalities. Most municipal-sewage charges are now so low that even substantial increases would be unlikely to raise serious ability-to-pay questions.[157] However, reducing or cutting off federal construction grants would force many municipalities to choose between a sudden, drastic sewer-rate hike and continued violation of EPA effluent standards (which must be met regardless of the availability of federal funds).[158] The continuation of grants (even at the 55 percent level that goes into effect in 1984, down from 75 percent) could offer an opportunity to promote more flexible, innovative ways of meeting quality standards if EPA were to create incentives to substitute nonstructural, least-cost approaches (such as nonpoint-source pollution control) for traditional, capital-intensive, secondary treatment plants.[159]

A third approach to federal involvement is to use federal funds to remedy disparities in the ability of different states or localities to finance their own needs. This approach handles the difficulty that state and local governments are having in maintaining basic public facilities, including water-supply and -treatment facilities, as a problem that has risen to nationwide significance.[160] Representatives of the Northeast and Midwest cite the fairness issue to support making federal assistance for repairing municipal facilities on which people's homes and livelihoods already depend a higher priority than assistance that promotes new growth.[161]

But any new proposal must define eligibility narrowly, or it will become essentially the same "subsidize everyone" type of water program. As a nation, the United States no longer can afford an approach that prefers buying off potential opponents to assure that funds are delivered to the deserving—rather than defining needs at the outset. If the country chooses to underwrite needy areas, Congress should fully define "local need" itself and not leave this to the discretion of Executive Branch agencies. With the recent history of federal-state conflict in water policy, the outlook is poor for any new water program that requires federal bureaucrats to tell states what their needs are.

Principles for Decision Making

After Congress answers some of the basic questions posed in this chapter and defines the goals for federal water investment, it will then be appropriate to consider the options for putting those goals into action. This section will not discuss specific proposals for grant formulas, state percentages, user-fee schemes, or the like; for those, the reader is directed to the recent profusion of more technical discussions.[162] Instead, some principles to guide specific implementation proposals are suggested.

The first principle is that funding from any source should support only the least-cost solution to a water problem—without regard to whether that solution includes a politically advantageous and visible structural proposal. Water funding is now authorized to build specific kinds of projects—dams or treatment plants—not to solve water problems as such. Of course, solutions may continue to include big structures, but a very poor return on society's water investments will persist so long as nonstructural and system-management improvements are not supported on the same basis as physical structures.

The second principle is that, as a general rule, all types of users should pay the full cost of getting water to them. It is a matter of common sense that users will not be able to pay for new or rebuilt water facilities unless they are charged for their present use on the basis of what replacement water, in the form of such facilities, would cost—that is, the marginal cost of new water.

The third principle is that any federal subsidy for water should recognize the first principle of least-cost problem solutions and should be explicit about its rationale for violating the second, user-pay principle. Where the federal government is itself the user—for instance, when water is required for national defense or for protecting endangered species—the user-pay principle is in fact observed. And where subsidies of state and local governments or private users are employed, the targeting of the subsidies must be narrow to ensure that they are given only to those for whom Congress expressly affirms a specific need. In other words, the historical subsidies in this area (whether or not justified in the past) promise to impose such a high cost on society if continued that further government intervention on equity grounds should be restricted to the neediest cases.

CONCLUSIONS: CROSSING THE WATERSHED

U.S. water policy has entered a period of fundamental change. This change may be deceptive because it is gradual, sometimes imperceptible, and often at variance with public rhetoric. But cumulatively it adds up to a distinct departure from past practices and mindsets. In the words of many policy experts, the nation is moving from an era of water development to an era of water management.

Several examples cited in this chapter mark that trend. Instead of developing new water supplies and facilities to meet new demands, existing supplies and facilities are being reallocated to different uses: the shift of Maryland's Bloomington Dam from flood control to water supply for the Washington, D.C., area, and the buy-outs of western agricultural water by urban, industrial, and energy users.

Another aspect of the trend to water management is the physical modification of water facilities to accommodate broader, newly recognized values. Florida provides a particularly dramatic example, perhaps because its natural systems were so extensively modified by earlier projects. The U.S. Army Corps of Engineers is actively involved there in attempting—by such means as shifting the Kissimmee River out of its government-constructed, artificial channel back into segments of the natural river and adjacent river floodplains—to re-create marshes, belatedly recognizing the importance of environmental values ignored by the narrow emphasis of the earlier development on economics alone.

A third manifestation of the transition to a management era is possibly the most central one: simply making existing uses work better. The Colorado River's salinity issue exemplifies this trend. In the proposed salinity-control measures, agricultural water use would be maintained in full but would be made more efficient by installing water-conservation measures on farms and in irrigation-district facilities. In the Salt River Project in Arizona, a vigorous use-monitoring program has reduced losses of water unaccounted for from nearly 30 percent in 1971 to less than 19 percent by 1981, with projected further reductions of up to 10 percent within a few years.[163] Similar results were obtained by the state of Idaho on one stretch of the Snake River.

Though these changes are quite diverse, they do seem to share one important characteristic. They are specific responses to local problems, not coordinated answers developed out of any overriding national theory. Ironically, as noted earlier, these changes often have occurred at the same time that an area was publicly calling for a return to subsidies or other policies of the development era. Arizona adopted a radical groundwater-conservation law and Tucson drastically hiked the prices charged for water while they were publicly fighting federal cost-sharing proposals that demanded higher state contributions. Boston organized its fragmented water utilities into an areawide entity, increasing water delivery efficiency and financing capability, while the East was asking for federal funds to repair its deteriorating road and public-utility systems. State and local governments are embracing innovative, forward-looking management far more widely and quickly than their public rhetoric might suggest.

This does not imply that no federal role in any of these areas is needed or warranted. Rather, it suggests that regional demands for the restoration of traditional water-development and water-treatment subsidies should be discounted somewhat and, more important, that any federal action should be tailored to recognize, complement, and reinforce the nascent efforts toward improved water management. Thus, a federal role in research, information transfer, and technical aid is clearly indicated. If any federal financial assistance is given, it should be targeted to areas where earnest and innovative efforts nonetheless leave a core of need that is clearly beyond state or local capability to address unaided. The federal government should not respond unthinkingly to plaints of incapacity or to vague promises of national benefits.

In fact, forced by diminishing federal water budgets, state and local governments are beginning to turn, of necessity, to the least-cost alternatives that national water-policy experts long urged to no avail. Similarly, the user-pay philosophy is winning adherents not by force of rationality but by unavoidable budgetary and practical necessity. Change is stemming simply from adaptation to new conditions. The United States no longer has the unending water surpluses, overflowing capital budgets, or clear policy consensus to continue as before. With new participants, limited funds, and overcommitted water resources becoming common across the country, individual areas are crafting answers responsive to local conditions.

This search for least-cost, user-supported actions that integrate quality and quantity, and sometimes transcend jurisdictional boundaries, cannot be mandated from Washington, D.C. But it can be either stimulated or discouraged by federal programs, and either nurtured or ignored at the state and local level. The challenge today for policy makers at all levels is to recognize the validity of, and learn about the potential of, the shift to water management, and to understand how management often can harmonize efficient and equitable use of water with environmental quality. Policy makers then will be able to see how best to apply these broader lessons to the water problems faced by each area of the United States.

FURTHER READING

Although it was completed over a decade ago and is now out of print, the 1973 report of the National Water Commission, *Water Policies for the Future,* continues to set much of the agenda for policy reform today. Its analyses are both comprehensive and detailed, and the many background papers prepared for the commission (if of uneven quality) are often important studies in their own right.

A classic, incisive statement on water-resource issues, which also remains appropos, is the short report issued by the National Academy of Sciences in 1966 entitled *Alternatives in Water Management* (Washington, D.C.: National Academy of Sciences, 1966). A different, stimulating, and sometimes controversial libertarian free-market perspective is offered by Terry Anderson's *Water Crisis: Ending the Policy Drought* (Washington, D.C.: Cato Institute, 1983).

On more specific issues, the Congressional Budget Office's report, *Efficient Investments in Water Resources: Issues and Options*

(Washington, D.C.: U.S. Government Printing Office, 1983) is a concise and thorough exploration of the cost-sharing issue, one that can be used both as an introduction to the issue and as a definitive analysis of its economic aspects. The recent series, *Water In the West* by Western Network (214 McKenzie St., Santa Fe, N. Mex. 87501), has useful, detailed, and generally objective summaries of many specific cases in the two titles available to date, "What Indian Water Means to the West" (1983) and "Water for the Energy Market" (1984). A third volume on urban water conflicts is forthcoming. A technical but very readable discussion of another, increasingly visible national issue is provided in *Groundwater Contamination in the United States* by Veronica I. Pye, Ruth Patrick, and John Quarles (Philadelphia: University of Pennsylvania Press, 1983).

Up-to-date sources on regional issues, though fairly common in the past, now seem more difficult to find. As might be expected, western-oriented sources predominate. Perhaps the best known is the absorbing story of the Colorado River, Philip Fradkin's well-written and thorough *A River No More: The Colorado River and the West* (New York: Knopf, 1981). Water issues are covered for all the Rocky Mountain states by the biweekly *High Country News* (224 Grand Avenue, Paonia, Colo. 81428). While its articles often have a clear environmentalist slant, they generally strive to bring out facts on all sides of an issue and provide much information not otherwise available. William Ashworth's volume, *Nor Any Drop to Drink* (New York: Simon and Schuster, 1982) offers a useful and readable variety of stories about water supply and quality problems across the country, though it is written in a dramatic, occasionally apocalyptic tone. The weekly *National Journal* (1730 M Street, NW, Washington, D.C. 20036) often gives its characteristic, objective, scholarly treatment to regional water issues, but it is more often a vital source of news and interpretation on national and congressional water politics.

Finally, the U.S. Geological Survey has undertaken the preparation of annual assessments of water issues, including both water quality and water quantity. The first volume, *National Water Summary 1983—Hydrological Events and Issues*, USGS Water Supply paper 2250 (Washington, D.C.: U.S. Government Printing Office, 1984) is a well-illustrated, informative document containing succinct statements of issues in each of the states as well as a national overview.

Chapter 8

Intergovernmental Relations and Environmental Policy

The Reagan administration declared a policy of decentralizing government functions to the state and local level, and, to many observers,
decentralization is the wave of the future.[1] However, American governmental history in the 20th century is characterized by centralization.
The debate over the proper balance of power among governments in
the United States is as old as the nation but particularly pertinent when
environmental problems are the debated subjects.

What level of government should have primary responsibility for dealing with emerging environmental issues? To what extent should local
perspectives influence assessments of risk? Can a cross-media approach
to pollution control be implemented more effectively at the federal or
the state level? Who should decide how the nation's water supplies are
managed? How can wildlife-protection programs be better coordinated
among different agencies and different levels of government?

Examples of jurisdictional conflicts among governments over environmental matters are easy to find:

- Six northeastern states filed suit against the federal Environmental Protection Agency (EPA) to force it to act to abate acid rain,
  blamed on emissions from midwestern states.[2]
- California and other coastal states filed lawsuits and applied political
  pressure to reduce federal oil and gas leasing in offshore waters.[3]
- The federal government cut off financial aid for highway construction to state and local governments that failed to adopt controls
  on automobile emissions required by the Clean Air Act.[4]
- California enacted a statute banning new nuclear power plants until
  a federally approved method exists for permanently storing high-
  level nuclear wastes.[5]
- Various states opposed federal plans for siting, within their boundaries, the MX missile system and other unpopular facilities.

419

- Federal and state governments jousted over regulation of the fungicide EDB (ethylene dibromide);[6] individual states' regulatory initiatives prompted concern about "regulatory Balkanization" and prodded the federal government into taking long-delayed regulatory action.
- The selectmen of Brimfield, Massachusetts, proposed forming a committee to consider secession from the state because the Massachusetts government overrode local zoning laws when awarding a permit to site a hazardous-waste-treatment facility in their town.[7]
- An environmentalist lawsuit stopped the Interior Department from delegating control of a wolf-management program to Minnesota; the state's program, which would allow sport hunting of the threatened gray wolf, was rejected by the Carter administration.[8]

The list of jurisdictional conflicts is almost endless. This is not surprising, since there are over 80,000 governmental units in the United States, and environmental problems have no respect for political boundaries.[9] Conflicts occur between the federal government and state governments, between the federal government and local governments, among neighboring states, between regions, and between state and local governments.

But for all the conflict, there is—and must be—a great deal of cooperation. The federal government relies on state and local administrative personnel to carry out air, water, and other pollution-control programs established by federal law. State governments often depend on the federal government to conduct research, to set nationally uniform standards, and to help fund state programs. Groups of states organize interstate compacts and informal regional policy and lobbying groups, all for the purpose of addressing common problems.

So environmental programs operate with ever present tension—a tension between the need for intergovernmental cooperation and the inherent conflicting interests of governments. That tension can be constructive, with the opposing parties stimulating each other to perform better, or destructive, with the conflict consuming everyone's energy in fights over turf and money rather than efforts to solve problems.

The problems of the future will be no easier—and, perhaps, more difficult—to deal with than those of the past. The focus now is how to emphasize the constructive aspects of intergovernmental tensions and minimize the destructive ones. Certainly different environmental statutes and programs have prompted experiments with varied approaches to intergovernmental relations. What are the lessons of these experiments?

MAJOR LESSONS

Although the question is simple, the answer is not. No single framework for intergovernmental relations guarantees success. Environmental problems differ too greatly, and too many uncontrollable variables are at work. So it is necessary to keep several caveats in mind when considering the lessons of experience from different environmental programs.

First, by its nature, a particular environmental problem may be solved more readily at a certain level of government. In the matter of noise pollution, for example, neighborhood problems are best controlled by local ordinances, but a standard for motorcycles or lawn mowers sold nationwide is more appropriately set at the federal level. The relative difficulty, complexity, or cost of controlling a problem also helps determine the most effective level of management.

Second, a program's effectiveness often is determined less by its statutory approach to intergovernmental structure and procedures than by other, often more prosaic factors—the type of leadership available and financial or historical considerations. Thus, comparing the effectiveness of different environmental programs and deducing how such programs' intergovernmental provisions enhance or impede effectiveness are troublesome. Success in one program might not transfer to other programs. For example, the threat posed by federal sanctions in the Clean Air Act probably prompted states to take stronger abatement action than they otherwise would have taken. But it is not at all clear that placing similar sanctions in the Coastal Zone Management Act would have caused states to make greater progress in protecting coastal resources than they have made. Comparing the effectiveness of these two laws would be an apples-and-oranges approach.[10]

Third, even though experience teaches much, new challenges always emerge beyond the scope of past experience. Experimentation with new and different responses must continue as problems change. The intergovernmental system itself is constantly in flux, not only in response to specific new problems but also because of broader demographic and economic changes in society.

Although these caveats hamper drawing conclusions, they need not interfere completely. In fact, four major lessons can be drawn.

First, despite the philosophical rhetoric of federalism lacing debate over intergovernmental relations in the environmental field, pragmatism reigns when decisions are made.[11] Politicians, environmentalists, business representatives, and other interest groups strive to locate regulatory authority where it will best serve their substantive goals at the same time they embellish their speeches with pronouncements of "states' rights" or "compelling national interests."

President Reagan, for example, professes to support greater state freedom from federal intrusiveness, but his Department of the Interior accelerated coal and offshore-oil leasing in the face of strident opposition by affected states and continues to oppose legislative efforts to give states a greater say in the leasing process. Industry often complains about burdensome federal regulations but recently pleaded with the U.S. Occupational Safety and Health Administration to establish federal regulations for labeling hazardous substances in the workplace; those regulations would preempt generally tougher state regulations. Environmentalists frequently champion forceful federal action but have sided with coastal states in challenging the Interior Department's Outer Continental Shelf (OCS) leasing program.[12]

Most observers recognize that the federal government does not have a monopoly on environmental virtue. This was evident even before the Reagan administration's frontal assault on environmental programs, for noteworthy shortcomings already existed in federal efforts to regulate airborne toxic substances, hazardous wastes, pesticides, and threats to occupational health. States could legitimately squawk that the federal government was prosecuting private polluters for noncompliance with pollution-control laws while some federal agencies were failing to reduce pollution at their own facilities.[13] Likewise, some states complain that the federal government is failing to curb other states' emissions of air pollutants, blamed for acid rainfall on distant states.

But most observers also recognize that, although the states have shed their "malevolent bunglers chrysalis,"[14] ample reasons nonetheless remain for having the federal government force state action. For example, Ohio has been notoriously slow to implement federal air-pollution-control laws, out of concern for the economic health of its coal-mining and other industries. In early 1984, some Oklahoma coal companies successfully sought federal enforcement of strip-mine controls in the state, contending that Oklahoma's laxness benefited competitors in the state who were not complying with the law.[15]

A second lesson of the past is that most environmental and resource-management programs are characterized by considerable bargaining, because the states and the federal government need one another in environmental partnerships. This bargaining often is directed at resolving tensions caused by conflicting demands for national uniformity and state flexibility. In programs providing for state action within a federal framework, federal officials often strive, for administrative ease and other reasons, to maximize uniformity and minimize state discretion. Some state officials may see benefits in some uniformity, but others may consider federally required policies inappropriate or environmentally counterproductive.

The relative strengths of the parties in such bargaining are determined by several factors. One major consideration is the arsenal of procedural weapons provided both to federal agencies and to the states by Congress. U.S. senators and representatives, sensitive to state and local concerns and simultaneously aware of national needs, vary regulatory procedures greatly from statute to statute. At one extreme, Congress may completely preempt the states from policy action, or at the other extreme, allow states to veto actions by federal agencies.

The attitudes that government officials bring to bargaining also greatly influence its outcome. Mutual trust and confidence go a long way in smoothing relations and enhancing program effectiveness. Conversely, when distrust is present, the small problems inherent in implementing complex programs become insurmountable hurdles—when federal officials insist on excessive review of state pollution-control actions even after a state develops what it believes to be a credible program, for example.

In addition, governments' administrative capabilities affect bargaining power. Bargaining often requires adequately trained personnel to negotiate agreements. Many state governments are not the sleepy backwaters they were decades ago, but, if a state is not well staffed to take advantage of negotiating opportunities, the hands of federal bargainers are strengthened.

The federal judiciary is still another influence in the bargaining process. Federal courts determine how far the national government may assert authority over the states. The courts also provide a forum for environmental groups, business interests, and citizens to challenge federal and state actions. Court decisions in lawsuits filed by both business groups and environmentalists can complicate federal agencies' relations with state and local governmental bodies.

A third important lesson is that federal funding has played a key role in the success of U.S. environmental programs. Making funds available and threatening to cut them off have been major leveraging tools for federal agencies. States have increased their spending on environmental programs but remain heavily dependent on federal funds. However, federal support for state environmental programs has declined in recent years, partly because of concern over rising federal deficits and partly as a result of the Reagan administration's environmental attitudes. Many states' ability and willingness to continue increasing their support for environmental programs are uncertain. Future dramatic reductions in funding for state programs will undermine the administrative structures and improvements carefully nurtured since the 1960s.

A fourth lesson of the "environmental decade" is that eliminating all intergovernmental conflict is an unrealistic and unwise goal. No matter how environmental programs are restructured, the differing constituency interests of the governments and agencies involved in many conflicts will endure. If conflict often is inevitable, then it must be used to forge creative solutions to difficult problems. Techniques are needed to reduce intergovernmental tensions constructively and creatively.

Attempts to stifle conflict by excluding governments from decisions in one forum simply transfer conflict to others. For example, under the 1953 Outer Continental Shelf Lands Act, states had no influence over OCS oil and gas leasing by the federal government, even though such leasing could significantly affect coastal resources. Federal efforts to speed OCS leasing in the 1970s were hamstrung by lawsuits brought by states unhappy about the leasing's environmental consequences. Congress finally recognized the importance of responding to the states' interests when, in 1978, it amended the 1953 act to give states a greater role in leasing decisions.

Intergovernmental conflicts in pollution-control programs can, however, be reduced by modifying those administrative procedures that were believed necessary when programs were first created but that, in practice, have proved difficult to administer and have made little contribution to environmental quality. EPA's approval of state plans to implement programs required by the Clean Air Act has been quite slow and cumbersome, causing even the most inconsequential changes in plans to be mired in administrative reviews.[16] In general, federal policy should encourage agencies to take greater administrative risks to promote state flexibility, keeping in reserve the powerful hand of the federal government to come down on overly lax state efforts.

In sum, then, clearly the lessons of different intergovernmental approaches to environmental regulations are neither startling nor esoteric. They provide no Rosetta stone. In fact, they may appear mundane. Perhaps the overriding lesson is equally mundane—that improving intergovernmental relations depends as much on making alterations in current types of programs as on developing marvelous new models. The balance of this chapter further supports these lessons, spins out some corollary lessons, and recommends changes.

THE PROGRAMS[17]

Most of the federal environmental statutes initiated in the 1970s represented a massive increase in the federal government's responsibility for environmental concerns and a substantial extension of its authority into areas previously the almost exclusive domain of others.[18] In many cases, however, these laws also increased the authority of state and local governments—as long as they conformed to federal guidelines[19]—although the patterns of federal involvement and the mechanisms by which other governments could gain power differed greatly among the programs.[20]

Regulatory Programs

The rapid appearance of environmental protection as a national political issue stimulated the increased involvement of the federal government in pollution problems during the early 1970s. New federal requirements were a reaction to the inadequacy of existing laws and institutions.[21]

Many state and local environmental-protection programs in the 1960s were weak, although some could claim noteworthy accomplishments.[22] When active programs did exist, the regulators often engaged in seemingly endless negotiations with polluters. Individual states and municipalities were subject to economic blackmail, with polluters warning of job losses and closed plants if strong pollution-control measures were taken. Ralph Nader's task force on air pollution, critical of many state and local efforts, reported that not a single air polluter was prosecuted in 10 states during 1968 and 1969.[23] Nader's task force was not much kinder to federal programs, characterizing the National Air Pollution Control Administration as a "disorganized band of government officials acting out a pollution control charade."[24] Whether or not such a characterization is appropriate, considerable truth rings in the task force's complaints about the weaknesses of both federal and state programs.

Republican and Democratic congressional and presidential candidates alike responded to public concern about environmental quality with a plethora of proposals for new federal laws. As enacted, these laws generally had the federal government set standards and oversee state efforts to comply. To keep regulators honest, ready access to the federal courts was provided for citizens' environmental groups.

Strengthened federal programs had much to recommend them: The federal government had the financial resources to assist states and localities with the cost of running their programs and building pollution-control facilities; federal standard setting established a minimum level for environmental protection, so that states no longer competed for economic development at the expense of environmental quality; federally established deadlines for action reduced foot dragging; federal regulators, in theory, could address interstate pollution; and federally funded research and development seemed more cost-effective than uncoordinated, underfunded research supported by individual states.[25] Environmental organizations and industry groups that preferred the uniformity of national requirements to the uncertainties and burdens of conflicting state laws both pushed for federal environmental action, although they disagreed strenuously over how zealous any preemptive federal actions should be.

Although the national laws represented a massive increase in federal responsibility and authority, much of this authority was delegable to the states. The amount of delegation, however, varied from statute to statute. Most of the legislation followed a general scheme by which states were obliged to develop programs to meet national standards by firm deadlines. Federal grants encouraged state and local action. States that failed to act were threatened with direct federal administration of programs, withdrawal of funds, and other sanctions.

The Clean Air Act typifies this approach to federal regulation.[26] Congress establishes deadlines for meeting standards for permissible levels of common pollutants in the air. EPA then establishes specifics for those standards, and the states are supposed to develop pollution-abatement programs to meet those standards by Congress's deadlines. EPA reviews, approves, and financially assists state programs, but, if a state fails to act or develops an inadequate program, EPA can develop its own program for the state. Both state and federal governments can take enforcement action against individual polluters. In addition, EPA establishes standards for emissions of pollutants from major new industrial sources and from new automobiles. The Clean Air Act also contains a sanction not found in other regulatory programs: areas that fail to meet air-quality standards by a statutory deadline may be denied federal highway grants.[27]

The Surface Mining Control and Reclamation Act (SMCRA) uses an approach similar to that of the Clean Air Act. It sets forth numerous, detailed performance standards for environmental protection that coal-mining operations must meet during a two-phase process. In the "interim" phase, mining operations must comply with some, but not all, of these standards.[28] All standards must be met in the "permanent" phase.

During the interim phase, states issue permits for new mining operations under their existing regulatory programs. However, those permits must require compliance with the interim federal standards.[29] The Office of Surface Mining (OSM) in the U.S. Department of the Interior does not issue permits during the interim phase, but OSM does inspect mining operations and enforce the statute.[30]

States wishing to assume primary responsibility for regulating surface mining of coal during the permanent phase must submit proposed programs to OSM for approval. SMCRA requires state program regulations to be "consistent with" OSM's regulations and the statute's stringent requirements. Should a state choose not to regulate surface mining of coal, fail to gain program approval, or fail to implement adequately an approved program, OSM implements a federal program.[31]

A third example of federal-state regulatory relations is the Occupational Safety and Health (OSH) Act of 1970.[32] This act established a federal regulatory scheme that may be supplemented by state regulation or that may be delegated to the states entirely. The OSH act requires the U.S. secretary of labor to promulgate occupational health and safety standards.[33] These federal standards are enforceable by the U.S. Occupational Safety and Health Administration and preempt state regulation of whatever problems they cover. However, states may, at any time, regulate safety and health issues for which there are no federal standards.[34] States also may assume partial or total responsibility for regulating occupational risks for which there are federal standards,[35] if the state standards and enforcement are "at least as stringent" as the federal standards.

To be delegated this regulatory responsibility, a state must submit a plan to be approved by the U.S. secretary of labor. After granting such a plan initial approval, the secretary may, but is not required to, retain concurrent jurisdiction over OSH issues covered in the plan for three years. The secretary may give final approval no less than three years after initial approval, if the criteria for approval are being satisfied. Even after granting final approval, the secretary retains oversight responsibility for the state program and can withdraw that approval if the state fails to comply substantially with the sanctioned plan.

Other environmental-protection laws also specify federal and state responsibilities for standard setting, permitting, enforcement, and funding (see box on federal statutes). The co-optive nature of these

Allocations of Authority to Federal and State Governments in Five Environmental-Protection Statutes*

Clean Water Act

Standard Setting—Subject to the approval of the Environmental Protection Agency (EPA), states establish ambient water-quality standards for bodies of water. If a state fails to establish an approved standard, EPA establishes the standard. EPA establishes industry-specific effluent limitations for point sources of pollution.

Permitting—Once a state program is approved by EPA, the state may issue permits for the discharge of pollutants into navigable waters. At a minimum, state permits incorporate EPA's effluent limits for different classes of dischargers. EPA may veto issuance of a state permit if it is not consistent with the act and may issue its own permit. If a state fails to adopt or adequately implement an approved program, permits are issued by EPA.

Enforcement—Where a state has an approved program, the state and EPA have concurrent enforcement responsibility. Where the state does not have an approved program, or fails to enforce its program's requirements effectively, EPA can take enforcement action against violations.

Federal Funds—Federal grants are available to states for administering and enforcing water-pollution control programs and for constructing publicly owned sewage-treatment plants.

_____
* This box provides only a selective summary of intergovernmental arrangements in these statutes.

Federal Sanctions—Failure of a state to develop or adequately implement an approved program can result in withdrawal of program approval, loss of program grants, and federal assumption of permitting and enforcement responsibility.

Resource Conservation and Recovery Act

Standard Setting—EPA sets minimum standards for generators, transporters, treaters, storers, and disposers of hazardous waste. These preempt state regulations. However, a state may establish more stringent standards and may regulate issues not covered by federal regulations.

Permitting—Once a state program is approved, the state issues permits. If a state fails to develop or adequately implement an approved program, EPA issues permits under a federal program.

Enforcement—The state enforces its approved program; however, EPA retains concurrent enforcement authority. If a state fails to develop or adequately implement an approved program, EPA enforces a federal program.

Federal Funds—Federal grants are available to states to develop and implement state programs.

Federal Sanctions—Failure of a state to develop or adequately implement an approved program results in withdrawal of program approval, loss of program grants, and federal administration of a federal program.

Federal Insecticide, Fungicide and Rodenticide Act

Standard Setting—EPA has responsibility for registering pesticides for general and/or restricted uses. (No unregistered pesticide may be sold or transported in the United States.) States may register pesticides for additional uses within the state only if EPA has not previously denied registration for such uses. States may regulate pesticide use more stringently than the federal registration but may not impose different labeling or packaging requirements.

Permitting—States with approved programs may certify applicators to use, or supervise the use of, restricted pesticides. (Pesticides registered for general uses may be applied for those uses without supervision by certified applicators.) If a state does not develop or adequately implement an approved program, EPA conducts the certification program.

Enforcement—States that have and are implementing adequate laws and enforcement procedures, or that have cooperative agreements with EPA for enforcing pesticide regulations, have primary enforcement responsibility. EPA may enforce the statute in emergencies and in instances where a state does not respond. EPA may also rescind a state's primary enforcement responsibilities if the state is not carrying out those responsibilities adequately.

Federal Funds—Federal grants are authorized to cover 50 percent of the cost of conducting programs for training and certifying applicators.

Federal Sanctions—If a state fails to develop or adequately implement certification or enforcement programs, EPA may rescind program approval and take over those responsibilities.

Surface Mining Control and Reclamation Act

Standard Setting—The Office of Surface Mining (OSM) sets minimum standards for surface mining and reclamation that preempt inconsistent state regulations; however, a state may establish more stringent standards and may regulate matters not covered by federal regulations.

Permitting—During a brief interim phase following the act's enactment, states were able to issue permits under existing programs so long as the states required compliance with selected federal standards. After a permanent state program is approved by OSM, the state issues permits.

Enforcement—OSM and the state enforce interim federal standards. The state enforces its approved permanent program. If a state fails to develop or adequately implement an approved program, OSM enforces a federal program, which includes issuance of federal, rather than state, permits. OSM may also issue a cessation order while a state program is in effect, if any federal inspection reveals a condition that creates an imminent danger to the public or to the environment.

Federal Funds—Federal grants to states for program development, administration, and enforcement may not exceed 80 percent of total costs in the first year, 60 percent in the second year, and 50 percent thereafter. Additional grants are authorized to cover the cost of state regulation of surface mining on federal land, if the state chooses to exercise this authority.

Federal Sanctions—Failure of a state to develop or adequately implement an approved program results in withdrawal of program approval, loss of program grants, and federal administration of a federal program.

Occupational Safety and Health Act

Standard Setting—The federal government sets minimum occupational health and safety standards that preempt state regulations; states may establish more stringent standards with federal approval and may regulate issues not covered by federal regulations.

Permitting—No permits are issued.

Enforcement—The state enforces its approved program. If the state fails to develop or implement satisfactorily its approved program, the U.S. Occupational Safety and Health Administration (OSHA) enforces a federal program. OSHA retains enforcement authority for federally established standards for at least three years following state-program approval, pending a determination that the state program is being implemented adequately.

Federal Funds—Federal grants not exceeding 90 percent of total costs are authorized to assist states in developing programs. Grants not exceeding 50 percent of total costs are authorized for program administration and enforcement.

Federal Sanctions—Failure of a state to develop or adequately implement an approved program results in withdrawal of program approval, loss of program grants, and federal administration of a federal program.

programs—their reliance on grants, on threats to withhold funds from other programs, and on threats of direct federal regulation—stems from constitutional limits on the federal government's power to directly force states to adopt legislation.[36] Those limits, combined with the reality that complete federal staffing of programs would be politically infeasible, dictate the "carrot-and-stick" structure of most environmental statutes.

When Congress's reliance on such approaches has been challenged, federal courts have given a liberal interpretation to congressional authority to regulate pollution, concluding that pollution involves interstate commerce and is covered by the Constitution's commerce clause. In addition, the courts have narrowly interpreted states' rights under the Tenth Amendment to the Constitution,[37] which reserves rights not delegated to the federal government to the states or to the people. Theoretically, the Tenth Amendment can serve as a buffer for states against federal requirements that states either take regulatory action themselves or submit to direct federal administration of programs. But even U.S. Supreme Court appointees with a states'-rights orientation have found little basis in the amendment for limiting the reach of federal environmental laws. For example, in 1981, the Supreme Court unanimously rejected a Tenth

Amendment challenge to the constitutionality of SMCRA. (The structure of SMCRA is similar to that of most federal pollution-control programs.)

Resource-Management Programs

During the 1970s, Congress passed several statutes that significantly altered the ground rules for managing federal lands. Different political forces lie behind each, though all potentially strengthen the role of states and local governments in managing those lands.

One such statute amended the 1953 Outer Continental Shelf Lands Act in response to pressure that resulted when, in the mid-1970s, the federal government greatly accelerated its leasing of OCS oil and gas resources in an attempt to solve problems brought on by the energy crisis. The 1953 act[38] gave the secretary of the interior authority to manage the OCS, including the right to approve leasing. Coastal states had no role in the process,[39] nor did they receive any revenues from the development of OCS resources off their states' coasts (as they did from onshore development).[40] These factors, plus concern over the environmental effects of offshore-oil drilling, stimulated widespread state opposition to accelerated federal OCS leasing in the 1970s. Finally, in 1978, Congress passed extensive amendments to the Outer Continental Shelf Lands Act.[41] These amendments were intended to accomplish several purposes. Among them were expediting OCS oil and gas development, ensuring such development occurred in a way that protected the environment, and giving affected coastal states a major role in the OCS decision-making process (see box on the OCS).[42]

A second statute that altered the course of federal land management was the Federal Land Policy and Management Act (FLPMA), passed in 1976.[43] This law was a response to concerns that the Interior Department's Bureau of Land Management (BLM) lacked the statutory authority necessary to manage effectively the lands under its jurisdiction (some 310 million acres in 1984)[44] and that the more than 3,000 laws affecting federal lands were antiquated, overlapping, and often inconsistent. Although FLPMA clarified and strengthened federal policy for managing BLM lands, it also enlarged the formal participation of state and local governments in BLM decisions.*

---

* The Resources Planning Act establishes a planning process for U.S. Forest Service lands that requires coordination with state and local plans.[45] These provisions do not give state and local governments as much influence as FLPMA does.

The two statutes used different techniques to give states new influence over federal resource-management actions. The Outer Continental Shelf Lands Act Amendments establish a process of consultation and coordination for offshore development, with a detailed planning procedure that gives the states bargaining power at two stages. The secretary of the interior must accept state recommendations in developing a five-year schedule for leasing OCS lands, if those recommendations are found to provide for a "reasonable balance" of state and national concerns.[46] The secretary also must accept similarly balanced state comments on subsequent individual lease sales and must consider, but not necessarily accept, local governments' comments channeled through the states.[47]

FLPMA establishes a comprehensive planning process for BLM—the first statutory planning process the bureau has had since it was created in 1946.[48] BLM now must coordinate its planning with state and local governments, and its "resource-management plans" must be consistent with state and local land-use plans (so long as this does not violate another federal law). FLPMA, unlike some federal laws, does not provide federal grants to support state and local planning efforts, nor does it require that state and local plans be formally approved by a federal agency.

Review-and-Comment Programs

A third approach to environmental protection is found in various statutes, executive orders, and Office of Management and Budget (OMB) directives that establish planning, assessment, and review processes. Many of these seek to increase the capability of state and local governments to conduct comprehensive resource planning and to review proposed federal actions for consistency with one another and with state and local plans. Two principal incentives stimulate states to participate in these programs—federal funding (in some cases) and the opportunity to influence proposed federal actions.

OMB's "Circular A-95," issued in 1969, is one example of a review-and-comment approach. The directive, which implemented provisions of the Demonstration Cities and Metropolitan Development Act of 1964 and the Intergovernmental Coordination Act of 1968, required that proposed federal grants and projects be reviewed by regional clearinghouses (such as regional councils of governments [COGs]).[49] The A-95 review process was intended to reduce duplication and conflict in the burgeoning numbers of federal programs and to foster the consideration of federal project impacts on state, regional, and local plans. A-95 preceded the major environmental statutes of the 1970s, but the review-and-comment procedures it established could be used for environmental ends. (A-95 was heavily criticized for its ineffectiveness and was succeeded in 1982 by another review process, discussed later in this chapter.)[50]

The National Environmental Policy Act (NEPA) is another vehicle for state and local review of proposed federal actions. This act enables state and local governments to review and comment on major federal actions that would significantly affect the quality of their environments.[51] The openness of the NEPA process to the public and the potential threat of litigation that the law also provides enhance the influence of such state and local comments on federal actions.

The Coastal Zone Management Act

In 1972, Congress enacted the Coastal Zone Management Act (CZMA)[52] because existing federal, state, and local programs were not preventing damage to the nation's coastal areas or resolving the increasingly incompatible demands being placed on those areas. Wise management of limited coastal resources clearly was of national interest, but most land-use decisions historically had been the responsibility of local governments (using authority granted by states). There was great reluctance to have the federal government dictate local decisions via some form of federally required land-use planning. CZMA's solution came in a program of comprehensive coastal land-use planning and regulation, with the states taking the lead role.

Using federal financial assistance, states have developed coastal-zone-management plans. The program is completely voluntary: the federal government imposes no sanctions for inaction, and no federal agency has the authority to draw up a coastal plan if a state fails to do so. States that elect to participate in the program must adopt plans that address issues of national interest (such as coastal access and wetlands protection), balance state and national interests in energy-facility siting, and satisfy other largely procedural conditions. The states, rather than the federal government, determine substantive policy respecting these issues,[53] and also determine what administrative mechanisms will be employed. Once the U.S. Department of Commerce approves a state's program, the state is eligible for annual program-administration grants.

CZMA gives states with Commerce Department-approved programs substantial bargaining power to ensure that federal actions affecting their coastal zones[54] do not conflict with state coastal program policies. One section of the law provides that federal agencies may not issue permits for activities affecting a state's coastal zone (including permits required for OCS development and production) unless the permit applicant certifies, and the state agrees, that the activity is consistent with the state's coastal policies.[55] The applicant may appeal an adverse decision to the secretary of commerce.

Another CZMA section states that federal activities (other than permit issuance) that "directly affect" a state's coastal zone must be consistent "to the maximum extent practicable" with state coastal program policies.[56] When a federal agency proposes a coastal zone activity, it must make an initial "consistency" determination. If an affected state disagrees with the determination, both parties may request the U.S. secretary of commerce to mediate the dispute. Mediation is not compelled, however, and the federal agency may proceed with its proposal despite the state's disagreement.[57] Of course, the state can file a lawsuit challenging the propriety of the federal agency's consistency determination.

Because of these provisions, CZMA is essentially a hybrid of features found in the federal program approaches discussed above. The law resembles the pollution-control statutes in the requirement that state programs be approved by the federal government to be eligible for federal aid, although CZMA gives states more discretion in program design than do those other federal statutes. CZMA also resembles federal resource-management laws, such as FLPMA, in its stipulations giving states influence over federal resource-development activities that affect them. Finally, like the review-and-comment procedures, CZMA's consistency requirements apply to all federal agencies.

In early 1984, the U.S. Supreme Court limited the reach of state power under one of CZMA's consistency provisions. In a 5-4 ruling in *Secretary of the Interior* v. *California*,[58] the Court held that the sale of a federal OCS lease does not directly affect a state's coastal zone. Moreover, the decision strongly suggested that, contrary to conventional wisdom, the consistency requirements do not apply to federal actions taken outside a coastal zone, even if spillover effects from the actions would adversely affect the coastal zone in violation of a state plan. This narrow reading of the "directly affecting" requirement threshold, however, may be reversed by legislation introduced in Congress.[59] Neither the decision nor the proposed legislation would alter the state's ability to influence the leasing process at the exploration, production, and development phases, where the lessee must apply for federal permits. (See box on the OCS.)

FUNDING

No government program can be implemented without adequate funding, regardless of the combination of federal and state leverage involved. Many state-level environmental programs rely on federal funds as a major source of support. However, the federal government's willingness to continue this role is uncertain. The budgets of EPA and other federal environmental agencies are likely to be considerably restrained in coming years.

President Reagan, if he is reelected, is almost certain to continue his administration's push to increase defense spending, and, no matter who is elected to the White House and Congress during the rest of the 1980s, federal deficits remain a concern in both the executive and legislative branches. These two emphases—on greater defense spending and simultaneous spending cuts to reduce federal deficits—may severely compromise the effectiveness of both federally managed programs and state programs that receive federal assistance. Moreover, it is not clear whether even environmentally sympathetic states will be willing or able to assume a substantially increased role in funding environmental programs. Most state governments had their fiscal conditions damaged during the early-1980s recession, although their situations are improving.

Federal Finances

The federal government provides financial support for states' environmental programs by giving grants. The importance of these grants cannot be understated. For example, in fiscal year 1982, federal funds constituted approximately 45 percent of state air-quality program budgets, about 46 percent of state water-quality program budgets, about 69 percent of state hazardous-waste program budgets, and about 48 percent of state water-supply program budgets.[60]

Despite their importance, EPA grants to states have been declining (in constant dollars) since 1979 (figure 8.1). In 1983, the inflation-adjusted total was just under half what it had been in 1975. The fall is due in part to federal budget pressures and in part to the Reagan administration's low regard for environmental programs.

In addition, EPA itself has never had enough personnel to get its job done; just as one program would get under way, new ones were enacted and demands on EPA staff multiplied. Between 1971 and 1980, the agency's permanent staff increased by 53 percent. But, under the Reagan administration, staff levels have been cut to the level of 1974,[61]

Figure 8.1
EPA Grants to States, 1971–1985

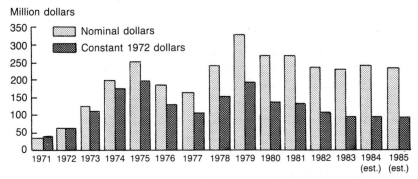

Inflation for 1984 and 1985 is based on estimates in the *Economic Report of the President.*

Source: American Environmental Safety Council.

Figure 8.2
EPA Staff Levels, 1971–1984

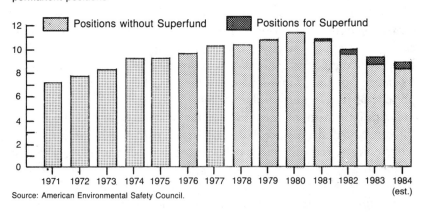

Source: American Environmental Safety Council.

Figure 8.3
EPA Workload, Compared with Other Federal Agencies, 1979

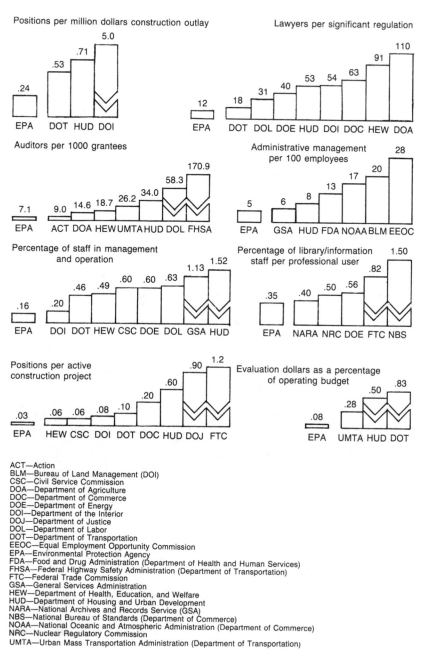

ACT—Action
BLM—Bureau of Land Management (DOI)
CSC—Civil Service Commission
DOA—Department of Agriculture
DOC—Department of Commerce
DOE—Department of Energy
DOI—Department of the Interior
DOJ—Department of Justice
DOL—Department of Labor
DOT—Department of Transportation
EEOC—Equal Employment Opportunity Commission
EPA—Environmental Protection Agency
FDA—Food and Drug Administration (Department of Health and Human Services)
FHSA—Federal Highway Safety Administration (Department of Transportation)
FTC—Federal Trade Commission
GSA—General Services Administration
HEW—Department of Health, Education, and Welfare
HUD—Department of Housing and Urban Development
NARA—National Archives and Records Service (GSA)
NBS—National Bureau of Standards (Department of Commerce)
NOAA—National Oceanic and Atmospheric Administration (Department of Commerce)
NRC—Nuclear Regulatory Commission
UMTA—Urban Mass Transportation Administration (Department of Transportation)

Source: U.S. Environmental Protection Agency.

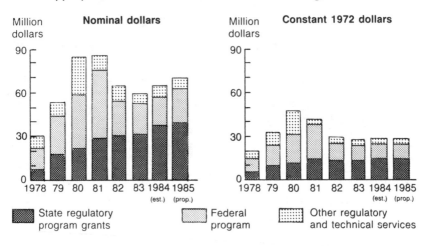

Figure 8.4
Appropriations for U.S. Office of Surface Mining, 1978–1985

Nominal dollars — Million dollars

Constant 1972 dollars — Million dollars

1978 79 80 81 82 83 1984 (est.) 1985 (prop.)

State regulatory program grants

Federal program

Other regulatory and technical services

Source: U.S. Department of the Interior.

Aiding the States

The federal government provides state and local governments significant financial support for environmental and natural-resource programs, spending $4.0 billion in 1983. The single largest category of federal aid in this area is the Environmental Protection Agency's sewage-treatment-plant construction program. In 1983, this one category comprised nearly three-fourths of total federal environmental and natural-resource program grants.

Other grant categories include pollution control and abatement, coastal-zone management, park and recreation land acquisition, historic preservation, fish and wildlife restoration and enhancement, and watershed and flood prevention. Excluding sewage-treatment grants, federal spending for state environmental and natural-resource programs fell 21 percent in constant dollars between 1980 and 1983, although increasing nominally from $1,019 million to $1,035 million. President Reagan's proposed 1985 budget includes $1,069 million in outlays for these grants.

Federal aid reductions are particularly severe in the Land and Water Conservation Fund (LWCF). The fund is financed primarily from Outer Continental Shelf oil and gas revenues; appropriations from it have provided states with over $2.75 billion dollars in matching funds since 1965. This money is used to acquire and develop outdoor recreation facilities, from parkland to swimming pools. Appropriations for LWCF grants to states peaked in 1979 at $369.8 million, fell to $174.7 million in 1981, were eliminated entirely in 1982, and restored at low levels in 1983 and 1984. The administration has proposed zero funding for state LWCF grants in 1985.
(Source: Office of Management and Budget and National Park Service.)

Figure 8.5
Coastal Zone Managment Program Appropriations, in
Nominal and Constant Dollars, 1974–1985

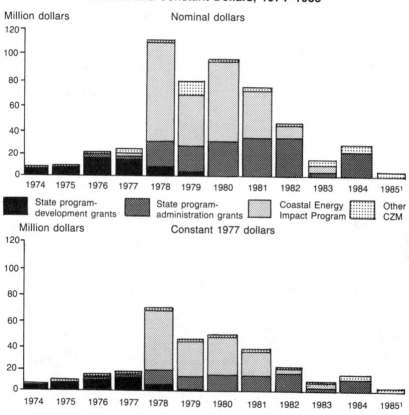

[1] Proposed 1985 budget

Source: U.S. Office of Ocean and Coastal Resource Management.

Figure 8.6
Bureau of Land Management Appropriations

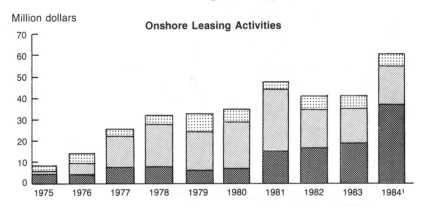

Million dollars

Onshore Leasing Activities

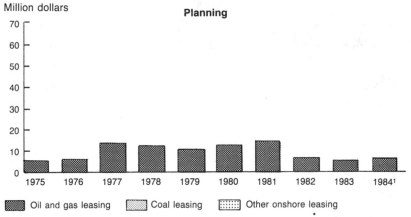

Million dollars

Planning

■ Oil and gas leasing   ▨ Coal leasing   ⬚ Other onshore leasing

[1] In 1984, responsibility for onshore-mineral resource evaluation, regulation, and lease supervision was transferred from the Minerals Management Service to BLM, which accounts for at least part of the increase.

Source: U.S. Bureau of Land Management.

Figure 8.7
Bureau of Land Management Onshore Oil and
Gas Leasing, 1977–1983

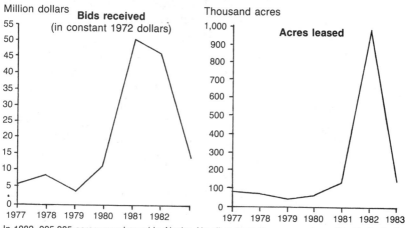

In 1982, 905,985 acres were leased in Alaska. No oil and gas leases were issued in Alaska in the other years shown.

Source: U.S. Bureau of Land Management.

Figure 8.8
Bureau of Land Management Coal Leasing, 1978–1983

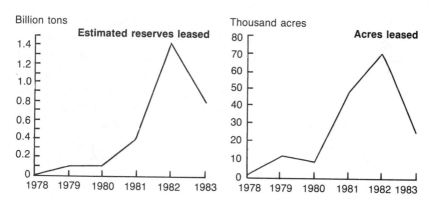

The BLM coal-leasing program was under a partial moratorium until 1981 and again in 1983.

Source: U.S. Bureau of Land Management.

even though several major programs have been added since that time (figure 8.2). Moreover, EPA has a lower worker-to-workload ratio than many other federal agencies (figure 8.3). Limited resources undoubtedly have slowed the agency's standard-setting efforts, made its careful oversight of state programs more difficult, and reduced its ability to provide technical assistance to the states.

Federal grants are also important to state programs that regulate surface mining. In 1983, federal dollars paid nearly 50 percent of the costs of these programs.[62] When adjusted for inflation, federal Office of Surface Mining (OSM) grants for states' coal programs increased by just over 10 percent from 1981 to 1984.[63] At the same time, funding for OSM's own programs was cut dramatically. Adjusted for inflation, the decrease from 1981 to 1984 was nearly 60 percent[64] (figure 8.4). Although OSM grants to states have not been cut back as EPA grants have been, both annual evaluations by OSM itself and outside criticisms of the agency reveal that federal and state programs are inadequate to address mining problems.[65] For example, OSM found that in fiscal year 1983, Tennessee conducted only 39 percent of the complete inspections and 13 percent of the partial inspections required by law. OSM later initiated federal enforcement of portions of Tennessee's program.[66]

Federal support for the coastal-zone-management (CZM) program has declined during the last few years. Federal support for state coastal programs was reduced dramatically in 1983, from $36.7 million to $5.6 million (figure 8.5). Although the Reagan administration proposed eliminating the state grants in fiscal year 1984, Congress restored funding at $21 million.[67] (The administration also proposed that there be no funding for state program administration in fiscal year 1985.[68]) Future funding of the CZM program may be affected by the fate of legislation, now before Congress, that would provide for the federal government to share OCS oil- and gas-lease revenues with coastal states.[69] Such revenue sharing might be seen an alternative to continued CZM grants.

As noted earlier, FLPMA does not provide federal support for state and local planning efforts. Funding for BLM's own planning has been greatly reduced while resource development on BLM lands has increased (figures 8.6, 8.7, and 8.8).

State and Local Finances

As noted, the ability and willingness of state and local governments to replace federal funds with their own are unclear. Many states have cut back environmental programs in recent years because of difficult financial situations; it is tempting to assign all of the blame for these cutbacks to reduced federal assistance. But state spending and revenues have been affected more by general economic conditions (economic stagnation, high unemployment, and high interest rates) than by cutbacks in federal aid.[70] Moreover, in compensating for reduced federal spending, many states have replaced cuts in grants to operating programs (such as environmental ones) more than they have replaced cuts in federal benefit programs for people.[71] Still, many state environmental officials have doubts about the future willingness of state legislatures to increase state funds to offset further declines in federal environmental grants.[72]

Even with a healthy national economy, state and local governments may be limited from raising taxes much farther or spending more money. In the early 1980s, many states raised taxes and cut spending to avoid budgetary deficits.[73] As a result of those moves and improvements in the national economy, some states are beginning to show surpluses in their budgets.[74] Still, despite the apparent quieting of the national tax rebellion of the 1970s, popular sentiment to curb state and local taxes and spending remains strong. Efforts continue to place tax- and spending-limitation measures on the 1984 ballot in several states,[75] and those efforts, as well as spending limitations already in place, could limit the growth of some states' pollution-control programs.

State and local governments have increased their reliance on user and permit fees to meet shortfalls between revenues and expenditures. A survey by the National League of Cities indicates that in fiscal year 1982, 27 cities created new user fees and 35 raised existing ones.[76] In the short run, however, most state environmental agencies cannot rely substantially on permit fees to fund their programs. Even when state agencies charge permit fees, the revenues collected are generally deposited in general funds.[77] Moreover, most such fees currently cover only a very small percentage of program costs. But state attitudes toward fees may change. For example, New York expects to raise about one-third of the administrative costs of its air, water, and hazardous-waste programs under its newly enacted Environmental Regulatory Fee law.[78] Similarly, New Jersey implemented a permit-fee system for water polluters designed to fund most of the state's environmental-program administrative costs as well as to reduce pollution.[79]

Creative partnerships with the private sector, especially for the construction and operation of such capital facilities as sewage-treatment plants, are yet another alternative to increases by state and local governments in taxes and spending. However, the feasibility of such partnerships depends to a great extent on provisions in the Internal Revenue Code, which Congress has the right to change at any time.[80]

As another alternative to raising taxes, many state and local governments sell revenue bonds to raise money for construction programs.[81] The uncertain fiscal condition of many municipalities and the default of the giant Washington Public Power Supply System (WPPSS) temporarily cast a shadow on this market. Although the market rebounded, it may become difficult for state and local governments to rely on both revenue bonds and traditional tax-exempt bonds if interest rates rise significantly or if Congress places ceilings on the use of those bonds.[82] Moreover, state and local governments will be under considerable financial pressure because of their need to fund reconstruction of aging roads, bridges, and similar structures.

In sum, although the extent to which states will be able to fill gaps created by cutbacks in federal funding is difficult to predict, there is good reason to doubt that many states will choose to, or be able to, compensate fully when drastic cutbacks are made with little advance warning.[83] If states are unable to do a good regulatory job because they have been given added responsibilities and fewer funds, the result could be a wide variation among states in applying environmental requirements—a result unacceptable to all interests affected by environmental regulations.[84]

POLITICS AND PRAGMATISM

Federal environmental programs and their mechanisms for intergovernmental relations emerge from a political caldron in which groups strive to achieve competing and often incompatible objectives. The programs are a product of a political tug-of-war among groups and of the personal values of executive- and legislative-branch policy makers. Members of Congress, business people, environmentalists, and state and local officials often express concern for fairness, cost-effectiveness, public participation, compelling national interests, states' rights, federalism, and a multitude of other noble objectives. But often these expressed concerns are mere code words, used to advance pragmatic interests.

The rhetoric is particularly noteworthy in the context of intergovernmental relations because it often masks someone's efforts to get authority located where it will best serve a political, economic, or other objective.[85] For example, state and local officials seek to maximize their influence over, and benefits from, federal programs, while minimizing the political and economic cost to their jurisdiction and their constituents. At all levels of government, business groups often try to minimize regulatory burdens, extract subsidies, and maximize their continuing influence over programs affecting them. Environmentalists want authority located where it will maximize environmental protection and their own continuing administrative influence. Except in budget squabbles, the goals of environmental groups are not primarily economic, although the organizations may advance economic arguments and form coalitions with business groups whose economic interests coincide with the environmental groups' objectives.

It vastly oversimplifies the creation of environmental programs to describe them solely in terms of group interaction and interests. Nevertheless, such a description helps explain the positions that different advocates adopt regarding specific program proposals. That description also helps explain why such diverse structures and procedures for intergovernmental relations are established in U.S. environmental laws.

Business interests in the early and mid-1970s often tended to favor state regulation of environmental problems, because states could be played off against one another and because considerable influence could be wielded on part-time, conservative state legislators and on overwhelmed state agencies.[86] Some states did take strong, effective steps to address environmental problems and, in doing so, were ahead of both the federal government and their neighboring states. In those circumstances, many business interests were happy to see federal authority preempt tougher state regulation.[87]

By the same token, environmentalists tended, during that period, to favor federal solutions. This preference was rooted in the states' generally poor environmental record in the 1960s, in the need for uniform standards to avoid the "competition in laxity"[88] that could arise from different states trying to attract economic growth with lenient environmental regulation,[89] and in the limited resources of the environmental community that made spreading its efforts across many state and local forums impractical, especially when a single victory in Congress could mean a victory across the entire nation.

Environmentalists seem to have changed their view of state governments and, while still favoring strong federal action, are prodding states to address concerns that have been downplayed or disregarded by the federal government. Several factors combined to produce this prodding: the administrative shortcomings of federal environmental programs that became obvious by the late 1970s; the Reagan administration's environmental attitudes in the 1980s; the greatly increased exploitation of federal land resources; and the perception of increased state competence and willingness to deal with environmental matters.

This more favorable assessment of the environmental responsiveness and administrative competence of state bureaucracies derives in part from substantial changes in many state governments during the last two decades. When environmental programs were first created, many state environmental agencies were either nonexistent or in poor shape. Low salaries and cumbersome civil-service procedures made attracting staff with the necessary training and competence very difficult.* While these problems remain, most state agencies now are far stronger than they were. They have grown in size and competence, and a state tradition of civil service, akin to that of federal civil service, is developing.[90] State environmental officials have formed professional organizations to share information and to influence federal legislation and federal agencies.

State administrative procedures also improved considerably in the last two decades, incorporating many of the safeguards found in federal environmental laws. Many states have adopted freedom-of-information, open-meeting, and administrative-procedure acts.[92] Many publish notices and rules in publications similar to the *Federal Register*. Such improvements increase the accountability of state governments and benefit those environmental groups organized to take advantage of them.

The new administrative procedures often reflect the increased openness and responsiveness of state legislatures, which now meet more often and for longer periods, and are served by much stronger staffs.[93] Since the U.S. Supreme Court's "one man-one vote" ruling of 1964 and the enactment of federal civil-rights laws, state legislatures are less dominated by part-time, rural legislators with a laissez-faire view of state government. A new breed of state legislator has developed—a full-time professional politician.[94] Together with state governors who now more commonly serve longer, multiple terms,[95] these activist legislators are beginning to demonstrate why states have been characterized as "laboratories for innovation."[96] Moreover, after the Watergate scandal, and at the prodding of Common Cause and other citizen groups, most states have adopted campaign- and lobbying-reform laws, as well as laws requiring financial disclosure by public officials.[97]

Business groups are recognizing increases in state activism; their percep-

---

* Many states have had difficulty hiring and retaining well-qualified personnel because of their low salary structures. Well before the economic downturn of recent years, many states reported vacancy rates of up to 20 percent. Many also reported severe turnover rates among their most experienced personnel, who made up almost 58 percent of those departing.[91]

tions are reflected in a journal article, headlined "Business Mobilizes as States Begin to Move into the Regulatory Vacuum."[98] However, the degree of assertiveness by individual states depends very much on the pull and tug of political forces, as is reflected in another journal article headline: "The States Can Do It, But Is There the Will?"[99] Many states have already answered this question by enacting laws forbidding their agencies from adopting standards any tougher than those of the federal government.[100] Such laws could be viewed positively as a meritorious effort to promote national consistency, but, more likely, they are a testimonial to states' fears of discouraging economic development if their environmental regulations are tougher than those of their neighbors.*

In 1980, Ronald Reagan campaigned for the presidency on a platform that stressed reduction of the federal government's role in American life—and in state and local affairs.[102] Candidate Reagan supported less federal regulation, reduced federal spending and taxation, a return of responsibility to state and local government, less reliance on governments at all levels and greater reliance on the marketplace and voluntary organizations to solve social problems, and greater attentiveness to the costs of environmental, health, and safety regulations.

However, the Reagan administration's policy for resource development on federal lands shows that its general concern for state authority can be subordinate to other, more specific policy objectives.[103] For example, under President Reagan's first secretary of the interior, James Watt, the federal government greatly increased the pace of natural-resource leasing, in part to help reduce looming federal budget deficits. Accelerated coal leasing in the Rocky Mountain region raised state opposition on environmental and socioeconomic grounds, but the Interior Department refused to accommodate state concerns[104] (figures 8.7 and 8.8 show increases in onshore energy leasing). This refusal was especially ironic since President Reagan had declared himself a "Sagebrush Rebel," allying himself with those westerners who sought greater state and local influence over management of western federal lands.†[105] The administra-

---

* These fears may be groundless. A recent study by The Conservation Foundation found no evidence that industry migrates from state to state in search of pollution havens.[101]

† It is ironic that the Federal Land Policy and Management Act (FLPMA), which gives state and local governments potentially significant influence in BLM decisions, helped trigger the Sagebrush Rebellion. FLPMA called for multiple-use management of federal lands, but its conservation-oriented elements were perceived as a threat by some traditional local users of federal rangelands.

tion raised even greater antagonism among coastal states with its accelerated OCS leasing program (figure 8.9 and OCS box).

The Reagan administration's program to speed the delegation of environmental programs to the states is wrapped in the rhetoric of federalism. But the simultaneous effort to cut federal grants for these programs, at a time when recession had placed many states in dire fiscal straits, suggests that the real motivation for the transfer was not so much abstract political theory as antipathy for environmental protection. The effort to speed delegation illustrates well the proposition that "federalism sometimes becomes a stalking-horse" for other political objectives.[106]

The subordination of the Reagan administration's state-oriented federalism to other objectives is apparent in the debate over federal regulations to label toxic and hazardous substances in the workplace.[107] A rigorous labeling regulation, developed over a period of eight years by the Occupational Safety and Health Administration, was proposed by the Carter administration shortly before it left office, but the proposal was withdrawn by the Reagan administration. The proposed regulation was sought by organized labor and opposed by industry. The Reagan administration's quashing of the proposal reflected distaste for regulation and a desire to minimize burdens on American business. In the vacuum left by federal inaction, organized labor and other groups persuaded 17 states and dozens of localities to adopt their own labeling requirements.[108]

Anxious about this regulatory balkanization, the chemical industry reversed itself and pushed the Reagan administration to issue a federal regulation. The administration resisted, then finally relented. However, the new federal proposal is substantially weaker than many of the state and local requirements it would preempt, as well as weaker than the one suggested by the Carter administration.[109] The labeling proposal suggests environmental concerns may be disserved by federal preemption when state and local governments are more determined to protect those concerns.[110]

A final example of the Reagan administration's subordination of states' rights is in congressional arguments over state authority to require more registration data on pesticides than is required by federal law.[111] California has exercised this authority, to the dismay of the chemical industry, which has experienced delays in the California registration process. In response, the industry sought an amendment to the Federal Insecticide, Fungicide and Rodenticide Act to deny this authority to California and like-minded states. Representative William Wampler (R.-Va.), support-

Figure 8.9
Bureau of Land Management Outer Continental Shelf
Oil and Gas Leasing, 1974–1983

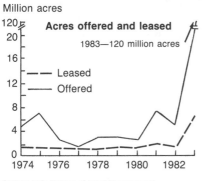

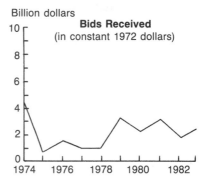

Source: U.S. Bureau of Land Management.

Mending Fences

William Ruckelshaus has made improved relationships with state and local governments an important goal of his second term as administrator of the U.S. Environmental Protection Agency (EPA). Two examples of this emphasis are a newly issued EPA policy on program delegation and oversight and new guidelines for EPA auditing of air-quality programs delegated to the states.

The EPA policy on delegation and oversight, signed by Ruckelshaus in April 1984, reflected the work of a task force whose members included both EPA officials and representatives of state and local governments. It remains to be seen how well the policy will be implemented in practice, especially since levels of federal funding for state and local programs remain uncertain.

EPA's newly published National Air Audit System (NAAS) provided standardized criteria for EPA regional offices to use when auditing state and local air pollution agencies. Developed in concert with organizations representing state and local air pollution officials, the guidelines are an effort to overcome the existing inconsistencies in auditing practices of EPA regional offices. The system is scheduled to be implemented in fiscal year 1984.

The sensitivity of states to EPA involvement in their affairs was illustrated by an episode in early 1984, when Ruckelshaus lambasted EPA enforcement officials for their failure to launch larger numbers of enforcement actions. State officials reportedly took umbrage at Ruckelshaus's outburst, because the EPA Administrator apparently had disregarded enforcement activity being undertaken by the states. Ruckelshaus later conceded that he did not have the states in mind when he made his speech, but he also reiterated that EPA must step in if states are not doing the job. EPA has since developed an intergovernmental task force to develop state-federal enforcement strategy.

ing the amendment, said, "Normally my position is that I support states' rights. But I'm not sure this is the issue. If you let each state operate on its own whim . . . it will work an impossible burden on pesticide producers." The Reagan administration, as a believer in greater state discretion, initially opposed the amended provision, saying it would "unduly and inappropriately preempt state law." But the White House dropped its opposition after being lobbied by congressional Republicans and the chemical industry.

Interest groups—by advocating competing environmental-quality, resource-development, and other policy objectives—often force government policy makers to improvise as they devise complex administrative and legal procedures to accommodate those objectives. The resulting mechanisms typically provide a series of pragmatic checks and balances among different levels and branches of government.

Consider, for example, the provisions of the Clean Air Act that are intended to protect the pristine air of large national parks and monuments through the "prevention of significant deterioration" of air quality. These provisions set very tight ceilings on how much the air of such areas can be dirtied. These "Class I ceilings" presumably protect important "air quality-related values," but the act recognizes that the ceilings may be insufficient in some cases and too stringent in others. To deal with this uncertainty, Congress included variance procedures for new sources of pollution. But these variances also represent a congressional effort to resolve disagreements within and between governments over environmental protection and energy development. The variance procedures show how convoluted such balancing processes can become:

> If the federal land manager demonstrates to the state that, despite meeting Class I ceilings, air quality-related values are adversely affected, a permit may not be issued [by the state]. If, on the other hand, the source convinces the federal land manager that, despite exceeding Class I ceilings, air quality-related values are not affected, the state may issue a permit reflecting specified incremental ceilings. . . . If the source and the federal land manager do not agree, the state may issue a permit containing a variance to the source. If the federal land manager does not concur with this proposed permit, the matter is referred to the President for a decision which is not judicially reviewable.[112]

A second example of the complex, pragmatic balancing of interests is the Nuclear Waste Policy Act,[113] which is intended to establish a national repository for long-term storage of high-level radioactive wastes. Because this decision is such a political hot potato, the act contains very detailed mechanisms for state and local participation in selecting a site.[114] The president is required to recommend a disposal site to Congress, but the state in which the site is located may disapprove the choice. The state's disapproval may be overridden by a congressional resolution adopted in accordance with detailed procedures specified in the act.[115]

Pragmatism in intergovernmental relations is nothing new. To be sure, when America's founders were drafting the Constitution in the late 1700s, they were not concerned with protecting western national parks from energy development or with the disposal of nuclear wastes. But the Constitution itself is a pragmatic document, forged from battles among different political constituencies, each seeking to protect its own interests. And much like intergovernmental relations in the environmental field, the forging of the Constitution occurred only with much bargaining. The next section examines bargaining and factors affecting it.

BARGAINING

Bargaining is a "given" in intergovernmental relations. It plays a prominent role in decisions to delegate regulatory programs, in federal oversight of programs administered by states, and in consultation, coordination, and "consistency" proceedings. It is influenced by the language of federal statutes and by the administrative capabilities of, and program funding available to, federal, state, and local governments. Perhaps it is influenced most strongly by the attitudes and perceptions of government officials.

Because their views are shaped by the previous failure of states to control pollution, federal officials often have little confidence in states' willingness or capability to take tough regulatory steps and insist that states adhere to federal priorities and procedures. These officials also have strong external incentives to make tough demands on states seeking program-management authority. They might be accused of "giving away the store" if they were to allow states too much leeway; environmentalists have been quite ready to sue on grounds of undue laxness. Federal officials often issue rules that are quite specific, to make them readily enforceable, and that are intended to restrain the worst possible abuses by states and by polluters.[116]

This specificity can reduce state flexibility. Under the Surface Mining Control and Reclamation Act, the Office of Surface Mining (OSM) adhered closely to strict statutory requirements in devising its first set of permanent regulations for approving permanent state regulatory

The OCS Leasing Controversy

For more than 30 years, coastal states and the U.S. Department of the Interior have battled intermittently over who should control development of the nation's offshore resources—primarily oil.[1] The recent focus of controversy is the Interior Department's Outer Continental Shelf (OCS) oil and gas leasing program. The controversy has spawned at least six lawsuits pitting coastal states and environmental groups against the Interior Department and the oil industry.[2] This lineup suggests that more pragmatic issues underlie the rhetorical cries of "states' rights" and "overriding national interests." Indeed, the controversy highlights how pragmatism and personality help shape intergovernmental relations and how efforts to sweep conflict under the rug generally fail.

Ironically, the OCS leasing controversy involves two federal laws that were intended in part to reduce federal-state conflict over OCS development by giving coastal states a greater role in the development process—the 1978 Outer Continental Shelf Lands Act Amendments (OCSLAA) and the 1972 Coastal Zone Management Act (CZMA).[3] During the Carter administration, Interior Secretary Cecil D. Andrus issued the first five-year schedule of OCS lease sales to be developed under the detailed criteria set forth in OCSLAA. This schedule accelerated the pace of OCS leasing and expanded its geographic scope as well. The states of California and Alaska, along with some environmental groups, successfully challenged the schedule in federal court on the grounds that the secretary had failed to consider all the required criteria.[4] But, by the time that court issued its decision on the

five-year schedule, another administration was in place, and another lawsuit—this time over an individual lease sale—had been decided.

The first OCS lease sale held under Interior Secretary James G. Watt's tenure involved lease tracts off the coast of central and northern California. California protested Watt's decision not to delete from the sale certain tracts that would have buffered sensitive habitat areas from potential oil spills. California sought to enjoin the lease sale under provisions of several federal laws and succeeded in U.S. district court on grounds that the Interior Department had not complied with CZMA's requirements.[5]

Though they proclaimed themselves states' rights advocates, President Reagan and Watt did little to accommodate California and other coastal states' concerns about the OCS leasing program. Watt appealed the adverse district court decision to the Ninth Circuit, lost,[6] and appealed again to the U.S. Supreme Court, where his successor, William Clark, won a significant victory in a 5-4 decision (*Secretary of the Interior* v. *California*).[7] And when Watt revised Andrus's five-year leasing schedule in 1982, he further accelerated the pace of lease sales and proposed offering for lease the entire billion-acre OCS in five years[8]—more than 50 times the scale of average annual leasing from 1974 through 1980 (figure 8.9). His revision prompted another lawsuit by states and environmentalists, which was unsuccessful.[9]

Although OCSLAA and CZMA were intended in part to give coastal states significant influence over OCS development, they failed to do so. In part, this failure was a result of vague language in the statutes. But even if these laws had clearly given states the power they sought, there could still have been struggles. Since officials' dispositions are crucial to bargaining, even a process that requires federal officials to be even more responsive to state concerns can be subverted if those administering it do not act in good faith. For example, Watt once declared that compromise was not part of his vocabulary,[10] a statement largely corroborated by his relationship with coastal states over OCS leasing. His successor, Clark, has pledged to pay greater heed to state concerns about leasing than was paid by Watt, notwithstanding the Supreme Court decision on CZMA's consistency provision that favors the federal government.[11]

Whether Clark truly makes good on his promises remains to be seen. Even if he does, the pragmatic issues fueling the OCS controversy will re-main. OCS development's social and environmental costs are borne primarily by adjacent coastal states, but almost all revenues from OCS leases and royalties go to the federal government (though proposed legislation could change this by sharing some OCS revenues with coastal states[12]). A large federal deficit and a desire to reduce U.S. dependence on oil imports encourage a federal policy to accelerate leasing, even at the expense of states' concerns; conversely, a desire to reduce environmental risks and minimize conflicts with other coastal-zone resources (for example, fishing and tourism) encourages states to slow or limit this federal effort.[13]

Federal-state tension over OCS development likely will remain. If the Interior Department and coastal states are unable to resolve it constructively through communication and negotiation, it will simply surface elsewhere—either in Congress[14] or the courts.

programs.[117] The OSM regulations virtually required that a state program be a carbon copy of the federal program to receive approval. Many states, believing they were to have "primacy" in implementing the strip-mining law, were incensed, and litigation over the regulations reached "unprecedented proportions in the field of environmental law."[118] The regulations have since been relaxed under the Reagan administration.[119]

State officials' attitudes also influence bargaining, and an attitude of dissatisfaction with, and resentment of, federal agencies is not uncommon. Because they dislike having a "distant federal bureaucracy" administering environmental programs affecting their governments, citizens, and businesses, states have a strong incentive to assume control of delegable programs.[120] Such control enables states to tailor national requirements more closely to their concerns, to integrate more efficiently new programs with existing state institutions, and to streamline permit-processing mechanisms to help simplify the regulatory maze for citizens, industry, and local governments. But the states have to bargain for this authority. They may have to accept some requirements they consider unrealistic, unscientific, economically inefficient, or otherwise flawed.

State officials have many complaints about the federal environmental programs in which they become partners. Many officials believe that the states function as little more than regional offices of federal environmental agencies.[121] As EPA Associate General Counsel William Pedersen observes: "One might argue that the opportunity afforded the states to operate some of these programs is more of an effort to conscript them into federal service than it is an acknowledgement of their autonomy."[122] Pedersen's statement highlights a certain schizophrenia present in environmental programs. A federal statute may state that allowing states flexibility in designing programs is one of its goals, yet it may simultaneously set forth highly restrictive conditions that state plans must meet for approval.[123] At the root of this problem is a congressional failure firmly to reconcile conflicting interests during the legislative process, a shortcoming that may reflect Congress's own dualistic nature (as both the legislative body of the national government and an assembly of representatives of states and localities).

States' complaints to the U.S. General Accounting Office are typical and include:

> EPA's adversarial attitude, widely varying EPA regional oversight practices and expectations, excessive duplication in EPA reviews of state actions, a focus on individual project or permit problem cases rather than an evaluation of overall state program effectiveness, and long delays in reporting the results of their reviews to the states.[124]

State officials' frustration with their federal partners is augmented by other problems, including delayed congressional appropriations and differences between federal and state fiscal years, both of which confuse state plans for federal funds. Late issuance by EPA of its regulations also causes antagonism, especially when the states are required to comply with tight deadlines. (The significance of these and other problems as obstacles to management of state environmental programs is shown in figure 8.10.)

The centrality of officials' attitudes to the bargaining process is reflected in the delegation of environmental programs to the states under the Reagan administration's federalism. During the 1970s, EPA had a reputation for being slow and cautious in delegating regulatory responsibilities to states. (As a practical matter, in many instances where authority was not formally delegated, states did much of the work anyway.) The OSM had a similar reputation for being tight-fisted in approving

Figure 8.10
Obstacles to Managing State Environmental Programs, 1980

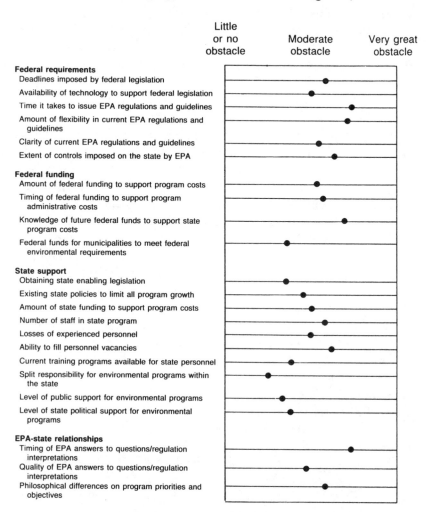

Based on survey responses by state environmental-program directors.

Source: U.S. Comptroller General.

state programs.[125] But the situation changed during the early 1980s under the Reagan administration. Between December 1981 and December 1983, the number of states fully authorized to conduct the Clean Air Act's program for "prevention of significant deterioration" increased from 17 to 36.[126] The number of states fully authorized to administer the program to control hazardous air pollutants leapt from 25 to 37 between 1981 and 1984 (figure 8.11).

Some of those delegations may have been on the verge of approval before December 1981, but the surge stemmed from the Reagan administration philosophy that a program *should* be delegated unless a state clearly lacks the staff or authority to ensure results compatible with national goals.[127] This philosophy contrasts with the Carter administration's view that programs *should not* be delegated unless a state clearly could meet national goals.[128] Obviously, determinations of capability are subject to interpretation and bargaining. In any case, the shift in the burden of proof from one administration to another, plus the Reagan administration's policy of giving EPA officials numerical goals for program delegations, were designed to speed transfers to the states. The rapid increase in delegation under the Reagan administration suggests that political appointees' philosophies and internal agency-management controls are at least as significant as formal statutory requirements in determining the extent to which programs are delegated.

If EPA was too slow to delegate programs before 1981, perhaps it has been too quick since then. Environmentalists fear that "premature delegation" to states is simply a way for the Reagan administration to ensure that certain statutes are not enforced,[129] especially since stepped-up delegations have been accompanied by decreased federal grants to the states.[130]

Although officials may administer the same statute differently, as the diametrical approaches of the Carter and Reagan administrations illustrate, this does not mean that statutory language and bargaining levers contained in legislation are unimportant. For example, the U.S. Department of Commerce seems to have shown greater leniency in approving state coastal zone-management programs than has been shown by federal pollution-control agencies in approving state pollution-control programs.

This leniency most likely stems from provisions of the Coastal Zone Management Act (CZMA) that limit federal bargaining leverage. Since CZMA's goals are very broad, the states are allowed wide latitude in program design. In part, this is a recognition of state and local governments' traditional preeminence in land-use planning. Also, because state participation in the coastal program is voluntary, overly stringent

Figure 8.11
Delegation of Selected Environmental Programs
to State and Territorial Governments, 1984

Program	Number of Delegations or Approvals	
	Full	Partial[1]
Clean Air Act		
PSD permits—for new and modified sources in areas classified for prevention of significant deterioration	36	10
NSPS permits—for sources required to meet new source performance standards	34	18
NESHAPS permits—for hazardous air pollutants	37	11
Clean Water Act		
NPDES permits—for point-source dischargers	15	21
Construction-grants management	4	51
404 permits—dredge-and-fill	0	—
Safe Drinking Water Act		
Drinking-water-standards enforcement	52	—
Underground-injection-wells control program	22	8
Coastal Zone Management Act		
Coastal-zone-management programs	28	—
Federal Insecticide, Fungicide and Rodenticide Act		
Applicator certification training	48	—
Restricted pesticide uses	48	0
Occupational Safety and Health Act		
Occupational safety and health programs	2 1	—
Resource Conservation and Recovery Act		
Interim program		
Phase I	45	—
Phase II	12	11
Final program	1	—
Surface Mining Control and Reclamation Act		
Regulatory programs	25[2]	—

[1] "Partial" has different meanings in different programs. See figure references for full explanation.

[2] Two states may soon have their approvals revoked. See figure references.

program-approval requirements would simply cause states to drop out without fear of subsequent federal intrusion. Because the states determine both the substantive policy and administrative structure of their programs, program-approval criteria are largely procedural (for example, requiring opportunities for public involvement). And the statute gives states wide flexibility in deciding how to meet those criteria.

One major drawback of a lenient approach to delegation is that states can end up with ineffective programs. Some states do, in fact, have poor programs that scarcely embody the comprehensive planning and regulatory tools that CZMA envisions,[131] whereas other state programs are quite good. However, stringent program-approval requirements do not necessarily guarantee quality programs. As is noted below, EPA's limited bargaining ability caused it to approve state plans for controlling air pollution that were widely acknowledged to be unrealistically optimistic, if not inadequate.

Moreover, the threat of a federally administered program if a state declines to develop its own program, or fails to adequately implement a delegated program, has proved somewhat unwieldy in practice. Federal agencies simply lack sufficient money and personnel to do a good job of administering programs entirely by themselves.

Evidence of the difficulties associated with federal program administration was provided in 1981, when the Idaho legislature voted to withhold all funding from the state's air-quality program.[132] The legislators complained about EPA second-guessing and duplicating state actions. EPA was forced to administer the state's program. A year later, the state legislature relented and reinstated the funding. Both state and federal officials concluded that the federal takeover "caused more problems than it solved."[133] EPA reportedly spent almost five times more money to maintain the Idaho program that year than the state would have spent to do the same job.[134] In another case, Iowa's environmental budget was cut 15 percent in 1982, triggering a loss of matching federal funds. The state then dropped its municipal water-monitoring program, returning responsibility to EPA. But EPA is managing to conduct only about 15 percent of the inspections previously performed by the state.[135]

Federal agencies recognize that they depend heavily on the states to implement controls, which gives the states some leverage in bargaining over program delegation and oversight. For example, in commenting on state implementation plans prepared under the Clean Air Act, the National Commission on Air Quality observed that EPA accepted virtually all of the states' projections to meet air-quality standards—even though officials at all levels of government acknowledged privately that the projections "often were based on imprecise emission inventories, inadequate projection techniques and, in general, were overly optimistic."[136]

Despite federal agencies' limited funding and staff, the agencies sometimes must administer a program, as a last resort, when a state is unable or reluctant to take essential regulatory action. For example, EPA's midwest regional office had to prepare a sulfur dioxide-control plan for Ohio in 1975 when the state government failed to prepare an adequate plan of its own. The *Wall Street Journal* observed that Ohio's "dismal record" is a product of its great dependence on heavy industry for its economic well-being.[137] Industries, unions, and miners join together to tilt state policies toward protection of jobs and away from protection of air quality.

In addition to officials' attitudes and statutory provisions, the administrative arrangements and fiscal capabilities of states and federal agencies affect the bargaining process. Even when federal officials personally bring positive attitudes to the program delegation and oversight process, the complex structure of their agencies may complicate relations with their counterparts in state and local agencies.

For example, within EPA's Washington, D.C., headquarters, there may be harmony or disharmony between the general counsel's office, the program offices, and the offices of EPA's administrator and deputy administrator. Differences also may exist among those offices and EPA's regional offices, with the latter caught in the middle of disputes between the states and Washington, D.C., and within and between EPA regional offices. By increasing uncertainty and producing delayed, contradictory, and quickly reversed policy decisions, the internal disputes within federal agencies sour federal officials' relations with state and local governments.

The effect of administrative arrangements on bargaining is clearer in the consistency processes of CZMA and FLPMA than in the pollution-control programs. As noted earlier, CZMA provides that federal activities "directly affecting" a state's coastal zone must be consistent "to the maximum extent practicable" with state policies and that federal agencies may not issue permits for activities affecting the coastal zone unless the state certifies that the activity is consistent with its coastal policies. With the exception of OCS lease sales (see OCS box), the consistency process generally helps resolve state and local concerns over federal actions by forcing coordination among the parties. State disagreements with federal agencies' consistency determinations are quite infrequent, probably occurring in fewer than 3 percent of the cases.[138]

The success of CZMA's consistency process for "federal activities" depends on negotiation to resolve disagreements before a federal agency makes its formal consistency determination. A state's position in such bargaining can be quite strong if its policies are clear and specifically forbid the proposed federal action. However, if a state's policies are vague and subject to conflicting interpretations by federal and state personnel, the state may be unable to find a credible rationale for discouraging the action, leaving the state little legal leverage and giving the federal agency dispensation to proceed as it wishes. Further difficulties arise because CZMA is silent on whether the state agency's or the federal agency's interpretation of a state's program is to receive more weight in determining consistency.[139] But, a state's position also may be strengthened by vagueness in its policies. A state's broad interpretation of general goals and policies may initiate a negotiating process and let the state bring to the bargaining political chits and other weapons.

FLPMA's consistency provisions, as noted, require that Bureau of Land Management (BLM) land-use plans be consistent with state and local plans, so long as those plans are consistent with federal law. But the potential influence of state and local governments may be undercut if their administrative organization prevents them from presenting BLM with coherent, consolidated positions on various issues.[140] Frequently the plans of different local governments and state agencies are inconsistent, and sometimes there are no "plans" in the sense of comprehensive land-use requirements. Instead, isolated policies with varying degrees of formality or simply programs with implicit policy statements in them constitute plans. A state fish-and-game department, for instance, may have a policy of protecting bighorn sheep habitat to promote sport hunting, but the policy may conflict with a state agricultural department policy endorsing cattle grazing. If BLM, in planning the management of an area that can support either bighorn sheep or cattle, is faced with such conflicting policies, it probably decides in line with its own preferences.

One additional factor apt to play an important role in determining how well consistency provisions of federal laws are implemented is the availability of adequate funding to state agencies. In the past, federal grants for state coastal programs helped states hire the capable personnel needed to develop and implement state plans, to review federal agency proposals, and to bargain effectively. But the federal support for state programs declined as the coastal program matured, and increased state support is uncertain[141] (see figure 8.5). A state's bargaining ability can also be undermined if a tight state budget or the election of a governor unsympathetic to environmental concerns (as happened in 1982 in California[142]) causes the state's own funding of environmental agencies to drop dramatically.

Similarly, FLPMA's consistency process can be undermined by a lack of funding. Since FLPMA, as does CZMA, relies on negotiation to tailor federal actions to state and local needs, sufficient competent personnel are needed on all sides. This can be costly. Although local governments receive payments in lieu of property taxes on federal lands within their boundaries,[143] FLPMA does not provide federal financial or technical assistance for state or local planning efforts. Furthermore, funds for planning within BLM itself have been reduced considerably, even as energy resource development accelerates (figures 8.6, 8.7, and 8.8). Without adequate federal funds, the whole planning and coordination process could wither. Indeed, a recent BLM memorandum reportedly criticized the quality of resource-management plans being prepared by BLM state offices, stating that the plans "do not provide an adequate planning base for future management action."[144]

The impact of the "A-95" review-and-comment process mandated by the OMB also strongly depended on the ability of state and local governments to speak with one voice and to staff and finance clearinghouses adequately.[145] This process apparently promoted the flow of information to state and local officials, but clearinghouses often were poorly funded, enabling federal agencies to take advantage of the chorus of conflicting comments received on proposed actions.

The Reagan administration abolished the A-95 process—which was widely criticized as ineffective and for generating undue paperwork—and substituted a process intended to give states greater flexibility in organizing review-and-comment mechanisms.[146] The stated purpose of the executive order establishing the new process is to advance President Reagan's goal of "restoring rightful authority to state and local governments."[147] But the executive order offers little improvement, according to political scientists George Gordon and Irene Fraser Rothenberg:

> While the Order does offer some possibility that reviewers can improve the quality and persuasiveness of their comments, there seems little guarantee that federal agencies will heed or respond to these reviews. This situation, coupled with a major reduction of financing for the system, suggests that the Order does little to improve (and may indeed exacerbate) chronic problems in the intergovernmental review process.[148]

The new system may not work well because many projects can be excluded from it; the federal share of funding for clearinghouses has been reduced and substitute state funds are not readily available; the Federal Regional Councils, which helped promote federal agency responsiveness at the regional office level, have been abolished; and OMB shows limited interest in policing federal agency compliance.

Intergovernmental relations under CZMA, FLPMA, and A-95 clearly demonstrate that coordination "inevitably advances some interests at the expense of others."[149] Gordon and Rothenberg remark that the design, objectives, and results of coordination processes can only be understood and evaluated in terms of political impacts.[150] In sum, politics, pragmatism, and bargaining are intertwined. This must be borne in mind as the future of intergovernmental relations is examined.

THE FUTURE

Greater realism must be introduced into the planning, budgeting, and overseeing of environmental programs if those programs are to be more effective and intergovernmental relations are to be enhanced. The search must continue for suitable mechanisms to protect environmental quality while reconciling and balancing conflicting government interests. Such concerns as administrative and economic efficiency, equitable treatment of states and polluters, and accountability must not be forgotten.[151]

Although many of the environmental problems facing the United States are becoming more complex, chances are that the nation will try to deal with new problems by using variants of the legal and administrative techniques adopted during the 1970s. Lessons can be learned from the past, but none of those approaches has revealed itself as a surefire road to success. If the weaknesses in those methods are not addressed, not only will they continue to be used in less-than-optimum ways in existing programs, but their clones, developed for more complex problems, will likely be hobbled by the same shortcomings. Moreover, even those approaches that have shown promise in addressing past and present problems may not be able to survive the future stresses caused by cutbacks in governmental funding. Certainly, the old approaches to environmental planning and management should be patched up, but entirely new ones probably also need to be devised.[152] Like several of the programs of the 1970s, many of the programs of the 1980s may be giant experiments.

A Role for Regional Solutions?

What promise is there in interstate regional arrangements for addressing environmental problems that do not respect state boundaries? Interstate compacts, river-basin commissions, and other multistate approaches have been used for many years, most notably to address regional water concerns. The pragmatism, politics, and bargaining that influence other federal-state mechanisms are also evident in the creation and operation of these multistate organizations. This is illustrated by recent efforts to establish a regional interstate compact to manage low-level radioactive wastes in the northeastern United States.

Congress enacted the Low-Level Radioactive Waste Policy Act in March 1980 after three states with dump sites threatened to close them or to restrict the acceptance of out-of-state wastes.[1] The act declares that disposal of low-level radioactive waste (for example, refuse from hospitals) is a state responsibility, but that it can be most safely and efficiently managed on a regional basis.[2] After January 1, 1986, any regional compact may limit the use of regional disposal facilities to wastes generated by signatory states. States are encouraged to form regional compacts, that is, arrangements for disposing of wastes on a regionwide basis. Pursuant to the compacts, one state may agree to be the disposal site for a while, and then another state will assume the disposal burden.

As of early 1984, compacts have been developed in the Northeast, Rocky Mountains, Central Plains, and Southeast; the compacts await congressional approval.[3] In the Northeast, only four states have joined the proposed compact, although 11 states from Maine to Maryland have been involved in the negotiations. The *Wall Street Journal* has described the bargaining among states:

A major sticking point is the principle that every state must be willing to accept a dump site. Rural states such as Vermont, New Hampshire and Maine, which have strong environmental concerns and little nuclear activity of their own, worry that they might get stuck with all the atomic waste for a region that includes New York, Pennsylvania, Massachusetts, and Maryland, among the biggest nuclear waste-producing states in the nation. . . .

A breakthrough came last month when New York's energy office recommended that states with little nuclear waste should be exempt from hosting a dump.

Massachusetts is another problem. The state has a law requiring voter approval of any proposed compact and dumpsite. Other states are understandably skittish about signing on with a partner whose voters could blow an agreement apart.

On top of this is Massachusetts' reputation for stonewalling negotiations with environmental objections. [A Massachusetts official] concedes his state's prickly reputation makes bargaining with other states difficult. "My concern is to get representatives of New York and Pennsylvania to sit down and talk with us."[4]

States can find methods of regional cooperation that are less binding than the responsibilities codified in interstate compacts. For example, many states are cooperating to continue the work of interstate river basin commissions, even though federal funding for six of these commissions was terminated in 1981.[5] The particular modes of regional cooperation established by states will depend on each state's calculation of the costs and benefits to it of working with its neighbors.

Delegation and Oversight

The federal government must pay more attention to the way its agencies oversee state pollution-control programs. This must be done so that both intergovernmental relations and overall program operations are enhanced. EPA, for example, could take many simple administrative steps to speed its decisions.[153] An EPA task force reports that a "glaring weakness" in all the agency's programs is the lack of a "well-conceived, clearly-defined policy" on oversight of states.[154] The agency also must decide how much discretion its national headquarters should allow its regional offices. As things are now, Washington's review of regional decisions lengthens the time required for delegation and oversight.

Better procedures are needed for giving states a role in the development of federal regulations that guide delegated programs. Early state involvement could identify opportunities for flexibility and innovation that otherwise might go unnoticed. Such involvement, which has been sought by the states, is potentially more useful now than in the past because of the considerable administrative experience that states have accumulated. Moreover, that involvement could be facilitated through the national organizations that state pollution-control officials have created to represent their views to Congress and to EPA.

Still, the greater involvement of, and consultation with, state officials is difficult for several reasons. First, in times of budget stringency, federal and state travel budgets get cut, making it almost impossible to convene all the desirable consultative meetings. Second, because states differ in their views, national umbrella organizations of state officials may have difficulty representing state interests. Third, state officials, whose agendas already are quite full, may lack time to participate meaningfully in developing federal regulations and guidance. One final problem is the frequency of very tight deadlines that federal agencies must meet. In the 1970s, much was accomplished because the deadlines were so short, but the rush to meet them probably also precluded some coordination with states that might have reduced misunderstandings.[155] The rather hasty work that resulted undoubtedly reduced the quality of federal and state decisions.

Unfortunately, the credibility and capability of federal agencies—the qualities that could be a cornerstone for experimentation and risk taking in, for example, deadline revisions—eroded badly under the Reagan administration. Thus, changes that might improve both federal-state relations and environmental quality are becoming politically and administratively more difficult.[156]

Management of Federal Resources

Attention must be paid to the pragmatic prerequisites for successful negotiation over the management of federal land. For states and localities, this means developing "one voice" with which all branches and agencies of a state or local government can speak to federal agencies.

Several western states already have established systems for coordinating state responses to federal land-management proposals and decisions. For example, Nevada recently enacted a statute authorizing state-level planning, in cooperation with local government, aimed at maximizing state and local influence in planning by the BLM. Utah adopted a different approach. Its governor issued an executive order establishing an Environmental Coordinating Committee composed of representatives from 19 state agencies and offices. The committee reviews proposed federal actions and regulations and comments on them. Disputes within the committee are mediated by the state's planning coordinator. To ensure a unified state position, Utah agreed to "memoranda of understanding" with BLM and the U.S. Forest Service under which those federal agencies will not accept comments from individual Utah state agencies in situations in which a single, unified state response would be expected.[157]

These developing mechanisms hold promise, but they are only partial solutions. First, most coordinate only state-level responses and do not involve local governments. Indeed, stimulating local planning efforts in western states often is quite difficult. Second, funding these coordination mechanisms requires additional fiscal commitments by states and local governments; they will find competition tough for a share of state and local budgets.

Another question to address is how much bargaining leverage the U.S. government should provide various governments in regard to federal land-management decisions. The extreme approach of total federal management with no state or local input is unrealistic. The likely consequences would be widespread political unrest, such as the Sagebrush Rebellion, and attempts to resolve management disagreements through litigation, as in the controversy over OCS oil and gas leasing. Even in managing Defense Department lands, situations arise in which some state and local influence is appropriate—for example, when a federal activity overloads local highways or competes for scarce resources such as water.

The other extreme—transferring federal lands to the states—also is unworkable. Wholly apart from the fact that those lands belong to the nation as a whole, to be managed for this and succeeding generations, the states currently are not capable of administering these lands. Most state land agencies have few employees and low budgets. Moreover, most states lack an adequate statutory framework to manage lands in the public interest and ensure environmental integrity.[158]

The question, again, is one of degree. In searching for an answer to how much say states and local governments should have in managing federal lands, it is important to consider the nature of the land involved. For instance, it may not be appropriate to give state and local governments as much bargaining power in national park management as in BLM land management. In part this is because national parks are usually established to preserve a nationally important natural or cultural feature, whereas BLM lands generally are managed for resource exploitation, frequently by local or regional interests. Defense Department lands, with their connection to national security, present another set of considerations when determining the extent to which federal policy should bend to local concerns. The other side of the coin, frequently overlooked, is the extent to which states and local governments should alter their policies to promote national goals for federal lands and resources. The most obvious problems of this kind are the threats to national parks from development on adjacent lands that are under the regulatory control of state or local governments.

Can Cooperation Replace Confrontation?

Many of our existing environmental programs seem to base the resolution of conflicts on litigation and other adversarial methods. Is there an opportunity to use more cooperative approaches? Would such a shift enhance environmental quality? In recent years, attention has moved to nonadjudicatory approaches, such as mediation, for resolving environmental disputes.[159]

Mediation, per se, simply means the assistance of a neutral, third party in a negotiation process. This process does not turn lions into lambs, but it does create an opportunity for parties to reach a voluntary, mutually acceptable solution to a problem. Among other factors, for mediation to work the parties must have sufficient incentives to reach, and implement, a voluntary settlement. Voluntary approaches for resolving environmental disputes have been used for about a decade. Although these approaches vary—in part because environmental disputes are so varied—they all involve some form of negotiation or joint problem-solving process. The use of mediation and other innovative dispute-resolution approaches has proceeded primarily on a case-by-case basis, with over 150 cases documented.[160]

These approaches are being incorporated into new state laws. For example, statutes in Massachusetts, Rhode Island, and Wisconsin authorize, or even require, negotiation of hazardous-waste-siting disputes.[161] A statute in Virginia specifies procedures for negotiation and mediation of intergovernmental disputes triggered by annexation proposals.[162] At the national level, the Administrative Conference of the United States (an independent federal agency that works to improve the legal procedures by which federal agencies administer programs) passed a resolution encouraging regulatory agencies, under certain circumstances, to consider using a negotiation process when developing proposed regulations.[163]

The promise of mediated solutions is that they offer "closure" for long-festering controversies and provide solutions to reconcile both environmental and economic objectives. Of course, negotiations are the essence of the political process. But they often have failed. The question is whether the experience with more recent attempts to mediate environmental disputes can provide methods to increase the chances of cooperative solutions.[164]

It is not yet clear how negotiation approaches can best be incorporated into programs and statutes. Perhaps the experience gained under the state statutes, described above, will provide useful insights. If that experience indicates that cooperative approaches can be integrated successfully into administrative practices, a major new opportunity opens up for improving governmental institutions' effective responses to future environmental problems.

Funds

The availability of financial resources to different governmental units clearly influences intergovernmental relations and society's ability to respond effectively to problems.

The federal government's fiscal resources are going to be strained by large deficits for years to come, limiting the prospects for substantially increased federal spending for pollution control. But, without such increases, too much of the nation's past investment in building up the institutional capacity of government agencies to address pressing environmental issues may be negated. Severely limiting spending can be shortsighted; those environmental effects that prove to be irreversible or very expensive to mitigate will cost far more to deal with tomorrow than to prevent today. Those who rush to assess the costs of governmental regulation should not forget its benefits.

Some programs can be run more cost-effectively by the federal government than by other governments. Research programs that study environmental problems, for example, usually cannot be funded by the states. Moreover, central coordination of such research offers benefits, such as providing an understanding of whether national environmental standards are too strict or too lenient, and makes it possible to collect, manage, and analyze environmental data on a national scale, so that some sense can be gained of the progress already made and of the problems emerging.

The federal government also must allocate sufficient funds to permit federal oversight of state programs and to assure a strong federal enforcement effort. As Ohio's failure to prepare a sulfur dioxide-control plan suggests, federal oversight of reticent state governments is essential. And, gripe as they may about federal intrusiveness, environmental regulators in many states know that the threat of federal enforcement action is a useful backstop—"the gorilla in the closet"[165]—when they negotiate with polluters in their states. When the polluters happen to be powerful local governments, the threat of federal enforcement is that much more important.

Because the federal government enrolled state governments in a nationwide effort to clean up environmental problems, it is both unfair and unwise to radically cut assistance for state programs and simultaneously expect states to shoulder a heavier share of the national burden. Underfunding of delegated programs and limited federal oversight could lead to inconsistent application of requirements. States also might choose simply not to operate delegated programs, leaving them for the federal government to take over. As noted earlier in this chapter, federal takeover would be unfortunate because polluters would have to deal with already-overwhelmed federal administrators, who might be less sensitive than state regulators to local conditions, and citizens would have less assurance that environmental laws were being enforced satisfactorily.

The federal government also needs to assist local governments technically to protect the billions of dollars invested in new public sewage-treatment plants. A recent study by the General Accounting Office found that over one-third of the treatment systems it assessed were significantly out of compliance with the terms of their permits; 69 percent of the violators were municipal plants.[166] One major need is for operator training in these sewage-treatment plants.

Additionally, the federal government must provide adequate funding to permit state and local governments, as well as its own agencies, to participate in interagency and intergovernmental coordination. Travel, mail, phone, publication, and other budget items necessary for coordination often are the first targets of budget cutters. However, the information learned and differences resolved through such exchanges may produce big payoffs in later program stages.

Although the future of state and local funding for environmental programs is quite uncertain, there are options state and local governments can pursue to increase the funding available to their environmental programs. One of the principal routes is use of user and permit fees. The Clean Air Act specifically encourages states to implement fees for permits, but states do not fully use this authority.[167] The Clean Water Act requires municipalities to impose user fees on users of publicly owned sewage-treatment plants, but many communities have had difficulty implementing this requirement.[168]

Many states, however, are making better use of the user-fee option. They are launching their own versions of the federal Superfund, which is comprised in part of levies collected on crude oil, petroleum products, and chemical feedstocks.[169] Pushing administrative and cleanup costs onto the creators of pollution problems (and ultimately onto the consumers of their products) not only can help state and local governments finance environmental programs but also, if the fees are closely related to waste generation, can encourage polluters to reduce wastes, increase recycling, and otherwise lessen the environmental impact of their activities.

These fee efforts notwithstanding, the financial circumstances of state and local governments, as well as the federal government, offer little prospect of future revenues keeping pace with environmental program needs. If environmental programs are to be improved—or just maintained at their current levels—alternative methods to implement portions of these programs, while reducing resource demands on government agencies, must be developed. Perhaps, the private sector and citizen organizations could assume more responsibility for overseeing society's pollution-control efforts.

SUMMING UP

The late 1970s and early 1980s have been a period of major adjustment in government activity at all levels. Soaring energy prices, double-digit inflation, tax rebellions, deepening federal deficits, reduced federal assistance to state and local governments, and the election of a conservative president who believes that the less government the better, all have produced wrenching changes. Heady optimism about the ability of the United States to tackle and resolve its environmental problems has been replaced rather abruptly by the frustrating realization that those problems are more complex and the nation's capacities more limited than once thought.

Through most of the 1970s, the federal government was the principal focus of interest-group efforts to shape national environmental policy and, through national policy, to shape state and local policies. The federal government's retreat in the 1980s from its commitment to environmental protection leaves a void that states and local governments have yet to fill satisfactorily. These governments will have to play a larger role in the future, but they will need federal support—both financial and political—to succeed. The federal government must continue to be the leader in the national—and that is the key word—effort to secure a clean and safe environment. At the same time, federal authorities must exercise this leadership carefully with a proper regard for the interests of its partners—states and local governments. Tension is inevitable, but it need not be hazardous to the health of intergovernmental relations.

FURTHER READING

For a historical perspective on the evolution of federal-state relations in the United States, see David Walker, *Toward a Functioning Federalism* (Boston: Little, Brown and Company, 1981) and U.S. Congress, Congressional Budget Office, *The Federal Government in A Federal System: Current Intergovernmental Programs and Options for Change* (Washington, D.C.: U.S. Government Printing Office, 1983). Some contemporary problems in current federal-state relations, and suggestions on how to overcome them, are advanced in three reports of the U.S. Advisory Commission on Intergovernmental Relations: *A Crisis of Confidence and Competence* (Washington, D.C.: U.S. Government Printing Office, 1980), *An Agenda for American Federalism: Restoring Confidence and Competence* (Washington, D.C.: U.S. Government Printing Office, 1981), and *Regulatory*

Federalism: Policy, Process, Impact and Reform (Washington, D.C.: U.S. Government Printing Office, 1984).

The development of federal-state-local relations in federal environmental regulatory programs is traced in J. Clarence Davies and Barbara Davies, *The Politics of Pollution*, 2d. ed. (Indianapolis: Bobbs-Merill, 1975); U.S. Advisory Commission on Intergovernmental Relations, *Protecting the Environment: Politics, Pollution, and Federal Policy* (Washington, D.C.: U.S. Government Priting Office, 1981), and U.S. Congress, Congressional Research Service, *Federal-State Relations in Transition: Implications for Environmental Policy*, Report prepared for Committee on Environment and Public Works, U.S. Senate, 97th Cong., 2d. Sess. (1982), Serial No. 97-7. Excellent overviews of some of the sticking points in federal-state relations, particularly in delegation of regulatory programs, are found in U.S. Comptroller-General, *Federal-State Environmental Programs—The State Perspective* (Washington, D.C.: U.S. General Accounting Office, 1980); in collections of articles in the Environmental Law Institute's *The Environmental Forum* (January 1983) and *Environmental Law Reporter* (December 1982); and in U.S. EPA's *EPA Journal* (January-February 1984).

The evolution and politics of laws governing federal lands are traced in Samuel Trask Dana and Sally Fairfax, *Forest and Range Policy*, 2d. ed. (New York: McGraw-Hill, 1980). Federal-state relations in both federal land and federal regulatory contexts are assessed in the symposium, "Federalism and the Environment: A Change in Direction," 12 *Envtl. L.*, No. 4 (Summer 1982). For a good review of the competing pressures on federal land managers, see Paul J. Culhane, *Public Lands Politics* (Baltimore: Johns Hopkins University Press for Resources for the Future, 1981).

For discussion of the Reagan administration's environmental policies, see the articles in Norman J. Vig and Michael E. Kraft, eds., *Environmental Policy in the 1980s: Reagan's New Agenda* (Washington, D.C.: Congressional Quarterly Press, 1984). The impact of Reagan administration economic policies on state and local governments is described in John L. Palmer and Isabel V. Sawhill, eds., *The Reagan Experiment* (Washington, D.C.: The Urban Institute, 1982) and Richard P. Nathan et al. *The Consequences of Cuts* (Princeton: Princeton University Press, 1983). See U.S. Comptroller-General, "Potential Impacts of Reducing the Environmental Protection Agency's Budget" (Washington, D.C.: General Accounting Office, 1982), for a discussion of the impacts of cuts in EPA's budget on state pollution-control programs, and see U.S. Congress, Congressional Budget Office, *Public Works Infrastructure: Policy Considerations for the 1980s* (Washington, D.C.: U.S. Government Printing Office, 1983) for an analysis of alternative federal and state approaches to financing sewage-treatment plants and other capital projects.

New approaches to environmental-dispute resolution are described in *Resolve* newsletter, published quarterly by The Conservation Foundation and available at no charge upon request. A wide range of alternatives to conventional regulatory strategies, placing greater emphasis on responsibilities assumed by the private sector, is explored in Eugene Bardach and Robert Kagan, eds., *Social Regulation: Strategies for Reform* (San Francisco: Institute for Contemporary Studies, 1982) and LeRoy Graymer and Frederick Thompson, eds., *Reforming Social Regulation* (Beverly Hills: Sage Publications, 1982).

References

CHAPTER 1: UNDERLYING TRENDS

Text References

1. U.S. Department of Commerce, Bureau of the Census, *Statistical Abstract of the United States: 1984*, 104th ed. (Washington, D.C.: U.S. Government Printing Office, 1984), Table 2, p. 6.
2. *Ibid.*, Table 7, p. 9.
3. *Ibid.*
4. U.S. Department of Health and Human Services, National Center for Health Statistics, *Vital Statistics of the United States, Vol. I, Natality* (Washington, D.C.: U.S. Government Printing Office, 1978), Table 1-6, pp. 1–9.
5. Population Reference Bureau, "1983 World Population Data Sheet" (Washington, D.C.: Population Reference Bureau, Inc., 2213 M Street, N.W., 1983).
6. U.S. Department of Commerce, Bureau of the Census, "Demographic Estimates for Countries with Populations of 10 Million or More" (Washington, D.C., U.S. Government Printing Office, 1981).
7. Population Reference Bureau, "1983 World Population Data Sheet."
8. Based on calculations of data from "World Population Data Sheet."
9. *Ibid.*
10. The Conservation Foundation, *State of the Environment: 1982* (Washington, D.C.: The Conservation Foundation, 1982), p. 14.
11. *The Numbers News* 4(4): 1-2 (1984).
12. Bureau of the Census, *Statistical Abstract*, Table 19, p. 18.
13. *Ibid.*, Table 23, pp. 20-25, and Table 20, p. 18.
14. *Ibid.*, Table 28, p. 27.
15. Richard L. Forstall and Richard A. Engels, U.S. Department of Commerce, Bureau of the Census, "Growth in Nonmetropolitan Areas Slows" (Washington, D.C.: Bureau of the Census, March, 1984), p. 2.
16. *Ibid.*, Table 2.
17. *Ibid.*, Table 3.
18. *Ibid.*
19. Bureau of the Census, *Statistical Abstract of the United States: 1983* (see ref. 1), Table 17, p. 15.
20. *Ibid.*
21. Forstall and Engels, "Growth in Nonmetropolitan Area Slows," Table 2, p. 1.
22. *Ibid.*, p. 2.
23. American Demographics 5(12):23 (1983).

24. *Ibid.*
25. Population Reference Bureau, "1983 World Population Data Sheet."
26. United Nations, Department of International Economics and Social Affairs, "Estimates and Projections of Urban, Rural, and City Populations 1950–2025: the 1980 Assessment" ST-ESA-#R-45 (New York: United Nations, 1982), Table 8, p. 61.
27. *Ibid.*
28. *Ibid.*
29. Lester R. Brown et al., *State of the World* (New York: W.W. Norton, 1984), pp. 8–11.
30. Normal Gall, "Can Mexico Pull Through," *Forbes*, Aug. 15, 1983, pp. 70–75; and "The Trouble with Living in Mexico City," *Manchester Guardian Weekly*, Jan. 29, 1984.
31. Congress of the United States, Congressional Budget Office, *The Economic Outlook: A Report to the Senate and House Committees on the Budget - Part I* (Washington, D.C.: U.S. Government Printing Office, 1984), p. 79.
32. Executive Office of the President, Council of Economic Advisors, *Economic Report of the President: 1984* (Washington, D.C.: U.S. Government Printing Office, 1984), pp. 220, 254.
33. *Ibid,* pp. 222–223.
34. *Ibid.,* p. 283.
35. John L. Palmer and Isabel V. Sawhill, eds., *The Reagan Experiment* (Washington, D.C.: The Urban Institute, 1982), p. 37.
36. Congressional Budget Office, *The Economic Outlook,* Figure II-19, p. 52.
37. *Ibid.,* Figure II-11, p. 36.
38. Congress of the United States, Congressional Budget Office, *Reducing the Deficit: Spending and Revenues Options: A Report to the Senate and House Committees on the Budget - Part III* (Washington, D.C.: U.S. Government Printing Office, 1984), p. 1.
39. Gregory B. Mills and John L. Palmer, *The Deficit Dilemma: Budget Policy in the Reagan Era* (Washington, D.C.: The Urban Institute Press, 1983), p. 50.
40. Congressional Budget Office, *The Economic Outlook,* p. 15.
41. *Ibid.,* p. 16.
42. U.S. Department of Commerce, Bureau of Industrial Economics, *1984 U.S. Industrial Outlook* (Washington, D.C.: U.S. Government Printing Office, 1984), p. 41.
43. *Ibid.*
44. Robert G. Healy, "America's Industrial Future: An Environmental Perspective" (Washington, D.C.: The Conservation Foundation, 1982), p. 30.
45. Herman Bluestone, U.S. Department of Agriculture, Economic Research Service, "Employment Growth in Metropolitan and Nonmetropolitan America: A Change in the Pattern" (AER Report No. 492) (Springfield, Va.: National Technical Information Service, undated), p. 1.
46. Bureau of Industrial Economics, *1984 U.S. Industrial Outlook,* p. 41.
47. *Ibid.,* p. 42.
48. "Sounding the Tocsin for Toxins," *Time,* July 25, 1983, p. 61.
49. The World Bank, *World Development Report 1983* (New York: Oxford University Press, 1983), p. 1.

50. *Ibid.*, p. 29.
51. *Ibid.*, p. 1.
52. Brown et al., *State of the World*, p. 84.
53. *Ibid.*, p. 74.
54. The World Bank, *World Development Report 1983*, p. 27.
55. *Ibid.*, p. 35.
56. Brown et al., *State of the World*, p. 2.
57. Robert Cameron Mitchell, "Public Opinion and Environmental Politics in the 1970's and 1980's" in Norman J. Vig and Michael E. Kraft, eds., *Environmental Policy in the 1980's: Reagan's New Agenda* (Washington, D.C.: Congressional Quarterly Press, 1984), p. 52.
58. "Watt's Departure is Helping Reagan," *Business Week*, Dec. 19, 1983, p. 14.
59. *Ibid.*
60. *Ibid.*
61. Paul Cramer, "Reagan Gets Bad Marks on the Environment: Public Does Not Want Pollution Laws Relaxed," ABC News/*Washington Post* Poll, April 1983, p. 4.
62. "A *New York Times/CBS Survey Found 58• Back Environmental Laws at Any Cost,"* Inside EPA Weekly Report*, April 29, 1983, p. 9
63. The following discussion is taken from Robert Cameron Mitchell, "Public Opinion and Environmental Politics in the 1970s and 1980s," pp. 54-57.
64. *Ibid.*, p. 55.
65. *Ibid.*, p. 56.
66. *Ibid.*, p. 60.
67. *Ibid.*, p. 62.
68. Organization for Economic Cooperation and Development, *The State of the Environment in OECD Member Countries* (Paris: OECD, 1979), p. 175.
69. *Ibid.*, p. 176.
70. *Ibid.*
71. U.S. Comptroller General, *Wastewater Discharges Are Not Complying with EPA Pollution Control Permits* (Washington, D.C.: General Accounting Office, 1983).
72. *Environmental Reporter—Current Developments*, Sept. 23, 1983, p. 903.
73. U.S. Environmental Protection Agency, Office of Water Program Operations, *1982 Needs Survey: Cost Estimates for Construction of Publicly-Owned Wastewater Treatment Facilities* (Washington, D.C.: U.S. Environmental Protection Agency, 1982).
74. Clean Water Act Amendments of 1981, 33 U.S.C.A. sec. 1251 et seq. (1983).
75. Jeffrey G. Miller, "Private Enforcement of Federal Pollution Control Laws, Part I," 13 ELR 10314 (1983).
76. *Ibid.*
77. *NRDC Newsline* 2(1):2 (1984).

Figure References

1.1 U.S. Department of Commerce, Bureau of the Census, *Statistical Abstract of the United States: 1984*, 104th ed. (Washington, D.C.: U.S. Government Printing Office, 1984), Table 7, p. 9.

1.2 U.S. Department of Commerce, Bureau of the Census, "Projections of the Population of the United States: 1982 to 2050," *Current Population Reports*, Series P-24, No. 922 (Washington, D.C.: Bureau of the Census, Oct. 1982).

1.3 Population Reference Bureau, "1983 World Population Data Sheet" (Washington, D.C.: Population Reference Bureau, Inc., 2213 M Street, N.W., 1983).

1.4 *Ibid.*

1.5 U.S. Department of Energy, Energy Information Administration, "1983 Annual Data and Summaries," *Monthly Energy Review* (Washington, D.C.: Energy Information Administration, March 1984), p. 21.

1.6 U.S. Department of Commerce, Bureau of Industrial Economics, *1984 U.S. Industrial Outlook* (Washington, D.C.: U.S. Government Printing Office, 1984), p. 29.

1.7 *Ibid.*, pp. 41-42.

1.8 "Opinion Roundup—Environmental Update," *Public Opinion*, February/March 1982, p. 32, and unpublished results of survey conducted by The Roper Organization.

1.9 Robert Cameron Mitchell, "Moving Backwards vs. Moving Forwards: Motivations for Collective Action," Working Paper No. D-140 (Washington, D.C.: Resources for the Future, 1984). Data are estimates (actual counts not available) for: (1) Defenders of Wildlife from 1965 through 1979, (2) The Wilderness Society from 1960 through 1973 and 1980 through 1981, (3) The Natural Resources Defense Council for 1980 through 1982, and (4) Environmental Action in 1982.

1.10 Kit D. Farber, Fredrick J. Dreiling, and Gary L. Rutledge, U.S. Department of Commerce, Bureau of Economic Analysis, "Pollution Abatement and Control Expenditures, 1972-1982" 64(2):24-25 (1984); and Gary L. Rutledge and Susan Lease-Trevathan, U.S. Department of Commerce, Bureau of Economic Analysis, "Pollution Abatement and Control Expenditures, 1972-81" 63(2):16-17 (1983).

1.11 *Ibid.*

1.12 *Ibid.*

1.13 U.S. Department of Commerce, Bureau of the Census, "Value of New Construction Put in Place" (Washington, D.C.: U.S. Department of Commerce, Sept. 1975), pp. 3-9; 1964-1972 data: Council of Environmental Quality, *Environmental Quality: 1976* (Washington, D.C.: Council on Environmental Quality, Sept. 1976), Table 1-9, p. 17; and 1973-1983 data: provided by U.S. Environmental Protection Agency, Office of Water Program Operations.

   The data for the EPA construction grants disbursements have been shifted forward approximately one-half year because these payments are made to grantees after they have actually made the investments shown in the top line on figure 1.13. The EPA data are plotted against the data in which the fiscal year began rather than against the year in which it ended.

1.14 Unpublished data provided by the American Environmental Safety Council, Washington, D.C.

1.15 Council on Environmental Quality, *Environmental Quality: 1982* (Washington, D.C.: U.S. Government Printing Office, 1982), p. 305. Typographical errors corrected by The Conservation Foundation.

CHAPTER 2: ENVIRONMENTAL CONTAMINANTS

Text References

Toxic Substances

1. The Conservation Foundation, *State of the Environment 1982* (Washington, D.C.: The Conservation Foundation, 1982), p. 51. These data only pertain to total suspended particulates and sulfur dioxide.

2. U.S. Environmental Protection Agency, Office of Planning and Evaluation, draft, *National Accomplishments in Pollution Control: 1970-1980* (Washington, D.C., U.S. Government Printing Office, May 1980), pp. 9-12.

3. Environmental Law Reporter; Erica Dolgin, ed., *Federal Environmental Law* (St. Paul: West Publishing Co., 1974); William H. Rogers, *Environmental Law* (St. Paul: West Publishing Co., 1977).

4. U.S. Department of Health and Human Services, National Institute for Occupational Safety and Health, Rodger L. Tatken and Richard J. Lewis, Sr., *Registry of Toxic Effects of Chemical Substances 1981-2* (Cincinnati, Ohio: U.S. Department of Health and Human Services, June 1983), p. xiii.

5. Appendix to RCRA Biennial Report, Unlisted (characteristic) hazardous wastes. (40 C.F.R. §26, Subpart C). Listed hazardous wastes (40 C.F.R. §261, Subpart D). 45 Fed. Reg. 78529, 78541, (1980) as amended at 46 Fed. Reg. 27477, (1981).

6. List of toxic pollutants published in Table 1, House Committee Print No. 95-30 of the House Committee of Public Works and Transportation incorporated by reference in Clean Water Act §307(a)(1).

7. U.S. Department of Health and Human Services, "Third Annual Report on Carcinogens—Summary" (Springfield, Va.: National Technical Information Service, 1983).

8. Ralph Althouse, James Huff, Lorenze Tomatis and Julian Wilbourn, World Health Organization, International Agency for Research on Cancer, *Chemicals and Industrial Processes Associated with Cancer in Humans*, IARC Monographs, Volumes 1-20 (Lyon, France: International Agency for Research on Cancer, Sept. 1979), p. 2.

9. National Research Council, *Toxicity Testing: Strategies to Determine Needs and Priorities* (Washington, D.C.: National Academy Press, 1984), p. 12.

10. National Agricultural Chemicals Association, "1981 Industry Profile Study" (Washington, D.C.: National Agricultural Chemicals Association, May 1982), Schedule 5-A, p. 7.

11. U.S. Department of the Interior, Bureau of Mines, *Mineral Commodity Summaries 1983* (Washington, D.C.: U.S. Government Printing Office, Jan. 1983), pp. 2-5.

12. U.S. International Trade Commission, *Synthetic Organic Chemicals United States Production and Sales, 1982* (Washington, D.C.: U.S. Government Printing Office, 1983), pp. 1-2.

13. U.S. Department of Health and Human Services, Food and Drug Administra-

tion, "Compliance Program Report of Findings FY 79 Total Diet Studies—Adult" (Springfield, Va.: National Technical Information Service, 1982), pp. 1-2.

14. Information provided by U.S. Department of Agriculture, National Residue Program.

15. R.A. Hall, E.G. Zook, and G.M. Meaburn, U.S. Department of Commerce, National Oceanic and Atmospheric Administration, National Marine Fisheries Service, *National Marine Fisheries Service Survey of Trace Elements in the Fishery Resource* (Washington, D.C.: U.S. Government Printing Office, March 1978), p. 1.

16. Christopher J. Schmitt, J. Larry Ludke, and David F. Walsh, "Organochlorine Residues in Fish: National Pesticide and Monitoring Program, 1970-74," *Pesticide Monitoring Journal* 14(4):136 (1981).

17. Edward D. Goldbert et al., "The Mussel Watch," *Environmental Conservation* 5(2):101-112.

18. State of California, Water Resources Control Board, John M. Ladd, Stephen P. Hayes et al., "California State Mussel Watch: 1981-83" (Water Quality Monitoring Report 83-6Ts) (Sacramento: Water Resources Control Board, Jan. 1984), p. 3.

19. U.S. Department of Commerce, National Oceanic and Atmospheric Administration, Ocean Assessments Division, Coastal and Estuarine Assessment Branch, "National Status and Trends Program" (Washington, D.C.: National Oceanic and Atmospheric Administration, April 1984), pp. 1-5.

20. Anne R. Yobs, "The National Human Monitoring Program for Pesticides," *Pesticides Monitoring Journal* 5(1):44-45 (1971); and F.W. Kutz, W.G. Johnson, A.R. Yobs, and G.B. Wiersman, U.S. Environmental Protection Agency, Office of Pesticides Programs, "The National Human Monitoring Program for Pesticides" (Washington, D.C.: U.S. Environmental Protection Agency, 1974) or *Laboratory Investigation* 30(3):380 (1974).

21. Marie Vahter, National Swedish Institute of Environmental Medicine and Dept. of Environmental Hygiene, "Assessment of Human Exposure to Lead and Cadmium Through Biological Monitoring" (Stockholm: Karolinska Institute, 1982), pp. 1-45.

22. National Academy of Sciences, Environmental Studies Board, Committee on Water Quality Criteria, *Water Quality Criteria 1972*, (Washington, D.C.: U.S. Government Printing Office, 1972), p. 251-252.

23. The Conservation Foundation, *State of the Environment 1982* (Washington, D.C.: The Conservation Foundation, 1982), pp. 121-122; U.S. Department of the Interior, Bureau of Mines, *Mineral Commodity Profiles*, "Lead" (Washington, D.C.: Bureau of Mines, 1983), p. 12.

24. Joseph L. Annest et al., Department of Health and Human Services, Public Health Service, Office of Health Research, Statistics and Technology, *Advance data; Blood Lead Levels for Persons 6 Months-74 Years of Age: United States, 1976-80; Number 79, May 12, 1982, p. 12.*

25. *U.S. Environmental Protection Agency, Office of Air Quality, Planning and Standards, National Air Quality and Emissions Trends Report, 1982* (Research Triangle Park: U.S. Environmental Protection Agency, 1984), pp. 62-63.

26. U.S. Environmental Protection Agency, Office of Air Quality Planning and

Standards, *National Air Quality and Emission Trends Report, 1981* (Research Triangle Park: U.S. Environmental Protection Agency, 1981), pp. 42-45.

27. U.S. Department of the Interior, Geological Survey, *National Water Summary, 1984 - Hydrological Events and Issues* (Washington, D.C.: U.S. Government Printing Office, 1984), pp. 46-49.

28. Information provided by Professor Stephen A. Norton, University of Maine, Department of Geological Sciences, 1984.

29. U.S. Environmental Protection Agency, Office of Research and Development, *Air Quality Criteria for Lead* (Washington, D.C.: U.S. Government Printing Office, 1977), pp. 7-9.

30. Global Environmental Monitoring System, Joint FAO/WHO Food and Animal Feed Contamination Monitoring Programme, *Summary and Assessment of Data Received from the FAO/WHO Collaborating Centres for Food Contamination Monitoring* (Uppsala, Sweden: National Food Administration, 1982), pp. 36, 49 and 75.

31. Marie Vahter, "Assessment of Human Exposure to Lead and Cadmium Through Biological Monitoring," p. 49.

32. *Ibid.*, pp. 103-104.

33. *Ibid.*, p. 63.

34. U.S. Environmental Protection Agency, *Air Quality Criteria for Lead*, pp. 1-5, 12-33, 12-34.

35. Marie Vahter, "Assessment of Human Exposure to Lead and Cadmium Through Biological Monitoring," p. 13.

36. R. Coleman, J. Lent, E. Burns, and P. Siebert, Energy and Environmental Analysis, Inc., "Atmospheric Cadmium: Population Exposure Analysis," prepared for U.S. Environmental Protection Agency, Office of Air and Waste Management, Office of Air Quality Planning and Standards, (Research Triangle Park: U.S. Environmental Protection Agency, 1978), p. 16.

37. *Ibid.*, p. 15.

38. *Ibid.*, pp 12-13.

39. U.S. Geological Survey, *National Water Summary, 1983—Hydrological Events and Issues*, p. 46.

40. Global Environmental Monitoring System, *Summary and Assessment of Data Received from the FAO/WHO Collaborating Centres for Food Contamination Monitoring*, pp. 44, 77.

41. John M. Ladd, Stephen P. Hayes, et al., "California State Mussel Watch: 1981-83."

42. U.S. Food and Drug Association, Bureau of Foods, Division of Chemical Technology, unpublished data.

43. Marie Vahter, "Assessment of Human Exposure to Lead and Cadmium Through Biological Monitoring," p. 51.

44. Lewis Carroll, *The Annotated Alice: Alice's Adventures in Wonderland and Through the Looking-Glass* (Middlesex, England: Penguin Books, Ltd., 1960, 1972), p. 90.

45. George W. Ware, *Fundamentals of Pesticides* (Fresno, Calif.: Thomson Publications, 1982), pp. 39, 40, 47 and 50.

46. U.S. Department of Health and Human Services, "Third Annual Report on Carcinogens. Summary," pp. iii-v.

47. *NRCS vs. Train*, No. 75-172, 8 ERC 2120 (D.D.C. June 9, 1976) Clean Water Act of 1977 33 U.S.C. §1251 et seq (1977).
48. George W. Ware, *Fundamentals of Pesticides*, p. 1.
49. *Ibid.*
50. U.S. Environmental Protection Agency, Office of Pesticide Programs, Benefits and Field Studies Division, Economic Analysis Branch, "Regulatory Impact Analysis of Registration Guidelines," draft (Washington, D.C.: U.S. Government Printing Office, Oct. 1981), pp. 10-11.
51. George W. Ware, *Fundamentals of Pesticides*, p. 1.
52. *Ibid.*, p. 52; J. Calvin Giddings, *Chemistry, Man, and Environmental Change* (New York: Canfield Press, 1973), pp. 382-383.
53. George W. Ware, *Fundamentals of Pesticides*, p. 226.
54. See, e.g., National Research Council, Committee on Prototype Explicit Analyses for Pesticides, *Regulating Pesticides* (Washington, D.C.: National Academy of Sciences, 1980), pp. 6-7, 84-89; specific chemicals listed in U.S. Department of Health and Human Services, Public Health Service, Centers for Disease Control, National Institute for Occupation Health, *Registry of Toxic Effects of Chemical Substances* (Cincinnati, Ohio: National Institute for Occupational Safety and Health, June 1983); and F.W. Mackison, R.S. Stricoff, and L.J. Patridge, Sr., *Occupational Health Guidelines for Chemical Hazards* (Washington, D.C.: U.S. Government Printing Office, Jan. 1981).
55. National Academy of Sciences, National Research Council, Environmental Studies Board, *Contemporary Pest Control Practices and Prospects: The Report of the Executive Committee* (Washington, D.C.: National Academy of Sciences, 1975), pp. 54-92. A somewhat more alarmist assessment is given in David Weir, *Circle of Poison* (San Francisco, Calif.: Institute of Food and Development Policy, 1981).
56. National Research Council, Commission on Natural Resources, Environmental Studies Board, *Regulating Pesticides* (Washington, D.C.: National Academy of Sciences, 1980).
57. U.S. Department of Agriculture, Economic Research Service, *Outlook and Situation*, "Inputs" (Washington, D.C.: U.S. Government Printing Office, 1983), Table 3, pp. 5, 7.
58. *Ibid.*, p. 4.
59. Theodore R. Eichers, U.S. Department of Agriculture, Economics and Statistics Service, "Farm Pesticide Economic Evaluation, 1981," AERS 464 (Washington, D.C.: U.S. Government Printing Office, 1981), p. 3.
60. Information provided by William Storck, business editor, *Chemical and Engineering News*, May 25, 1984.
61. U.S. Department of Agriculture, *Outlook and Situation* 'Inputs," p. 3.
62. International Trade Commission, *Synthetic Organic Chemicals 1978* (Washington, D.C.: U.S. Government Printing Office, 1979), and previous annual issues; American Chemical Society, Committee on Environmental Improvement, *Cleaning Our Environment: A Chemical Perspective* (Washington, D.C.: American Chemical Society, 1978), p. 335.
63. U.S. Department of Agriculture, *Outlook and Situation* 'Inputs," p. 8.
64. *Ibid.*
65. George W. Ware, *Fundamentals of Pesticides*, pp. 52, 55; Office of Science

and Technology, David Pimental, *Ecological Effects of Pesticides on Non-Target Species* (Washington, D.C.: U.S. Government Printing Office, 1971).

66. U.S. Department of Agriculture, Economic Research Service, T.R. Eichers and W.S. Serletts, "Farm Pesticide Supply-Demand Trends, 1982" (Washington, D.C.: U.S. Government Printing Office, 1982), pp. 14-15; Edward H. Smith, David Pimentel, eds., *Pest Control Strategies* (New York: Academic Press, Inc., 1978).

67. Global Environmental Monitoring System, Joint Food and Agricultural Organization/World Health Organization Food and Animal Feed Contamination Monitoring Program based on, "Index and Summary 1965-1978," *Pesticide Residues in Food*, FAO Plant Production and Protection paper 11 (Rome: Food and Agricultural Organization, 1978).

68. Information provided by U.S. Department of Agriculture, National Residue Program.

69. *Chemical Regulation Reporter*—"Current Reports," September 30, 1983, p. 859; October 14, 1983, pp. 896-897; and February 3, 1984, p. 1598; also *Chemical Regulation Reporter*, "Current Reports," March 2, 1979, p. 2202.

70. Lawrie Mott, "Pesticides in Food: What the Public Needs to Know" (San Francisco: National Resources Defense Council, 1984), p. iv.

71. *Ibid.*, Table 2.

72. Robert J. Gillian et al., "Pesticides in the Nation's Rivers, 1975-1980, and Implications for Future Monitoring," draft, USGS Water Supply Paper (Reston, Va.: Geological Survey, forthcoming).

73. *Ibid.*, Table 1.

74. *Ibid.*, Table 2.

75. *Ibid.*, p. 1.

76. Brian W. Cain and Christine M. Bunck, "Residues of Organochlorine Compounds in Starlings (Starnus vulgaris), 1979" *Journal of Environmental Monitoring and Assessment* 3:170 (1983).

77. Donald White, "Nationwide Residues of Organochlorine Compounds in Wings of Adult Mallards and Black Ducks, 1976-77," *Pesticide Monitoring Journal* 13(1):12-16 (June 1979).

78. *Chemical Regulation Reporter*, "Current Reports," Feb. 3, 1984, p. 1599; and *Pesticide and Toxic Chemical News*, Jan. 11, 1984, pp. 10-11.

79. U.S. Department of the Interior, Fish and Wildlife Service, "Fish and Wildlife Service Releases Texas, New Mexico Pesticide Study" News Release (Albuquerque: U.S. Department of the Interior, 1983) p. 2.

80. *Chemical Regulation Reporter*, "Current Reports," Feb. 3, 1984, p. 1599; and *Pesticide and Toxic Chemical News*, Jan. 11, 1984, pp. 10-11.

81. Fredrick W. Kutz et al., U.S. Environmental Protection Agency, "Toxic Substance Residues and Metabolites in Human Blood and Urine from a General Population Survey," Table 1.

82. Samuel S. Epstein et al., *Hazardous Waste in America* (San Francisco: Sierra Club Books, 1982); The Conservation Foundation, *The State of the Environment 1982*, p. 121.

83. *U.S. Federal Register* No. 48 (1 February 1983); "Environmental News," U.S. Environmental Protection Agency May 9, 1983.

84. *Chemical Regulation Reporter*, "Current Reports," June 15, 1979, pp. 420-421.

85. Steven J. Eisenreich et al., "Airborne Organic Contaminants in the Great Lakes Ecosystem," *Environmental Science and Technology* 15(1):30-38 (1981); and Robert V. Thomann and John P. Connolly, "Model of PCB in the Lake Michigan Lake Trout Food Chain," *Environmental Science and Technology* 18(2):65-71 (1984).

86. Global Environmental Monitoring System, *Summary and Assessment of Data Received from the FAO/WHO Collaborating Centres for Food Contamination Monitoring*, p. 34.

87. *Chemical Regulations Reporter*, "Current Reports," Sept. 21, 1979, pp. 969-970.

88. Donald White, "Nationwide Residues of Organochlorine Compounds in Wings of Adult Mallard and Black Ducks 1976-77," p. 15.

89. Council on Environmental Quality, *Environmental Quality—1979*, (Washington, D.C.: U.S. Government Printing Office, 1979), pp. 448-449.

90. Information provided by U.S. Environmental Protection Agency, Exposure Evaluation Division, "National Human Adipose Tissue Survey (NHATS)."

91. U.S. Environmental Protection Agency, Office of Water Regulations and Standards, "An Exposure and Risk Assessment for Benzene" Final Draft Report (Washington, D.C.: U.S. Environmental Protection Agency, 1980) pp. 3-1, 3-22, 3-24, 3-25.

92. U.S. Environmental Protection Agency, *Intermedia Pollutants—Benzene* (Washington, D.C.: U.S. Environmental Protection Agency, July 1982), p. 3-3.

93. *Environment Reporter*, "Current Developments," December 16, 1983, p. 1435.

94. *Chemical Regulation Reporter*, "Current Reports," December 16, 1983, p. 1342.

95. Robert Kayser et al. "Intermedia Priority Pollutant Guidance Documents," p. 4-1, 4-2.

96. Research Triangle Institute, "Once a Blessing Now a Curse," *Hypotenuse*, July-August 1983, p. 12.

97. U.S. Environmental Protection Agency, Office of Pesticides and Toxic Substances, *Support Document Asbestos-Containing Materials in Schools: Health Effects and Magnitude of Exposure* (Washington, D.C.: U.S. Environmental Protection Agency, Oct. 1980), pp. 19, 35.

98. "Killer in the Classroom," *The New York Times*, Nov. 13, 1983.

99. *Ibid.*; Research Triangle Institute, *Hypotenuse*, pp. 10-19; U.S. Environmental Protection Agency, Office of Toxic Substances, "Fifteen Toxic Chemicals Subject to Imminent Regulations," *Toxic and Hazardous Substances* (Washington, D.C.: U.S. Environmental Protection Agency, April 1976), pp. 83-84.

100. National Research Council, Commission on Life Sciences, Board on Toxicology and Environmental Health Hazards, Committee on Nonoccupational Health Risks of Asbestiform Fibers, *Nonoccupational Health Risks of Asbestiform Fibers* (Washington, D.C.: National Academy Press, 1984), pp. 220-223.

101. U.S. Environmental Protection Agency, Office of Management Systems and Evaluation and Office of Pesticides and Toxic Substances, "Asbestos in Schools Program Review" (Washington, D.C.: U.S. Environmental Protection Agency, Dec. 1983); "On Asbestos Peril E.P.A. Report Cites Failure to Inspect and Report Risks," *New York Times*, Feb. 1, 1984.

102. "Killer in the Classroom," *The New York Times.*
103. *Ibid.*; "Final School Asbestos Rule Issues Requires Inspection, But no Reporting," *Chemical Regulation Reporter*, May 28, 1982, p. 317.
104. "On Asbestos Peril: EPA Report Cites Failure to Inspect and Report Risks," *New York Times.*
105. National Research Council, Commission on Life Science, Board on Toxicology and Environmental Health Hazards, *Toxicity Testing: Strategies to Determine Needs and Priorities* (Washington, D.C.: National Academy Press, 1984), p. 3.
106. *Ibid.*, p. 33.
107. *Ibid.*, p. 3.
108. Information provided by Henry P. Lau, U.S. Environmental Protection Agency, Office of Toxic Substances, May 22, 1984.
109. *Ibid.*
110. National Research Council, "Toxicity Testing," p. 13.
111. *Ibid.*, p. 11.
112. *Ibid.*
113. *Ibid.*, p. 196.

Hazardous Wastes

114. Office of Technology Assessment, *Technologies and Management Strategies for Hazardous Waste Control* (Washington, D.C.: U.S. Government Printing Office, 1983), p. 122.
115. Westat, Inc., *Final Report: National Survey of Hazardous Waste Generators and Treatment, Storage and Disposal Facilities Regulated under RCRA in 1981*, prepared for U.S. Environmental Protection Agency, Office of Solid Waste (Rockville, Md.: Westat, Inc., April 1984), pp. 230-1.
116. Comprehensive Environmental Response, Compensation, and Liability Act §103; 42 U.S.C.A. §9603(C)(d) (1983).
117. Office of Technology Assessment, *Technologies and Management Strategies of Hazardous Waste Control*, p. 116.
118. Resource Conservation and Recovery Act, §1004(5), 42 U.S.C.A. §6903 (1983).
119. 40 C.F.R. §261, Subpart C & D (1983) and Office of Technology Assessment, *Technologies and Management Strategy for Hazardous Waste Control*, pp. 271-277.
120. 42 U.S.C.A. ⁸6903(27)(1976) and U.S. Comptroller General, *Information on Disposal Practices of Generators of Small Quantities of Hazardous Wastes* (Washington, D.C.: General Accounting Office, 1983), p. 14.
121. 40 C.F.R. §261-6 (1983). 45 Fed. Reg. 33094 (1980); and 48 Fed. Reg. 14472 (1983).
122. U.S. Comptroller General, *Hazardous Waste Management Programs Will Not be Effective: Greater Efforts are Needed* (Washington, D.C.: General Accounting Office, 1979), p. 5.
123. Booz-Allen and Hamilton, Inc., and Putnam, Hayes, & Bartlett, Inc., *Hazardous Waste Generation and Commercial Hazardous Waste Management Capacity: An Assessment*, prepared for U.S. Environmental Protection Agency, Office of Water and Waste Management, series SW-894 (Washington, D.C.: U.S. Environmental Protection Agency, 1980), pp. III-2,3.

124. Westat, Inc., "National Survey of Hazardous Waste Generators and Treatment, Storage, and Disposal Facilities Regulated under RCRA in 1981. Preliminary Highlights of Findings," prepared for U.S. Environmental Protection Agency (Rockville, Md.: Westat, Inc., Aug. 1983).

125. Westat, Inc., *Final Report: National Survey of Hazardous Waste Generators and Treatment, Storage and Disposal Facilities Regulated under RCRA in 1981*, pp. 2-3.

126. Philip Shabecoff, "Hazardous Waste Exceeds Estimates," *New York Times*, August 31, 1983.

127. Westat, Inc., *Final Report: National Survey of Hazardous Waste Generators and Treatment, Storage and Disposal Facilities Regulated under RCRA in 1981*, p. 2.

128. *Ibid.*, p. 150.

129. Office of Technology Assessment, *Technologies and Management Strategies for Hazardous Waste Control*, pp. 120-122.

130. Westat, Inc., *Final Report: National Survey of Hazardous Waste Generators and Treatment, Storage and Disposal Facilities Regulated under RCRA in 1981*, p. 71.

131. Chemical Manufacturers' Association, *Hazardous Waste Survey for 1981 and 1982* (Washington, D.C.: Chemical Manufacturers' Association, undated), p. 2.

132. Westat, Inc., *Final Report: National Survey of Hazardous Waste Generators and Treatment, Storage and Disposal Facilities Regulated under RCRA in 1981*, p. 155.

133. Information provided by U.S. Environmental Protection Agency, Office of Solid Waste and Emergency Response, 1984.

134. Westat, Inc., *Final Report: National Survey of Hazardous Waste Generators and Treatment, Storage and Disposal Facilities Regulated under RCRA in 1981*, pp. 139-140.

135. Information provided by U.S. Environmental Protection Agency, Office of Solid Waste and Emergency Response, 1984.

136. Westat, Inc., *Final Report: National Survey of Hazardous Waste Generators and Treatment, Storage and Disposal Facilities Regulated under RCRA in 1981*, pp. 75-78.

137. *Ibid.*, p. 89.

138. *Ibid.*, pp. 104, 205.

139. *Ibid.*, pp. 78-81.

140. *Ibid.*, p. 146.

141. U.S. Comptroller General, "Interim Report on Inspection, Enforcement, and Permitting Activities at Hazardous Waste Facilities" (Washington, D.C.: General Accounting Office, 1983), pp. 6-9.

142. Information provided by U.S. Environmental Protection Agency, Office of Solid Waste and Emergency Response, 1984.

143. Westat, Inc., *Final Report: National Survey of Hazardous Waste Generators and Treatment, Storage and Disposal Facilities Regulated under RCRA in 1981*, pp. 213-224.

144. Richard C. Fortuna, "Same Wastes, New Solutions," speech prepared for a Bureau of National Affairs conference, Sept. 1983 (Washington, D.C.: Hazardous Waste Treatment Council, 1919 Pennsylvania Ave., 1983), p. 16.

145. "New York Task Force Questions Earlier Waste Estimate," *Hazardous Waste Report* 5(14):10-11 (1984).

146. Information provided by U.S. Environmental Protection Agency, Office of Solid Waste and Emergency Response, 1984.

147. State of California, "Draft Hazardous Waste Management Plan," prepared by California Hazardous Waste Treatment Council (Sacramento: Hazardous Waste Management Council, 1219 K St., Suite 101, 1984).

148. Westat, Inc., *Final Report: National Survey of Hazardous Waste Generators and Treatment, Storage and Disposal Facilities Regulated under RCRA in 1981*, p. 213.

149. See, for example, Bette Hileman, "Hazardous Waste Control," *Environmental Science and Technology* 17(17):281A (1983).

150. U.S. Environmental Protection Agency, Office of Solid Waste and Emergency Response, *Hazardous Waste Sites: National Priorities List* (Washington, D.C.: U.S. Environmental Protection Agency, 1983).

151. U.S. Environmental Protection Agency, Office of Water, Office of Drinking Water, "Surface Impoundment Assessment National Report," (Washington, D.C.: U.S. Environmental Protection Agency, Dec. 1983), pp. 17, 85.

152. Clean Water Action, "Maryland Profile: Surface Impoundments," mimeo (Washington, D.C.: Clean Water Action, 1984).

153. "California May Close Surface Impoundments Near Water Supplies," *Hazardous Waste Report* 5(17):9 (1984), and 49 Fed. Reg. 20238 (1984).

154. Information provided by U.S. Environmental Protection Agency, Office of Drinking Water, 1984, and 49 Fed. Reg. 20238 (1984).

155. Office of Technology Assessment, *Technologies and Management Strategies for Hazardous Waste Control*, pp. 191-2.

156. Westat, Inc., *Final Report: National Survey of Hazardous Waste Generators and Treatment, Storage and Disposal Facilities Regulated under RCRA in 1981*, p. 100.

157. Information provided by U.S. Environmental Protection Agency, Office of Drinking Water, 1984.

158. Patrick Sullivan, "An Assessment of Class I Hazardous Waste Injection Wells," prepared as a A.A.A.S./E.P.A. Engineering Fellow (Muncie: Ball State University, 1983), p. 15. Sullivan says 273 additional wells are scheduled for permitting by 1986. The EPA Office of Drinking Water stresses that these are not all new wells.

159. Information provided by U.S. Environmental Protection Agency, Office of Drinking Water, 1984.

160. Letter from David E. Click, U.S. Geological Survey, Water Resources Division to Clifford L. Jones, Pennsylvania Department of Environmental Resources, March 17, 1980.

161. Information provided by U.S. Environmental Protection Agency, Office of Drinking Water, 1983; and "Ohio EPA Study Says Waste Management Unit's Wells Leaked," *Wall Street Journal*, April 6, 1984.

162. Patrick Sullivan, "An Assessment of Class I Hazardous Waste Injection Wells."

163. Office of Technology Assessment, *Technologies and Management Strategies for Hazardous Waste Control*, p. 194.

164. Information provided by U.S. Environmental Protection Agency, Office of Solid

Waste and Emergency Response, 1983.

165. "Text of EPA Draft 'Son of Superfund' Report," *Inside EPA Weekly Report*, Feb. 3, 1984, Special Supplement, p. 3.

166. The Conservation Foundation, *State of the Environment: 1982* (Washington, D.C.: The Conservation Foundation, 1982), p. 153.

167. This includes 133 sites in the first update to the list proposed in August 1983 and seven for which rulemaking is in process as well as 406 which are now on the list by final rule.

168. "Text of EPA Draft 'Son of Superfund' Report," *Inside EPA*, p. 1.

169. U.S. Environmental Protection Agency, *Hazardous Waste Sites: National Priorities List*.

170. U.S. Environmental Protection Agency, Office of Solid Waste and Emergency Response, *Hazardous Waste Sites: National Priorities List*.

171. Fred C. Hart Associates, "Assessment of Hazardous Waste Mismanagement Damage Cases," prepared for U.S. Environmental Protection Agency, Office of Solid Waste (Washington, D.C.: U.S. Environmental Protection Agency, Dec. 1982), p. 5.7.1.

172. Information provided by U.S. Environmental Protection Agency, Office of Solid Waste and Emergency Response, 1984.

173. Information provided by U.S. Environmental Protection Agency, Office of Solid Waste and Emergency Response, 1984.

174. Gene Lucero, "Constraints on Private Party Cleanup at Superfund Sites." See, *Inside EPA Weekly Report*, April 27, 1984, p. 11.

175. Association of State and Territorial Solid Waste Management Officials, *State Cleanup Programs for Hazardous Substance Sites and Spills*, prepared for the U.S. Environmental Protection Agency (Washington, D.C.: ASTSWMO, 1983), p. 9.

176. *Inside EPA Weekly Report*, Feb. 3, 1984 and "GAO Says EPA May Have Underestimated Costs in 'Son of Superfund Report,' " *Inside EPA Weekly Report*, March 9, 1984.

177. "Superfund Needed for Cleanup of 1,000 Sites, Costs Unpredictable," *Hazardous Waste Report* 5(8):8 (1983).

178. James R. Janis and Gilah Langner, "The Fundamental Issue: How Clean is Clean?" *Hazardous Waste Report*, Special Supplement, undated.

179. CERCLA, §104; 42 U.S.C.A. §9604 (1983). Testimony of Richard C. Fortuna regarding Superfund Authorization before the U.S. Congress. House. Energy and Commerce Committee, Subcommittee on Commerce, Transportation and Tourism, Nov. 16, 1983, p. 2.

180. *Pesticide and Toxic Chemicals News*, Feb. 1, 1984, pp. 8-9, 12-13, 15-17.

181. Association of State and Territorial Solid Waste Management Officials, *State Cleanup Programs for Hazardous Substance Sites and Spills*, Exhibit 3-1.

182. New Jersey Department of Environmental Protection, *Management Plan 1983-1986 for Hazardous Waste Site Cleanups in New Jersey* (Trenton: Department of Environmental Protection, Aug. 1983), pp. 1-3.

183. The Steering Committee on Hazardous Waste Cleanup, *Clean Sites: A Plan to Accelerate Hazardous Waste Cleanup* (Washington, D.C.: The Conservation Foundation, 1984).

184. U.S. Environmental Protection Agency, *Report to Congress: Disposal of Hazardous Waste* (Washington, D.C.: Environmental Protection Agency, 1974), p. 4.

Air Quality

185. The Conservation Foundation, *State of the Environment 1982* (Washington, D.C.: The Conservation Foundation, 1982), pp. 62-65.
186. Robert W. Crandall, *Controlling Industrial Pollutions: The Economics and Politics of Clean Air* (Washington, D.C.: The Brookings Institution, 1983), p. 17.
187. Thomas Hauser, Donald R. Scott, and M. Rodney Midgett, "Air Monitoring: Research Needs," *Environmental Science and Technology* 17(2):86-96 (1983); U.S. Comptroller General, *Problems in Air Quality Monitoring System Affect Data Reliability* (Washington, D.C.: U.S. General Accounting Office, 1982).
188. The Conservation Foundation, *State of the Environment - 1982*, pp. 51, 53.
189. U.S. Environmental Protection Agency, Office of Air Quality, *National Air Quality and Emissions Trends Report, 1981* (EPA-450/4-83-011) (Research Triangle Park: U.S. Environmental Protection Agency, April, 1981), pp. 22-24.
190. "Sagging Economy Leads to Improved Air Quality," *Air/Water Pollution Report*, April 4, 1983.
191. Lester R. Brown et al., *State of the World* (New York: W. W. Norton, 1984), p. 145; and "Smoke Stirs Curbs on Wood Stoves," *The Washington Post*, March 31, 1984.
192. National Commission on Air Quality, *To Breath Clean Air* (Washington, D.C.: U.S. Government Printing Office, 1981), p. 74.
193. *Environment Reporter—Current Developments*, March 16, 1983, p. 2044; and 49 Fed. Reg. 10408 (1984).
194. "Environmental Health Groups Object to EPA's Proposed PM 10 Standard," *Air/Water Pollution Report*, March 7, 1983, p. 82
195. Council on Environmental Quality, *Environmental Quality: 1982* (Washington, D.C.: U.S. Government Printing Office, 1982), Table A-57, p. 292.
196. *Ibid.*, p. 34.
197. Monitoring and Assessment Research Center, "Air Pollution Concentrations in Selected Urban Areas: 1973-1980," preliminary report prepared for United Nations Environment Program, Global Environment Monitoring Systems (GEMS) and World Health Organization (London: Monitoring and Assessment Research Center, 1983).
198. The Conservation Foundation, *State of the Environment 1982*, p. 53.
199. U.S. Environmental Protection Agency, *National Air Quality and Emissions Trend Report, 1981*, p. 4.
200. U.S. Environmental Protection Agency, Office of Air Quality, *National Air Pollutant Emission Estimates, 1970-1981* (EPA-450/4-82-012) (Research Triangle Park: U.S. Environmental Protection Agency, 1982), p. 31.
201. *Ibid.*, pp. 30-31.
202. *Ibid.*, p. 34.
203. Monitoring and Assessment Research Center, "Air Pollution Concentrations in Selected Urban Areas: 1973-1980," Table 7.

204. The Conservation Foundation, *State of the Environment 1982*, p. 54.
205. U.S. Environmental Protection Agency, Office of Air Quality, *National Air Pollutant Emission Estimates, 1970-1981*, Table 4, p. 7.
206. Council on Environmental Quality, *Environmental Quality: 1982*, p. 35.
207. The Conservation Foundation, *State of the Environment 1982*, p. 57.
208. U.S. Environmental Protection Agency, *National Air Quality and Emissions Trend Report, 1981*, p. 30.
209. *Ibid.*, p. 32.
210. Council on Environmental Quality, *Environmental Quality: 1982*, p. 30.
211. *Ibid.*, p. 35.
212. T. D. Hartwell et al., *Study of Carbon Monoxide Exposure of Residents of Washington, D.C. and Denver, Colorado, part 1*, prepared for U.S. Environmental Protection Agency, Office of Monitoring Systems and Quality Assurance (Research Triangle Park: Research Triangle Institute, September 1983), p. 12.
213. The Conservation Foundation, *State of the Environment 1982*, p. 55.
214. Information provided by U.S. Environmental Protection Agency, Monitoring and Data Analyses Division.
215. U.S. Environmental Protection Agency, Office of Air Quality, *National Air Pollutant Emission Estimates, 1970-1981*, Table 6, p. 9.
216. *Ibid.*, p. 32.
217. *Ibid.*
218. Council on Environmental Quality, *Environmental Quality: 1982*, p. 26.
219. *Ibid.*, Table 2-5, p. 27.
220. *Ibid.*
221. William Drozdiak, "West Germans Fear a Calamity As Acid Rain Damages Forests," *The Washington Post*, December 28, 1983.
222. The Conservation Foundation, *State of the Environment 1982*, pp. 67, 70.
223. Interagency Task Force on Acid Precipitation, *Annual Report: 1982* (Washington, D.C.: Council on Environmental Quality, 1983), p. 22.
224. U.S. Department of the Interior, Geologic Survey, "Impacts of Acid Rain: Downward Trend in Northeast, Up in South and West" (news release) (Washington, D.C.: U.S. Dept. of the Interior, September 8, 1983).
225. Interagency Task Force on Acid Precipitation, *Annual Report: 1983*, draft (Washington, D.C.: Council on Environmental Quality, forthcoming).
226. William C. Malm and John V. Molena, "Visibility Trends in the National Parks in the Western United States" (unpublished paper) (Fort Collins, Colo.: National Park Service, 1983); and Lowell L. Ashbaugh et al., "A Residence Time Probability Analysis of Sulfur Concentrations at Grand Canyon National Park (unpublished paper) (Fort Collins, Colo.: National Park Service, undated).
227. William C. Malm and John V. Molena, "Visibility Trends in the National Parks in the Western United States," p. 15.
228. John Trijonis, "Visibility in California," *Journal of the Air Pollution Control Association* 32(2):167 (1982).
229. R. B. Castow and C. D. Keeling, "Atmospheric Carbon Dioxide Concentration, the Observed Airborne Fraction, the Fossil Fuel Airborne Fraction, and the Difference in Hemispheric Airborne Fractions," in B. Bolen, ed., *SCOPE 16: Global Carbon Modelling* (London: John Wiley and Sons, 1981).

230. National Research Council, Board on Atmospheric Sciences and Climate, *Changing Climate* (Washington, D.C.: National Academy Press, 1983), p. 15.
231. G. M. Woodwell et al., "Global Deforestation: Contribution to Atmospheric Carbon Dioxide," *Science* 222(4628):1081 (1983).
232. National Research Council, *Changing Climate*, p. 22.
233. *Ibid.*, p. 33.
234. *Ibid.*, pp. 34, 52, figure 1.1.4.
235. U.S. Environmental Protection Agency, Office of Policy and Resources Management, Strategic Studies Staff, "Can We Delay a Greenhouse Warming?" (Washington, D.C., U.S. Environmental Protection Agency, Sept. 1983), pp. 1-7, 1-8; and National Research Council, *Changing Climate*, p. 30.
236. National Research Council, *Changing Climate*, p. 81.
237. U.S. Environmental Protection Agency, "Can We Delay a Greenhouse Warming?" p. 7-7.
238. Walter Orr Roberts, "It's Time to Prepare for Global Climate Changes," *The Conservation Foundation Letter*, April 1983.
239. National Research Council, *Causes and Effects of Changes in Stratospheric Ozone: Update 1983* (Washington, D.C.: National Academy Press, 1984).
240. Thomas H. Maugh, "What is the Risk from Chlorofluorocarbons," *Science* 223(4640):1052 (1984).
241. *Ibid.*, p. 1051.
242. *Ibid.*, p. 1052.
243. *Ibid.*
244. John D. Spengler and Ken Sexton, "Indoor Air Pollution: A Public Health Perspective," *Science* 221(4605):9-10 (1983).
245. National Research Council, Committee on Indoor Pollutants, *Indoor Pollutants* (Washington, D.C.: National Academy Press, 1981).

Water Quality

246. The Conservation Foundation, *State of the Environment 1982* (Washington, D.C.: The Conservation Foundation, 1982), p. 97.
247. U.S. Comptroller General, *Costly Wastewater Treatment Plants Fail to Perform as Expected* (Washington, D.C.: U.S. General Accounting Office, Nov. 1980).
248. Veronica I. Pye, Ruth Patrick, and John Quarles, *Groundwater Contamination in the United States* (Philadelphia: University of Pennsylvania Press, 1983), pp. 49-52.
249. U.S. Environmental Protection Agency, *America's Clean Water: The States' Evaluation of Progress, 1972-1982*, prepared by the Association of State and Interstate Water Quality Pollution Administrators (Washington, D.C.: U.S. Environmental Protection Agency, Feb. 1984), p. 4.
250. U.S. Environmental Protection Agency, *America's Clean Water*.
251. *Ibid.*, pp. 4-5.
252. U.S. Environmental Protection Agency, *America's Clean Water*.
253. *Ibid.*, Appendix, "Louisiana," p. 1.
254. U.S. Environmental Protection Agency, Office of Water Regulations and Standards, *National Water Quality Inventory: 1982 Report to Congress* (EPA

440/2-84-006) (Washington, D.C.: U.S. Environmental Protection Agency, Feb. 1984), p. 10.

255. U.S. Environmental Protection Agency, "Report Surveys Water Quality for Fish," *EPA Journal* 10(3):25 (1984).

256. Richard A. Smith and Richard B. Alexander *A Statistical Summary of Data from the U.S. Geological Survey's National Water Quality Networks*, Open-File Report 83-533 (Reston, Va.: U.S. Geological Survey, 1983).

257. U.S. Department of the Interior, U.S. Geological Survey, *National Water Summary 1983—Hydrologic Events and Issues*, Water Supply Paper 2250 (Washington, D.C.: U.S. Government Printing Office, 1984), pp. 46-47.

258. The Conservation Foundation, *State of the Environment 1982*, p. 96.

259. U.S. Geological Survey, *National Water Summary 1983*, p. 46.

260. U.S. Environmental Protection Agency, *National Water Quality Inventory*, pp. 21-22.

261. U.S. Environmental Protection Agency, "Report Surveys Water Quality."

262. U.S. Geological Survey, *National Water Summary 1983*, pp. 48-49.

262. John Clapper, Garrett Power and Frank R. Shrivers, Jr., *Chesapeake Waters: Pollution, Public Health, and Public Opinion, 1607-1972* (Centerville, Md.: Tidewater Publishers, 1983), p. 167.

264. U.S. Geological Survey, *National Water Summary 1983*, pp. 48-49.

265. *Ibid.*

266. Edwin H. Clark II, Jennifer A. Haverkamp, and William Chapman, *Eroding Soils: the Off-Farm Impacts*, draft (Washington, D.C.: The Conservation Foundation, forthcoming).

267. U.S. Environmental Protection Agency, "Report Surveys Water Quality."

268. U.S. Geological Survey, *National Water Summary 1983*, pp. 48-49.

269. The Conservation Foundation, *State of the Environment-1982*, p. 103.

270. U.S. Geological Survey, *National Water Summary 1983*, pp. 48-49.

271. *Ibid.*

272. Information provided by Frank Wood, The Salt Institute, May, 1984.

273. Information provided by Richard A. Smith, U.S. Geological Survey, Feb., 1984.

274. U.S. Geological Survey, *National Water Summary 1983*, pp. 48-49.

275. *Ibid.*

276. Richard A. Smith and Richard B. Alexander, *Evidence for Acid-Precipitation-Induced Trends in Stream Chemistry at Hydrologic Benchmark Stations*, Geological Survey Circular 910 (Reston, Va.: U.S. Geological Survey, 1983), p. 1.

277. *Ibid.*

278. U.S. Geological Survey, *National Water Summary 1983*, p. 55.

279. U.S. Environmental Protection Agency, *Chesapeake Bay Program Technical Studies: A Synthesis* (Washington, D.C.: U.S. Environmental Protection Agency, Sept., 1982).

280. *Ibid*, p. i.

281. U.S. Geological Survey, *National Water Summary 1983*, p. 46.

282. *Ibid.*

283. U.S. Environmental Protection Agency, "Report Surveys Water Quality."

284. U.S. Geological Survey, *National Water Summary 1983*, p. 46.

285. *Ibid*, pp. 51-59.

286. U.S. Environmental Protection Agency, *National Water Quality Inventory*, pp. 21-22.

287. U.S. Environmental Protection Agency, *America's Clean Water*, p. 16.

288. U.S. Environmental Protection Agency, "Report Surveys Water Quality."

289. Council on Environmental Quality, *Contamination of Groundwater by Toxic Organic Chemicals* (Washington, D.C.: U.S. Government Printing Office, 1981), pp. 36-37.

290. Veronica I. Pye, Ruth Patrick and John Quarles, *Groundwater Contamination in the United States*, pp. 115-162.

291. *Ibid*, p. 212.

292. *Ibid*.

293. U.S. Geological Survey, *National Water Summary 1983*, p. 75.

294. National Academy of Sciences, National Academy of Engineering, *Water Quality Criteria 1972* (Washington, D.C.: U.S. Government Printing Office, 1972), p. 88.

295. Veronica I. Pye, Ruth Patrick and John Quarles, *Groundwater Contamination in the United States*, p.63.

296. *Ibid*., p. 193.

297. U.S. Geological Survey, *National Water Summary 1983*, pp. 80-239.

298. *Ibid*.

299. *Ibid*.

300. The discovery of Trichloroethylene (TCE) in Bedford, Massachusetts prompted the closure of wells there. Residents were forced to buy water from neighboring towns, until TCE was also found in the water supply of one of those towns. Increased pumpage may have accounted for a faster rate in which contaminants spread within one aquifer. Council on Environmental Quality, *Contamination of Groundwater by Toxic Organic Chemicals* (Washington, D.C.: Council on Environmental Quality, Jan. 1981), pp. 21-22.

301. Wayne B. Solley, Edith B. Chase and William B. Mann IV, *Estimated Use of Water in the U.S. in 1980*, Geological Survey Circular 1001 (Reston, Va.: U.S. Geological Survey, 1983), p. 12.

302. U.S. Environmental Protection Agency, Office of Drinking Water, *National Statistical Assessment of Rural Water Conditions* (Washington, D.C.: U.S. Environmental Protection Agency, 1983), p. 8.

303. *Ibid*.

304. U.S. Geological Survey, *National Water Summary 1983*, pp. 51-55.

305. *Ibid*.

306. U.S. Comptroller General, Report to the Administrator, Environmental Protection Agency, *Wastewater Dischargers Are Not Complying with EPA Pollution Control Permits* (Washington, D.C.: U.S. General Accounting Office, Dec., 1983).

307. U.S. Environmental Protection Agency, *America's Clean Water*, p. 10.

308. Veronica I. Pye, Ruth Patrick and John Quarles, *Groundwater Contamination in the United States*, pp. 54, 59.

309. U.S. Environmental Protection Agency, Office of Water Program Operations, *Report to Congress on Control of Combined Sewer Overflow in the United States* (Washington, D.C.: U.S. Environmental Protection Agency, 1978), Table 5-1, pp. 5-4 to 5-6.

310. Council on Environmental Quality, *Annual Report: 1979* (Washington, D.C.: U.S. Government Printing Office, 1979), p. 112.
311. *Ibid.*, p. 115.
312. Information provided by Leonard P. Gianessi and Henry M. Peskin, Resources for the Future, Jan. 11, 1984.
313. Council on Environmental Quality, *Environmental Quality: 1982* (Washington, D.C.: U.S. Government Printing Office, 1982), Table A-61, p. 295.
314. Veronica I. Pye, Ruth Patrick and John Quarles, *Groundwater Contamination in the United States*, p. 54.
315. U.S. Environmental Protection Agency, *The Report to Congress: Waste Disposal Practices and Their Effects on Groundwater*, Executive Summary (Washington, D.C.: U.S. Environmental Protection Agency, 1977).
316. U.S. Environmental Protection Agency, *America's Clean Water*, p. 7.
317. U.S. Environmental Protection Agency, *National Water Quality Inventory*, p. 14.
318. U.S. Environmental Protection Agency, Office of Water, "Status of Regulations Under Development-Update," Feb. 29, 1984, pp. 3-4.
319. U.S. Geological Survey, *National Water Summary 1983*, p. 58.
320. Philip C. Metzger, *To Master A Thirsty Future: An Analysis of Water Management Efforts in Tucson, Arizona* (Washington, D.C.: The Conservation Foundation, 1984).
321. U.S. Environmental Protection Agency, Office of Drinking Water, *Surface Impoundment Assessment National Report* (Washington, D.C.: U.S. Environmental Protection Agency, Dec. 1983), Table 4.1, p. 9.
322. Council on Environmental Quality, *Environmental Statistics* (Springfield, Va.: National Technical Information Service, 1978), p. 213.
323. U.S. Geological Survey, *National Water Summary 1983*, p. 175.
324. Veronica I. Pye, Ruth Patrick and John Quarles, *Groundwater Contamiantion in the United States*, p. 57.
325. U.S. Geological Survey, *National Water Summary 1983*, p. 46.
326. U.S. Comptroller General, *Wastewater Dischargers Are Not Complying*, ; and U.S. Environmental Protection Agency, *National Water Quality Inventory*.
327. U.S. Comptroller General, *Wastewater Dischargers Are Not Complying*, p. 7.
328. *Ibid.*, p. ii.
329. *Ibid.*, p. 8.
330. U.S. Environmental Protection Agency, *America's Clean Water*, p. 10.
331. *Ibid.*, p. 11.
332. *Ibid.*
333. U.S. Environmental Protection Agency, "Report Surveys Water Quality."
334. U.S. Geological Survey, *National Water Summary 1983*, p. 55.
335. Edwin H. Clark II, Jennifer A. Haverkamp, and William Chapman, *Eroding Soils*.
336. Veronica I. Pye, Ruth Patrick and John Quarles, *Groundwater Contamination in the United States*, p. 143.
337. U.S. Geological Survey, *National Water Summary 1983*, pp. 74-239.
338. Colorado Department of Health, *Public Comments on Groundwater Quality Protection Issues and Alternatives*, Aug. 1983.
339. U.S. Environmental Protection Agency, Water Planning Division, Office of

Water Program Operators, *Final Report of the Nationwide Urban Runoff Program*, Executive Summary (Washington, D.C.: U.S. Environmental Protection Agency, Dec., 1983), p. 4.

340. *Ibid.*, p. 6.

341. U.S. Environmental Protection Agency, *Final Report of the Nationwide Urban Runoff Program*.

342. *Ibid.*, p. 7.

343. *Ibid.*, p. 9.

344. *Ibid.*

345. *Ibid.*, p. 5.

346. U.S. Geological Survey, *National Water Summary 1983*, p. 215.

347. *Ibid.*, pp. 74-239.

348. U.S. Environmental Protection Agency, Office of Water Program Operations, *Report to Congress: Nonpoint Source Pollution in the U.S.* (Washington, D.C.: U.S. Environmental Protection Agency, Jan. 1984), Table 1-2, pp. 1-5.

349. *Ibid.*

350. *Ibid.*

351. Veronica I. Pye, Ruth Patrick and John Quarles, *Groundwater Contamination in the United States*, pp. 64-65.

352. U.S. Environmental Protection Agency, *Inside EPA Weekly Report*, Feb. 3, 1984, p. 10.

353. U.S. Department of the Interior, Geological Survey, *Basic Ground-Water Hydrology*, Water Supply Paper 2220 (Reston, Va.: U.S. Government Printing Office, 1983), pp. 66-67.

354. Louis Harris and Associates, *A Survey of American Attitudes Toward Water Pollution*, Study No. 822033 (Washington, D.C.: Louis Harris and Associates, Inc., undated), p. 4.

355. U.S. Environmental Protection Agency, *A Groundwater Protection Strategy for the Environmental Protection Agency* (Washington, D.C.: U.S. Environmental Protection Agency, Jan. 1984), pp. 18-28.

Waste Production

356. U.S. Environmental Protection Agency, *Environmental Outlook 1980* (Washington, D.C.: U.S. Government Printing Office, July 1980).

357. Donna M. Lacombe, "An Overview of Solid Waste Generation in the United States," prepared for U.S. Department of Energy (Los Alamos, N.Mex.: Los Alamos Scientific Laboratory, Dec. 1979), p. 12.

358. *Ibid.*

359. U.S. Environmental Protection Agency, *Environmental Outlook 1980*, pp. 68-110.

360. *Ibid.*, pp. 68-110.

361. Donna M. Lacombe, "An Overview of Solid Waste Generation in the United States," p. 3.

362. U.S. Environmental Protection Agency, *Environmental Outlook 1980*, p. 511.

363. *Ibid.*, pp. 534, 563, 575.

364. UNESCO, International Hydrological Programme, *Aquifer Contamination and Protection* in Veronica Pye, Ruth Patrick, and John Quarles, *Groundwater Con-*

tamination in the United States (Philadelphia: University of Pennsylvania Press, 1983), p. 56.

365. U.S. Environmental Protection Agency, *Environmental Outlook 1980*, pp. 262-288.
366. JRB Associates, *Solid Waste Data: A Compilation of Statistics on Solid Waste Management Within the United States*, prepared for U.S. Environmental Protection Agency (McLean, Va.: JRB Associates, Aug. 1981); Donna Lacombe, "An Overview of Solid Waste Generation in the United States."
367. *Municipal Sewage Treatment: A Comparison of Alternatives*, Final Report prepared for the Council on Environmental Quality and the U.S. Environmental Protection Agency (Washington, D.C.: U.S. Government Printing Office, 1974), pp. 87-125.
368. Information provided by the U.S. Coast Guard, Washington, D.C., Feb. 1984.
369. Council on Environmental Quality, *Environmental Trends* (Washington, D.C.: U.S. Government Printing Office, 1981), p. 266.

Figure References

Toxic Substances

2.1 Environmental Law Reporter; Erica Dolgin, ed., *Federal Environmental Law* (St. Paul: West Publishing Co., 1974); William H. Rogers, *Environmental Law* (St. Paul: West Publishing Co., 1977).
2.2 U.S. Department of the Interior, Bureau of Mines, *Mineral Commodity Profiles*, "Lead" (Washington, D.C.: Bureau of Mines, 1983), Table 11, p. 15.
2.3 Unpublished data provided by U.S. Food and Drug Administration, Bureau of Foods, Division of Chemical Technology, "Adult Total Diet Studies." U.S. Environmental Protection Agency, Office of Air Quality, Planning and Standards, *National Air Quality and Emissions Trends Report, 1982* (Research Triangle Park: U.S. Environmental Protection Agency, 1984), pp. 62, 63.
2.4 John M. Ladd, Stephen P. Hayes et al., States Water Resources Control Board, *California State Mussel Watch 1981-83* (Sacramento: California Water Resources Control Board, 1982), p. 20.
2.5 U.S. Department of the Interior, Bureau of Mines, *Mineral Facts and Problems* 'Cadmium'' (Washington, D.C.: U.S. Government Printing Office, 1980), Table 8, p. 10.
2.6 Unpublished data provided by U.S. Food and Drug Administration, Bureau of Foods, Division of Chemical Technology, "Adult Total Diet Studies."
2.7 International Trade Commission,'Synthetic Organic Chemicals 1970'' (Washington, D.C.: U.S. Government Printing Office, 1979), and previous anual issues.
2.8 Information provided by U.S. Environmental Protection Agency, Exposure Evaluation Division, "National Human Adipose Tissue Survey (NHATS)."
2.9 Pesticide residues in fish and birds, 1966-1976
    Fish: U.S. Fish and Wildlife Service, Columbia National Fisheries Research Laboratory, Columbia, Mo., unpublished data. Starlings, 1968: "Nationwide Residues of Organochlorines in Starlings, 1974," Donald H. White, *Pesticides*

Monitoring J. 10:15 (1976). 1970-1976: "Nationwide Residues of Organochlorines in Starlings, 1976," Donald H. White, *Pesticides Monitoring J.* 12:197 (1979). Waterfowl, 1966: Based on "Occurrences of PCB in National Fish and Wildlife Monitoring Program," Charles R. Walker, U.S. Fish and Wildlife Service. 1969: "Nationwide Residues of Organochlorines in Wings of Adult Mallards and Black Ducks, 1972-1973," Donald H. White and Robert G. Heath, *Pesticides Monitoring J.* 9:184 (1976). 1972-1976: "Nationwide Residues of Organochlorines in Wings of Adult Mallards and Black Ducks, 1976," Donald H. White, *Pesticides Monitoring J.* 13:16 (1979). For data later than 1977, see Council on Environmental Quality, *State of the Environment: 1982*, Table A-51, p. 289; Table A-53, p. 290; Table A-49, p. 287.

2.10 Information provided by U.S. Environmental Protection Agency, Exposure Evaluation Division, "National Human Adipose Tissue Survey (NHATS)" data.

2.11 Interdepartmental Task Force on PCBs, "Polychlorinated Biphenyls and the Environment" (Washington, D.C.: U.S. Government Printing Office, 1972), pp. 6, 7. 1972-1973: Monsanto Industrial Chemicals Company, unpublished data.

2.12 Pesticide residues in fish and birds, 1966-1976
Fish: U.S. Fish and Wildlife Service, Columbia National Fisheries Research Laboratory, Columbia, Mo., unpublished data. Starlings, 1968: "Nationwide residues of Organochlorines in Starlings, 1974," Donald H. White, *Pesticides Monitoring J.* 10:15 (1976). 1970-1976: "Nationwide Residues of Organochlorines in Starlings, 1976," Donald H. White, *Pesticides Monitoring J.* 12:197 (1979). Waterfowl, 1966: Based on "Occurrences of PCB in National Fish and Wildlife Monitoring Program," Charles R. Walker, U.S. Fish and Wildlife Service. 1969: "Nationwide Residues of Organochlorines in Wings of Adult Mallards and Black Ducks, 1972-1973," Donald H. White and Robert G. Heath, *Pesticides Monitoring J.* 9:184 (1976). 1972-1976: "Nationwide Residues of Organochlorines in Wings of Adult Mallards and Black Ducks, 1976," Donald H. White, *Pesticides Monitoring J.* 13:16 (1979). For data later than 1977, see Council on Environmental Quality, *State of the Environment: 1982*, Table A-51, p. 289; Table A-53, p. 290; Table A-49, p. 287. Also, unpublished data provided by U.S. Food and Drug Administration, Bureau of Foods, Division of Chemical Technology, "Adult Total Diet Studies."

2.13 Information provided by U.S. Environmental Protection Agency, Exposure Evaluation Division, "National Human Adipose Tissue Survey (NHATS)."

2.14 Production of selected industrial chemicals, 1950-1978: Benzene, vinyl chloride, acrylonitrile, phthalates: International Trade Commission, *Synthetic Organic Chemicals 1978, 1979, 1980, 1981, 1982* (Washington, D.C.: U.S. Government Printing Office, 1979) and previous annual issues. Asbestos, 1955: U.S. Bureau of Mines, *Mineral Facts and Problems* (Washington, D.C.: U.S. Government Printing Office, 1976), p. 120. 1960-1978: U.S. Bureau of Mines, *Asbestos* (Mineral Commodity Profiles) (Washington, D.C.: U.S. Government Printing Office, 1979), p. 1. PCBs, 1960-1971: Interdepartmental Task Force on PCBs, *Polychlorinated Biphenyls and the Environment* (Washington, D.C.: U.S. Government Printing Office, 1972), pp. 6, 7. 1972-1972: Monsanto Industrial Chemicals Company, unpublished data.

One gallon of benzene equals 7.31 pounds. Data for asbestos are for primary demand; 1978 asbestos data are estimated. PCB data include only that produced for domestic sale. Data for benzene, phthalates, acrylonitrile, and vinyl chloride include only that produced by the original manufacturers; they exclude intermediate products.

2.15 National Research Council, *Nonoccupational Health Risks of Asbestiform Fibers* (Washington, D.C.: National Academy Press, 1984), Table 7-6, p. 220. This source provides a somewhat fuller description of the particular measurements included in the figure.

2.16 National Research Council, *Toxicity Testing: Strategies to Determine Needs and Priorities* (Washington, D.C.: National Academy Press, 1984), p. 12.

Hazardous Wastes

2.17 The basis for the 56 million ton estimate, prepared by an EPA contractor for an environmental impact statement on the implementation of the hazardous waste section of RCRA, is described in U.S. Comptroller General, *Hazardous Waste Management Programs Will Not Be Effective: Greater Efforts are Needed* (Washington, D.C.: U.S. General Accounting Office, 1979), p. 5.

The 41 million ton estimate is made in Booz-Allen and Hamilton, Inc., and Putnam, Hayes, & Bartlett, Inc., *Hazardous Waste Generation and Commercial Hazardous Waste Management Capacity: An Assessment* prepared for the U.S. Environmental Protection Agency, Office of Water and Waste Management, series SW-894 (Washington, D.C.: U.S. Environmental Protection Agency, 1980), pp. III-2-3.

The 250 million ton estimate is reported in Office of Technology Assessment, *Technologies and Management Strategies for Hazardous Waste Control* (Washington, D.C.: U.S. Government Printing Office, 1983), p. 120.

The 264 million ton estimate is made in Westat, Inc., *Final Report, National Survey and Disposal Facilities Regulated under RCRA in 1981*, prepared for U.S. Environmental Protection Agency, Office of Solid Waste (Rockville, Md.: Westat, Inc., April 1984), p. 123. For 150 million ton initial estimate see Westat's "Preliminary Highlights of Findings," August 1983, Figure 7.

2.18 The total number of treatment, storage, and disposal facilities exceeds the total number of sites because a site may use more than one management method. Westat, *Final Report*, pp. 65-66 and 139-142; and "Preliminary Highlights," Figure 7b.

2.19 Westat, *Final Report*, Figures 15-17 and 32-34.

2.20 Westat, *Final Report*, Figure 11.

2.21 Item 1 is noted in U.S. Comptroller General, *Hazardous Waste Facilities with Interim Status May Be Endangering Public Health and Environment* (Washington, D.C.: U.S. General Accounting Office, 1981), p.11. Items 2 through 11 are found in Westat, *Final Report*, 2-5, p. 12; 6, p. 59; 7-8, p. 75; 9, p. 92; 10-11, p. 89. Information for items 12-15 was provided by the U.S. Environmental Protection Agency, Office of Solid Waste and Emergency Response, 1984.

2.22 U.S. Environmental Protection Agency, Office of Solid Waste and Emergency

Response, *Hazardous Waste Sites: National Priorities List* (Washington, D.C.: EPA, 1983).

2.23 EPA's Draft "Son of Superfund" Report, published in *Inside EPA*, Feb. 3, 1984, as a special supplement includes the estimates of 16,000-22,000, 1,400-2,200, and 546. The state estimates of 7,113 and 33 are made in Association of State and Territorial Solid Waste Management Officials, *State Cleanup Programs for Hazardous Substance Sites and Spills*, prepared for the U.S. Environmental Protection Agency (Washington, D.C.: ASTSWMO, 1983), p. 9.

The 100 and 100-170 estimates of likely cleanups are made in Gene Lucero's paper on "Constraints on Private Party Cleanup at Superfund Sites," see *Inside EPA Weekly Report*, April 27, 1984, p.11. The estimates of 196 emergency removals and 6 NPL sites cleaned up were provided by the U.S. Environmental Protection Agency, Office of Solid Waste and Emergency Response, 1984.

Air Quality

2.24 U.S. Environmental Protection Agency, Office of Air Quality Planning and Standards, *National Air Pollutant Emission Estimates, 1970-1981* (Research Triangle Park: U.S. Environmental Protection Agency, Sept. 1982), pp. 5-9, Tables 2-6.

2.25 Council on Environmental Quality, Council on Environmental Quality, *Environmental Quality: 1982* (Washington, D.C.: U.S. Government Printing Office, 1983) pp. 22-25, Appendix B, pp. 315-318; Weston Inc. analysis of the U.S. Environmental Protection Agency's air quality data bank, SAROD (Storage and Retrieval of Aerometric Data) previous CEQ annual reports, and unpublished data.

PSI is designed for the daily reporting of air quality to advise the public of potentially acute, but not chronic, health effects. PSI is not used to rank air pollution problems in various cities. To properly rank the air pollution problems in different cities, one should rely not just on air quality data but should also analyze data on population characteristics, daily population mobility, transportation patterns, industrial composition, emission inventories, meteorological factors, and the spatial representativeness of air monitoring sites.

The PSI analysis for 1974-1981 is based on standards applicable during 1981, not on standards applicable at the time of monitoring. The primary standard for ozone was relaxed in 1979 from 160 to 240 micrograms per cubic meter per hour.

Note that the average PSI values do not represent an average SMSA, but an average of 23 SMSAs.

2.26 Information provided by U.S. Environmental Protection Agency, Office of Air Quality Planning and Standards, (Research Triangle Park: U.S. Environmental Protection Agency, May 1984).

Data for ambient trends were taken from EPA's National Aerometric Data Bank (NADB). This information is submitted to EPA by state and local governments and various federal agencies. For a monitoring site to be included in this analysis the site had to contain at least 5 out of the 7 years of data in the period 1975 to 1982 and each of these years had to satisfy annual data com-

498 STATE OF THE ENVIRONMENT

pleteness criteria. For a more complete discussion of criteria and procedures used to select data for ambient trends see *National Air Quality and Emissions Trends Report, 1981*, p. 17-19.

The number of monitoring sites used to generate data for 1982 ambient trends analysis were: TSP—1076, SO₂—351, CO—196, SO₂—276, O₃—193.

2.27 U.S. Environmental Protection Agency, Office of Air Quality Planning and Standards, *National Air Quality and Emissions Trends Report, 1982* (Research Triangle Park: U.S. Environmental Protection Agency, Sept. 1982), Table 3-1, p. 30, Table 3-2, p. 39, Table 3-3, p. 47, Table 3-4, p. 51, Table 3-5, p. 60. From time to time EPA updates its emissions estimates for the criteria pollutants (TSP, SO₂, NO₂, CO, and VOC). In the process they revise all the data in the time series.

2.28 Monitoring and Assessment Research Center, "Air Pollution Concentrations in Selected Urban Areas, 1973-1980," Preliminary Report prepared for the United Nations Environmental Programme and the World Health Organization (London: Monitoring and Assessment Research Center, 1983), Statistical Appendix. Data are annual average sulfur dioxide concentrations.

Data for selected urban areas from around the world were taken from the UNEP-sponsored Global Environmental Monitoring System (GEMS). Only data collected from monitoring sites located in central city commercial areas were chosen for the graphic: 19 sites for SO₂, 20 sites for suspended particulate matter (SPM). Each site had to have representative data for 5 or more years to be selected.

2.29 Research Triangle Institute, "Study of Carbon Monoxide Exposure of Residents of Washington, D.C. and Denver, Colorado," Draft Final Report, Part I, prepared for the U.S. Environmental Protection Agency, Office of Monitoring Systems and Quality Assurance (Research Triangle Park: Research Triangle Institute, Sept. 1983), pp. 177-178.

2.30 U.S. Department of Energy, *Acid Rain Information Book*, Final Report, 2nd ed. (Springfield, Va.: National Technical Information Service, May 1983), pp. 2-17.

2.31 William C. Malm and John V. Molenar, "Visibility Trends in National Parks in the Western United States" (Fort Collins: National Park Service, Oct. 1983), Figure 4, p. 21.

2.32 *Ibid.*, Figure 6, p. 24.

2.33 *Carbon Dioxide Production—Institute for Energy Analysis, Oak Ridge Associated Universities, Carbon Dioxide Review, 1982*, edited by William C. Clark (New York: Oxford University Press, 1982), p. 378.

Data from R.M. Rotty Institute for Energy Analysis, Oak Ridge Assoc. Universities, pp. 456-460.

2.34 *Atmospheric Concentrations of Carbon Dioxide—Institute for Energy Analysis, Oak Ridge Associated Universities, Carbon Dioxide Review, 1982*, edited by William C. Clark (New York: Oxford University Press, 1982), pp. 456-460.

Data from Bacastow and Kneeling, Scripps Institute of Oceanography, p. 434.

2.35 *Mean Global Temperature—Institute for Energy Analysis, Oak Ridge Associated Universities, Carbon Dioxide Review, 1982*, edited by William C. Clark (New York: Oxford University Press, 1982), pp. 448-456.

Water Quality

2.36 Association of State and Interstate Water Pollution Control Administrators, *America's Clean Water: The States' Evaluation of Progress 1972-1982* (Washington, D.C.: Association of State and Interstate Water Pollution Control Administrators, 1984).

2.37 U.S. Department of the Interior, Geological Survey, *National Water Summary 1983, Hydrologic Events and Issues* USGS Water Supply Paper 2250 (Washington, D.C.: U.S. Government Printing Office, 1984), p. 47.

2.38 U.S. Department of the Interior, Geological Survey, *National Water Summary 1983*, p. 47.

2.39 Council on Environmental Quality, *Environmental Quality: 1982* (Washington, D.C.: U.S. Government Printing Office, 1982), Table A-61, p. 295.

2.40 Edwin H. Clark, "Estimated Effects of Nonpoint Source Pollution" (Washington, D.C.: The Conservation Foundation, forthcoming).

2.41 Association of State and Interstate Water Pollution Control Administrators, *America's Clean Water*, p. 11.

2.42 U.S. Environmental Protection Agency, "National Urban Runoff Program. Draft Summary." (Washington, D.C.: U.S. Environmental Protection Agency, 1984), Table 6-21, p. 6-53.

Waste Production

2.43 For agricultural wastes: Donna M. Lacombe, "An Overview of Solid Waste Generation in the United States," prepared for U.S. Department of Energy (Los Alamos, N.Mex.: Los Alamos Scientific Laboratory, Dec. 1979), p. 584; for mining wastes: *Ibid.*, p. 543; for air pollutants: U.S. Environmental Protection Agency, *Environmental Outlook 1980* (Washington, D.C.: U.S. Government Printing Office, July 1980), pp. 68-110; for point source water pollutants: *Ibid.*, pp. 262-288; for nonpoint source water pollutants: *Ibid.*, pp. 350-377; for residential and commercial solid wastes: "Waste Paper: The Future of a Resource," Franklin Resources Ltd., p. 7; for industrial solid wastes: JRB Associates, *Solid Waste Data: A Compliation of Statistics on Solid Waste Management Within the United States*, prepared for U.S. Environmental Protection Agency (McLean, Va.: JRB Associates, Aug. 1981) and Donna Lacombe, "An Overview of Solid Waste Generation in the United States'; for hazardous wastes: U.S. Environmental Protection Agency, *Environmental Outlook 1980* (Washington, D.C.: U.S. Government Printing Office, July 1980); for demolition: JRB Associates, *Solid Waste Data: A Compliation of Statistics on Solid Waste Management Within the United States*, prepared for U.S. Environmental Protection Agency (McLean, Va.: JRB Associates, Aug. 1981); Donna Lacombe, "An Overview of Solid Waste Generation in the United States"; for oil spills: Information provided by the U.S. Coast Guard, Washington, D.C., Feb. 1984.

CHAPTER 3: NATURAL RESOURCES

Text References

Water

1. U.S. Department of the Interior, Geological Survey, *National Water Summary 1983—Hydrologic Events and Issues*, Water Supply Paper 2250 (Washington, D.C.: U.S. Government Printing Office, 1984).
2. *Ibid.*, p. 12.
3. "Great Salt Lake, High and Rising, Nears Record Level Set in 1878," *Washington Post*, May 16, 1984.
4. U.S. Geological Survey, *National Water Summary 1983*, pp. 12-13.
5. *Ibid.*, pp. 8, 240.
6. "Report Surveys Water Quality for Fish," *EPA Journal* 10(3):25 (1984).
7. Council on Environmnental Quality, *Environmental Trends* (Washington, D.C.: U.S. Government Printing Office, 1981), figure 10-8, p. 217.
8. Wayne B. Solley, Edith B. Chase, and William B. Mann IV, *Estimated Use of Water in the U.S. in 1980*, Geological Survey Circular 1001 (Reston, VA: U.S. Geological Survey, 1983), p. 47; and U.S. Department of Commerce, Bureau of the Census, *Statistical Abstract of the United States: 1984*, 104th ed. (Washington, D.C.: U.S. Government Printing Office, 1984), Table 2, p. 6.
9. Wayne B. Solley, Edith B. Chase and William B. Mann IV, *Estimated Use of Water in the U.S. in 1980*, pp. 47, 36.
10. *Ibid.*, p. 16.
11. *Ibid.*, p. 16.
12. *Ibid.*, p. 8.
13. *Ibid.*, p. 36.
14. *Ibid.*, p. 27.
15. *Ibid.*, p. 19.
16. *Ibid.*, p. 15.
17. *Ibid.*, p. 11.
18. *Ibid.*, pp. 20, 23.
19. *Ibid.*, p. 47.
20. *Ibid.*, p. 20.
21. *Ibid.*, p. 47.
22. *Ibid.*, p. 47.
23. Gordon Sloggett, *Prospects for Groundwater Irrigation: Declining Levels and Rising Costs*, Agricultural Economic Report Number 478 (Washington, D.C.: U.S. Department of Agriculture, 1981), p. 8.
24. U.S. Water Resources Council, *The Nation's Water Resources, 1975-2000, Vol. 1* (Washington, D.C.: U.S. Government Printing Office, 1978), p. 18.
25. *Ibid.*
26. *Ibid.*
27. U.S. Geological Survey, *National Water Summary 1983*, pp. 89, 92, 120, 227.
28. *Ibid.*, pp. 33-34.

29. U.S. Water Resources Council, *The Nation's Water Resources, 1975-2000*, p. 12.
30. U.S. Geological Survey, *National Water Summary 1983*, pp. 30-31.
31. U.S. Water Resources Council, *The Nation's Water Resources, 1975-2000*, p. 16.
32. *Ibid.*
33. U.S. Geological Survey, *National Water Summary 1983*, p. 27.
34. Philip Fradkin, *A River No More, The Colorado River and the West* (New York: Alfred A. Knopf, 1981).
35. Environmental Defense Fund, *Trading Conservation Investments for Water* (Berkeley, Calif.: Environmental Defense Fund, 1983), p. 48.

Land Use

36. U.S. Department of Agriculture, *Soil and Water Resources Conservation Act, 1980 Appraisal, Part I, Soil, Water, and Related Resources in the United States: Status, Condition, and Trends* (Washington, D.C.: U.S. Department of Agriculture, 1981), p. 72. Excluding the Great Lakes and large estuaries, there are 60 million acres of inland water.
37. United Nations, Food and Agriculture Organization, *FAO Production Yearbook, 1981*, Statistics Series No. 40 (Rome: Food and Agriculture Organization, 1982), Tables 1 and 3, pp. 45-56, 61-71. See also Population Reference Bureau, "1983 Data Sheet."
38. U.S. Department of the Interior, Bureau of Land Management, *Public Land Statistics 1982* (Washington, D.C.: U.S. Government Printing Office, April 1983), p. 5.
39. *Ibid.*, pp. 10-12.
40. *Ibid.*, p. 9.
41. James A. Lewis, U.S. Department of Agriculture, Economics, Statistics, and Cooperatives Service, "Landownership in the United States, 1978," Agriculture Information Bulletin No. 435 (Washington, D.C.: U.S. Department of Agriculture, 1980), p. 3. Updating information provided by U.S. Department of Interior, Bureau of Land Management, May 1984.
42. *Ibid.*, p. 4.
43. *Ibid.*, p. 5.
44. U.S. Department of Agriculture, *Soil and Water Resources Conservation Act, 1980 Appraisal Part I*, p. 21.
45. Information provided by U.S. Department of Agriculture, Economic Research Service, May 1984.
46. H. Thomas Frey, U.S. Department of Agriculture, Economic Research Service, *Major Uses of Land in The United States: 1978*, Agricultural Economics Report No. 487 (Washington, D.C.: U.S. Department of Agriculture, 1981), pp. 2-3.
47. *Ibid.*, p. 12.
48. *Ibid.*, p. 16.
49. *Ibid.*, p. 4.
50. H. Thomas Frey, U.S. Department of Agriculture, Economic Research Service, "Expansion of Urban Areas in the U.S.: 1960-1980," Staff Report – AGES830615 (Washington, D.C.: U.S. Government Printing Office, June 1983), p. ii.

51. Information provided by Geography Division, U.S. Department of Commerce, Bureau of the Census; and U.S. Department of Agriculture, Soil Conservation Service, *Available Federal Data on Agricultural Land Use*, Technical Paper II, prepared by the Research Staff of the National Agricultural Lands Study (Washington, D.C.: U.S. Department of Agriculture, 1981), Table 1, p. 8. The 1982 National Resources Inventory, using different definitions, identified 46.6 million acres of urban and built-up land. This is much closer to the Census Bureau's estimate of urban land.

52. H. Thomas Frey, "Expansion of Urban Areas in the U.S.: 1960-1980," pp. 11-13.

53. U.S. Department of Agriculture, *Soil and Water Resources Conservation Act, 1980 Appraisal Part I*, p. 50.

54. James Horsfield and Norman Landgren, *Cropland Trends Across the Nation*, Agricultural Economic Report No. 494 (Washington, D.C.: U.S. Department of Agriculture, Dec. 1982), pp. 2-11.

55. U.S. Department of Agriculture, *Soil and Water Resources Conservation Act, 1980 Appraisal, Part I, Soil, Water, and Related Resources in the United States: Status, Conditions and Trends* (Washington, D.C.: U.S. Department of Agriculture, 1981), p. 49

56. Philip M. Raup, "Competition for Land and the Future of American Agriculture," in Sandra S. Batie and Robert G. Healy, eds., *The Future of American Agriculture as a Strategic Resource* (Washington, D.C.: The Conservation Foundation, 1980), p. 49.

57. Council on Environmental Quality, *Environmental Statistics 1978* (Springfield, Va.: National Technical Information Service, 1979), p. 33; Information provided by U.S. Department of Agriculture, Economic Research Service, May 1984.

58. Philip M. Raup, "Competition for Land and the Future of American Agriculture," pp. 52-53.

59. Merle C. Prunty, "Agricultural Lands: A Southern Perspective," paper prepared for Agricultural Lands Study Workshop, Memphis, Tennessee, October 3, 1979 (Mississippi State, Miss.: Southern Rural Development Center, 1979), pp. xi, 17.

60. M. B. Lapping, G. E. Penfold, and S. MacPherson, "Right-to-Farm Laws: Do they Resolve Land Use Conflicts?" *Journal of Soil and Water Conservation* 38(6):465-67 (1983).

61. See generally, Gordon Bradley, ed.,*Land Use and Forest Resources in A Changing Environment: The Urban/Forest Interface* (Seattle, Wash.: University of Washington Press, forthcoming).

62. *Ibid.*

Cropland, Forestland, and Rangeland

63. H. Thomas Frey, U.S. Department of Agriculture, Economic Research Service, *Major Uses of Land in the United States, 1978*, Agricultural Economic Report No. 487 (Washington, D.C.: U.S. Government Printing Office, Aug. 1982), p. 2.

64. U.S. Department of Agriculture, *Agricultural Statistics, 1983* (Washington,

D.C.: U.S. Government Printing Office, 1984), pp. 398-399. Crop value information is given for crops which cover over 97 percent of the total acreage planted; the real total value is therefore probably just slightly higher. 1982 data for sugarbeets and sugarcane were not available; in 1981 the value of these two crops was about $1.5 billion.

65. U.S. Department of Agriculture, *Agricultural Statistics, 1983*, p. 402. The figure given includes value of cattle, calves, sheep, lambs, milk, and wool. Other livestock products and their values are: hogs, $10 billion; chickens and turkeys, $6 billion; eggs, $3.5 billion.

66. U.S. Department of Commerce, Bureau of the Census, *1981 Annual Survey of Manufactures: Statistics for Industry Groups and Industries*, April, 1983, p. 8. Data are combined for the Lumber and Wood Products industry group and the Paper and Allied Products industry group.

67. Estimates of original extent of prairie: A. W. Kuchler, *Potential Natural Vegetation of the Conterminous United States* (Special Publication 36) (New York: American Geographical Society), cited in P.G. Risser et al., *The True Prairie Ecosystem* (Stroudsburg, Pa.: Hutchinson Ross, 1981), p. 13. Precise estimates of remaining prairie are unavailable. A.A. Auclair, "Ecological Factors in the Development of Intensive-Management Ecosystems in the Midwestern United States," *Ecology* 57:431-444 (1976), documented the conversion of 92 percent of the prairie in a southern Wisconsin location to cropland/pasture rotation in the century between 1833 and 1934, as well as the virtual absence of any prairie in the area today.

68. H. Thomas Frey, *Major Uses of Land*, p. 3; U.S. Department of Agriculture, *Agricultural Statistics, 1983*, p. 383.

69. U.S. Department of Agriculture, *Agricultural Statistics, 1983*, p. 422; United States Department of Agriculture, *Agricultural Statistics, 1982* (Washington, D.C.: U.S. Government Printing Office, 1983), p.430.

70. Harold F. Breimyer, "A Disguised 'Bonanza' for Farmers," *New York Times*, Dec. 4, 1983.

71. U.S. Department of Agriculture, *Agricultural Statistics, 1983*, p. 381.

72. U.S. Department of Agriculture, *1983 Handbook of Agricultural Charts*, Agricultural Handbook No. 619 (Washington, D.C.: U.S. Government Printing Office, 1984), Chart 163, p. 58.

73. U.S. Department of Agriculture, *Agricultural Statistics, 1983*, p. 381.

74. Dale E. Hathaway, "The Internationalization of U.S. Agriculture," in E.N. Castle and K.A. Price, eds. *U.S. Interests and Global Natural Resources* (Washington, D.C.: Resources for the Future, 1983), pp. 90-102.

75. U.S. Department of Agriculture, *Agricultural Statistics, 1983*, p. 400.

76. United Nations, Food and Agricultural Organization, *FAO Production Yearbook, 1981*, Statistics Series No. 40 (Rome: Food and Agricultural Organization, 1982), Tables 1 and 3. FAO figures for persons engaged principally in agriculture are lower than agricultural employment as reported either by the U.S. Census Bureau or the U.S. Depart4143⁶ment of Agriculture. They are also lower than "agricultural population" reported by FAO, which includes non-workers dependent on agricultural workers. On the other hand, it should be noted that FAO includes workers employed in forestry, hunting, and fishing

in the "agricultural" category. In the United States such inclusions have little effect on the total numbers.

77. U.S. Department of Agriculture, *Agricultural Statistics, 1983*, p. 394.

78. U.S. Department of Agriculture, *Agricultural Statistics, 1983*, pp. 402-404.

79. *Ibid.*, p. 30; and information provided by U.S. Department of Agriculture, Crop Reporting Service, May 1984.

80. "Fertilizer Prices Soar as Controls Go Off," *Business Week*, Nov. 3, 1973, p. 24; "Tough Times Ahead for Fertilizer Users," *Business Week*, March 2, 1974, p. 18; "Why Fertilizer is in Such Short Supply," *Business Week*, Oct. 6, 1974, p. 84.

81. U.S. Department of Agriculture, *Agricultural Statistics, 1982*, pp. 421, 426, 437.

82. Data from the National Resources Inventory, reported in Pierre R. Crosson and Ruth B. Haas, "Agricultural Land," in Paul R. Portney, ed., *Current Issues in Natural Resource Policy* (Washington, D.C.: Resources for the Future, 1982), pp. 263-265.

83. Michael F. Brewer and Robert F. Boxley, "Agricultural Land: Adequacy of Acres, Concepts and Information," *American Journal of Agricultural Economics* 63:881 (1981).

84. Information provided by U.S. Department of Agriculture, Soil Conservation Service, May 1984.

85. Robert G. Healy and James L. Short, *The Market for Rural Land: Trends, Issues, Policies* (Washington, D.C.: The Conservation Foundation, 1981), p. 19.

86. *Ibid.*, pp. 28-9.

87. Pierre R. Crosson and Anthony T. Stout, *Productivity Effects of Cropland Erosion in the United States* (Baltimore: Johns Hopkins University Press for Resources for the Future, 1983), pp. 42-3, 55; Office of Technology Assessment, *Impacts of Technology on U.S. Cropland and Rangeland Productivity* (Washington, D.C.: U.S. Government Printing Office, 1984), pp. 34-5; R. Neil Sampson, "Soil Conservation," *Sierra* 68(6):40 (1983).

88. Lester R. Brown et al., *State of the World 1984* (New York: W.W. Norton, 1984), pp. 57-62.

89. U.S. Department of Agriculture, Soil Conservation Service, *National Summary, 1982 NRI*, preliminary (Washington, D.C.: U.S. Department of Agriculture, April 1984), Table 9a.

90. Information provided by U.S. Department of Agriculture, Soil Conservation Service; and U.S. Department of Agriculture, *Basic Statistics 1977 National Resources Inventory* (Washington, D.C.: U.S. Department of Agriculture, Dec. 1982), p. 55.

91. U.S. Department of Agriculture, Soil Conservation Service, *National Summary, 1982 NRI*, preliminary, Table 9a.

92. R. Neil Sampson, "Soil Conservation," p. 40; Council on Environmental Quality, *Environmental Quality: 1980*, p. 315.

93. U.S. Department of Agriculture, Soil Conservation Service, *National Summary, 1982 NRI*, Table 19a.

94. U.S. Department of Agriculture, *Basic Statistics 1977 National Resources Inventory*, p. 55; Council on Environmental Quality, *Environmental Quality: 1980* (Washington, D.C.: U.S. Government Printing Office, 1980), p. 314.

95. U.S. Office of Technology Assessment, *Impacts of Technology on U.S. Cropland of Rangeland Productivity* (Washington, D.C.: U.S. Government Printing Office, 1982), p. 138.

96. Sandra S. Batie, *Soil Erosion: Crisis in America's Croplands?* (Washington, D.C.: The Conservation Foundation, 1983), p. 76.

97. Office of Technology Assessment, *Impacts of Technology*, p. 146.

98. National Conservation Tillage Information Center, *1982 National Survey Conservation Tillage Practices* (Washington, D.C.: National Conservation Tillage Information Center, 1983), pp. 2-3, 5. The 1970's number is from Office of Technology Assessment, *Impacts of Technology on U.S. Cropland and Rangeland Productivity*, 1982, p. 98.

99. National Conservation Tillage Information Center, *1983 National Survey Conservation Tillage Practices, Executive Summary*, 1984, p. 4.

100. William Cronon, *Changes in the Land* (New York: Hill and Wang, 1983), pp. 108-126.

101. Marion Clawson, "Forests in the Long Sweep of American History," *Science* 204(4398):1169 (1979); and H. Thomas Frey, *Major Uses of Land*, p. 3.

102. United Nations, Food and Agriculture Organization, *FAO Production Yearbook, 1981*, Table 1, p. 45.

103. Dwight Hair, *America's Renewable Resources: A Supplement to the 1979 Assessment of the Forest and Rangeland Situation in the United States*, review draft (Washington, D.C.: U.S. Forest Service, Feb. 1983), p. 14.

104. National Forest Products Association, "Increased Wood Products Exports: A Bonus for the Industry and Nation" (Washington, D.C.: National Forest Products Association, undated), p. 41.

105. National Forest Products Association and U.S. Department of Agriculture, Foreign Agricultural Service, "USA Wood for the World Today and Tomorrow" (Washington, D.C.: National Forest Products Association, undated).

106. U.S. Department of Agriculture, Forest Service, *U.S. Timber Production, Trade, Consumption, and Price Statistics, 1950-81*, Miscellaneous Publication 1424 (Washington, D.C.: U.S. Forest Service, 1981), Table 3, p. 10.

107. Dwight Hair, *America's Renewable Resources*, pp. 17-18; D.R. Darr and G.L. Lindell, "Prospects for U.S. Trade in Timber Products: Implications," *Forest Products Journal* 30(6):20 (1980).

108. U.S. Department of Agriculture, Forest Service, *An Assessment of the Forest and Rangeland Situation in the United States*, FS-345 (Washington, D.C.: U.S. Forest Service, Jan. 1980), pp. 376-380.

109. *Ibid*, p. 376; The Conservation Foundation, *State of the Environment 1982* (Washington, D.C.: The Conservation Foundation, 1982), pp. 232, 233.

110. Information provided by Survey directors at Forest Experiment Stations, including: Northeast, South, Southeast, North Central, Pacific Northwest, and Intermountain, A rough summary of the softwood situation is as follows: Substantial excess of growth over cut: Lake States, most of Northeast, Southern Rockies, Northern Rockies National Forests (because of roadless area review and evaluation process). Slight excess of growth over cut: Pacific Northwest, Maine. Growth and cut about equal: Southeast, South Central. Cut in excess of growth: Southern industrial lands, Northern Rockies private holdings. Documentary support sent by the survey leaders includes: Joseph E. Barnard

and Douglas S. Powell, "Some Preliminary Results of the 1982 Forest Inventory of Maine," May 6, 1983 ; Thomas J. Considine Jr. and Thomas S. Frieswyk, *Forest Statistics for New York, 1980*, Resource Bulletin NE-71, 1982; Douglas S. Powell and Thomas J. Considine Jr., *An Analysis of Pennsylvania's Forest Resources*, Resource Bulletin NE-69, 1982; William A. Bechtold and Raymond M. Sheffield, *Forest Statistics for Florida, 1980*, Resource Bulletin SE-58, 1981; John B. Tansey, *Forest Statistics for Georgia, 1982*, Resource Bulletin SE-69, 1983; Raymond M. Sheffield, *Forest Statistics for South Carolina, 1978*, Resource Bulletin SE-50, 1979; John S. Spencer, Jr., and Jerold T. Hahn, *Michigan's Fourth Forest Inventory: Timber Volumes and Projections of Timber Supply*, Resource Bulletin NC-72, 1983; Pamela J. Jakes and W. Brad Smith, *A Second Look at North Dakota's Timber Lands, 1980*, Resource Bulletin NC-58, 1982; Staff, Renewable Resources Evaluation Research Work Unit, *Forest Statistics for Arkansas Counties*, Resource Bulletin SO-76, 1980; Staff, Renewable Resources Evaluation Research Work Unit, *Forest Statistics for Tennessee Counties*, Resource Bulletin SO-89, 1982; Charles E. Thomas and Carl V. Bylin, *Louisiana Mid-Cycle Survey Shows Change in Forest Resource Trends*, Resource Bulletin SO-86, 1982.

111. William Cronon, *Changes in the Land*, pp. 159-160; and Carl Reidel, *The Yankee Forest: A Prospectus* (New Haven, Conn.: Yale University, 1978), pp. 13-16.

112. Karl R. Hosford, "The Lands Nobody Wanted," *Michigan Natural Resources Magazine* 52(6):53 (1983).

113. R. Eugene Turner et al., in "Bottomland Hardwood Forest Land Resources of the Southeastern United States," in J.R. Clark and J. Benforado, eds., *Wetlands of Bottomland Hardwood Forests*, (New York: Elsevier Scientific Publishing Co., 1981), p. 17; and R.S. Fecso et al., *Management Practices and Reforestation Decisions for Harvested Southern Pinelands*, Staff Report No. AGES821230 (Washington, D.C.: U.S. Forest Service, Dec. 1982), pp. 11-12.

114. U.S. Department of Agriculture, Forest Service, *An Analysis of the Timber Situation in the United States: 1952-2030* (Washington, D.C.: U.S. Forest Service, 1980), Appendix 3, Tables 11, 34, 40.

115. Philip Shabecoff, "Widespread Ills Found in Forests in Eastern U.S.," *New York Times*, Feb. 26, 1984; and Leslie Roberts, "Studies Probe Unexplained Decline in Eastern Forests," *BioScience* 34(5):291-292 (1984).

116. For two good discussions of the history and future of prescribed burning, see: Stephen J. Pyne, "Fire Policy and Fire Research in the United States Forest Service," *Journal of Forest History* 25(2):64-77 (1981); Von J. Johnson, "Prescribed Burning: Requiem or Renaissance?', *Journal of Forestry* 82(2):82-90. Johnson, on p. 88, indicates that up to 21.2 million acres of southeastern woodland was subjected to controlled burning, per year, in the late 1960's. This acreage is more than four times the *national* acreage burned by wildfires during that time period.

117. U.S. Department of Agriculture, Forest Service, *Forest Insect and Disease Conditions in the United States, 1982* (Washington, D.C.: U.S. Forest Service, 1983), p. i.

118. *Ibid.*, p. 1. Fifteen of these states are considered "generally infested" with gypsy moths.

119. See, for example, U.S. Department of Agriculture, Forest Service, *Forest Insect and Disease Conditions in the United States, 1980*, p. 30, *1981*, p. 45, *1982*, p. 44, which show a very large southern pine beetle outbreak in 1980, very little infestation in 1981, and some expansion of infestation in 1982.

120. Before 1971: U.S. Department of Agriculture, Forest Service, *The Outlook for Timber in the United States* (Washington, D.C.: U.S. Government Printing Office, 1974). 1971-1978: U.S. Department of Agriculture, Forest Service, *1978 Report, Forest Planting, Seeding, and Silvical Treatments in the United States* (Washington, D.C.: U.S. Government Printing Office, 1979). Since 1978: U.S. Department of Agriculture, Forest Service, *Forest Planting, Seeding, and Silvical Treatments in the United States, 1979 Report* (Washington, D.C.: U.S. Government Printing Office, Feb. 1981), and *1980 Report* (Washington, D.C.: U.S. Government Printing Office, Sept. 1981); U.S. Department of Agriculture, Forest Service, *1981 U.S. Forest Planing Report* (Washington, D.C.: U.S. Government Printing Office, Sept. 1982), and *1982 Report* (Washington, D.C.: U.S. Government Printing Office, July 1983).

121. U.S. Department of Agriculture, Forest Service, *1982 U.S. Forest Planting Report*, p. 4.

122. Marion Clawson, *The Economics of U.S. Nonindustrial Private Forests* (Washington, D.C.: Resources for the Future, 1979), p. 1.

123. U.S. Department of Agriculture, Forest Service, *Forest Planting, Seeding and Silvical Treatments in the United States 1979*, p. 2, and *U.S. Forest Planting Report(s)* from 1980, 1981, 1982.

124. Marion Clawson, *The Economics of U.S. Nonindustrial Private Forests*, p. 88.

125. *Ibid.*, p. 91.

126. Jack P. Royer and H. Fred Kaiser, "Reforestation Decisions on Harvested Southern Timberlands," *Journal of Forestry* 81(10):658 (1983); and R.S. Fecso et al., *Management Practices and Reforestation Decisions for Harvested Southern Pinelands*, p. 60.

127. H. Thomas Frey, *Major Uses of Land*, p. 9; U.S. Department of Agriculture, *Agricultural Statistics, 1983*, p. 383.

128. Robert G. Healy, "Animal Agriculture and the Demand for Southern Land," unpublished manuscript (Washington, D.C.: The Conservation Foundation, undated), p. 8.

129. United States Department of Agriculture, *Agricultural Statistics, 1983*, p. 383.

130. U.S. Department of Agriculture, Forest Service, *An Assessment of the Forest and Rangeland Situation in the United States*, pp. 296-297.

131. Cass Peterson, "Antelopes May Roam to Home," *Washington Post*, Dec. 12, 1983.

132. Frederic H. Wagner, "Livestock Grazing and the Livestock Industry," in Howard P. Brokaw, *Wildlife and America* (Washington, D.C.: U.S. Government Printing Office, 1978), p. 137.

133. *Ibid.*, pp. 124-126.

134. United States Department of Agriculture, Forest Service, *An Assessment of the Forest and Range Land Situation in the United States*, FS-345, Jan. 1980, p. 287.

135. *Ibid.*, pp. 280, 282.

136. *Ibid.*, pp. 254-255.

137. *Ibid.*, p. 254.
138. U.S. Department of Agriculture, Soil Conservation Service, *National Summary 1982 NRI*, Table 34a.

Wildlife, Wildland and Critical Areas

139. The term *ecosystem services* has been used to describe the various functions of wild organisms and ecosystems which are of value to humanity but generally considered free goods or, in some cases, poorly identified and underutilized. See Daniel B. Tunstall, "Draft Background Document on Wildlife Resources," prepared for Organization for Economic Cooperation and Development, Environment Directorate, Environment Committee, Group on the State of the Environment, draft (Paris: Organization for Economic Cooperation and Development, April 1983), pp. 23-26.
140. U.S. Department of the Interior, Fish and Wildlife Service, *A Summary of Selected Fish and Wildlife Characteristics of the 50 States* (Washington, D.C.: Fish and Wildife Service, March 1983), Table E.1, p. 71.
141. Page Chichester, "Help for the Unhunted," *Defenders* 59(1):3 (1984).
142. Daniel A. Poole and James B. Trefethen, "Maintenance of Wildlife Populations," in Howard P. Brokaw, ed. *Wildlife and America* (Washington, D.C.: U.S. Government Printing Office, 1978), p. 339.
143. *Ibid.*, p. 341.
144. U.S. Department of the Interior, *A Summary of Selected Fish and Wildlife Characteristics*, Table C.1, p. 27. The actual harvest for the 26 eastern states in their most recent reporting years was 1,706,462 deer. In almost all cases harvest was reported for 1980, with 4 states reporting data for the 1980-81 season, 2 for 1981, and 2 for 1978-79.
145. Ted Williams, "Resurrection of the Wild Turkey," *Audubon* 81(1):71 (1984).
146. U.S. Department of the Interior, *A Summary of Selected Fish and Wildlife Characteristics*, Table C.6, p. 32.
147. Williams, "Resurrection of the Wild Turkey," p. 71.
148. U.S. Department of Agriculture, Forest Service, Wildlife and Fisheries Staff, *Wildlife and Fisheries Report 1980* (Washington, D.C.: U.S. Department of Agriculture, undated), pp. 52, 54; and *Wildlife and Fish Habitat Management in the Forest Service 1981* (Washington, D.C.: U.S. Department of Agriculture, Aug. 1983), p. 4; information also provided by U.S. Forest Service.
149. Information supplied by Regional Wildlife Biology staff, U.S. Forest Service, Milwaukee, Wis.
150. *Ibid.*; *Sierra Club and Defenders of Wildlife v. James Watt*, U.S. D.Ct., D. Minn., Civ. No. 5-83-254; decision by Judge Miles Lord, reprinted in "In Favor of the Wolf," *Defenders* 59(2):10-15 (1984); information provided by Defenders of Wildlife.
151. Chandler S. Robbins, Danny Bystrak, and Paul H. Geissler, *The Breeding Bird Survey: Its First 15 Years, 1965-1979*, Fish and Wildlife Survey, draft (Washington, D.C.: U.S. Department of the Interior, 1983). See the text and figures referring to the particular birds discussed.

152. Council on Environmental Quality, *Environmental Quality: 1982* (Washington, D.C.: U.S. Government Printing Office, 1983), p. 260.
153. Paul A. Opler, "The Parade of Passing Species: A Survey of Extinctions in the U.S.," in Folkerte and Mason, eds., *Environmental Problems*, 2d ed. (Dubuque: William C. Brown and Co., 1979); U.S. Department of the Interior, Fish and Wildlife Service, Endangered Species Program, *Endangered Species Technical Bulletin* 8(10):3 (1983).
154. Endangered Species Act of 1973, 16 U.S.C.A. §§1531-1543 (1983).
155. *Endangered Species Technical Bulletin* 8(10):3 (1983), 9(2):3 (1984); also information provided by Endangered Species Program staff.
156. See monthly *Endangered Species Technical Bulletins*. For a comparison with 1979, see Council on Environmental Quality, *Environmental Trends*, p. 167.
157. Greta Nilsson, *The Endangered Species Handbook* (Washington, D.C.: The Animal Welfare Institute, 1983), pp. 119-120. Seventy-three percent of the animals (almost 90 percent of invertebrates) appearing on 26 state lists, and virtually all of the plants on 9 state lists, were not listed by the federal government, according to Nilsson's tabulations. The percentages are perhaps slightly exaggerated because species on more than one state list are counted each time they appear.
158. *Endangered Species Technical Bulletin* 9(2):8 (1984).
159. *Endangered Species Technical Bulletin* 8(1):12 (1983) and 9(3):8 (1984).
160. *Endangered Species Technical Bulletin* 8(12):1,6 (1983).
161. Daniel B. Tunstall, "Draft Background Document on Wildlife Resources," Annex, pp. 9-10.
162. *Endangered Species Technical Bulletin* 9(2):8 (1984).
163. Philip Shabecoff, "Endangered Species Act Marks a Decade of Gains," *New York Times*, Dec. 28, 1983.
164. Clark E. Pell, " 'Return a Gift to Wildlife' Program—A Successful First Year," *The Conservationist*, Jan.-Feb., 1984, p. 5.
165. Peter E. Nye, "Still Soaring—DEC's Eagle Program," *The Conservationist*, Nov.-Dec., 1983, 38(3), p. 23.
166. "Forest Service Puts Up a Wall to Save a Rare Alpine Flower," *New York Times*, Sept. 22, 1983.
167. *Endangered Species Technical Bulletin* 8(11):5.
168. "As the Old Growth Goes, So Goes the Spotted Owl," *Wild Oregon*, Winter 1983, 10(4), pp. 10-11.
169. 16 U.S.C.A. §§3101-3233 (Supp. 1984).
170. National Association of State Park Directors, *Annual Information Exchange*, January 1983, in U.S. Department of the Interior, National Park Service, *Federal Recreation Fee Report, 1982* (Washington, D.C.: U.S. Department of Interior, 1983), p. 43.
171. *Ibid.* Both the variety of state parks and the intensity of visitation are documented in the *Information Exchange*.
172. Based on Council on Environmental Quality, *Environmental Quality: 1979* (Washington, D.C.: U.S. Government Printing Office, 1979), Table A-17, p. 699.
173. Information provided by National Park Service, Land Resources Division. Vir-

tually all the acquired acres had been authorized for inclusion earlier. Essentially no new acres have been authorized for inclusion in the National Park System since 1980.

174. Based on a Conservation Foundation analysis of Park Service data.

175. For a good recent account of urban wildlife, see Bayard Webster, "Wildlife Returns to Parts of Urban America," *New York Times*, Dec. 27, 1983.

176. Information provided by U.S. Department of Agriculture, Economic Research Service.

177. U.S. Department of the Interior, Fish and Wildlife Service, "Annual Report of Lands Under Control of the U.S. Fish and Wildlife Service as of September 30, 1983" (Washington, D.C.: U.S. Department of the Interior, 1983), p. 3; also see previous annual issues.

178. Council on Environmental Quality, *Environmental Quality: 1979*, pp. 417-418. In 1978, the Fish and Wildlife Service categorized 90 percent of its refuges, comprising over 25 percent of refuge acreage, as being for migratory birds. The service no longer classifies its refuges by purpose.

179. 16 U.S.C.A. §§1131-1136 (Supp. 1984).

180. *Ibid.*, §1131(c) (Supp. 1984).

181. "Wilderness Fact Sheet, Jan. 17, 1983," provided by U.S. Forest Service, Recreation staff; 16 U.S.C.A. §1132 (Supp. 1984).

182. J. Harrison, K. Miller and J.A. McNeely, "The World Coverage of Protected Areas: Development Goals and Environmental Needs," *Ambio* 11(5):238-245 (1982), pp. 241-243; International Union for the Conservation of Nature and Natural Resources, *1982 United Nations List of National Parks and Protected Areas* (Gland, Switzerland: IUCN, 1982).

183. Mason Walsh, Jr. and William D. Blair, Jr., "Year in Review: Private Action in the Public Interest" (The Nature Conservancy Annual Report 1982) *The Nature Conservancy News*, 33(2):9 (1983).

184. The Trust for Public Land, *Annual Report 1983* (San Francisco: The Trust for Public Land, 1983).

185. Information provided by the National Audubon Society, March 1984.

186. Mason Walsh, Jr. and William D. Blair, Jr., "Year in Review," p. 4; Frank D. Boren and William D. Blair, Jr., "Year in Review: A National Perspective for the '80's" (The Nature Conservancy Annual Report 1980), *The Nature Conservancy News*, 31(3):7 (1981); Mason Walsh, Jr., and William D. Blair, Jr., "Year in Review: The Nature Conservancy at Thirty" (The Nature Conservancy Annual Report 1981) *The Nature Conservancy News*, 32(2):4 (1982).

187. Nye, "Still Soaring."

188. Mason Walsh, Jr., and William D. Blair, Jr., "Year in Review."

189. Russell A. Cohen, "The National Natural Landmark Program: A Natural Areas Protection Technique for the 1980s and Beyond," 3 *U.C.L.A. J. Envtl. L. and Pol.* 126 (1982).

190. U.S. Department of the Interior, Fish and Wildlife Service, *Fish and Wildlife Service Resource Problems* (Washington, D.C.: U.S. Fish and Wildlife Service, July 1983), p. 5. The seven problems are: soil erosion/sediments, wildlife disturbance, flow decrease, wildfires, land development, flow increase/floods, fertilizer runoff. U.S. Department of the Interior, National Park Service, *State of the Parks: 1980* (Washington, D.C.: National Park Service, May 1980), p. viii.

191. Examples of these measures include the federal Coastal Zone Management Act (16 U.S.C.A. §1451-1464 (1980)), under which 28 states and territories have developed approved programs, and §404 of the Clean Water Act (33 U.S.C.A. §1344 (1980)) to regulate discharges of dredged and fill material in wetlands. In addition, most coastal states have programs designed to protect coastal wetlands, while a few states regulate inland wetlands. See, Jon A. Kusler, *Our National Wetland Heritage* (Washington, D.C.: Environmental Law Institute, 1983).

192. Among many sources, see Eugene P. Odum, "Foreword," in J.R. Clark and J. Benforado, eds., *Wetlands of Bottomland Hardwood Forests* (Amsterdam: Elsevier Scientific, 1981), p. xii.

193. W.E. Frayer, T.J. Monahan, D.C. Bowden, F.A. Graybill, *Status and Trends of Wetlands and Deepwater Habitats in the Conterminous United States, 1950's to 1970's* (Fort Collins: Colorado State University, April, 1983), pp. 26-27.

194. U.S. Department of Agriculture, Forest Service, *An Assessment of the Forest and Range Land Situation in the United States* (Washington, D.C.: U.S. Department of Agriculture, 1980), p. 218.

195. J.R. Clark and J. Benforado, *Wetlands of Bottomland Hardwood Forests*, p. 1; Mark M. Brinson, Bryan L. Swift, Reuben C. Plantico, and John S. Barclay, *Riparian Ecosystems: Their Ecology and Status* (Kearneysville, W.Va.: U.S. Fish and Wildlife Service, Sept. 1981), p. 10.

196. Brinson et al., *Riparian Ecosystems*, p. 9.

197. Council on Environmental Quality, *Environmental Quality: 1982*, table A-16, p. 258.

198. Frayer et al., *Status and Trends of Wetlands and Deepwater Habitats*, pp. 20, 21, 26, 29.

199. *Ibid.*, pp. 20-23.

200. Council on Environmental Quality, *Environmental Quality: 1979*, p. 453; U.S. Environmental Protection Agency, *Chesapeake Bay: A Framework for Action* (Annapolis: U.S. Environmental Protection Agency, Region 3, Sept. 1983), pp. 23, 25; U.S. Department of Commerce, National Oceanic and Atmospheric Administration, National Marine Fisheries Service, *Fisheries of the United States, 1982* (Current Fisheries Statistics No. 8300), April 1983, p. 3.

201. Council on Environmental Quality, *Environmental Quality: 1979*, p. 457.

202. Frayer et al., *Status and Trends of Wetlands and Deepwater Habitats*, pp. 23-25.

203. Council on Environmental Quality, *Environmental Quality: 1979*, pp. 468-469.

204. U.S. Department of Commerce, National Oceanic and Atmospheric Administration, National Ocean Service, Office of Oceanography and Marine Services, Ocean Assessments Division, Strategic Assessment Branch, *Strategic Assessment of the Nation's Estuaries: Synthesis and Application of Existing Data Bases* (Washington, D.C.: National Oceanic and Atmospheric Administration, June 1983), p. 50.

205. U.S. Environmental Protection Agency, *Chesapeake Bay: A Framework for Action*, pp. xvi, 23, 25.

206. U.S. Department of the Interior, Coastal Barriers Task Force, *Final Environmental Impact Statement: Undeveloped Coastal Barriers* (Washington, D.C.: U.S. Department of Interior, May 1983), pp. II-10-11, A4, A50-A53, A67-A74.

207. *Ibid.*, pp. IV-7-14, A36-38.

208. Wesley Marx, *Acts of God, Acts of Man* (New York: Coward, McCann and Geoghegan, 1977), p. 86 and photo section.

209. Coastal Barriers Task Force, *Final Environmental Impact Statement*, pp. IV-14, A-92.

210. 16 U.S.C.A. §§3501-3510 (Supp. 1984).

211. Coastal Barriers Task Force, *Final Environmental Impact Statement*, p. F-14.

212. Edward Bullard, "Continental Shelves: Their Nature and History," *Oceanus* 19(1):3-7 (1975); Brian J. Skinner, *Earth Resources*, 2d ed. (Englewood Cliffs, N.J.: Prentice-Hall, 1976), p. 16; and Robert S. Dietz, "The Underwater Landscape," in C.P. Idyll, ed., *Exploring the Ocean World* (New York: Crowell, 1969), p. 31.

213. National Marine Fisheries Service, *Fisheries of the United States, 1982*, pp. 1-3.

214. *Ibid.*, p. 6.

215. *Ibid.*, pp. 75-6.

216. 16 U.S.C.A. §§1801-1882 (Supp. 1984).

217. National Marine Fisheries Service, *Fisheries of the United States*, p. 8.

218. Of course, only a simplified version of fisheries economics is presented here. The interested reader might consult any of a number of texts, including David H. Cushing, *Fisheries Resources of the Sea and their Management* (New York: Oxford University Press, 1975).

219. New England Fishery Management Council, *Final EIS and Regulatory Impact Review for the American Lobster* (Homarus americanus) *Fishery Management Plan* (Saugus, Mass.: New England Fishery Management Council, March, 1983), pp. iii, 4, 26-33, 96. National Marine Fisheries Service, *Fisheries of the United States, 1982*, p. ix. (The small increase in catch per trap observed in the late 1970s may result from two factors: new technologies permitting a substantial trap fishery in the previously underexploited waters more than three miles offshore, and changes in water temperature favoring lobster reproduction. Fishery models tend to assume that all factors, except fishing, which affect the stock's population dynamics are exogenously determined and constant. This is of course untrue. Natural fluctuations in currents, water temperature, water chemistry, prey or predator populations, etc. may have dramatic effects on particular species. Human activities ranging from polluting coastal waters, to altering spawning habitat for estuary dependent or anadromous species, to changing fishery regulations on fish which eat or are eaten by the species in question, may also have serious consequences.)

220. National Marine Fisheries Service, *Fisheries of the United States*, p. 60.

221. Information provided by National Marine Fisheries Service, Juneau, Alaska.

222. *Ibid.*

223. *Clemon W. Fay, Richard J. Neves, and Garland B. Pardue, Alewife/Blueback Herring* "Species Profiles" series (FWS/OBS-82/11.9) (Washington, D.C.: U.S. Department of the Interior, Fish and Wildlife Service, Oct., 1983), pp. 12-13.

224. S. Gordon Rogers and Michael J. Van Den Ayle, *Atlantic Menhaden* "Species Profiles" series, FWS/OBS-82/11.11 (Washington, D.C.: U.S. Department of the Interior, Fish and Wildlife Service, Oct., 1983), p. 9.

225. U.S. Congress. Senate. Committee on Commerce and National Ocean Policy Study, *A Legislative History of the Fishery Conservation and Management Act,*

94th Congress (Washington, D.C.: U.S. Government Printing Office, Oct. 1976), pp. 360, 633.

226. National Marine Fisheries Service, *Fisheries of the United States*, p. 1.

227. Information provided by National Marine Fisheries Service, May 1984.

228. National Marine Fisheries Service, *Fisheries of the United States*, p. 62.

229. Information provided by National Marine Fisheries Service, May 1984.

230. Council on Environmental Quality, *Environmental Quality: 1982*, p. 304; National Marine Fisheries Service, *Fisheries of the United States*, p. 25.

231. P. R. Ehrlich, A. H. Ehrlich, and J. P. Holdren, *Ecoscience*, 3rd ed. (San Francisco: W. H. Freeman, 1977), p. 354.

232. Gwen Struik, "Commercial Fishing in New Zealand: An Industry Bent on Extinction," *The Ecologist* 13(6):213-221 (1983), p. 214.

233. John D. Ardill, "Fisheries in the Southwest Indian Ocean," *Ambio* 12(6):341-344 (1983), p. 343.

Energy

234. U.S. Department of Energy, Energy Information Administration, *1982 Annual Energy Review* (Washington, D.C.: U.S. Government Printing Office, April 1983), p.3.

235. *Ibid.*, p. 221.

236. *Ibid.*, p. 7.

237. *Oliphant Washington Service*, May 3, 1984, p. ES-6.

238. U.S. Department of Energy, Energy Information Administration, *Monthly Energy Review*, Jan. 1984. (Washington, D.C.: U.S. Government Printing Office, April 1984), p.71.

239. *Monthly Energy Review*, Dec. 1983, pp. 25, 27.

240. *Ibid.*, p. 26.

241. U.S. Department of Energy, Energy Information Administration, *State Energy Data Report 1960-1981* (Washington, D.C.: U.S. Government Printing Office, June 1983), p. 15.

242. U.S. Department of Energy, *1982 Annual Energy Review*, p.195.

243. U.S. Department of Energy, Energy Information Administration, *Housing Characteristics, 1981* (Washington, D.C.: U.S. Government Printing Office, Aug. 1983), p. 2.

244. *Monthly Energy Review*, Dec. 1983, p.9.

245. Information provided by U.S. Commerce Department, Bureau of the Census, Population Division, May 24, 1984.

246. *Ibid.*

247. *Monthly Energy Review*, Dec. 1983, p.29.

248. *Monthly Energy Review*, Jan. 1984, p.14.

249. *Ibid.*

250. U.S. Department of Energy, *1982 Annual Energy Review*, pp. 9, 191, 197.

251. Eric Hirst et al., "Recent Changes in U.S. Energy Consumption: What Happened and Why?," *Annual Review of Energy 1983* (8):194.

252. J. Erich Evered, EIA Administrator, in *Energy Conservation Digest*, Dec. 19, 1983, p. 9.

253. Bernard J. Frieden and Kermit Baker, "The Record of Home Energy Conser-

vation: Saving Bucks, not BTU's,"*Technology Review* 86:24 (1983).
254. Office of Technology Assessment, *Industrial Energy Use* (Washington, D.C.: U.S. Government Printing Office, June 1983), p. 90; *International Economic Consequences of High-Priced Energy*, a statement by the Research and Policy Committee of the Committee for Economic Development (New York: Committee for Economic Development, Sept. 1975), p. 74.
255. Steven J. Marcus, "Conservation in Industry is Spreading,"*New York Times*, Sept. 30, 1983, quoting Dr. Philip S. Schmidt, Univ. of Texas.
256. U.S. Department of Energy, Energy Information Administration, *1981 International Energy Annual* (Washington, D.C.: U.S. Government Printing Office, Sept. 1982.)
257. U.S. Department of Energy, Energy Information Administration, *1982 Annual Energy Review*, p. 141; and Harry Perry, "Coal in the United States: A Status Report,"*Science* 222(4622):378 (1983).
258. *Monthly Energy Review*, Dec. 1983, pp. 3-4.
259. *Monthly Energy Review*, Dec. 1983, p.3.
260. *Ibid.*, p. 19.
261. *Ibid.*, p. 4.
262. *Monthly Energy Review*, Dec. 1983, pp. 6-9.
263. Harry Perry, "Coal in the United States: A Status Report," pp. 377-384.
264. U.S. Department of Energy, Energy Information Administration, *1983 Annual Outlook for U.S. Coal* (Washington, D.C.: U.S. Government Printing Office, Nov. 1983), p. vii.
265. U.S. Department of Energy, Energy Information Administration, *1982 Annual Energy Review*, pp. 7, 57; and *Monthly Energy Review*, Dec. 1983, pp. 11, 42.
266. *Ibid.*, p. 57.
267. U.S. Department of Energy, U.S. Department of Agriculture, "A Biomass Energy Production and Use Plan for the United States, 1983-90." Agriculture Economic Report No. 505 (Washington, D.C.: U.S. Government Printing Office, Nov. 1983), p.1.
268. Adela M. Bolet et al., *Ethanol: National Security Implications*, Georgetown University, Center for Strategic and International Studies, Significant Issues Series 5(7):5 (1983); American Petroleum Institute, *Two Energy Futures: A National Choice for the 80s* (Washington, D.C.: American Petroleum Institute, Oct. 1982), p.107.)
269. Bolet, *Ethanol: National Security Implications*, p. 33.
270. *Ibid.*
271. American Petroleum Institute, *Two Energy Futures*, p. 108.
272. U.S. Department of Energy, Energy Information Administration, *Housing Characteristics, 1981* (Washington, D.C.: U.S. Government Printing Office, Aug. 1983), p.14.
273. American Petroleum Institute, *Two Energy Futures*, p. 110.
274. *Ibid.*
275. U.S. Department of Energy, *1982 Annual Energy Review*, p. 183.
276. Information provided by Renewable Energy Institute, May 1984.
277. U.S. Department of Energy, *1982 Annual Energy Review*, p. 181.

278. American Petroleum Institute, *Two Energy Futures*, p. 108.
279. *Ibid.*
280. U.S. Department of Energy, *1982 Annual Energy Review*, p. 181; *Monthly Energy Review*, Dec. 1983, p. 9.
281. Electric Power Research Institute, *Electricity Today's Technologies, Tomorrow's Alternatives*, rev. ed. (Los Angeles: William Kaufmann, Inc., 1982), p. 36.
282. American Petroleum Institute, *Two Energy Futures*.
283. Daniel Deudney and Christopher Flavin, *Renewable Energy The Power to Choose* (New York: W.W. Norton & Co., 1983), p.112.
284. U.S. Department of Energy, Energy Information Administration *Estimates of U.S. Wood Energy Consumption from 1949 to 1981* (Washington, D.C.: U.S. Government Printing Office, Aug. 1982).
285. U.S. Department of Energy, *Housing Characteristics*, p.14.
286. U.S. Department of Energy, Energy Information Administration, *Residential Energy Consumption Survey: Consumption and Expenditures: April 1980 through March 1981. Part 1: National Data* (Washington, D.C.: U.S. Government Printing Office, Sept. 1982), p.17.
287. Deudney and Flavin, *Renewable Energy; The Power to Choose*, p.115.
288. Frieden and Baker, "The Record of Home Energy Conservation," p.27.
289. Frederic Golden, "Heat Over Wood Burning," *Time*, Jan. 16, 1984, p. 67.
290. Lester R. Brown et al., *State of the World 1984: Worldwatch Institute Report on Progress Toward a Sustainable Society* (New York: W.W. Norton and Co., 1984), p. 4.
291. *Monthly Energy Review*, Dec. 1983, p. 96.
292. *Ibid.*, p. 89.
293. *Ibid.*, p. 98.
294. *Ibid.*, p. 97.
295. Massachusetts Institute of Technology, Center for Energy Policy Research, unpublished briefing booklet for "The Future of Natural Gas" Conference, March 14-15, 1983, p. 6a.
296. U.S. Department of Energy, *1982 Annual Energy Review*, Dec. 1983, p. 95.
297. *Ibid.*, pp. 195, 199.
298. Frieden and Baker, "The Record of Home Energy Conservation," p. 26.
299. *Monthly Energy Review*, Sept. 1983, p. x, Table E-8.
300. U.S. Department of Energy, Energy Information Administration, *International Energy Prices 1978-1982.* (Washington, D.C.: U.S. Government Printing Office, Jan. 1984), p. 39.
301. *Ibid.*, pp. 40-43.
302. *Ibid.*, p. 49.
303. *Ibid.*, p. 51.
304. *Ibid.*, pp. 54-57.
305. *Ibid.*, p. 56.
306. *Ibid.*, pp. 59, 61.
307. Keizai Koho Center, Japan Institute for Social and Economic Affairs, "Japan 1983: An International Comparison" (Tokyo: Keizai Koho Center, Sept. 1983), p. 52.
308. U.S. Department of Energy, *1982 Annual Energy Review*, p. 83.

Recreation

309. U.S. Department of the Interior, National Park Service, ''The 1982-1983 Nationwide Survey: Summary of Selected Findings'' (Washington, D.C.: National Park Service, April 1984), Table 2. Outdoor recreation was defined broadly in the survey, and includes everything from playing or watching outdoor sports to hunting to driving for pleasure.

310. U.S. Department of the Interior, Fish and Wildlife Service, *1980 National Survey of Fishing, Hunting, and Wildlife-Associated Recreation* (Washington, D.C.: U.S. Government Printing Office, 1982), p. 5. Wildlife-associated recreation includes fishing, hunting, and non-consumptive activity such as watching, feeding or photographing wildlife. *Ibid.*, p. 2.

311. U.S. Department of the Interior, Heritage Conservation and Recreation Service, *The Third Nationwide Outdoor Recreation Plan: The Executive Report* (Washington, D.C.: U.S. Government Printing Office, 1979), p. 1.

312. Outdoor Recreation Policy Review Group, *Outdoor Recreation for America—1983* (Washington, D.C.: Resources for the Future, Inc., 1983), p. 3.

313. *Ibid.*, p. 5.

314. Council on Environmental Quality, *Environmental Quality: 1979* (Washington, D.C.: U.S. Government Printing Office, 1979), pp. 421-422.

315. See D. Cole, ''Controlling the Spread of Campsites at Popular Wilderness Destinations,'' *Journal of Soil and Water Conservation* 37(5):291 (1982); R. Washburne and D. Cole, ''Problems and Practices in Wilderness Management: A Survey of Managers,'' research paper INT-304 (Ogden, Ut.: U.S. Department of Agriculture, Forest Service, Intermountain Forest and Range Experiment Station, 1983), pp. 4-6, 14.

316. 16 U.S.C.A. §528 (1974), 43 U.S.C.A. §1701(a)(7) (Supp. 1984).

317. 16 U.S.C.A. §1 (1974).

318. National Park Service, ''1982-1983 Survey,'' Table 5.

319. *Ibid.*

320. Outdoor Recreation Policy Review Group, *Outdoor Recreation for America*, pp. 9-13.

321. H. Cordell and J. Hendee, *Renewable Resources Recreation in the United States: Supply, Demand, and Critical Policy Issues* (Washington, D.C.: American Forestry Association, 1982), pp. 48-55.

322. National Park Service, ''1982-1983 Survey,'' Table 2.

323. Outdoor Recreation Resources Review Commission (ORRRC), ''National Recreation Survey,'' in *Outdoor Recreation Resources Review Commission Study Reports* (Washington, D.C.: U.S. Government Printing Office, 1962), study report 19, p. 124; National Park Service, ''1982-1983 Survey,'' Table 2.

324. Outdoor Recreation Resources Review Commission, ''National Recreation Survey,'' p. 124.

325. National Park Service, ''1982-1983 Survey,'' Table 2.

326. Information provided by U.S. Forest Service, April, 1984.

327. Outdoor Recreation Resources Review Commission, ''National Recreation Survey,'' p. 248; National Park Service, ''1982-1983 Survey,'' Table 2.

328. Information provided by National Ski Areas Association, April, 1984.

329. Roderick Nash has documented the dramatic shift in American attitudes toward

wilderness, from viewing it as something to be feared and conquered to something to be appreciated and preserved. Roderick Nash, *Wilderness and the American Mind*, 3rd ed. (New Haven: Yale University Press, 1982).

330. See, e.g., National Park Service, "Public Use of the National Park System, Calendar Year Report 1973" (Washington, D.C.: National Park Service, 1974), p. 21.

331. Backcountry areas are those that may be reached only on foot, horseback, or by boat. National Park Service, "National Park Statistical Abstract 1983" (Denver: National Park Service, 1984), pp. 35-36.

332. Outdoor Recreation Resources Review Commission, "National Recreation Survey," p. 120; National Park Service, "1982-1983 Survey," Table 2.

333. *Ibid.*

334. See United States Department of Agriculture, Forest Service, *Report of the Forest Service Fiscal Year 1983* (Washington, D.C.: U.S. Forest Service, 1984), p. 117.

335. See, e.g., National Park Service, "Statistical Abstract 1983," p. 38.

336. U.S. Department of Agriculture, Forest Service, *Report of the Forest Service Fiscal Year 1977* (Washington, D.C.: Forest Service, 1978), p. 69; Forest Service, *1983 Report*, p. 124.

337. Forest Service, *1983 Report*, p. 124.

338. Fish and Wildlife Service, *1980 Survey*, p. 11.

339. *Ibid.*, pp. 10-11.

340. *Ibid.*, p. 11.

341. *Ibid.*, p. 20.

342. *Ibid.*, pp. 21-22.

343. U.S. Department of Agriculture, Forest Service, *An Assessment of the Forest and Range Land Situation in the United States* (Washington, D.C., Forest Service, 1980), pp. 105-106.

344. *Ibid.*, p. 114.

345. *Ibid.*

346. National Campground Owners Association, "Private Sector Campground Data," in U.S. Department of the Interior, National Park Service, *Federal Recreation Fee Report 1982* (Washington, D.C.: National Park Service, 1983), p. 64.

347. Fish and Wildlife Service, *1980 Survey*, p. 26.

348. Aggregate statistics on local park visitation are essentially nonexistent, but a moment's reflection should affirm their substantial contribution to outdoor recreation.

349. For most states, visitation figures cover the period from July 1, 1981, to June 30, 1982. National Association of State Park Directors, "Annual Information Exchange 1983," in U.S. Department of the Interior, National Park Service, *Federal Recreation Fee Report 1982* (Washington, D.C.: National Park Service, 1983), p. 43.

350. Information provided by the National Park Service, Recreation and Resources Assistance Division, April, 1984.

351. Forest Service, *An Assessment of the Forest and Range Land Situation*, p. 114.

352. *Ibid.*

353. Among the three federal agencies, the Park Service has the most reliable

statistics, as well as the longest reporting period. However, it keeps fewer statistics than the Forest Service. The Corps also keeps fairly reliable statistics about visitation to developed portions of lands under its jurisdiction, but does little in the way of aggregating his data. Its data on dispersed visitation is less reliable. Finally, the Forest Service also keeps fairly detailed statisitics at the service-wide level, but these are probably less accurate than Park Service figures or the Corps' figures for its developed areas, since two-thirds of the recreation on Forest Service land is dispersed.

354. Forest Service, *1983 Report*, p. 29.
355. *Ibid.*
356. *Ibid.*, p. 119.
357. *Ibid.*
358. Forest Service, *1983 Report*, p. 13.
359. U.S. Department of Agriculture, Forest Service, *Report of the Forest Service Fiscal Year 1982* (Washington, D.C.: U.S. Forest Service, 1983), p. 17.
360. Department of the Army, Office of the Chief of Engineers, *78-79 Recreation Statistics* (Washington, D.C.: U.S. Government Printing Office, 1981), p. 12.
361. Information provided by U.S. Army Corps of Engineers, Natural Resources Management Branch, April, 1984.
362. *Ibid.*
363. National Park Service, "Public Use of the National Parks 1971-1980: A Statistical Report" (Denver: National Park Service Statistical Office); National Park Service, "Statistical Abstract 1983," p. 2. The Park Service defines a visit as "the entry of any person, except Service personnel, onto lands or waters administered by the National Park Service." 'Statistical Abstract 1983," p. 38. Visits may be recreational (i.e., for recreation purposes) or non-recreational. Non-recreational visits include persons going to and from inholdings, through traffic, tradespeople with business in the park, and non-Service government personnel with business in the park. Entries by Service personnel, their families, and by concessioner-employees are not reported as visits. *Ibid.*, p. 37.
364. National Park Service, "Statistical Abstract 1983," p. 2. Prior to 1971, the Park Service did not distinguish between recreational and non-recreation visits. The 1971 change significantly inflated visitation statistics system-wide, and made a comparison of pre- and post-1971 data difficult. National Park Service, "Public Use of the National Park System Calendar Year Report 1975" (Washington, D.C.: U.S. Government Printing Office, 1975), p. 18.
365. *Ibid.*, p. 17.
366. Information provided by U.S. Department of the Interior, National Park Service, Natchez Trace Parkway Unit, October, 1983.
367. National Park Service, "Statistical Abstract 1983," pp. 6, 13.
368. *Ibid.*, p. 7.
369. A. Galipeau, "Changes in National Park Service Visitation Volume 1971-1981" (Denver: National Park Service, undated document), p. 1.
370. The number of areas under the Corps' jurisdiction rose by more than a third between 1977 and 1983, from roughly 3,100 to 4,200. Information provided by Army Corps of Engineers, Natural Resources Management Branch, April, 1984.
371. National Park Service, "1982-1983 Survey," Table 2.

372. Department of the Interior, National Park Service, "National Park Service Releases Preliminary Findings of 1982-83 Nationwide Recreation Survey" (news release, April 19, 1984).
373. National Park Service, "1982-1983 Survey," Table 2.
374. *Ibid.*
375. Fish and Wildlife Service, *1980 Survey*, p. 23.
376. *Ibid.*, p. 13.
377. National Park Service, "1982-1983 Survey," Table 4.
378. U.S. Department of the Interior, Heritage Conservation and Recreation Service, *The Third Nationwide Outdoor Recreation Plan* (Washington, D.C.: U.S. Government Printing Office, 1979), Appendix I (Survey Summary), pp. 17, 33.
379. On the whole, nonparticipants and participants who didn't have an activity they "particularly enjoyed" may well have been deterred more frequently, or by different factors, than avid participants. In the 1977 survey, *all* respondents were asked what constraints kept them from visiting parks and recreation areas. However, the population of 1977 survey respondents is likely skewed by "avidity bias," because the response rate to the survey was only 54 percent, and it is probable that nonparticipants refused to be interviewed more frequently than participants. National Park Service, "1982-1983 Survey," p. 7; Heritage Conservation and Recreation Service, *Third Nationwide Outdoor Recreation Plan*, pp. 6, 17.

Figure References

Water

3.1 U.S. Water Resources Council, *The Nation's Water Resources 1975-2000* (Washington, D.C.: U.S. Government Printing Office, 1978), Vol. I, Summary, p. 12; Wayne B. Solley, Edith B. Chase, and William B. Mann IV, USGS Circular 1001 (Washington, D.C.: U.S. Geological Survey, 1983), p. 47.
3.2 Wayne B. Solley, Edith B. Chase, and William B. Mann IV, *Estimated Use of Water in the United States in 1980*. USGS Survey Circular 1001 (Washington, D.C.: U.S. Geological Survey, 1983), p. 47.
3.3. *Ibid.*, p. 47.
3.4. *Ibid.*, pp. 8-27; and Council on Environmental Quality, *Environmental Statistics* (Springfield, Va.: National Technical Information Service, 1978), p. 214.
3.5 Wayne B. Solley, Edith B. Chase, and William B. Mann IV, *Estimated Use of Water in the United States in 1980*; U.S. Water Resources Council, *Second National Water Assessment, The Nation's Water Resources: 1975-2000* (Washington, D.C.: U.S. Government Printing Office, Dec. 1978), Vol 2, Part IV, p. 19; U.S. Environmental Protection Agency, Office of Drinking Water, *Planning Workshop to Develop Recommendations for a Groundwater Protection Strategy, Appendices* (Washington, D.C.: U.S. Environmental Protection Agency, June 1980), Table 1, 2, pp. II 3-4.
3.6 U.S. Department of the Interior, Geological Survey, *National Water Summary 1983*, Water Supply Paper 2250 (Washington, D.C.: U.S. Government Printing Office, 1984), p. 31.

3.7 Wayne B. Solley, Edith B. Chase, and William B. Mann IV, *Estimated Use of Water in the United States in 1980*, p. 33.

3.8 U.S. Geological Survey, *National Water Summary 1983*, p. 27.

Land Use

3.9 U.S. Department of the Interior, Bureau of Land Management, *Public Land Statistics 1982* (Washington, D.C.: U.S. Government Printing Office, 1983), p. 9.

3.10 Council on Environmental Quality, *Environmental Statistics* (Springfield, Va.: National Technical Information Service, 1979), Table 1-12, p. 29; (1978): H. Thomas Frey, "Major Uses of Land in the United States: 1978" (Washington, D.C.: U.S. Department of Agriculture, Economic Research Service, 1981), Table 2, p. 3. 'Specialized uses'' includes urban land for all years.

3.11 H. Thomas Frey, "Major Uses of Land in the United States: 1978" (Washington, D.C.: U.S. Department of Agriculture, Economic Research Service, 1982), Appendix, Table 1, pp. 17-18.

3.12 James Horsfield and Norman Landgren, "Cropland Trends Across the Nation" (Washington, D.C.: U.S. Department of Agriculture, Economic Research Service, 1982), Figure 1, p. 17. Original map showed one dot equaling a 10,000 acre increase or decrease, in counties with net increases or decreases in cropland acreage; for figure 3.12, envelopes were drawn around concentrations of dots (at least 30,000 acre change clustered on the original map). Because areas indicated do not correspond to county lines, they should be considered approximate.

Cropland, Forestland, and Rangeland

3.13 U.S. Department of Agriculture, *Agricultural Statistics 1982* (Washington, D.C.: U.S. Government Printing Office, 1982), Table 584, p. 407; U.S. Department of Agriculture, *Agricultural Statistics 1983*, Table 574, p. 401.

Up to 1980, the indexes are from *Agricultural Statistics 1982*. 1981 and 1982 indexes are from *Agricultural Statistics 1983* and are reindexed to 1967.

3.14 U.S. Department of Agriculture, *Agricultural Statistics 1983*, p. 381.

3.15 U.S. Department of Agriculture, *Economic Indicators of the Farm Sector, Production and Efficiency Statistics, 1982* (Washington, D.C.: U.S. Government Printing Office, 1984), p. 29 (fertilizer), p. 35 (labor), p. 20 (land), and p. 33 (machinery, measured by tractor horsepower). Irrigation: see U.S. Geological Survey, *Estimated Use of Water in the United States in 1975*, USGS Circular 765 (Washington, D.C.: U.S. Government Printing Office, 1977), p. 38 and previous quinquennial surveys; 1980 estimated at 83 billion gallons per day, a 3.7 percent increase between 1975 and 1980; see also U.S. Water Resources Council, *Second National Assessment*. Pesticides: U.S. Department of Agriculture, *Quantities of Pesticides Used by Farmers in 1964*, Agricultural Economic Report No. 131, p. 9; U.S. Department of Agriculture, *Farmers' Use of Pesticides in 1971… Quantities*, Agricultural Economic Report No. 252, pp. 6-10, including data for 1966; U.S. Department of Agriculture, *Farmers' Use of Pesticides in 1976*, Agricultural Economic Report No. 418, pp. l9, 15;

U.S. Department of Agriculture, *Inputs: Outlook and Situation*, IOS-2, Oct. 1983, pp. 4-5 for 1982 data. 1967 use estimated by linear regression using 1966, 1971, and 1976 values. 1982 use, reported only for major field crops, increased by average ratio of all crop use to major field crop use as reported in 1971 and 1976.

When necessary, all figures were re-indexed to 1967.

3.16 U.S. Department of Agriculture, *Agricultural Statistics 1982*, Tables 587, 586, 591, pp. 408-410; *Agricultural Statistics 1983*, Tables 581, 577, 576, pp. 402-404. When necessary, all figures were re-indexed to 1967.

3.17 U.S. Department of Agriculture, *Agricultural Statistics 1982 and 1983*, p. 1 (wheat), p. 15 (rye), p. 30 (corn), p. 38 (oats), p. 43 (barley), p. 129 (soybeans).

3.18 U.S. Department of Agriculture, Soil Conservation Service, "National Resources Inventory 1982," preliminary (Washington, D.C.: U.S. Government Printing Office, April 1984), Table 9a.

3.19 U.S. Department of Agriculture, Forest Service, *U.S. Timber Production, Trade, Consumption, and Price Statistics*, Misc. Pub. No. 1424 (Washington, D.C.: Forest Service, July 1983), p. 10.

3.20 Area burned by wildfire: U.S. Department of Commerce, Bureau of the Census *Historical Statistics of the U.S. Colonial Times to 1970* (Washington, D.C.: U.S. Government Printing Office, 1975), p. 537; U.S. Department of Agriculture, Forest Service, *1981 Wildlife Statistics* (Washington, D.C.: Forest Service, Feb. 1984), and previous annual issues; Area defoliated by spruce budworm: Council on Environmental Quality, *Environmental Quality: 1982* (Washington, D.C.: U.S. Government Printing Office, Dec. 1980), Table A-8, p. 250; U.S. Department of Agriculture, *Forest Insect and Disease Conditions in the United States, 1982* (Washington, D.C.: U.S. Government Printing Office, April 1983), Tables 2 and 3, p. 41, and previous annual issues; Area defoliated by gypsy moth: same as spruce budworm, except Table 1, p. 40 in 1982 *Conditions* report; Forest acres planted and seeded: U.S. Department of Agriculture, Forest Service, *The Outlook for Timber in the U.S.*, Forest Research Report 20 (1950-1970) (Washington, D.C.: U.S. Government Printing Office, 1974); and U.S. Department of Agriculture, Forest Service, *Forest Planting, Seeding, and Silvical Treatments in the U.S. 1980 Report*, Forest Service Report FS-368 (Washington, D.C.: U.S. Government Printing Office), and previous years to 1971; U.S. Department of Agriculture, Forest Service, *1982 U.S. Forest Planting Report* (Washington, D.C.: U.S. Government Printing Office, July 1983), (1981-82).

3.21 U.S. Department of Agriculture, Soil Conservation Service, "National Resources Inventory 1982," preliminary (Washington, D.C.: U.S. Government Printing Office, April 1984), Table 34a.

Wildlife, Wildland, and Critical Areas

3.22 Council on Environmental Quality, *Environmental Quality: 1982*, Table A-21, p. 262. 1982 data provided by U.S. Department of Agriculture, Forest Service, Wildlife and Fisheries staff.

3.23 Data provided ca. 1978 by states to U.S. Department of Agriculture, Forest Service. Summary of state data provided by U.S. Department of Agriculture, Forest Service, Rocky Mountain Forest and Range Experiment Station, April, 1984. States reporting populations much smaller (at least 2 orders of magnitude) than typical for a given species were excluded, namely: Nev., S.C. (black bear); Hawaii (mule deer); Ore., Colo. (white-tail deer); Hawaii (mourning dove); Neb., Nev., Pa., S.C., Tex. (common elk); Va. (ring-necked pheasant); Wash. (pronghorn antelope).

3.24 Council on Environmental Quality, *Environmental Quality: 1982*, Table A-25, p. 266, using data from the Breeding Bird Survey. Errors in addition were corrected.

3.25 Council on Environmental Quality, *Environmental Quality: 1982*, Table A-18, p. 260.

3.26 U.S. Department of the Interior, Fish and Wildlife Service, *Endangered Species Technical Bulletin* 9(2):8 (1984).

3.27 Number of species endangered and threatened: *Ibid*. Total number of species: Council on Environmental Quality, *Environmental Trends* (Washington, D.C.: U.S. Government Printing Office, 1981), p. 149.

3.28 State Parks: National Recreation and Parks Association, *State Park Statistics, 1970* (Washington, D.C.: National Recreation and Park Association, 1971), p. 9; U.S. Department of Commerce, Bureau of the Census, *Statistical Abstract of the United States: 1976* (Washington, D.C.: U.S. Government Printing Office, 1977), p. 216; National Recreation and Parks Association, *State Park Statistics, 1975* (Washington, D.C.: National Recreation and Parks Association, 1976), p. 28; National Association of State Park Directors, "Inventory," in U.S. Department of the Interior, *Federal Recreation Fee Report 1980* (Washington, D.C.: U.S. Department of the Interior, Heritage Conservation and Recreation Service, 1981), p. 72; National Association of State Park Directors, "1983 Annual Information Exchange," in U.S. Department of the Interior, *Federal Recreation Fee Report 1982* (Washington, D.C.: National Park Service, 1983), pp. 44-45.

For comparability, National Association of State Park Directors data was supplemented as follows. 1980: 1983 figure for Colorado added to total due to absence of 1980 data for Colorado. 1980, 1983: Acres under authority of Baxter State Park Authority (Maine) and Department of Environmental Conservation (New York—Adirondack and Catskill preserves) are not included in N.A.S.P.D. surveys. 1970 acreages for these agencies were added to 1980 and 1983 figures. Land reclassifications or reporting differences between N.A.S.P.D. and N.R.P.A. data may exaggerate the apparent jump in state park acreage between 1975 and 1980.

National Parks: U.S. Department of the Interior, *National Park Service, Index of the National Park System and Affiliated Areas as of January 1, 1975* (Washington, D.C.: National Park Service, 1975); "Updated Addenda of October 22, 1976" for the *Index, 1975*; information provided by U.S. Department of the Interior, National Park Service; analysis to account for acreage revisions drawn from a Conservation Foundation report on the National Park

System, forthcoming. Acres shown are authorized for inclusion in the National Park System; some 1.3 million of the acres within authorized National Park boundaries are owned by public agencies other than the National Park Service, and 3.2 million such acres are privately owned.

State Wildlife Areas: H. Thomas Frey, "Major Uses of Land in the United States: 1978" (Washington, D.C.: U.S. Department of Agriculture, Economic Research Service, 1982), Table II, p. 30; Council on Environmental Quality, *Environmental Statistics* (Springfield, Va.: National Technical Information Service, 1979), Table 2-12, p. 50; information provided by U.S. Department of Agriculture, Economic Research Service, January, 1984.

National Wildife Refuges: U.S. Department of the Interior, Division of Realty, "Annual Report of Lands Under Control of the U.S. Fish and Wildlife Service as of Sept. 30, 1983" (Washington, D.C.: U.S. Department of the Interior, 1983), p. 3, and previous annual issues.

National Wilderness Preservation System: Council on Environmental Quality, *Environmental Statistics* (Springfield, Va.: National Technical Information Service, 1979), Table 2-7, p. 44; U.S. Department of Agriculture, Forest Service, Recreation Management Staff, "Wilderness Fact Sheet," February 15, 1979, December 31, 1980, and January 17, 1983; unpublished data from Forest Service, National Park Service, U.S. Fish and Wildlife Service, and Bureau of Land Management.

3.29 J. Harrison, K. Miller and J.A. McNeely, "The World Coverage of Protected Areas: Development Goals and Environmental Needs," *Ambio* 11(5):242-243 (1982); International Union for the Conservation of Nature and Natural Resources, *1982 United Nations List of National Parks and Protected Areas* (Gland, Switzerland: IUCN, 1982).

3.30 U.S. Congress, Office of Technology Assessment, *Wetlands: Their Use and Regulation* (Washington, D.C.: U.S. Government Printing Office, March 1984), p. 92.

3.31 Council on Environmental Quality, *Environmental Quality: 1982*, Table A-16, p. 258; 16 U.S.C.A. §1274; information provided by U.S. Department of the Interior, National Park Service. The 9th Circuit Court has ruled that, pending appeal, the areas designated by Secretary Andrus in January 1981 will remain in the system. *County of Del Norte et al., v. United States of America et al.* D.C. Ct. 81-0567 (9th Cir. May 11, 1984).

3.32 U.S. Congress, Office of Technology Assessment, *Wetlands: Their Use and Regulation*, p. 93.

3.33 U.S. Department of the Interior, Coastal Barriers Task Force, *Final Environmental Impact Statement: Undeveloped Coastal Barriers* (Washington, D.C.: U.S. Department of the Interior, May 1983), pp. IV-14, F-14.

3.34 Council on Environmental Quality, *Environmental Quality: 1982*, Table A-27, p. 267 (through 1982); U.S. Department of Commerce, National Marine Fisheries Service, *Fisheries of the United States, 1982* (Current Fisheries Statistics 8300) (Washington, D.C.: National Oceanic and Atmospheric Administration, April 1983), pp. iv, 3.

3.35 New England Fishery Management Council, *Final Environmental Impact Statement and Regulatory Impact Review for the American Lobster* (Homarus americanus) *Fishery Management Plan* (Saugus, Mass.: New England Fishery Management Council, March 1983), p. 29; National Marine Fisheries Service, *Fisheries of the United States, 1982*, Current Fisheries Statistics No. 8300, April 1983, pp. ix, 61.

> Fishing effort is measured in "trap equivalents'—the traps set by inshore fishermen plus an estimate of the trap value of trawling efforts offshore. Offshore effort was negligible until the mid 1950s, peaking at about 25 percent to 30 percent of total effort in the early 1970s; it now accounts for less than 5 percent of total effort.

3.36 Council on Environmental Quality, *Environmental Quality: 1982*, Table A-75, p. 304; National Marine Fisheries Service, *Fisheries of the United States, 1982*, Current Fisheries Statistics No. 8300, p. 25.

Energy

3.37 U.S. Department of Energy, Energy Information Administration, *1982 Annual Energy Review* (Washington, D.C.: U.S. Government Printing Office, April 1983); U.S. Department of Energy, Energy Information Administration, *Monthly Energy Review*, Dec. 1983 (Washington, D.C.: U.S. Government Printing Office, March 1984), p. 11.

3.38 U.S. Department of Energy, *1982 Annual Energy Review*, , p. 9; *Monthly Energy Review*, Dec. 1983, pp. 26-29.

3.39 *Monthly Energy Review*, Dec. 1983, p. 21.

3.40 U.S. Department of Energy, Energy Information Administration, *Housing Characteristics, 1981* (Washington, D.C.: U.S. Government Printing Office, Aug. 1983), p. 2.

3.41 U.S. Department of Energy, *1982 Annual Energy Review*; *Monthly Energy Review*, Dec. 1983, p. 3.

3.42 *Monthly Energy Review*, Dec. 1983, pp. 36-37.

3.43 *Ibid.*, p. 183.

3.44 U.S. Department of Energy, Energy Information Administration, *Estimates of U.S. Wood Energy Consumption from 1949 to 1981* (Washington, D.C.: U.S. Government Printing Office, Aug. 1982, p. 95.

3.45 U.S. Department of Energy, *1982 Annual Energy Review*, p. 171; *Monthly Energy Review*, Dec. 1983.

3.46 U.S. Department of Energy, *Housing Characteristics*, 1981, p. 87.

3.47 U.S. Department of Energy, Energy Information Administration, *International Energy Prices 1978-1982* (Washington, D.C.: U.S. Government Printing Office, Jan. 1984), pp. 56-57.

3.48 Population data from Population Referecne Bureau, "1982 World Population Factsheet;" consumptive data from U.S. Department of Energy, *1982 Annual Energy Review*, p. 83.

Recreation

3.49 U.S. Department of the Interior, National Park Service, "The 1982-1983 Nationwide Recreation Survey: Summary of Selected Findings" (document dated April 1984 accompanying Department of the Interior press release of April 19, 1984), p. 7.

The survey was designed to reflect the non-institutionalized United States population 12 years old and older.

3.50 1960: Outdoor Recreation Resources Review Commission, "National Recreation Survey," in *Outdoor Recreation Resources Review Commission Study Reports*, study report 19 (Washington, D.C.: U.S. Government Printing Office, 1962), pp. 120, 198 and 248;

1982: National Park Service, "1982 National Recreation Survey Summary," p. 3.

3.51 National Park Service Data: National Park Service, "National Park Statistical Abstract 1983" (Denver: National Park Service Statistical Office, 1984), p. 2; National Park Service, "National Park Statistical Abstract 1979" (Denver: National Park Service Statistical Office, 1980), p. 2.

Corps of Engineers Data: Information provided by U.S. Army Corps of Engineers, Natural Resources Management Branch, April 1984.

U.S. Forest Service Data: U.S. Department of Agriculture, Forest Service, *Report of the Forest Service Fiscal Year 1982* (Washington, D.C.: Forest Service, 1983), p. 119; U.S. Department of Agriculture, Forest Service, *Report of the Forest Service Fiscal Year 1981* (Washington, D.C.: Forest Service, 1982), p. 102.

3.52 U.S. Department of the Interior, National Park Service, "National Park Statistical Abstract 1983" (Denver: National Park Service Statistical Office, 1984), p. 7.

3.53 1960: U.S. Department of the Interior, National Park Service, "Public Use of the National Parks; A Statistical Report 1954-1964" (National Park Service, Bureau of Statistics Analysis, February 1966).

1982: Information provided by National Park Service, Denver Statistical Office, September 1983.

Visits to the George Washington Memorial Parkway do not include automobile traffic on the parkway itself, but do include visits to areas administered as part of the parkway unit, such as Great Falls Park, Turkey Run Farm, and the Clara Barton House. Information provided by National Park Service, George Washington Memorial Parkway unit, November 1983.

CHAPTER 4: IDENTIFYING ISSUES

Text References

1. "Conference on Environmental Research and Management Priorities for the 1980s," *Ambio* 12(2):58 (1983); J. F. Coates Inc., *Clues to the Domestic Environmental Agenda for the Next Three Decades*, prepared for the U. S. Environmental Protection Agency, Office of Strategic and Scientific Studies (Washington, D.C.: J. F. Coates Inc., February 8, 1983); survey working papers for the Coates report; Ministere de l'Environnement et Ministere de l'Urbanisme et du Logement, "Consultation Prospective sur l'Environnement" (Paris: Ministere de l'Environnement, November 1982); University of Michigan, Program in Technology Assessment, "Survey of Emerging Environmental Issues" (Ann Arbor: University of Michigan, summer 1983); Congressional Clearinghouse for the Future, "Environment: The Future Agenda as seen by the Committees and Subcommittees of the United States House of Representatives" (Washington, D.C.: Congressional Clearinghouse for the Future, undated); and an unpublished Conservation Foundation survey of major environmental issues, 1983.
2. *Sierra Club* v. *Sigler*, 695 F. 2d 957, (5th Cir. 1983).
3. 48 *Fed. Reg.* 36486 (1983).
4. "Towards a New Kind of Economic Growth," *Ambio* 12(2):66 (1983).
5. "Conference on Environmental Research and Management Priorities for the 1980s," *Ambio* 12(2):59 (1983).
6. Arthur H. Westing, "The Environmental Aftermath of Warfare in Vietnam," 23 *Nat. Res. J.* 368 (1983).
7. Hugh Sidey, "Coming to Terms with Nukes," *Time*, December 5, 1983, p. 44.
8. Russell E. Train, "The 1983 Marshall Lecture of the Natural Resources Defense Council," Washington, D.C., September 29, 1983 (Washington, D.C.: Natural Resources Defense Council, 1983).
9. Testimony of Peter S. Thacher, to U.S. Congress, House, Committee on Foreign Affairs, Subcommittee on Western Hemisphere Affairs, February 23, 1984.
10. Information provided by Joseph F. Coates.
11. John Naisbitt, *Megatrends* (New York: Warner Books, 1982), pp. 4-5.
12. David J. Rose, "Community and Change: Thinking in New Ways about Large and Persistent Problems," *Technology Review* 83(4):54 (1981).

Six Surveys Identifying Major Environmental Issues

1. R. D. Munro,"Environmental Research and Management Priorities for the 1980s," *Ambio* 12(2):60 (1983).
2. Ministere de l'Environnement et Ministere de l'Urbanisme et due Logement, "Consultation Prospective sur l'Environnement" (Paris: Ministere de l'Environnement, November 1982), pp. 1-4.

47 Issues

1. J. F. Coates Inc., *Clues to the Domestic Environmental Agenda for the Next Three Decades*, prepared for the U.S. Environmental Protection Agency, Office of Strategic and Scientific Studies (Washington, D.C.: J. F. Coates Inc., February 8, 1983), p. 87; survey working papers for the Coates report.
2. L. E. Obeng, "The Control of Pathogens from Human Waste and Their Aquatic Vectors," *Ambio* 12(2):106 (1982).
3. J. F. Coates Inc., *Clues to the Domestic Environmental Agenda for the Next Three Decades*, pp. 15, 55.
4. Mary F. Lyon, "The Cryptic Spread of Mutant Genes," *Ambio* 12(2):75 (1982).

CHAPTER 5: RISK ASSESSMENT AND RISK CONTROL

Text References

1. There are also many naturally occurring toxics. See Bruce N. Ames, "Dietary Carcinogens and Anticarcinogens," *Science* 221(4617):1256-64 (1983).
2. National Research Council, *Risk Assessment in the Federal Government: Managing the Process* (Washington, D.C.: National Academy Press, 1983).
3. William W. Lowrance, *Of Acceptable Risk* (Los Altos, Calif.: William Kaufman, Inc., 1976), p. 8.
4. Devra Lee Davis et al., "Basic Science Forcing Laws and Regulatory Case Studies: Kepone, DBCP, Halothane, Hexane, and Carbaryl" (Washington, D.C.: Environmental Law Institute, 1980), p. 1.
5. Toxic Substances Control Act, 15 U.S.C.A., §2603(e) (1982).
6. Davis et al., "Basic Science Forcing Laws and Regulatory Case Studies," pp. 132-33.
7. Thomas R. Bartman, "Deciding What to Regulate: Priority-Setting at OSHA," 2 *Va. J. Nat. Resources L.* 102 (1982).
8. Toxic Substances Control Act, 15 U.S.C.A., §2605(e) (1982).
9. *Natural Resources Defense Council v. Train*, 8 ERC 2120-2136 (1976).
10. *Environment Reporter—Current Developments*, September 23, 1983, p. 900.
11. U.S. Comptroller General, "Delays in EPA's Regulation of Hazardous Air Pollutants" (Washington, D.C.: General Accounting Office, 1983), pp. 8-12.
12. U.S. Environmental Protection Agency, Office of Pesticide Programs, "Status Report on Rebuttable Presumption Against Registration (RPAR) or Special Review Chemicals, Registration Standards and Data Call-In Programs" (Washington, D.C.: U.S. Environmental Protection Agency, Sept. 1983).
13. U.S. Department of Health and Human Services, Public Health Service, Center for Disease Control, "Ten Leading Causes of Death in the United States, 1977" (Atlanta: Center for Disease Control, July, 1980), p. 15.
14. *Ibid.*
15. Dorothy Rice et al., "The Current Burden of Illness in the United States," Occasional Paper (Washington, D.C.:National Academy of Science, 1976), p. 17.
16. On inability to select most serious risks, see Jurgen Schmandt, "Regulation

and Science," Working Paper No. 25 (Austin: University of Texas, Lyndon B. Johnson School of Public Affairs, 1983), pp. 27-8.

17. Quoted in Michael E. Kraft, "The Use of Risk Analysis in Federal Regulatory Agencies: An Exploration," *Policy Studies Review* 1(4):671-2 (1982).

18. In 1980, EPA published a bibliography of more than 30 methods for assigning priorities to chemicals. U.S. Environmental Protection Agency, Office of Pestidices and Toxic Substances, "Chemical Selection Methods: An Annotated Bibliography," T115-80-001 (Washington, D.C.: U.S. Environmental Protection Agency, 1980).

19. Dorothy Nelkin, "Workers at Risk," *Science* 221(4620): 125 (1983).

20. Paul Slovic et al., "Rating the Risks: The Structure of Expert and Lay Perceptions," in Christoph Hohenemser and Jeanne X. Kasperson, *Risk in the Technological Society* (AAAS Selected Symposium; 65) (Boulder: Westview Press, 1982), pp. 153-4.

21. For discussion see Edwin Levy and David Capp, "Risk and Responsibility: Ethical Issues in Decisionmaking," in W. Cragg, ed., *Contemporary Moral Problems* (Toronto: McGraw-Hill Ryerson, 1983), p. 495.

22. James C. Miller, III, "Comparative Data on Life-Threatening Risks," *Toxic Substances Journal* 5(1):3-14 (1983). The difference in rates for motorcycle accidents may be due to different bases for the estimates, but the article does not make clear what the basis of each of the estimates is.

23. For other criticisms of this approach see Baruch Fischoff, et al., *Acceptable Risk* (Cambridge: Cambridge University Press, 1981), pp. 79-100.

24. Council on Environmental Quality, *Environmental Quality, The Seventh Annual Report* (Washington, D.C.: U.S. Government Printing Office) p.4.

25. See Robert Nilsson, "Aspects on the Toxicity of Cadmium and its Compounds," Ecological Research Committee Bulletin No. 7 (Stockholm: Swedish Natural Science Research Council, 1970).

26. See Interdepartmental Task Force on PCBs, *Polychlorinated Biphenyls and the Environment* (Springfield, Va.: National Technical Information Service, 1972). pp. 124-5.

27. See Alexander I. Kucherenko and Jan W. Huismans, "The International Register of Potentially Toxic Chemicals (IRPTC) of UNEP," *Environmental Conservation* 9(1):59-73 (1982).

28. International Institute for Applied Systems Analysis, *Environmental Impacts of Electrical Generation: A Systemwide Approach* (PR-76-013) (Laxenburg, Austria: IIASA, 1976).

29. U.S. Nuclear Regulatory Commission, *Reactor Safety Study: An Assessment of Accident Risks in U.S. Commercial Nuclear Power Plants*, Report WASH-1400, NUREG 75/014 (Washington, D.C.: U.S. Nuclear Regulatory Commission, October, 1975).

30. Risk Assessment Review Group, "Report to the U.S. Nuclear Regulatory Commission," NUREG/CR-0400 (Washington, D.C.: U.S. Nuclear Regulatory Commission, Sept. 1978), p. vii.

31. *Ibid.*, p. vi.

32. Based on information provided by the National Highway Traffic Safety Administration, Federal Accident Reporting System.

33. Gulf South Insulation v. United States Consumer Product Safety Commission, 701 F.2d 1137 (5th cir., April 17, 1983). See also Edward W. Lawless, Martin v. Jones, and Richard M. Jones, "Comparative Risk Assessment: Toward an Analytical Framework" (Draft final report to National Science Foundation under NSF Grant No. PRA-8018868, no date), p. 57.

34. Congress of the United States, Office of Technology Assessment, *Assessment of Technologies for Determining Cancer Risks from the Environment* (Washington, D.C.: U.S. Government Prining Office, 1981), p. 122.

35. *Ibid.*, pp. 114-15.

36. *Toxic Substances Journal* 2(2) 138-149 (1980).

37. Lawless et al., "Comparative Risk Assessment," p. 57.

38. William H. Harris and Judith S. Levey, eds., *The New Columbia Encyclopedia* (New York: Columbia University Press, 1975).

39. 45 Fed. Reg. 5001 (1980).

40. *Southern Oregon Citizens Against Toxic Sprays, Inc. v. Clark*, 720 F. 2d 1475; *Paul Merrell v. J.R. Block*, No. 881-6138-E (D. Or., filed April 18, 1983); and *Save Our Ecosystems v. Watt*, No. 83-6090-E (D. Or., filed May 20, 1983). Also see *Chemical Regulation Reporter*, Dec. 16, 1983, p. 1339.

41. See the entire issue of *Toxic Substances Journal* 4(1) (1982).

42. The phrase is found in the Clean Air Act as amended, §108(f)(1)(c). For a discussion see Robert D. Friedman, *Sensitive Populations and Environmental Standards* (Washington, D.C.: The Conservation Foundation, 1981), pp. 2-3.

43. Asbestos and smoking interact synergistically in causing bronchogenic lung cancer but not lung mesothelioma. Bernard D. Goldstein, "Toxic Substances in the Atmospheric Environment," *Journal of the Air Pollution Control Association* 33(5):457 (1983).

44. National Research Council Committee on Medical and Biologic Effects of Environmental Pollutants, Subcommittee on Airborne Particles, *Airborne Particles* (Baltimore: University Park Press, 1979), pp. 147-166.

45. Herbert Inhaber, *Energy Risk Assessment* (New York: Gordon Breach Science Publications, 1982). See also, John P. Holdren et al., *Risk of Renewable Energy Sources: A Critique of the Inhaber Report*, ERG 79-3 (Berkeley: University of California, 1979).

46. International Institute for Applied Systems Analysis, *Options*, 1983/2, p. 5.

47. National Research Council, *Risk Assessment in the Federal Government*, p. 33.

48. *Ibid.*, p. 36.

49. Gregory L. Campbell and D. Warner North, "Perchloroethylene: A Case Study of the Application of Decision Analysis to the Determination of the Risk Posed by A Toxic Chemical" (Palo Alto: Decision Focus, Inc., March 1981), p. 7-5.

50. Frances M. Lynn, "The Interplay of Science and Values in Assessing Environmental Risks," Ph.D. dissertation, (Chapel Hill: University of North Carolina, School of Public Health, 1983).

51. *Ibid.*

52. Ralph Althouse, et al., "Chemicals and Industrial Processes Associated with Cancer in Humans" (Lyon, France: International Agency for Research on Cancer, Sept. 1979), p. 3.

53. 45 Fed. Reg. 5001 (1980).

54. Fischoff et al., "Lay Foibles and Expert Fables in Judgements about Risks," in T. O'Riordan and R. Kerry Turner, ed., *Progress in Resource Management and Environmental Planning*, Vol. 3 (New York: John Wiley, 1981), p. 1983.
55. U.S. Environmental Protection Agency, Office of Policy Planning and Evaluation, Toxics Integration Task Force, Risk Management Subcommittee, *"Final Report," (Draft)* (Washington, D.C.: U.S. Environmental Protection Agency, 1984) p. 8.
56. National Research Council, *Risk Assessment in the Federal Government*, p. 107. For arrangements in other agencies see *Ibid.*, pp. 93-131.
57. Information provided by the National Highway Traffic Safety Administration.
58. 44 Fed. Reg. 39858-79 (1979).
59. Office of Science and Technology Policy, Interagency Staff Group, "Review on the Mechanisms of Effect and Detection of Chemical Carcinogens," 2nd draft (Washington, D.C.: Office of Science and Technology Policy, undated).
60. *Pesticide and Toxic Chemical News*, Oct. 26, 1983, pp. 3-5.
61. *Inside the Administration*, Jan. 27, 1984, p. 7.
62. Administrative Procedure Act, 5 U.S.C.A. §553(c) (1976).
63. American Industrial Health Council, "Proposals for Improving the Science Base for Chronic Health Hazard Decision-making" (Washington, D.C.: American Industrial Health Council, Dec. 2, 1981), p. 14.
64. Clean Air Act, §109(d)(2); 42 U.S.C.A. §7409(a)(2)(A) (1983).
65. Clean Air Act, §117(c), 42 U.S.C.A. §7417 (a) (1983). See also U.S. Comptroller General, *Delays in EPA's Regulations of Hazardous Air Pollutants* (Washington, D.C.: Government Printing Office, 1983), pp. 28-35.
66. Federal Insecticide, Fungicide, and Rodenticide Act, §25(d), 15 U.S.C.A. §2077 (1982).
67. Centaur Associates, Inc., "Siting of Hazardous Waste Management Facilities and Public Opposition," prepared for the U.S. Environmental Protection Agency, Office of Water and Waste Management, SW 809 (Washington, D.C.: U.S. Environmental Protection agency, 1979), p. 9.
68. 46 Fed. Reg. 13193-98 (1981).
69. Susan J. Tolchin and Martin Tolchin, *Dismantling America: The Rush to Deregulate* (Boston: Houghton Mifflin, 1983), pp. 44-56.
70. J. Clarence Davies, "The Reagan Adminsitration and Environmental Institutions" in Norman J. Vig and Michael E. Kraft, eds., *Environmental Policy in the 1980's: Reagan's New Agenda* (Washington, D.C.: Congressional Quarterly Press, 1984). Tolchin and Tolchin, *Dismantling America*.
71. For a general discussion of Congress and risk assessment, see Michael E. Kraft, "The Political and Organizational Setting for Risk Analysis" in Vincent J. Covello, ed., *Contemporary Issues in Risk Analysis: Social and Behavioral Sciences* (New York: Plenum, 1984).
72. Industrial Union Department, AFL-CIO v. American Petroleum Institute, 10 ELR 20489 (June, 1980).
73. *American Textile Manufacturers Institute, Inc. v. Donovan*, 101 S.Ct. 2478 (June, 1981).
74. *Gulf South Insulation v. United States Consumer Product Safety Commission*, 701 F. 2d 1137 (5th Cir., April 7, 1983).
75. See Norman J. Vig and Patrick J. Bruer, "The Courts and Risk Assessment,"

Policy Studies Review 1(4)716:27 (1982). Also Norman J. Vig, "The Courts: Judicial Review and Risk Assessment," in Susan G. Hadden, ed., *Risk Analysis, Institutions, and Public Policy* (Port Washington, N.Y.: Associated Faculty Press, 1984).

76. Vig and Bruer, "The Courts and Risk Assessment," p. 723.
77. *Ibid.*
78. *Ibid.*, p. 724.
79. Nicholas A. Ashford, C.W. Ryan, and C.C. Caldart, "Law and Science Policy in Federal Regulation of Formaldehyde," *Science* 222(4626)894:900 (1983).
80. *Gulf South Insulation v. United States Consumer Product Safety Commission*, 701 F. 2d 1146.
81. William D. Ruckelshaus, "Science, Risk and Public Policy," *Science* 221(4615)1027:28 (1983).
82. National Research Council, *Risk Assessment in the Federal Government*, p. 6.
83. For other efforts at categorization see Rae Zimmermann, "The Management of Risk" in J. Menkes and V. Covello, eds., *Contemporary Issues in Risk Management* (New York: Plenum, forthcoming), pp. 6-7. For a list of 38 statutes requiring some form of risk analysis, see, Michael E. Kraft, "The Political and Organizational Setting for Risk Analysis," Appendix I.
84. §409(c)(3)(A), 21 U.S.C.A. §348(c)(3)(A) (1982).
85. Clean Air Act, §109, 42 U.S.C.A. §7409 (1983).
86. Clean Air Act, 42 U.S.C.A. §7412 (1983).
87. Richard A. Merrill, "Regulating Carcinogens in Food: A Legislator's Guide to the Food Safety Provisions of the Federal Food, Drug, and Cosmetic Act," 77 *Mich. L. Rev.* 171 (1978). See also, Peter Barton Hutt, "Public Policy Issues in Regulatory Carcinogens in Food," *Food Drug Cosm. L.J.*, Oct. 1978, p. 542.
88. Hutt, "Public Policy Issues," p. 542.
89. Clean Water Act of 1977, §301(b), 33 U.S.C.A. §1311(b)(1)(A) (1978).
90. J. Clarence Davies, Sam Gusman, and Frances Irwin, *Determining Unreasonable Risk Under the Toxic Substances Control Act* (Washington, D.C.: The Conservation Foundation, 1979).
91. Safe Drinking Water Act, §1412(a)(2), 42 U.S.C.A. §300g-1(a)(2) (1982).
92. Ruckelshaus, "Science, Risk, and Public Policy."
93. David A. Doniger, Richard A. Liroff, and Norman L. Dean, "An Analysis of Past Federal Efforts to Control Toxic Substances" (Washington, D.C.: Environmental Law Institute, 1978), pp. 38-9.
94. John D. Graham & James W. Vaupel, "The Value of a Life: What Difference Does It Make?" in Richard J. Zeckhauser and Derek Leebaert, eds., *What Role for Government?* (Durham: Duke University Press, 1983), pp. 184-5.
95. John D. Graham, "Some Explanations for Disparities in Lifesaving Investments," *Policy Studies Review* 1(4)692:704 (1982).
96. Roger Dower, "How Uncle Sam Values Human Health Risks," *Environmental Forum*, Jan. 1984, pp. 14-18. On other difficulties see E.J. Mishan, *Cost-Benefit Analysis*, 3d ed. (New York: Praeger, 1976); and Daniel Swartzman, Richard A. Liroff, and Kevin G. Croke, eds., *Cost-Benefit Analysis and Environment Regulations* (Washington, D.C.: The Conservation Foundation, 1982). Cost-effectiveness analysis is frequently used in some types of regulatory decision making about risks. (Letter from Don R. Clay to J.C. Davies, 4/9/84).

97. National Research Council, *Risk Assessment in the Federal Government*, p. 7.

98. National Research Council, *Chloroform, Carbon Tetrachloride and Other Halomethanes: An Environmental Assessment* (Washington, D.C.: National Academy Press, 1978), p. 109.

99. For a discussion of pesticide use in the UDCs see David Bull, *A Growing Problem* (Oxford, England: OXFAM, 1982). Chapter 3 deals with pesticides and malaria.

100. See J. Clarence Davies and Frances H. Irwin, "Costs and Benefits of the Premanufacture Notification Program Under the Toxic Substances Control Act," research paper, (Washington, D.C.: The Conservation Foundation, 1981).

101. Robert W. Crandall and Lester B. Lave, eds., *The Scientific Basis of Health and Safety Regulation* (Washington, D.C.: The Brookings Institution, 1981), p. 14. Also see Jurgen Schmandt, "Regulation and Science," p. 27.

102. Fischoff et al., *Acceptable Risk*, pp. 61-78.

103. Off the record meeting on Cuba, October 16, 1962, 6:30-7:55 p.m., p. 25, Presidential Recordings, Presidential Office File,, Papers of President John F. Kennedy, John F. Kennedy Library, Boston, Mass.

104. Crandall and Lave, eds., *The Scientific Basis of Health and Safety Regulation*, p. 14.

105. National Research Council, *Toxicity Testing: Strategies to Determine Needs and Practices* (Washington, D.C.: National Academy Press, 1984).

106. U.S. Environmental Protection Agency, Office of Toxic Substances, "Preliminary Assessment of the Environmental Problems Associated with Vinyl Chloride and Polyvinyl Chloride: Report on the Activities and Findings of the Vinyl Chloride Task Force" (Washington, D.C.: U.S. Environmental Protection agency, Sept. 1974), p. 1.

107. Nick Nichols, "Conservatism in Risk Assessment," draft, unpublished paper (Washington, D.C.: U.S. Environmental Protection Agency, Sept. 1983), p. 9. Early in 1984, EPA altered its policy, directing that: "Exposure assessments, where possible, should be based on actual monitoring rather than modeling alone," and "risk assessments should include realistic assumptions about exposure as well as 'worst case' assumptions." Memo, Alvin L. Alm to Assistant Administrators, EPA, Jan. 25, 1984.

108. *Ibid.*, p. 13.

Figure References

5.1 National Research Council, *Risk Assessment in the Federal Government: Managing the Process* (Washington, D.C., National Academy Press, 1983), p. 21.

5.2 Edward V. Lawless, Martin V. Jones, and Richard M. Jones, "Comparative Risk Assessment: Toward an Analytical Framework" (Draft final report to National Science Foundation, Grant No. PRA-8018868, no date), p. 85, adapted from Paul Slovic, et al. "Facts and Fears: Understanding Perceived Risk," briefing presented to General Electric, June 4, 1981, p. 7.

5.3 *Ibid.*

5.4 George Su, K.A. Wurzel, "A Regulatory Framework for Setting Air Emission Limits for Non-Criteria Pollutants," mimeo, (Lansing: Michigan Department of Natural Resources, 1983).

5.5 Lorenz K. Ng and Devra Davis, *Strategies for Public Health: Promoting Health and Preventing Disease* (New York: Van Nostrand, 1980), pp. 214-15.

The Tacoma Smelter

1. *New York v. Gorsuch*, 554 F. Supp. 1060 (Dist. Ct. N.Y. 1983).
2. 48 Fed. Reg. 3312 (1983).
3. Bureau of National Affairs, *Environment Reporter—Current Developments*, July 15, 1983, p. 395.
4. §112(b)(1)(B), 42 U.S.C.A. §7412 (1983).
5. *Environment Reporter—Current Developments*, July 15, 1983, p. 395.
6. *Environment Reporter—Current Developments*, May 6, 1983, p. 395.
7. U.S. Environmental Protection Agency, Office of Health and Environmental Assessment, "Health Assessment Document for Inorganic Arsenic," EPA-600/8-83-021A (Research Triangle Park: U.S. Environmental Protection Agency, June 1983).
8. U.S. Environmental Protection Agency, Office of Air Quality Planning and Standards, "Inorganic Arsenic Emissions from High-Arsenic Primary Copper Smelters—Background Information for Proposed Standards," EPA-450/3-83-009a (Research Triangle Park: U.S.Environmental Protection Agency, April 1983).
9. U.S. Environmental Protection Agency, "Health Assessment Document for Inorganic Arsenic," p. 2-1.
10. *Ibid.*, p. 2-26.
11. *Air and Water Pollution Report*, Nov. 7, 1983, p. 423.
12. *Environment Reporter—Current Developments*, May 6, 1983, p. 6.
13. *Environment Reporter—Current Developments*, July 15, 1983, p. 395.
14. *Air and Water Pollution Report*, Nov. 7, 1983, p. 423.
15. *Environment Reporter—Current Developments*, Aug. 5, 1983, p. 669.
16. *National Journal* 15(49):2530 (1983).

EDB

1. U.S. Environmental Protection Agency, Office of Pesticide Programs, "Ethylene Dibromide: Position Document 2/3" (Washington, D.C.: U.S. Environmental Peotection Agency, Dec. 1980), p. 134.
2. *Chemical Regulation Reporter*, Sept 30, 1983, p. 859.
3. *Ibid.*
4. *Ibid.*
5. Journal of the Association of Official Analytical Chemists 40:163-209 (1957).
6. National Cancer Institute, "Memorandum of Alert" Oct. 16, 1974. See also, U.S. Environmental Protection Agency, Office of Pesticide Programs, "Ethylene Dibromide: Position Document 2/3," p. 8.
7. *Chemical Regulation Reporter*, Aug. 5, 1983, p. 573.
8. U.S. Environmental Protection Agency, Office of Pesticide Programs, "Ethylene Dibromide (EDB): Position Document 4 (Washington, D.C.: U.S. Environmental Protection Agency, Sept. 27, 1983), p. 103. See also, *Chemical Regulation Reporter*, Sept. 30, 1983, p. 859 and Oct. 14, 1983, p. 896-7.

9. "Patchwork of State Standards Complicates Federal EDB Effort," *Washington Post*, March 23, 1984.
10. U.S. Environmental Protection Agency, Office of Pesticide Programs, "Ethylene Dibromide: Position Document 2/3," pp. 66-67.

Zero Risk from Natural Disasters?

1. Department of the Army, Baltimore District, Corps of Engineers, "Metropolitan Washington, D.C. Area Water Supply Study: Maryland, Virginia and the District of Columbia," final report (Baltimore: Corps of Engineers, Sept. 1983), pp. 29-30.

CHAPTER 6: CONTROLLING CROSS-MEDIA POLLUTANTS

Text References

1. Personal communication, Langdon Marsh, February 15, 1984; and Merrill Heit, Catherine S. Klusek, and Kevin M. Miller, "Trace Element, Radionuclido, and Polynuclear Aromatic Hydrocarbon Concentrations in Uniondale Mussels from Northern Lake George," *Environmental Science and Technology* 14(4):465 (1980).
2. Message to Congress, Richard M. Nixon, July 9, 1970. Council on Environmental Quality, *Environmental Quality: The First Annual Report of the Council on Environmental Quality* (Washington, D.C.: U.S. Government Printing Office, 1970), pp. 306-7.
3. National Research Council, *Toxicology Testing: Strategies to Determine Needs and Priorities* (Washington, D.C.: National Academy Press, 1984), p. 33.
4. James C. Dickerman, "A Systems Approach to Waste Management," in Donald Huisingh and Vicki Bailey, eds., *Making Pollution Prevention Pay: Ecology with Economy as Policy* (New York: Pergamon Press, 1982), p. 104.
5. State of California, Air Resources Board, Stationary Source Division, "Air Pollution Impacts of Hazardous Waste Incineration: A California Perspective. A Report to the California Legislature" (Sacramento: Air Resources Board, Dec. 1983), p. 57.
6. Blair T. Bower, G.P. Larson, A. Michaels, and W.M. Phillips, *Waste Management: Generation and Disposal of Solid, Liquid and Gaseous Waste in the New York Region, A Report of the Second Regional Plan* (New York: Regional Plan Association, 1968).
7. Allen V. Kneese and Blair T. Bower, *Environmental Quality and the Residuals Management* (Baltimore: Johns Hopkins University Press, 1979), p. 68.
8. Michael A. Gruber, Office of Policy Analysis, Integrated Environmental Management Division, "The Industry Approach to Integrated Environmental Management: Rationale, Objectives, and Methods" (Washington, D.C.: U.S. Environmental Protection Agency, undated), pp. 1-2.
9. Battelle Columbus Laboratories, "Development of Cross-Media Evaluation Methodology," prepared for Council of Environmental Quality and the

Environmental Protection Agency (Columbus: Battelle, Jan. 1974.)

10. State of California, Hazardous Substance Task Force, "Toxics Management in California: An Identification of Issues," draft. (Sacramento: Department of Environmental Affairs, Oct. 1983), pp. 64-5. Also Blair T. Bower, "Formulation and Implementation of Environmental Policies for Integrated Waste Management, including Management of Toxic Wastes," unpublished draft (Washington, D.C.: Resources for the Future, 1983), p. 13.

11. JRB Associates, Inc., "Inventory of Air Pollution Control, Industrial Wastewater Treatment and Water Treatment Sludge," prepared for U.S. Environmental Protection Agency, (McLean: JRB Associates, Inc., 1983), p. 4-27.

12. Information provided by U.S. Environmental Protection Agency, Office of Research and Development.

13. JRB Associates, Inc., "Inventory of Air Pollution Control, Industrial Wastewater Treatment and Water Treatment Sludges," Table 5-1.

14. National Research Council, Commission of Natural Resources, *Multimedium Management of Municipal Sludge* (Analytical Studies for the U.S. Environmental Protection Agency) (Washington, D.C.: National Academy of Sciences, 1977). p.24.

15. Stephen W. Bailey and David C. Zimomra, "Nationwide Survey of Heavy Metals in Municipal Sludge" in C.P. Huang, ed., *Industrial Waste Proceedings of the Thirteenth Mid-Atlantic Conference* (Ann Arbor: Ann Arbor Science, 1981), pp. 18-19.

16. U.S. Comptroller General, *Information on Ocean Disposal of Municipal and Industrial Waste* (Washington, D.C.: General Accounting Office, 1983), pp. 18-21.

17. D.V. Feliciano, "Sludge on Lands: Where We Are, But Where Are We Going?" *Journal Water Pollution Control Association* 54:1259-66 (1982).

18. Information provided by U.S. Environmental Protection Agency, Integrated Environmental Management Program, August 1983.

19. U.S. Comptroller General, *Information on Disposal Practices of Generators of Small Quantities of Hazardous Wastes* (Washington, D.C.: General Accounting Office, 1983.), p. 14.

20. *Ibid.*, pp. 14, 23.

21. C. Stephen Kim, et al. "Love Canal: Environmental Studies," in Joseph Highland, ed., *Hazardous Waste Disposal: Assessing the Problem* (Ann Arbor: Ann Arbor Science, 1982), pp. 83-94.

22. Fred C. Hart Associates, *Assessment of Hazardous Waste Mismanagement Damage Case Histories*, prepared for U.S. Environmental Protection Agency, Office of Solid Waste (Washington, D.C.: U.S. Environmental Protection Agency, Dec. 1982), Table 5-2.

23. Veronica I. Pye, Ruth Patrick, and John Quarles, *Groundwater Contamination in the United States* (Philadelphia: University of Pennsylvania Press, 1983), pp. 123, 138.

24. U.S. Environmental Protection Agency, Office of Water Quality, Office of Drinking Water, *Surface Impoundment Assessment, National Report* (Washington, D.C.: U.S. Environmental Protection Agency, Dec. 1983), p. 2, 8.

25. U.S. Comptroller General, *Cleaning Up the Environment: Progress Achieved*

but Major Unresolved Issues Remain, Vol. 1 (Washington, D.C.: General Accounting Office, 1982), pp. 49-50.

26. Charles L. Stratton et al., "Environmental Assessment of Polychlorinated Biphenyls (PCBs) Near New Bedford, Mass. Municipal Landfill," prepared for U.S. Environmental Protection Agency, Office of Toxic Substances (Springfield, Va.: National Technical Information Service, 1978).

27. State of California, Air Resources Board, "Air Pollution Impacts of Hazardous Waste Incineration: A California Perspective. A Report to the California Legislature," p. iii.

28. Richard W. Gerstle and Diane N. Albrinck, "Atmospheric Emissions of Metals from Sewage Sludge Incineration," *Journal of the Air Pollution Control Association* 32(11):1119 (1982).

29. John R. Cline and Thomas T. Shen, "Measurement and Monitoring of Non-Criteria Toxic Contaminants in Air," *Journal of the Air Pollution Control Association* 33(10)947 (1983).

30. State of California, Air Resources Board, "Air Pollution Impacts of Hazardous Waste Incineration: A California Perspective. A Report to the California Legislature," pp. 75-77.

31. For a summary of the program, see Chapter 2 of Allen V. Kneese and Blair T. Bower, *Environmental Quality and Residuals Management* (Baltimore: Johns Hopkins University Press, 1979).

32. National Research Council, Commission on Natural Resources, *Multimedium Management of Municipal Sludge*, p. 4.

33. Robert K. Bastien, "EPA Comprehensive Review of Municipal Sludge Management Alternatives," mimeo (Washington, D.C.: U.S. Environmental Protection Agency, Office of Water, undated), pp. 3-4.

34. U.S. Comptroller General, *Information on Ocean Disposal of Municipal and Industrial Waste*, p. 27.

35. The Royal Commission on Environmental Pollution, *Tenth Report: Tackling Pollution Experience and Prospects* (London: Her Majesty's Stationary Office, 1984), p. 53.

36. Federal Water Pollution Control Act, §405(d), 33 U.S.C.A. §1345 (1978).

37. Marine Protection Research, and Sanctuaries Act of 1972, §102, 33 U.S.C.A. §1412(a)(G) (1978).

38. RCRA, §1002, 42 U.S.C.A. §6901(b)(3) (1983).

39. Monica E. Campbell and William M. Glenn, *Profit from Pollution Prevention: A Guide to Industrial Waste Reduction and Recycling* (Toronto: Pollution Probe Foundation, 1982), pp. 1-2.

40. Gregory S. Wetstone and Armin Rosencranz, *Acid Rain in Europe and North America: National Responses to an International Problem* (Washington, D.C.: Environmental Law Institute, 1983), pp. 97-99, Figure 4.

41. Edward A. Keller, *Environmental Geology* (Columbus, Ohio: Charles E. Merrill Publishing Company, 1976), p. 54. Also see Bette Hileman, "Water Quality Uncertainties," *Environmental Science and Technology* 10(4):125A (1984).

42. National Research Council, Committee to Review Methods for Ecotoxicology, *Testing for Effects of Chemicals on Ecosystems* (Washington, D.C.: National Academy Press, 1981), p. 16-18.

43. "Currents," *Environmental Science and Technology*, 17(11):512A (1983).

44. S.J. Eisenreich, et al. "Assessment of Airborne Organic Contaminants in the Great Lakes Ecosystem. A Report to the Science Advisory Board's Ecological and Geochemical Aspects Expert Committee of the International Joint Commission" (Minneapolis: University of Minnesota, Environmental Engineering Program, 1980).

45. F. Moriarty, *Ecotoxicology: The Study of Pollutants in Ecosystems* (London: Academic Press, Inc. 1983), p. 11.

46. U.S. Environmental Protection Agency, Office of Water Regulations and Standards, "An Exposure and Risk Assessment for Cyanide." For information about the Office of Toxic Integration's Working File of Materials Balance/Exposure Assessments," as further referenced in footnotes 47, 50, 65 66, 67, and 69, contact U.S. Environmental Protection Agency, Walter Kovalick, Director, Integration staff, Office of Toxics Integration, Office of Pesticides and Toxic Substances.

47. U.S. Environmental Protection Agency, Office of Water Regulations and Standards, "An Exposure and Risk Assessment for Arsenic."

48. National Research Council, Committee to Review Methods for Ecotoxicology, National Research Council, *Testing for Effects of Chemicals on Ecosystems* (Washington, D.C.: National Academy Press, 1981) p. 16-30.

49. Office of Technology Assessment, *Technologies and Management Strategies for Hazardous Waste Control* (Washington, D.C.: U.S. Government Printing Office, 1983) pp. 153-154.

50. U.S. Environmental Protection Agency, Office of Water Regulations and Standards, "An Exposure and Risk Assessment for Mercury."

51. U.S. Environmental Protection Agency, *Chesapeake Bay Program Technical Studies: A Synthesis* (Annapolis: U.S. Environmental Protection Agency, Chesapeake Bay Program, 1982).

52. Bert Bolin and Robert B. Cook, eds., *The Major Biogeochemical Cycles and Their Interactions*, SCOPE 21 (New York: John Wiley and Sons, 1983), p. xv.

53. "Love Canal: The Facts (1892-1980)," *Hooker Factline*, No. 11, (Houston: Hooker Chemical, Division of Occidental Petroleum, June 1980).

54. Bette Hileman, "Hazardous Waste Control: Are We Creating Problems for Future Generations, *Environmental Science and Technology*, 17:7 (281A) (1983).

55. Jane Kay, "TCE Can of Worms Opened Wide," April 21, 1983, and "Report Details Waste Dumping at Hughes Pits," May 30, 1982, *The Arizona Daily Star*.

56. Elizabeth M. Rupp et al., "Composite Hazard Index for Assessing Limiting Exposures to Environmental Pollutants: Application Through a Case Study," *Environmental Science and Technology* 12:7(806) (1978).

57. Robert V. Thomann and John P. Connolly, "Model of PCB in Lake Michigan Lake Trout Food Chain," *Environmental Science and Technology* 18(2):65 (1984).

58. "Combined Pollutants: Double Trouble!" *International Wildlife*, July-August, 1983, p.24-D.

59. James R. Janis and Gilah Langer, "The Fundamental Issue: How Clean is Clean?," *Hazardous Waste Report*, p. 12.

60. U.S. Comptroller General, *Delays in EPA's Regulation of Hazardous Air*

Pollutants (Washington, D.C.: General Accounting Office, 1983), p. 20.

61. U.S. Comptroller General, *Cleaning Up the Environment: Progress Achieved But Major Unresolved Issues Remain*, Vol. I, p. 50.

62. State of New York, Department of Environmental Conservation, "Division of Water Policy and Delegation Memo (83-Water-38)," (Albany: New York Department of Environmental Conservation, August 8, 1983).

63. California Institute of Technology, Department of Environmental Heath Engineering, *Mass Balance Determinations for Pollutants in Urban Regions*, prepared for U.S. Environmental Protection Agency, Environmental Monitoring and Support Laboratory (Springfield, Va.: National Technical Information Service, August 1978), pp. 9-10.

64. Robert Kayser, Doreen Sterling, Donn Viviani, eds., U.S. Environmental Protection Agency, Office of Pesticides and Toxic Substances, Chemical Coordination Staff, "Intermedia Priority Pollutant Guidance Documents," mimeo (Washington, D.C.: U.S. Environmental Protection Agency, July, 1982), "Benzene," p. 33.

65. U.S. Environmental Protection Agency, Office of Water Regulations and Standards, "An Exposure and Risk Assessment for Lead."

66. U.S. Environmental Protection Agency, Office of Water Regulations and Standards, "EPA: Arsenic: A preliminary materials balance"; U.S. Environmental Protection Agency, Office of Water Regulations and Standards, "OAQPS—Arsenic: Human Exposure to Atmospheric Arsenic'; and U.S. Environmental Protection Agency, Office of Water Regulations and Standards, "EPA: An Exposure and Risk Assessment for Arsenic.

67. "EPA Draft Study Shows 38 Gallons Per 200 Drum Shipment Lost in Transport," *Inside EPA Weekly Report*, October 28, 1983, p. 11; and Mark Abkowitz et al., "Assessing the Risks and Costs Associated with Truck Transport of Hazardous Wastes," Draft Final Report, prepared for U.S. Environmental Protection Agency, Office of Solid Waste (Washington, D.C.: U.S. Environmental Protection Agency, undated).

68. U.S. Environmental Protection Agency, "Investigation of Selected Potential Environmental Contaminants: Acrylonitrile."

69. U.S. Environmental Protection Agency, "Proceedings of the Workshop on Transport and Fate of Toxic Chemicals in the Environment," EPA-600/9-81-024 (Washington, D.C.: U.S. Environmental Protection Agency December 1981).

70. "Program Report," The National Center for Intermedia Transport Research, UCLA, 5531 Boelter Hall, Los Angeles, California 90024.

71. National Research Council, Commission on Natural Resources, *Nonfluorinated Halomethanes in the Environment* (Washington, D.C.: National Academy of Sciences, 1978).

72. Elizabeth Rupp et al., "Composite Hazard Index for Assessing Limiting Exposures to Environmental Pollutants: Application through a Case Study," *Environmental Science and Technology* 12:7(807) (1978).

73. State of New Jersey, Department of Environmental Protection, Office of Science and Research, "Program Plan," (Trenton: New Jersey Department of Environmental Protection, undated), p. 4.

74. National Research Council, Committee to Review Methods for Ecotoxicology,

Testing for Effects of Chemicals on Ecosystems (Washington, D.C.: National Academy Press, 1981), pp. 5-7, 11.

75. National Science Foundation, *Long-Term Ecological Measurements: Report of a Conference*, Woods Hole, Mass., March 16-18, 1977 (Springfield, Va.: National Technical Information Services 1977), p. 1.

76. See Council on Environmental Quality, "Interagency Task Force on Environmental Data and Monitoring" (Springfield, Va.: National Technical Information Service, 1980), pp. 4-6, 34.

77. Thomas J. O'Shea and J. Larry Ludke, U.S. Department of the Interior, Fish and Wildlife Service, "Monitoring Fish and Wildlife for Environmental Pollutants" (Washington, D.C.: U.S. Government Printing Office, 1979), p.4.

78. State of New Jersey, Department of Environmental Protection, Office of Science and Research, "Program Plan," p. 6.

79. Anne E. Giblin, *Comparisons of the Processing of Elements of Ecosystems II. Metals* (Ithaca: Cornell University, Ecosystems Research Center, 1982), pp. 2, 12, 18.

80. U.S. National Committee for SCOPE, "Interim Report to the SCOPE Executive Committee," New Delhi, India, Feb. 6-8, 1983 (Paris: Scientific Committee on Problems of the Environment, 1983).

81. The Conservation Foundation, "National Ecological Research Center: Draft Concept Paper" (Washington, D.C.: The Conservation Foundation, 1983), pp. 1-7.

82. National Research Council, *Toward an International Geosphere-Biosphere Program: A Study of Global Change*, A Report of a Workshop, July 25-29, 1983 (Washington, D.C.: National Academy Press, 1983), pp. 22 and 24.

83. *Ibid.*, p.1. and National Aeronautics and Space Administration and California Institute of Technology, Jet Propulsion Laboratory, "Global Change: Impacts on Habitability: A Scientific Basis for Assessment," a report by the Executive Committee of a Workshop held at Woods Hole, Mass., June 21-26, 1982. National Aeronautics and Space Administration, "Technical Memorandum 85629" (Washington, D.C.: National Aeronautics and Space Administration, 1983).

84. Council on Environmental Quality, "Interagency Task Force on Environmental Data and Monitoring," pp. 16 and 18.

85. Michael D. Gwynne, "The Global Environment Monitoring System (GEMS) of UNEP," *Environmental Conservation* 9(1):35-36 (1982).

86. Michael A. Gruber, U.S. Environmental Protection Agency, Office of Policy Analysis, Integrated Environmental Management Division, "The Industry Approach to Integrated Environmental Management: Rationale, Objectives, and Methods" (Washington, D.C.: U.S. Environmental Protection Agency, undated); and Robert Currie, U.S. Environmental Protection Agency, Office of Policy Analysis, Integrated Environmental Management Division, "The Geographic Approach to Integrated Environmental Management: Rationale, Objectives and Methods" (Washington, D.C.: U.S. Environmental Protection Agency, undated).

87. State of Michigan, Department of Natural Resources, Groundwater Quality Division, "Site Assessment System (SAS) for the Michigan Priority Ranking

System Under the Michigan Environmental Response Act," (Lansing: Michigan Department of Natural Resources, Nov. 1983), pp. 1-91.

88. Gruber, "The Industry Approach to Integrated Environmental Management: Rationale, Objectives, and Methods," p. 2.

89. Richard A. Liroff, "Impact Statement Preparation by the U.S. Environmental Protection Agency," in *Decision Making in the Environmental Protection Agency, Selected Working Papers, Vol. IIb* (Washington, D.C.: National Academy of Sciences, 1977), pp. 286-302.

90. State of New York, Department of Environmental Conservation, "In the Matter of the Applications of Consolidated Edison Company of New York, Inc., Applicant: Decision" (Albany: Department of Environmental Conservation, Sept. 14, 1983).

91. State of Illinois. Environmental Protection Agency, "Towards A Multimedia Toxics Control Strategy: An Interim Progress Report" (Springfield: Department of Environmental Protection, Oct., 1983), p. 2.

92. Information provided by Illinois Department of Environmental Protection, Nov. 1983.

93. State of Colorado, Department of Natural Resources, "Colorado's Joint Review Process for Major Energy and Mineral Resource Development Projects," (Denver: Department of Natural Resources, Dec. 1980), p. 3.

94. An example of the work which has been done is the Habitat Suitability Indexes. See, for instance, P.J. Sousa, U.S. Department of the Interior, Fish and Wildlife Service, "Habitat Suitability Index Models: Lewis' Woodpecker," FWS.OBS-82/10.32 (Washington, D.C.: U.S. Department of Interior, 1982).

95. State of New York, Department of Environmental Conservation, "Division of Water Policy and Delegation Memo" (83—Water—38), (Albany: Department of Environmental Conservation, August 8, 1983).

96. U.S. Environmental Protection Agency, Integrated Environmental Management Program, "Briefing Materials on Philadelphia Demonstration Project" (Washington, D.C.: U.S. Environmental Protection Agency, Jan. 6, 1983).

97. Office of Technology Assessment, *Technological and Management Strategies for Hazardous Waste Control*, p. 145.

98. *Ibid.*, pp. 143-44.

99. *Ibid.*, p. 142.

100. Huisingh and Bailey, *Making Pollution Prevention Pay*, p.2.

101. Robert G. Healy, *American's Industrial Future: An Environmental Perspective* (Washington, D.C.: The Conservation Foundation, 1982), p. 22.

102. Office of Technology Assessment, *Technologies and Management Strategies for Hazardous Waste Control*, p. 143.

103. Paul Palmer, "Chemical Recycling: Making It Work, Making It Pay," in Huisingh and Bailey, *Making Pollution Prevention Pay*, pp. 82-83.

104. Office of Technology Assessment, *Technologies and Management Strategies for Hazardous Waste Control*, p. 155.

105. 40 C.F.R., §761.75 (1982).

106. Richard W. Gerstle and Diane N. Albrinck, "Atmospheric Emissions of Metals from Sewage Sludge Incineration," *Journal of the Air Pollution Control Federation*, 32(11):1119 (1982).

107. Office of Technology Assessment, *Technologies and Management Strategies for Hazardous Waste Control*, p. 170.
108. "NBS to Patent New Process to Remove SO₂ and NOˣ from Industrial Gas Streams," *Journal of the Air Pollution Control Association* 32(11):1156 (1982).
109. National Governors' Association, State Integrated Toxics Management, "Benefits of State Integrated Toxics Management (SITM)," Issue Brief #1 (Washington, D.C.: National Governors' Association, Aug. 1982).
110. State of California, Hazardous Substances Task Force, "Toxics Management in California: An Identification of Issues," draft (Sacramento: Resources Agency, Oct. 1983), pp. 61-65.
111. U.S. Environmental Protection Agency, Office of Pesticides and Toxic Substances, "Status Report Chemical Activities," 3rd. ed. (Washington, D.C.: U.S. Environmental Protection Agency, 1982).
112. Robert Kayser, Doreen Sterling, Donn Viviani, eds., U.S. Environmental Protection Agency, Office of Pesticides and Toxic Substances, Chemical Coordination Staff, "Intermedia Priority Pollutant Guidance Documents." As stated earlier in note 46, for information about the Office of Toxic Integration's Working File of Materials Balance/Exposure Assessments," contact Director, Integration Staff, Office of Toxics Integration, Office of Pesticides and Toxic Substances, U.S. Environmental Protection Agency.
113. Stuart L. Sessions, U.S. Environmental Protection Agency, Office of Policy Analysis, Regulatory Policy Division, "Permitting System Reforms in the United States" (Washington, D.C.: U.S. Environmental Protection Agency), p. 9.
114. Information provided by Iowa Department of Water, Air and Waste Management, Water Coordinator, November 1983.
115. David D. Doniger, "Federal Regulation of Vinyl Chloride: A Short Course in the Law and Policy of Toxic Substances Control." 7 *Ecology L. Q.* 500, 501, 504 (1978).
116. Clean Air Act, §111(a)(1)(c), 42 U.S.C.A. §7412 (1983).
117. Letter from Landgon Marsh, Executive Commissioner of the New York Department of Environmental Conservation to Edwin Clark The Conservation Foundation, Oct. 13, 1983.

Figure References

6.1 The Conservation Foundation
6.2 Information on atmospheric and industrial point sources from Thomas McHerdtke et al., "U.S. Heavy Metal Loadings to the Great Lakes: Estimates of Point and Nonpoint Contributions," Great Lakes Environmental Planning Study, Contribution No. 12 (Ann Arbor: Great Lakes Commission, Jan. 1980). Information on municipal point sources and rural and urban runoff from Great Lakes Science Advisory Board, 1980 Annual Report (Ann Arbor: Great Lakes Commission, 1981). Table prepared by The Conservation Foundation for The Conservation Foundation and Environmental Research and Technology, Inc., "Review of Policy Issues: Discussion of Cross-Media Pollution and Nonpoint Source Air and Water Pollution." Prepared for U.S. Environmental Protection Agency, 1983. Table 11.

6.3 U.S. Environmental Protection Agency, Office of Water Regulations, "An Exposure and Risk Assessment for Mercury." More recent information for some sources and transfers of mercury is available in Robert Kayser, Doreen Sterling, Donn Viviani, eds., U.S. Environmental Protection Agency, Office of Pesticides and Toxic Substances, Chemical Coordination Staff, Intermedia Priority Pollutants Guidance Documents, mimeo, "Mercury."

6.4 California Institute of Technology, Department of Environmental Health Engineering, Mass Balance Determinations for Pollutants in Urban Regions, prepared for U.S. Environmental Protection Agency, Environmental Monitoring and Support Laboratory (Springfield, Va.: National Technical Information Service, August 1978), p.68, figure 11.

6.5 Adapted from Toxic Substances Program, Inform, 381 Park Avenue South, New York, N.Y. 10016.

Shifting Wastes in Tennessee

1. The material presented here is drawn from three sources. They are Robert H. Harris, Joseph V. Rodrick, Robert K. Rhamy, Stavros S. Papadopulos, "Adverse Health Effects at a Tennessee Hazardous Waste Disposal Site," draft, prepared for Fourth Annual Symposium on Environmental Epidemiology, University of Pittsburgh, 1983 (Princeton: Princeton University, Center for Energy and Environmental Studies, 1983); U.S. Congress, House Committee on Interstate and Foreign Commerce, Subcommittee on Oversight and Investigations, *Oversight-Resources Conservation and Recovery Act*, Hearing, 95th Cong., 2d sess., Oct. 30, 1978, Serial No. 95-183; Samuel S. Epstein, Lester O. Brown, and Carl Pope, *Hazardous Waste in America* (San Francisco: Sierra Club Books, 1982), pp. 47-68.

PCBs Pervade Fishing Port

1. The material presented here is drawn from three sources. They are Grant Weaver, "PCB Contamination In and Around New Bedford, Mass." *Environmental Science and Technology* 18(2):22A-27A (1984); "PCBs—Persistent, Pervasive, Perplexing," *Impact* (Tennessee Valley Authority, Office of Natural Resources), September 1983; U.S. Environmental Protection Agency, Office of Pesticides and Toxic Substances, Chemical Coordination Staff, Intermedia Priority Pollutants Guidance Documents, "Polychlorinated Biphenyls" (Washington, D.C.: U.S. Environmental Protection Agency, 1982).

CHAPTER 7: WATER RESOURCES

Text References

1. "The Browning of America," *Newsweek*, Feb. 23, 1981, p. 27. See also Thomas Y. Canby, "Water: Our Most Precious Resource," *National Geographic* 158(8):144-79 (1981).

2. U.S. Department of the Interior, Geological Survey, *National Water Summary 1983*, p. 26; *Congressional Quarterly*, April 18, 1981, p. 673.

3. See U.S. Department of the Interior, Geological Survey, *National Water Summary 1983*, pp. 120, 172, and descriptions of state issues generally, pp. 74-238; see also discussions of specific issues in text at note 16 and 22.
4. Sura 4:31.
5. Arthur Maass and Raymond Anderson, *And the Desert Shall Rejoice: Conflict, Growth and Justice in Arid Environments* (Cambridge: MIT Press, 1978), p. 395.
6. Plato, *The Laws* 844a-845e; Aristotle, *Politics* 1330a-b.
7. 44 Fed. Reg. 27963 (1979).
8. See, e.g., National Water Commission, *Water Policies for the Future* (Washington, D.C.: U.S. Government Printing Office, 1973), p. 1; letter to the editor from Sen. Daniel P. Moynihan, *Wall Street Journal*, May 13, 1982.
9. See, e.g. "Ending the Southwest's Water Binge," *Fortune*, Feb. 23, 1981.
10. Montana Code Ann. §85-2-402 (3) (1978).
11. Philip L. Fradkin, *A River No More: The Colorado River and the West* (New York: Alfred A. Knopf, Inc., 1981), pp. 251-259; U.S. Water Resources Council, *1975 Water Assessment, Summary Report* (Washington, D.C.: U.S. Government Printing Office, July 1977 (Upper Colorado Region), December 1977 (Lower Colorado Region).
12. R. H. Coase, "The Problem of Social Cost," *Journal of Law and Economics*, Vol. III, Oct. 1960.
13. "Unneighborly Suit Ignores S.D. Role," *Sioux Falls Argus-Leader*, Aug. 21, 1982.
14. Harvey Banks et al., "Prospects for Developing New Water Supplies," paper presented to the conference on "Impacts of Limited Water Supplies for Agriculture in the Arid West," organized by the University of California—Davis, held at Asilomar, Calif., Sept. 28-Oct. 1, 1982; "Local Policies Promote Unified Planning," *Water Information News Service*, Dec. 23, 1983, pp. 1-5.
15. See, e.g., California State Assembly, Office of Research, "A Marketing Approach to Water Allocation," report prepared for the California State Assembly, Sacramento, Calif., Feb. 1982; State of Idaho, Department of Water Resources, "Rules and Regulations: Water Supply Bank" (Boise: Department of Water Resources, Oct. 1980).
16. "An Analysis—The Colorado in Flood—Was the Bureau to Blame?" *High Country News*, Oct. 3, 1983. See also "Floods Along Colorado River Set Off a Debate over Blame', *New York Times*, Sept. 13, 1983; U.S Congress, House, Committee on Interior and Insular Affairs, *Oversight Hearings on Colorado River Management*, 98th Cong., 1st Sess., Ser. No. 98-20, Sept. 7-8, 1983 (Washington, D.C.: U.S. Government Printing Office, 1983).
17. See, generally, Helen Ingram et al., "Replacing Confusion with Equity: Alternatives for Water Policy in the Colorado River Basin" (Tucson: University of Arizona, undated). See also "Tamed Colorado Defies the River Oracles," *Washington Post*, Feb. 26, 1984.
18. U.S. Army Corps of Engineers, *Kowanesque Lake Reformulation Study* (Baltimore: Corps of Engineers, March 1982); U.S. Army Corps of Engineers, *Washington Metropolitan Area Water Supply Study* (Baltimore: Corps of Engineers, Sept., 1983), pp. 45-48.

19. "Charles County Crisis: Wells Are Running Dry," *Washington Post*, Jan. 15, 1984.
20. Jack Hirshleifer et al., *Water Supply: Economics, Technology, and Policy* (Chicago: University of Chicago Press, 1960), pp. 255-288; U.S. Army Corps of Engineers, "Northeastern United States Water Supply (NEWS) Study," Public Issuance Nov. 11, 1977.
21. John J. Boland, "Water/Wastewater Pricing and Financial Practices in the United States," Technical Report 1 MMI 19-83 prepared for Agency for International Development (Washington, D.C.: MetaMetrics, Inc., August 17, 1983), pp. 1.8-1.22; "Maintaining Integrity in Aging Systems: Boston's Approach," *Journal of the American Water Works Association*, Nov. 1982, pp. 554-559.
22. "Flooding Poses Threat to Everglades' Ecology," *New York Times*, Sept. 25, 1983; "Caught in an Everglades Range War," *Wall Street Journal*, May 18, 1983; "Natural Water Flow in East Everglades Urged By Official," *Miami Herald*, Oct. 17, 1982; Robert Cahn, "Maintaining the Everglades' Delicate Balance," *Christian Science Monitor*, June 14, 1982.
23. M. Herron, "The Rush is on to Find New Gold in Falling Water," *Smithsonian*, Dec. 1982, pp. 87-90.
24. Allan R. Talbot, *Settling Things: Six Case Studies in Environmental Mediation* (Washington, D.C.: The Conservation Foundation, 1983), pp. 41-53.
25. One standard reference on the basic physical principles governing water pollution is Thomas R. Camp, *Water and Its Impurities* (New York: Reinhold Publishing Corporation, 1963).
26. Philip L. Fradkin, *A River No More*, p. 297.
27. *Ibid.*, pp. 188, 200; State of Colorado, Department of Natural Resources, "The Availability of Water for Oil Shale and Coal Gasification Development in the Upper Colorado River Basin," Summary Report, a report to the U.S. Water Resources Council (Denver: Colorado Department of Natural Resources, Oct. 1979), Tables 4.1-4.3.
28. U.S. Department of the Interior, Bureau of Reclamation, *Water Assessment for the Lower Colorado River Region—Emerging Energy Technology Development* (Boulder City, Nev.: Bureau of Reclamation, Aug. 1981), Table 9, p. 4-2.
29. U.S. Department of the Interior, Bureau of Reclamation, "Salinity Update" (Washington, D.C.: Bureau of Reclamation, Jan. 1983).
30. The Colorado River Salinity Control Act of 1974, 43 U.S.C.A. §§1571-1597 (Supp. 1984).
31. "Water-Short Colorado May Be Dammed If It Builds, Dammed If It Doesn't," *National Journal*, July 17, 1982, p. 1259.
32. U.S. Congress, Senate, Committee on Energy and Natural Resources, Subcommittee on Water and Power, Hearing, *Colorado River Basin Salinity Control Act Amendments*, 97th Cong. 2d sess, June 22, 1982 (Washington, D.C.: U.S. Government Printing Office, 1982), p. 33.
33. *Ibid.*, p. 18.
34. State of North Carolina, Governor's Coastal Water Management Task Force, *Final Report* (Raleigh: North Carolina Dept. of Natural Resources and Community Development, 1982).

35. "Pesticide Reported In Florida Drinking Water," *New York Times*, Nov. 20, 1983; "Florida," *From the State Capitals*, July 1983, January 1984; "Florida: Poisonous Paradise," *Clean Water Action News*, Fall 1983, p. 10; Philip C. Metzger, *To Master A Thirsty Future: An Analysis of Water Management Efforts in Tucson, Arizona* (Washington, D.C.: The Conservation Foundation, May 1984).

36. K.J. DeCook, "Water Rights Conflicts in Use of a Common-Pool Aquifer, Santa Cruz Valley, Arizona" (Tucson: University of Arizona, Water Resources Research Center, 1977), p. 5.

37. "Pentagon Waste Sites Represent Huge, Neglected Crisis, Critics Say," *Wall Street Journal* July 22, 1983.

38. U.S. Department of the Interior, Geological Survey, *Estimated Use of Water in the United States in 1980*, USGS Circular 1001 (Reston, Va.: U.S. Geological Survey, 1983), Table 22, p. 47.

39. Correspondence from William Eichbaum, Assistant Secretary for the Maryland Department of Health and Mental Hygiene, Feb. 15, 1984.

40. Grant McConnell, *Private Power and American Democracy* (New York: Random House, 1970); Theodore S. Lowi, *The End of Liberalism: The Second Republic of the United States* (New York: W.W. Norton, 1979); John E. Chubb, *Interest Groups and the Bureaucracy: The Politics of Energy* (Palo Alto: Stanford University Press, 1983).

41. Hugh Heclo, "One Executive Branch Too Many?" in Anthony King, ed., *Both Ends of the Avenue* (Washington, D.C.: American Enterprise Institute, 1983), p. 36; Grant McConnell, *Private Power and American Democracy*, pp. 119-127; and John E. Chubb, *Interest Groups and the Bureaucracy*, p. 20.

42. Hugh Heclo, "One Executive Branch Too Many?', p. 40; C. Lindblom, *The Policy-Making Process* (New York: Prentice-Hall, 1980), pp. 64-70; Theodore S. Lowi, *The End of Liberalism*, pp. 50-63; and Grant McConnell, *Private Power and American Democracy*, p. 124.

43. 44 Fed. Reg. 27963 (1979).

44. *Environment Reporter—Current Developments*, Aug. 28, 1981, p. 540.

45. Theodore S. Lowi, *The End of Liberalism*, pp. 50-63; and Grant McConnell, *Private Power and American Democracy*, p. 124.

46. U.S. Department of the Interior, "Interim Report Acreage Limitation," Executive Summary (Washington, D.C.: U.S. Department of the Interior, March 1980).

47. See Court and Administration Proceedings arising under the National Environmental Policy Act, p. 2 (memorandum to Council of Environmental Quality Chairman Russell Train from Council of Environmental Quality General Counsel Timothy Atkeson, March 22, 1973).

48. California Environmental Policy Act, Calif. Pub. Res. Code §§21000-21176 (Deering 1976 and Supp. 1982); Massachusetts Environmental Policy Act, Massachusetts Ann. Laws ch. 30 §61-62H (Michie/Law Coop. 1973 and Supp. 1981); Washington State Environmental Policy Act, Washington Rev. Code Ann. §43.21C.010-.910 (Supp. 1981), as supplemented by 1981 Washington Laws chs. 278, 290.

49. "Supreme Court Protects Snail Darter from TVA," 8 ELR 10156 (1978); *Ten-*

546 STATE OF THE ENVIRONMENT

nessee Valley Authority v. Hill, 8 ELR 20524 (1978); Richard A. Liroff, "NEPA—Where Have We Been and Where Are We Going?," *American Planning Association Journal,* April 1980, pp. 157-158.

50. For a positive example, see U.S. Army Corps of Engineers, "Memorandum of Agreement Among Alabama, Georgia, Florida, and the United States Army Corps of Engineers. Mobile District Regarding the Apalachicola-Chattahoochee-Flint River System" (Mobile, Ala.: U.S. Army Corps of Engineers, 1983).

51. Environmental Law Institute, *Groundwater: Strategies for State Action* (Washington, D.C.: Environmental Law Institute, 1984), p. 24.

52. This is done under the aegis of the State's 1981 water policy, State of Florida. Department of Environmental Regulation rule in chapters 17-40, especially §§17-40.04-40.05 (Tallahassee: Department of Environmental Regulation, 1981).

53. State of Arizona, Department of Water Resources, Tucson Active Management Area, *Groundwater Management Plan, First Management Period 1980-1990* (Turf Industries Section Industrial Program Chapter (April 1984); Lee Wilson and Associates, Inc., *Water Supply Alternatives for El Paso,* a report prepared for El Paso Water Utilities Public Service Board. Nov. 1981; U.S. Congress, Senate, Committee on Environment and Public Works, Subcommittee on Water Resources, Hearings, *Water Resources Policy Issues,* 97th Congress, 1st session (Washington, D.C.: U.S. Government Printing Office, 1984), pp. 281-283.

54. Information provided by staff of the Washington State Department of Ecology, Aug. 24, 1983.

55. Testimony of Robert Neufeld, Secretary of South Dakota Department of Water and Natural Resources, before the U.S. Congress. Senate. Committee on Environment and Public Works, Subcommittee on Water Resources. Hearings, *Water Resources Policy Issues,* pp. 189-190, 266-279.

56. Personal communications with Conservation Foundation staff.

57. State of New Jersey, Department of Environmental Protection, "New Jersey Statewide Water Supply Master Plan," (Trenton: New Jersey Department of Environmental Protection, April 1982); John McPhee, *The Pine Barrens* (New York: Farrar, Strauss, and Giroux, Inc, 1981).

58. Rae Zimmerman, *The Administration of Regulation: Permit and Licensing Activities for Water Resource Management in New York and New Jersey* (New York: New York University, OWRT grant No. 14-34-001-8405, April 1980), pp. 44-61.

59. "Wheat Farmer Stuns the West with Water Suit," *The Washington Post,* Sept. 12, 1982.

60. 458 U.S. 941, 102 S.Ct. 3456 (1982).

61. John Folk-Williams, *What Indian Water Means to the West* (Santa Fe, N.Mex.: Western Network, 1983); Connie Boris and John Krutilla, *Water Rights and Energy Development in the Yellowstone River Basin: An Integrated Analysis* (Baltimore: Johns Hopkins University Press, 1980).

62. For analyses of the instream flow issue, see, e.g., A. Dan Tarlock, "Recent Developments in the Recognition of Instream Uses in Western Water Law," 1975 Utah L. Rev. 871; A. Dan Tarlock, "The Recognition of Instream Flow Rights: 'New' Public Western Water Rights" 25 *Rocky Mnt. Min. L. Inst.* 24

(1979); Comment, "Maintenance of Minimum Instream Flows in South Dakota," 23 *S. D. L. Rev.* (Winter 1978); Alan B. Lilly, "Protecting Streamflows in California," 8 *Ecology L. Q.* 697 (1980); Harold A. Ranquist, "Res Judicata—Will it Stop Instream Flows from being the Wave of the Future?," in 20 *Natural Resources J.* 121 (1980), p. 121; Richard L. Dewsnup and Dallin W. Jensen, *Promising Strategies for Reserving Instream Flows*, prepared for Fish and Wildlife Service, Western Energy and Land Use Team, (Springfield, Va.: National Technical Information Service, Oct. 1977), pp. 1-3; James L. Huffman, *The Allocation of Water to Instream Flows*, Final Report DOI-OWRT, Grant 14-34-0001-8403 (Portland, Ore.: Lewis and Clark Law School, July 1980); Rick A. Thompson, "Statutory Recognition of Instream Flow Preservation: A Proposed Solution for Wyoming," 17 *Land and Water L. Rev.* 139 (1982).

63. John-Folk Williams, *What Indian Water Means to the West; and* Connie Boris *and* John Krutilla, *Water Rights and Energy Development in the Yellowstone River Basin*.

64. Ariz. Rev. Stat. Ann. §§45-401 to -636 (Supp. 1981-82).

65. See, e.g., "Foes of Canal Built Success on Two Points," *Los Angeles Times*, June 10, 1982; Editorial, "California's Canal Vote," *Denver Post*, June 14, 1982; William Kahrl, "It's Rethinking Time on Water," *Los Angeles Times*, Nov. 4, 1982.

66. See, e.g., Water Law Study Commitee, *The Impact of Recent Court Decisions Concerning Water and Interstate Commerce on Water Resources of the State of New Mexico*, a report to Governor Toney Anaya (Albuquerque: University of New Mexico School of Law, 1984); Gail Bingham, "Metropolitan Water Roundtable Formed to Build Consensus on Meeting Denver's Long-term Water Needs," *Resolve*, Summer 1982, pp. 5-7.

67. Lawrence Mosher, "Water Politics As Usual May Be Losing Ground in Congress," *National Journal*, July 19, 1980, p. 1189.

68. Advisory Commission on Intergovernment Relations, *The Federal Role in the Federal System: The Dynamics of Growth* (Washington, D.C.: ACIR, March 1981), p. 31; *Environment Reporter—Current Developments*, May 28, 1982, p. 101.

69. *Environment Reporter—Current Developments*, Sept. 30, 1983, p. 940.

70. *Environment Reporter—Current Developments*, Jan. 21, 1983, p. 1629.

71. Civ. No. 80-730 HB (D.Ct. N.M.), Jan. 17, 1983.

72. "Michigan Acts to Prevent Diversion of Water," *New York Times*, Oct. 23, 1983.

73. "Exxon's Taking of Hudson Water Leads to Inquiry," *New York Times*, Oct. 5, 1983; "Exxon is Faulted on Use of Hudson," *New York Times*, Oct. 15, 1983; "Exxon is Sued by New York Over Use of Hudson Water," *New York Times*, April 26, 1984.

74. U.S. Army Corps of Engineers, "Memorandum of Agreement Among Alabama, George, Florida, and the U.S. Army Corps of Engineers . . ."; U.S. Water Resources Council, "Vol. 4: South Atlantic-Gulf Region" of *Water Resources 1975-2000* (Washington, D.C.: U.S. Government Printing Office, 1978), pp. 25-34 *passim* and 35-41; "A Pipeline that is Inciting a Water War," *Business Week*, Oct. 26, 1981; "Decision to Sell River's Water Angers Missouri Basin

States," *New York Times*, June 1, 1982; 'South Dakota Sets Stage for Interstate Water Wars," *Albuquerque Journal*, June 13, 1982; Edward R. Kaynor, *Connecticut River Diversion: A Case Study in Water Allocation Policy*, OWRT Project Completion Report C-7178 (Amherst: University of Massachusetts Water Resources Research Center, July 1978).

75. Testimony of Robert Neufeld before the Senate, Committee on Environment and Public Works, Subcommittee on Water Resources, Hearings, *Water Resources Policy Issues*, p. 191.

76. U.S. Environmental Protection Agency, *Chesapeake Bay: A Framework for Action* (Annapolis: U.S. Environmental Protection Agency, 1983), pp. 60-72, 130-137; "Great Lakes Need Wise Dispute Resolutions," *Conservation Foundation Letter*, Nov. 1983; U.S. Comptroller General, *A More Comprehensive Approach is Needed to Clean Up the Great Lakes* (Washington, D.C.: General Accounting Office, 1982).

77. Lee Wilson and Associates, Inc., *Water Supply Alternatives for El Paso*.

78. Terry L. Anderson et al., "Privatizing Groundwater Basins; A Model and Its Application," in Anderson, ed., *Water Rights* (Cambridge, Mass.: Ballinger Publishing Co., 1983); Florida Statutes 1981, §373.069 *et. seq.*; New Mexico Stat. Ann. §72-12-1 et. seq.; Philip C. Metzger, *To Master a Thirsty Future: An Analysis of Water Management Efforts in Tucson, Arizona*.

79. U.S. Department of the Interior, Geological Survey, *National Water Summary 1983—Hydrologic Events and Issues*, USGS Water Supply Paper 2250 (Washington, D.C.: U.S. Government Printing Office, 1984), pp. 26, 27.

80. *Ibid.*, p. 28.

81. "American Survey: Water in the West," *The Economist*, May 14, 1983, pp. 41-50.

82. Wells A. Hutchins, *Water Rights Laws in the Nineteen Western States*, misc. pub. 1206 (Washington, D.C.: U.S. Department of Agriculture, 1971); *Mason v. Hoyle*, 56 Conn 255, 14 att. 786 (Sup. Ct. of Errors of Conn. (1888)); see also other cases cited in Charles J. Meyers and A. Dan Tarlock, *Water Resource Management* (Mineola, N.Y.: The Foundation Press, 1979), pp. 52-75.

83. William E. Cox and Leonard A. Shabman, "Interbasin-Interstate Transfer of Water in the South," and "Steirer Describes Evolution of Southern Water Law," from *Rural Postcript*: "Proceedings of the Conference," 'Future Waves: Water Policy in the South," Nov. 18-19, 1982 (Mississippi State: Mississippi State University, Southern Rural Development Center, 1982).

84. Leonard Shabman and William Cox, "Costs of Water Management Institutions: The Case of Southeast Virginia," paper presented at a Resources for the Future seminar held at the National Academy of Sciences, Nov. 17, 1983, to be published in a forthcoming compendium of water policy case studies by Resources for the Future.

85. "Indian Water Rights Clouding Plans for the West's Economic Development," *National Journal*, Oct. 30, 1982, pp. 1841-1845. See also Anne E. Ross, "Water Rights: Aboriginal Water Use and Water Law in the Southwestern United States: Why the Reserved Rights Doctrine Was Inappropriate," 9 *Amer. Ind. L. Rev.* 198-201, 208-209 (1981); Mary Wallace, "Papago Participation in the Formulation of SAWRSA," paper to be included in the forthcoming book prepared

under a grant from the Ford Foundation by Helen Ingram, Lee Brown et al., *Water and Poverty in the Southwest.*

86. See, e.g., *Colville Confederated Tribes v. Walton*, 647 F. 2d 42 (9th Cir. 1981).

87. E.g., John Baden and Richard Stroup, "Property Rights, Environmental Quality, and the Management of National Forests," in Garrett Hardin and John Baden, eds., *Managing the Commons* (San Franscisco: W.H. Freeman and Co., 1977), pp. 232-234.

88. Richard W. Behan, "The Privatization Alternative for the Future of the Federal Public Lands: A Penultimate Comment," paper presented to the annual meeting of the Western Political Science Association, Seattle, March 25, 1983 (Flagstaff: Northern Arizona University School of Forestry, 1983); Christopher K. Leman, "The Revolution of the Saints: The Ideology of Privatization and its Consequences for the Public Lands," paper presented at the conference titled "Selling the Federal Forests" University of Washington, Seattle, April 22-23, 1983 (Seattle: University of Washington Press, forthcoming).

89. Ariz. Rev. Stat. Ann. §§45-401 to -636 (Supp. 1981-82).

90. State of Arizona, Department of Water Resources, "Progress Report: Implementation of the 1980 Groundwater Management Code" (Phoenix: Department of Water Resources, undated).

91. Ariz. Rev. Stat. §§45-564 to -568 (Supp. 1981-1982).

92. See, e.g., Charles J. Meyers and A. Dan Tarlock, *Water Resource Management*, pp. 366-380, and refs. cited therein.

93. Discussion condensed from Richard A. Solomon, *The Federal State Regional Corporation*, Report to the National Water Commission (Springfield, Va.: National Technical Information Service, 1971), and from the discussion in the National Water Commission report itself, pp. 427-433.

94. *Ibid.*

95. John Folk-Williams, "Negotiation Becomes More Important in Settling Indian Water Rights Disputes in the West," *Resolve*, Summer 1982, p. 5.

96. See, e.g., Water Law Study Committee, *The Impact of Recent Court Decisions*; Gail Bingham, "Metropolitan Water Roundtable'; John Folk-Williams, *What Indian Water Means to the West*; personal communications with Conservation Foundation staff.

97. Charles J. Meyers and A. Dan Tarlock, *Water Resource Management*, p. 394; and references on interstate compact, p. 380.

98. Gary W. Hart, *Institutions for Water Planning*, background paper NWC-L-71-017, prepared for the National Water Commission (Springfield, Va.: National Technical Information Service, 1971), pp. 2-3; Jerome C. Muys, *Interstate Water Compacts*, background paper NWC-L-71-001, prepared for the National Water Commission (Springfield, Va.: National Technical Information Service, 1971), p. 38.

99. Delaware River Basin Commission Act, 75 Stat. 688 (Sept. 27, 1961); Susquehanna River Basin Commission Act, 84 Stat. 1509 (Dec. 24, 1970).

100. Executive Order 12319, 46 Fed. Reg. 45591 (1981).

101. U.S. Comptroller General, *Federal Interstate Compact Commissions: Useful Mechanisms for Planning and Managing River Basin Operations* (Washington, D.C.: General Accounting Office, 1983); National Water Commission Report,

Water Policies for the Future (Washington, D.C.: U.S. Government Printing Office, 1973), pp. 422-423.

102. *Ibid.*

103. Information provided by staff of the Interstate Commission on the Potomac River Basin, Dec. 28, 1982.

104. Personal communications with author.

105. Gary W. Hart, *Institutions for Water Planning*, pp. 98-99 109-112; and National Water Commission Report, *Water Policies for the Future*, pp. 417-418.

106. See, generally, David R. Zwick, ed., *Water Wasteland* (Washington, D.C.: Center for Study of Responsive Law, 1971).

107. Terry L. Anderson, *Water Crisis: Ending the Policy Drought* (Washington, D.C.: The Cato Institute, 1983).

108. *Ibid.*

109. *Ibid.*; John Neary, "The Great Southwest Water War," *Saturday Review* 4:19 (Sept. 3, 1977), "In New Mexico, Water is Valuable Resource—And So Is Water Boss," *Wall Street Journal*, May 1, 1980.

110. Helen Ingram, Lee Brown et al., *Water and Poverty in the Southwest*.

111. Terry L. Anderson, *Water Crisis: Ending the Policy Drought*, pp. 73-91.

112. Philip C. Metzger and Jennifer A. Haverkamp, "Instream Flow Protection: Adaptation to Intensifying Demands" (Washington, D.C.: The Conservation Foundation, 1983).

113. "Dakota Dispute Opens War on Midwest Water," *Los Angeles Times*, Oct. 23, 1982; "It's Not Only the Russians Who Regard the MX as a Threat," *National Journal*, Aug. 23, 1980, p. 1400; see also "Nature Lovers, How Western Slope Cowboys Became Inflamed Environmentalists," *Rocky Mountain News*, Feb. 7, 1982.

114. Civ. No. 80-K-624, U.S. D. Ct. Colo. (1983).

115. Report by the U.S. Comptroller General, *Water Supply Should Not be an Obstacle to Meeting Energy Development Goals* (Washington, D.C.: General Accounting Office, 1980).

116. Frederick R. Anderson et al., *Environmental Improvement Through Economic Incentives* (Baltimore: Johns Hopkins University Press, 1977), pp. 157-158.

117. U.S. Congress, Congressional Budget Office, "Efficient Investments of Water Resources: Issues and Options" (Washington, D.C.: U.S. Government Printing Office, 1983), pp. 1-7; Edward R. Osann et al., *Shortchanging the Treasury: The Failure of the Department of the Interior to Comply with the Inspector General's Audit Recommendations to Recover the Costs of Federal Water Projects* (Washington, D.C.: National Wildlife Federation, 1984); "Water Projects Await Funding as Debate Over Cost-sharing Stalls Action on Capitol Hill," *Congressional Quarterly*, July 30, 1983, p. 1553; "Remarks of William R. Gianelli, Asst. Secretary of the Army-Civil Works, on Federal Water Project Cost Sharing and Financing Policies," speech to the California Water Resources Association, San Diego, Calif., Aug. 18, 1983, pp. 2-4.

118. U.S. Water Resources Council, *The Nation's Water Resources* (Washington, D.C.: U.S. General Printing Office, 1968), pp. 2-2, 2-3.

119. U.S. Congress. Congressional Budget Office,'The Federal Government in a Federal System: Current Intergovernmental Programs and Options for Change" (Washington, D.C.: U.S. Government Printing Office, 1983), p. 129.

120. "States Bite Federal Tax Cut," *Business Week*, July 26, 1982, p. 21.

121. U.S. Department of Agriculture, "A History of Federal Water Resources Programs, 1800-1960" (Washington, D.C.: U.S. Department of Agriculture, June 1972).

122. *Ibid.*

123. Congressional Budget Office, "Efficient Investments in Water Resources: Issues and Options" (Washington, D.C.: U.S. Government Printing Office, 1983), pp. 1-7.

124. "Environmentalists Fault Western Water Projects," *The Washington Post*, May 22, 1984; Edward R. Osann et al., *Shortchanging the Treasury*.

125. "Water Projects Await Funding as Debate over Cost-sharing Stalls Action on Capitol Hill." *Congressional Quarterly*, July 30, 1983, p. 1553; "Remarks of William R. Gianelli, Asst. Secretary of the Army-Civil Works, on Federal Water Project Cost Sharing and Financing Policies," speech to the California Water Resources Association, San Diego, Calif., Aug. 18, 1983, pp. 2-4.

126. U.S. Comptroller General, *Water Project Construction Backlog—A Serious Problem with no Easy Solution* (Washington, D.C.: General Accounting Office, 1983); "Governors Seek a Water Policy That Has Something for Everyone," *National Journal*, March 18, 1978, p. 432.

127. Lawrence Mosher, "Water Politics as Usual May Be Losing Ground in Congress," p. 1190.

128. *Congressional Quarterly*, "Water Projects Await Funding as Debate over Cost-Sharing Stalls Action on Capitol Hill," p. 1553; and "The Pork-Barrel Politics of Western Water Pose a Dilemma for Reagan's Budget Plans," *Wall Street Journal*, Feb. 11, 1982.

129. "Reagan Revises Water-Project Policy," *The Washington Post*, Jan. 25, 1984.

130. B. Joseph Tofani, President of the Water Resources Congress, quoted in "Water Crisis is Predicted Unless Congress and States Get Together on Water Policy," *Congressional Quarterly*, April 18, 1981, p. 673.

131. Congressional Budget Office, *Efficient Investments in Water Resources*, Figure 1, p. 22.

132. *Ibid*, p. xiii.

133. Edward Osann, Executive Director of the Coalition for Water Project Review, quoted in *Congressional Quarterly*, 'Water Crises is Predicted Unless Congress and States Get Together on Water Policy," p. 678.

134. Congressional Budget Office, "Efficient Investments in Water Resources: Issues and Options," p. 56; "Remarks of William R. Gianelli," pp. 2-4); Wes Watkins, "The Funding of Water Resources Development," *ICWP Washington Report*, May 1983.

135. See, e.g., Jean Gimpel, *The Medieval Machine* (Baltimore, Md.: Penguin Press, 1976), pp. 248-252.

136. Labor-Management Group, *A Consensus on Rebuilding America's Vital Public Facilities: Highways, Bridges, Urban Water Supply, Wastewater Treatment*, Oct. 1983, pp. 21-24. Copies of this report can be obtained by writing to: Infrastructure Report, c/o Union Pacific Corporation, 345 Park Ave., New York 10154.

137. U.S. Water Resources Council, *The Nation's Water Resources*, pp. 4-3-1, 4-3-2, 4-3-6; see also Philip C. Metzger, "Nationally Significant Studies of Water

552   STATE OF THE ENVIRONMENT

Policy: A Review of Major Water Policy Studies and Assessment of Present Issues," (Washington, D.C.: The Conservation Foundation, June 1983), p. 9.
138. Statement of George Peterson, Urban Land Institute, before 1983 ASWIPCA conference, quoted in *Water Information News Service*, Apr. 19, 1983, p. 5.
139. Report by the U.S. Comptroller General, *Report to the Administrator, Environmental Protection Agency. Wastewater Dischargers Are Not Complying with EPA Pollution Control Permits* (Washington, D.C.: U.S. Government Printing Office, 1983), p. i.
140. Statement of Brig. Gen. C.E. Edgar III, Deputy Director of the Army Corps of Engineers, June 27, 1983, in U.S. Congress, Senate Committee on Environment and Public Works, Subcommittee on Water Resources, Hearings, *Omnibus Water Resources Legislation, Part 3*, 98th Cong., 1st Sess. (Washington, D.C.: U.S. Government Printing Office, 1984), p. 6.
141. "Area Jurisdictions Reach Agreement on Sharing Water for Rest of Century," *The Washington Post*, Feb. 21, 1981; Department of the Army, Baltimore District, Corps of Engineers, *Metropolitan Area Water Supply Study* Final Report (Baltimore: U.S. Army Corps of Engineers, Sept. 1983), p. 43.
142. Letter from Daniel P. Sheer, Director, Interstate Commission on the Potomac River Basin, to Assistant Secretary of the Army-Civil Works William Gianelli, March 19, 1982; see also testimony of Daniel P. Sheer, June 28, 1983, in Hearings, *Omnibus Water Resources Legislation*, p. 220.
143. John J. Boland, "Water/Wastewater Pricing and Financial Practices in the United States," pp. 4.7, 4.11.
144. *Ibid.*, pp. ix-x, 4.26.
145. *Ibid.*, p. viii.
146. Congressional Budget Office, *Efficient Investments in Water Resources*, Table 4, p. 15; and see, generally, U.S. Comptroller General, *Federal Charges for Irrigation Projects Do Not Cover Costs* (Washington, D.C.: General Accounting Office, March 1981).
147. *Ibid.*
148. Rodney Smith, *Financing Western Water Investment* (Washington, D.C.: Council of State Planning Agencies, 1984).
149. John J. Boland, "Water/Wastewater Pricing and Financial Practices in the United States," p. 5.7.
150. Information provided by Orange County Water District, May 15, 1984.
151. Comment of Wyoming Governor Herschler on proposed federal cost sharing policy, quoted in *Water Information News Service*, April 19, 1983, p. 2.
152. Interstate Conference on Water Problems, Cost-Sharing Task Force, "Water Resources Financing Proposal," draft (Washington, D.C.: Interstate Conference on Water Problems, March 31, 1983), p. 4.
153. U.S. Department of the Interior, "Potential Modifications in Eight Proposed Western Colorado Projects for Future Energy Development, Special Report" (Washington, D.C.: U.S. Department of the Interior, Water And Power Resources Service, June 1980).
154. Warren Viessman, "Water Resources Development: Water Projects Cost-Sharing and Financing," Issue Brief No. IB81173 (Washington, D.C.: Library of Congress, February 16, 1982), pp. 6-9; American Public Works Association, *Changing Directions in Water Management*, proceedings of the National Water Sym-

posium, an infrastructure financing policy symposium. Nov. 17-19 (Washington, D.C.: American Public Works Association, 1983), pp. 38, 49.

155. A. K. Biswas, "Long Distance Mass Transfer of Water," in *Water Supply and Management* 5(3) 1981, pp. 245-251; see also Philip L. Fradkin, *A River No More*, p. 256.

156. National Water Commission Report, *Water Policies for the Future*, p. 495.

157. John J. Boland, "Water/Wastewater Pricing and Financial Practices in the United States," pp. 5.6, 5.8, 5.9.

158. *Ibid.*; U.S. Environmental Protection Agency, National Municipal Policy," Jan. 27, 1984.

159. Northeast/Midwest Institute, *Building a Water Policy Consensus: Key Issues for the Eighties* (Washington, D.C.: Northeast/Midwest Institue, 1982), pp. 5-9.

160. Labor Management Group, *A Consensus on Rebuilding America's Vital Public Facilities...*, p. 8; American Public Works Association, *Changing Directions in Water Management*, p. 4.

161. Northeast/Midwest Institute, *Building a Water Policy Consensus...*, pp. 5-9.

162. See, e.g.,Interstate Conference on Water Problems, Cost-Sharing Task Force, "Water Resources Financing Proposal"; U.S. Department of Agriculture, "A History of Federal Water Resources Programs, 1800-1960'; Warren Viessman, "Water Resources Development: Water Projects Cost-Sharing and Financing"; American Public Works Association, *Changing Directions in Water Management*, pp. 21-26, 33-49; and Utah Water Research Laboratory, *A Study of Feasibility of State Water User Fees for Financing Water Development*, OWRT project no. B-122-Utah (Logan: Utah Water Resource Research Laboratory, 1978); and Rodney Smith, *Financing Western Water Investment*.

163. Salt River Project, *Annual Report 1981-82* (Phoenix: Salt River Project, 1982), pp. 10-11, 18; information provided by Watershed Division, Salt River Project.

Figure References

7.1 U.S. Army Corps of Engineers, *Washington Metropolitan Area Water Supply Study*. Final Report (Baltimore: U.S. Army Corps of Engineers, Sept. 1983), p. 47.

7.2 U.S. Department of Interior, Bureau of Reclamation, "Salinity Update" (Washington, D.C.: U.S. Department of Interior, Jan. 1983).

7.3 U.S. Department of Interior, Geological Survey, "Water Resources of Lower Colorado River-Salton Sea Area as of 1971," Summary Report, Professional Paper 486-A (Reston, Va.: U.S. Geological Survey, 1976).

7.4 U.S. Congress, Congressional Budget Office, "Efficient Investments in Water Resources: Issues and Options" (Washington, D.C.: U.S. Government Printing Office, Aug. 1983), p. 22.

7.5 *Ibid.*, p. 15. For urban flood protection the Bureau of Reclamation and Soil Conservation Service reported the activity but no cost sharing percentage; for commercial harbors the same two agencies reported no activity; the Soil Conservation Service reported no activities or cost showing for hydroelectric power, water quality improvement, or inland waterways. Finally, the Congressional

Budget Office estimates that non-federal cost sharing could be as high as 11 percent for inland waterways.

7.6 Walter B. Langbein, "Dams, Reservoirs, and Withdrawals for Water Supply—Historic Trends." Open File Report 82-256 (Reston, Va.: U.S. Geological Survey, 1982).

7.7 U.S. Army Corps of Engineers, *Washington Metropolitan Area Water Supply Study*, p. 37.

Yakima Valley: Dousing the Flames of Conflict

1. Michael H. Glantz, "Consequences and Responsibilities in Drought Forecasting: The Case of Yakima, 1977," *Water Resources Research* 18(1):3 (1982); U.S. Bureau of Reclamation, "Yakima River Basin Water Enhancement Project, Plan of Study" (Boise, Idaho: U.S. Bureau of Reclamation, May 1981); Northwest Power Planning Council, November 1982), Section 900; Paul Mongillo and Lee Faulconer, *Yakima Fisheries Enhancement Study Final Report* (Olympia: Washington State Department of Game, U.S. Water and Power Resources Service Contract No. 7-07-10-S0038, October 1980); John Q. Ressler, "Graphic Display of Water Rights and Water Resource Information for the Yakima River Basin as an Aid to Decision-Making," OWRT Project No. A-075-WASH (Ellensburg, Wash.: Central Washington State College, Oct. 1976).

Hispanics, Indians, Anglos: A Struggle over Water Rights

1. "Bitter Water Battle Nears End in New Mexico," *New York Times*, December 9, 1983; "The Aamodt Case Pits Rural New Mexicans Against Each Other," *High Country News*, March 5, 1984; see also John Neary, "The Great Southwest Water War," *Saturday Review*, September 3, 1977; "In New Mexico, Water Is Valuable Resource—And So Is Water Boss," *Wall Street Journal*, May 1, 1980; and Albert Utton, Charles T. DuMars, and Marily O'Leary, *Pueblo Indian Water Rights: Vortex in the Struggle for a Precious Resource* (Tucson: University of Arizona Press, 1984).

CHAPTER 8:
INTERGOVERNMENTAL RELATIONS AND ENVIRONMENTAL POLICY

Text References

1. John Naisbett, *Megatrends: Ten New Directions Transforming Our Lives* (New York: Warner Books, Inc. 1982), pp. 97-129.
2. "6 Eastern States Sue EPA Over Over Acid Rain," *New York Times*, March 2, 1984.
3. See box, p. 452, and accompanying footnotes.
4. See, e.g., EPA's proposed imposition of sanctions on Fresno County, California, 49 Fed. Reg. 2269 (1984).
5. The constitutionality of the statute was upheld by the U.S. Supreme Court

in *Pacific Gas and Electric v. State Energy Resources Conservation and Development Commission*, 103 S. Ct. 1713, 13 ELR 20519 (1983).

6. Federal-state haggling over EDB is traceable in headlines of news stories: "Florida Officials Remove Products After Tests Show EDB Contamination," *Washington Post*, December 22, 1983; "EPA Turns Down Action on EDB-Tainted Foods," *Washington Post*, December 24, 1983; "EPA Would Consider Interim EDB Guide," *Washington Post*, December 30, 1983; "EPA Under Pressure to Act on Pesticide," *New York Times*, January 12, 1984; "Florida Relaxes Ban on Items With EDB; It and California Accept New U.S. Rules," *Wall Street Journal*, February 6, 1984; "Three Dissatisfied States Want to Tighten EDB Guidelines," *Washington Post*, February 6, 1984; "Stringent EDB Standards Are Set by New York and Five Other States," *New York Times*, February 24, 1984; "A Cancer Scare Pits the States Against the EPA," *Business Week*, February 20, 1984, page 38; "Patchwork of State Standards Complicates Federal EDB Effort," *Washington Post*, March 23, 1984. For a good summary of the issue's evolution through late January 1984, see Marjorie Sun, "EDB Contamination Kindles Federal Action," *Science* 223(4635):464-466 (1984).

7. See "Massachusetts Town Weighs Seceding Over a Waste Site," *New York Times*, February 19, 1984.

8. O. Cusack, "Reprieve for Minnesota's Wolves," *Sierra* 69(2):38-40 (1984).

9. There are 50 state governments, 3,041 counties, 19,076 municipalities, 16,734 townships, 14,851 school districts, and 28,588 special districts. See U.S. Department of Commerce, Bureau of the Census, *Governmental Organization, Volume I, 1982 Census of Governments* (Washington, D.C.: U.S. Government Printing Office, 1984).

10. The burgeoning academic literature on "implementation" reviews the numerous factors (political, economic, etc.) influencing the likelihood of success in carrying out policy. See, e.g., "Symposium on Successful Policy Implementation," *Policy Studies Journal* 8(4) (1980).

11. On the limits of pragmatism, see Christopher K. Leman and Robert H. Nelson, "The Rise of Managerial Federalism," 12 *Envtl L.* 981-1029 (1982).

12. For example, the Natural Resources Defense Council was a co-plaintiff with California and other states in lawsuits challenging 5 year OCS leasing schedules prepared by Secretaries Andrus and Watt. *California v. Watt*, 668 F. 2d. 1290 (D.C. Cir. 1981), *California v. Watt*, 712 F. 2d. 584 (D.C. Cir. 1983).

13. For example, as of November 1, 1977, 17 percent of the major federal facilities subject to the Clean Air Act were out of compliance with air quality standards or emission limitations, and over one-third of these noncomplying facilities were not anticipated to be in compliance by the July 1, 1979 statutory deadline. See Administrator of the Environmental Protection Agency, *Annual Report to the Congress: Progress in the Prevention and Control of Air Pollution in 1977."* U.S. Senate Document No. 95-100, 95th Cong., 2d Sess. (Washington, D.C. U.S. Government Printing Office, 1978), p. 103. See also U.S. Comptroller General, *DOD Can Make Further Progress in Controlling Pollution From Its Sewage Treatment Plants* (Washington, D.C.: U.S. General Accounting Office, 1984), p. iii.

14. Sally Fairfax, "Old Recipes for New Federalism," 12 *Envtl. L.* 980 (1982).

15. See "Interior Prepares to Crack Down on States with Deficient Strip-Mining Programs," *Wall Street Journal*, February 14, 1984. See also 49 Fed. Reg. 7560 (1984), and 49 Fed. Reg. 14674 (1984).

16. See Lawrence Mosher, "Reagan's Environmental Federalism—Are the States Up to the Challenge?" *National Journal* 14 (5):187 (1982). There was a backlog of 643 SIP revisions awaiting review in August 1981. EPA made a special effort to reduce the backlog. Even though 273 additional revisions had been received by November 1981, the total backlog had been reduced to 159. See U.S. Senate. Committee on Environment and Public Works, Subcommittee on Toxic Substances and Environmental Oversight, *The Impact of the Proposed EPA Budget on State and Local Environmental Programs*, 98th Cong., 1st Sess. (Washington, D.C.: U.S. Government Printing Office, 1983), p. 338. See also William F. Pedersen, Jr., "Why the Clean Air Act Works Badly," 129 *U. Pa. L. Rev.* 1059-1109 (1981). Some environmentalists are concerned that the reduction was achieved by turning the process into a rubber-stamp operation.

17. This is a selective review of federal environmental programs, sufficient to convey our principal lessons.

18. The increased federal involvement in environmental matters was part of a larger federal role in a host of policy areas. This increased federal activity is traced in Congressional Budget Office, "The Federal Government in a Federal System: Current Intergovernmental Programs and Options for Change," (Washington, D.C.: U.S. Government Printing Office, 1983), p. 15. The problems arising from the increased federal involvement in many policy areas are described in Advisory Commission on Intergovernmental Relations, *A Crisis of Confidence and Competence* (Washington, D.C.: U.S. Government Printing Office, 1980).

19. Numerous analyses have been produced describing the origins of the major federal pollution control programs. See, e.g., Advisory Commission on Intergovernmental Relations, *Protecting the Environment: Politics, Pollution, and Federal Policy* (Washington, D.C.: U.S. Government Printing Office, 1981), and the sources cited therein.

20. The intermingling of federal and state roles in environmental and other programs has been likened to the mixing of ingredients in a marble cake. The "marble cake" recipe was first cooked up by political scientist Morton Grodzins. His formulation is cited in Sally Fairfax, 12 *Envtl. L.* 945, 946 (1982).

21. See, generally, Library of Congress, Congressional Research Service, "Federal-State Relations in Transition: Implications for Environmental Policy," a report prepared for U.S. Senate. Committee on Environment and Public Works. 97th Cong., 2d Sess., Serial No. 97-7 (Washington, D.C.: U.S. Government Printing Office, 1982).

22. Leman and Nelson cite as examples of strong state and local action Seattle's clean-up of Lake Washington in the 1950s, Oregon's clean-up of the Willamette River in the 1960s, and California's efforts to abate air pollution. Leman and Nelson, *supra* note 11, pp. 1020-1021. For the general condition of state and local programs, see generally, J. Clarence Davies and Barbara Davies, *The Politics of Pollution*, 2d ed. (Indianapolis: Bobbs-Merrill, 1975).

23. John C. Esposito, *Vanishing Air* (New York: Grossman Publishers, 1970), p. 200.

24. *Ibid.*, p. 152.

25. For recent discussion of the rationale for this federal involvement see: Turner T. Smith, "Opening Address: Reflections on Federalism," 12 ELR 15068 (1982); Lewis Crampton, Chair, State/Federal Roles Task Force, "Final Report of the State/Federal Roles Task Force," submitted to U.S. EPA Deputy Administrator Alvin Alm, September 14, 1983; and Advisory Commission on Intergovernmental Relations, "Regulatory Federalism: Policy, Process, Impact and Reform," (Washington, D.C.: U.S. Government Printing Office, 1982). References in these footnotes to ACIR's "Regulatory Federalism" are to a 1982 summary of the report's findings and recommendations. The full report was published in February 1984.

26. 42 U.S.C.A. §§7401 *et seq*. The description in the text of the Clean Air Act is a selective one. For a more complete description, see Bradley I. Raffle, "The New Clean Air Act—Getting Clean and Staying Clean," *Environment Reporter*, Monograph No. 26 (May 19, 1978); John Quarles, "Federal Regulation of New Industrial Plants," *Environment Reporter*, Monograph No. 28 (May 4, 1979); and Phillip D. Reed and Gregory S. Wetstone, eds. *Air and Water Pollution Control Law: 1981* (Washington, D.C.: Environmental Law Institute, 1981).

27. Clean Air Act, 42 U.S.C.A. §7506 (1984).

28. 30 U.S.C.A. §1252(c) (Supp. 1984).

29. 30 U.S.C.A. §1252(b) (Supp. 1984). The regulations implementing this section varied from the statute's mandatory approach, thus allowing the states greater flexibility and avoiding a Tenth Amendment challenge. See W. Eichbaum and H. Babcock, "A Question of Delegation: The Surface Mining Control and Reclamation Act of 1977 and State-Federal Relations, An Inquiry Into the Success With Which Congress May Provide Detailed Guidance for Executive Agency Action," *86 Dick. L. Rev.*, 615, 635-40 (1982).

30. 30 U.S.C.A. §1252(e) (Supp. 1984).

31. 30 U.S.C.A. §§1253, 1254 (Supp. 1984).

32. 29 U.S.C. A. §651 (Supp. 1984). Some readers may quibble with characterization of the OSH Act as an environmental protection law. For purposes of this discussion, we interpret "environmental protection" broadly.

33. 29 U.S.C.A. §655 (Supp. 1984).

34. 29 U.S.C.A. §667 (Supp. 1984).

35. *Ibid*.

36. For a review of federal devices to promote state action in both environmental and nonenvironmental programs, see Advisory Commission on Intergovernmental Relations, "Regulatory Federalism," *supra* note 25.

37. See Grover Rees III, "The Fall of the House of *Usery*, " *Regulation* 7(3):33 (1983); and Cynthia Colella, "The Supreme Court in 1982: Retolling the Tenth Amendment Death Knoll?" *Intergovernmental Perspective*, Vol. 8, No. 4/Vol 9, No. 1 (Winter 1983), p. 16. See also *Hodel v. Virginia Surface Mining and Reclamation Association*, 452 U.S. 264, 11 ELR 20569 (1981).

38. 43 U.S.C.A. §1331 (Supp. 1984).

39. Pub. L. No. 83-212, §5(a)(1), 67 Stat. 462 (1953), codified as amended at 43 U.S.C.A. §§1331-56 (1976 and Supp. 1984).

40. However, states do own the resources beneath the seabed from the shore out a distance of three miles, and of course receive revenues from developing these resources. See the Submerged Lands Act, 43 U.S.C.A. §§1331-56 (1976 and

Supp. 1984). Also, in 1976, Congress enacted the Coastal Energy Impact Program to provide federal assistance to states that were adversely affected by OCS activities. See 16 U.S.C.A. §1456 (1984).

41. Pub. L. No. 95-372, 92 Stat. 629 (1978), codified at 43 U.S.C.A. §§1331-56 (Supp. 1984).

42. 43 U.S.C.A. §1332 (1984). For an analysis of this legislation and the long-running dispute between the federal government and coastal states over off-shore oil development, see D. Miller, "Offshore Federalism: Evolving Federal-State Relations in Offshore Oil and Gas Development," 11 *Ecology L. Q.* 401 (1984).

43. 43 U.S.C.A. §§1701-1784 (1984). Sen. Rep. No. 583, 94th Cong., 1st Sess. 24 (1975). 43 U.S.C.A. §§1701-1784 (1984). The legislative history discusses factors leading to the statute's adoption.

44. U.S. Executive Office of the President, Office of Management and Budget, *Budget of the United States Government, Fiscal Year 1985*, Appendix, page I-M1.

45. 16 U.S.C.A. §1604 (Supp. 1984).

46. 43 U.S.C.A. §1344(a) (Supp. 1984).

47. 43 U.S.C.A. §1345 (Supp. 1984).

48. 43 U.S.C.A. §1712 (Supp. 1984).

49. 41 Fed. Reg. 2052 (1976).

50. Executive Order 12372, 47 Fed. Reg. 30959 (1982).

51. 42 U.S.C.A. §§4321 *et seq.* See Richard A. Liroff, "NEPA-Where Have We Been and Where Are We Going?" *American Planning Association Journal* 46(2):154-161 (1980) and the sources cited therein.

52. 16 U.S.C. §§1451-64 (1976 and Supp 1984).

53. 16 U.S.C. §§1454, 1455 (Supp. 1984).

54. The coastal zone includes "land affected by the coastline" (as defined by the state and subject to federal approval, and extends out from shore a distance of three miles—to the near border of the Outer Continental Shelf. However, the statutory definition of the coastal zone excludes federal land. 16 U.S.C.A. §1453 (Supp. 1984).

55. 16 U.S.C.A. §1456(c)(3) (Supp. 1984).

56. 16 U.S.C.A. §1456(c)(1) (Supp. 1984)

57. This result is implicit. See comment to 15 C.F.R. §930.42(c), 44 Fed. Reg. 37149 (1979).

58. 104 S. Ct. 656 (1984), 14 ELR 20129 (1984).

59. H.R. 4589, introduced by Representatives Panetta, D'Amours, and Studds; S. 2324, introduced by Senator Packwood.

60. See National Governors' Association Committee on Energy and Environment, "The State of the States: Management of Environmental Programs in the 1980's" (Washington, D.C.: National Governors' Association, 1982), p. 2.

61. American Environmental Safety Council/Save EPA, "Environmentalists' Ideas on EPA's Budget," Briefing Package (Washington, D.C.: AESC, 1521 New Hampshire Ave., June 3, 1983).

62. Information provided by Budget Division, Office of Surface Mining, March 1984.

63. Calculated using implicit price deflators for state and local government pur-

chases (1981-83) and Reagan administration forecasts for inflation in 1984. See *Economic Report of the President* (Washington, D.C.: U.S. Government Printing Office, 1984), Appendix B, pp. 197 and 225.

64. Calculated using implicit price delators for federal non-defense purchases (1981) and Administration forecasts for inflation in 1984. See *Economic Report of the President*, Appendix B, pp. 197 and 225.

65. See, e.g., Public Lands Institute, *Still Stripping the Law on Coal* (Denver: Public Lands Institute, 1720 Race St., 1984); U.S. Department of Interior, Office of Surface Mining, "Annual Report Tennessee Permanent Program," (Knoxville: Office of Surface Mining, Oct. 1983).

66. U.S. Department of Interior, Office of Surface Mining, "Annual Report Tennessee Permanent Program," pp. 4, 40. The Office of Surface Mining plans to institute federal enforcement for those portions of Tennessee's program that the state has enforced inadequately. The state has been working to respond to criticisms of its efforts. See 49 Fed. Reg. 15495 (1984).

67. Executive Office of the President, Office of Management and the Budget, *Budget of the United States Government*, Fiscal Year 1985, p. 8-51.

68. *Ibid.*, fiscal year 1984, pp. 8-54.

69. For example, a version of the revenue sharing introduced in 1983 (H.R. 5) provides states that have approved CZM programs with a larger share of OCS revenues, and requires that states use a portion of revenue sharing funds for CZM purposes. H.R. 5, §§4 and 5.

70. See, generally, John L. Palmer and Isabel V. Sawhill, eds., *The Reagan Experiment* (Washington, D.C.: The Urban Institute, 1982), and Richard P. Nathan et al., *The Consequences of Cuts* (Princeton: Princeton University Press, 1983).

71. Nathan, *The Consequences of Cuts, supra* note 70, p. 191.

72. See U.S. Comptroller General, *Potential Impacts of Reducing the Environmental Protection Agency's Budget* Washington, D.C.: General Accounting Office, 1982), p. 12; comments by Maryland official William Eichbaum in "On Delegation to the States," *Environmental Forum* 1(9):11 (1983); and S. William Becker, "Air Quality and Federalism," *Environmental Forum* 1(9):16-19 (1983).

73. See Congressional Budget Office, "Balancing the Federal Budget and Limiting Federal Spending: Constitutional and Statutory Approaches," (Washington, D.C.: U.S. Government Printing Office, 1982). See Also "States, Their Budgets Already Pruned, Turn to Tax Increases," *Washington Post*, January 26, 1983; "The States Search for Fiscal Light in Gloom of Recession," *Washington Post*, July 13, 1982; Rochelle Stanfield, "State Taxes are Up, But Don't Worry—Federal Taxes are Down By Much More," *National Journal* 15(26):1320 (1983); and National Conference of State Legislatures, "State Fiscal Conditions Entering 1983," (Washington, D.C., 1983).

74. See "The Taxpayer Rebellion is Coming Back," *Business Week*, September 19, 1983, p. 33; "Record Surpluses at the State and Local Levels Ease Worry Over Washington's Budget Deficit," *Wall Street Journal*, December 6, 1983; and "Local Government Surpluses Will Keep the Heat Off Credit," *Business Week*, December 19, 1983, p. 18.

75. See "The Taxpayer Rebellion is Coming Back," *Business Week*, September 19, 1983, p. 33; and Rochelle L. Stanfeld, "The Taxpayer's Revolt is Alive

or Dead in the Water—Take Your Pick,'' *National Journal* 15(50):2568-2572 (1983).

76. See "States Put Their Bite on the Federal Tax Cut," *Business Week*, July 26, 1982, p. 21. See also Stanfield, "America's Oldest Largest Cities Seem to Have Found a Formula for Survival," *National Journal* 15(46):2357-2362 (1983).

77. See National Governors' Association Committee on Energy and Environment, "The State of the States: Management of Environmental Programs in the 1980's," *supra* note 60, p. 3.

78. See "State is Billing Companies on Antipollution Costs," *New York Times*, October 8, 1983.

79. See Philip R. Yeany, "Permit Fees for New Jersey's Surface and Groundwater Dischargers," *Environmental Forum* 2(9):21-25 (1984).

80. For discussion of these and other financial arrangements for capital facilities, see Association of State and Interstate Water Pollution Control Administrators, "Innovative Financing for the Clean Water Program: Technical Exchange Seminar Proceedings," and "Innovative Financing for the Clean Water Program: The State Perspective," (Washington, D.C.: ASIWPCA, 1983). See also "Wastewater Treatment" in Congressional Budget Office, *Public Works Infrastructure: Policy Considerations for the 1980s* (Washington, D.C.: U.S. Government Printing office, 1983), pp. 55-70. A New Jersey court recently struck down New Jersey's formula for assessing fees, declaring it represented an "arbitrary and haphazard distribution of administrative expenses." A new formula will have to be developed to satisfy the court. See *Air/Water Pollution Report*, May 7, 1984, p. 177.

81. In the early 1970s, the annual volume of municipal bonds was $22 billion. It increased to about $45 billion in 1977, reamining about that level until 1982, when it leaped to $78 billion. Whereas revenue bonds constituted only about 30% of new bond issues in the early 1970s, they constituted about 70% by the early 1980s. See Philip Dion, "Whoops—Default in the Northwest Has Municipal Bond Market on Edge," *National Journal* 15(39):1953 (1983).

82. See "The Fallout from 'Whoops,'" *Business Week*, July 11, 1983, pp. 82, 86; Rochelle L. Stanfeld, *supra* note 76, page 2361; "Exorcising the Fear of Municipal Bond Defaults," *Fortune*, 109(2):178 (1984); and Rochelle L. Stanfeld, "State, Local Governments Divided Over Limitations on Revenue Bonds," *National Journal* 16(1):21-23 (1984).

83. See sources cited *supra*, note 72.

84. See Library of Congress, Congressional Research Service, "Federal-State Relations in Transition: Implications for Environmental Policy," *supra* note 21, page VII. Looking at a wide range of intergovernmental programs, environmental and nonenvironmental, David Walker has argued that the intergovernmental system is overloaded with responsibility. See *Toward a Functioning Federalism* (Boston: Little, Brown and Company, 1981).

85. See Smith, *supra* note 25, 12 ELR 15068 (1982).

86. See sources cited *supra*, notes 22 and 23.

87. But it may also be the case that even if federal enforcement is tougher than state enforcement, national corporations may prefer it to the burden of complying with a multitude of different, though weaker, plans, in the many states where they do business. See Gary Nothstein, *The Law of Occupational Safety*

and Health (New York: Free Press, 1981) and M. Rothstein *Occupational Safety and Health Law* (St. Paul: West Publishing Company, 1982), cited in Richard S. Fischer, "Cooperative Federalism and Worker Protection: The Failure of the Regulatory Model, *60 Tex. L. Rev.* 945, n. 66 (1982). Moreover, the preferences of corporations marketing or manufacturing products in one state may not always coincide with those operating in many states. This can produce diverse responses within individual industries to regulatory proposals, and can make it difficult to generalize about the attitude of "industry," per se. For a good discussion of diverse industry attitudes, see Jerry Mashaw and Susan Rose-Ackerman, "Federalism and Regulation" in George Eads and Michael Fix, eds., *The Reagan Regulatory Strategy: An Assessment* (Washington, D.C.: Urban Institute Press, 1984).

88. "Competition in laxity," is Justice Brandeis's phrase, cited in Leman and Nelson, *supra* note 11, p. 1021.

89. For a recent example of such business activity, see Jonathan Lash, "A Cooperative Venture in Jeopardy," *Environmental Forum* 1(9):38 (1983).

90. See David Broder, "The New Federalism Fades Away and With it An Opportunity,"*Washington Post*, April 14, 1982.

91. See, e.g., Comptroller-General of the United States, *Federal-State Environmental Programs—The State Perspective* (Washington, D.C.: U.S. General Accounting Office 1980), pp. 60, 63.

92. See Advisory Commission on Intergovernmental Relations, *In Brief: Citizen Participation in the American Federal System* (Washington, D.C.: U.S. Government Printing Office, 1979).

93. In 1960, 15 states limited their governors to two year terms, but now only four do. In 1960, 16 states prohibited their governors from succeeding themselves, but now only 5 do. The number of states relying on legislative sessions every other year has dropped from 41 in 1960 to 14 in 1980, and all but six "find ways" to meet annually. See Neal R. Peirce, "The States Can Do It But Is There the Will?," *National Journal* 14(9):375 (1982). See also David Broder, *supra* note 90, and Alan Ehrenhalt, "Power Shifts in State Capitols as Professional Lawmakers Take Over Leadership Spots," *Congressional Quarterly*, September 3, 1983, p. 1767.

94. See Ehrenhalt, *supra* note 93, p. 1767.

95. See statistics cited *supra* note 93, from Pierce, p. 375.

96. The characterization of states as laboratories for innovation derives from U.S. Supreme Court Justice Louis D. Brandeis: "It is one of the happy incidents of the federal system that a single courageous State may, if its citizens choose, serve as a laboratory and try novel social and economic experiments without risk to the rest of the country." *New State Ice Co. v. Liebmann*, 285 U.S. 262, 311 (1932) (Brandeis, J., dissenting). Cited in Leman and Nelson, *supra* note 11, p. 1020.

97. Forty states have adopted campaign finance reform laws since 1972, 42 states have adopted lobbying reform laws since 1972, and 44 states have adopted laws requiring financial disclosure by public officials. See the following reports issued by Common Cause in September 1983: "Campaign Finance Reform in the States," 'Open Government in the States," 'Lobbying Law Reform in the States," and "Conflict of Interest Legislation in the States."

98. *National Journal* 14(31):1340 (1982). See also "State Regulators Rush in Where Washington No Longer Treads," *Business Week*, September 19, 1983, pp. 124-131.

99. *National Journal* 14(9):374 (1984).

100. See David Currie, "State Pollution Statutes, 48 *U. Chi. L. Rev.*, 44 (1981).

101. Christopher J. Duerksen, *Environmental Regulation of Industrial Plant Siting: How to Make it Work Better* (Washington, D.C.: The Conservation Foundation, 1983) p. 71.

102. See Timothy J. Conlan and David B. Walker, "Reagan's New Federalism: Design, Debate, and Discord," *Intergovernmental Perspective*, Vol. 8, No. 4/Vol. 9, No. 1 (Winter 1983) pp. 6-22.

103. C. Boyden Gray, Counsel to Vice-President George Bush, has written: "The ideal of local control . . . must be balanced against the need for a strong central government to promote commerce and other federal interests. That is why the presumption in favor of state and local regulation must be rebuttable." See "Regulation and Federalism," *Yale Journal on Regulation* 1(1):95-96 (1983).

104. See, e.g., Linowes Commission, *Fair Market Value Policy for Federal Coal Leasing* (Washington, D.C.: U.S. Government Printing Office, 1984) pp. 93-98.

105. *Arizona Republic*, November 21, 1980, at A-12 (quoted in J. Leshy, "Unraveling the Sagebrush Rebellion: Law, Politics and Federal Lands," 14 *U.C.D. L. Rev.* 317 354-55 (1980).

106. Leman and Nelson, *Managerial Federalism, supra* note 11, p. 985.

107. Except where otherwise indicated, the discussion in the text of chemical labeling is based on "The Battle Over Chemical Labeling," *New York Times*, September 12, 1982, and Daniel W. Gottlieb, "Business Mobilizes as States Begin to Move into the Regulatory Vacuum," *National Journal* 14(31):1342.

108. Michael Wines, "Auchter's Record at OSHA Leaves Labor Outraged, Business Satisfied," *National Journal* 15(40):2012 (1983).

109. Three states filed suit against OSHA, complaining about the federal rule's weakness relative to state regulations. See "Three States Say OSHA Rule on Chemicals Weakens Their Laws," *New York Times*, January 1, 1984.

110. By way of contrast, in the federal energy conservation program for home appliances, federal preemption of state appliance standards is not absolute. At least 22 states have petitioned for exemption from the federal standard. See "Governors Urge DOE to Quickly Approve Appliance Standard Exemptions," *Inside Energy with Federal Lands*, February 13, 1984, p. 7.

111. The discussion in the text of pesticide control is based on "White House Flip-Flop and Flap," *Washington Post*, August 7, 1982, and "Pesticides: Testing House on States' Rights," *Washington Post*, July 31, 1982.

112. George H. Pain, "Prevention of Significant Deterioration of Air Quality," in Gregory Wetstone, ed., *Air and Water Pollution Control Law: 1980* (Washington, D.C.: Environmental Law Institute, 1980), p. 31.

113. 42 U.S.C.A. §10101 (1983).

114. States' rights under the NWPA are summarized in James H. Davenport, "A Repository State's Federal Statutory Rights Under the Nuclear Waste Policy Act of 1982," *Western Natural Resource Litigation Digest Commentary* (Winter 1984), pp. 22-28. Federal grants are available to help states participate in the

site selection process and to help them and local governments to mitigate the impacts of the waste site.

115. 42 U.S.C.A. §§10135, 10136 (1983).
116. ACIR, *Regulatory Federalism*, *supra* note 25, pp. 32-33.
117. See Eichbaum & Babcock, *supra* note 29.
118. See Eichbaum and Babcock, *ibid.*
119. See David A. Thomsson,'Regulatory Reform Under the Surface Mining Control and Reclamation Act of 1977: Redefining Priorities and Restoring the States' Role," 3 *Va. J. Nat. Resources L.* 285 (1984).
120. See U.S. Environmental Protection Agency, Office of Policy and Resource Management, Office of Management Systems and Evaluation, Program Evaluation Division, "Improving Delegations of EPA Programs to the States," (Washington, D.C.: U.S. Environmental Protection Agency, Dec. 1982), p. 8; and "GAO Says States May Seek Delegation of Programs To Lure Industry Away From Other Areas," *Air/Water Pollution Report*, February 21, 1983, p. 62. See also Eichbaum and Babcock, *supra* note 29, at 622; T. Edgmon and D. Menzel, "The Regulation of Coal Surface Mining in a Federal System," 21 *Nat. Resources J.* 245, 256-259 (1981); Mark A. Rothstein, "OSHA Review," 34 *Vand. L. Rev.* 112 (1981).
121. William F. Pedersen, Jr., "Federal-State Relations in the Clean Air Act, the Clean Water Act, and RCRA: Does the Pattern Make Sense?" 12 ELR 15072 (1982). This state role in federal programs has been labeled "managerial federalism" by Leman and Nelson, *supra* note 11.
122. Pedersen, *supra* note 120, 12 ELR 15069 (1982).
123. Eichbaum and Babcock, *supra* note 29, have detailed this schizophrenia present in SMCRA.
124. Comptroller-General of the United States, *Potential Impacts* study, *supra* note 72, p. 20.
125. For example, OSM rejected eight states' programs. See Mosher, *supra* note 16, p. 186. Two former Department of the Interior officials attribute OSM's approach to strict language written by Congress. See Eichbaum and Babcock, *supra* note 29.
126. Figures from EPA Management Accountability System.
127. See "On Delegation to States," *supra* note 72, p. 10; and Joseph A. Cannon, "Delegation to States: Realizing A Long Delayed Mandate," *Environmental Forum* 1(9):39 (1983).
128. *Ibid.*
129. See William Butler, "The 'New Federalism'—Can it Really Work in Implementing Environmental Statutes?" 12 ELR 15098 (1982).
130. See Lash, *supra* note 89.
131. U.S. Congress. House. Committee on Merchant Marine and Fisheries, *Oversight Hearings on the Coastal Zone Management Act*, H.R. Rept. 1012, 96th cong. 2d Sess., p. 31.
132. The paragraph in the text is based on "Idaho Acts to Reclaim State Air Program After 8 Months of EPA Management," *Inside EPA Weekly Report*, March 12, 1982, p. 9; and "Idaho Legislators Revive State Air Program," *Journal of the Air Pollution Control Association* 32(5):567 (1982).
133. *Inside EPA; Ibid.*

134. See Becker, *supra* note 72, p. 18.

135. See Mosher, *supra* note 16, p. 185.

136. National Commission on Air Quality, *To Breathe Clean Air* (Washington, D.C.: U.S. Government Printing Office, 1981), p. 117. This acceptance of inadequate plans later became an issue when EPA considered imposing sanctions on states for their failure to meet national ambient air quality standards by statutory standards. States which in good faith had carried out their plans argued that if EPA knew the plans would be inadequate, EPA should not have initially approved them. See S. William Becker, "The Air Administrators—News from STAPPA-ALAPCO," *Journal of the Air Pollution Control Association* 33(4):284 (1983).

137. The paragraph in the text is based on "Ohio's Past May Lead to Tougher U.S. Stand on Acid Rain Control," *Wall Street Journal*, December 23, 1983.

138. Testimony of John V. Byrne, Administrator, National Oceanic and Atmospheric Administration, before U.S. Congress. House. Merchant Marine and Fisheries Committee, Subcommittee on Oceanography, House March 26, 1984.

139. See 15 C.F.R. §930 (1983).

140. See National Governors' Association, Subcommittee on Range Resource Management, "Partnership/Stewardship: Making Federalism Work in Public Land Management" (Washington, D.C.: National Governors' Association, 1980) p. 8; R. Cowart, S. Fairfax, C. Wilson, "Beyond the Sagebrush Rebellion: Enhancing State and Local Authority in Public Lands Management," draft report, prepared for the Western Conference, Council of State Government, 1983. On the other hand, some environmentalists contend that extending FLPMA's consistency requirements to state and local policies and programs will, given BLM's historical decentralization and deference to local concerns, lead to greater local control of BLM land use decisions. See Natural Resources Defense Council et al., "Comments on Proposed Rulemaking Amendments to the BLM's Planning Regulations, 46 Fed. Reg. 54778 (1981)," January 21, 1982.

141. The future of the CZM program may be tied to the fate of OCS revenue sharing proposals currently before Congress.

142. D. Weber, "Evolution of an Agency," *California Lawyer* 4(2):25-27 (1984).

143. 31 U.S.C.A. §6901 (1983).

144. "Quality and Timeliness of Resource Management Plans of Concern to BLM," *Inside Energy with Federal Lands*, (April 23, 1984), p. 13.

145. The discussion in the text of A-95 and Executive Order 12372 is based entirely on George J. Gordon and Irene Fraser Rothenberg, "From A-95 to Executive Order 12372: Intergovernmental Coordination in Flux," prepared for delivery at the 1983 annual meeting of the American Society for Public Administration, April 1983 (Normal, Ill.: Illinois State University, 1983). See also Irene Fraser Rothenberg, "National Support for Regional Review: Federal Compliance and the Future of Intergovernmental Coordination," in *Publius* 13(1)43-58 (1983), and Irene Fraser Rothenberg, "Regional Coordination of Federal Programs: Has the Difficult Grown Impossible?" in *Journal of Policy Analysis and Management*, (forthcoming 1984).

146. E.O. 12372, 47 Fed. Reg. 30959 (1982).

147. Cited in Gordon and Rothenberg, *supra* note 144, p. 6.

148. *Ibid.*, p. 13.

149. *Ibid.*, p. 22, quoting, Harold Seidman, *Politics, Position and Power: The Dynamics of Federal Organization*, 3d ed. (New York: Oxford University Press, 1980), p.204.

150. *Ibid.*

151. For discussion of accountability, equity, and efficiency, see Advisory Commission on Intergovernmental Relations, "An Agenda for American Federalism: Restoring Confidence and Competence" (Washington, D.C.: U.S. Government Printing Office, 1981), chapter 3.

152. It has been argued that intergovernmental relations in a tool box—"a collection of implements that can be used by various actors to accomplish their respective objectives." See Dubnick, Gitelson, and Anderson, "The Federal Tool Box: Administrative Craftsmanship in Intergovernmental Regulation," (paper presented at the 1981 Annual Meeting, American Political Science Association, New York City), p. 9. Carrying this metaphor further, we might consider which tools can find wider application and which have proven ill-suited to the jobs assigned them. We also have to consider inventing new tools.

153. EPA Delegation Study, *supra* note 119. The study's options are listed in "Staff Calls for Streamlined Review Procedures to Speed State Delegation," *Inside EPA Weekly Report*, December 24, 1982. See also the suggestions in Anthony D. Cortese, "Improving the Federal/State Environmental Partnership," *Environmental Forum* 1(9):39 (1983), p. 39.

154. Cover memo from Lewis Crampton accompanying EPA Task Force Report, *supra* note 25, p. 2. In a cooperative effort with state and local officials, EPA recently issued new guidance for overseeing air quality programs. See U.S. Environmental Protection Agency, Office of Air Quality Planning and Standards, "National Air Audit System Guidelines for FY84," (Research Triangle Park: U.S. Environmental Protection Agency, 1983). Also, on April 4, 1984 EPA Administrator William Ruckelshaus approved new EPA policies on delegation and oversight. See 'Ruckelshaus Signs Delegation Oversight Policies for State Environmental Programs," *Air/Water Pollution Report*, April 16, 1984, p. 144.

155. See, e.g., Eichbaum and Babcock, *supra* note 29, at 621-622.

156. In practice, EPA's current oversight of states it trusts the most may be quite discreet, cordial, and constructive. But evidence of proven approaches worth emulating is difficult to find in the studies prepared for EPA's task force on state-federal roles.

157. This and other coordinating arrangements are discussed in more detail in a report by L. Wilson for the National Governors' Association, Subcommittee on Range Resource Management, *Wanted: State Initiative in Public Land Planning* (Washington, D.C.: National Governors' Association, 1981). The Nevada Law is found in Nev. Rev. Stat. §§321.735-321.7355.

158. J. Wald and E. Temkin, "The Sagebrush Rebellion: The West Against Itself—Again," 2 *U.C.L.A. J. Envtl. Pol'y. L.* 187, 201 (1982). See also Public Lands Institute, *Trust Land Administration in the Western States* (Denver: Public Lands Institute, 1720 Race St., 1981). Arizona Governor Bruce Babbitt has noted that the constitutions of most western states require that state trust lands be managed for their maximum economic value. See "Federalism and the Environment: An Intergovernmental Perspective of the Sagebrush Rebellion," 12 *Envtl. L.*, 847, 850 (1982).

159. See, e.g., Allan R. Talbot, *Settling Things: Six Case Studies in Environmental Mediation* (Washington, D.C.: The Conservation Foundation, 1983).

160. These different approaches and circumstances are analyzed in a book on dispute resolution by Gail Bingham, forthcoming from The Conservation Foundation in 1984.

161. These and other statutory developments are described in *Resolve*, a quarterly newsletter on environmental dispute resolution, available at no charge from The Conservation Foundation.

162. See Roger Richman, "Structuring Interjurisdictional Negotiation: Virginia's Use of Mediation in Annexation Disputes, *Resolve* (Summer 1983), p. 1.

163. See Philip J. Harter, "Regulatory Negotiation: The Experience So Far," *Resolve* (Winter 1984), p. 1.

164. It is worth noting that the 1972 amendments to the Federal Water Pollution Control Act were a reaction to the failure to produce any solutions on the part of intergovernmental conferences set up to resolve water-quality problems. Davies and Davies, *supra* note 22, p. 210.

165. See Alvin Alm, "EPA Forges New Relationship With States," *EPA Journal* 10(1):3 (1984). See also Mosher, *supra* note 16, p. 185.

166. "EPA Enforcement Cuts Linked to New Violations," *Washington Post*, December 6, 1983. Municipalities constituted 69 percent of those in significant noncompliance. Those deemed in significant noncompliance exceeded the allowable limit for at least one pollutant by 50 percent or more at least four months in a row. See also "EPA Says Municipalities Must Comply With Water Act Despite Funding Problems," *Environment Reporter—Current Developments*, January 27, 1984, p. 1643.

167. See 42 U.S.C.A. §7410 (1983). The Natural Resources Defense Council expressed concern about EPA's failure to press this requirement when it reviewed state implementation plans. See August 6, 1979 letter from NRDC's Frances Dubrowski to EPA's Assistant Administrator for Air, Noise and Radiation and to all of EPA's Regional Administrators. For a recent summary of states' fee authority and whether it is used, see the National Governors' Association report, *supra* note 60, p. 6.

168. 33 U.S.C. §1284(b)(1) (1984) and A. Myrick Freeman, "Air and Water Pollution Policy" in Paul Portney et al., *Current Issues in U.S. Environmental Policy* (Baltimore: Johns Hopkins University Press for Resources for the Future, 1978), p. 65.

169. See Elaine C. Warren, "State Hazardous Waste Funds and CERCLA: Conflict or Complement?', 13 ELR 10348 (1983); see also John Quarles, "Federal Regulation of Hazardous Wastes," (Washington, D.C.: Environmental Law Institute, 1982), p. 170.

Figure References

8.1 Information provided by American Environmental Safety Council/Save EPA (based on EPA budget documents).

8.2 *Ibid.*

8.3 *Ibid.*

8.4 Information provided by U.S. Department of the Interior, Office of Surface Mining, Budget Division, February 1984.

Beginning in 1982, the Mining Institute was transferred from the Office of Surface Mining to the Bureau of Mines. In 1980, the Institute was funded at $10 million; in 1981, at $9.6 million. *Ibid.*

8.5 U.S. Department of Commerce, National Oceanic and Atmospheric Administration, Office of Ocean and Coastal Resource Management, "Summary of Financial Assistance Programs FY 1974-1982" (Washington, D.C.: National Oceanic and Atmospheric Administration, Nov. 1983); information provided by Office of Ocean and Coastal Resource Management, March 1984.

Authorization for program development grants expired after FY 1979. The Coastal Energy Impact Program was created by legislation passed in 1976.

8.6 FY 1975-83: U.S. Congress. House Committee on Appropriations. Subcommittee on Interior and Related Agencies. *Hearings, Part 1 Budget Justifications* (Washington, D.C.: U.S. Government Printing Office), issues for years 1977-1984.

FY 1984: Information provided by House Appropriations Committee, Interior Subcommittee Staff, March 1984.

8.7 1977-1982: U.S. Department of the Interior, Bureau of Land Management, *Public Land Statistics* (Washington, D.C.: U.S. Government Printing Office), issues for years 1977-1982.

1983: Information provided by Bureau of Land Management, Office of Public Affairs, March 1984.

8.8 1973-1980: U.S. Department of Interior, Bureau of Land Management, "Coal Leasing Activity Since 1973" (Washington, D.C.: Bureau of Land Management, March 1984).

1981-1983: Linowes Commission, *Fair Market Value Policy for Federal Coal Leasing* (Washington, D.C.: U.S. Government Printing Office, 1984), p. 68.

From 1971 to 1981, there was a moratorium on lease offerings initiated by the Bureau of Land Management (BLM). During that time, competitive leasing occurred at the request of existing lessees where necessary to prevent shutdowns and subsequent unemployment, to ensure that isolated "pockets" of federal coal would be mined when efficient to do so, or because of other hardship or emergency. In 1983, Congress imposed a new moratorium on BLM-initiated coal leasing because of concerns that the government did not receive fair market value for the coal offered in the 1982 Powder River basin lease sale.

8.9 U.S. Department of the Interior, Minerals Management Service, "Outer Continental Shelf Lease Offerings Statistics" (Washington, D.C.: U.S. Department of Interior, Jan. 1984).

Three lease sales have been held thus far in 1984. A total of 113.3 million acres were offered for lease. As of May 25, leases had been issued for only the first two sales. Approximately 1.9 million acres were leased for a total bonus bid of $367.1 million. Information provided by U.S. Department of the Interior, Minerals Management Service.

8.10 Comptroller General of the United States, *Federal-State Environmental Programs—The State Perspective* (Washington, D.C.: U.S. General Accounting Office, 1980), p. 17.

8.11 Partial delegation in the PSD program may mean either that the state is conducting only some of the activities involved in the program or that it is essentially conducting the program except for EPA's formal sign-off.

Under NSPS and NESHAPS, comparison of delegation figures is difficult, since delegation occurs on a standard-by-standard basis, and since different numbers of standards are applicable in different states. For example, South Dakota and Wyoming have no NESHAPS sources, and so are excluded from that program. In addition, new standards may be added as new sources begin operating, so the percentage of delegated standards may decline, even though the state is administering the same number of standards. Because of these factors, a more precise breakdown of the NSPS and NESHAPS programs' delegation status follows:

Percentage Delegated	NSPS	NESHAPS
75-99	16	7
50-74	1	2
25-49	0	2
1-24	1	0

Partial delegation in the NPDES program means the state has assumed responsibility for NPDES permits only or for NPDES permits and either federal facilities or pretreatment programs.

Partial delegation in the underground-injection control program means the state has assumed responsibility for regulating only certain classes of injection wells.

Partial delegation under RCRA Phase II means the state issues permits for either storage facilities or storage and incineration facilities. Full delegation means the state issues permits for storage, incineration and landfill facilities.

The Office of Surface Mining (OSM) recently instituted federal enforcement of portions of Tennessee's and Oklahoma's approved programs that were not being adequately implemented by those states. OSM has not yet revoked its approval of these programs, though revocation may be forthcoming.

Clean Air Act: Information provided by U.S. Environmental Protection Agency, Office of Air Quality Management and Standards, Control Programs Development Division, Standards Implementation Branch, May 1984; U.S. Environmental Protection Agency, Office of Policy, Planning and Evaluation, February 1984.

Clean Water Act: Information provided by U.S. Environmental Protection Agency, Office of Water Enforcement and Permits, Permits Division, May 1984; U.S. Environmental Protection Agency, Office of Water Program Operations, Municipal Construction Division, May 1984; U.S. Army Corps of Engineers, Civil Works, Environmental Programs, March 1984; U.S. Army Corps of Engineers, Civil Works, Environmental Programs, March 1984.

Safe Drinking Water Act: Information provided by U.S. Environmental Protection Agency, Office of Drinking Water, State Programs Division, March 1983; U.S. Envirnmental Protection Agency, Office of Drinking Water, May 1984.

Coastal Zone Management Act: U.S. Department of Commerce, National Oceanic and Atmospheric Administration, Office of Ocean and Coastal Resource Management, "CZM Information Exchange," (Washington, D.C.: Office of Ocean and Coastal Resource Management, April 1984), p. 22.

Federal Insecticide, Fungicide and Rodenticide Act: Information provided by U.S. Environmental Protection Agency, Office of Pesticides and Toxic Substances, March 1984.

Occupational Safety and Health Act: Information provided by U.S. Department of Labor, Occupational Safety and Health Administration, Office of State Programs, March 1984.

Resource Conservation and Recovery Act: Information provided by U.S. Environmental Protection Agency, Office of Solid Waste, Permits and State Programs Division, State Programs Branch, May 1984.

Surface Mining Control and Reclamation Act: Information provided by U.S. Department of the Interior, Office of Surface Mining Reclamation and Enforcement, Office of Budget and Administration, Planning and Budget Division, February and May, 1984.

The OCS Leasing Controversy

1. See D. Miller, "Offshore Federalism: Evolving Federal-State Relations in Offshore Oil Development," 11 *Ecology L.Q.* 401 (1984).
2. See, e.g., *California v. Watt,* 668 F. 2d 1290 (D.C. Cir., 1981), 16 ERC 1561; *California v. Watt,* 712 F. 2d 584 (D.C. Cir. 1983), 19 ERC 1281; *Secretary of the Interior v. California,* 464 U.S., 104 S. Ct. 656 (1984), 14 ELR 20129; *Conservation Law Foundation v. Watt,* 560 F. Supp. 561 (D. Mass. 1983), 18 ERC 1904; *Kean v. Watt,* 18 ERC 1921, No. 82-2420 (D. N.J. September 7, 1982); *California v. Watt,* 17 ERC 1711 (C.D. Cal. June 9, 1982); and *Clark v. California,* 464 U.S., 20 ERC 1256 (1983).

3. 43 U.S.C.A. §§1451-64 (Supp. V., 1981); 16 U.S.C.A. §§1331-56 (1982). The federal-state relations aspects of these laws and court decisions interpreting them is discussed in Miller, *supra* note 1.
4. *California v. Watt*, 668 F. 2d 1290 (D.C. Cir. 1981), 16 ERC 1561.
5. *California v. Watt*, 520 F. Supp. 1359 (C.D. Cal. 1981), 16 ERC 1729.
6. *California v. Watt*, 683 F. 2d 1253 (9th Cir. 1982), 17 ERC 1857.
7. *Secretary of the Interior v. California*, 464 U.S., 104 S. Ct. 656, 14 ELR 20129 (1984). The Interior Department argued that a lease sale does not directly affect the coastal zone because it causes no physical effects and because further government approvals must be given before oil production may begin. California argued that the lease sale set in motion a chain of events which resulted in definite coastal zone impacts. See T. Berger and J. Saurenman, "The Role of Coastal States in Outer Continental Shelf Oil and Gas Leasing: A Litigation Perspective," 3 *Va. J. Nat. Resources L.*, 35 (1983).
8. U.S. Department of the Interior, Minerals Management Service, "Outer Continental Shelf Lease Offerings Statistics," table revised 1/6/84.
9. *California v. Watt*, 712 F. 2d 584 (D.C. Cir. 1983), 19 ERC 1281.
10. Watt is quoted by *Washington Post* reporter Dale Russakoff on NBC's *Meet the Press* broadcast, January 9, 1983. See broadcast transcript, p. 8.
11. See "Clark Acts to Stem Issue Over Offshore Leasing," *Washington Post*, January 13, 1984.
12. S. 800, 98th Cong. 2d Sess. (1984).
13. OCS revenues are second only to income tax receipts as a source of federal revenue, earning $10.5 billion in fiscal 1983. Information provided by Budget Division, Minerals Management Service, February 1984.
14. H.R. 4589, 98th Cong., 2d Sess. (1984) and S. 2324, 98th Cong., 2d Sess. (1984) are two legislative efforts to reverse the Supreme Court decision on the CZMA's consistency provisions.

A Role for Regional Solutions?

1. Congressional Quarterly, Inc., *1980 CQ Almanac* (Washington, D.C.: Congressional Quarterly, Inc., 1981), p. 494.
2. The act, Pub. L. No. 96-205 (March 13, 1980), 94 Stat. 84, is codified at 42 U.S.C.A. §2021 b *et seq.* (Supp. 1984).
3. See "Proposal for Multistate Pacts on Nuclear Waste Hits Snags," *Wall Street Journal*, February 21, 1984.
4. *Ibid.*
5. Library of Congress, Congressional Research Service, "Federal-State Relations in Transition: Implications for Environmental Policy," a report prepared for U.S. Senate. Committee on Environment and Public Works. 97th Cong., 2d Sess., Serial No. 97-7 (Washington, D.C.: U.S. Government Printing Office, 1982), p. 86.

Index

of 1970s, 3-4, 237
obstacles to state management
   of, *455*
for point-source pollution,
   117-119
politics of, 444-451
and public opinion of, *28*
regional solutions for, 463
regulatory, 425-431
resource management, 431-432
review and comment, 432-433
see also Legislation (for specific
   enabling acts)
Environmental quality
of air, 9, 85-105
assessment of, 8-11
balanced with economy, 7-8
characteristics of new problems
   with, 3
contaminants of, 37-132
controllability of, 276-279
and the economy, 20-27
and environmental expen-
   ditures, 31-33
global climate, 7
irreversibility and immediacy
   of, 245-246
and land use, 9
and population trends, 19-20
and public opinion of, 27-31
and waste production, 129-132
of water, 9, 105-129, 373-383
see also Air quality; Land use;
   Water quality
Environmental Regulatory Fee
   law, 443
Environmental Response, Compensation, and Liability Act,
   Comprehensive, 68, 80, 83
Expenditures
available from BLM leasing
   programs, *439, 449,* 452-453
balanced with risk reduction,
   305
for energy, 215-220
and enforcement of com-
   pliance, 36
EPA grants to states, *436*

federal, 10-11, 89, 435-442
federal appropriations for Office of Surface Mining, *438*
federal BLM appropriations,
   440
federal, for water-resources
   projects, *405*
future availability of, 467-469
nonfederal, for federal water-
   resource projects, *405*
for pollution control, by
   government, 33, *32, 34, 35*
for pollution control, international, 31n
for pollution control, by sector,
   32
for pollution control, by type,
   32
for pollution control, U.S.,
   31-33
related to compliance, 33-36
state and local, 442-444
for wastewater treatment, *34*
for water quality of Colorado
   River, *372*
for water used, 401-414
for water supplies of the coterminous U.S., *135*
see also Economy

Farmland. See Cropland
Federal government. See
   Government
Federal Insecticide, Fungicide and
   Rodenticide Act, 277, 339,
   428, 448
Federal pollution-control statutes.
   See Legislation
Financing. See Expenditures
Finland, 183
Fisheries. See Wildlife, fisheries
Fishery Conservation and
   Management Act, 197-198,
   201
Florida, 16, 125, 150, 184, 191,
   195, 277, 366, 371, 381,
   387, 407, 414
Folk-Williams, John, 394